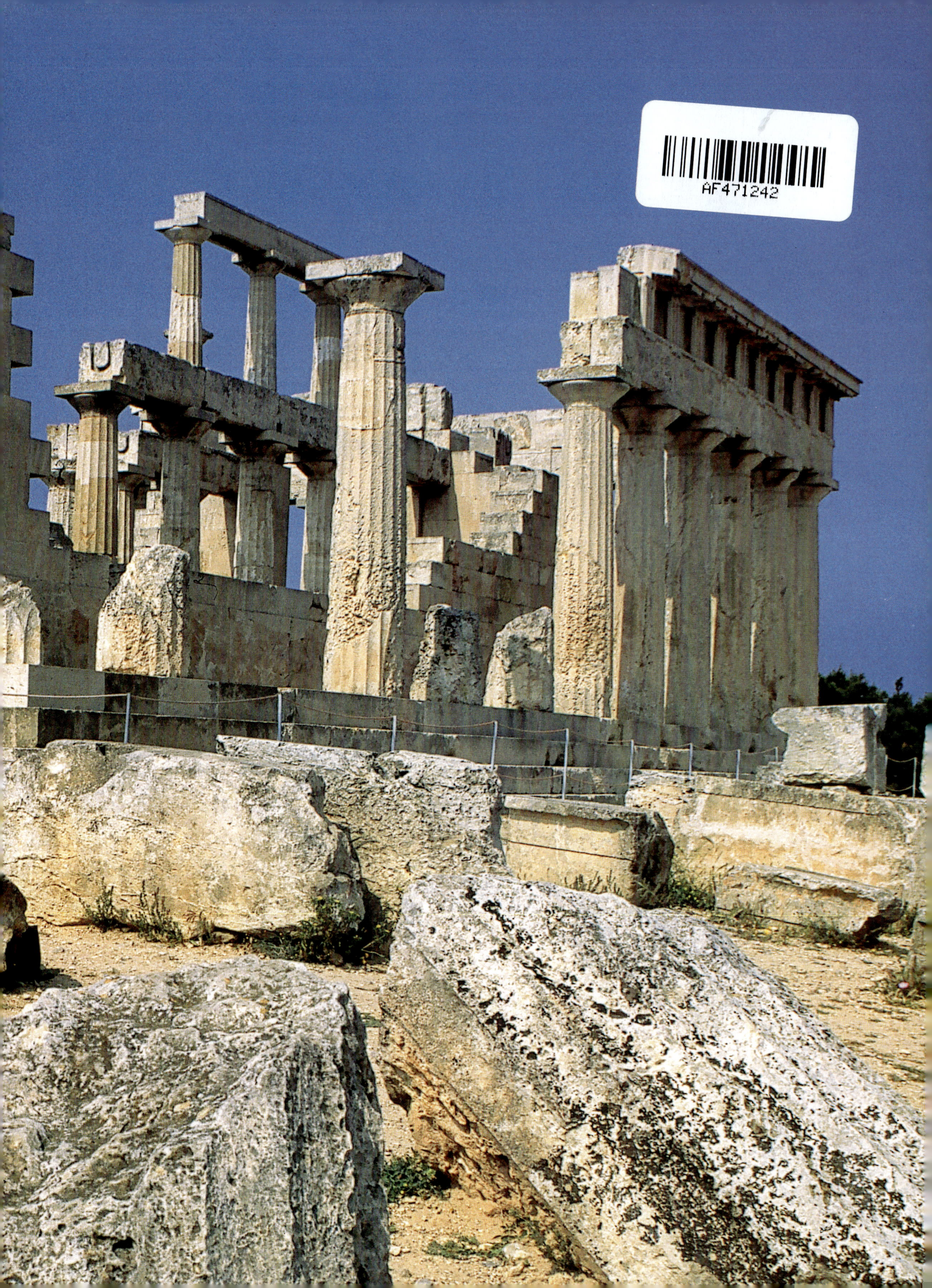

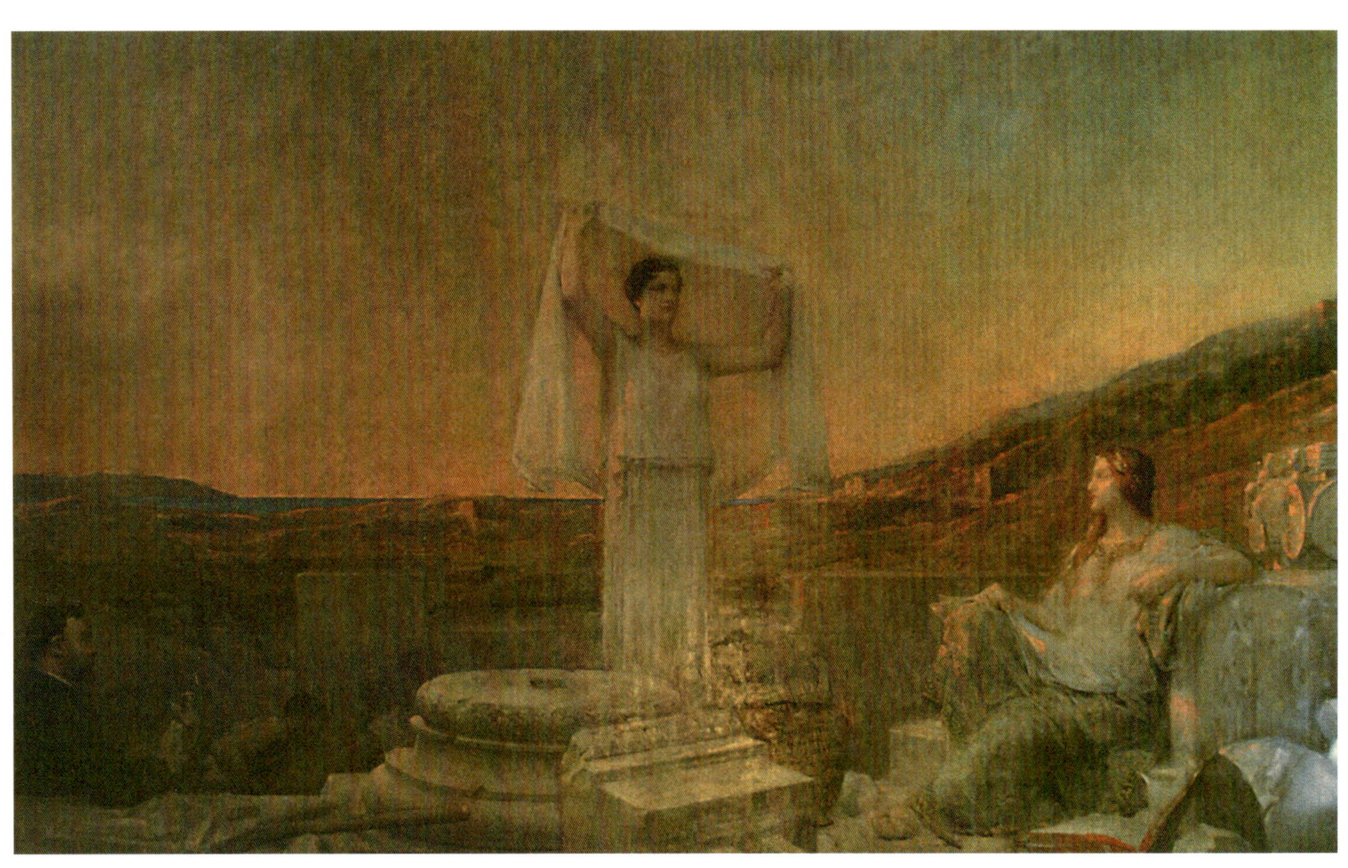

Published by Grange Books
an imprint of Grange Books Plc
The Grange
Kingsnorth Industrial Estate
Hoo, nr Rochester
Kent ME3 9ND
www. Grangebooks.co.uk
ISBN: 1-840139-463

TREASURES OF GREECE

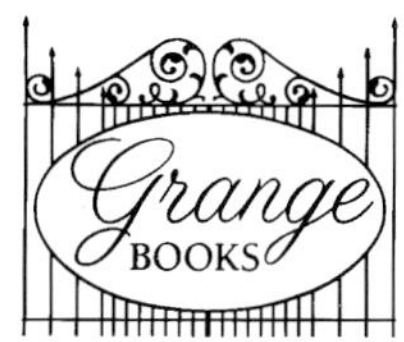

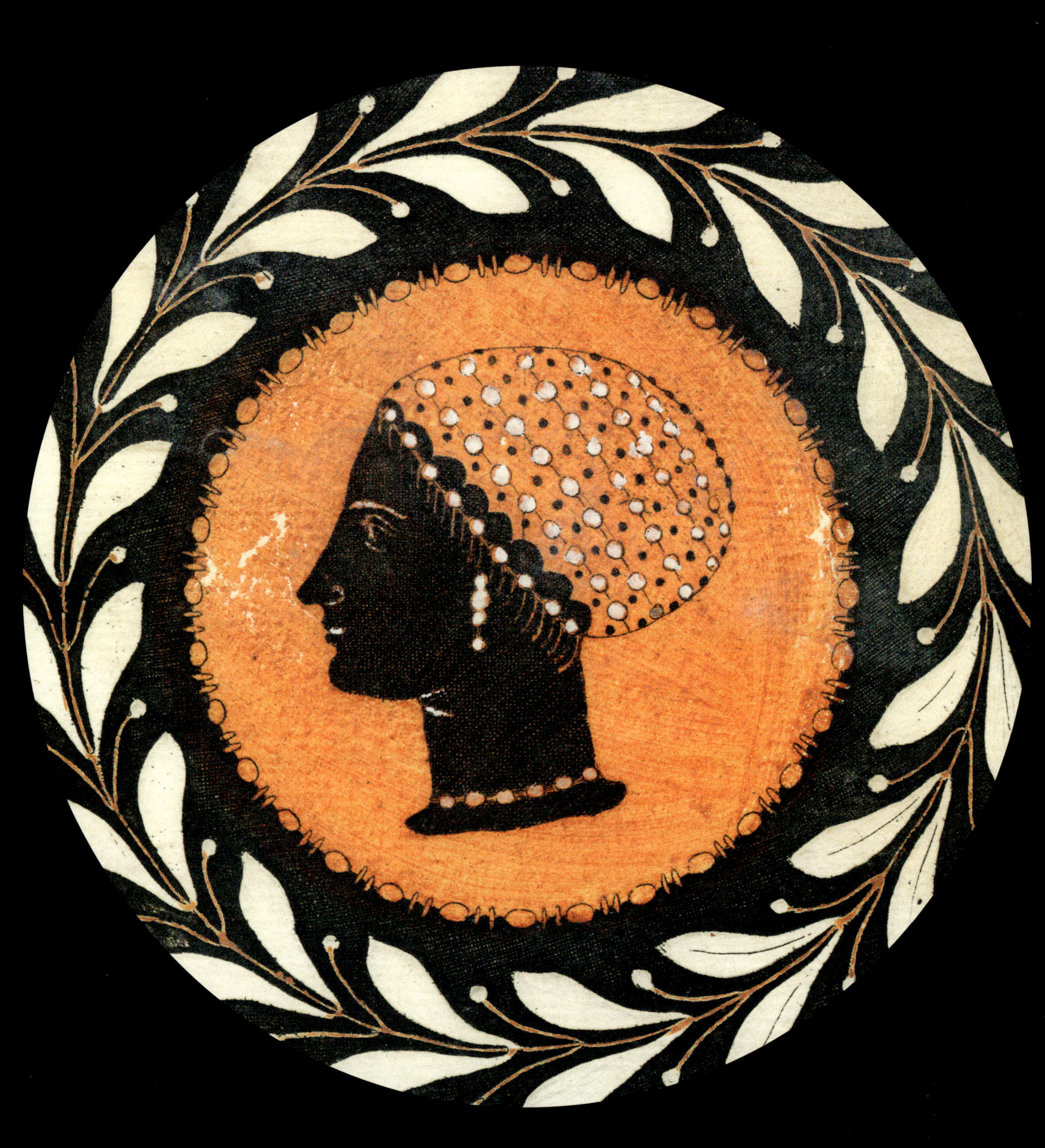

TREASURES OF GREECE

FOREWORD
PIERRE BRUNEL
TEXT
EMMANUELLE LE POMMELET
TRANSLATED BY
DEREK JOHNSTON

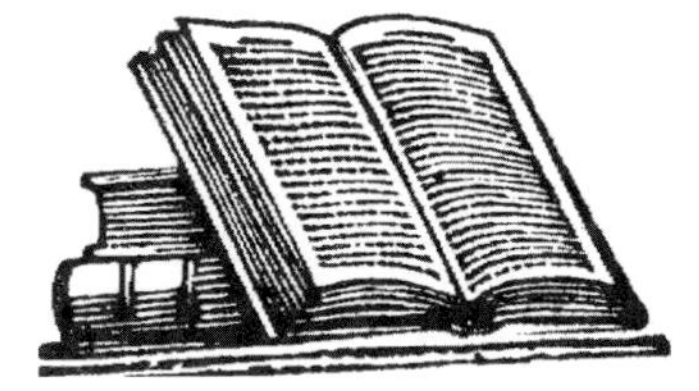

FOREWORD

THE GREEK MIRACLE

We owe the expression to Ernest Renan, I believe. It is a simple formula and seems obvious. It is not however clear to what extent it gets rid of all the ambiguities in which this prestigious civilization is still wrapped. This magnificent book tells us why.

The ideal clarity of line revealed in Greek pillars set against a background of trees is no doubt the "first prayer" that Paul Valéry talks of in his poetry; but were those Greeks really making "wonderful strides" along "the road to reason"? Greek history brings us the proof that all was not light, all was not reasonable in the struggles between Greeks and Barbarians, between Greek themselves, even between Greeks inhabiting the same city. Athenian democracy has been widely praised, perhaps even too highly praised, but it still fell into the traps of personal power and demagogy. And it was not just pure chance that saw Athens absorbed, even relegated to the shade; though at least it was not, like its mythical rival the island of Atlantis, swallowed up by the sea!

In the eyes of the Greeks, or at any rate the Athenians, the besetting sin was a loss of a sense of proportion, *hubris*. In 1934, Thomas Mann, in a greater Germany absorbed by its own demons, described it as the desire to steal one of its dimensions from space itself. Hellenic mythology and 5th century tragedy are full of such instances, where individuals have lost their sense of proportion and where their actions come to haunt them, bringing the condemnation of both men and gods. We think of Sisyphus and his gigantic architecture, Ajax driven mad and, turning to history itself, Alexander setting out from Macedonia to conquer Asia.

The struggles between Greeks and Persians, powerfully evoked in Aeschylus' *Persians*, is not so much the struggle between proportion and its lack, between civilization and barbarism, as a warning against a possible future error, against making the very mistake committed by one's adversary. The Destiny weighing so heavily on the Greek soul was not just the inexorable wheel of the Olympians' chariots; human also played their part, through their excess and their straying from the sober paths of realism and reason.

I should be tempted to say there is no such thing as a miracle. Renan believed in miracles for as long as it took him to say a short prayer on the Acropolis, it had nothing to do with the sorts of prayers he had learned as a seminarian in Saint-Sulpice! Before him, Friedrich Hölderlin had contrasted the cities of the Euphrates, which overpowered freely breathing beings, with the spring at the foot of Mount Parnassus, Spirit and Nature, the grace that had blessed the children of Hellas. But he knew that weeds now grew in ruined Athens, knew that an everlasting lament descended from the mountain on which Hercules was burnt, and that amongst the islands of Poseidon's archipelago you could hear the anger of the powerful sea-god as, in his rage, he still pursued Ulysses.

We see Greece against a backdrop of a blue sky, but we should also look at it against the background of a bottomless pit. The Greek miracle seemed effortless, but was achieved through struggle and distress. Greece today may have been deserted by her gods, all that remains on their statues is an enigmatic smile, but modern Greece can still inspire artists and writers as she did in the time of her glory in Antiquity.

Through the images of this book, which has no labyrinthine detours, I see the Titans and the giants of Hesiod's *Theogony* rise up out of the rocks. I see also the perfect proportions of the temples, the theaters and the stadiums. My imagination is stirred and my memory pricked by paintings on vases; they could appear rigid and sterile if they did not carry so powerful a mythological charge. I see ancient forms in their stone cloaks, but I also see the pilgrims of modern Greece, not to mention Chateaubriand, Goethe or Byron, who died there. For it is now impossible to escape the dimensions of History, even when dreaming of an eternal Greece. What is important is what remains, what can be preserved in the silence of a museum or in an art album.

"May the deep meaning of what remains be made visible": it was Höderlin's dream; and the vision of that lover of Greece, who eventually slipped out of reason, is today realized in a book of images which was not just produced for art lovers, but for all who try to come to some sense of the human destiny.

Pierre BRUNEL

CONTENTS

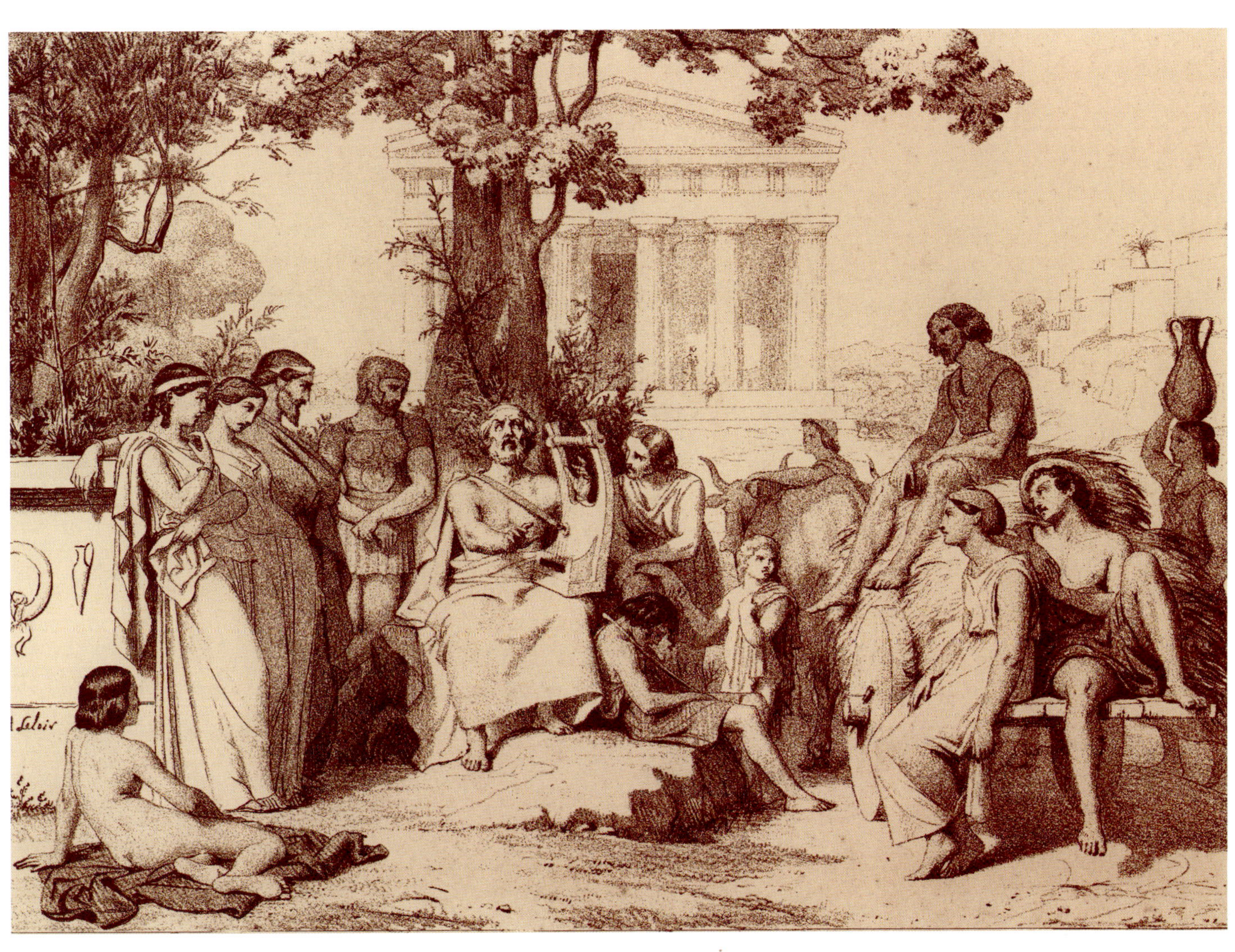

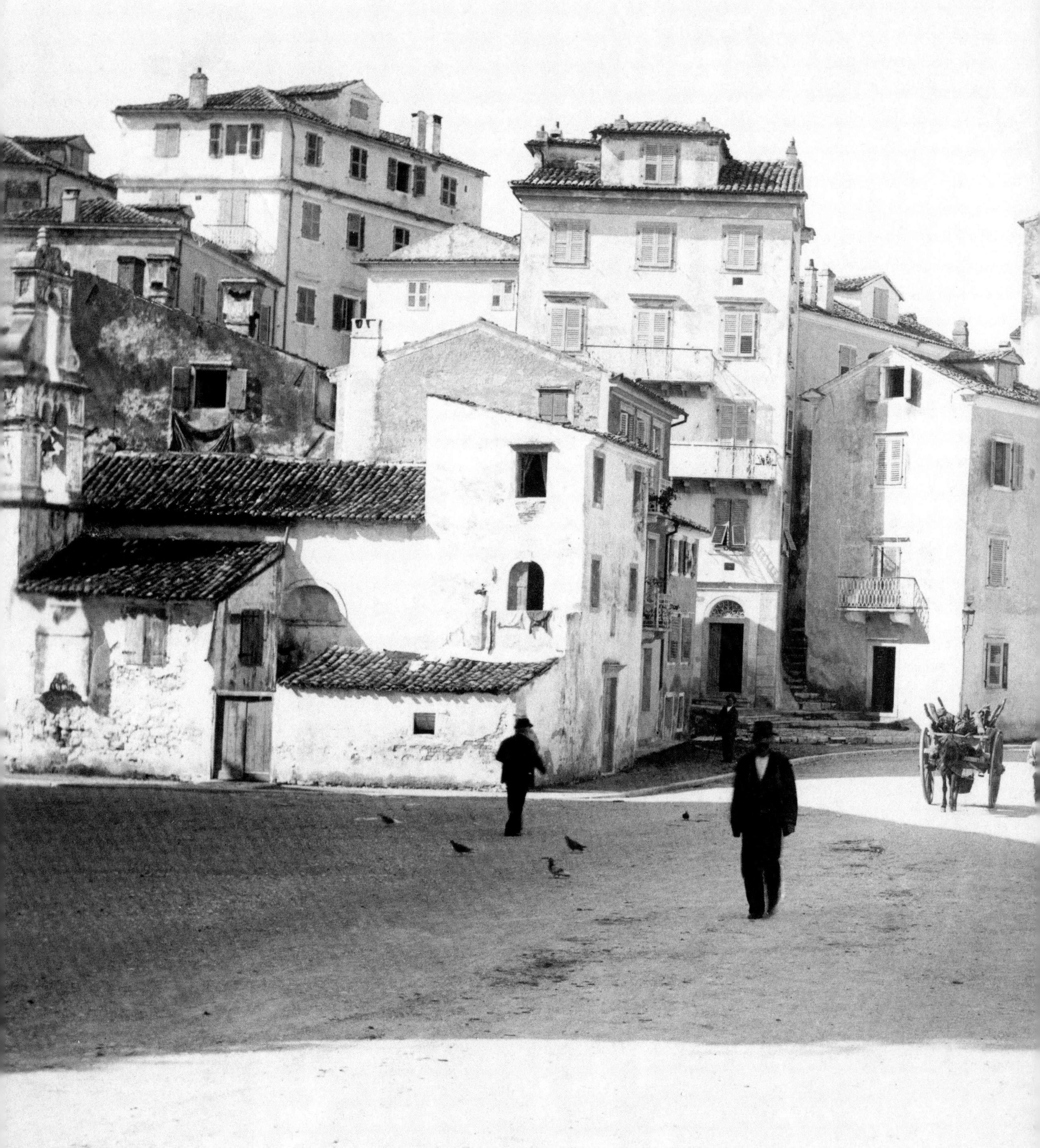

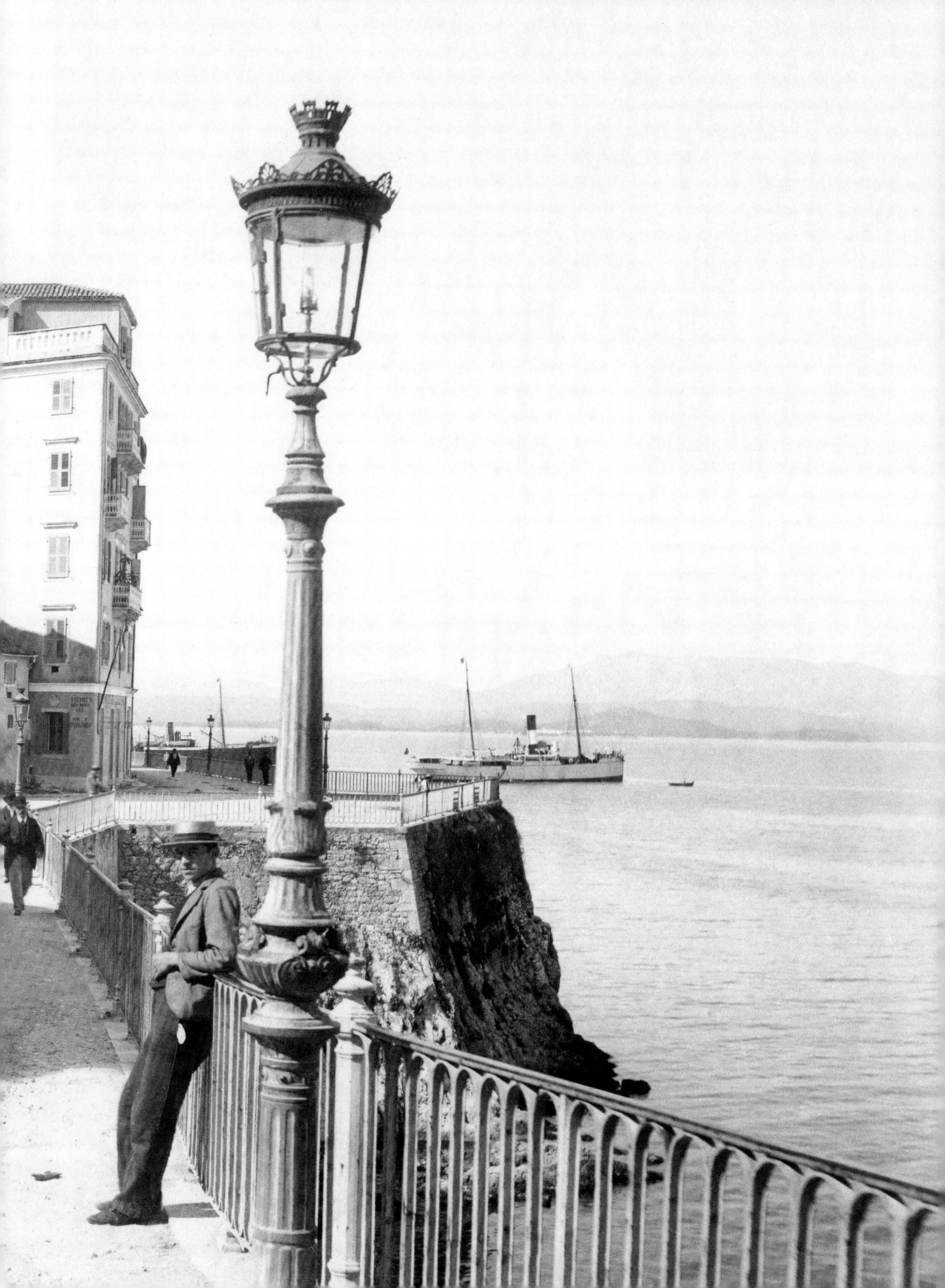

TRAVELING IN GREECE

"The further you travel the stronger grows the painful impression that, town by town, country by country, you are losing a wonderful world, which you created in youth through reading, looking at pictures and by dreaming. The world inside a child's head is so rich, so wonderful, that it is hard to say if it is the larger-than-life result of things learned, or if it is the recalling to memory of a previous existence and the magical geography of an unknown planet." (Gérard de Nerval, *Travels in the East*, 1843)

Such are the marvels of Greece: it has stirred up passions and excited the imagination! Landscapes are dreamed of before they are encountered. Travelers there dare to allow dream and reality to meet, they look to the horizon with great expectations. The seeds of this desire were sown when they first read Homer, Pausanias, Thucydides or many another... So, ever since the Middle Ages, scholars and artists, armed with classical culture, have followed one another along the roads of Greece, seeking the gods, the heroes and the great ones of Antiquity. The accounts of their travels are rich in mythological and historical references. These writers tell us of a pilgrimage to the sources, to the roots of humanity itself, but also of a journey of the mind, through dream and myth, which has universal and symbolic importance. Each one of them has a personal and unique bond with this country and each journey through it, as difficulties are overcome, takes on the coloring of an initiation into life itself. Raymond Queneau claimed to have come back from Greece completely changed, even though he had had no expectations of any sort when he set out.

There has been no shortage of writers! Over two hundred travelers described the site at Delphi between the 15th century and the archaeological investigations of the 19th. Over the same period one can point to about one hundred for Olympus and about four hundred for Delos. The number of such accounts rises from the 18th century on, the taste for the exotic was on the increase; they really take off from the early 19th century, the age of Romanticism. The search for "Elsewhere" becomes a constant preoccupation and travel writing becomes a major literary form: Chateaubriand, Lord Byron, Lamartine and Flaubert all indulged themselves."I could recognize neither Greek roads nor Roman ways in the Peloponnesus... Yet Pausanius and Peutinger's map show several in the area I passed through, especially near Mandinia. Berger followed them very well in his Roads of Empire." (François-René de Chateaubriand, *Journey from Paris to Jerusalem*, 1811)

The descriptions are sometimes tinged with the disappointment of not finding what one has been looking forward to, meeting a continent which the writer seems to know yet does not recognize. Disappointed by the landscapes, and by a people who, beneath the Ottoman yoke, do not compare with the proud and free figures who were their forebears, the traveler longs to bring back a time that has vanished, sighs for a paradise that is nowhere to be found. "I longed to glimpse the immortal gods, who had inspired such noble geniuses, so many noble virtues! I tried to call the laughing phantoms that your fathers had imagined out of the empty sea and the arid soil, and I thought, as I looked at the Cyclades, so sad and so bare, at the deserted coasts and inhospitable bays, that the curse of Neptune had struck forgetful Greece..." (Gérard de Nerval)

As for painters, they compose canvases reflecting and intensifying the image Europeans have of Ancient Greece, a Golden Age, an Age of the Sublime and of Virtue. They show noble ruins set in fertile and luxurious growth.

They take these ruins out of their real context and construct a universe that never existed, idealized memory and expectations of a country. However some writers could be surprised and delighted by the Greece they discovered. Struck by the eastern feel of the country, they were also touched by the subjection of the Greek people. Chateaubriand is a case in point; he tried to make French public opinion responsive to this question. No one was as enflamed as Lord Byron: not content with the pen he took up arms. His passion and courage led to his death during the siege of Missolonghi in 1827. During the second half of the 19th century, many Europeans came to play their part in the rebuilding of Greece, which had been independent since 1830. Full of folk images, they had been under a spell before they arrived. This was the heyday of archaeological investigations, when classical remains were brought to light, and often plundered as well!

With its grandiose landscapes, its exceptional climate, its ancient splendors, Greece has become increasingly attractive. Though a lost paradise for some, it quickly became a mass tourist destination in the second half of the 20th century. Drawn by travel posters where the blues of sky and sea take over from classical ruins, these visitors rarely step away from the tourist trail or leave the beaches. The sea surrounds this land of torturous and sinuous outlines, offering an abundance of sites for the holiday of your dreams. Hundreds of islands, each with its own flavor, surround a continent as it steps out into the Mediterranean, prolonged by the Peloponnesus peninsula to which it is joined by the Isthmus of Corinth. The green Ionian Islands, Corfu, with its Venetian hues amongst them, contrast with the drier, windier Cyclades, with their blue and white villages, out in the Aegean Sea. Matchless Santorini, its volcanic cliffs all the colors of the rainbow, must not be missed. The same may be said for the Dodecanese, Rhodes, the Island of the Sun, being the jewel of its crown.

The interior is less attractive than the coast. Mountains occupy 80% of the land. They have their own personality: dry in the south (Mount Taigetos), or green and austere in the north (the Pindos range). The people took refuge in these mountains during the Ottoman occupation and it was there that the folk and regional traditions survived. In this harsh, fragmented land the plains are tiny, so much so that the Thessalonian plain in Macedonia, and that of Larissa in Thessalia, appear enormous.

Water, land, air and fire have forged the landscapes of Greece. They have fashioned a land that is both harsh and full of light, gentle and wild, a place of legends. These primordial elements have given birth to gods who are sometimes compassionate, sometimes irate. The land is often arid, yet the three fundamental food sources of Mediterranean civilization, the vine, the olive tree and corn, all grow there. Ancient terraces, built and worked on the sides of mountains, now barely endure: a few stone walls and dusty earth.

The sea is everywhere, yet there is a shortage of water. The islands know this contradiction well. Summer's heat dries up even the rivers in the Vikos gorges in the north. The harsh winds touch the islands of the Cyclades; the Ancients called them Zephyrus and Boreas. Fire smolders beneath the earth's crust and blazes out where the European meets the African tectonic plate. Many islands were born out of this explosive underground activity; many others have disappeared... like Atlantis perhaps, though some people whisper it is now called Santorini...

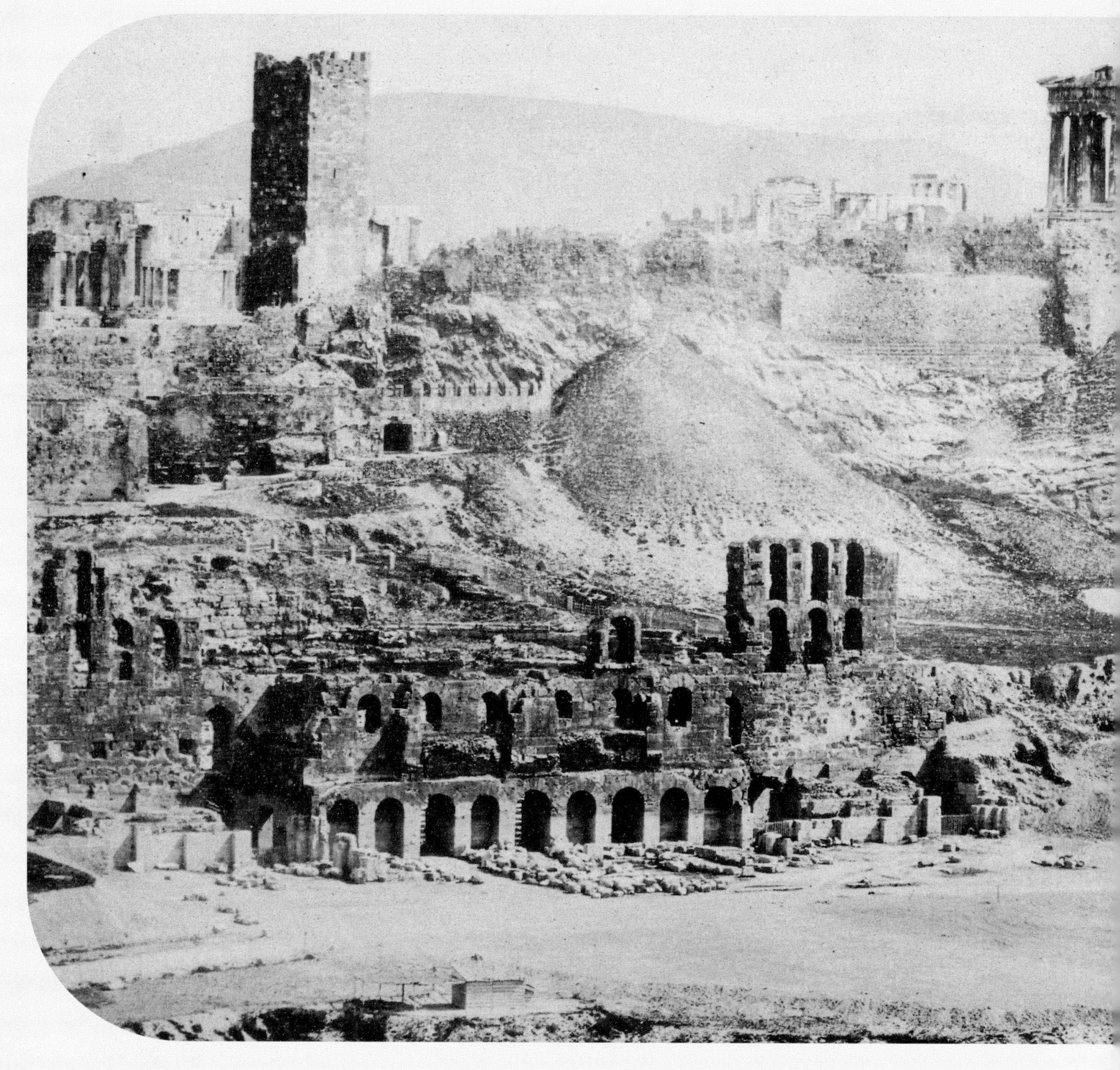

ATHENS IN THE 19TH CENTURY

Dimitri Constantin photographed the Acropolis in about 1860. From him we receive a powerful impression of what the site was like in the second half of the 19th century. Modern photos are taken from roughly the same point, but show a totally different view. The ruins are not set in luxuriant green surroundings, as visiting artists like to imagine them. The land is arid, rocky and bare. The sepia tone expresses well the atmosphere that reigns over the old stones of these ruins, over the rocky promontory of this holy site, even over the distant and austere mountains. This work speaks powerfully to visitors wistful for days of past glory: the ruins appear petrified under a divine curse and we are moved by their harsh beauty.

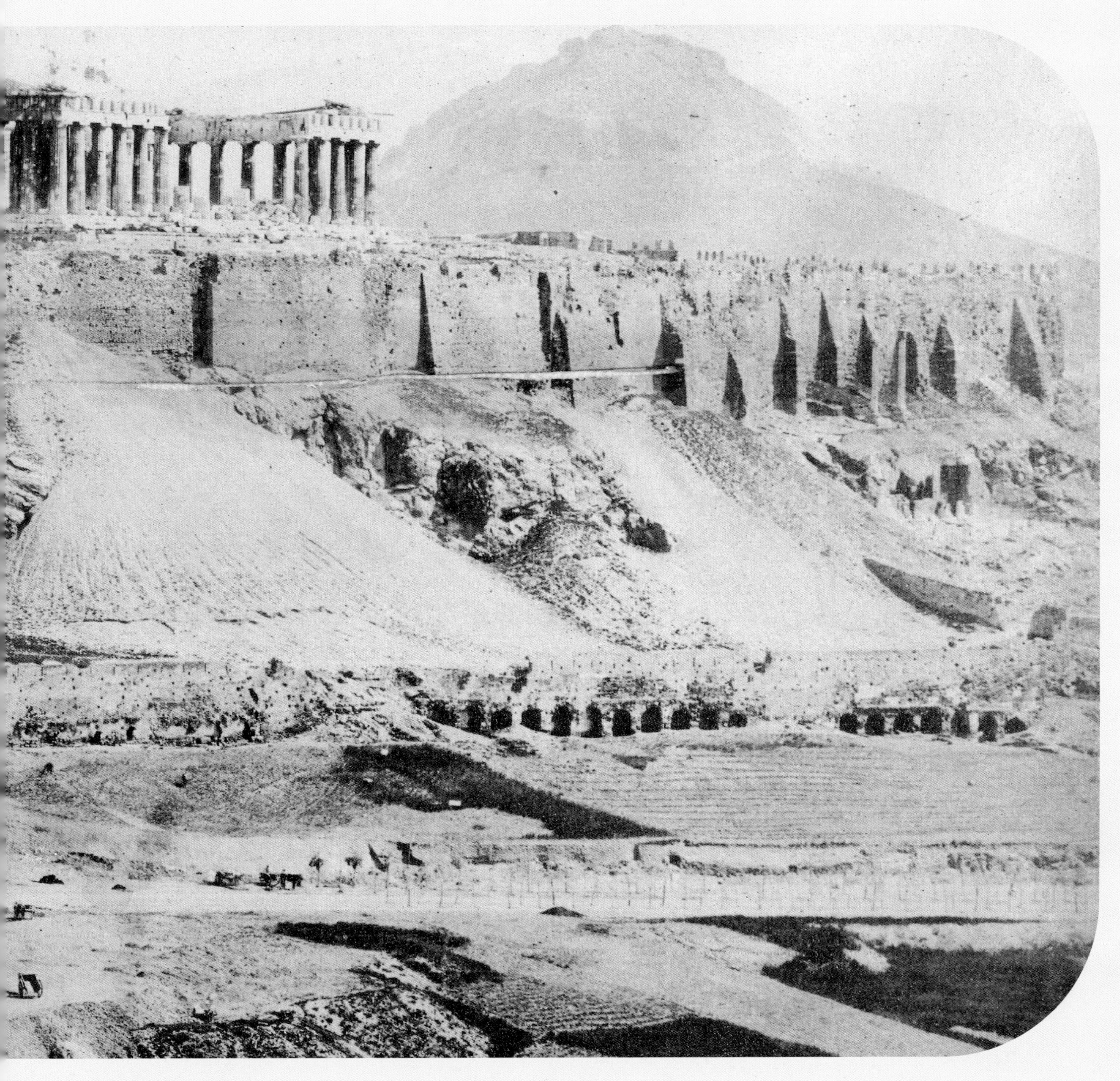

THE SHINING EXAMPLES OF ANTIQUITY

Whether they be philosophers, historians geographers, mathematicians, poets, orators or military leaders, the great figures of Greek antiquity have stimulated the minds of generations of scholars. Their stories, their writings, their inventions or their destinies have inspired many a dream. To know them is to be truly educated, said the humanists of the Renaissance. As for the Romantic writers of the 19th century, could anyone forget the way they paid homage to their ancient models? The names of Plato, Homer, Sophocles, Euripides, Aeschylus, Diogenes, Aristotle, Alexander the Great, Thales, Pericles, Pythagoras, Herodotus, Thucydides, Sappho, Aspasia etc. still ring in our ears, still an inspiration to us all. FOLLOWING PAGES

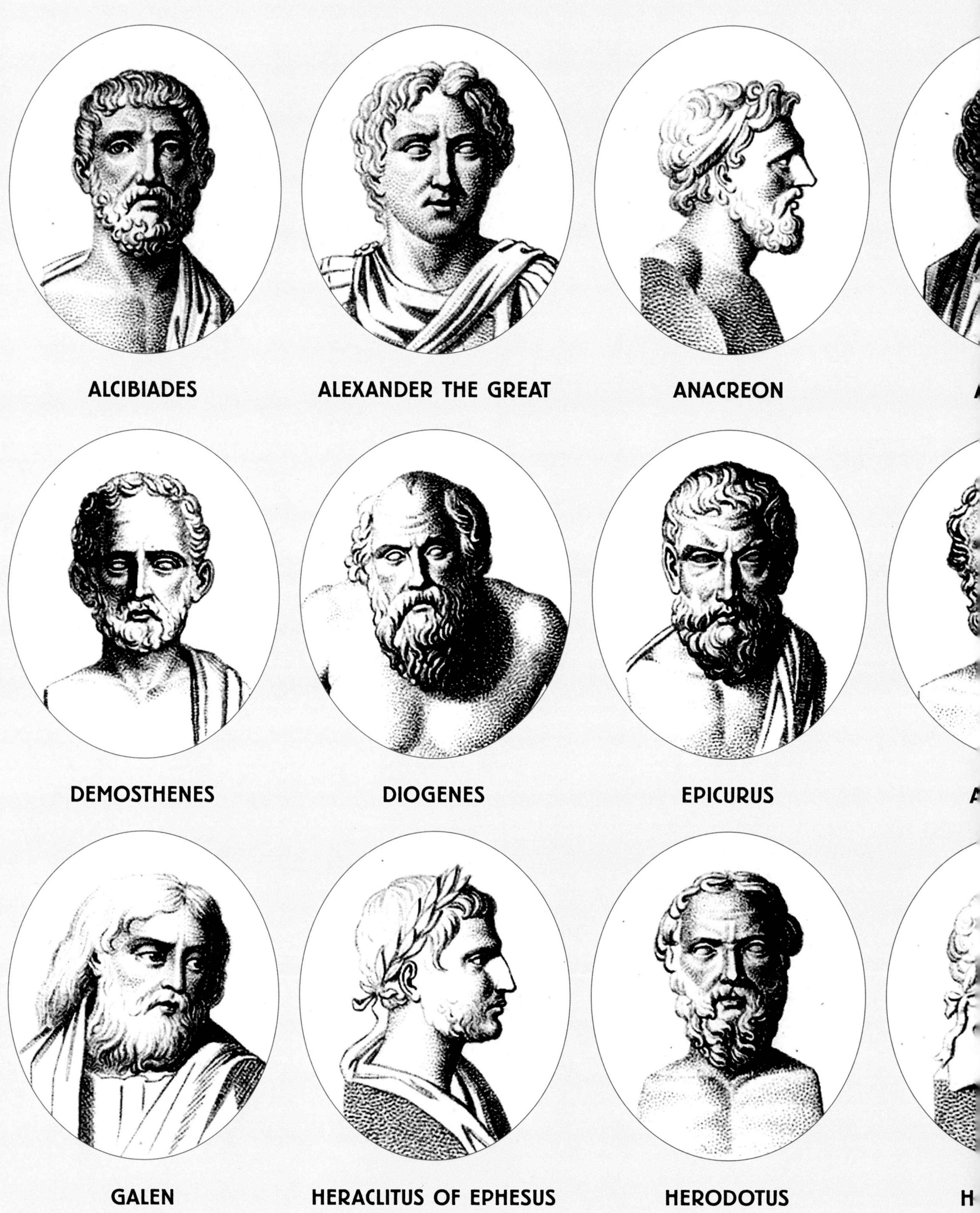
ALCIBIADES
ALEXANDER THE GREAT
ANACREON
DEMOSTHENES
DIOGENES
EPICURUS
GALEN
HERACLITUS OF EPHESUS
HERODOTUS

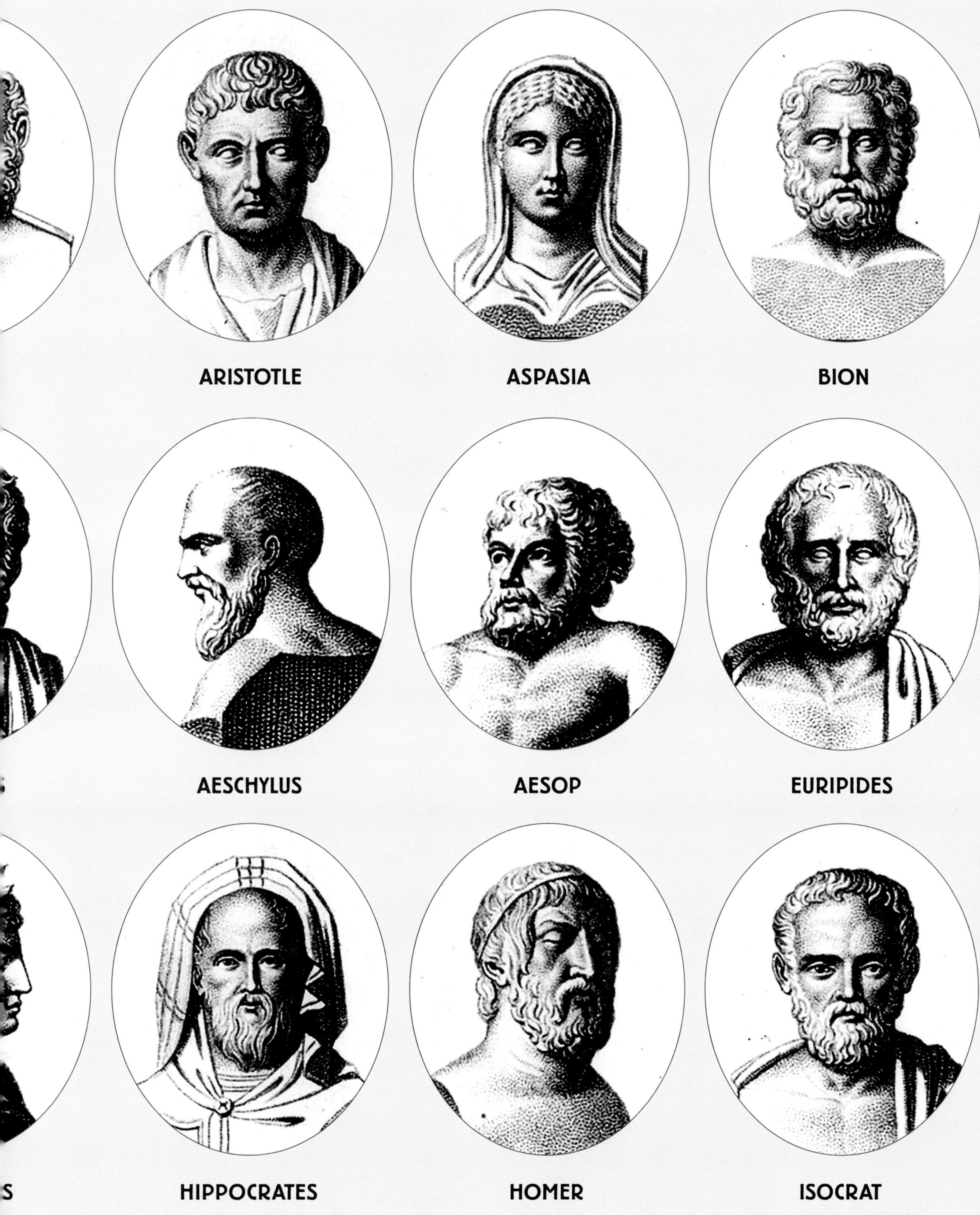
ARISTOTLE
ASPASIA
BION
AESCHYLUS
AESOP
EURIPIDES
HIPPOCRATES
HOMER
ISOCRAT

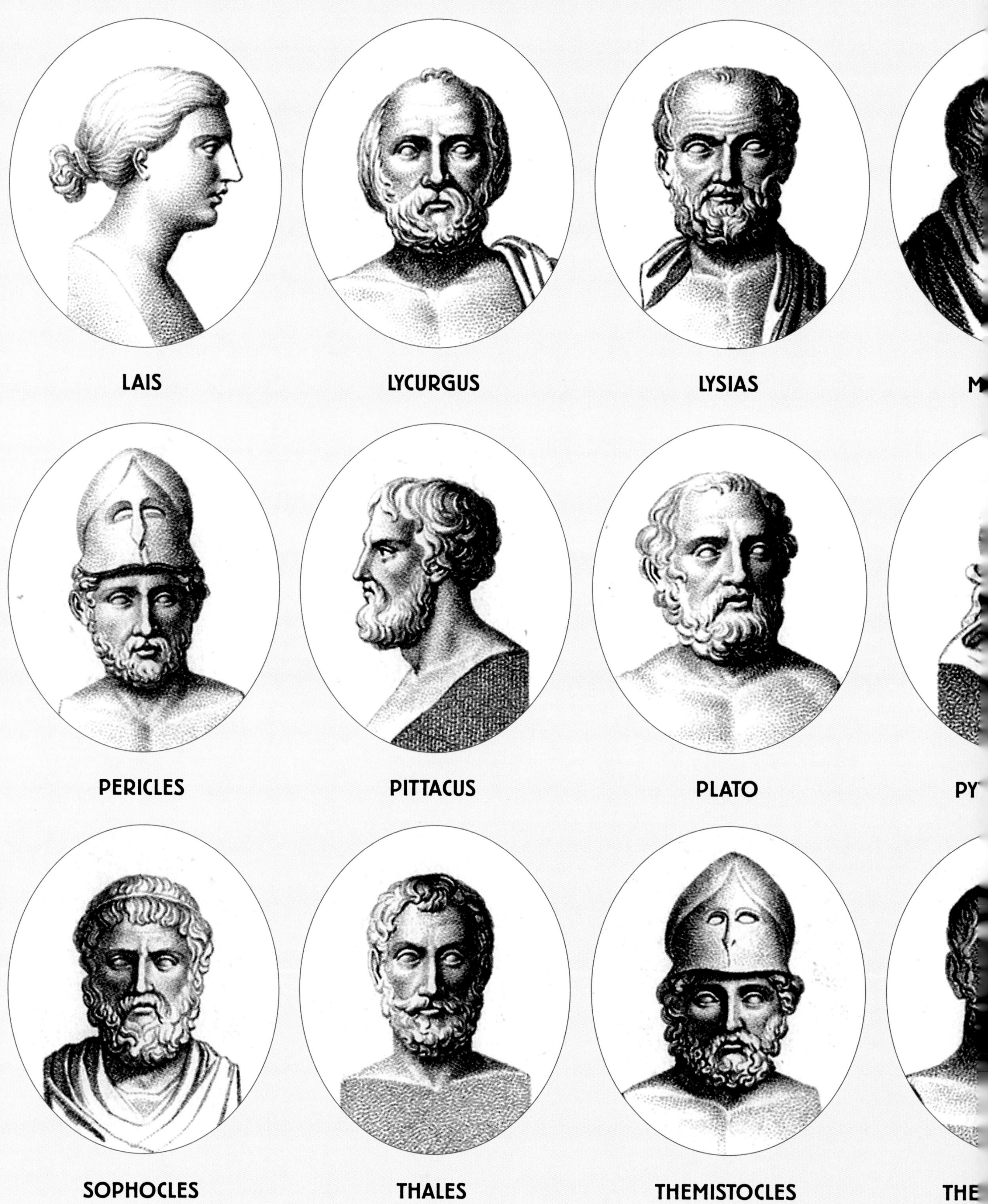
LAIS
LYCURGUS
LYSIAS
PERICLES
PITTACUS
PLATO
SOPHOCLES
THALES
THEMISTOCLES

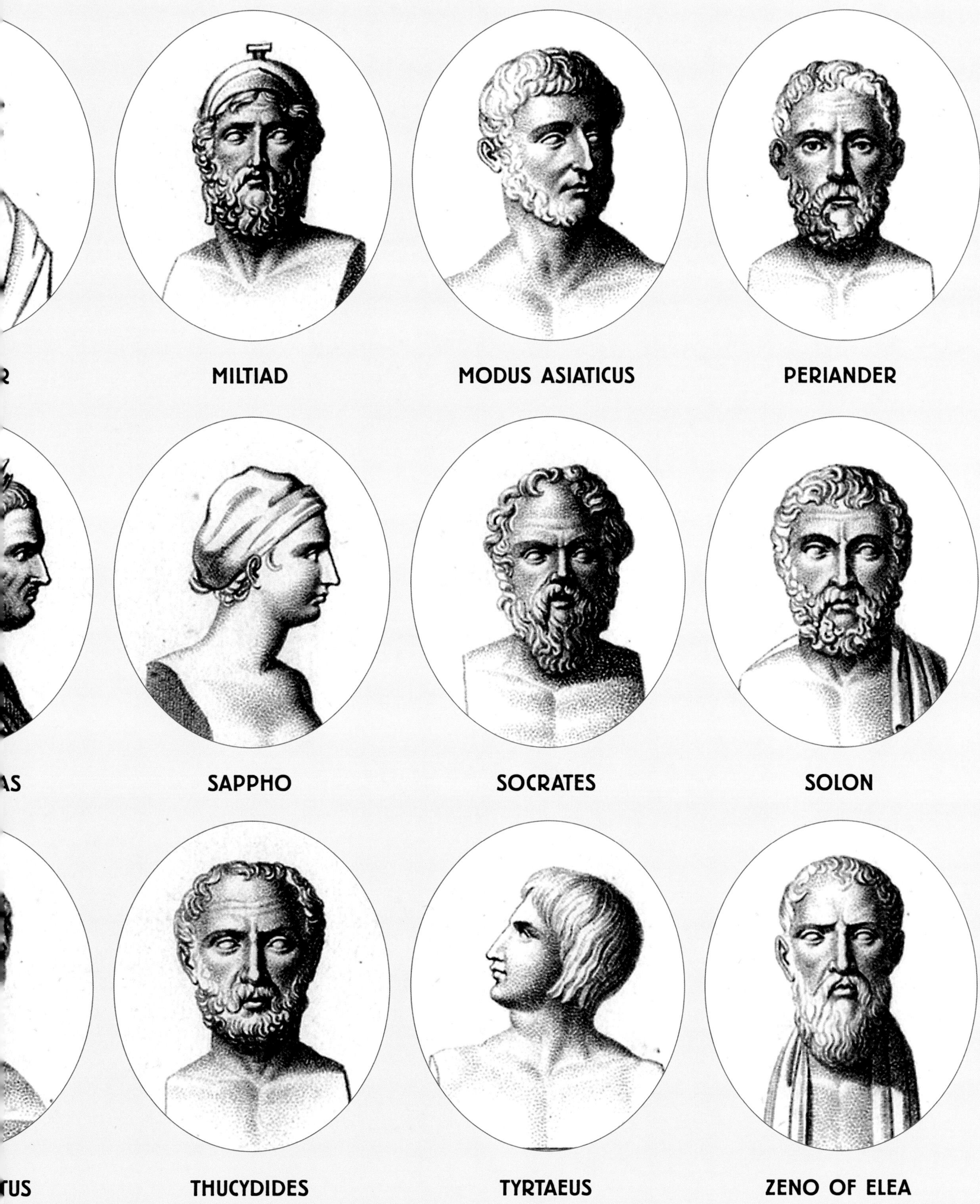
MILTIAD
MODUS ASIATICUS
PERIANDER
SAPPHO
SOCRATES
SOLON
THUCYDIDES
TYRTAEUS
ZENO OF ELEA

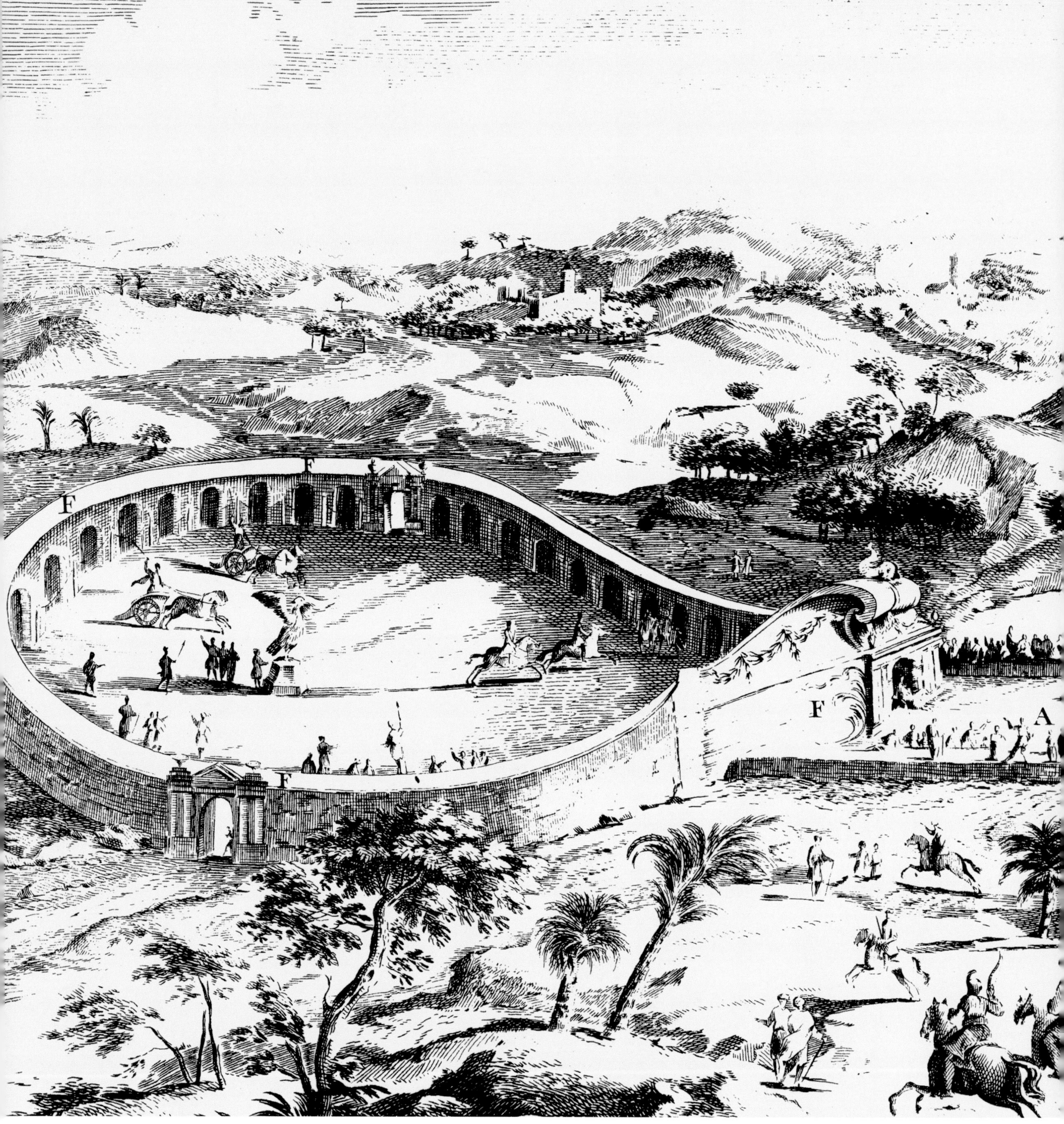

IN THE FOOTSTEPS OF PAUSANIAS

The rich stories which this 2nd century scholar has left us offer a striking picture of Ancient Greece. Many travelers have tried to follow in his footsteps as he journeyed throughout Greece and visit the sites and monuments he had described. But these have all either disappeared or are in ruins and we can only see them by an act of imagination. This plate is of a painting by Rigaud and was inspired by a new translation of Pausanias published in 1731. This is how the artist imagined the racecourse at Olympia.

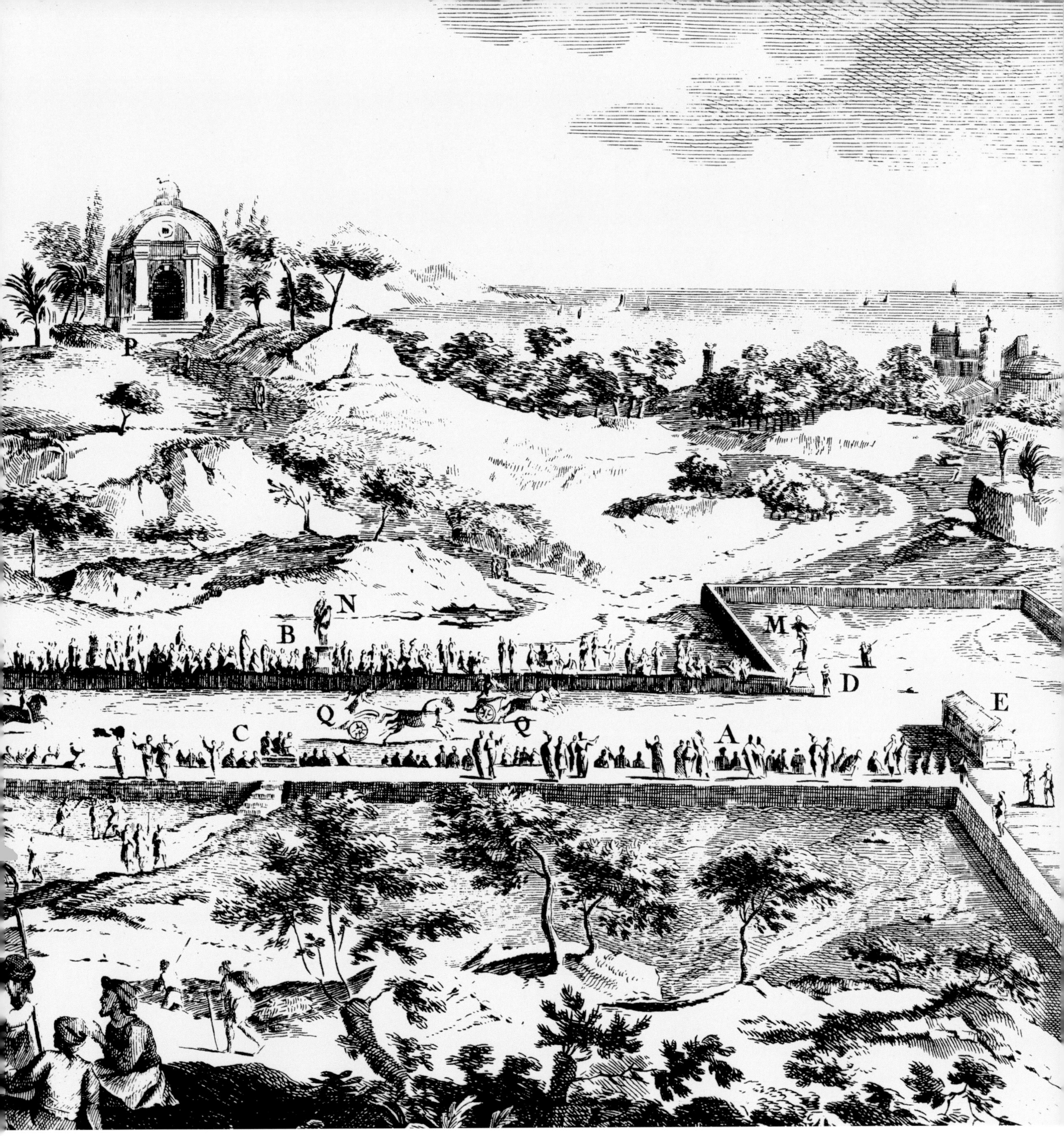

Note how he painted the door to the horses' stalls; see how he imagines its shape. Present-day reconstructions, suggest a flat and rectangular base; they show the stable compartments shaped like the prow of a ship jutting out into the stadium. The narrow door would seem to be incorrect. Coming out of their stalls one by one, starting with the furthest away and ending with the nearest, the chariots would all arrive at the starting line at the same time. The start was given by a device which caused a bronze eagle with outstretched wings to appear before the spectators sitting on the terraces beside the track. The chariots then made a circuit around the central wall of earth.

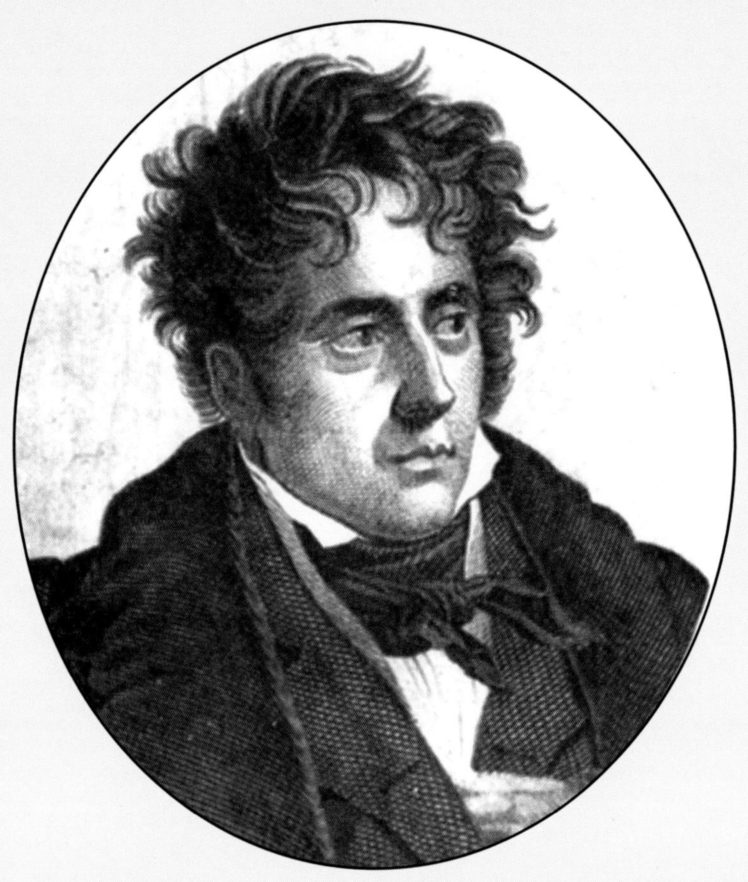

In 1805 the French writer René de Chateaubriand visited Greece as part of a journey to the sources of European civilization. Out of his notes and impressions grew the book A Journey from Paris to Jerusalem (1811). This work is one of many such volumes telling of travels in the east, and with this writer, it naturally sounded a romantic note. His book inspired many other young Romantics to set out for exotic places.

Like many of those who have traveled there in imagination, before ever setting foot on Greek soil, Chateaubriand was at first disappointed. In a letter from Constantinople, he wrote, "Never try to see Greece, except through the eyes of Homer. Trust nobody else." As an admirer of past greatness, he was dismayed by the ruins of a lost civilization, but also troubled, bitter and frustrated by the subjugation of the Greek people. Touched by events which would soon trouble the country he tried to draw international attention to the cause of Greek independence and denounced crimes committed by the Turks against Christians. He spoke in the Upper House of the French parliament demanding the intervention of the European powers in favor of a nation which was struggling to win its independence. He demonstrated his love of Greece and his belief in the greatness of the Greek nation in the 19th century by rewriting the prefaces to his books as they were re-issued; in the new prefaces he pleaded in favor of Greece.

CHATEAUBRIAND AND GREEK INDEPENDENCE

"Are the Greeks rebels? No. Are they a people we can negotiate with? Yes. Do they fulfill the social conditions required by law, in order to be recognized by other nations? Yes. Is it possible to help them without troubling the world, without being divided ourselves, without taking up arms, without endangering the existence of Turkey? Yes, and it could be done in three months, by a single demand made in the name of the major European powers, or by separate demands all making the same stipulation. This is the sort of diplomatic work that should be signed in blood..."

"Heroic Greece is rising from its ashes: to make sure she triumphs, we need nothing more that the benign approval of Christian princes... Let us, ordinary citizens as we are, redouble our efforts in favor of Greece; let us uphold her cause before the whole world; let us struggle for her, let us take into our homes her exiled children, as we have received hospitality amongst their ruins."

"When I was in Greece, she was sad, but peaceful; the silence of subjugation reigned over her ruined monuments; liberty had not yet sounded her call to new beginnings... How deplorable that I should think I was painting a picture of desolation as I described the ruins of Argos, Mycenae and Lacedemonia. But if one were to compare my tales to the ones coming out of Greece today, it would seem that I was traveling through a Greece of prosperity and splendor!" *A Journey from Paris to Jerusalem*

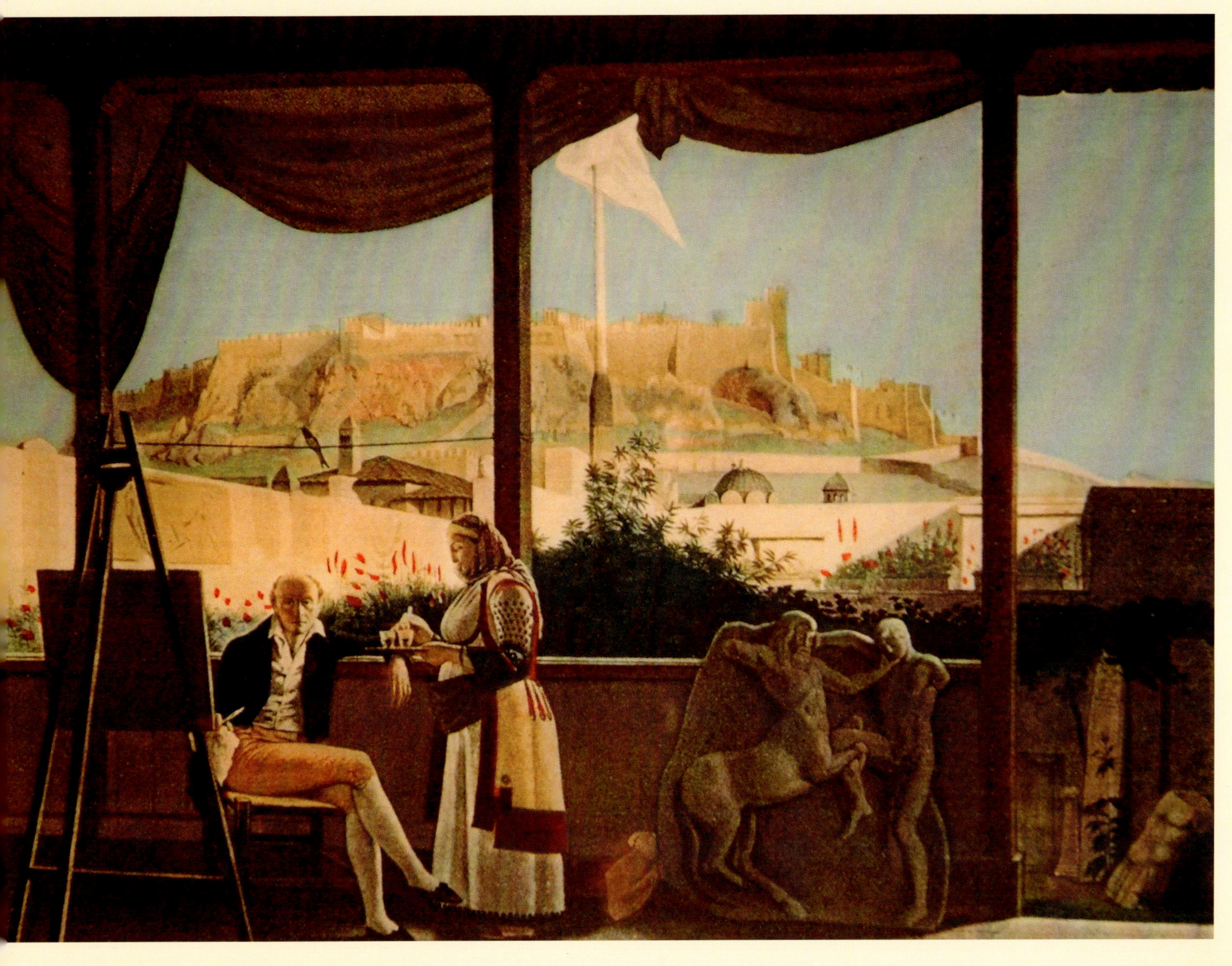

CONSUL FAUVEL

During his visit to Athens in 1806, Chateaubriand was put up by François Fauvel, the French consular official who had been living in the city for many years. He welcomed the writer to his magnificent residence which had an astounding view out over the Acropolis. During his stay the consul acted as Chateaubriand's guide to the city and to its ruins, and his guest appreciated his broad education and admired his talents both as artist and antiquary. Fauvel was an enthusiastic historian and made important contributions to many discoveries concerning the sites of Olympia and Marathon.

Lord Byron, who knew the consul well, recorded that they disagreed on the subject of Greek independence. Byron noted how the consul had lived in Greece, mainly in Athens, for over thirty years, praised his talent and his charisma, saying that all who met him were charmed by his manner. Byron alleged that Fauvel had stated in his hearing that the Greeks did not deserve independence, claiming that they were decadent people, both individually and collectively. But Byron believed this decadence could be reversed... but only in ways that Fauvel would not approve of.

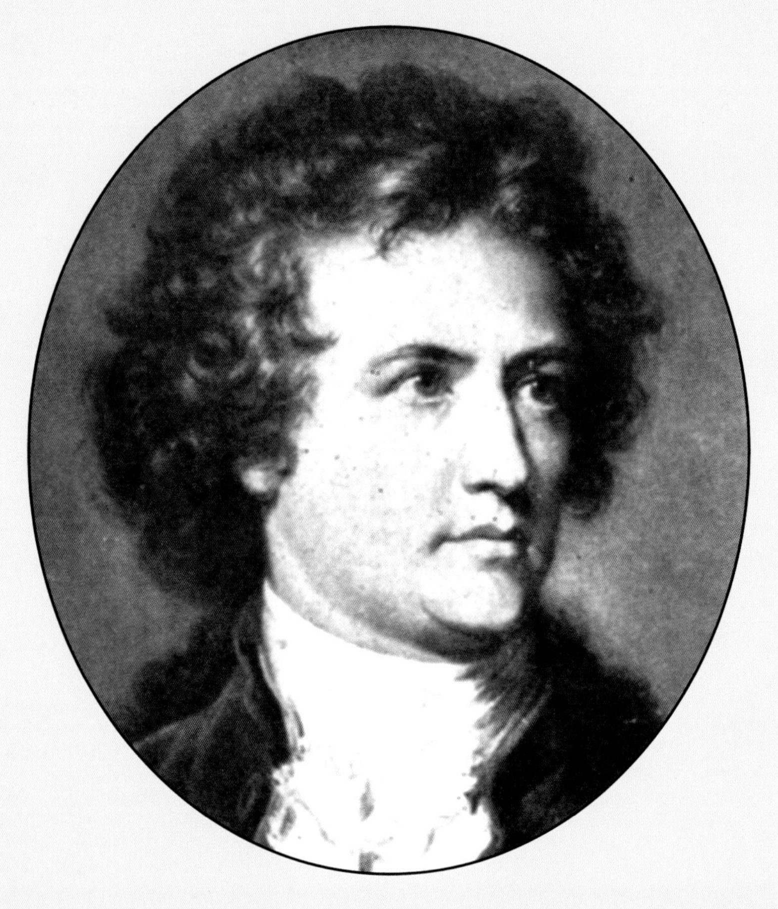

GOETHE AND THE WOMEN OF GREEK MYTHOLOGY

Goethe was the master of all forms of writing: novels, poetry, theater, short stories, journalism and scientific articles.

His education had made him a model of the perfectly rounded gentleman: a Renaissance ideal. He had mastered the ancient languages: Latin, Greek and Hebrew.

He had had a thorough grounding in Homer and the Greek tragic writers; he had absorbed classical influences before brilliantly re-using them. In 1786 he set out on his travels, visiting Sicily with the *Odyssey* in his hand. He stayed in Rome for almost a year and made a verse translation of Iphigenia at Tauris.

In 1798 he decided to write a long poem on Achilles, seeking to supply the missing link between the *Iliad* and the *Odyssey*. He next invested in two magazines, one devoted to archaeology and another to the Arts and antiquity. He finished a second version of the Faust legend, for which he resurrected the beautiful Helen of Troy. She became for him the inspiration for all his thoughts on the subject of classical antiquity. The poet pondered the idea of mythological woman.

Helen is no longer held in time, but becomes the principle of the eternal feminine: an inspiration and ageless muse come from classical Greece, who crosses all ages and thrives as each artist gives her free rein. Goethe makes her the wife of Faust. The fruit of this union of Greek beauty and German intelligence is Euphorion. This allegorical figure personifies romantic poetry and Goethe has given him the handsome qualities of Lord Byron.

HELEN OF TROY

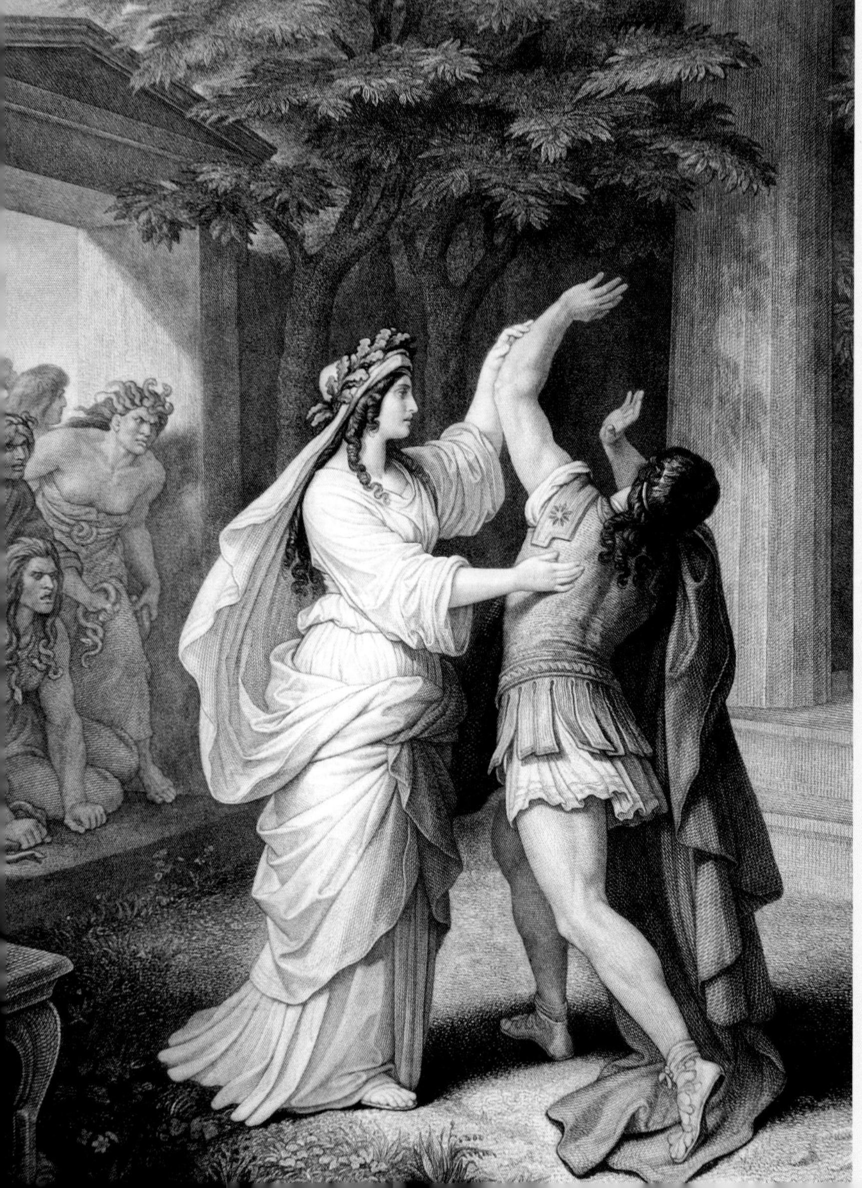

IPHIGENIA AT TAURIS

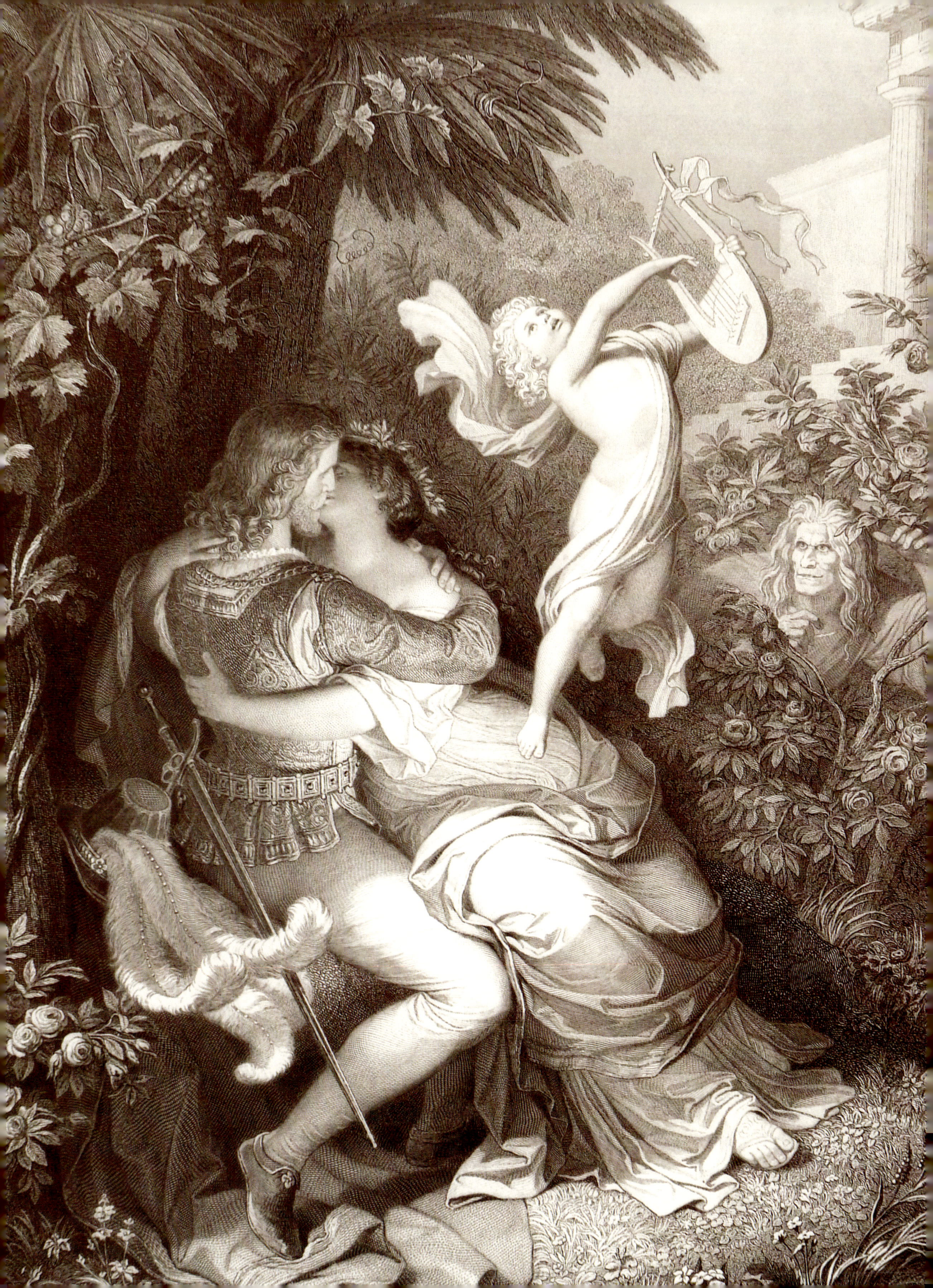

LORD BYRON AND ROMANTIC GREECE

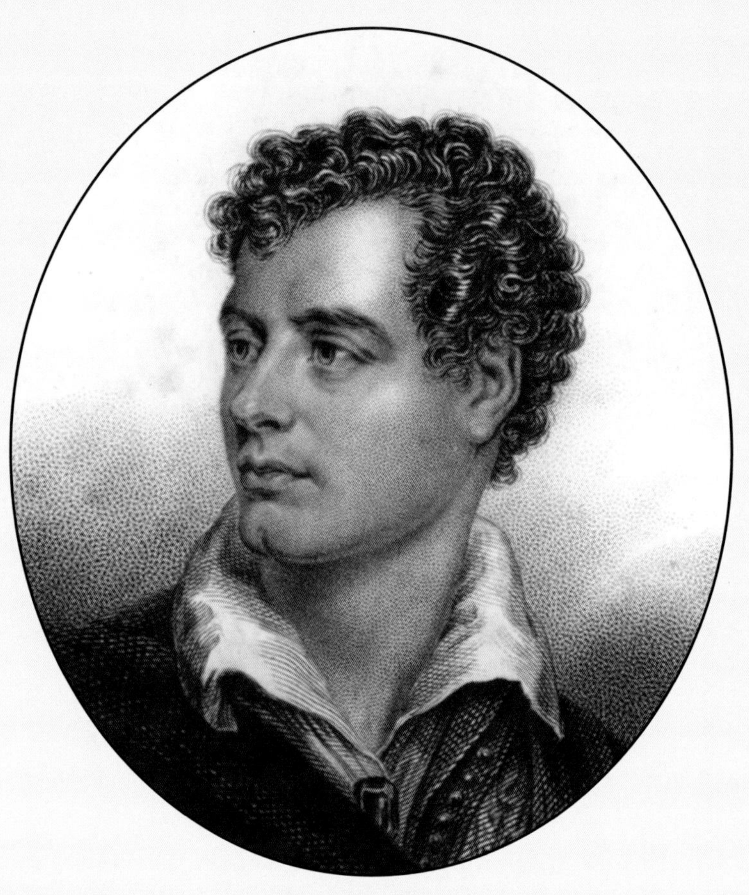

The handsome English poet (1788-1824) was fascinated by the East, and between 1810 and 1812, traveled in Portugal, Spain, Greece and Turkey. He stayed a while in Athens in 1811, living in a Franciscan convent and left a sign of his visit, his signature carved into the marble of the Temple of Poseidon on Cape Sounion.

Nevertheless he raged against those who did not respect such places which had already been so sacrilegiously abused! He condemned Lord Elgin's plundering and campaigned for the return of the Parthenon friezes to Athens. Once back in London, Lord Byron started writing Childe Harold's Pilgrimage, which gave his impressions of his journey and which guaranteed his success: he had become one of the leading writers of the Romantic Movement.

The poet was dismayed by the subjection of Greece, but was enthusiastic about the landscape, the monuments and the people. In spite of the Turkish yoke he recognized the Greek yearning for independence and their pride in their nation. Even though their detractors only perceived in them a slave mentality, a mere shadow of their glorious ancestors, the Greeks rebelled against the Turks in 1821, proving Byron right. Byron soon matched forceful words with deeds and joined the freedom struggle. As head of the Greek armed forces he tried to unite different factions, but died of a fever, on the 19th April at Missolonghi.

"Yet are thy skies as blue, thy crags as wild;
Sweet are thy groves, and verdant are thy fields,
Thine olive ripe as when Minerva smiled,
And still his honeyed wealth Hymettus yields...
Yet to the remnant of thy splendid past
Shall pilgrims, pensive, but unwearied, throng;
Long shall the voyager, with th' Ionian blast,
Hail the bright clime of battle and of song...
But, midst the throng in merry masquerade,
Lurk there no hearts that throb with secret pain,
Even through the closest searment half betrayed?
To such the gentle murmurs of the main
Seem to re-echo all they mourn in vain...
And long to change the robe of revel for the shroud!
(*Childe Harold's Pilgrimage*)

Byron sensed that the Greeks had never lost the hope of being freed, that they would welcome whoever came to them with an army and that, when the day of vengeance arrived, the Ottoman could hope only for the mercy of heaven.

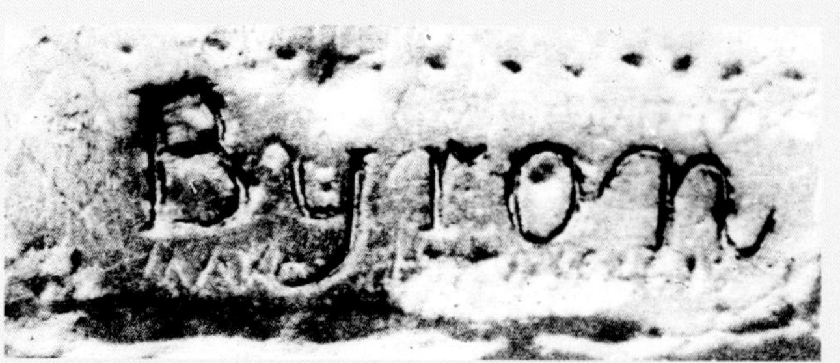

BYRON'S SIGNATURE AT SOUNION

THERESA MACRI

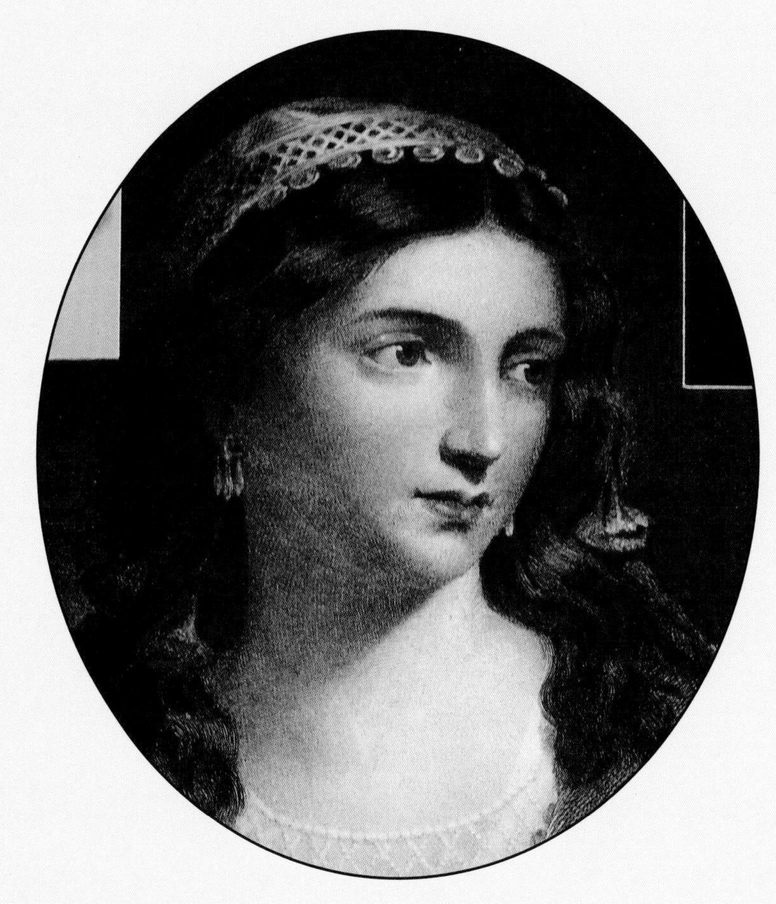

When in Athens Lord Byron stayed with Mrs Tarsia Macri, the widow of the English consul. He admired her three beautiful daughters, whom he called the three Graces. He was particularly attracted to Theresa, who was just fifteen, appears to have been in love with her, and it is agreed that the relationship was a chaste and tender one. He dedicated a poem about a child of Athens to her. His memory of this young girl recalls the story of the virgin of Athens.

THE FRANCISCAN CONVENT IN ATHENS

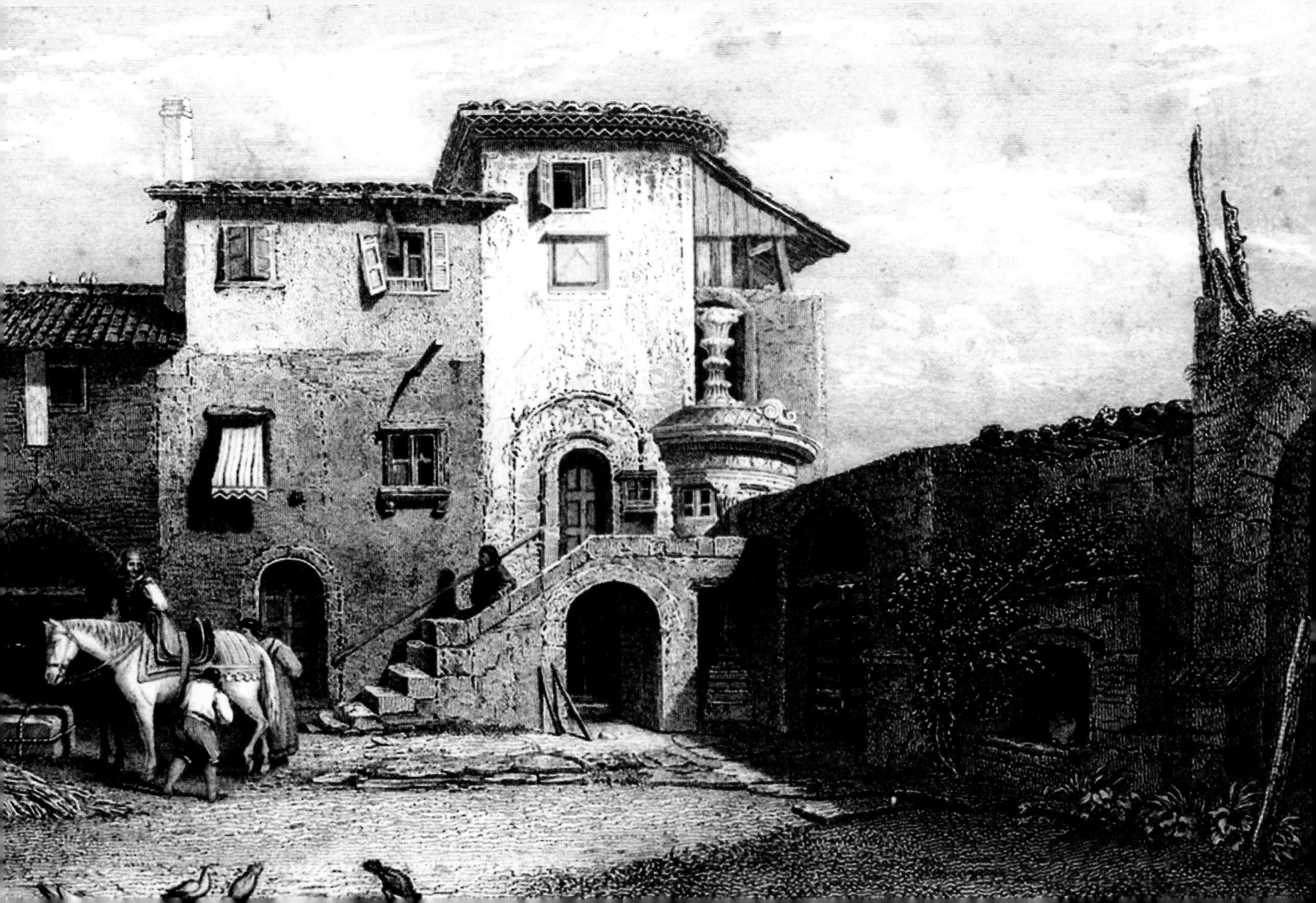

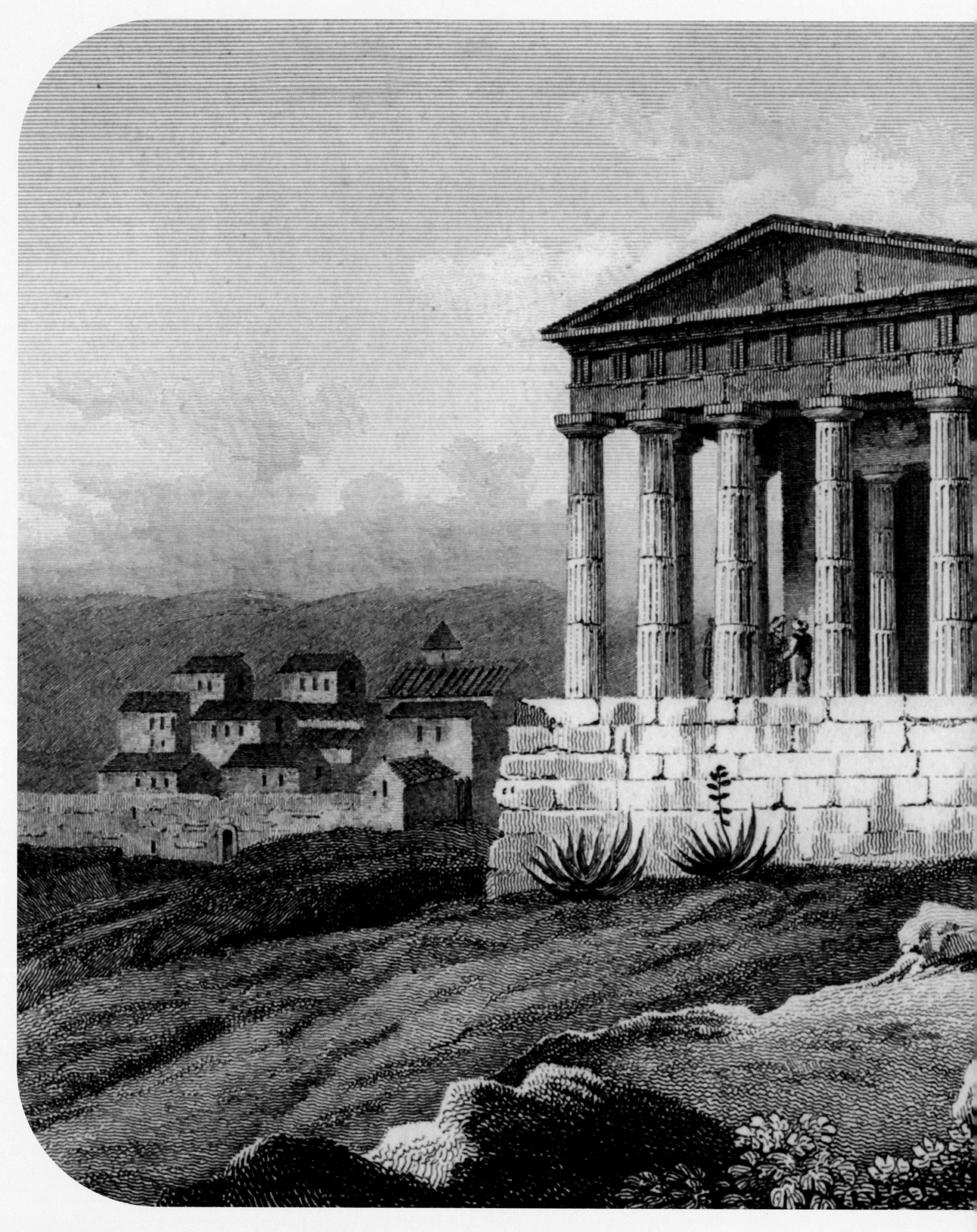

ATHENS: THE TEMPLE DEDICATED TO THESEUS

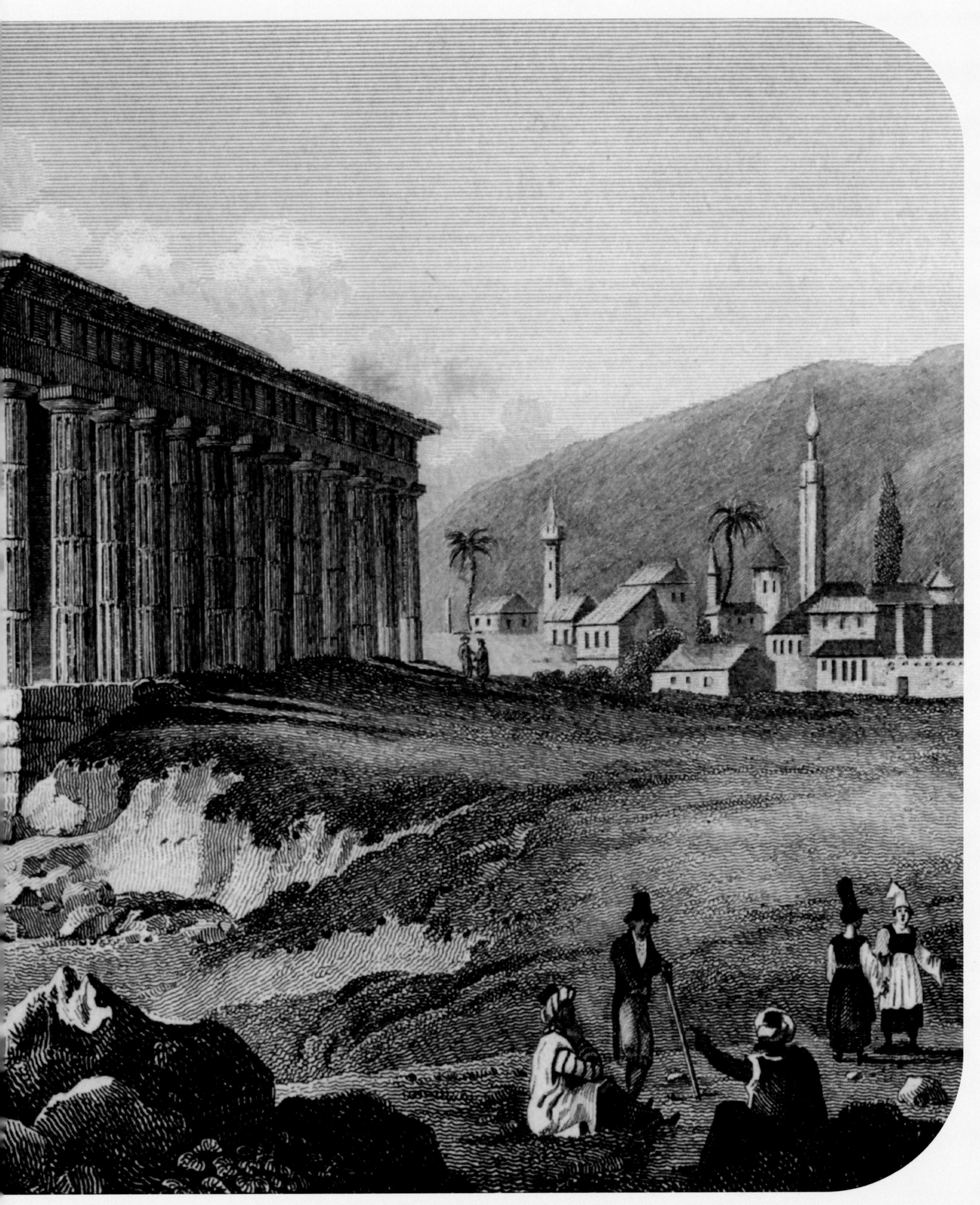

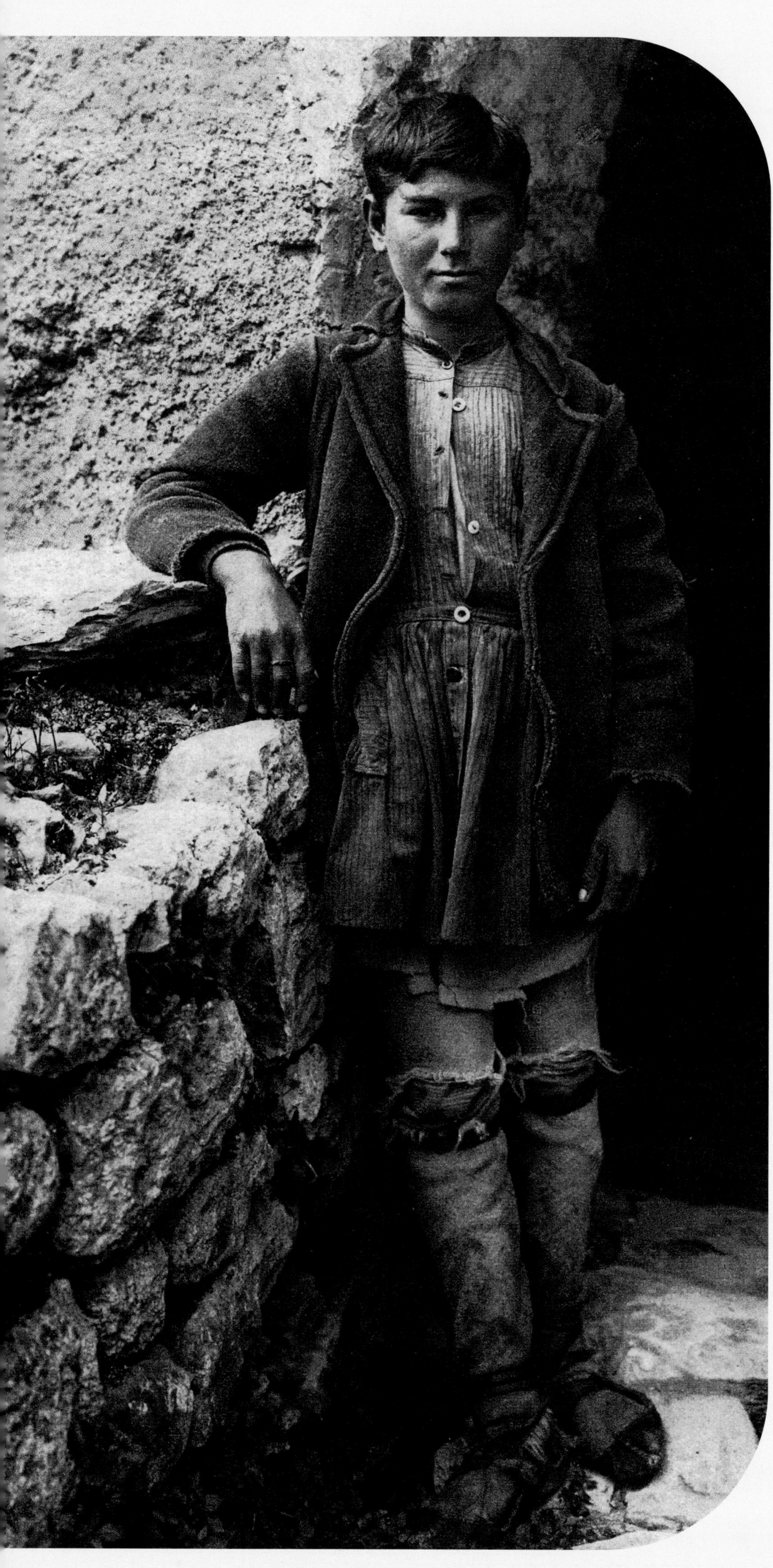

EARLY PHOTOGRAPHS OF GREECE

YOUNG GREEK SHEPHERD

THE STADIUM AT DELPHI
FACING PAGE: TOP

METEORS
THE VILLAGE OF KASTRAKI
FACING PAGE: BOTTOM

TRADITIONAL COSTUMES
FOLLOWING PAGES

TRADITIONAL DANCERS
PAGES 36-37

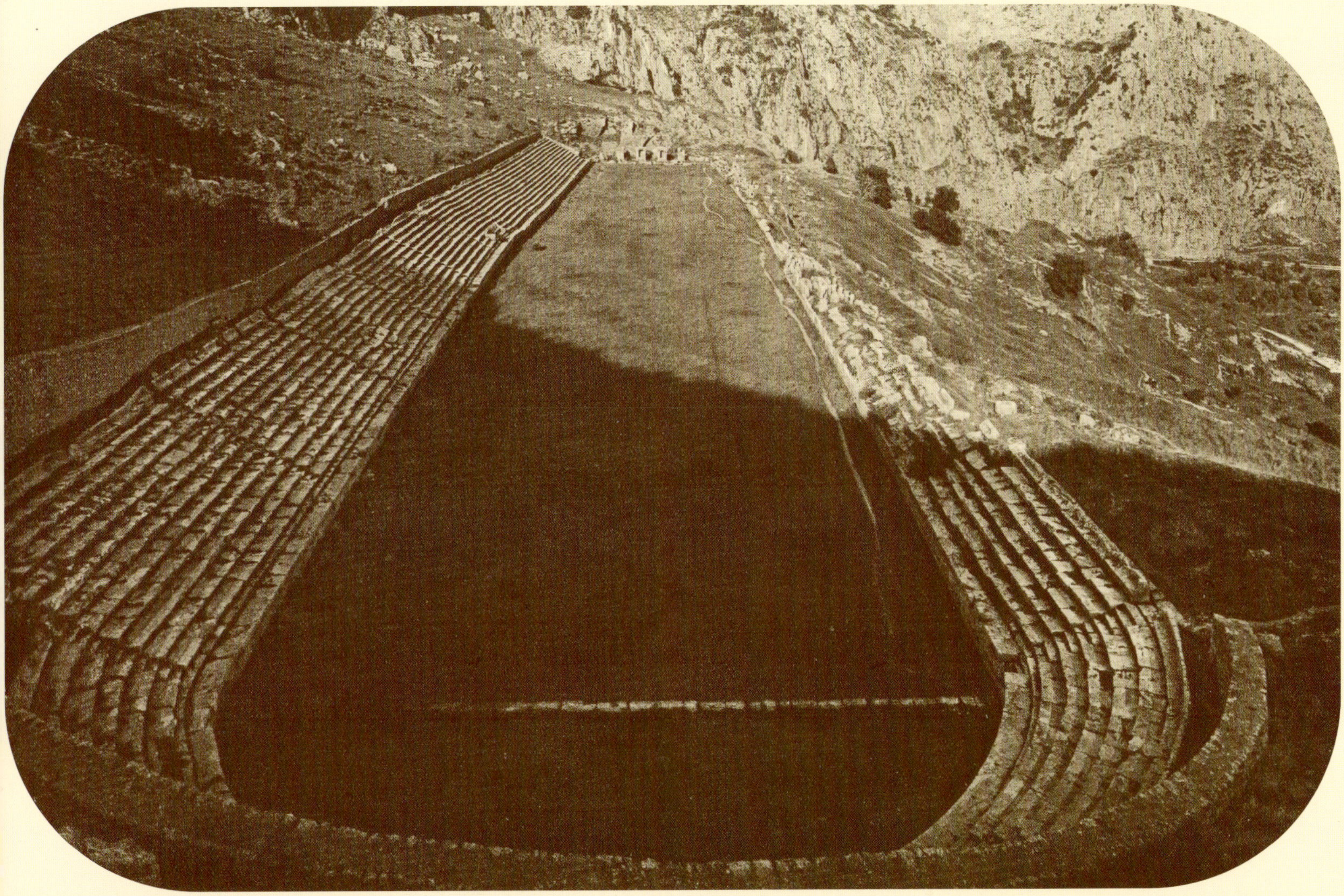

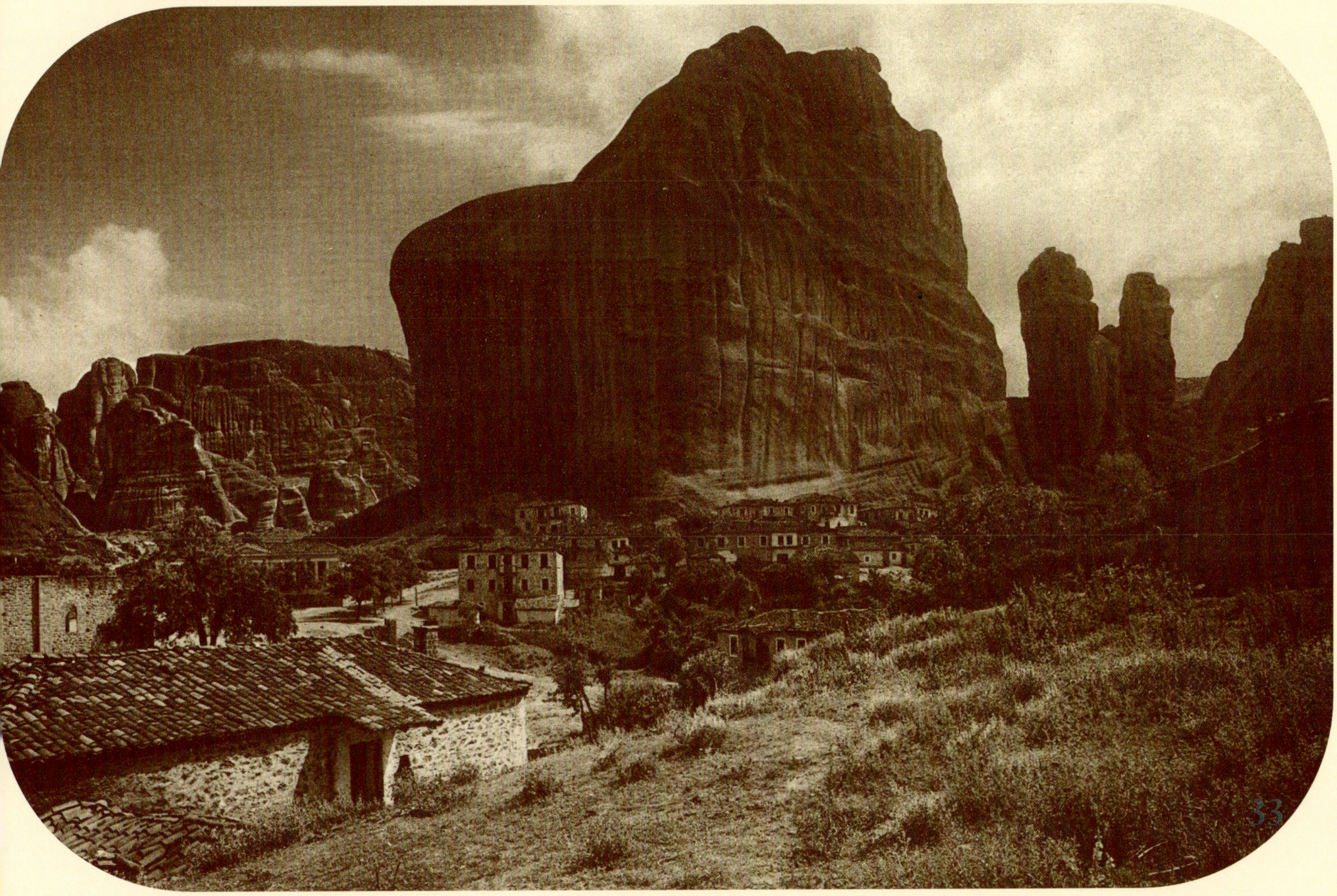

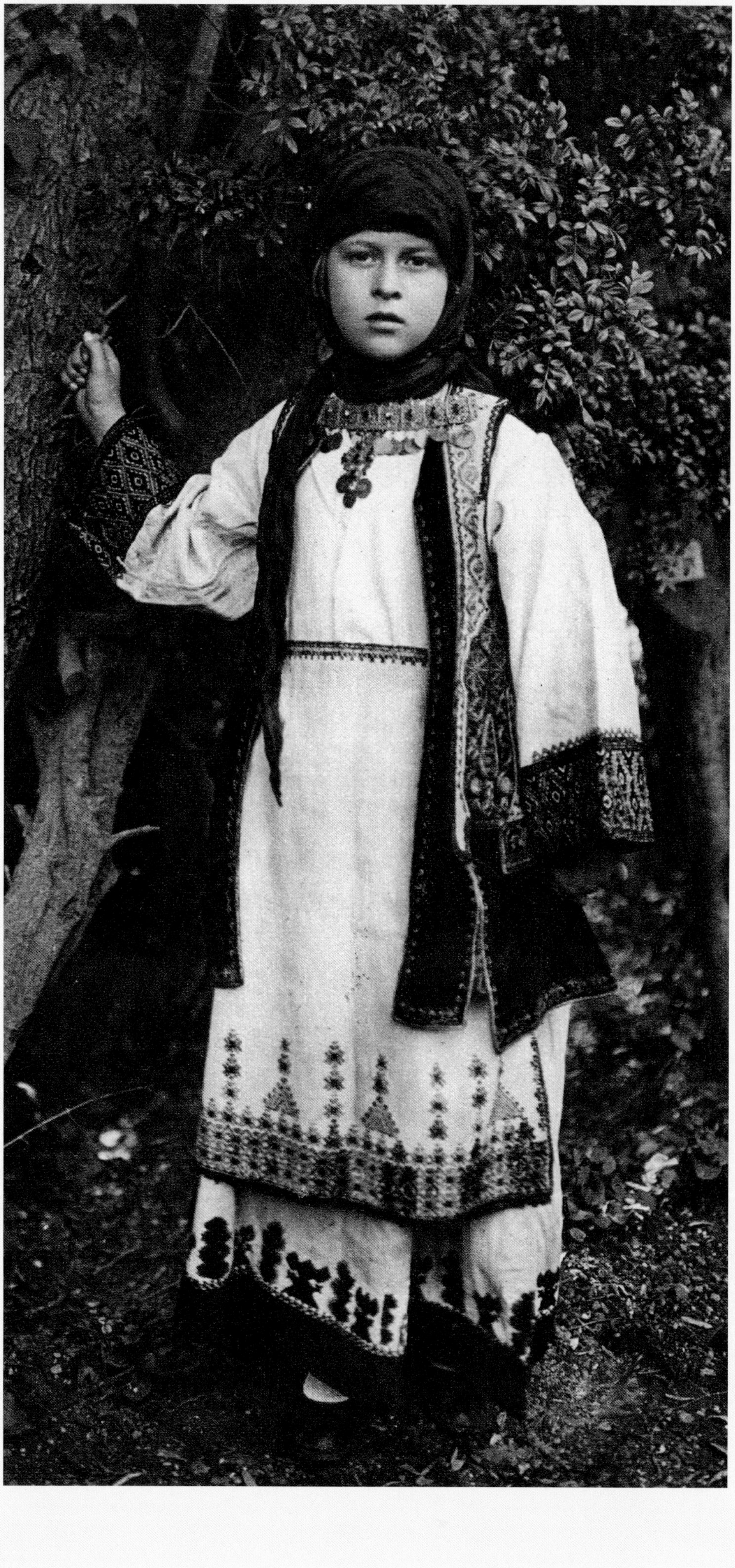

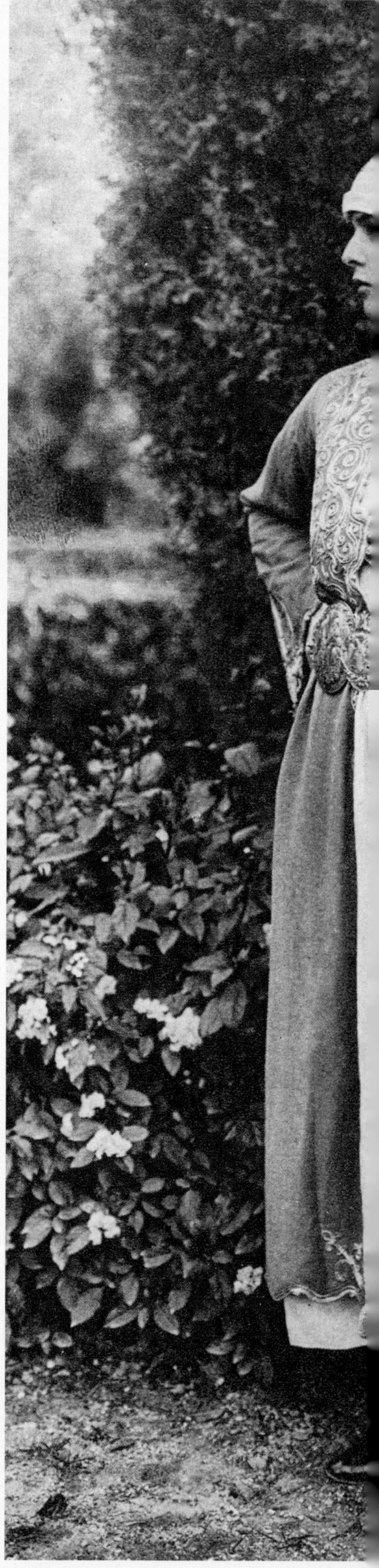

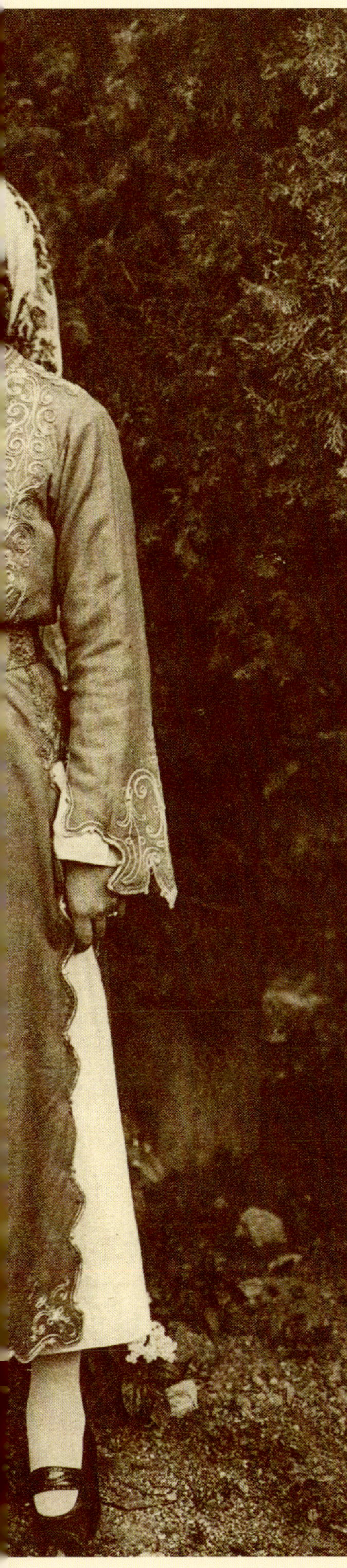

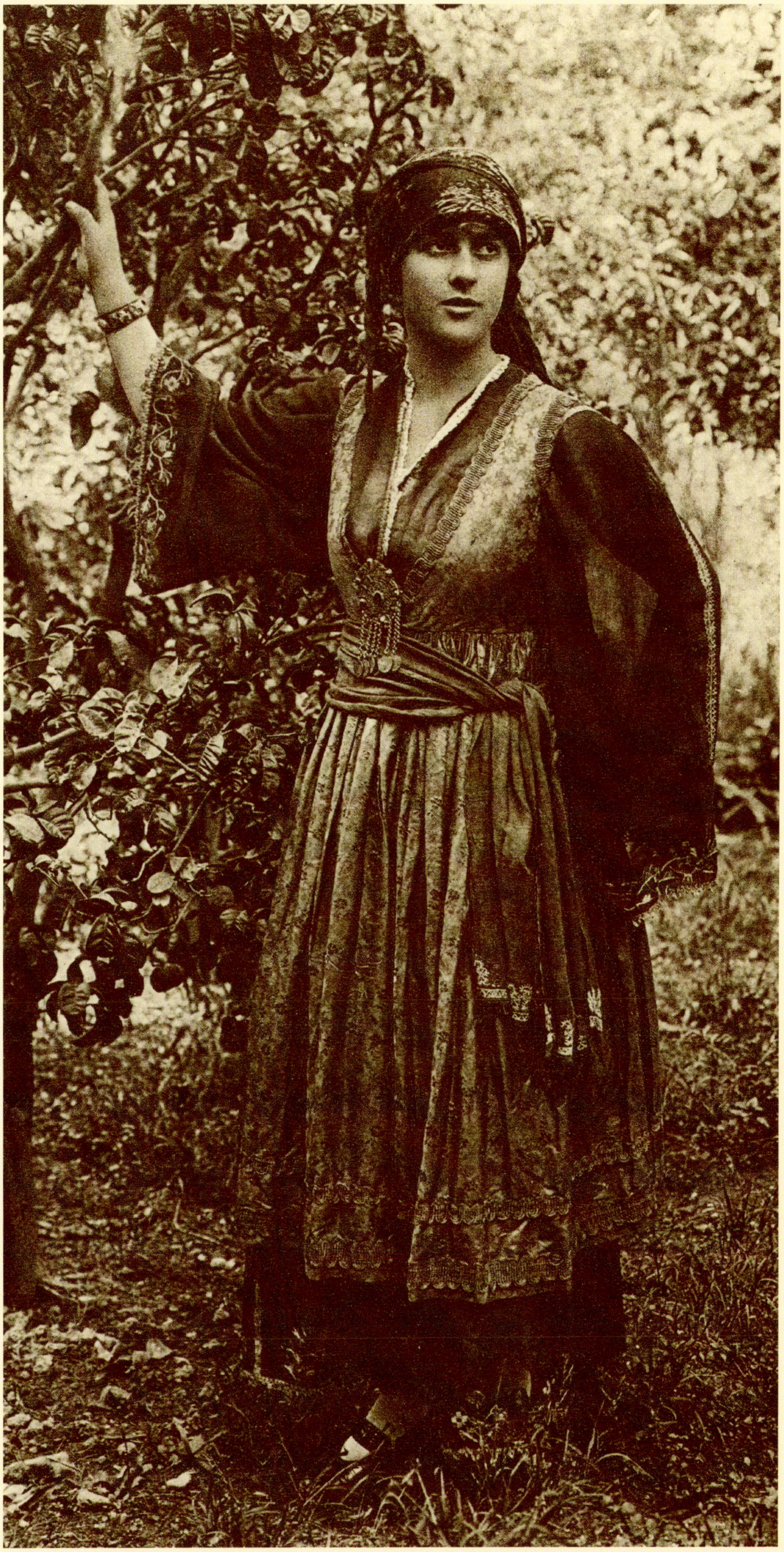

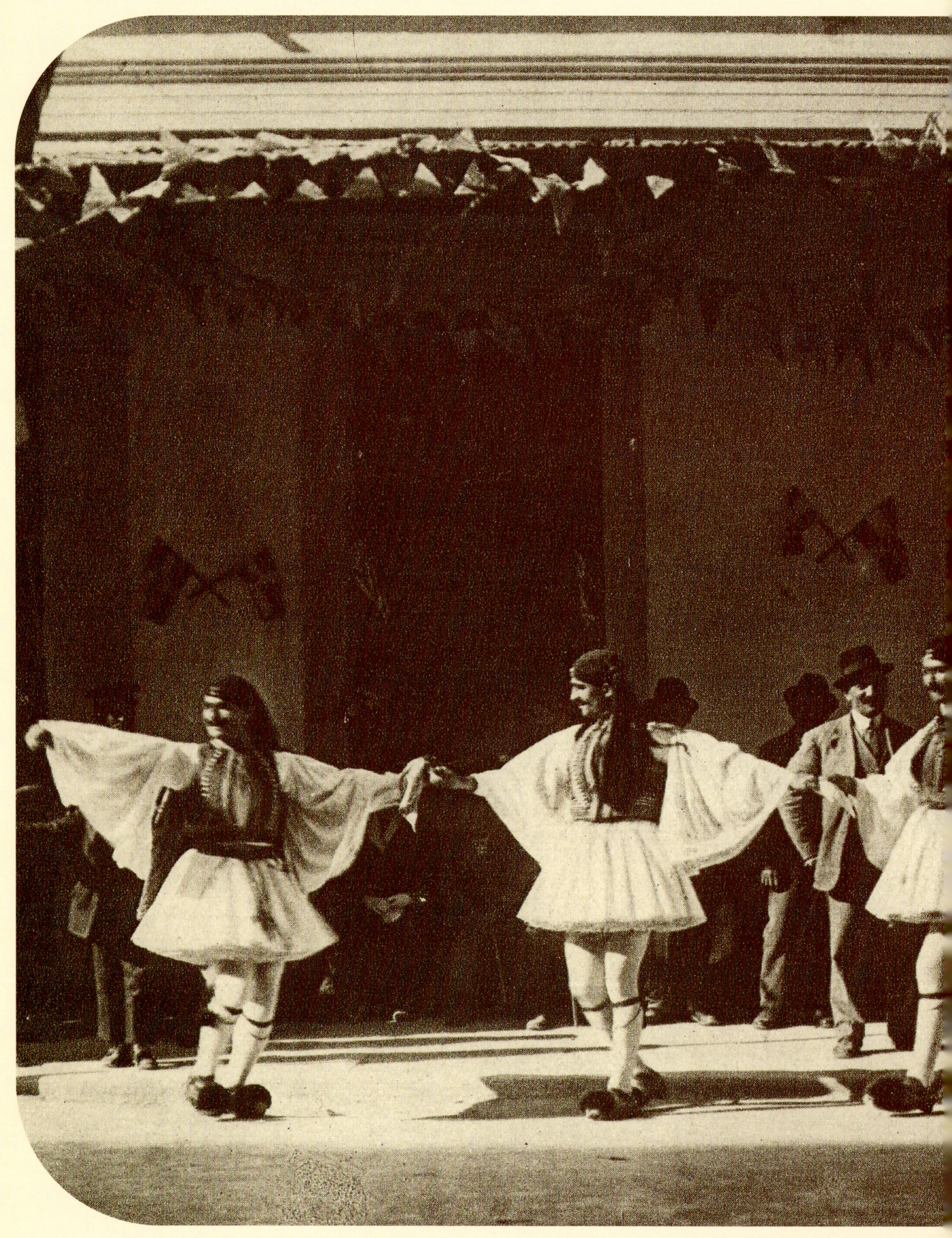

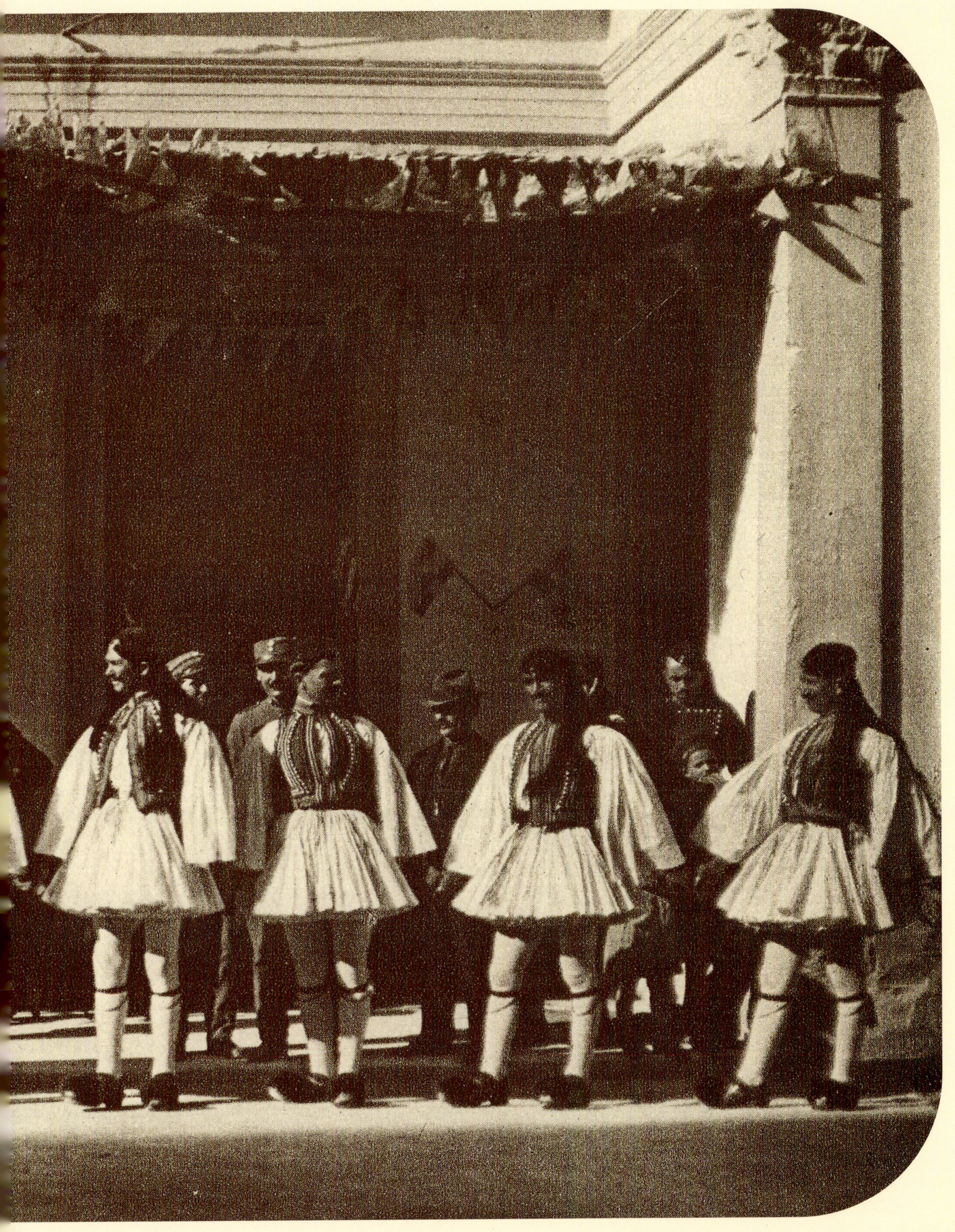

THE GODS HAVE DECIDED TO DWELL IN GREECE

The Greeks imagined gods dwelling on the snow-covered summit of Mount Olympus, which rises to 9554 feet on the borders of Thessaly and Macedonia. Only a huge mountain like Mount Olympus could contain such giants. However Zeus, the king of the gods, can make the very foundations of that great mountain tremble, such is his power! The clouds that always hide the summits of the highest peak in Greece from human eyes also hide a huge fortress and its majestic gates. These gates open to reveal imposing architecture, designed by the ingenious Hephaestus, the blacksmith god. Sheltered behind this wall, the palace of Zeus is set upon the highest peak. Its walls and pillars are made of gold and bronze, as are its furnishings. The luxurious palaces of his subject gods are built on lesser mountain crests. Up there an amphitheater of huge rocky peaks form the natural thrones of the gods. From these heights the gods look down on the world. Zeus is often alone on the highest peak as he meditates haughtily and in silence. But the Immortals often gather to feast in the golden palace of the king of the skies; they consult together and deliver judgment. The gods experience the full range of human emotions, often in exaggerated form as befits their extraordinary status.

Thus the squabbles of the royal couple Zeus and Hera were legendary and rocked heaven to its very foundations. At the center of this disorderly family, the king of the gods keeps order with an iron grip: he restrains the ambitions of some, the ill will and jealousies of others; he fights off the plots of his peers who are trying to depose him and uses his thunderbolt to punish them. Hera, who has intrigued against her husband, suffers the humiliating punishment of being chained to the sky by the wrists and weighed down by two anvils fastened to her ankles. Hephaestus, the blacksmith god, knows how dangerous it is to resist the master of Mount Olympus. So he advises Hera to submit: "Face the ordeal, Mother; put up with it, whatever it costs. May my eyes never see you, whom I love, suffer savage beatings!" (The *Iliad*)

During banquets, Hephaestus, who is peace-loving and given to pleasure, strives to preserve harmony and good will amongst the gods. Seated at golden tables in the palace of Zeus the gods of the Greek pantheon enjoy the most appetizing dishes, nectar and ambrosia. In welcoming the young Dionysus, for whom Hestia discreetly steps aside, the Immortals discover wine that gladdens their hearts. They enjoy the singing of the Muses and the beautiful music that Apollo draws from his lyre. They are amused by the gaiety and barbed wit of mischievous Hermes.

Athena, Zeus' favorite daughter, sits on his right hand, grave and reserved. Well away from the goddess of reason and intelligence, Ares is brooding. The god of war resents his father's warm and exclusive love for her. He too would like to use the aegis, the terrifying weapon that Zeus only lends, as a wonderful privilege, to Athena. He sits, envious and aggrieved, next to Aphrodite, the only member of the divine family who does not despise him. The beautiful goddess of love is flirting with her lover, ignoring Hephaestus, her lame and ugly husband.

Artemis, the patron of the hunt, Demeter, the goddess of the harvests and Poseidon, the sea-god, are also present at the banquet.

Hades, the lord of the Underworld, is the only god not present at the feast. He never leaves Hell. Access to his kingdom is by the cavern of Acherusia in Epirus, an impressive opening in the ground, and by the river Acheron that disappears underground in Thesprotia. Hell is the kingdom of Hades, the Sky is under the rule of Zeus and the Seas are the place where Poseidon reigns; that leaves the Earth to be carved up and struggled over by all the gods. Legends tell how the Immortals fought over little bits of it: pride and greed forcing them into conflict. Soon every city, region or island in Greece would be known for the special veneration accorded to a member of the pantheon. In return the gods spoke on their behalf and protected them.

Athena and Poseidon strove for mastery of Attica: Athena promised them the olive tree, the symbol of abundance and nourishment; the god of the sea offered nothing better than a spring of salty water, from which no one could drink. The choice was easy and the goddess became the patron of the city of Athens, which received her name.

Poseidon was truly unlucky in his quarrels. He also lost the island of Aegina to Zeus, that of Naxos to Dionysus and the region of Argolis to Hera. He is furious with his colleagues, feeling victimized by their plotting; when he appeals to their judgment they never decide in his favor. He is in dispute with Helios over Corinth, but is only given the isthmus; the sun god gets the Acropolis. The inhabitants of the isthmus console the sea god by instituting, not far from the city, in his sacred wood, and in his honor, the pan Hellenic games.

Helios is in love with a daughter of Poseidon, named Rhodes and marries her on the island that bears her name. He is the father of the local population and founded its maritime and commercial prosperity; it is now called the Island of the Sun.

Every plot of this sacred land has fired the fertile imagination of its inhabitants and of its poets, and received the mark of its gods. The interests and concerns of the Immortals combine to link each one of them with some region.

Hephaestus is particularly fond of the island of Lemnos since he landed there and was cared for by the inhabitants, having been flung out off Olympus by his mother Hera. Ares was judged on a hill in Athens and gave his name to the Areopagus. The citizens set up a special court there to hear criminal cases. Aphrodite had scarcely been born from the foam when she came ashore on the island of Cythera, now known as the island of Love. Delphi became sacred to Apollo, who was born nearby.

Arcadia, which is rich in legends, honors Zeus on Mount Lycaeus and they still point out, on Mount Cyllene, the cave where Hermes was born. The region has many memories of both Artemis, the goddess of the hunt, and of Pan who loved to roam its wild and mountainous countryside.

At Delphi you may see the stone that Rhea gave Cronos, her husband, to swallow instead of her newly-born Zeus. Having been saved, the latter soon overthrew his father. On Mount Ida the Cretans show you the place where Zeus was born and also his tomb. This gave rise to the belief that all Cretans are liars; for, according to the Greeks, Zeus is immortal.

The dancing and singing of the Muses haunt the woods of Mount Helicon in Boeotia; there many offerings in their honor have been discovered in the valley and in the forest. Here Hesiod received from them the gift of poetry, while tending his sheep in that sacred place.

Every single valley, rock, spring, river or clump of trees tells the story of some adventure or visit by a god…

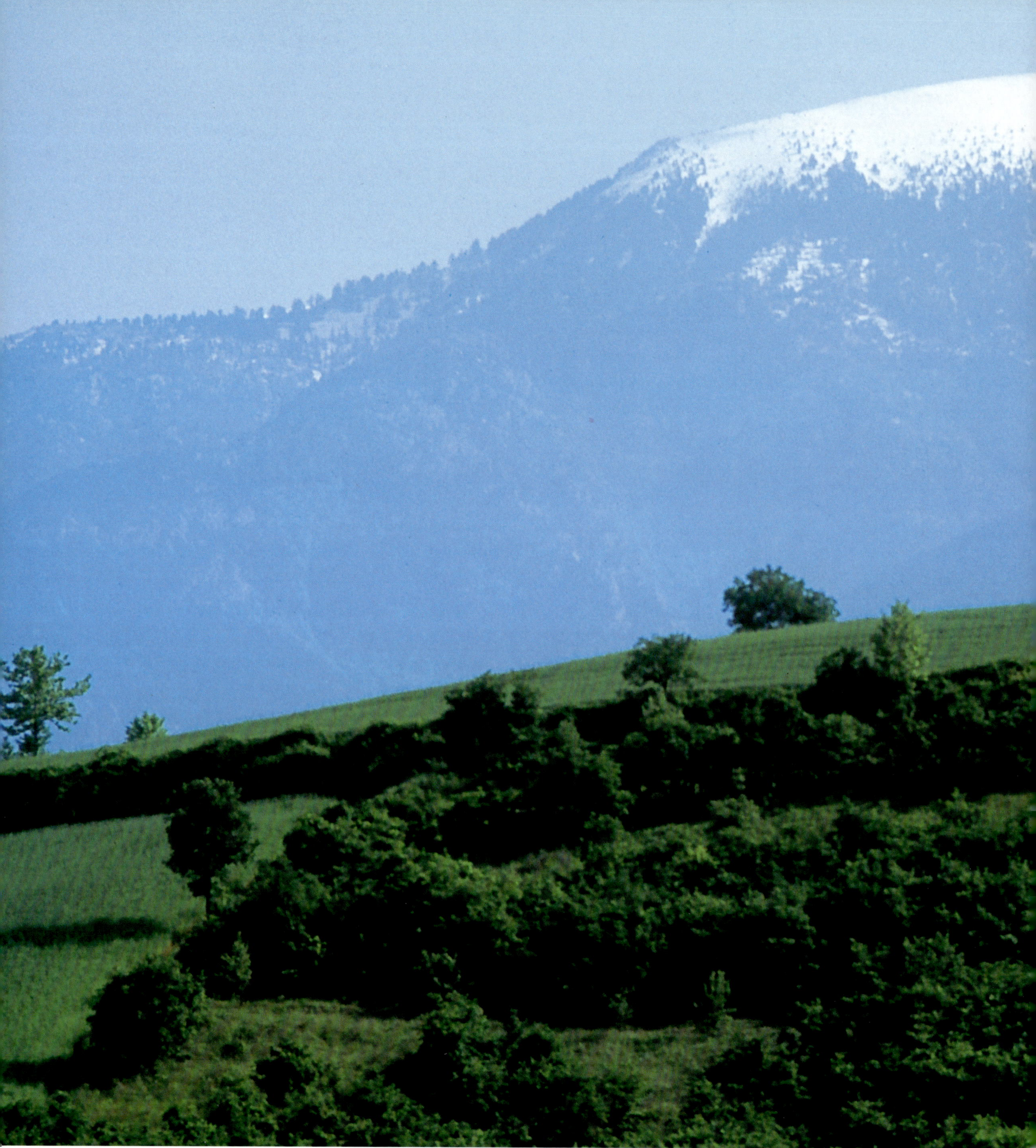

MOUNT OLYMPUS

The highest peak in Greece is 9674 feet high and most impressive! It is part of a mountain range of the same name which forms the border between Thessaly and Macedonia, along the coast of the Aegean Sea. Its huge, imposing mass with steep and dizzying precipices forms a harsh and wild landscape. Above the tree line there is bare rock and more or less permanent snow.

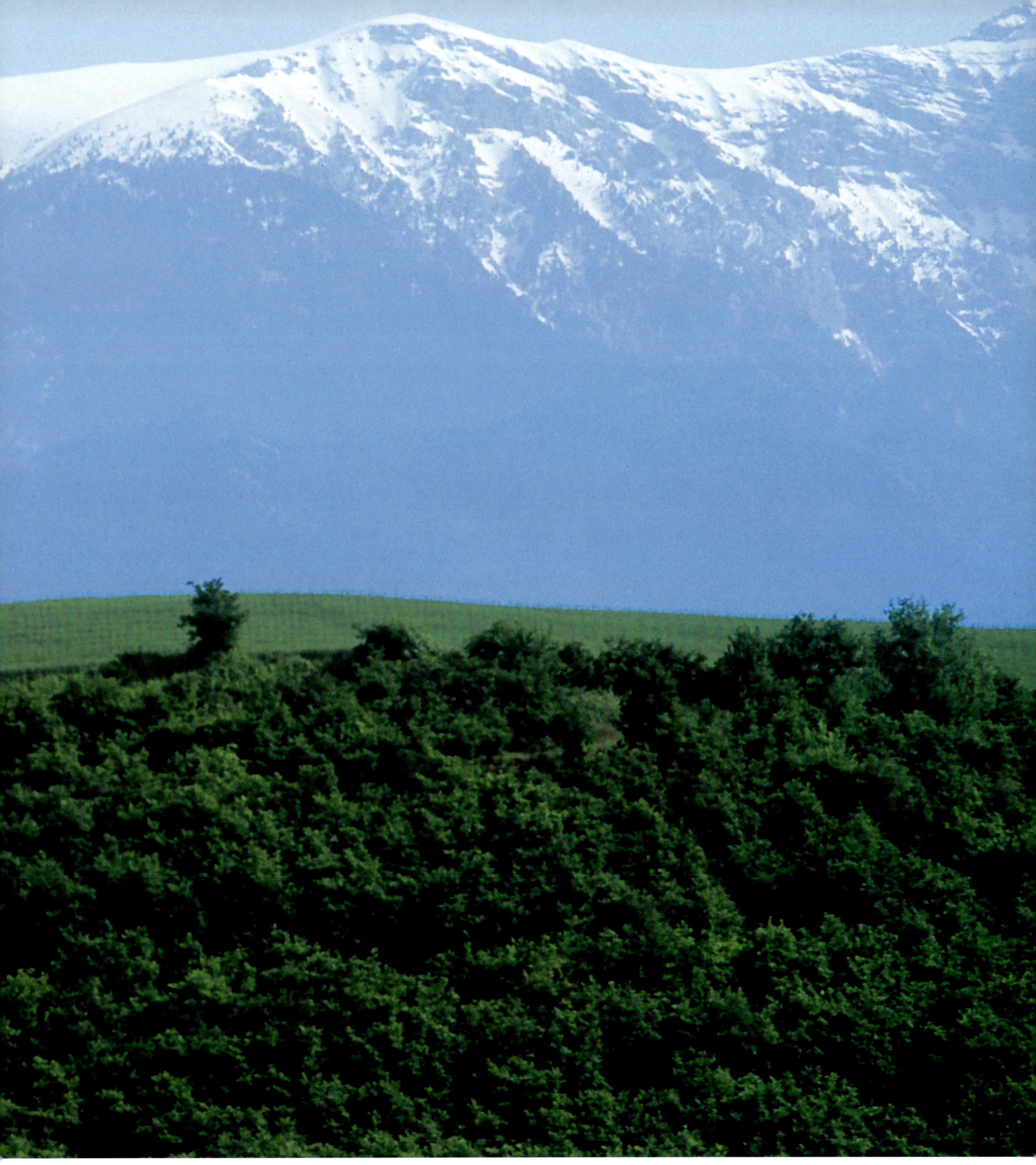

The Ancients imagined this inaccessible summit as the abode of the gods, protected from human gaze by persistent cloud. Olympus is both a real geographical site and a symbol of the heavens over which Zeus reigns; for he has chosen the highest spheres as his dwelling, the upper limits of the sky where shines the Ether, the purest, clearest and most incorruptible of light. No one doubts that above those clouds, the sun, reflecting off the snows of Mount Olympus, offers a most dazzling light.

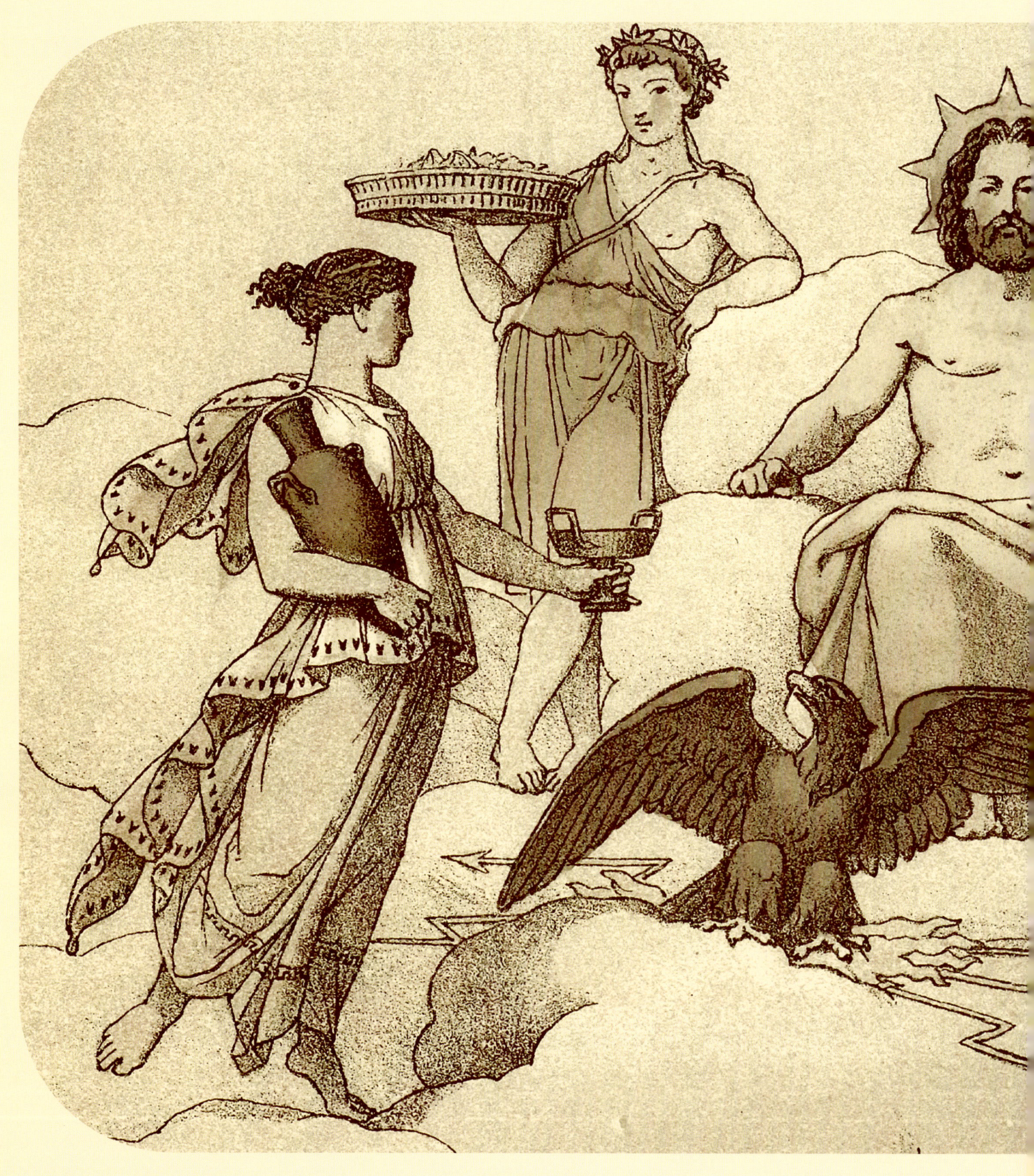

THE BURDEN OF POWER

On top of Mount Olympus, Zeus sits enthroned with his wife Hera. Zeus has surrounded himself with trusted, faithful and devoted servants who carry out his orders as king of the gods. Hermes and Iris, winged, swift and zealous messengers, hover about the royal couple. They deliver the divine orders and carry out the most delicate tasks. Zeus particularly depends on his son Hermes, who must defend his father from the machinations and fickle moods of Hera; she is, after all, more

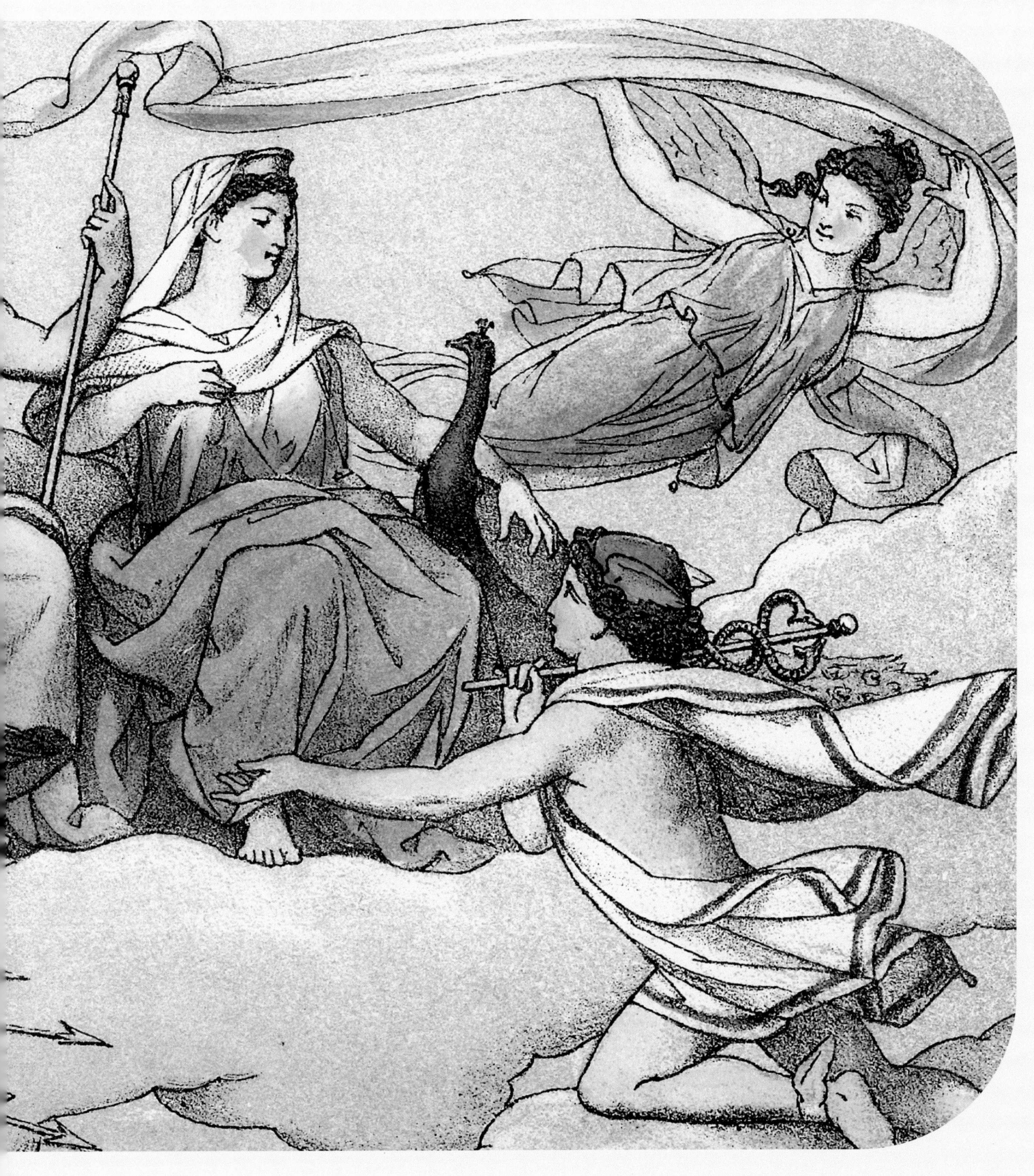

inclined to question his authority than to support it. He is thus the go-between, particularly in his father's love-life. So this cunning mediator negotiates with the Sun, the Moon and Sleep, ensuring that Hera will not wake up, thus guaranteeing Zeus an extremely long night of love with Alcmene. Ganymede stands at the right hand of Zeus. The king of the gods loved this young man and made him the cupbearer of Mount Olympus; he pours nectar into his lover's cup who thus keeps him by his side for ever. Ganymede has taken over this job from Hebe, who stands nearby. This obliging daughter of Zeus and Hera is responsible for the management of the palace.

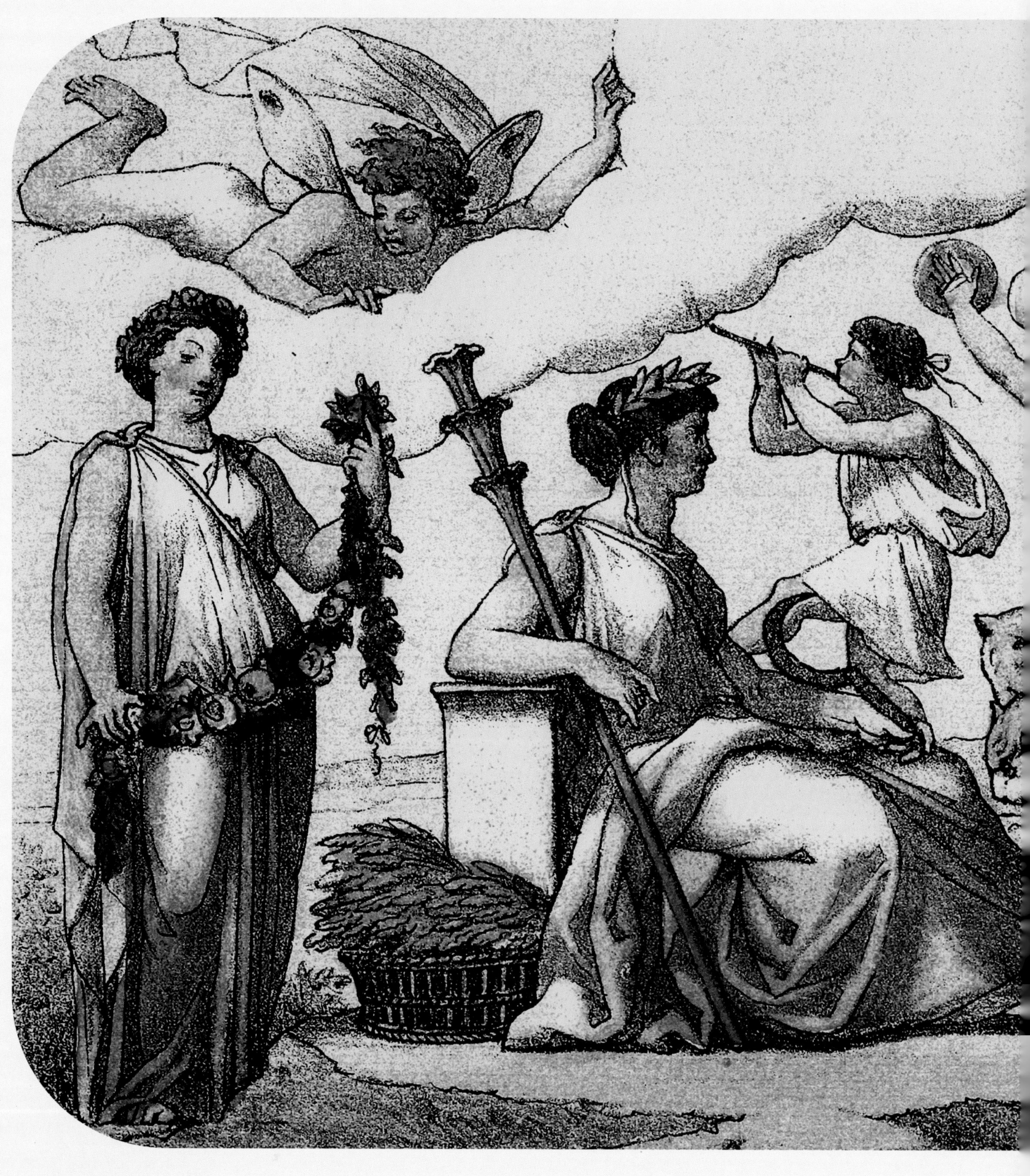

GODS OF THE COUNTRYSIDE

Demeter, the great goddess of corn and the harvest, is seated on the left, at the bottom. You can see her torch, the symbol of her mysterious power over the depths of the earth where the grain matures and germinates miraculously. In her left hand she is carrying a sickle, an agricultural tool with which the ears of corn are cut. There is a basket at her feet; it is full of corn symbolizing the great benefits she offers the human race, and she is crowned with an ear of corn.

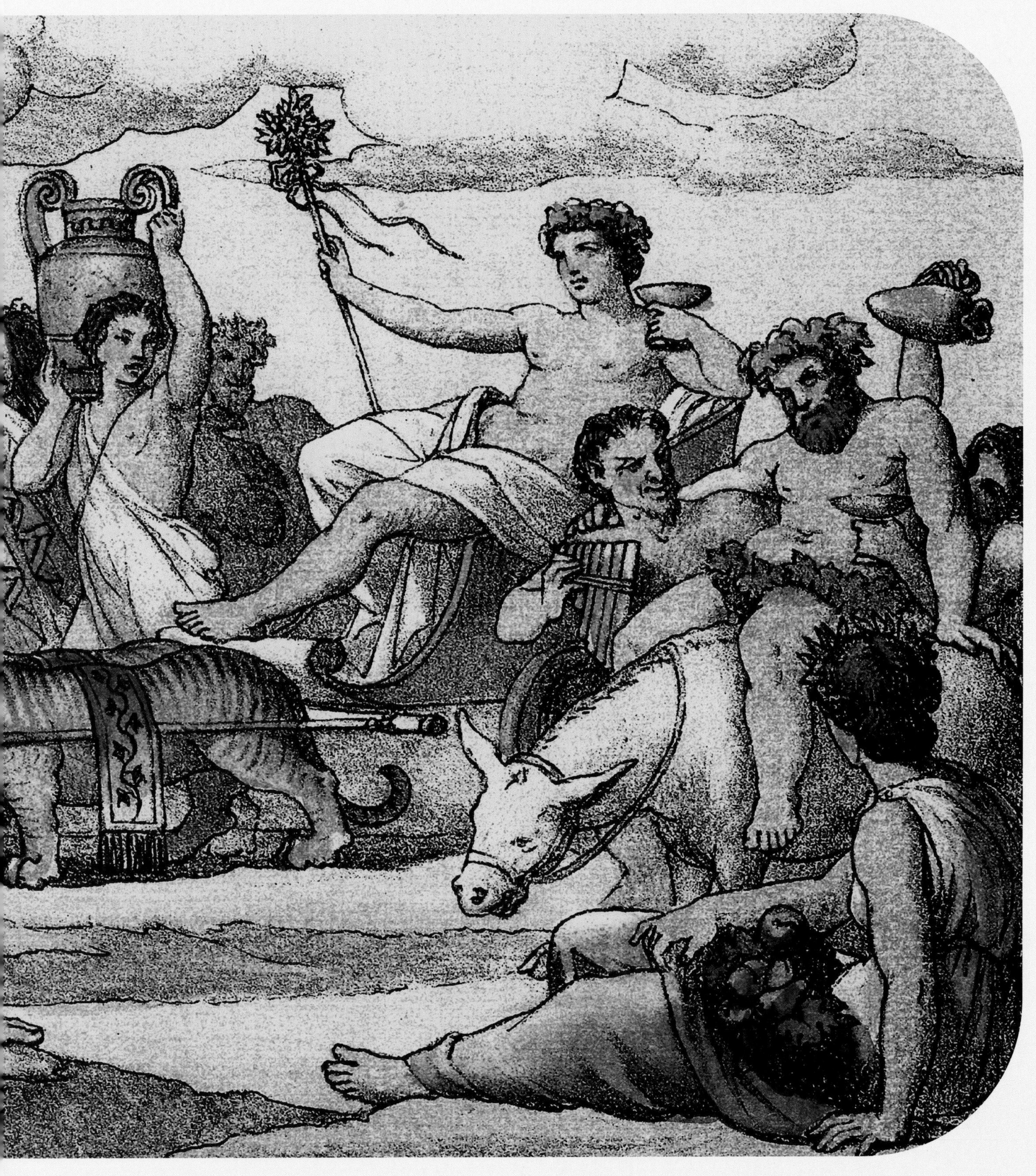

She is watching a joyful and colorful procession: Dionysus, the god of the vine and of mystical madness, is coming in a chariot pulled by wild beasts: he has no problem mastering animal energy, just as he releases savage longings. The god proudly displays his thyrsus garlanded with ivy and vine branches. Behind him come his followers the Maenads, making music, singing and dancing around a wine jar carried triumphantly by a young man. Silenus, the wise old satyr, has taken too much nectar and is so drunk he can scarcely stay upright on his donkey. He is held up by Pan, the god of shepherds, who is recognizable by his flute.

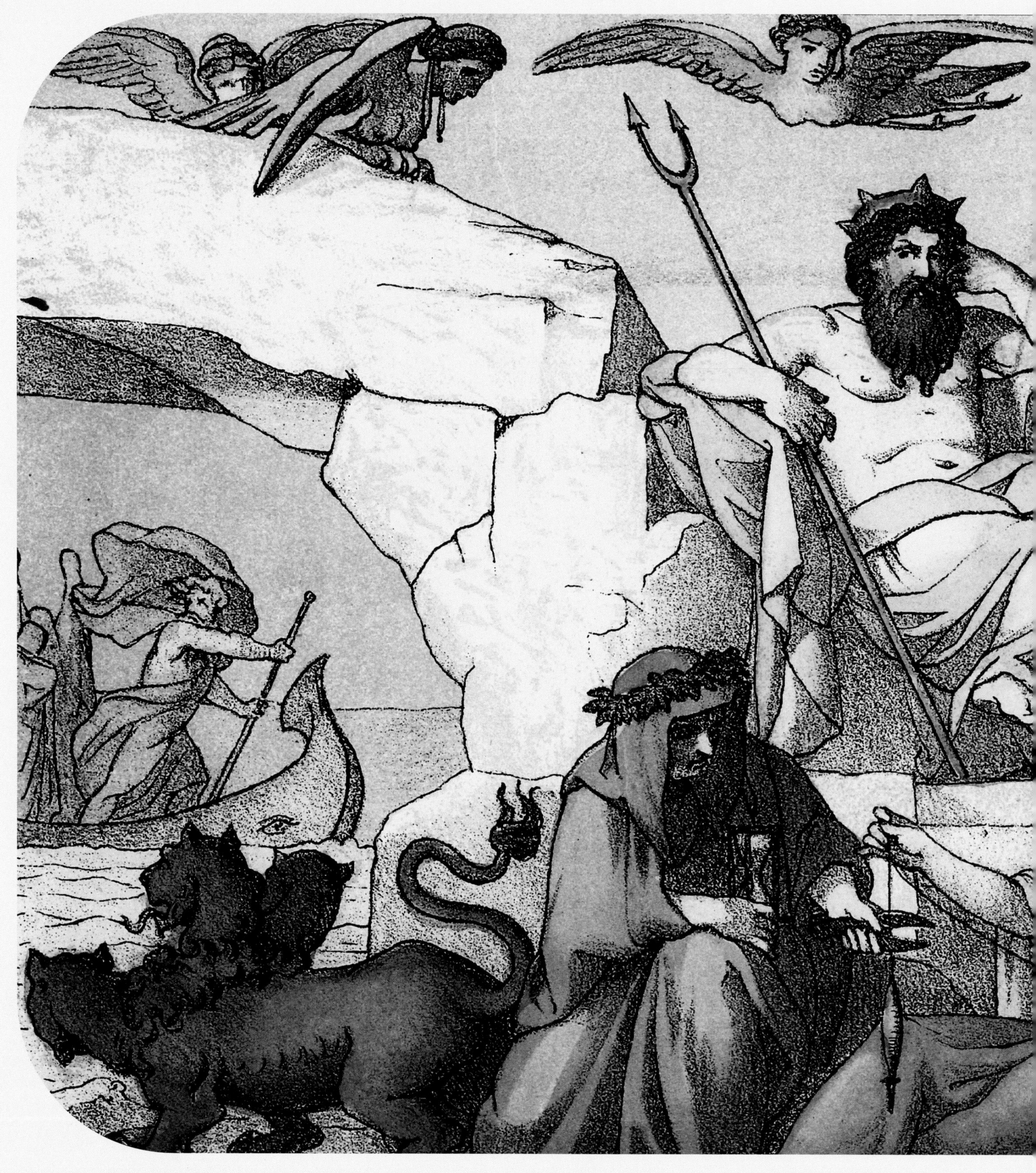

THE KINGDOM OF THE DEAD

Hades ruled over the dead with his queen Persephone, daughter of Demeter, whom he had carried away to the underworld and Cerberus, the monstrous dog, guarded the entrance to those places. Only the dead passed through and Charon ferried them across the river Styx, as long as they could give him a coin. But nobody was allowed back out again. The dead were judged by the wise men Minos, Aeacus and Radamanthys.

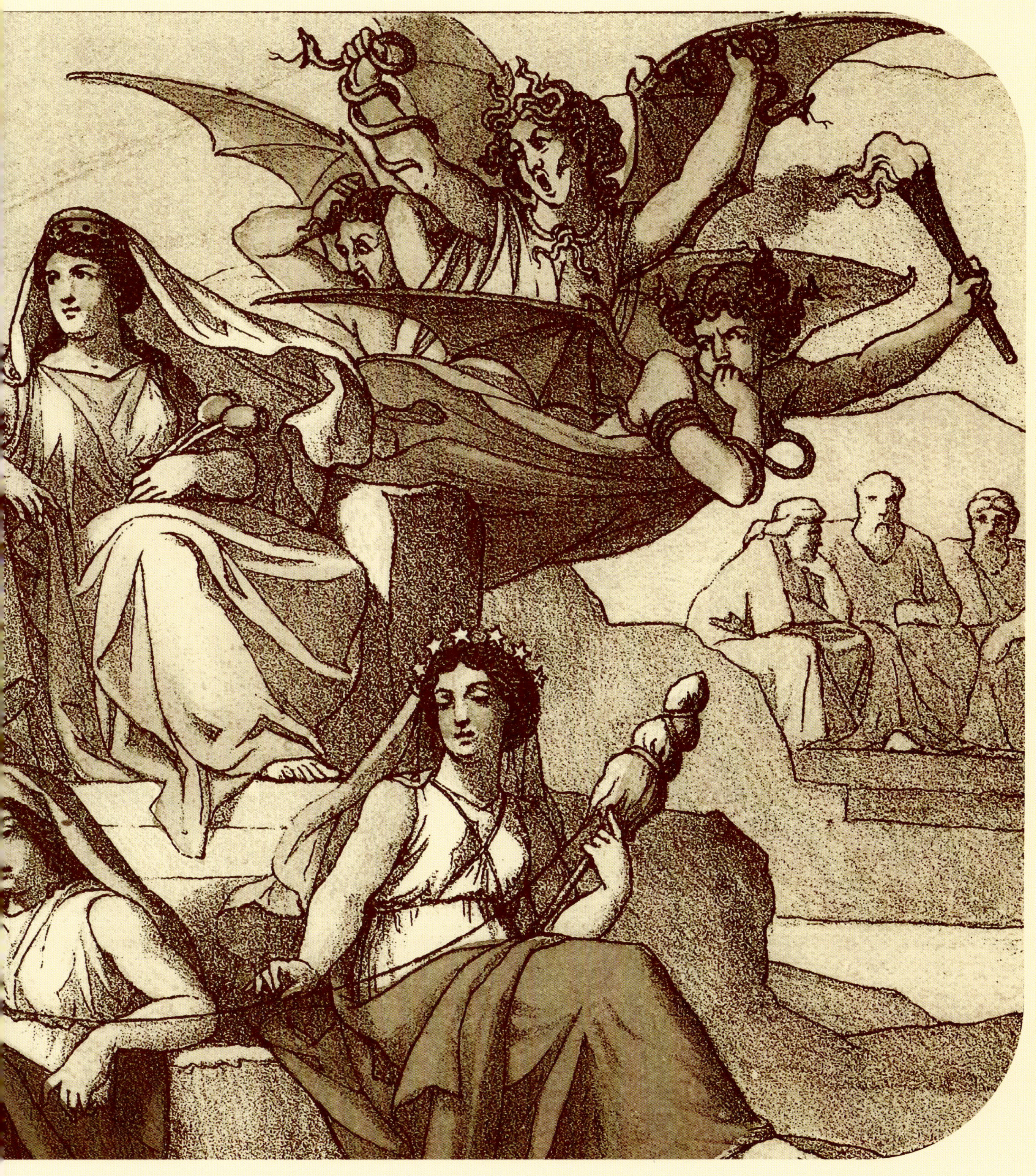

Souls of the dead were thrown into Tartarus, taken to the fields of asphodel or to the Elysian Fields. Collaborating with the dread work of Hades, the three inflexible Fates used to spin out the thread of human life and cut it when life's allotted time was over. The Hounds of Hades were terrifying, female, red robed demons who swarmed over battle fields. They uttered bloodthirsty cries and threw long shadows as they quarreled over their prey. Their long avid nails lacerated bodies and finished off the wounded. They greedily sucked their blood and then dragged the corpses off to Hades.

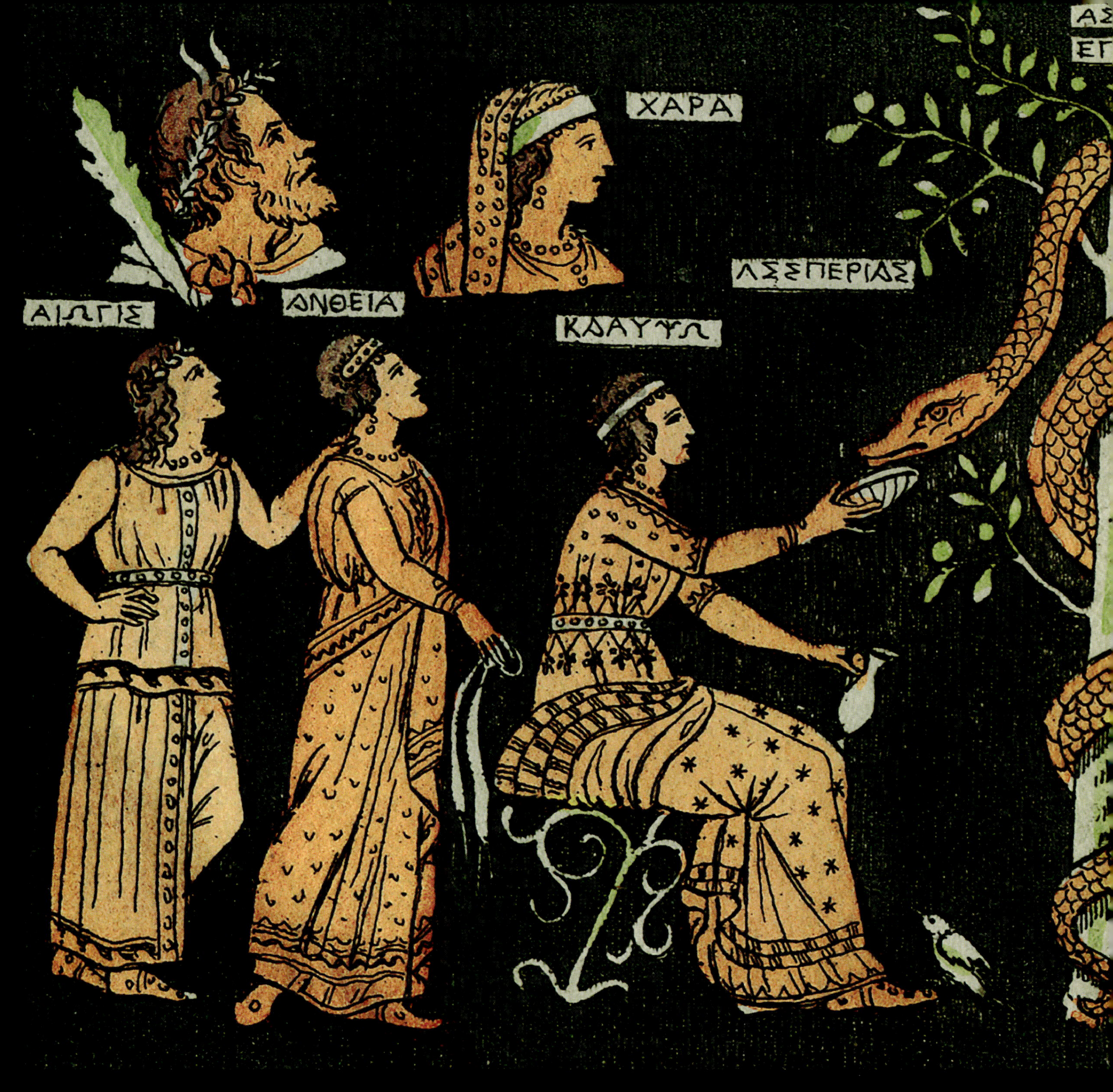

THE WEDDING OF THETIS AND PELEUS

When the mortal Peleus married the divine Thetis, Mount Pelion welcomed unusual guests: all the gods were invited to the ceremony and left Mount Olympus to attend the feast! It was not unusual for a locality to claim such prestigious company. The Olympians easily succumbed to the attractions of a feast. They also turned up for the marriage of Cadmus and Harmony in the city of Thebes. This was a sumptuous banquet! The honorable company was delighted with the nectar and the singing of the Muses. Zeus and Poseidon were particularly happy with the occasion.

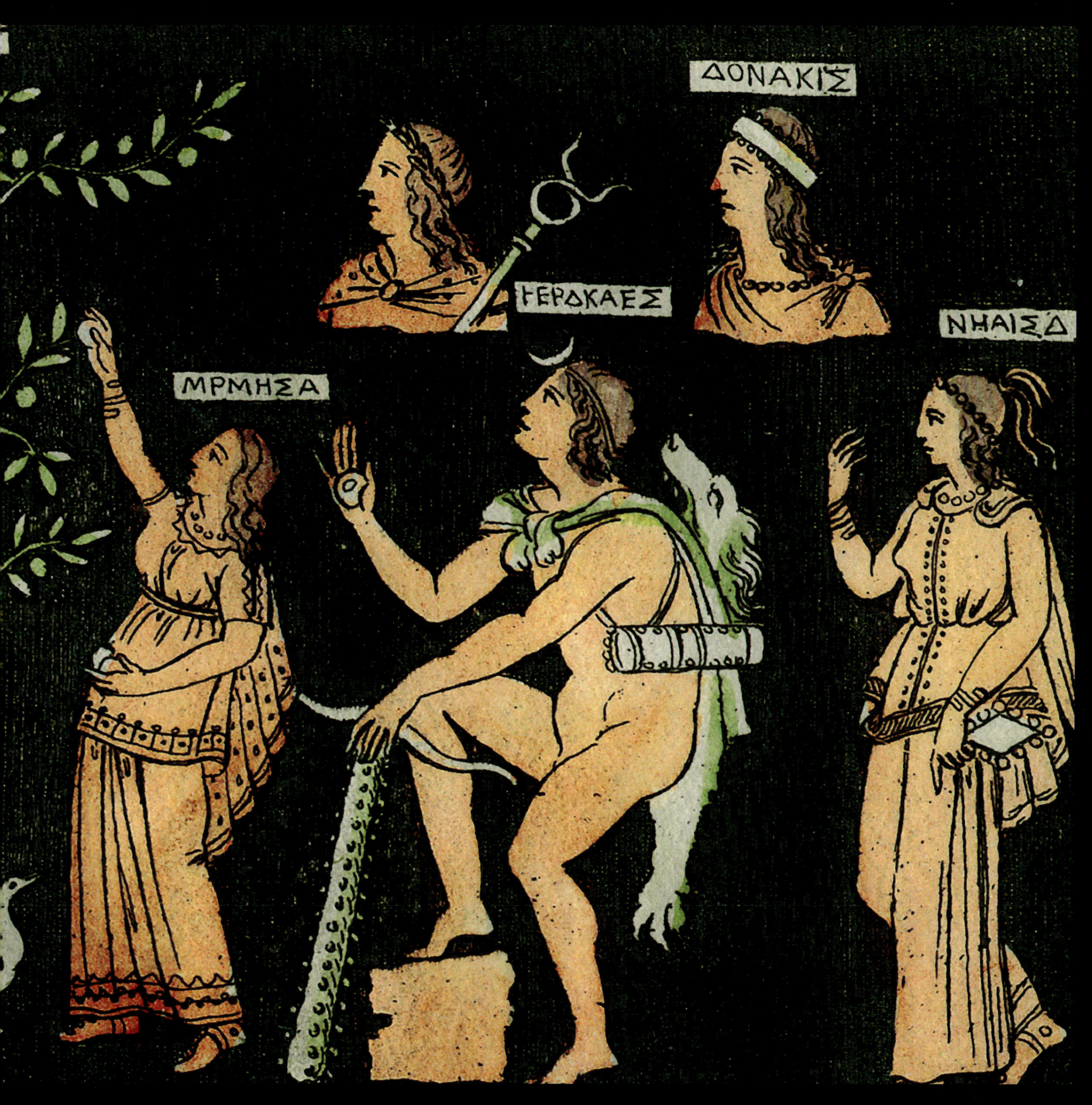

They had both been in love with Thetis, but learned that she was fated to bear a son who would be more powerful than his father. From that day on the Nereid was deserted by all her divine suitors. From now on only a mortal would agree to marry her. Peleus, the devout king of Thessaly, set out to woo the beautiful girl. But she was a wild lass and tried to get away from him by repeatedly changing form. But Peleus did not give up and Thetis soon gave in. Poseidon offered an unusual wedding gift: two immortal horses. This team would become even more famous when it drew the chariot of the most illustrious hero of the War of Troy. Achilles would be born of the love between Thetis and Peleus. As for Eris, Discord, she was not invited to the feast but threw a poisoned gift in among the guests: the famous apple which would cause the Trojan War.

BROTHERLY RIVALRY

This black-figured water jar dating from the 6th century BC reminds us of the amusing tussles between Hermes and Apollo. Hermes, the last born of the children of Zeus, is in his cradle at the center of the tableau. The precocious baby has been making his presence felt amongst the Olympians, exercising his talents, but also seeking the recognition of his peers. His first escapade was to steal his brother's herd of cows.

Apollo has discovered who is responsible and has come to the cave on Mount Cyllene to confront the rascal, who is pretending to be asleep! Apollo looses his temper, while Maia protests that her little baby must be innocent: he is too young to steal cattle and is anyway fast asleep. As a wise and all-powerful judge, Zeus does not allow himself to be hoodwinked by his son. Hermes quickly owns up, but then, full of guile, offers his services to his father. His astuteness and deviousness amuse the king of the gods who appoints him the divine herald. Ambitious Hermes has got what he wanted: he is now the twelfth god and moves to live on Mount Olympus.

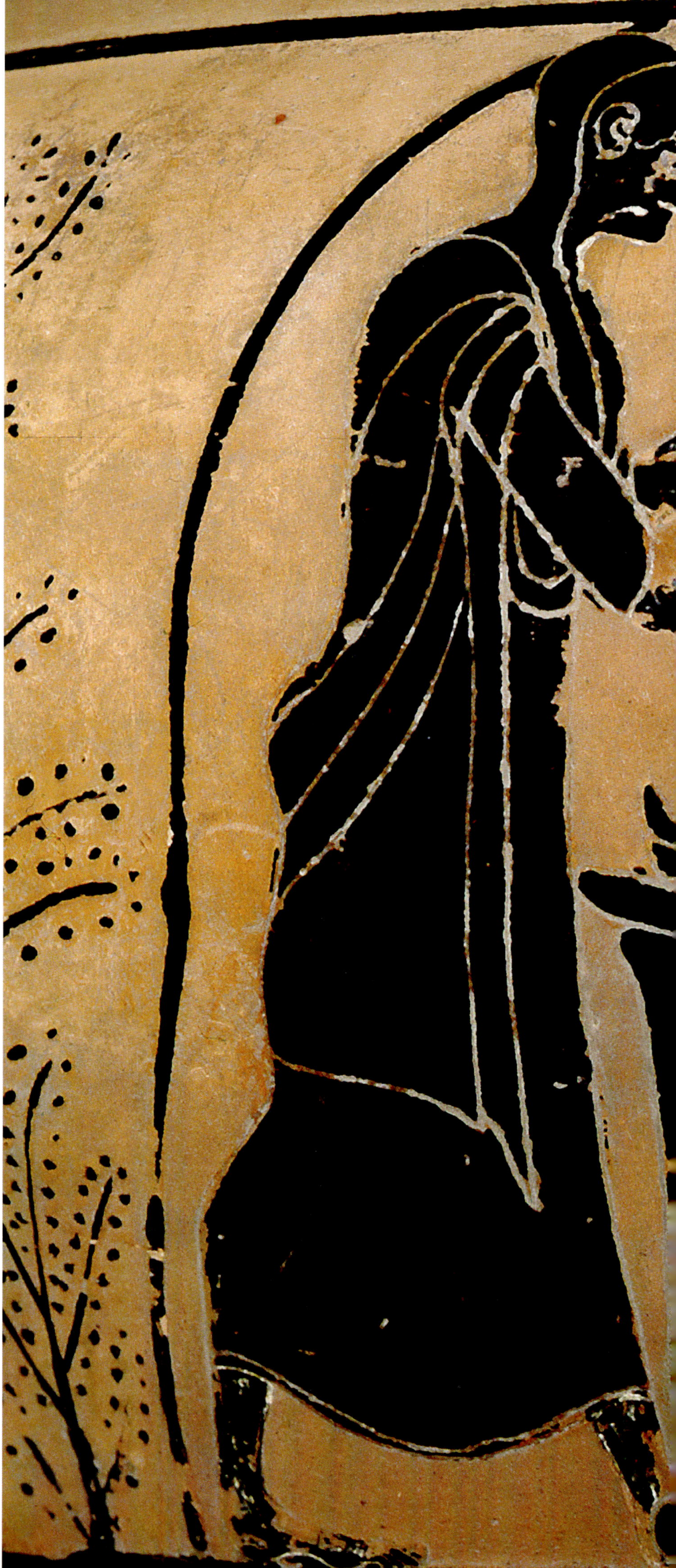

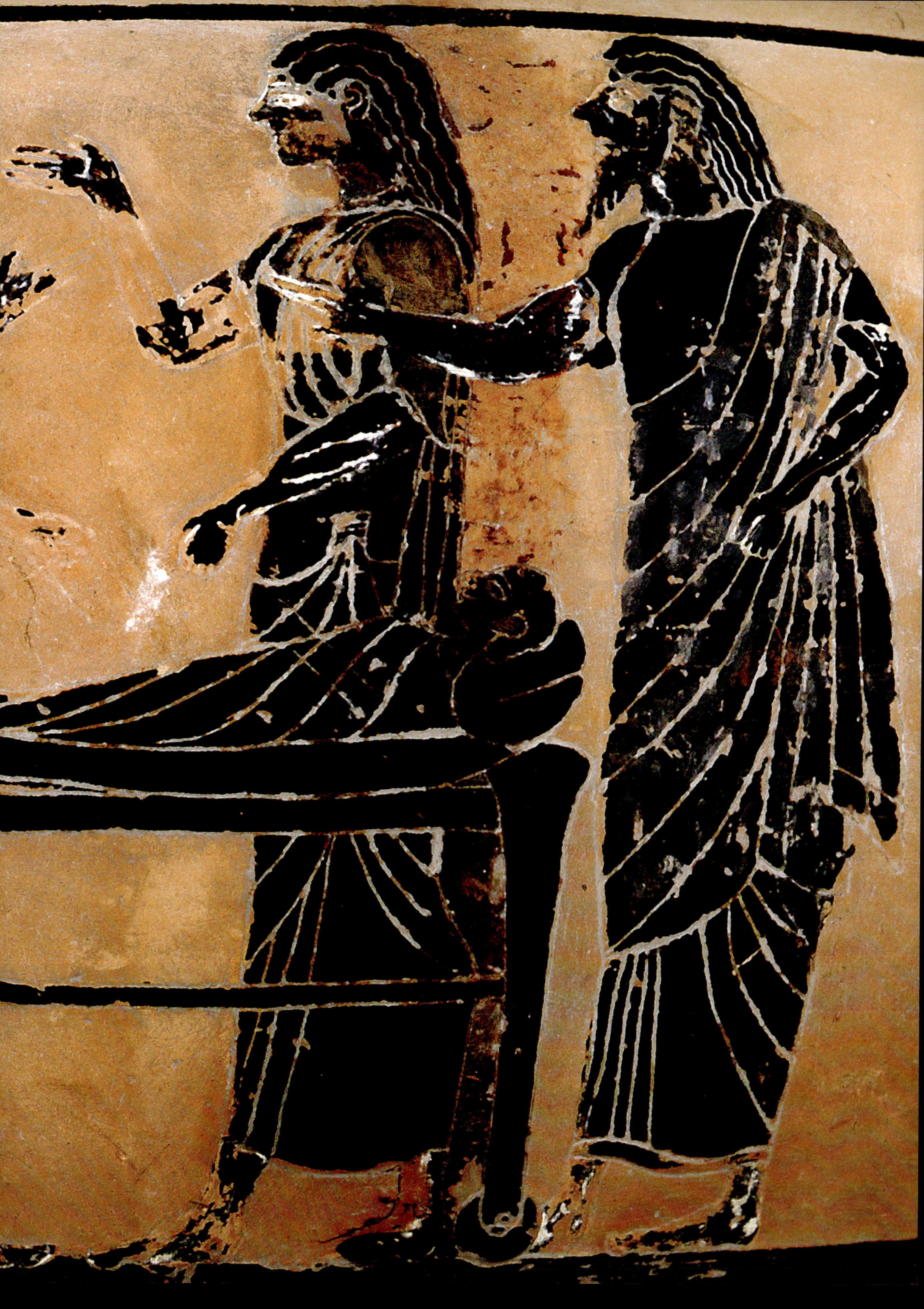

ATHENA BUILDS THE ACROPOLIS

This illustration is from the 5th century BC; in it Athena is represented as the chief builder of the city of Athens; she has just become its patron goddess. She has beaten off the claims of Poseidon in the competition to win the city. Both citizens and Immortals have chosen the goddess who gave the city an olive tree, in preference to Poseidon, who only offered a spring of salty water and some untrained horses; both of which were of little use to the inhabitants! Delighted with her achievement, Athena is now the divine architect busy beautifying the city. She is bringing giants to the huge building site where they are toiling to raise the defensive walls around the Acropolis. Soon this holy hill, strewn with stone blocks, will be the site where the citizens will construct magnificent buildings to her glory: the Parthenon, the Erechtheum and the temple of Athena Nike. The city will become more like its divine patron; Athens was considered to be a wise, just, gallant and victorious city. Its riches and beauty impressed foreign visitors, reminding all of the technical and artistic talents of Athena.

THE ACROPOLIS

The holy hill and its ruins are one of the treasures of contemporary Athens and many come to admire them. Below the enclosure is the Odeon, the Roman theater of Herod Atticus which was built in 161 AD.

FOLLOWING PAGES

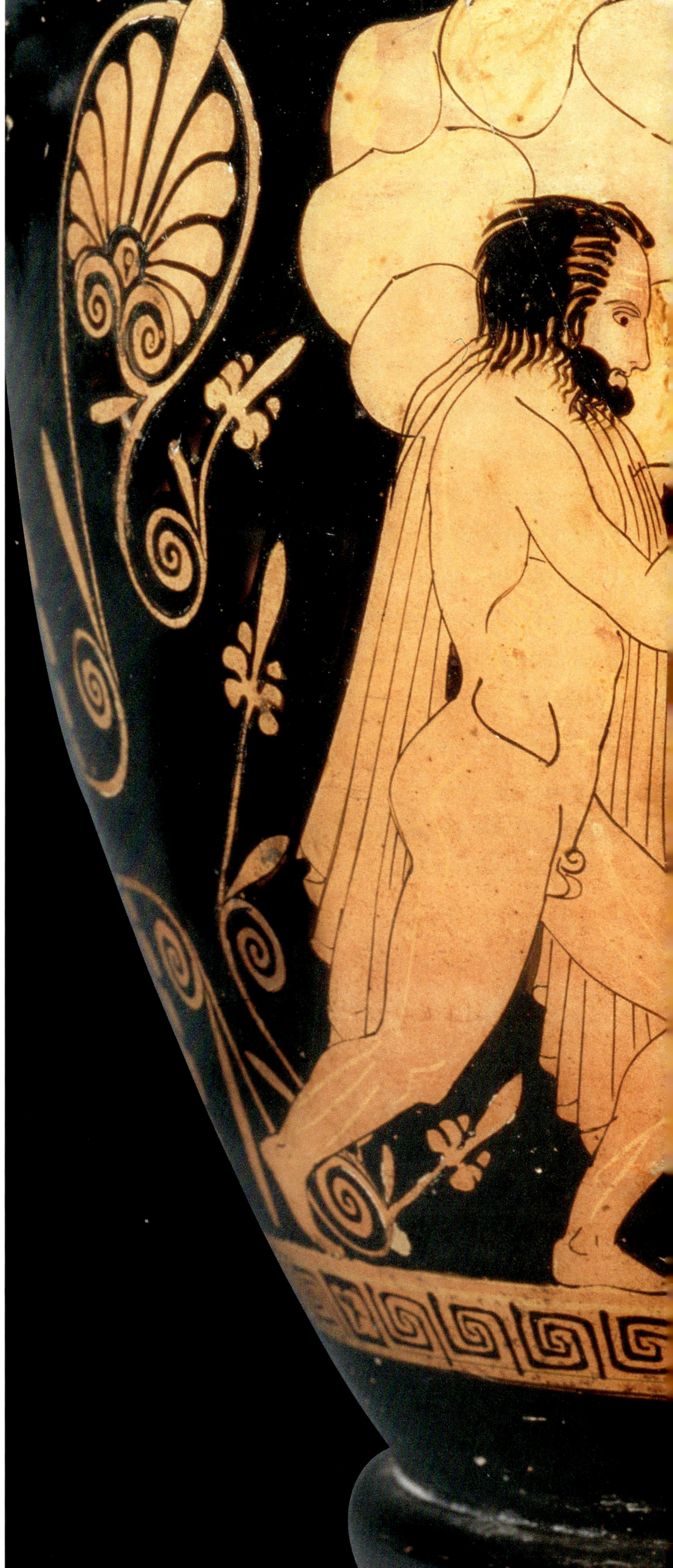

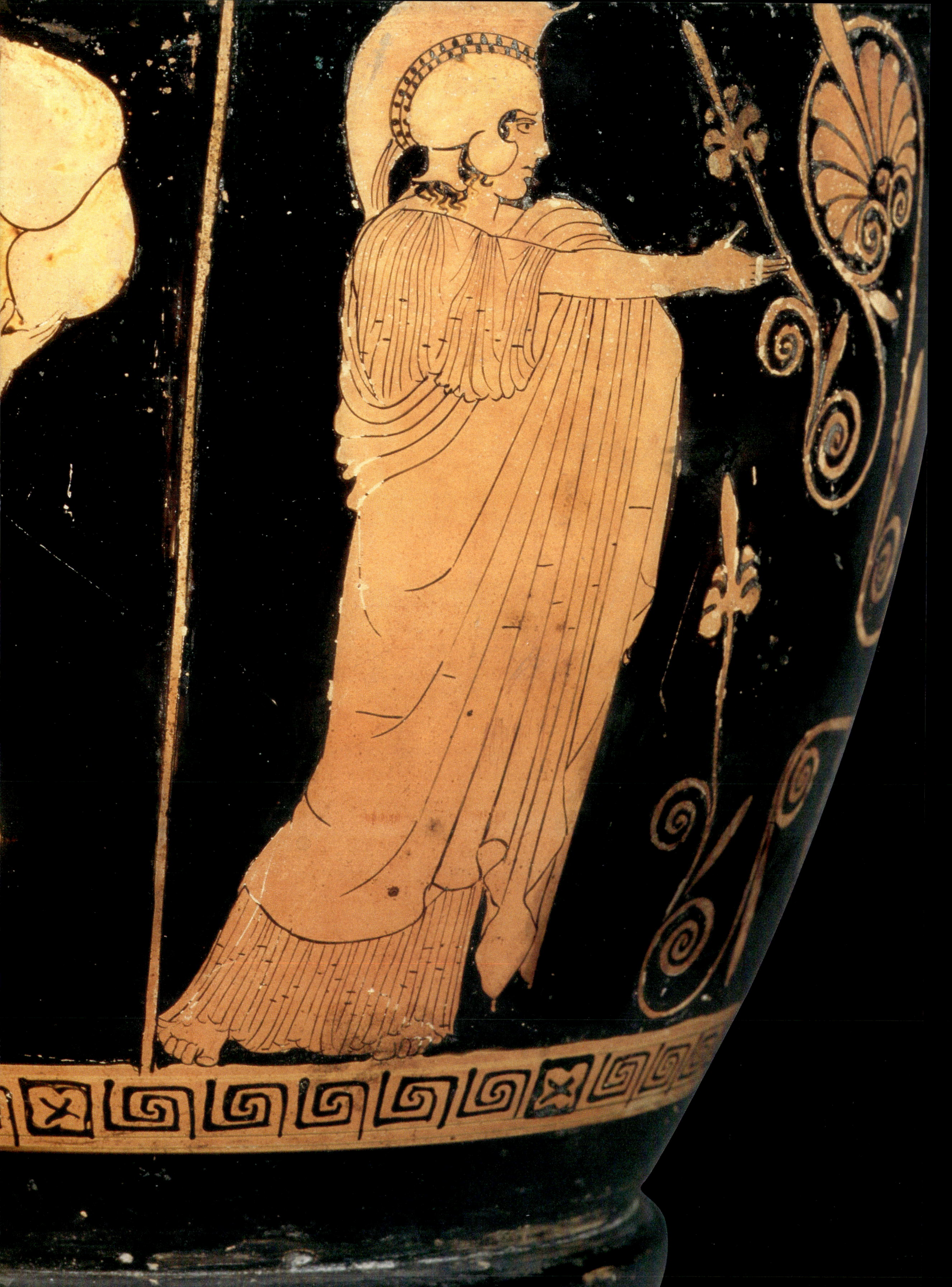

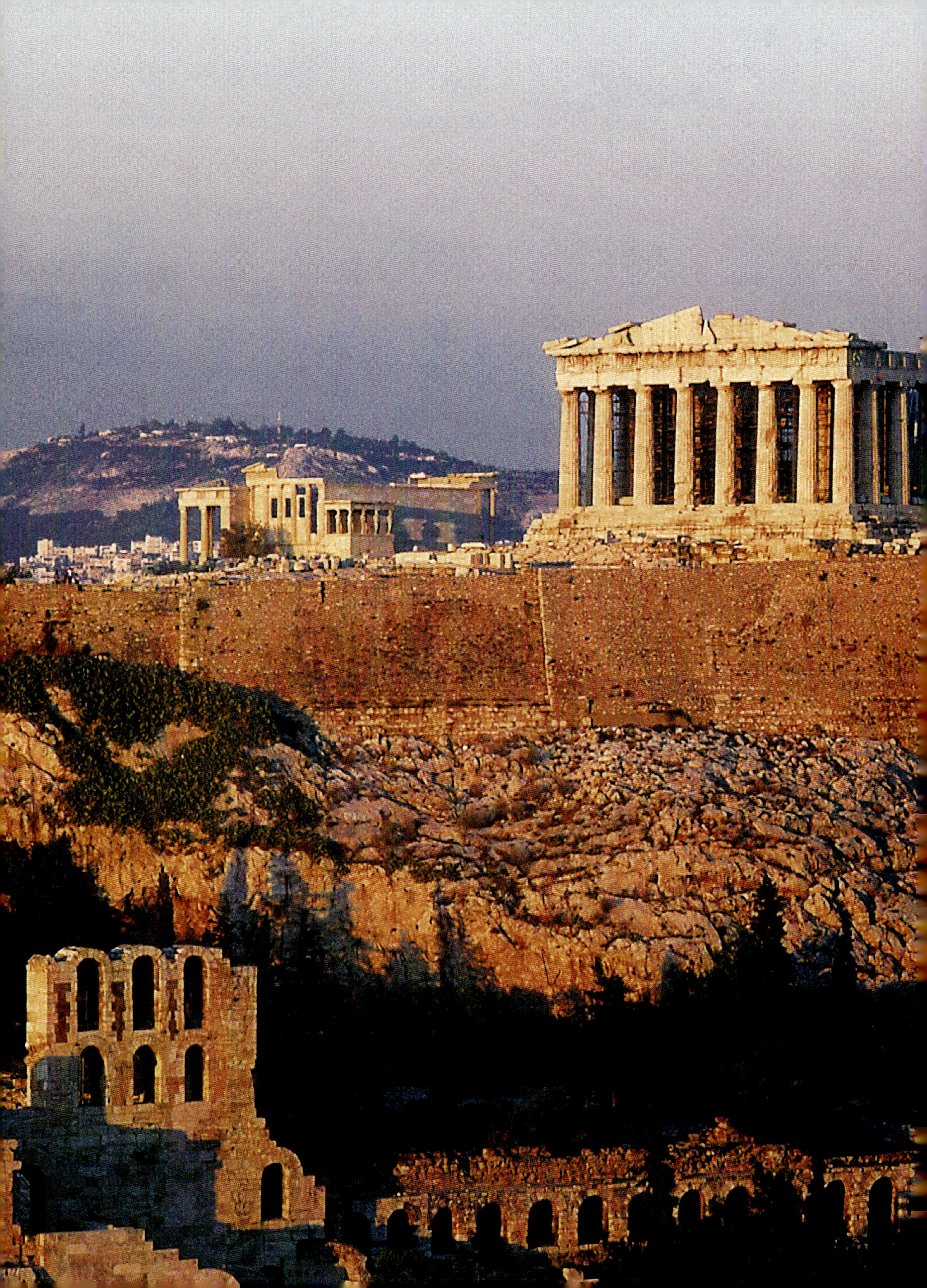

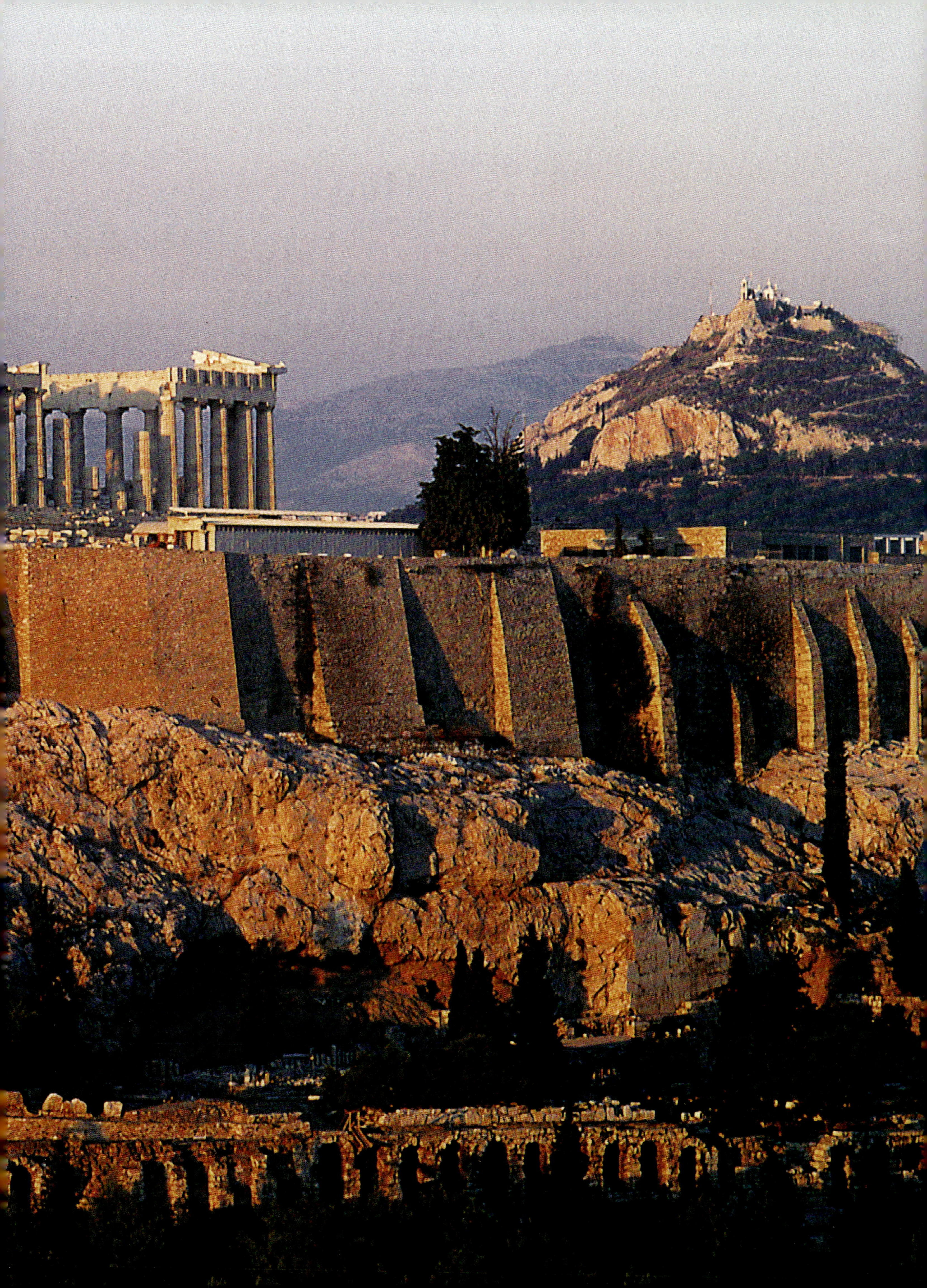

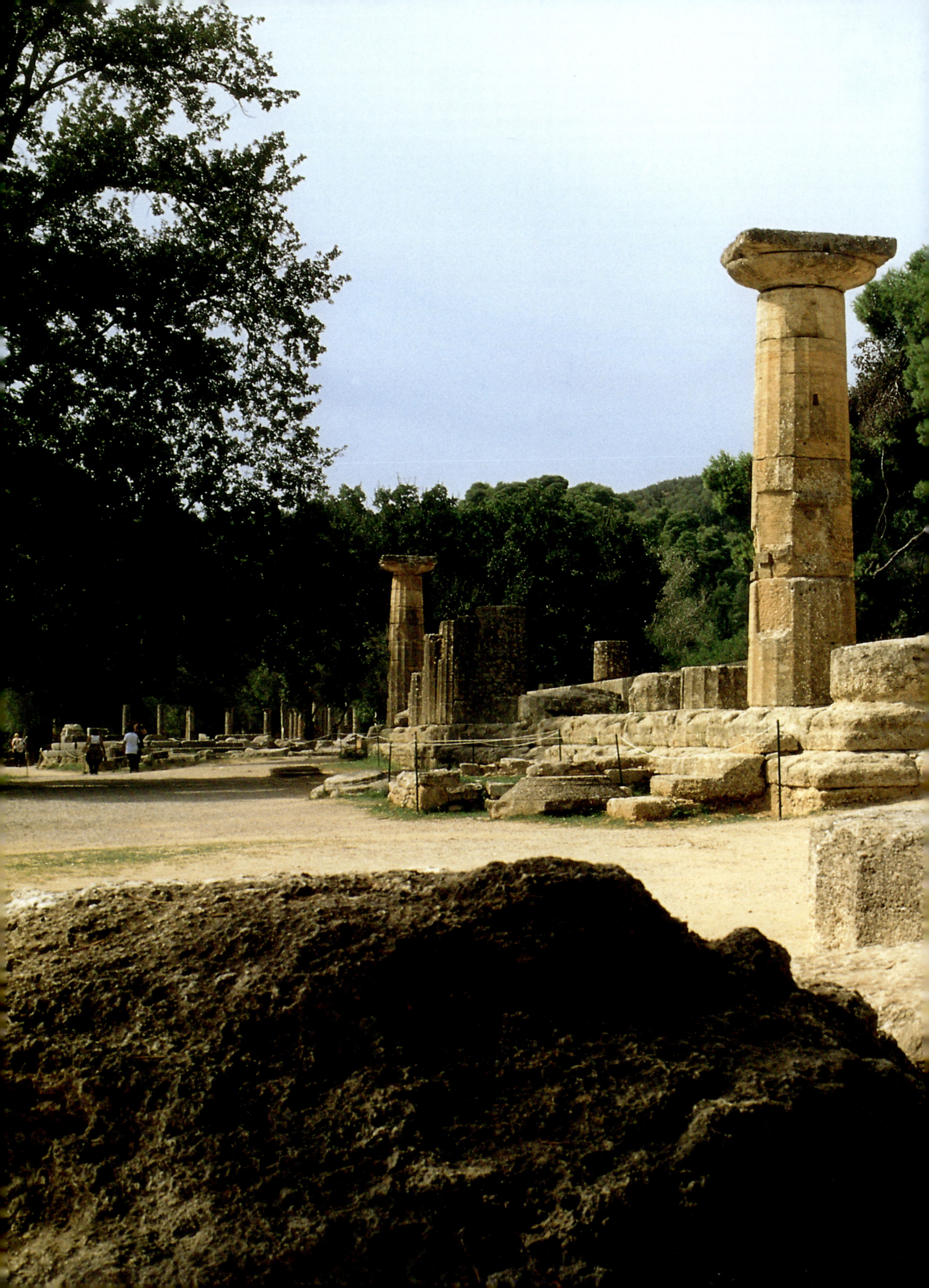

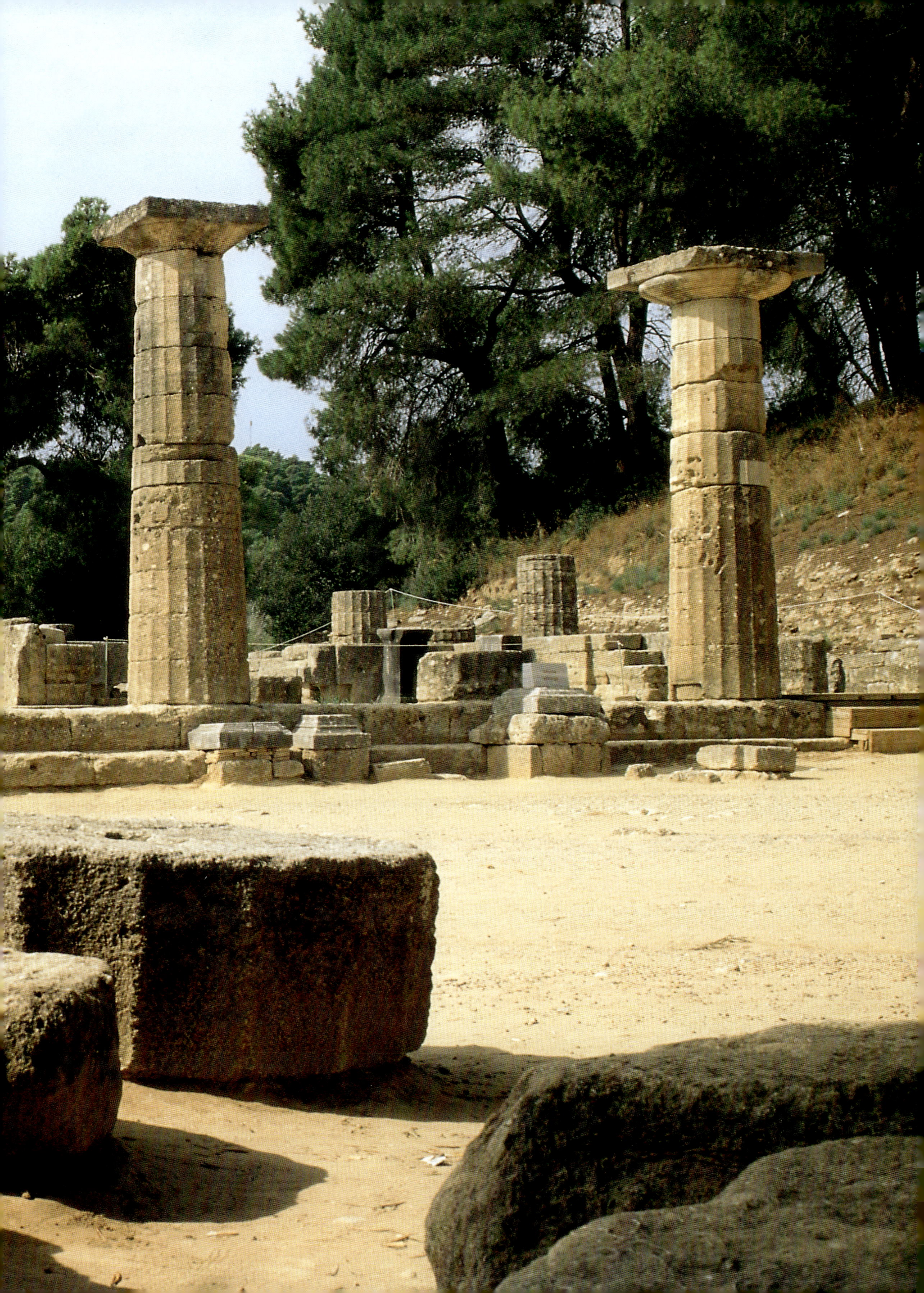

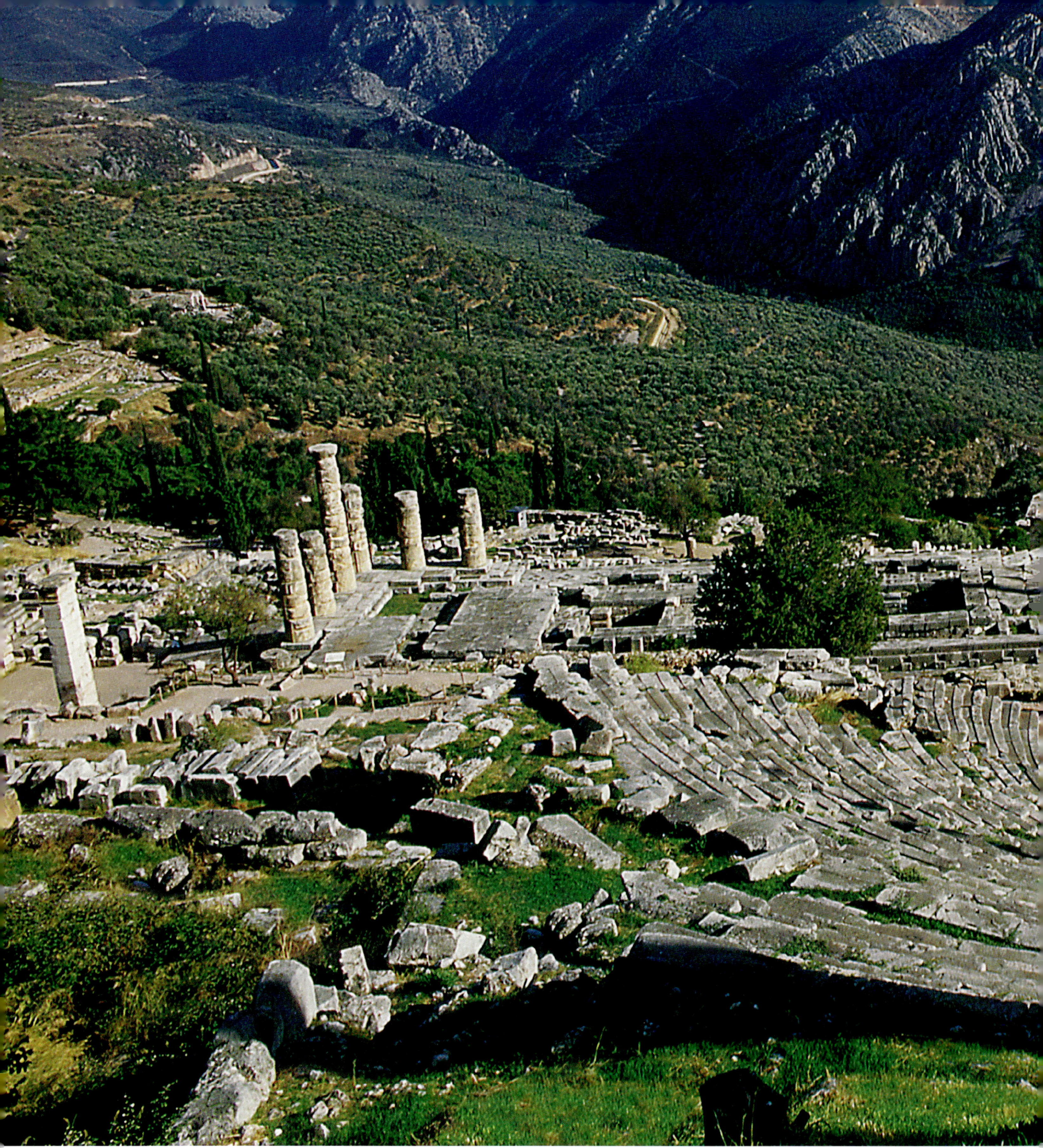

DELPHI, THE LAND OF APOLLO

The name of Apollo is indelibly linked with the sanctuary of the oracle of Delphi. This place was promised to the young god by his father Zeus and welcomed him when he returned from his visit to the lands of the Hyperboreans. Apollo took over the oracle when he killed its guardian, the serpent Python, a bloody monster who was terrorizing the locality. In this way he took vengeance for his mother Leto, hunted by the same dragon whilst pregnant with the divine twins.

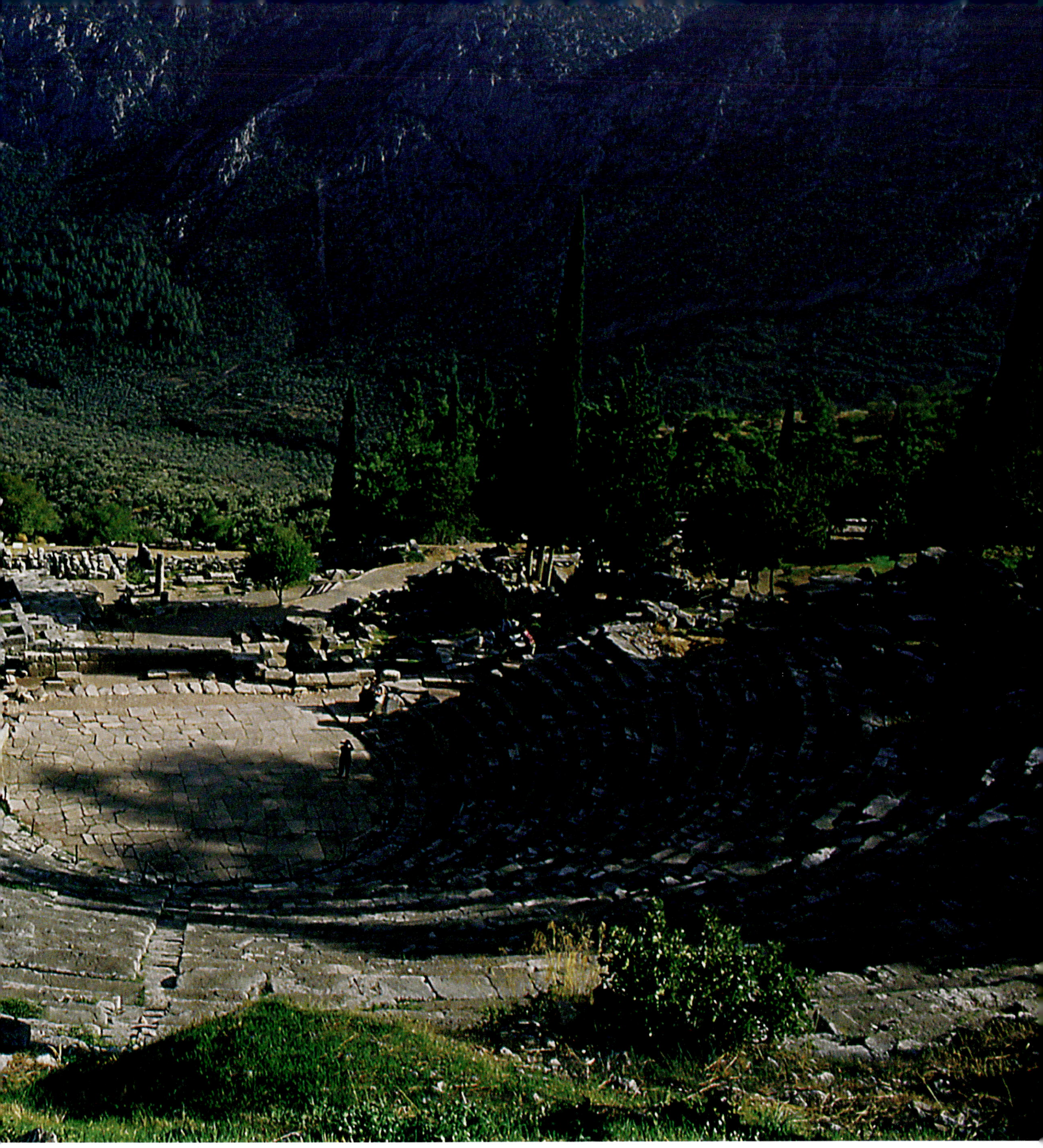

From now on he will be the master of the most spectacular and majestic site in Greece, considered to be the navel of the world. His sanctuary is set in an amphitheater of rocky cliffs, overlooking a majestic valley where olive trees cascade down to the sea. Apollo will soon have to defend his property. Hercules came to consult the Pythia, but was outraged when she refused to speak to him. So he tried to steal her tripod to inaugurate his own oracle elsewhere. The god of prophecy pursued him and engaged him in a fight. Seeing the struggle, Zeus hurled his thunderbolt to separate his two sons. It was thanks to the decision of Zeus that the oracle remained at Delphi.

HEROIC JOURNEYS

After long journeys strewn with traps and pitfalls, the Greek heroes show they are men of strength, courage and quality, rising above the ordinary. They thus win extraordinary status amongst human beings, even immortality. We should all like to see ourselves as these admirable beings, we can identify with them more easily than with gods! Indeed their stories have inflamed the imaginations of many a writer who tell how their travels in Greece were something of a personal eye-opener. So when Heinrich Schliemann, the archaeologist, was attacked by a pack of wild dogs on the island of Ithaca it reminded him of the monsters encountered by Hercules, Theseus, Jason, Ulysses and so many others... The cinema would later latch on to these resourceful and victorious heroes: they were great box-office attractions! Hercules would feature in as many epic films as variations could be found on his labors. Others would be invented, so great was the craze for his adventures. He has even confronted colossal difficulties in New York! We shall only mention the adventures of the best-known heroes here.

Hercules was born following the illicit love affair between Zeus and Alcmene and thus was destined to be the victim of Hera's fury. Zeus' wife even drove him mad so that she might get him to kill his very own children. Sullied by these crimes, he placed himself in the service of Eurystheus who ordered him to perform twelve apparently impossible tasks. These would all allow the hero to atone for his crimes and become pure again. The first six were in the Peloponnesus: he overcame the Nemean Lion (and thereafter wore its skin), the Lernean Hydra, the Boar of Erymanthus, the Hind of Mount Ceryneia, and the Stymphalian Birds in Arcadia. He also cleaned the stables of King Augeias in Elis. The remaining six labors were carried out all over the then known world. Hercules captured the famous Cretan Bull, and the Mares of Diomedes, King of Thrace. He stole the Girdle of Hippolyte, Queen of the Amazons in Scythia and the Cattle of Geryon on an island in the extreme west. To perform this task Hercules had to undertake a long journey through Libya, where he killed various monsters; he then set up two pillars framing the straits between Africa and Europe (the Rocks of Gibraltar and Ceuta). He returned to Greece, by following the coasts of Spain, Gaul and Italy. On the plain of Crau, between Marseille and the Rhone Valley, he was attacked by the Liguri. Zeus sent his son a shower of stones with which, since he had no other ammunition, he routed his enemies. His hard labors are not however at an end! He was initiated into the Eleusian Mysteries so that be could go down to the kingdom of the dead where he had to tie up Cerberus and bring him up to earth. He overpowered the dog and emerged from Hades at Troezen. He finally set off to steal the Golden Apples of the Hesperides, west of Libya...

Flushed with success, Hercules came one day to dine at the home of young Theseus at Troezen. The child took up an axe to kill the wild animal that had entered the building; the brave boy was squaring up to split the lion skin worn by the family's guest: a veritable hero in the making! Soon fabulous animals, thieves and murderers were once again endangering travelers on the roads of Greece, for Hercules was now the slave of Omphale in Lydia. Theseus, by now a young man, had discovered the secret of his birth and decided to join his father Aegeus in Athens.

His mother Aethra advised against taking the road via the Isthmus of Corinth, which was plagued by bandits. Wishing to emulate Hercules, Theseus was not fazed by such perils; he also wished the free the world of evildoers! So he killed the giant Periphetes at Epidaurus and took possession of the club he used to attack passers by. Near Corinth the bandit Sinis suffered the same fate as his victims: Theseus cut him in pieces. He also killed Phaea, the dreadful sow terrorizing the region of Crommyon. Near Megara, our hero hurled cruel Scyron over a cliff; Scyron used to force travelers to wash his feet before he threw them into the void. He then beat Cercyon at wrestling; that thug used to challenge all those who traveled along the road between Megara and Eleusis. Finally our hero confronted fierce Procrustes. Having brought peace and security back to the region, Theseus was now the hero of Attica and soon became King of Athens.

Hercules was also involved with the adventures of Jason. He was for a short period a member of the Argonauts' expedition in search of the Golden Fleece. Having left Thessaly, Jason and his companions first stopped on Lemnos where they comforted the women of the island who were being neglected by their husbands. They next visited the island of Samothrace, this was suggested by Orpheus so that the crew could be initiated into the cult of the great gods. They entered the Hellespont, crossed the Marmara Sea, sailed along the coast of Mysia, visited the land of the Bebryces, landed on the Thracian coast, where they accidentally left Hercules behind... He would no doubt have distracted attention from the heroic qualities of Jason! They sailed along the eastern shores of the Black Sea, beyond the Caucasus Mountains and arrived in Colchis. Once they had stolen the Golden Fleece, they returned in their ship the Argo, up the Danube and from there to the Adriatic. At the mercy of the unforeseeable, the ship sailed up the Po and down the Rhone before returning to the Mediterranean. The crew sailed around Sardinia, along the Italian and Sicilian coasts, landed on Corfu, got lost in Libya and finally returned to Iolcus, having first called in at Crete.

However, the heroic journey to end all heroic journeys is still the *Odyssey* as told by Homer: Ulysses left conquered Troy to return home to Ithaca which he would not see for another ten years... Many have tried to plot his wanderings on a map, in spite of the caustic remarks of Eratosthenes (3rd century BC); according to him, "Ulysses' route will be finalized the day they find the saddler who stitched the wineskin for the Aeolian winds!" In the second century BC Crates of Malos contended that he sailed out into the Atlantic, Aristarchus of Samos, said the Red Sea. A century later Strabo maintained that the poet had checked his facts thoroughly before composing his work. In 1927, in *The Navigations of Ulysses*, Victor Bérard claimed that Homer had used Phoenician sailing manuals, but this is totally unverifiable. According to him, having left Troy, Ulysses landed in Thrace (the land of the Ciconians), then stopped off at Djerba (the land of the Lotus Eaters), and arrived in the Bay of Naples (land of the Cyclops, though others place it in Sicily). Out from the bay are the Aeolian Islands, in the Lipari Archipelago. Our hero next reached Sardinia, where the Laestrygon giants lived. From there he headed for the promontory of Mount Circeo in modern Lazio where he met the enchantress Circe. Then somewhere between the mouth of the Tiber and the Bay of Naples he consulted the soul of the soothsayer Tiresias. Ulysses next sailed to the Sorrento peninsula (the island of the Sirens), went through the Straits of Messina, where Charybdis and Scylla terrorized sailors and came ashore in Sicily, the Island of the Sun. Having lost his crew, Ulysses came alone to the home of beautiful Calypso, at the foot of Mount Atlas, facing Gibraltar. When she finally agreed to leave him go, he got to Corfu, the island of the Phaeacians, and from there home to Ithaca. This theory is unsustainable today. There is perhaps a kernel of truth in the story of Ulysses' wanderings, but the essential truth of his journey is in a symbolic and imaginative forging of the self.

HERCULES AS A PROMISING YOUNG HERO

We can read the promise of a glorious and heroic destiny on the smooth face of this young man. He seems to be smiling faintly and he confidently looks to the horizon. He is already wearing on his proud head the skin of the Nemean lion, the first victim of his twelve labors.

It was when fighting that monster that he carved his famous club, out of the trunk of a wild olive tree. His other weapons, his bow, his arrows, his breastplate and shield were given to him by Zeus, Athena and Hephaestus.

But Hercules did not need these weapons to kill the wild beast terrorizing the region of Nemea. Our hero blocked up one entrance to the lion's den and entered by the second. He thus trapped the animal and squeezed it to death with his bare hands. He then flayed it and donned its skin, using the head as a helmet. Hercules is still at the start of a prestigious career…

THE TWELVE LABORS OF HERCULES

1- THE NEMEAN LION
2- THE LERNEAN HYDRA
3- THE WILD BOAR OF ERYMANTHUS
4- THE HIND WITH HOOVES OF BRASS
5- THE STYMPHALIAN BIRDS
6- THE STABLES OF AUGEIAS
7- THE CRETAN BULL
8- THE MARES OF DIOMEDES
9- THE GIRDLE OF QUEEN HIPPOLYTE
10- THE CATTLE OF GERYON
11- THE DOG CERBERUS
12- THE GOLDEN APPLES FROM THE GARDEN OF THE HESPERIDES

HERCULES AND THE LERNEAN HYDRA

A monster born from the union of Echidna and Typhon grew and prospered near the city of Lernaea This water serpent was raised by Hera with the sole aim of harming Hercules, because she had sworn to destroy him. The beast, which had many heads (one of them was immortal), was terrorizing the countryside. Its repellent breath immediately floored both men and beasts. As his second task, Eurystheus ordered Hercules to remove the hydra. Having already brought back the body of the Nemean lion, the hero willingly accepted this new challenge. He attacked the extraordinary serpent with his flaming arrows; then, with a little curved sword, cut off each of its heads. To prevent these growing again, his nephew Iolaus burned the flesh of each wound as a head was cut off. Finally Hercules cut off the immortal head which he imprisoned beneath a rock. The hero triumphantly dipped his arrows in the poisonous blood of the monster. In this way he kept a souvenir of his exploit, but the poisoned arrows also became fearful weapons against future enemies. FOLLOWING PAGES

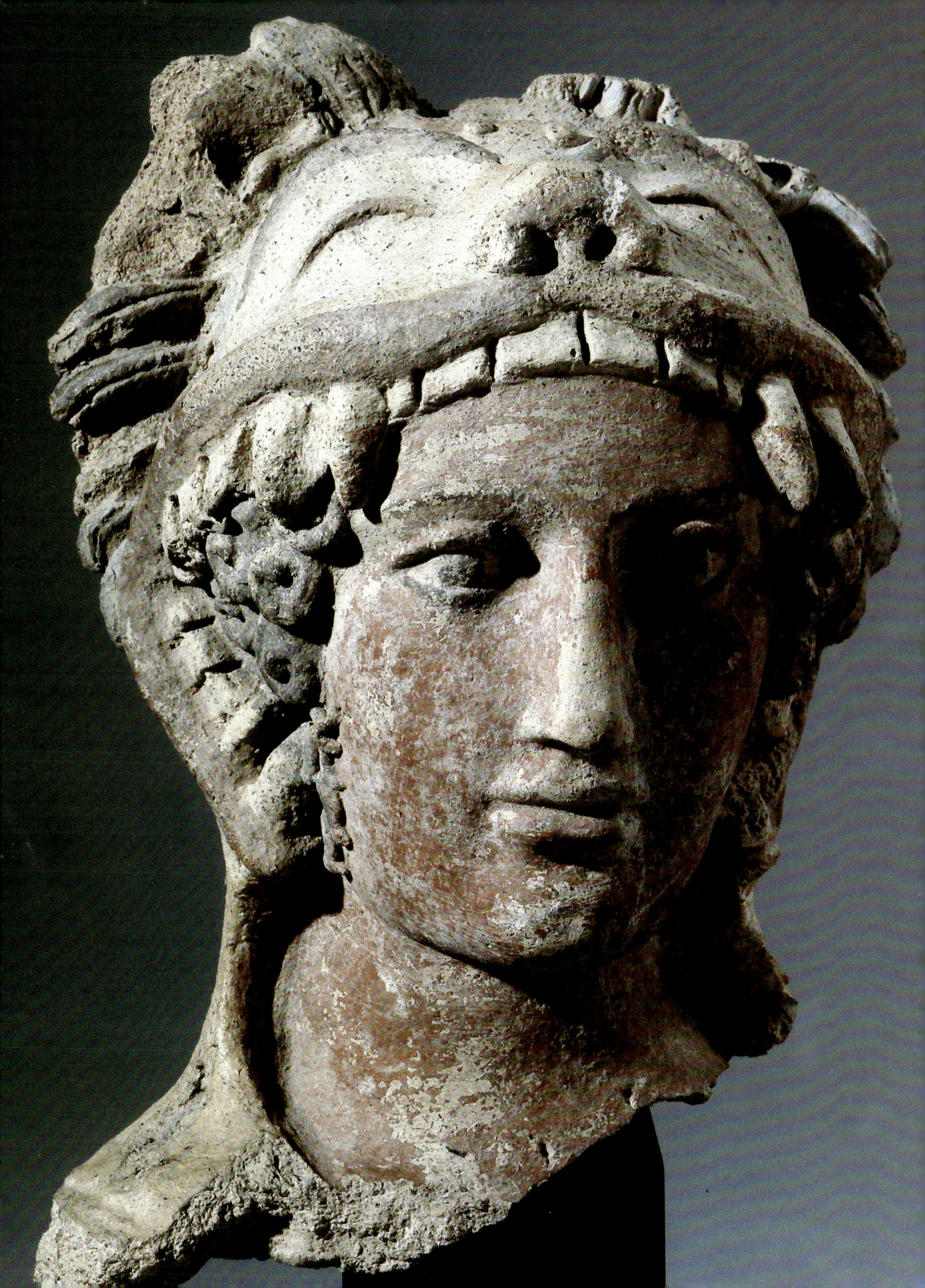

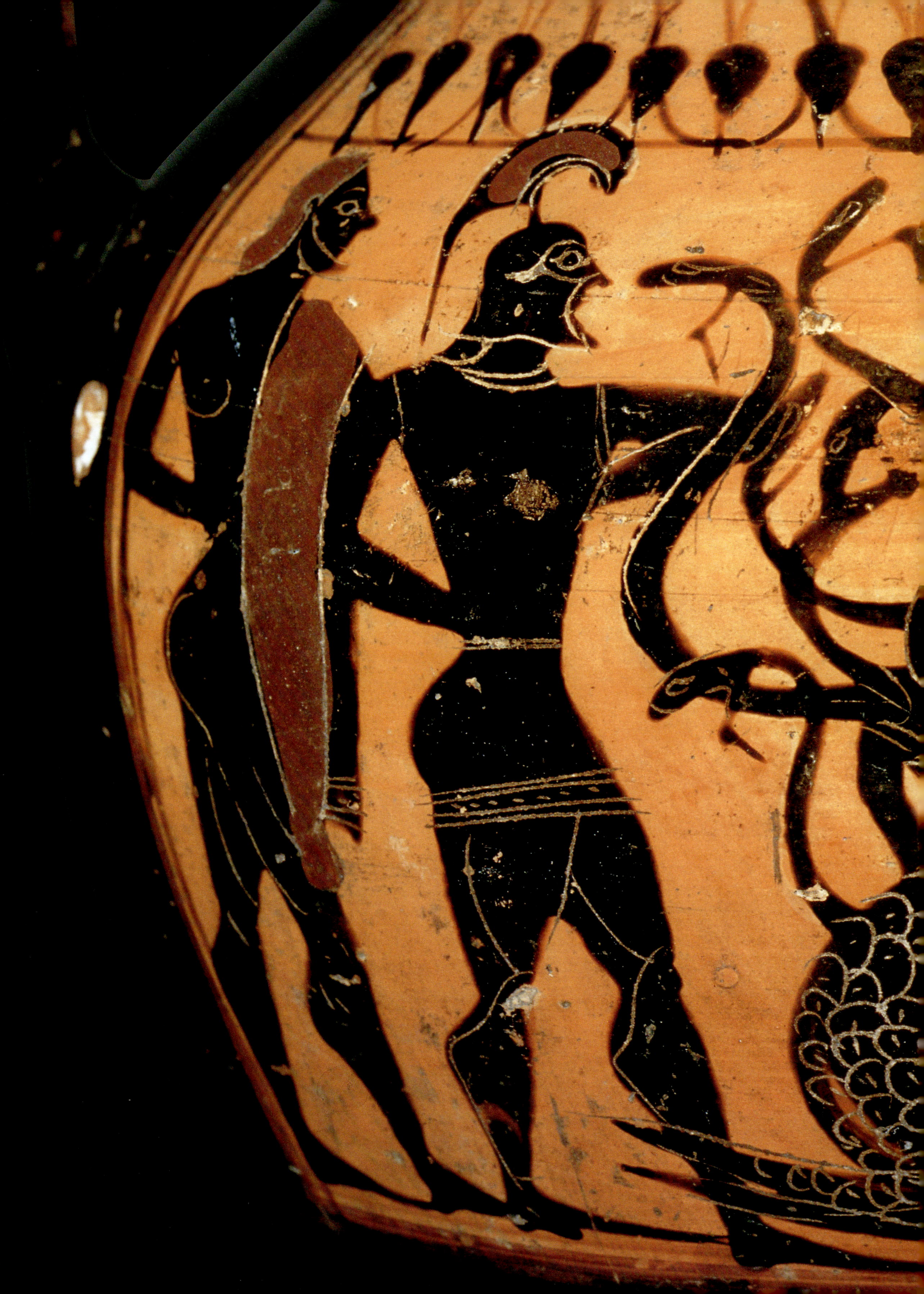

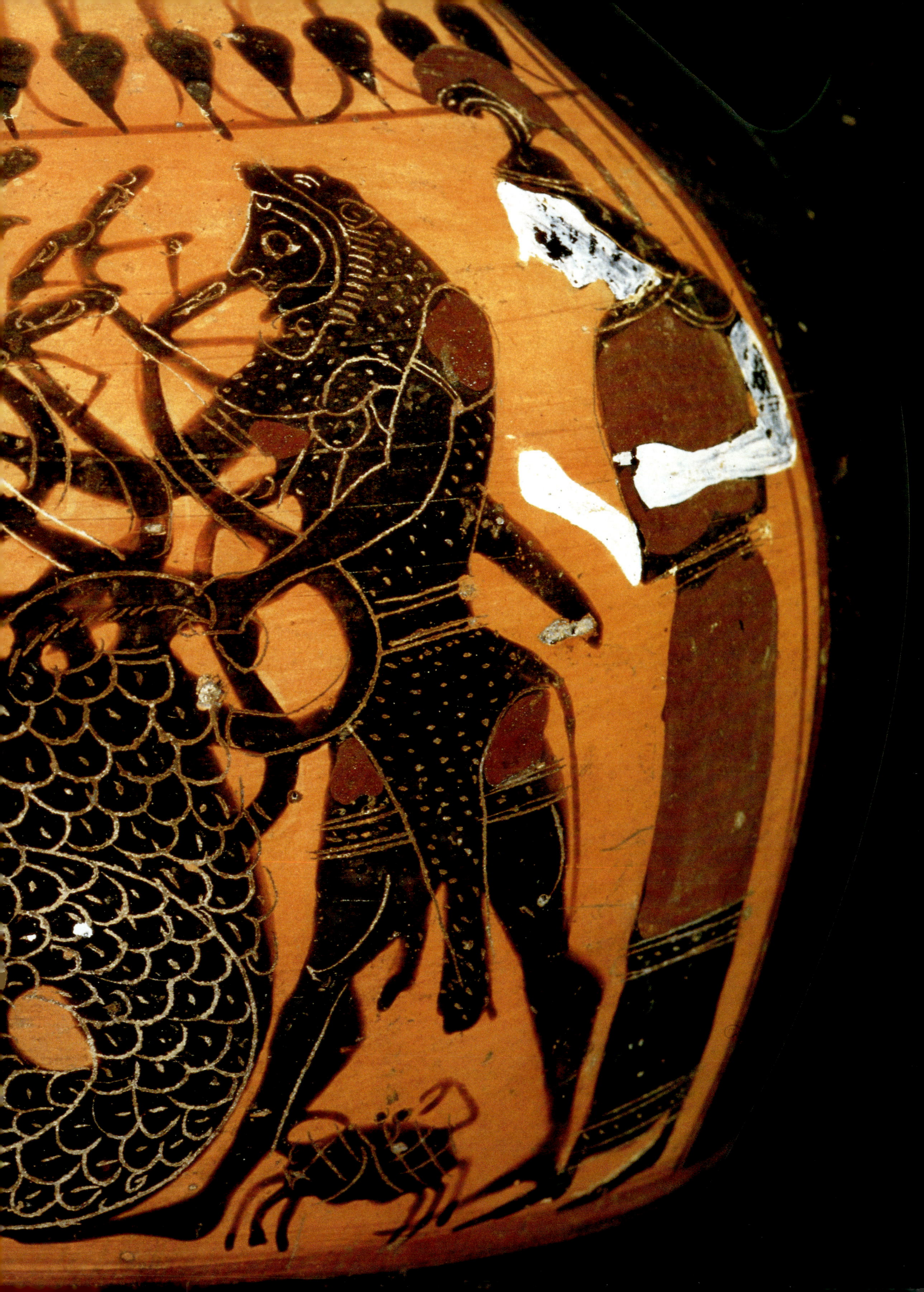

HERCULES EXHAUSTED!

Our hero's expression is unusual: he seems overcome by the weight of the years and the trials he has borne. Bearded, bulky and old, he has removed the skin of the Nemean lion and is leaning on his club. He leans his head to one side, in an exhausted trance. Hercules seems weary of fighting. But he has not faced all those dangers in vain, for the Delphic oracle has promised that the reward for his labors will be immortality! Our hero has cleared Greek soil, and elsewhere, of monsters and brigands; he has hunted down those who tricked him; he has re-established justice in many lands. So Hercules looks forward to a well merited rest which is still some way off; his sufferings are not over. He will soon undergo the ultimate test. Deianeira fears he no longer loves her and is concocting a love potion which is in fact a poison. Held in a tunic which is burning up his body, Hercules will seek to hasten his death and end his torment by mounting onto a funeral pyre. Then a thunderbolt will split the skies, he will be carried away to Mount Olympus where he will at last become immortal; he will be reconciled with Hera, marry Hebe and become a god.

PERSEUS KILLING THE GORGON

This scene depicts the greatest exploit of Perseus, son of Zeus and Danae. He faces the fearsome Gorgon who turns all those who look at her to stone. Here however, she appears to be less fierce than the grimacing masks, surrounded by serpents, which were so common in the Roman period. This hybrid monster, half-woman and half-animal, stands motionless, an easy prey. To equip himself for the expedition, Perseus first went to the Graeae. He forced them to give him the information he needed when he stole their single eye and single tooth. Mad with anxiety they told him how to lay his hands on everything he needed: the helmet of Hades which made him invisible, a pair of winged sandals and a satchel. Hermes also gave him a bronze sickle. Once he was ready for battle he crept up on the Gorgons while they slept, he flew up into the air above Medusa and, looking at her reflection in the shield held out by Athena, he beheaded the monster without looking into her eyes. Pegasus, the winged horse, sprang out of her severed neck. Perseus put the Gorgon's head in his satchel and returned home. FOLLOWING PAGES

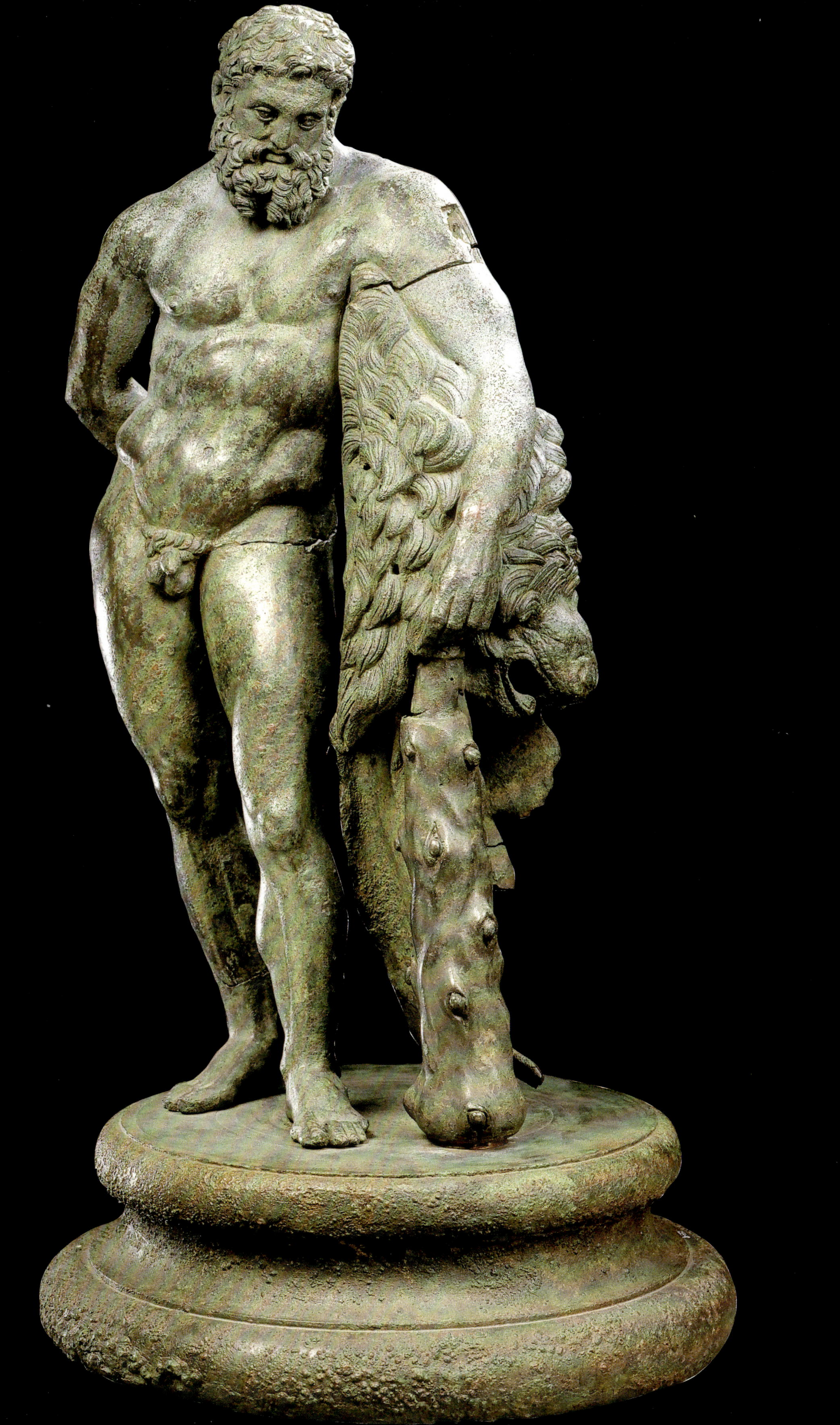

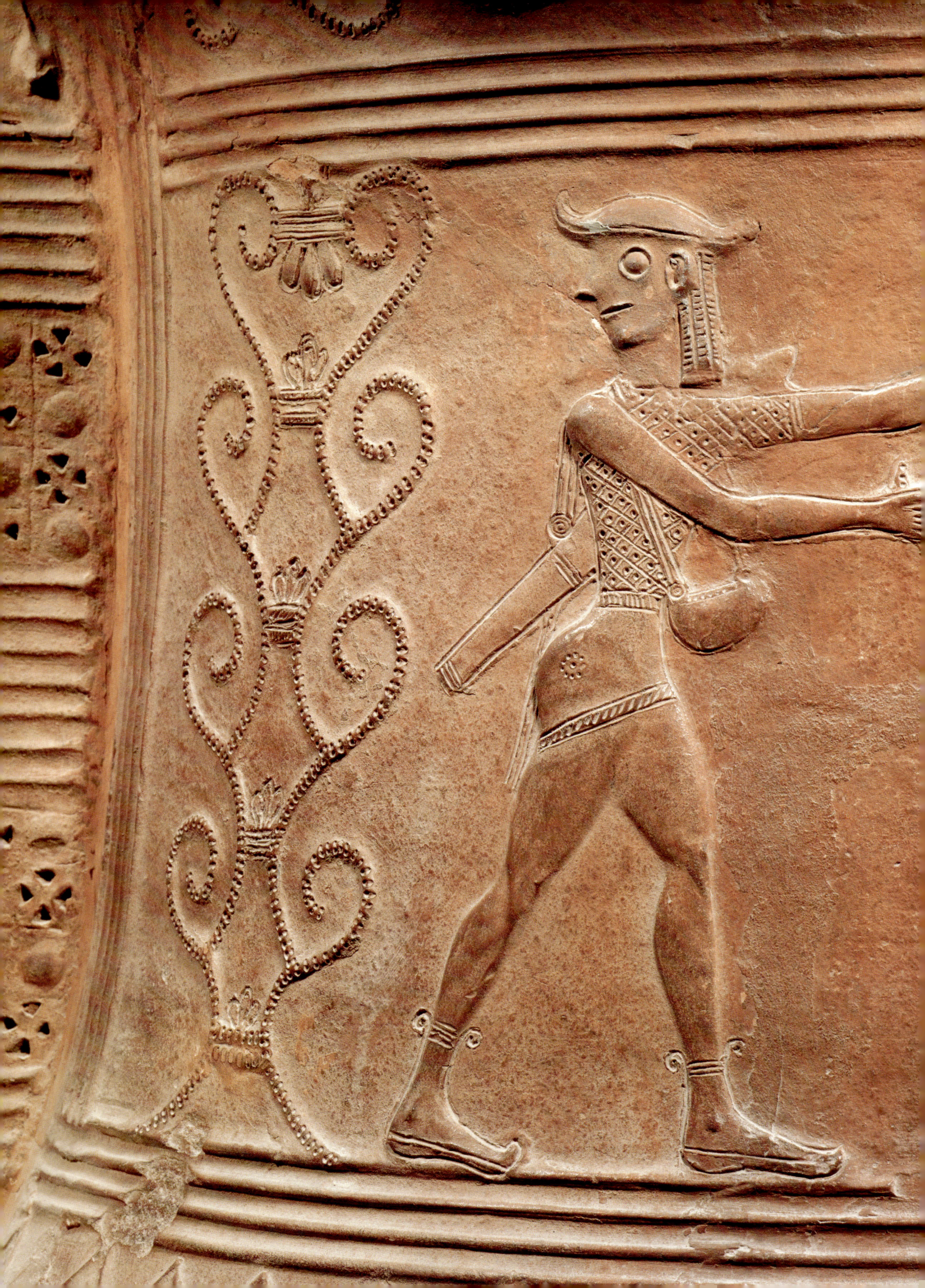

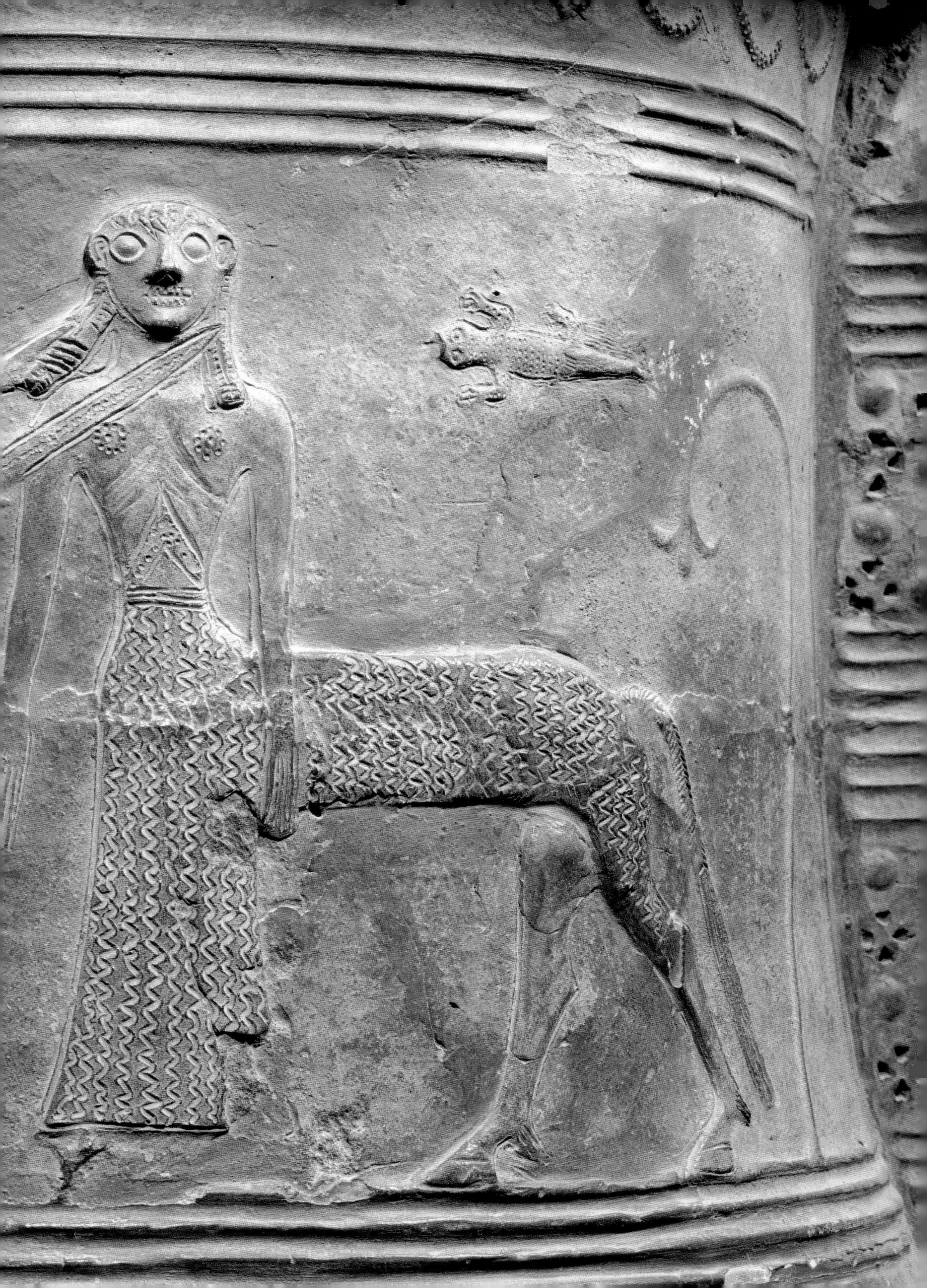

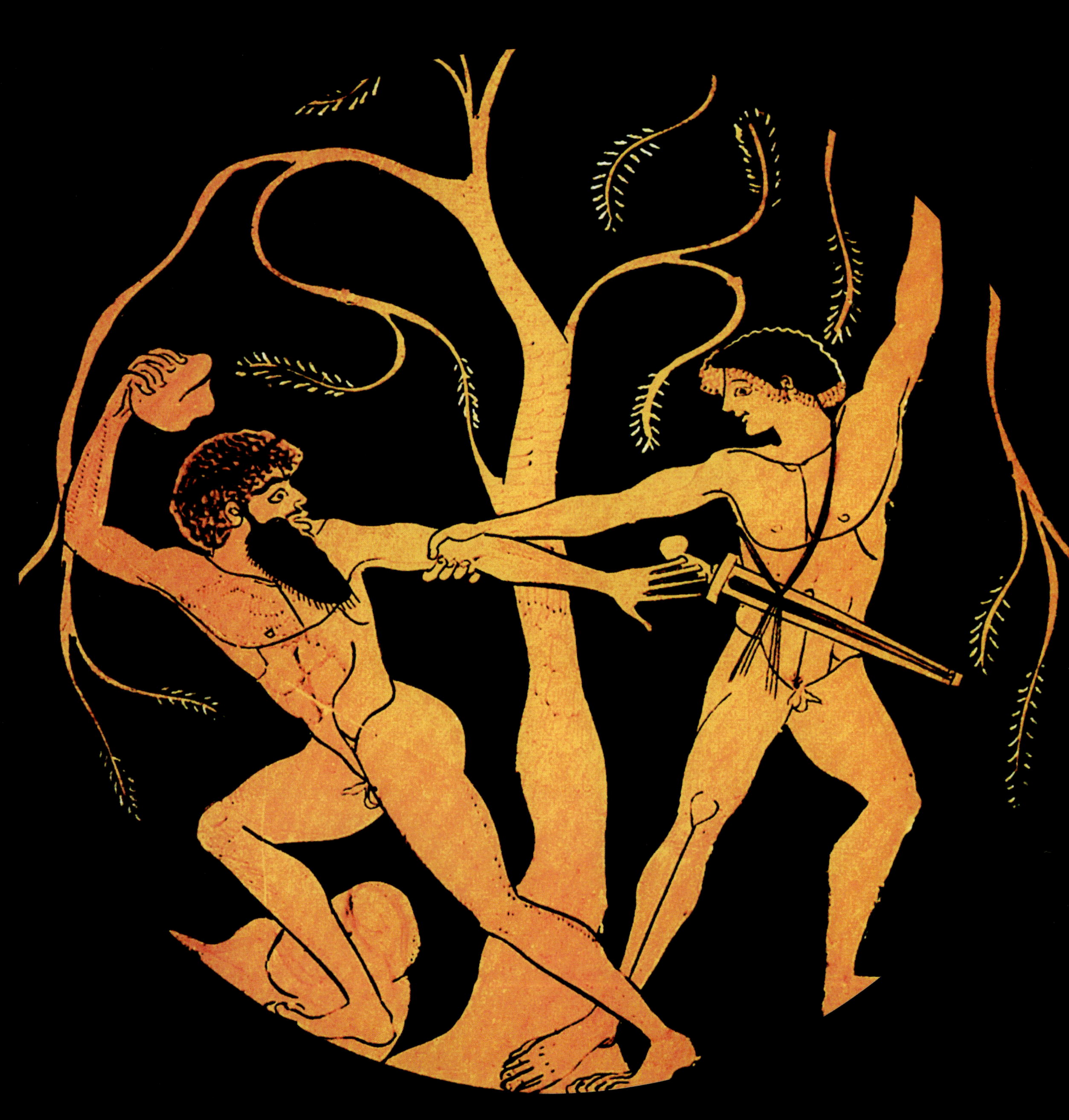

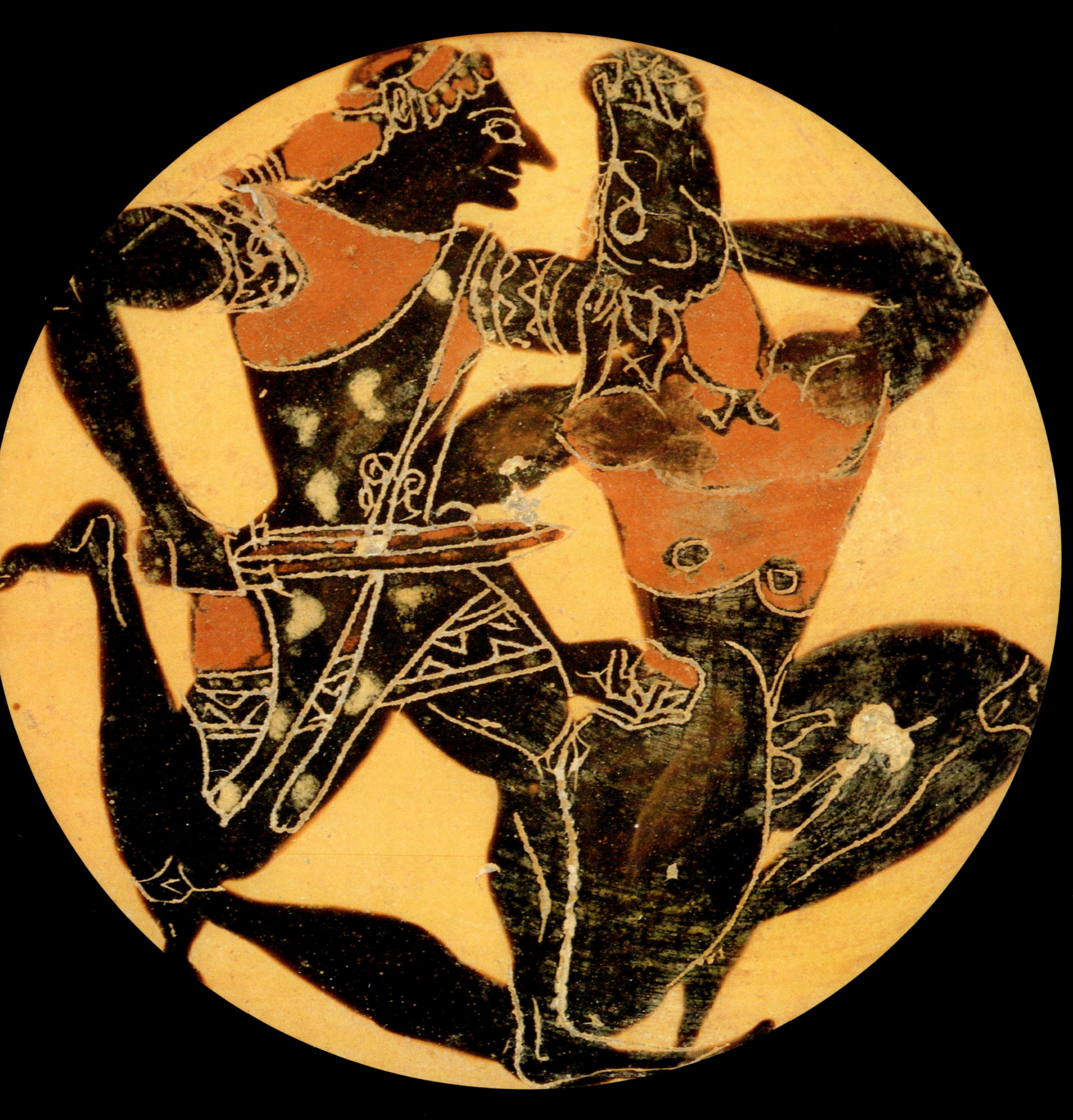

THESEUS FIGHTING THE BRIGAND SINIS

Theseus was still a very young man when he discovered the secret of his birth and set out for Athens to meet his father Aegeus. In an effort to match the exploits of the legendary Hercules he cleared the road to Athens of monsters and brigands. That was how he came across the giant Sinis who was a son of Poseidon who terrorized travelers near Corinth. He used to stretch them between two pine trees he had bent together. When he had secured the unfortunate travelers he allowed the trees to straighten up in opposite directions and the trees tore out their limbs. Theseus was the winner in their encounter and made the executioner suffer the same fate as his victims. PAGE 70

THESEUS AND THE MINOTAUR

When he had finally arrived at his father's palace, Theseus was first of all recognized by Medea the king's wife. This young hero, who has just proved his worth and whose heroic reputation has preceded him, upset the old sorceress so much she tried to poison him. But Aegeus recognized the sword he had left with Theseus' mother Aethra. Once he had been recognized and welcomed by his father, Theseus helped the king consolidate his grip on power. Soon came the time when Athens had to pay its heavy tribute to Minos. Every nine years, the city underwent a dreadful trial: it had to supply seven young men and seven young women, who were offered as victims to the Minotaur. Theseus volunteered as a member of the crew which set sail for Crete. He felt he would be able to confront the monstrous bull and to break the deadly cycle of human sacrifices.

Our hero received unexpected help from Ariadne, the daughter of King Minos. Having been captivated by his good looks she supplied him with a ball of thread which he unraveled as he went deeper into the labyrinth. At its very center awaited his greatest test. Theseus challenged and overcame the Minotaur in an epic struggle which has inspired many artists, and the scene has been depicted many times. To get out of the maze again, all our hero had to do was to follow the thread. PAGE 71

THE ABDUCTION OF ANTIOPE

Hercules was looking for the bravest and best to accompany him on his latest adventure. With the two heroes working together, the mission should be successful. They set off to capture the girdle of Hippolyte, the queen of the Amazons. These young warrior women were not at all fierce and made the strangers welcome; Hercules easily got his hands on his trophy. As for Theseus, he received presents from the beautiful Antiope. Theseus was smitten, invited her on board his boat and immediately set sail, carrying off the young Amazon. She would give him a son Hippolyte, but he later abandoned her for Phaedra. Some say that it was during a pitched battle that Hercules captured his girdle and Theseus carried off his precious plunder. Antiope's abduction made the Amazons furious; they marched on Athens to wage merciless war on Theseus.
OPPOSITE PAGE

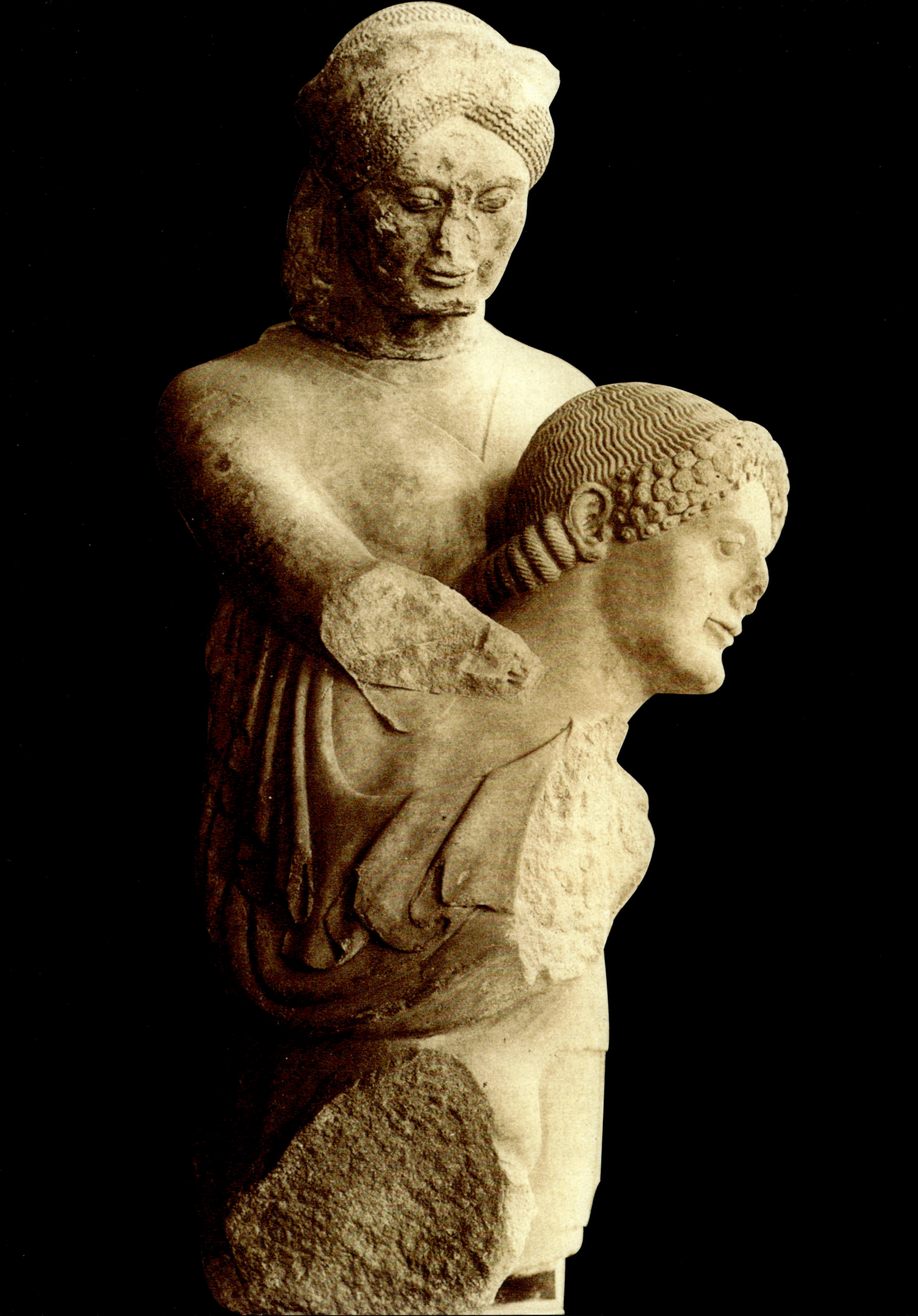

JASON PRESENTS PELEUS WITH THE GOLDEN FLEECE

As Hermes looks on with approval, Jason, accompanied by Medea, introduces himself to the king of Iolcus. He has returned from the dangerous expedition to Colchis with the Argonauts. He has overcome all the hazards of the journey and, as a token of his success, he offers Peleus the prize of his quest: the Golden Fleece. This trophy was supposed to help Jason regain his kingdom: the usurper Peleus had promised the rightful heir to give up the throne in exchange for the famous fleece. In fact the tyrant thought he was dispatching the young man to a certain death.

Jason prepares to take over the reins of power, but is quickly tricked as Peleus goes back on his word. According to some sources, he was forced into exile, because his wife Medea planned to kill Peleus. She persuaded his daughters to indulge in a strange ceremony, which was supposed to make their father young again, but it is in fact a deadly trick. The gullible girls cut Peleus up and boiled him in a cauldron. He did not, alas, return to life.

ULYSSES CONFRONTS HIS WIFE'S SUITORS

Ulysses returns at last to the island of Ithaca after an absence of twenty years. The journey back was hazardous, as Poseidon, who was his sworn enemy, used every opportunity to thwart him, and he wandered for many long years across the seas. He has had to overcome many dangers, escape being eaten by Polyphemus, dodge the spells of Circe, the charms of Calypso and the fatal lure of the Sirens. He has faced adverse winds and dreadful storms, eventually glimpsing the longed for shores of his kingdom. But Ulysses' troubles are not yet at an end!

Disguised as a beggar he enters his own palace full of suitors; they are all fighting to claim his wife Penelope in marriage, and to get their hands on his kingdom. She has bravely made them wait, by tricking them: she has promised to remarry as soon as she has finished weaving her tapestry; but what she wove by day, she unraveled by night. Ulysses reveals his true identity during an archery contest which he won. The master lets them all see who he is and chases the intruders away; he pierces them with his arrows and reestablishes his authority over the kingdom of Ithaca. PAGES 78-79

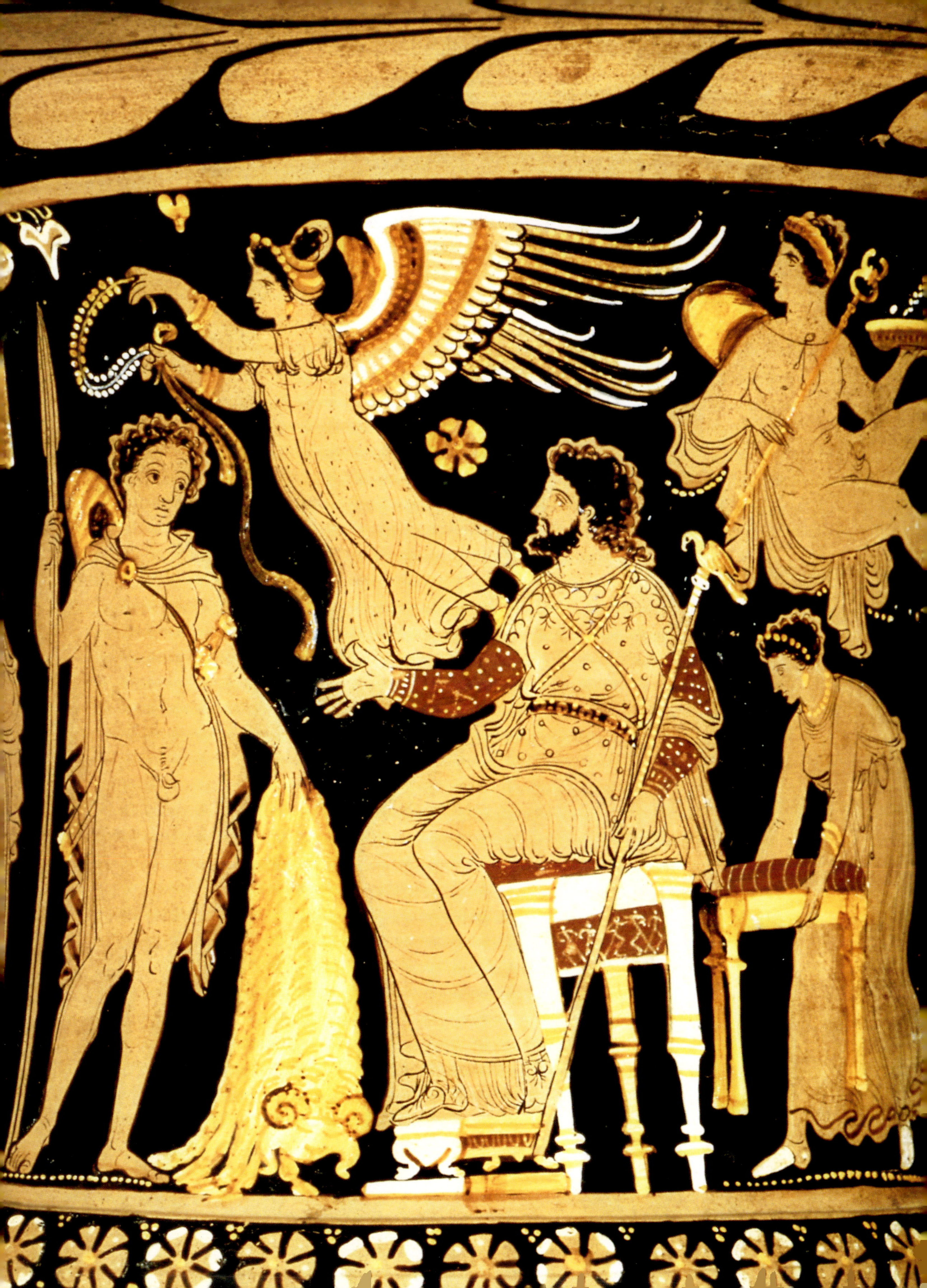

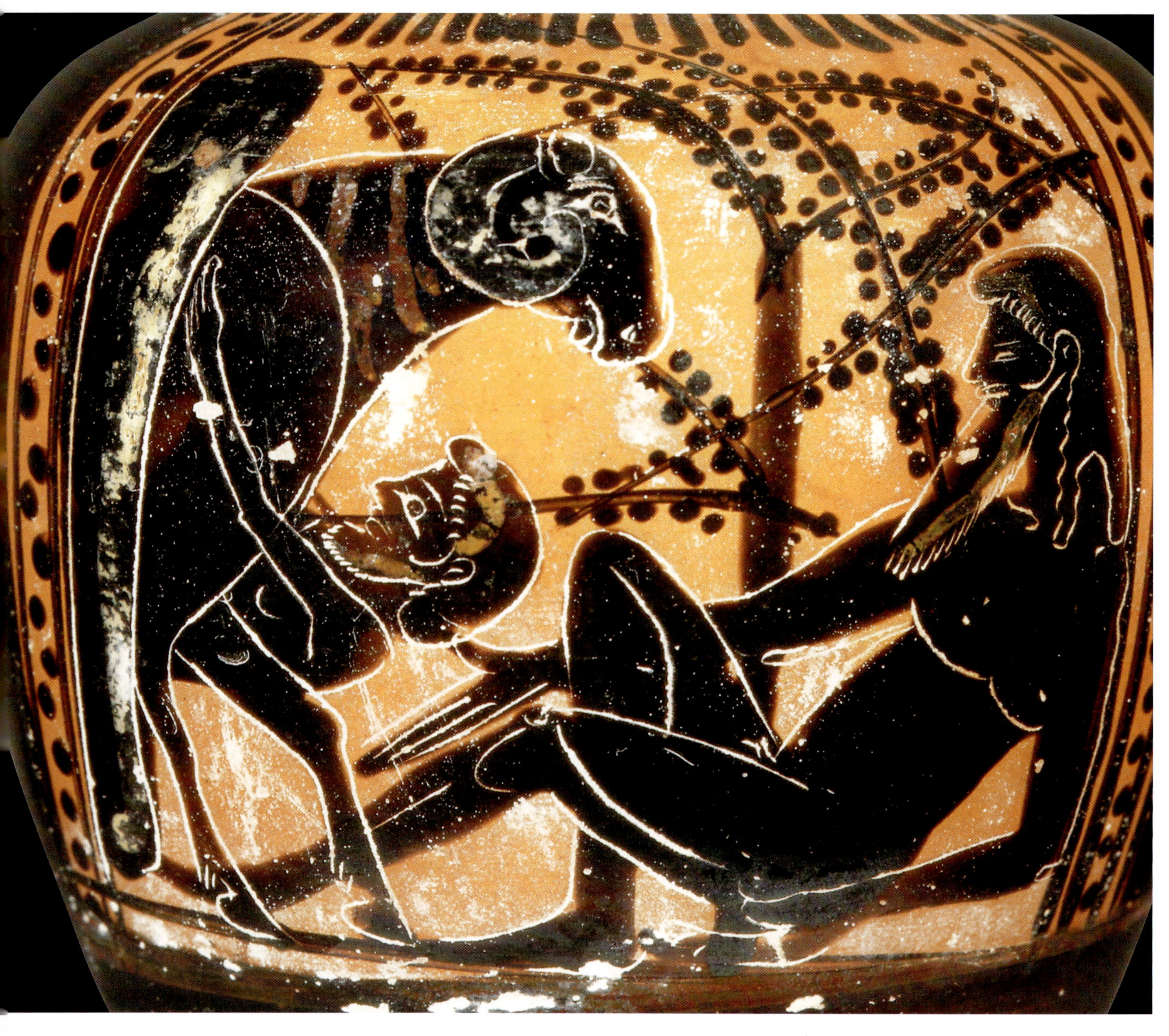

ULYSSES ESCAPES FROM THE CYCLOPS

The *Odyssey*, or return of Ulysses, is a famous story. It takes the hero ten years to return home from Troy to Ithaca. Many adventures extend his journey. During one such exploit, he lands on the island of the Cyclops, who are one-eyed giants. One of them, Polyphemus, shuts Ulysses and his companions up in a cave as he proposes to eat them. But Ulysses, who has told his jailer that his name is "No man", makes him drunk and when he has fallen into a drunken stupor, gouges his eye out with a stake. The other Cyclops come running at his cries, but leave without harming Ulysses when the giant tells them "No man" has injured him. Ulysses and his men escape by hanging under the bellies of his sheep. The giant sits at the entrance to the cave and runs his hand over the backs of all the sheep as they leave the cave for pasture; he is unaware that his captives are hanging beneath. But our hero has now provoked the anger of Poseidon who was the father of Polyphemus. He is not going to get back to Ithaca in a hurry…

ULYSSES AND THE SIRENS

The wanderings of Ulysses bring him face to face with many dangers but also with irresistible charms. So he must foil the spells of the sorceress Circe, only to succumb to the attractions of the nymph Calypso. When he leaves the embraces of Circe, and their son, she advises him to be cautious. He must beware of the Sirens as he sails past the bay of Naples, particularly off the peninsula of Sorrento. Nobody can resist the bewitching call of their singing. These demonic half-women and half birds use their voices to draw sailors into their clutches. The hypnotized sailors fling caution to the winds and are shipwrecked on the rocks from which those beautiful sounds appear to come. There they become easy prey and are devoured by the Sirens. Warned by Circe, Ulysses orders his crew to block their ears with wax. He on the other hand wants to hear their bewitching singing; so he has himself lashed to the mast of his ship, and his companions must under no pretext untie him. Now he hears the alluring pull of their silken voices and experiences a passionate longing to leave his ship and join them. But Ulysses' ship continues on its way, without being lured into this ambush. The Sirens recognize that, for the first time ever, they have failed, and in despair throw themselves into the sea and perish.

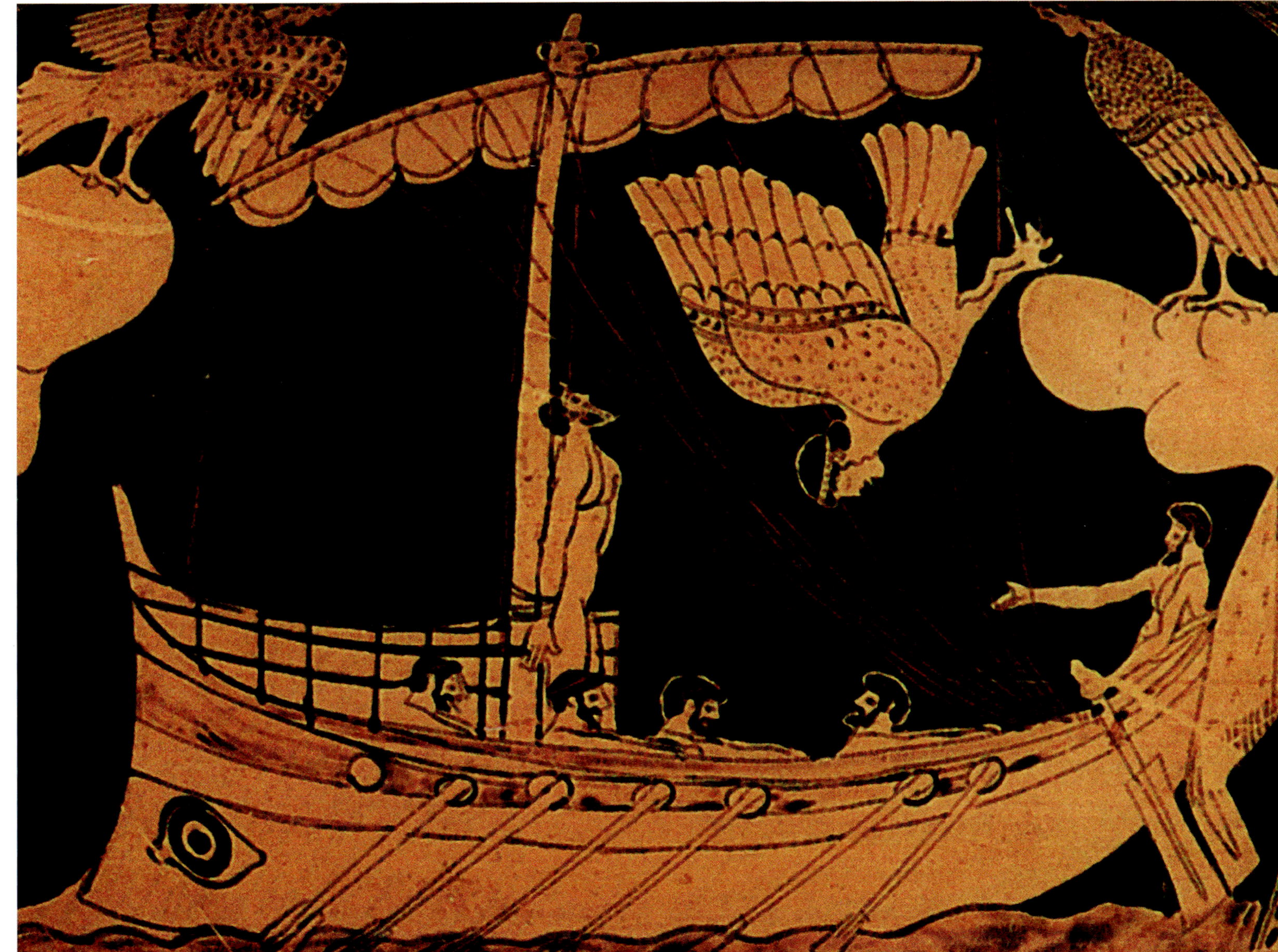

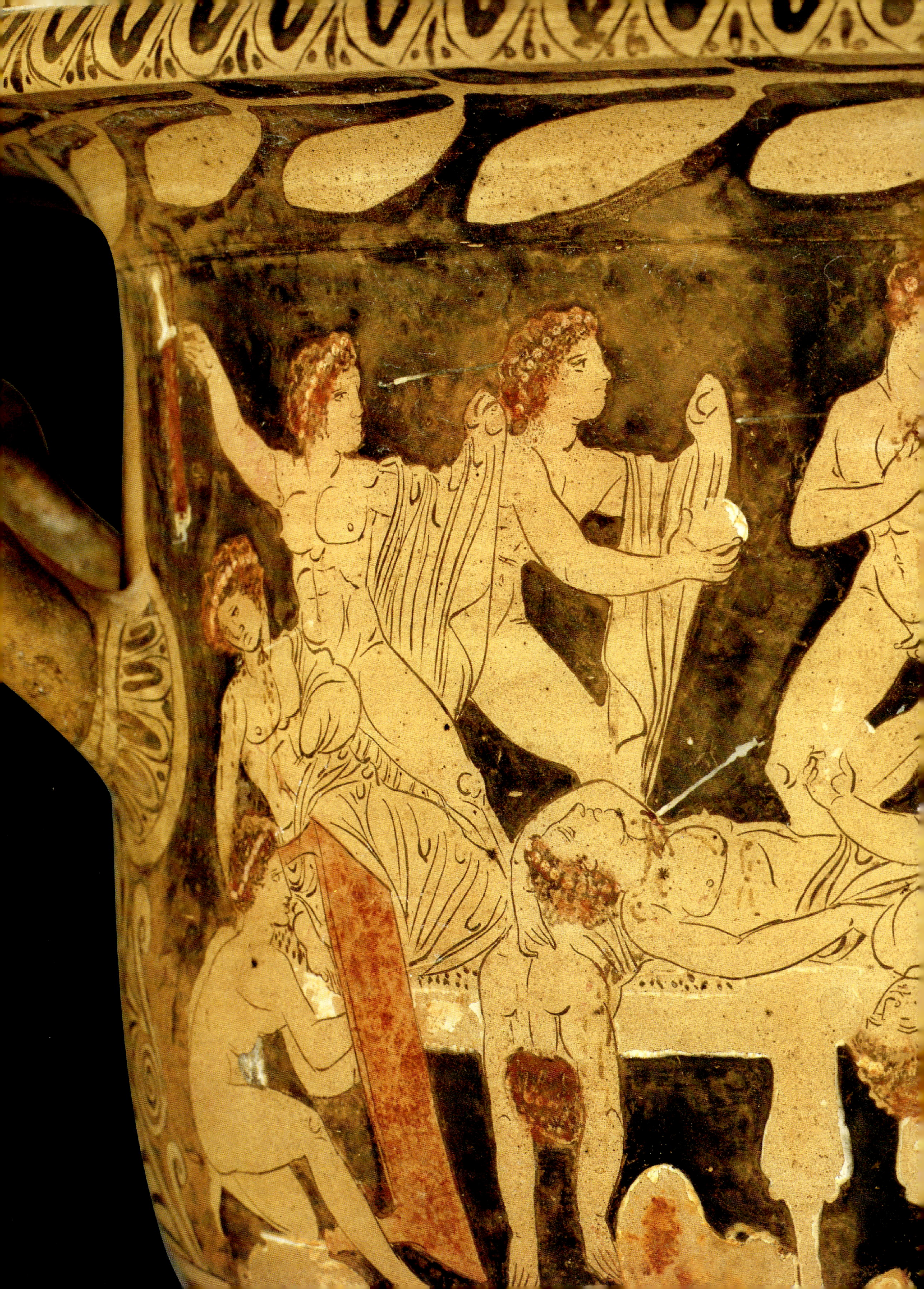

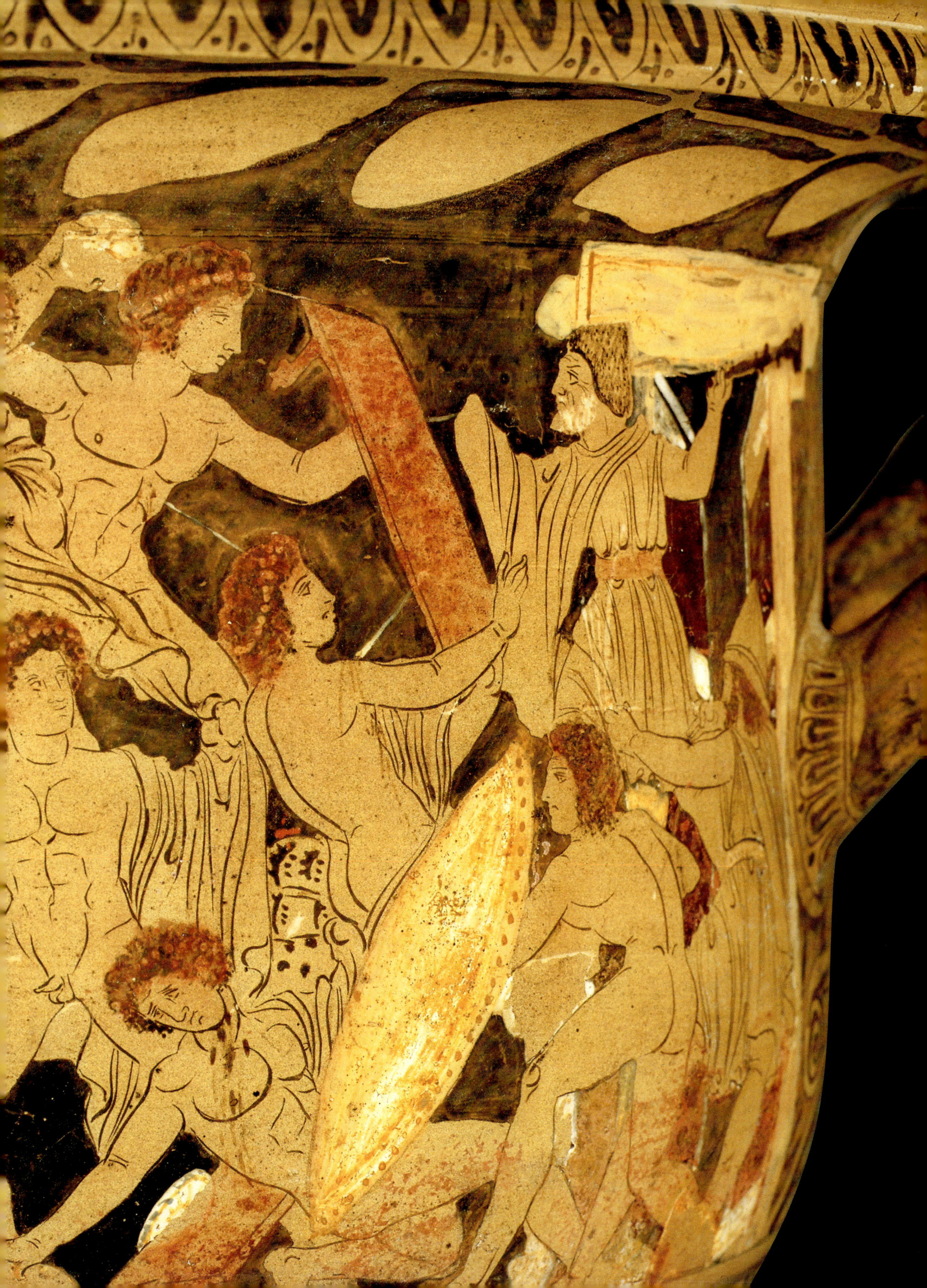

KINGS AND PALACES

Greek soil, the crucible of Hellenic identity, has been trodden underfoot and occupied by successive waves of immigration. These invasions have determined the sudden upsurges, failures and mutual enriching of primitive civilizations. According to myth, Ionians, Achaeans, Aeolians and Dorians mixed together and, when faced by the barbarians, soon recognized they had a common Greek identity. Archaeology can throw some light on how these different ethnic groups arrived and merged, and on the cultural endowments and technical skills which each one of them brought.

About 2700 BC, the first massive wave of immigration arrived from Anatolia in Asia Minor and took over continental Greece, the islands and Crete (Crete in particular still bears traces of primitive Neolithic settlement). The invaders brought with them skills from eastern societies. Thus we find early signs of cities and work in bronze. From this human core will develop a brilliant civilization, firstly in the Aegean Sea, then in Crete, finally in continental Greece.

The first region to flourish was the Archipelago of the Cyclades, which was the bridge between Anatolia in the east and Greece. These islands, among them Paros, Tinos and Syros, are rich in marble quarries, so we find traces of remarkable artistry: many statuettes with beautiful, clear and delicate lines; oval faces, almost abstract in realization, signs of real aesthetic sensitivity. The statuettes of the harp player or the flute player and the female figures with their stylized curves are full of grace and harmony. They tell us the worship of the fertility goddess, the Great Mother, was widespread in the Aegean region. These works are intensely moving and have inspired artists such as Brancusi. Cycladian culture declined about 2000 BC when the area was subjected to Cretan influence, which was then in full flower.

This is the beginning of the great period of Cretan and Minoan civilization. Minoan comes from the word for king, minos; the name Greek mythology has given to a legendary king. The palaces of Cnossos and Phaestos were built, evidence of strong central power. The early buildings disappeared about 1700 BC; following natural disasters, or else invasions, we are not sure. But they were quickly rebuilt and in even more luxurious style at Mallia, Phaestos, Kato Zakro and Cnossos. This latter city, at the very center of the network of roads stretching out to the provinces, was soon the most powerful city on the island. The wealth of Cretan society depended on flourishing means of production. The farmers were already growing corn, vines and olive trees, fig and pomegranate trees were also known. These people were also adept at animal husbandry, bee keeping, hunting and fishing. Ceramics, cabinet making, engraving and gold work were all practiced; they created objects of great refinement. The design of luxury items, with gold and precious stones, together with the sale of agricultural produce, was the basis for profitable trade. The Cretans were intrepid sailors and soon established a sea empire all over the Mediterranean. They set up trading posts and had contact with the people of Phoenicia, Egypt, Sicily and Greece.

Their vast palaces reflect an exceptional civilization: with many rooms built around a central yard and linked by corridors and stairs. This network of buildings of course calls to mind the story of the labyrinth of Daedalus, built to enclose the Minotaur. Cretans were concerned for comfort and hygiene and built sophisticated baths and toilets: fresh water was piped in and wastewater discharged by an ingenious system of drains. Colored and lively frescoes covered the palace walls. They show how these people lived and how their elegantly dressed young ladies looked. Friezes dug up at Santorini, depicting young boxers and a fisherman, show how Cretan culture flourished on that island. The earthquake and volcanic eruption which destabilized the entire region in 1450 BC weakened Crete and exposed it to the ambitions of the marauding Mycenaeans...

Mycenaeans were from the mainland of Greece which had developed differently from the Aegean islands. In the 3rd millennium BC influences from the east had developed side by side with the growth of local civilizations: bronze work, ceramics, and sea trade had helped the growth of the city of Lerni in the Bay of Navplion. However this part of Greece was more exposed than the islands and saw its progress inhibited by new barbarian invaders, the Ionians perhaps. About 2000 BC, they swept down from the north and violently overran the country. This intrusion resulted in a cultural recession. Nevertheless the newcomers learned from those already there, assimilated new techniques, myths and religious traditions. The coming together of these peoples resulted, about 1580 BC, in a new (Mycenaean) civilization. The name came from the most powerful city, Mycenae. At about the same time the Achaeans arrived in the land and quietly infiltrated into the population.

This emerging society profited from its contacts with Crete. The Mycenaeans were skilful, audacious and learned quickly; they took ideas from Crete and adapted them. The mainland was soon covered in rich palaces in the capitals of the various kingdoms: Mycenae, Tiryns, Athens, Pylos and Thebes. These cities were always at war with each other, were built on elevated positions and enclosed by gigantic walls. A very hierarchical and bureaucratic society gradually developed around the wanax, or king. This sovereign was assisted by the General of the Army, officers, administrators and accountants, as well as by a powerful clergy. As in Crete the fortresses were decorated with dazzling frescoes depicting processions of women, warriors and horses. Domed tombs have revealed numerous funerary objects. They show Cretan influences certainly; but also bear witness to the genius of the Achaeans. Gold masks, necklaces, jewelry and diadems, cups, carved drinking vessels, goblets, daggers whose handles are incrusted with precious stones... so many things have been found! These silver and gold items are so expertly made; they are unchallenged masterpieces of local skill! Finally, composite Linear B writing was used on the mainland and was both syllabic and ideographic; it derived from Cretan Linear A. Only the former has been deciphered revealing a Hellenic dialect; the Mycenaeans were already Greeks!

Trade, plunder and wars allowed this powerful civilization to spread out into the Mediterranean basin, from Macedonia to southern Italy, even as far as Asia Minor and Syria. In the 15th century BC the Achaeans were no longer happy to admire the masters of Crete, they took over the island, then occupied Rhodes. About 1230 BC they set out to conquer the rich city of Troy. Homer, who immortalized this epic story in the *Iliad*, named the Greek leaders: the expedition was led by Agamemnon, King of Mycenae! About 1200 BC this culture disappeared. Several factors could explain this disappearance: earthquakes, popular revolts or invasion by the Dorians. After the Ionians, the Achaeans and the Aeolians, this latest group arrived and settled during the 2nd millennium BC. This was the last Indo-European wave of immigrants. The assimilation of these groups, who all had common origins, was the beginning of the Greek identity.

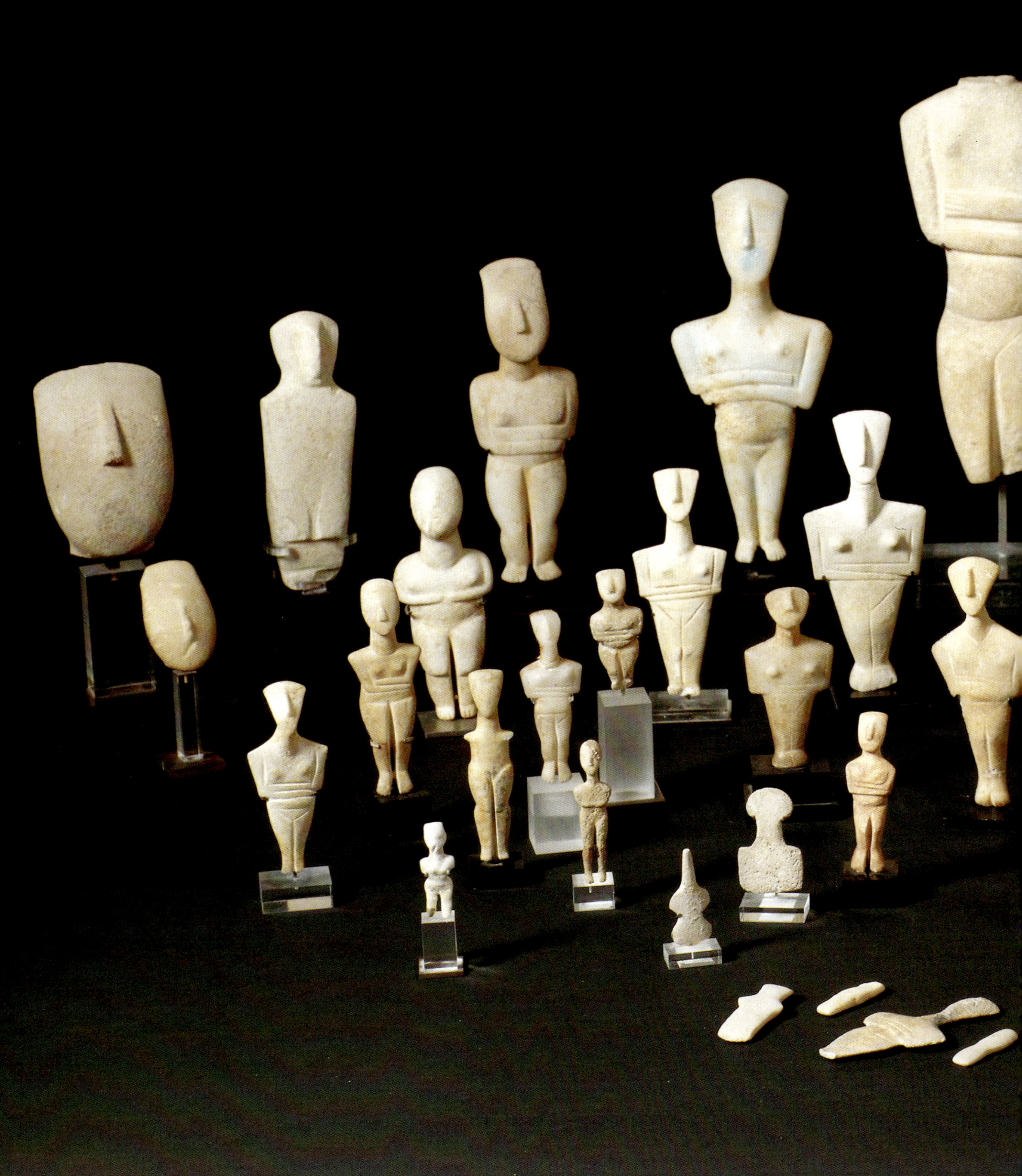

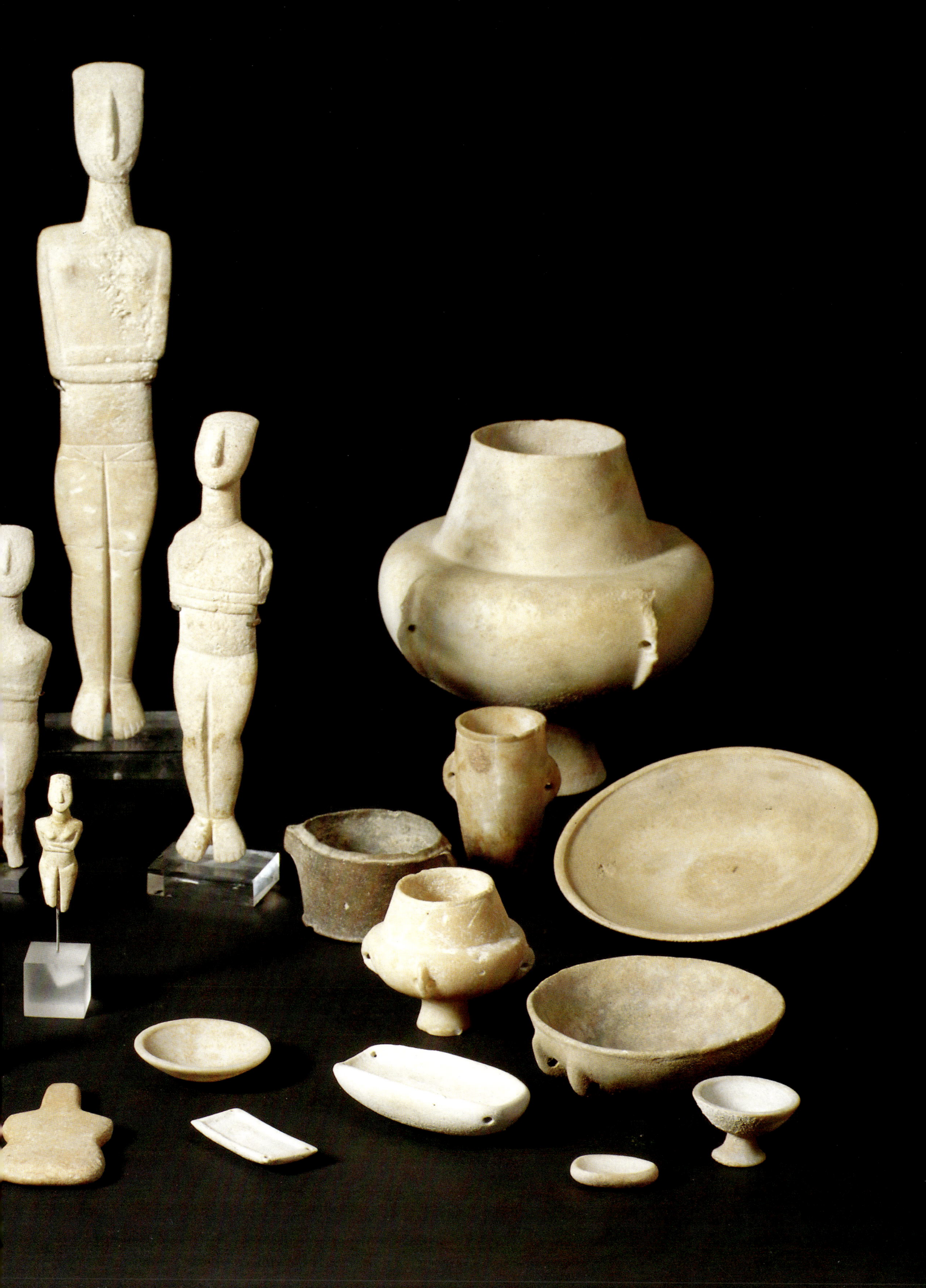

AEGEAN STATUETTES

These little statues from the Cyclades were discovered towards the end of the 18th century. They are between two inches and five feet high and archaeologists at first took little interest in them. Early judgments were negative since the classical ideal was fashionable at the time and made no allowance for other forms of art. However, about 1880, these marble idols attracted the attention of scholars and the wider public. Early rudimentary figures from the Cyclades are dated from between 3000 and 2600 BC; they were soon replaced (between 2600 and 2100 BC) by more refined examples of work. Craftsmen had now acquired greater technical skill: noses appeared on oval or triangular faces. We now see arms, often crossed in front of the body, and legs with greater detail and clearness.

These stylized figures were often female and were thought by many to be representations of the Great Earth Mother. But men also figured. The most famous of them is the violin player of Keros and great technical skill is apparent in this work. PREVIOUS PAGES

AT PRAYER

This little statue is from Crete and shows either a priestess or a member of the public at prayer. It is dated between 1110 and 800 BC. It has a classical design, often seen on coins and seals from Knossos. With raised arms and conically shaped skirt the young woman is calling on a god or goddess. Such a prayer scene might often be seen in a sacred enclosure, at the foot of a tree.

The worshippers danced around the tree trunk and brought offerings for the god. In Minoan Crete and Mycenaean Greece, trees were often objects of worship as the Immortals lived in them, but they soon detached themselves from plants and took on human form. This young woman is seeking a divine revelation: gods and goddesses would appear in the air, often showing themselves amongst the leaves or sitting on a branch.

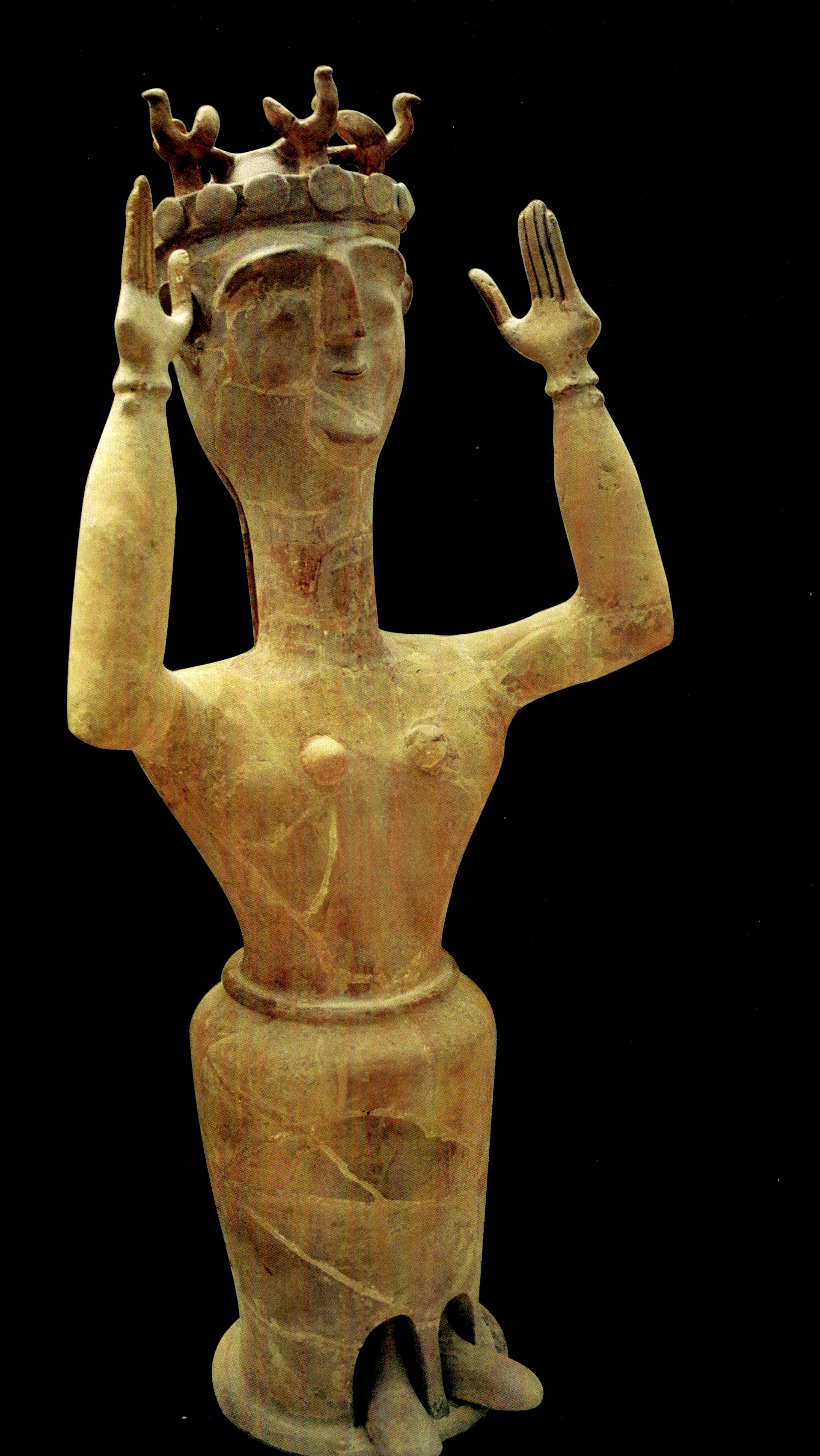

A HOUSE AT KNOSSOS

The splendor of Cretan civilization is evident in the dwellings built by Cretan merchants, who had amassed fortunes through overseas trade. This model demonstrates the art of their architects and shows how they had achieved a degree of complexity and refinement in buildings dated between 1650 and 1400 BC.

This house has a ground floor, generally used for storing the wine press and wine jars. Above are the living quarters which have a colonnade opening onto a terrace and balcony; so they are very open to the outside world.

THE DOLPHIN FRESCO

The palace at Knossos was discovered and investigated by the British archaeologist Sir Arthur Evans. It had been built about 2000 BC and was a complex and sophisticated structure. The fragments of mural painting which have been uncovered there suggest a pleasurable, colorful and festive lifestyle. Minoan artists depicted nature as abundantly rich: full of partridges, cats and dolphins. There are also hunting scenes and games involving bulls. The island's nobility come to life in these scenes; we admire the beauty of their young women and the magnificent build of their athletes, such as "the Parisian woman" or "the Prince with lilies". The dolphin fresco discovered in the queen's quarters was reconstructed by the archaeologist on site where visitors can come and admire it. FOLLOWING PAGES

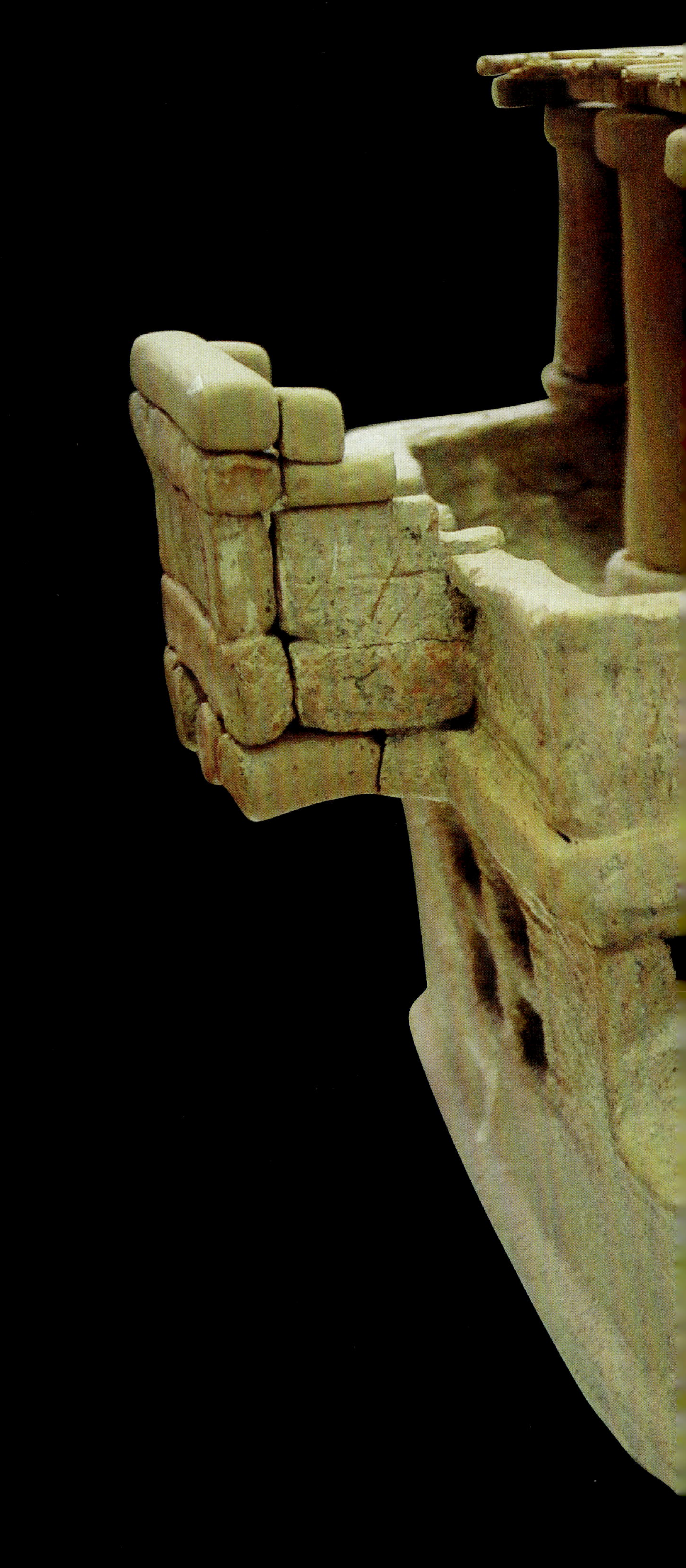

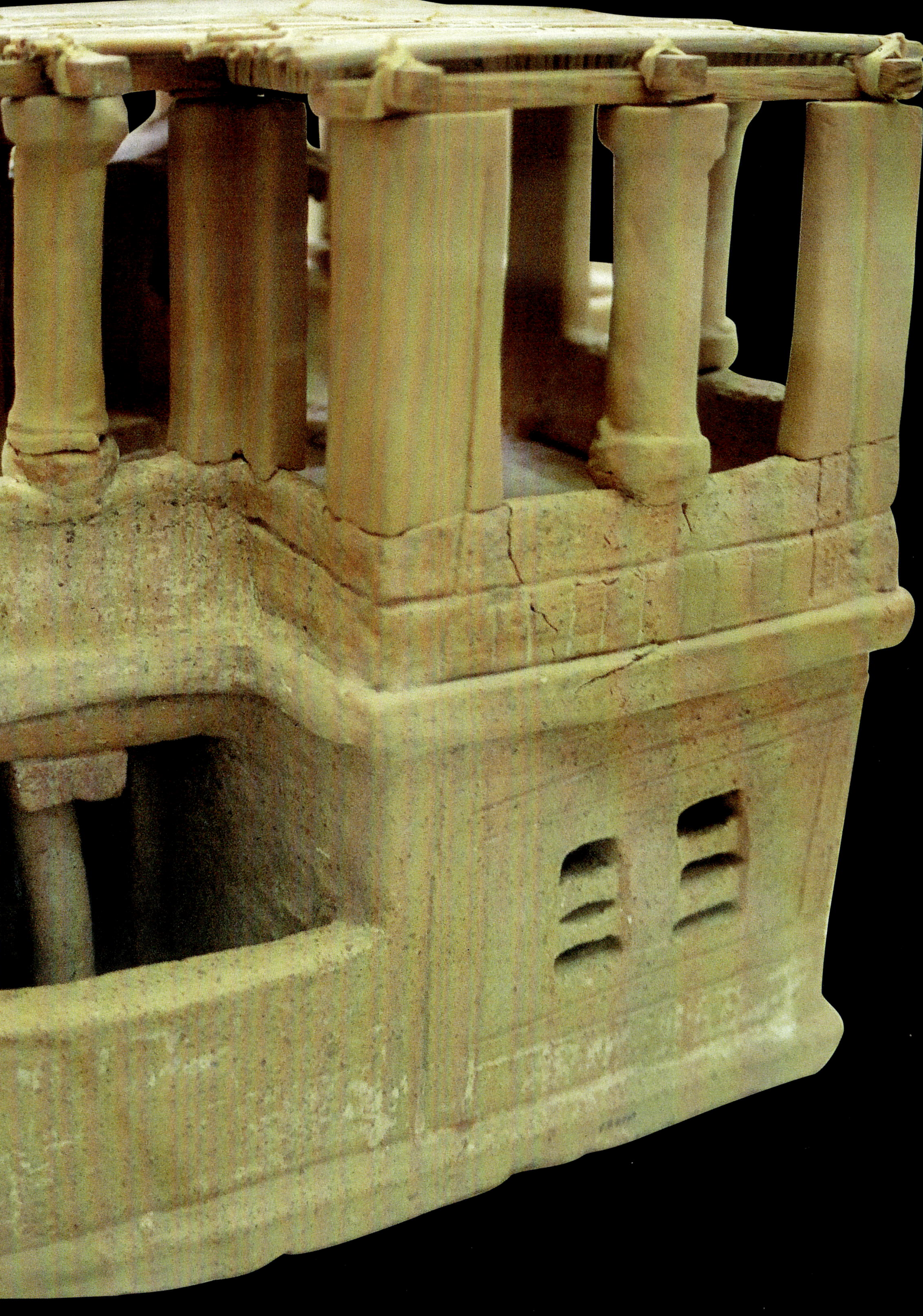

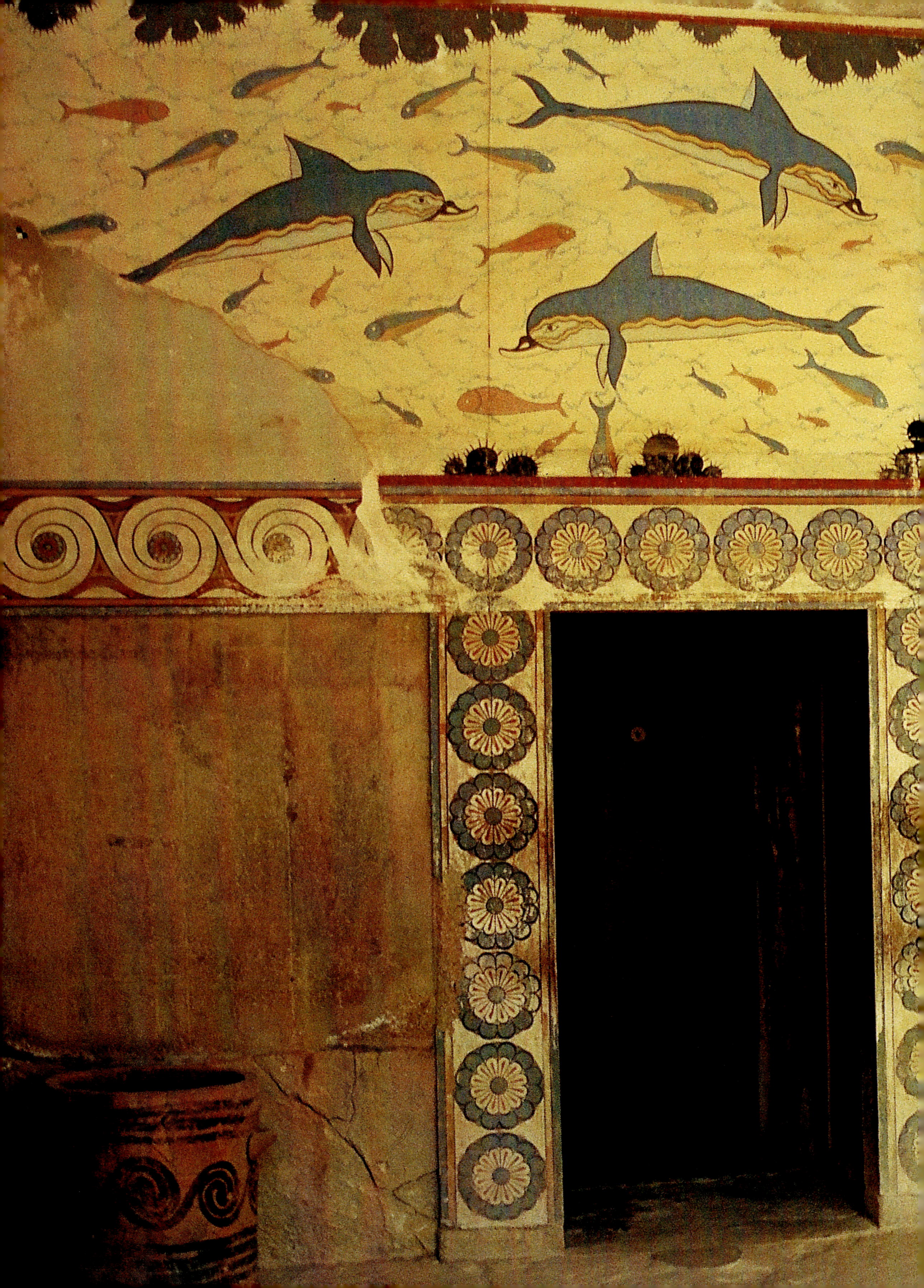

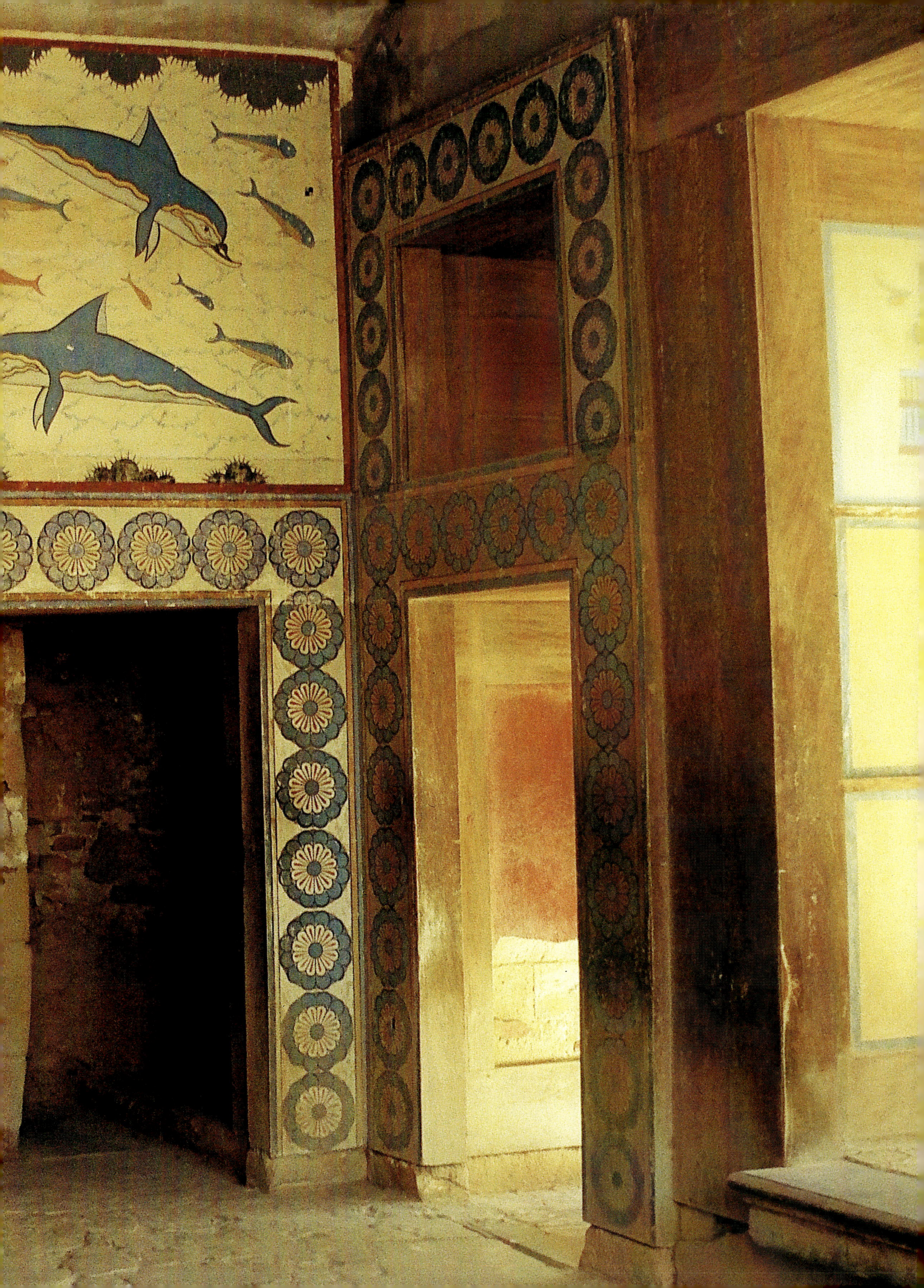

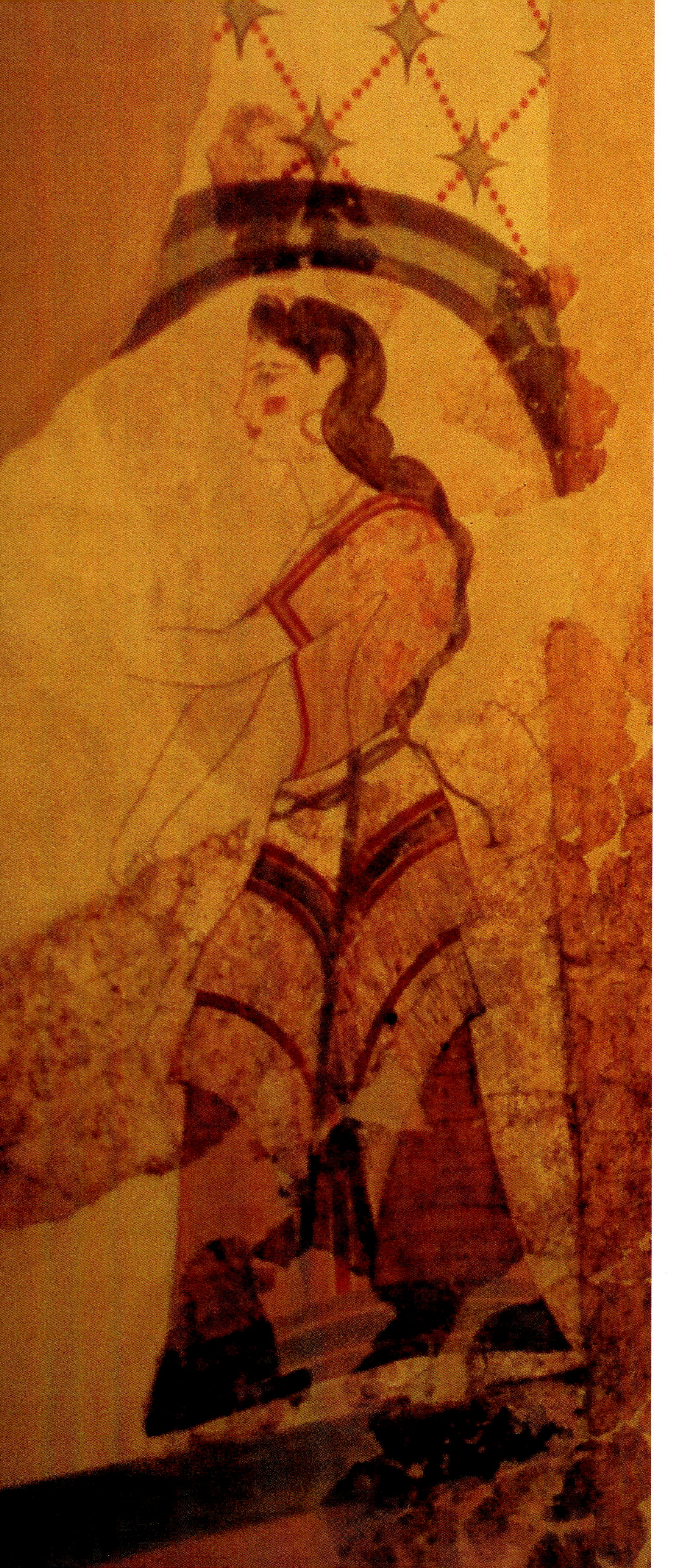

THE FRESCOES OF SANTORINI

In 1967 the ruins of a Bronze Age city were discovered at Akrotiri on the island of Thira, better known as Santorini. They had been preserved beneath the ashes of a volcanic explosion which occurred about 1450 BC. Archaeologists found magnificent frescoes; similar in style and content to Cretan paintings.

The young woman in profile is closely related to the aristocratic beauties of Crete. She displays all the elegance of her rank: a beautiful dress, jewels and elaborate hair styling.

To the right the wall is decorated with papyrus. These suggest the plant and floral arrangements which appear to have been highly prized and receive their finest expression in the so-called Spring fresco. Other paintings which are now well known were discovered in the buried city: blue monkeys, boxers, antelopes and a fisher-man. Cretan and Egyptian influences are striking. The island appears to have been a meeting place for all the peoples of the eastern Mediterranean; a major center of economic and cultural exchange in the Aegean archipelago in the middle of the 2nd millennium BC.

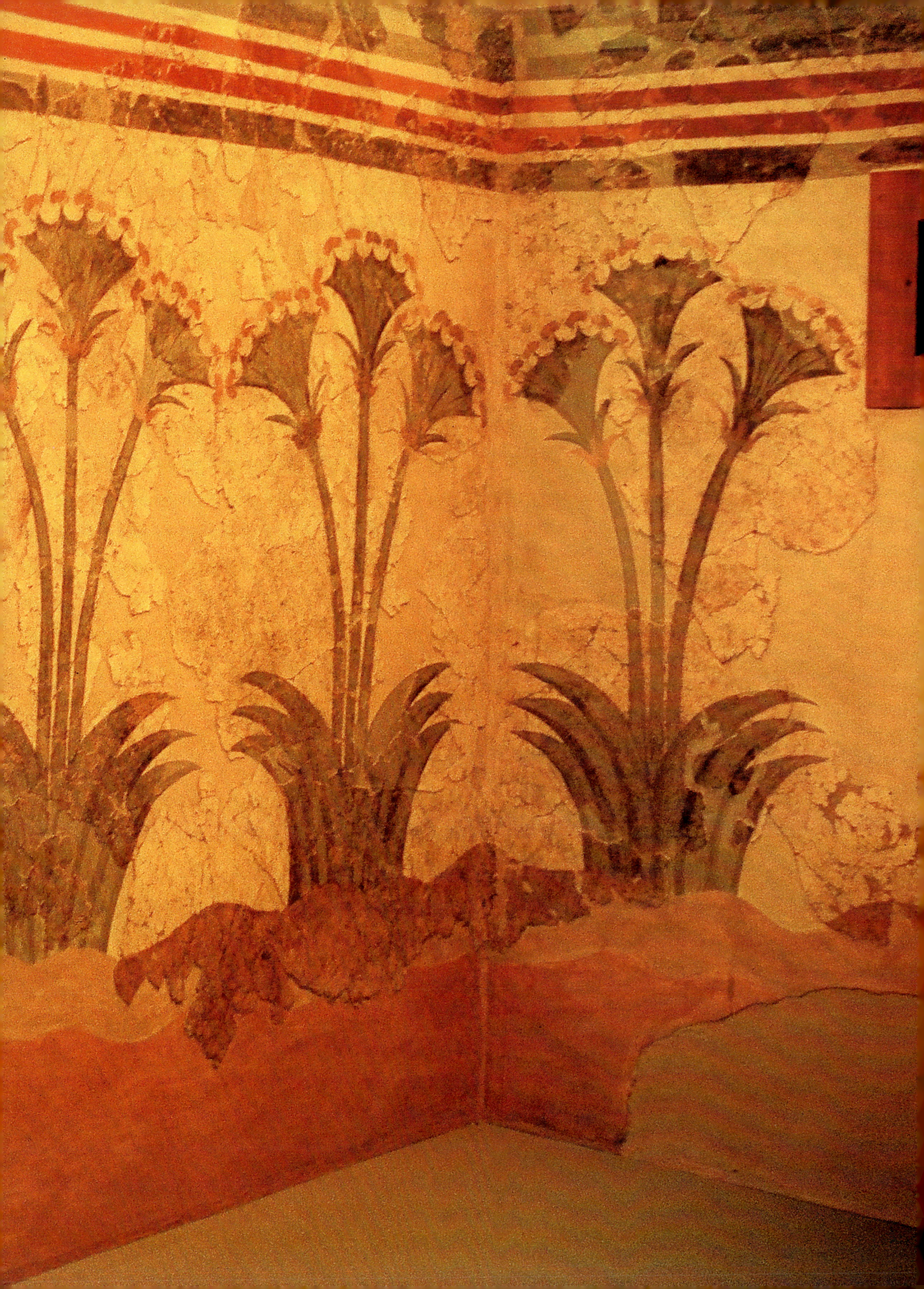

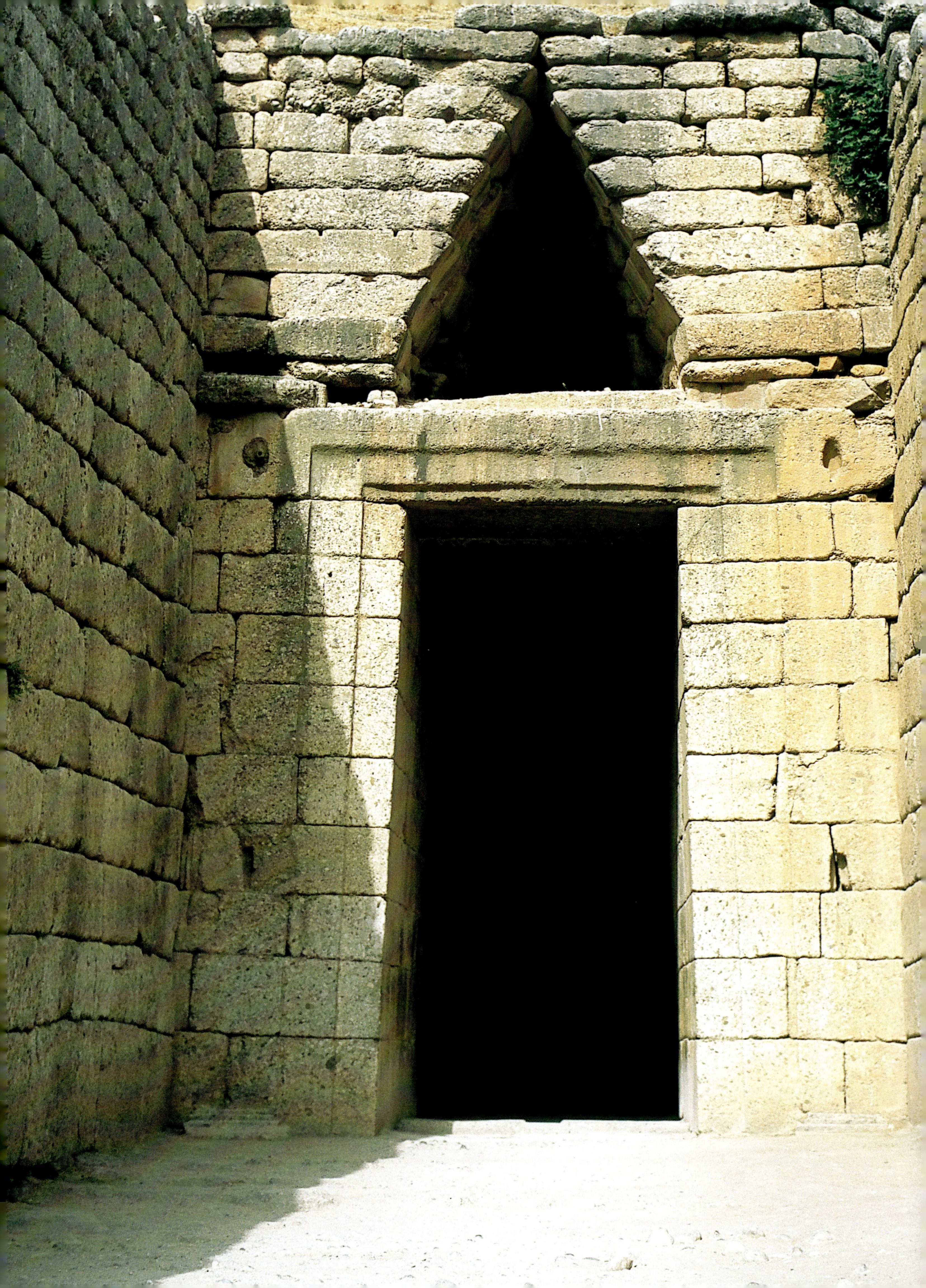

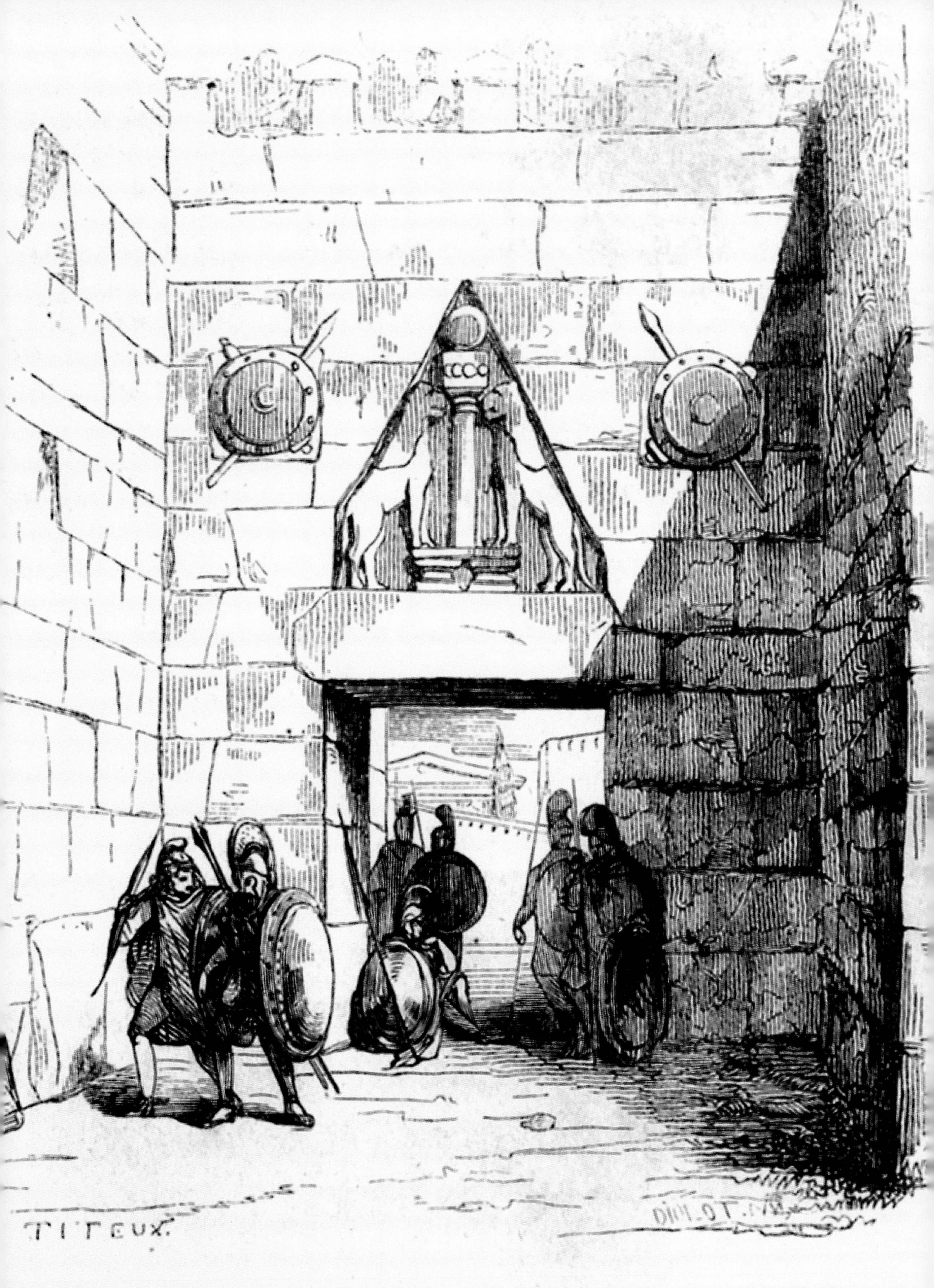
TITEUX.

THE TREASURE OF ATREUS AND THE LION GATEWAY AT MYCENAE

These two architectural items from the site at Mycenae are obviously related and have a harmonious symmetry. The first door opens into a tomb with a tholos, long considered to be the tomb of the legendary Agamemnon, while the second is the entrance to the palace of Atreus. One opening has a colossal single stone lintel surmounted by a triangle which serves to distribute the weight of the walls. The other is decorated with two lions. They face each other on either side of an altar bearing a sacred pillar. The huge fortification walls of massive stones, was built about 1350 or 1330 BC. PREVIOUS PAGES

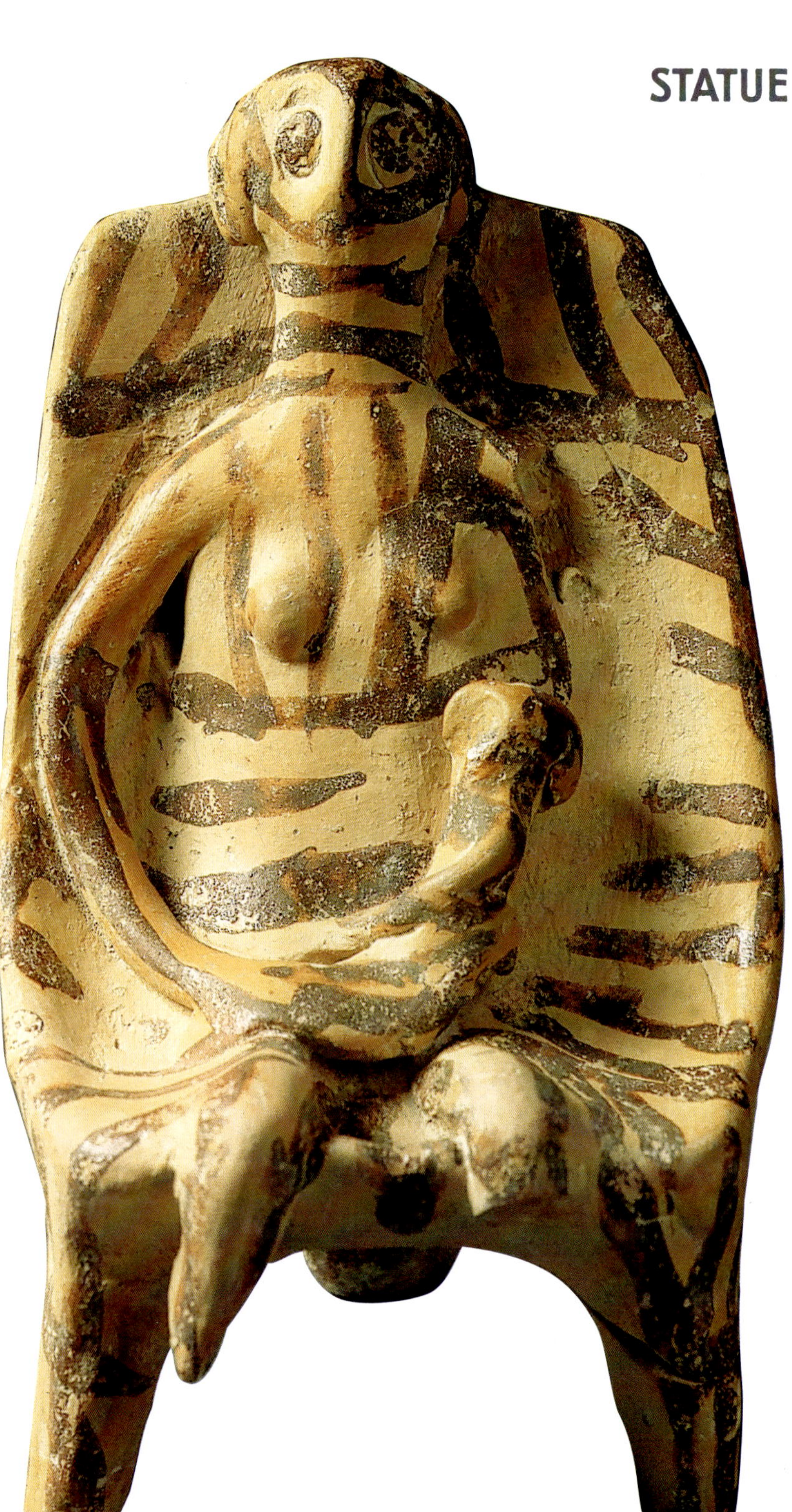

STATUE OF A CHILD-REARING WOMAN

This baked clay statuette represents a mother sitting in splendor and dignity carrying her newly-born child in her arms. It comes from Mycenae and was made about 1360 BC by a craftsman with experience of Cretan techniques. He has used that knowledge to depict this little figure of a mother rearing her child, a form which paid tribute to the cherishing role of women who give life and raise children.

THE MASK OF AGAMEMNON

A great amount of material has been found in the graves of Mycenae, amongst them this golden funeral mask, the symbol of royal immortality. We can see that the civilization which flourished on the site we now call Agamemnon's palace, was rich indeed. Agamemnon was the glorious king celebrated by Homer, who describes in the *Iliad* a kingdom where gold is plentiful. So when, in 1876, Heinrich Schliemann found this finely sculpted mask, he thought he was looking at the face of the great king; that he had discovered the treasure of the sons of Atreus and the tombs of the heroes of Troy. Greatly moved, he sent a telegram to the King of Greece saying, "Today I gazed upon the face of Agamemnon". But he badly wanted what he had found to correspond with what he had read. The mask was in fact made between 1600 and 1500 BC, several centuries before the Greeks assembled before Troy. Nevertheless it is still named after that legendary king. FOLLOWING PAGES

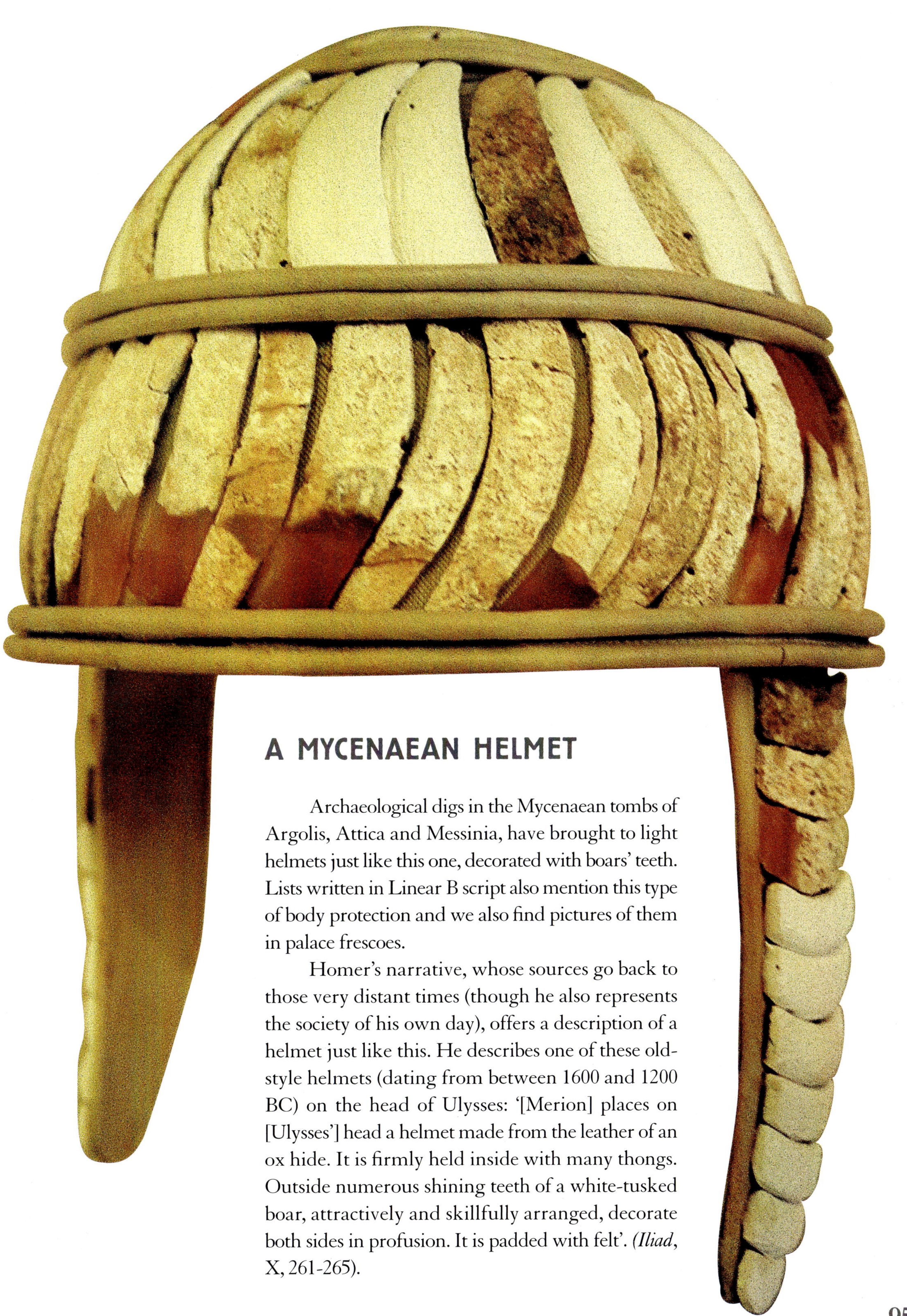

A MYCENAEAN HELMET

Archaeological digs in the Mycenaean tombs of Argolis, Attica and Messinia, have brought to light helmets just like this one, decorated with boars' teeth. Lists written in Linear B script also mention this type of body protection and we also find pictures of them in palace frescoes.

Homer's narrative, whose sources go back to those very distant times (though he also represents the society of his own day), offers a description of a helmet just like this. He describes one of these old-style helmets (dating from between 1600 and 1200 BC) on the head of Ulysses: '[Merion] places on [Ulysses'] head a helmet made from the leather of an ox hide. It is firmly held inside with many thongs. Outside numerous shining teeth of a white-tusked boar, attractively and skillfully arranged, decorate both sides in profusion. It is padded with felt'. *(Iliad*, X, 261-265).

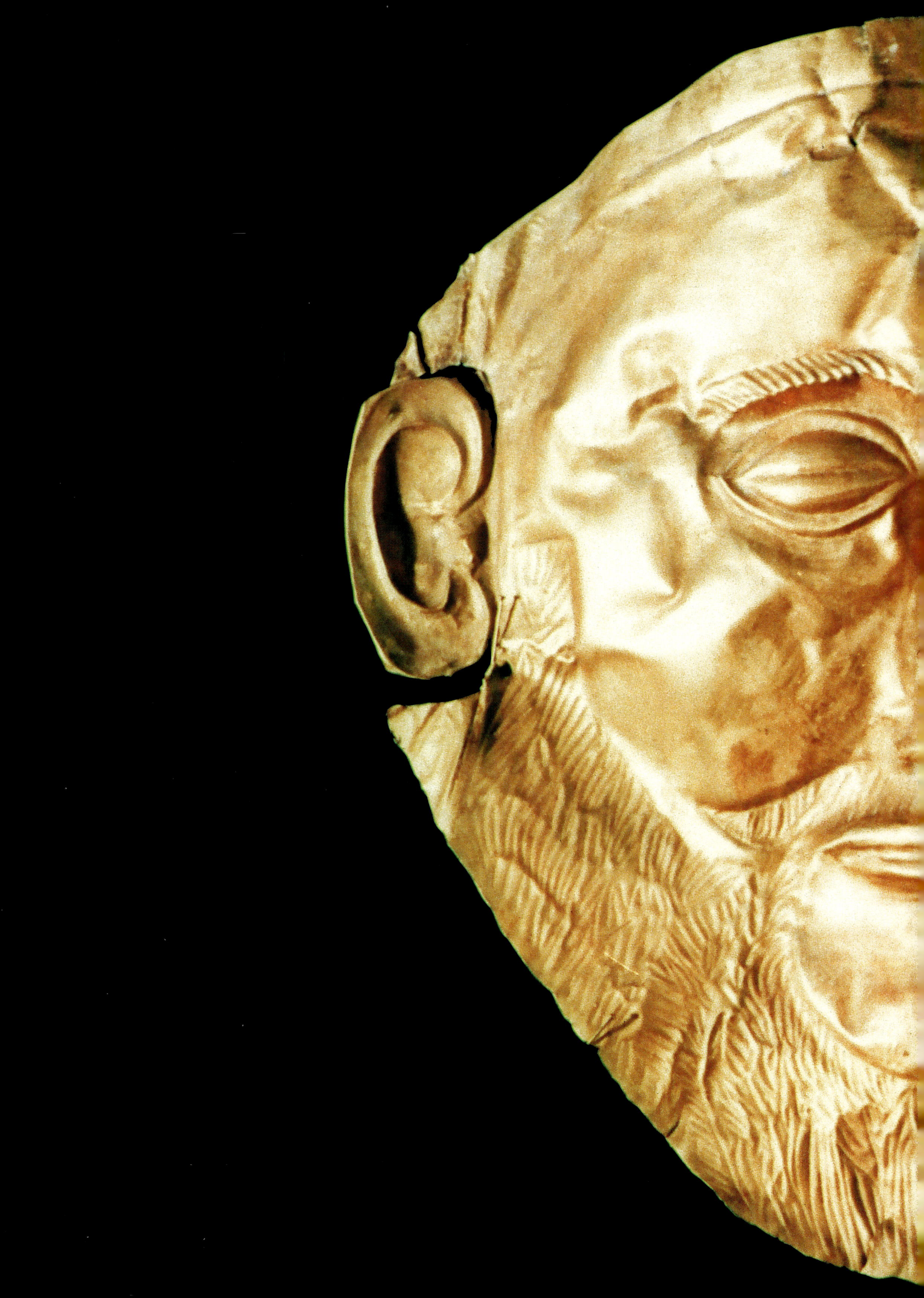

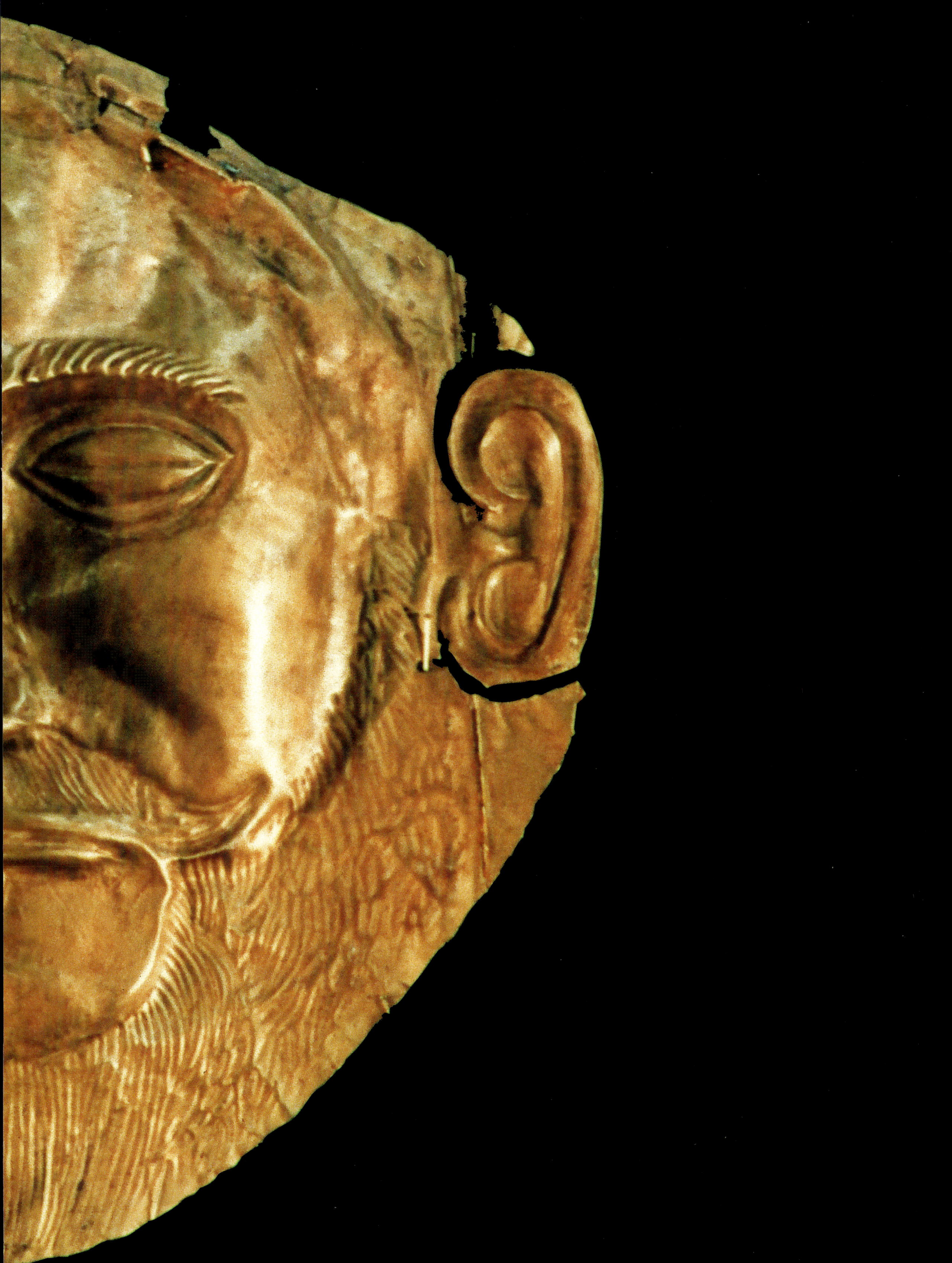

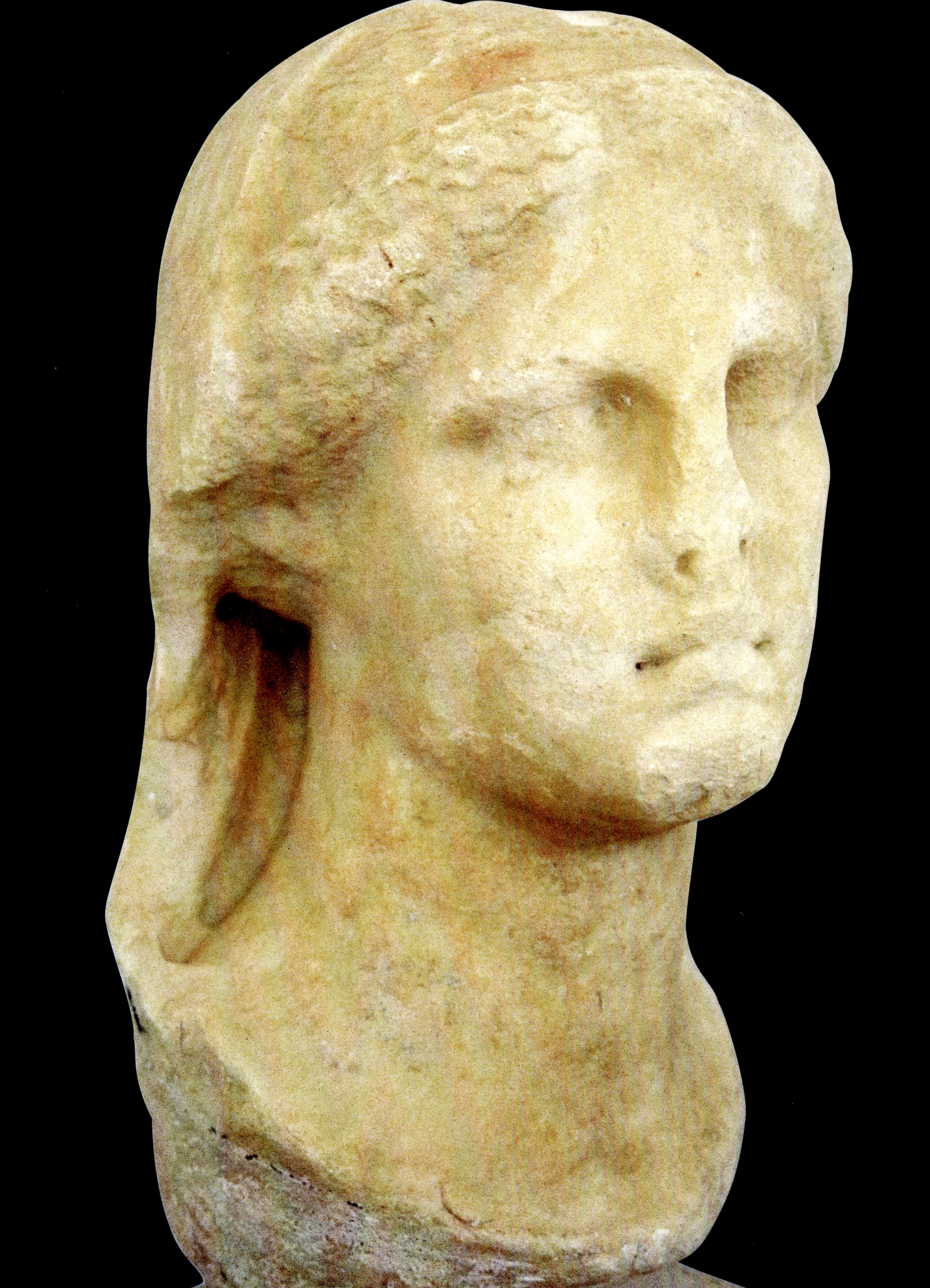

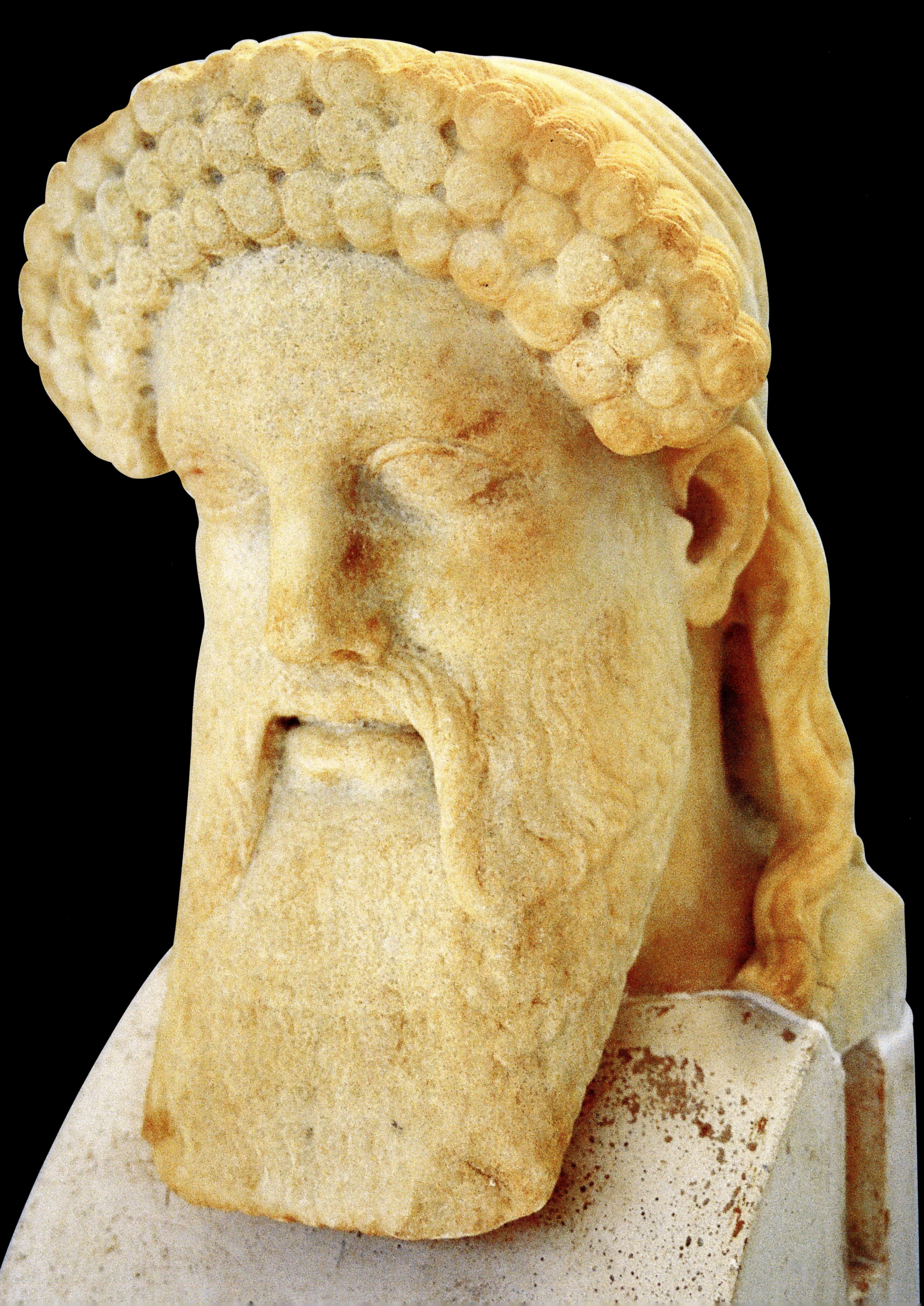

PILGRIMS IN CLASSICAL GREECE: SACRED SPACE

By and large popular religious devotion was expressed in the open air, and has left few signs of its fervor, we can however guess popular zeal from some exceptional remains: altars, temples, statues. If you visit the best-preserved and most impressive ancient sites today, you will be admiring the great sanctuaries of the classical period of the 5th century BC. You will retrace the steps of Greek pilgrims of ancient times as you explore Athens, Delphi, Epidaurus, Corinth, Olympus, Delos...

Each of these places has preserved a famous sanctuary, and its prime purpose was to honor a particular god or goddess. An altar was of course enough to create a sacred space, indeed it was the only essential element needed for Greek worship. Priests and people would gather at the time set for the ceremonies around a fire on which the sacrificial victims were burnt. Gradually rich and popular sites were equipped with prestigious buildings. The temples themselves became sumptuous offerings given to the eternal gods and to express the devotion of mere mortals. This building was the "home" of the deity and contained a statue in his or her image: the altar was always outside, usually to the east. In this manner cities displayed their power and ambitions: the politics of grandeur. So Pericles, in the 5th century BC, decorated the Acropolis with the most beautiful of architecture.

In the center of that city's sacred sanctuary, the Erechtheum sheltered the statue of Athena Polias, while the Parthenon had another image of the goddess. At Olympus, in the temple of Zeus, king of the gods, stood the famous gold and ivory statue of Phidias, one of the seven wonders of the ancient world: Zeus sitting on his throne with winged victory in his hand. At Epidaurus, in the "house" of the god Asclepius, there was a stone image enhanced with gold and ivory. The sanctuary at Delphi is built around the temple of Apollo; he had another in his honor at Corinth and a further one at Delos, the island dedicated to him. In the sacred wood of Poseidon, near Corinth, little more than the altar remains. Its size (8 feet by 130 feet) confirms the magnificence of the sacrifices offered during the Isthmian Games. Pilgrims would go to the great sanctuaries, in procession for a major feast or holiday, alone to make a personal vow or petition. When they arrived, they prayed and presented their offering to the god or goddess.

To altar and temple were added other buildings which today would be considered secular, but which, in those times, had a religious use. The sanctuaries were quickly supplied with an infrastructure that sometimes spilled out beyond the sacred enclosure or temenos. They had to host the games that were often organized on holidays in honor of the gods. After the sacred rituals, gymnastic, musical and theatrical competitions were held. These required a stadium, a gymnasium, a palestra (where the athletes trained), baths, a theater (very fine examples have been preserved at Epidaurus, Athens, Delphi, Delos, Dodona) and hostels to lodge all those taking part. All these activities contributed to the status of the Immortals. By their examples of courage and excellence, by outperforming themselves and others, athletes and artists expressed dedication and reverence to the gods who alone would select the winners.

The great sanctuaries were for all Greeks. Each Pan Hellenic sanctuary was famous for a precise reason. It attracted citizens form every corner of the Greek world, they came as individuals or representing their cities: to Olympus, Delphi, Asclepius, Corinth and Nemea to enjoy the games; to Delphi looking for advice from the oracle of the god; to Eleusis to be initiated into the divine mysteries, to Epidaurus in the hope of a cure.

Sick people crowded to Epidaurus, into the sacred enclosure of the divine doctor Asclepius. It was built in the 6th century BC. Its healing function required specific buildings in addition to those already mentioned. We find fountains, ritual basins and baths there; all bearing witness to the cleansing power attributed to water. The patients would arrive, purify themselves, sacrifice to the god of healing, offering cakes and animals (a cock, a pig, a ram...) Then they spent the night in the portico. This was a long colonnaded gallery, open on one side. The patients would be visited in a dream by the god of healing. He would place his hands on the part of the body to be treated, or would direct what should be done when the patient woke up. Doctor-priests interpreted the dreams, carried out the treatment or operated. In the 4th century BC religious fervor was particularly intense and there were many miracles. The site grew bigger and a theater was added. Games in honor of Aesculapius were celebrated every four years. Delphi was the most famous of the sanctuaries with an oracle. People came to make inquiries of the Pythia, the priestess of Apollo. She used to prophesy in the god's temple, seated on a tripod set above a sacred rift in the ground, from which arose vapors representing the divine inspiration that would govern the priestess's replies. Enquirers did not want her to predict the future or to state their personal fate; when faced with a grave decision, they were concerned to know which of their choices would be approved and if the god's favor would accompany them in their undertakings. The huge number of "treasures", ex-voto offerings given by cities, assert the wealth of the sanctuary; these little buildings, with a porch in front are built on either side of the sacred way which winds steeply upwards to the temple of Apollo.

The sanctuaries of the mystery religions offered all the emotions of a mystical experience. In Eleusis, near Athens, they promised to reveal the secrets of happiness in the afterlife, an alluring program that tempted many to be initiated! This vision of salvation was born from agrarian worship offered to Demeter and centered on the image of the grain of wheat that is reborn out of the ground in which it has been buried. The mystae came into the Telesterion, an enclosed and mysterious building. By torchlight they traveled on a journey that represented their passage through the Underworld, strewn with obstacles and inhabited by monsters; they learned means of overcoming the snares on the way and gaining access to the Elysian Fields.

Citizens were not however regular attenders at these great sanctuaries. Everyday worship took place in the setting of the family and within the city where they lived. They did not need to set out on dangerous roads to ask for divine help and guidance. In the first place they prayed to the god of their city, who defended the borders of their civilized, familiar space against the wild world outside. Every year the young men of Tanagra carried out the rite performed by Hermes to protect the city from epidemic: one of them walked around the city walls carrying a ram on his shoulders. Cities had a full calendar of religious feasts and competed with one another in building temples. The glory of Athens was there to be seen: even foreigners might take part in the Pan Athenian Games in honor of the city's goddess. Competitions were held, and then a solemn procession went up the Sacred Way, from one of the town gates as far as the Acropolis, the most holy place in the city. The procession carried a peplos, an embroidered tunic to the great statue of Athena. The whole of Athenian society turned out for the occasion. The magistrates and priests were followed by animals for the sacrifice, finally came the people and representatives of the city's colonies. A sacrifice of many oxen was offered to the goddess to earn her continued support in the future. Blood flowed and the citizens shared the cooked meat in a community meal.

THE PILGRIM GOD

The god of medicine, Asclepius, is disguised beneath the outward appearance of this traveler. Like a pilgrim to one of the great sanctuaries, he is wearing a long cloak and a hat to protect him from harsh weather. But he is not carrying the usual pilgrim's staff to ward off aggressive animals. A serpent has wound itself around this staff; this is the famous caduceus. It reveals to us that this is the god Asclepius and symbolizes the mysterious knowledge, said to have come out of the earth, by means of which he cured the sick. Asclepius traveled far and wide, visiting the sick and recommending that they visit his great sanctuary at Epidaurus. Pilgrims came from all over Greece to visit the sanctuaries, which were there to serve all Greeks, from every city. It was usual to travel on foot, but the roads were long and badly surfaced. The journey was in itself experienced as an initiation rite. Such an expedition required a great degree of courage and was in practice a form of homage offered by the pilgrims to the god. Once they had arrived at a sanctuary the pilgrims presented themselves before the gods in a humble, fervent and respectful manner. They expressed their devotion by offering prayers and making donations, obviously hoping to receive help and special favors in return.

THE PANATHENIAN FESTIVAL

Every year the city of Athens commemorated the victory of the gods over the giants. This festival took place at the end of July and every fourth year was especially lavish. Its high point was the parade carrying a tunic, embroidered with motifs representing the slaying of giants, to the city's goddess, Athena. The people took the sacred Way across the city to the Acropolis. The procession left the ceramic district, crossed the agora, stopping to honor the gods before various altars. The procession then climbed the hill, entering the citadel by the main entrance, the Propylaea Gate. The participants passed on their right the temple of Athena of Victories, built between 427 and 424 BC, to celebrate the victories of Athens over the Persians. The magistrates, priests, citizens and allies passed before the bronze statue of Athena Promachos, who has led the city to Victory. It had been carved by Phidias and, being thirty feet high, towered over the faithful. They continued along the side of the Parthenon, which was built by the architect Ictinos for Pericles. It was finished in 438 BC, and its central chamber housed a gold and ivory statue of the goddess. Finally the procession came to the plateau in front of the Erechtheum. It was built between 421 and 395 BC; this sanctuary housed the olive tree given by Athena to the city and the cults of Athena, Poseidon and the legendary king, Erectheus. The maidens who had embroidered the tunic draped it around the ancient olivewood statue of Athena Polias. The blood of sacrificed oxen soon trickled down from the sacred plateau to the bottom of the citadel. FOLLOWING PAGES

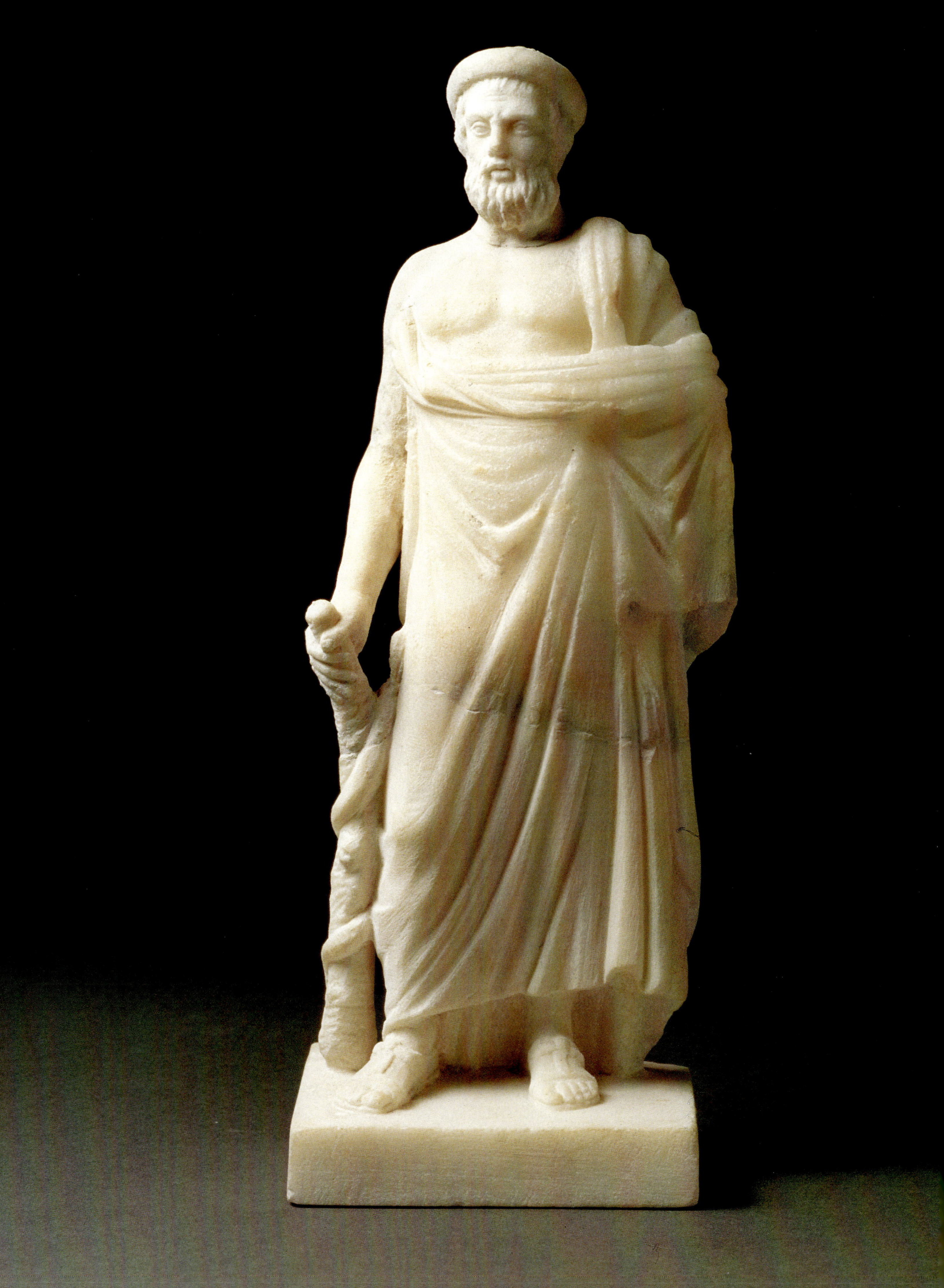

MODEL OF THE ACROPOLIS

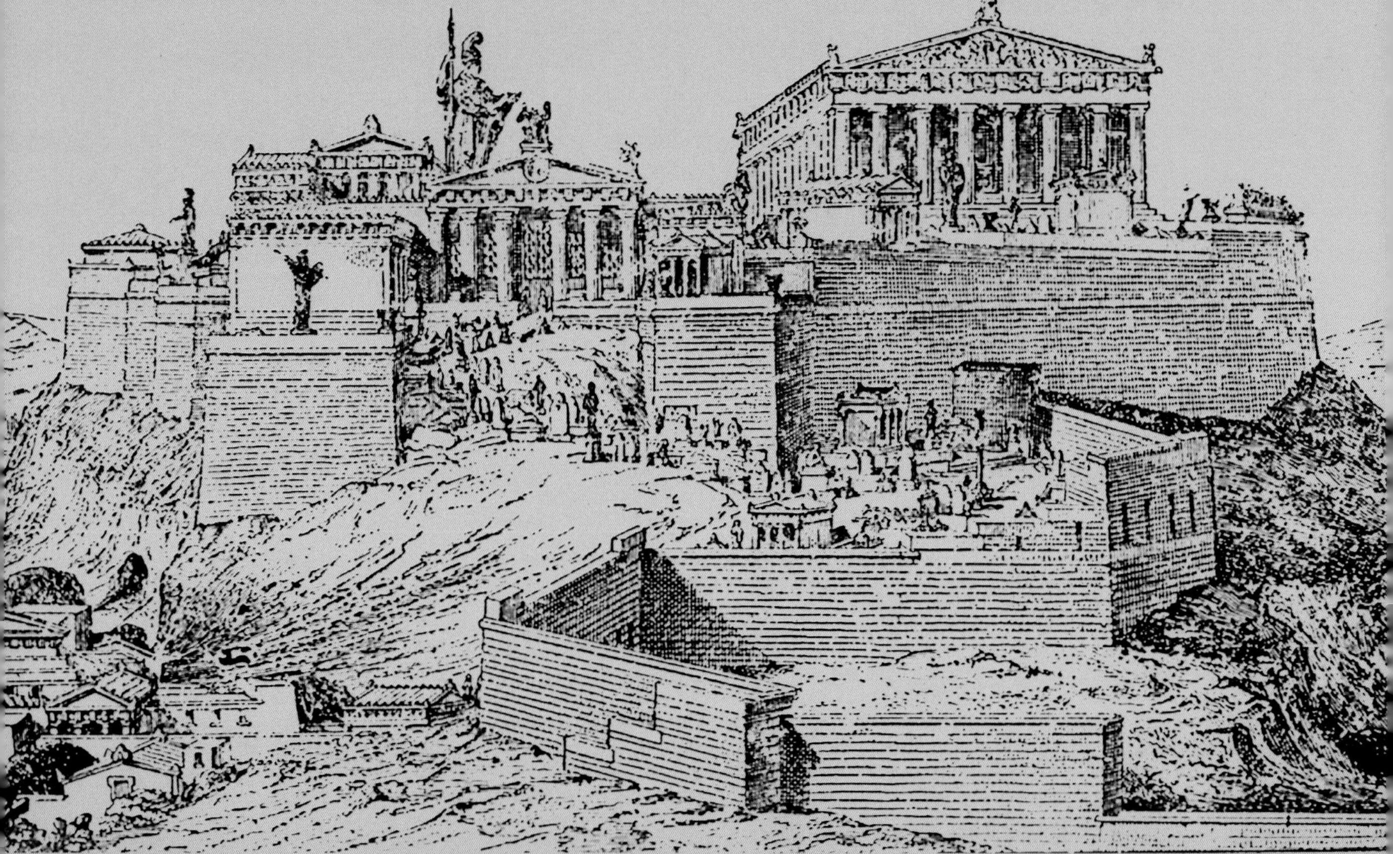

STREET MAP OF ATHENS

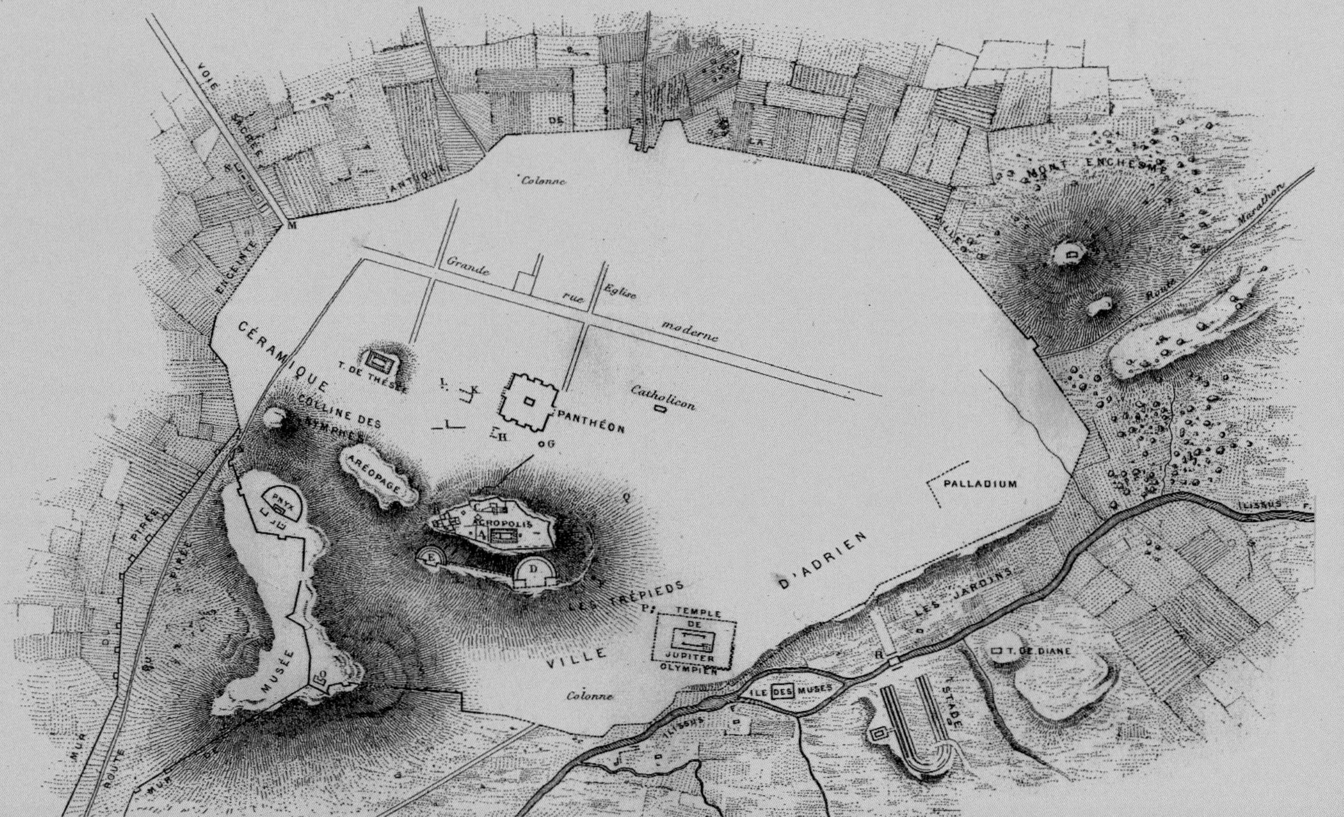

THE ACROPOLIS

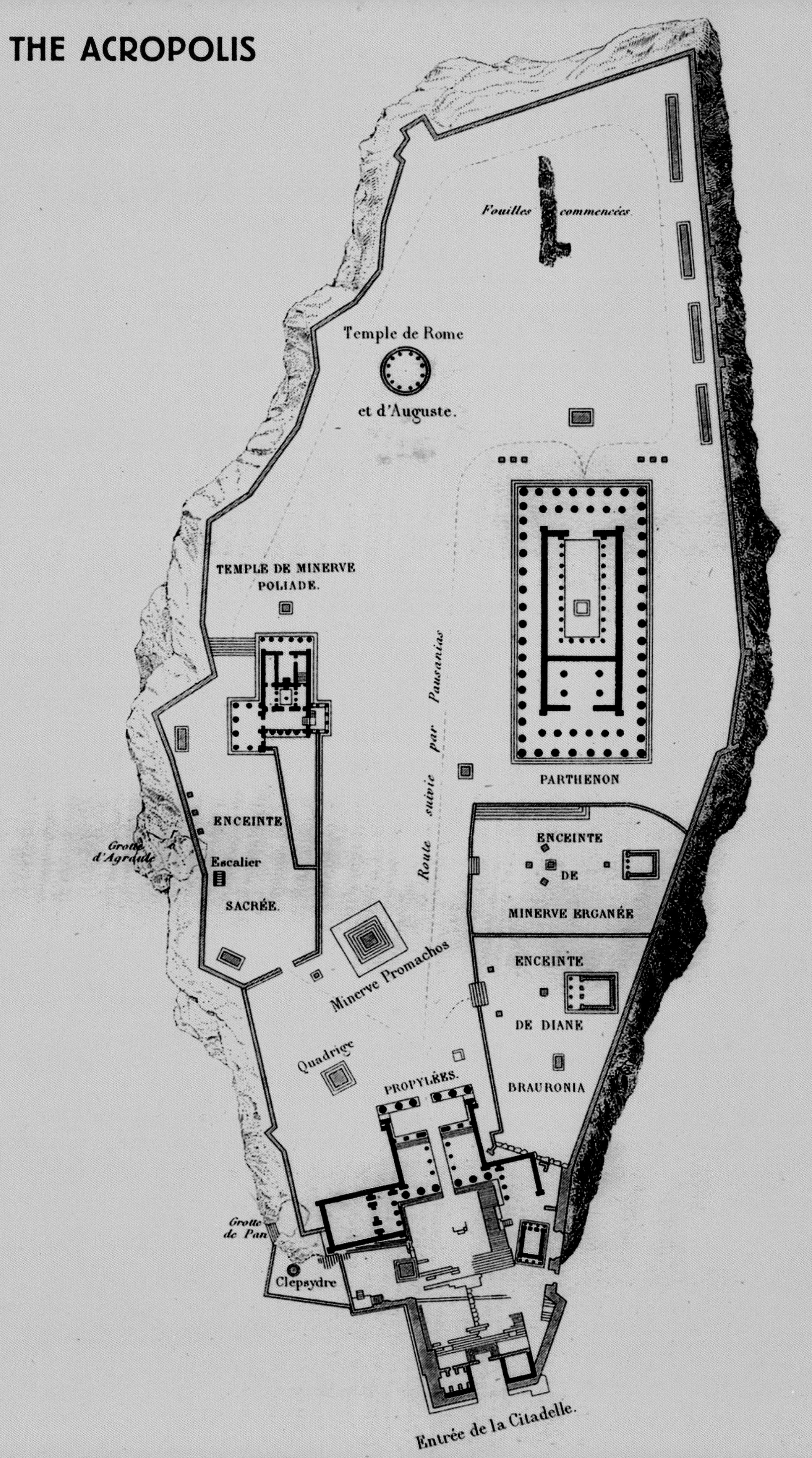

ATHENA PROMACHOS

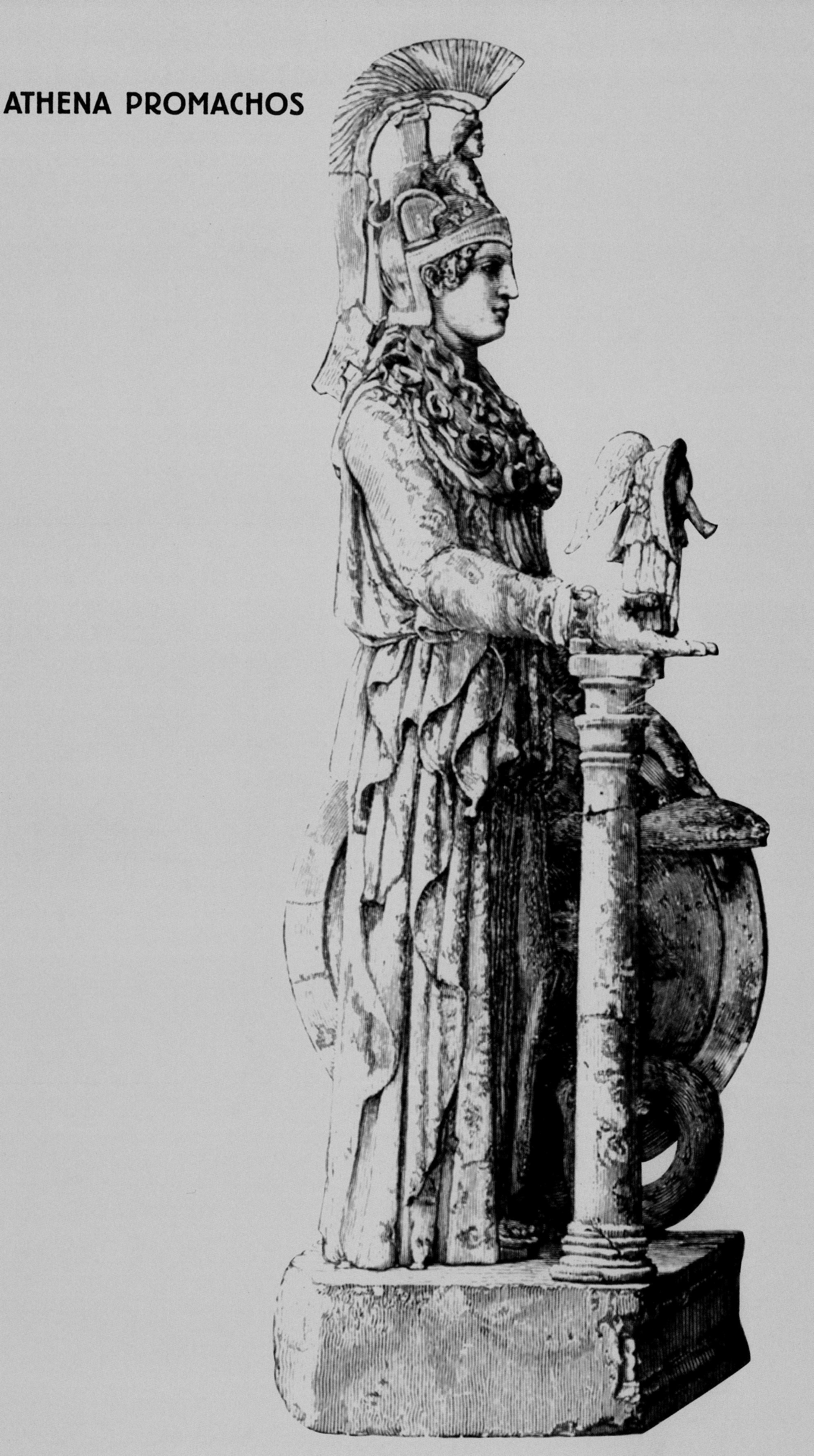

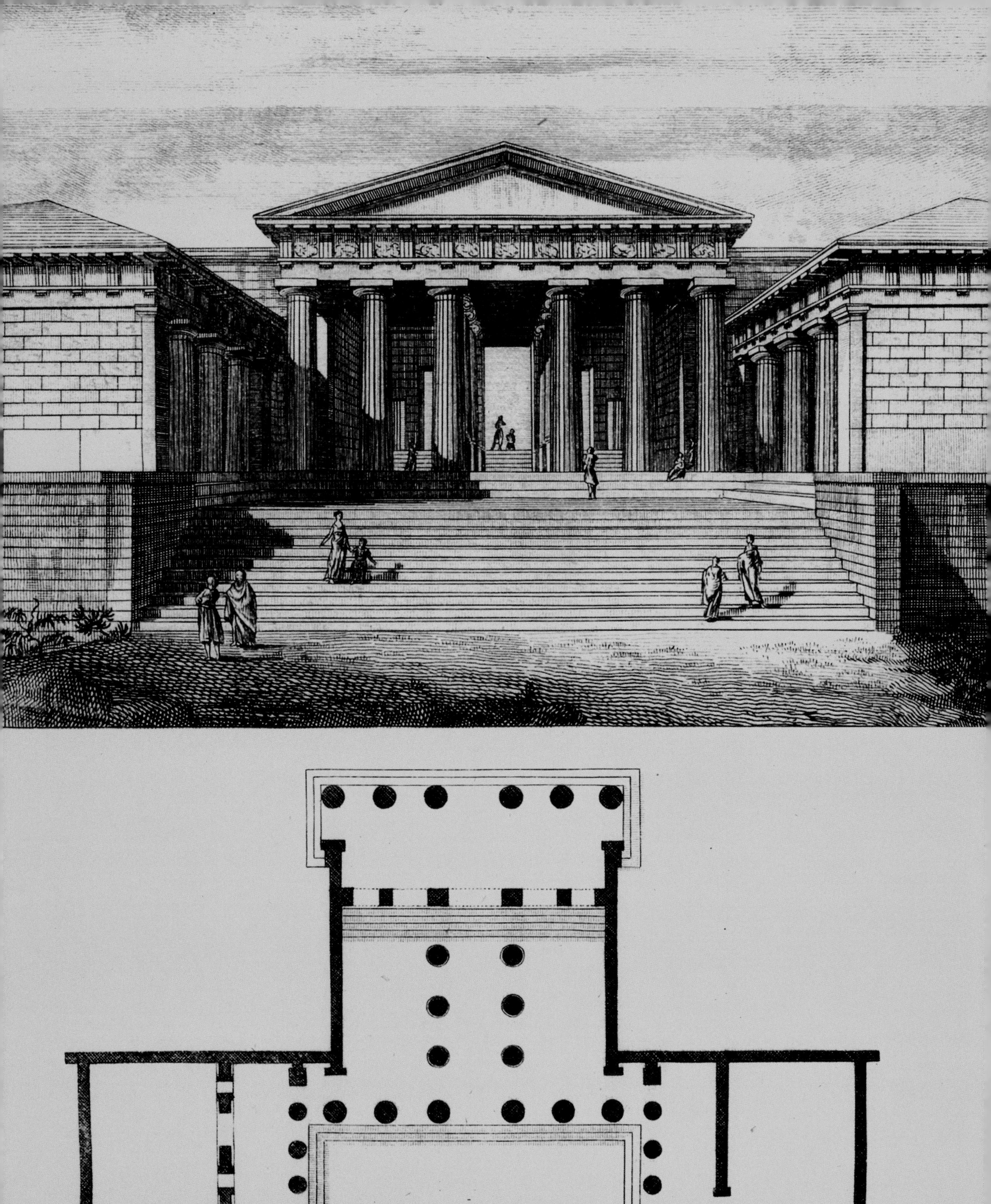

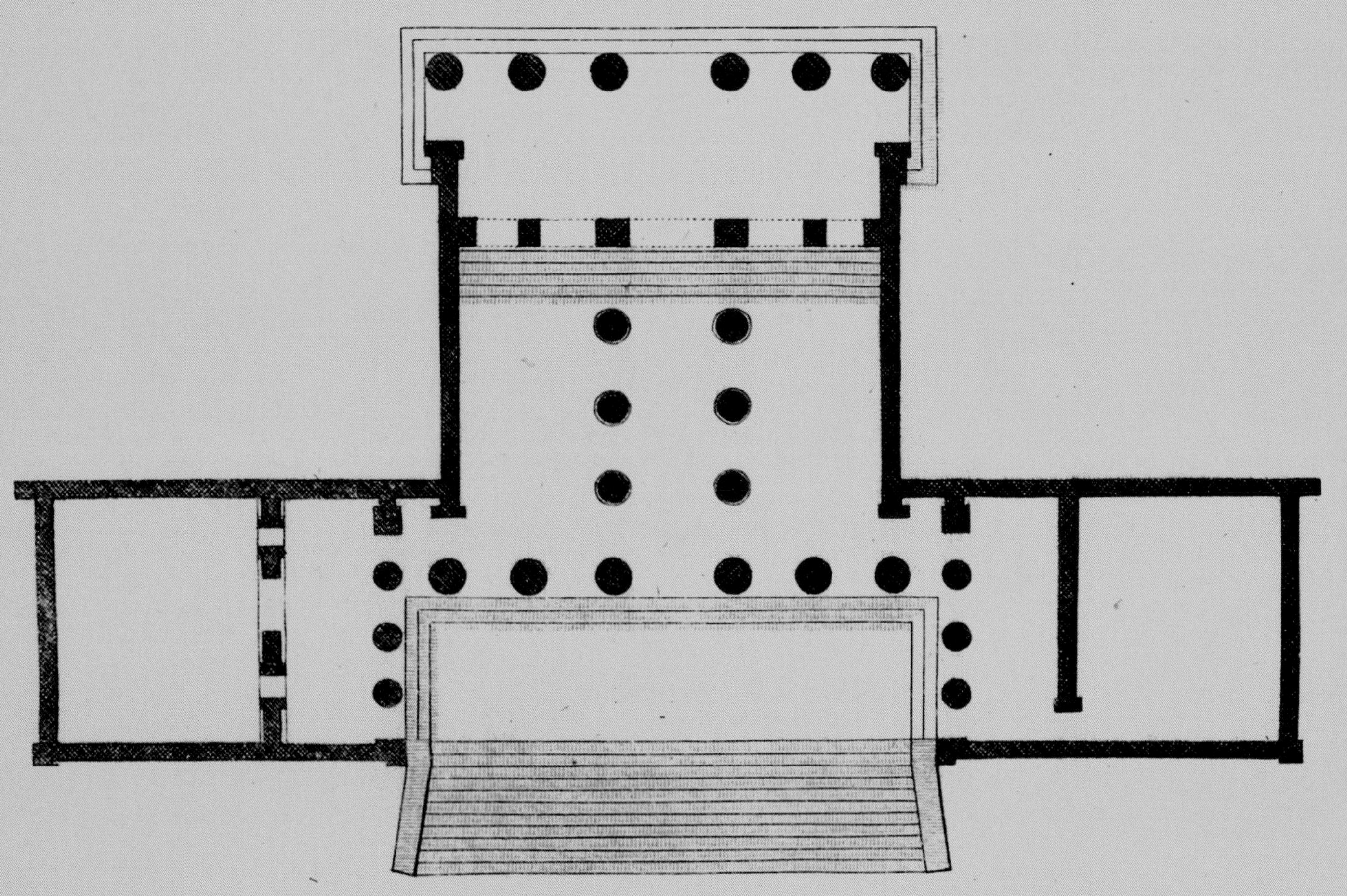

MODEL OF THE PROPYLAEA

THE SANCTUARY OF ARTEMIS AT BRAURON

In this little town in Attica the worship of Artemis had an unusual characteristic. The goddess, who had been brought from Tauris by Iphegenia and Orestes, was famous for her cruelty. Young Spartan boys were whipped until they bled before her altar. The founding myth at Brauron confirms her savagery. She had unleashed the plague against the Athenians who had killed a she bear. The bear was fond of human company and followed people about freely until a thoughtless girl annoyed her. The bear attacked the child and was killed promptly by her brothers. Artemis agreed to lift the curse provided that young Athenian girls, aged between five and ten, spent some time in her service in Brauron. They acted the part of the she-bear, served the rituals and, dressed in saffron colored cloaks, danced during the Brauron festival. A rite of passage completed their initiation; in this way the young worshippers left behind the untamed world of childhood and entered upon life as civilized persons. In spite of her fierce airs the goddess was in fact the benevolent protector of little girls and guided them towards marriage. The doorway, which is now incomplete, doubtless led to a banqueting hall.

THE TEMPLE OF APOLLO AT CORINTH

The temple of Apollo dominates the city of Corinth. It was built between 550 and 525 BC and is one of the oldest in Greece. Only seven out of thirty-six Doric columns remain from the vast colonnade around the building.

FOLLOWING PAGES

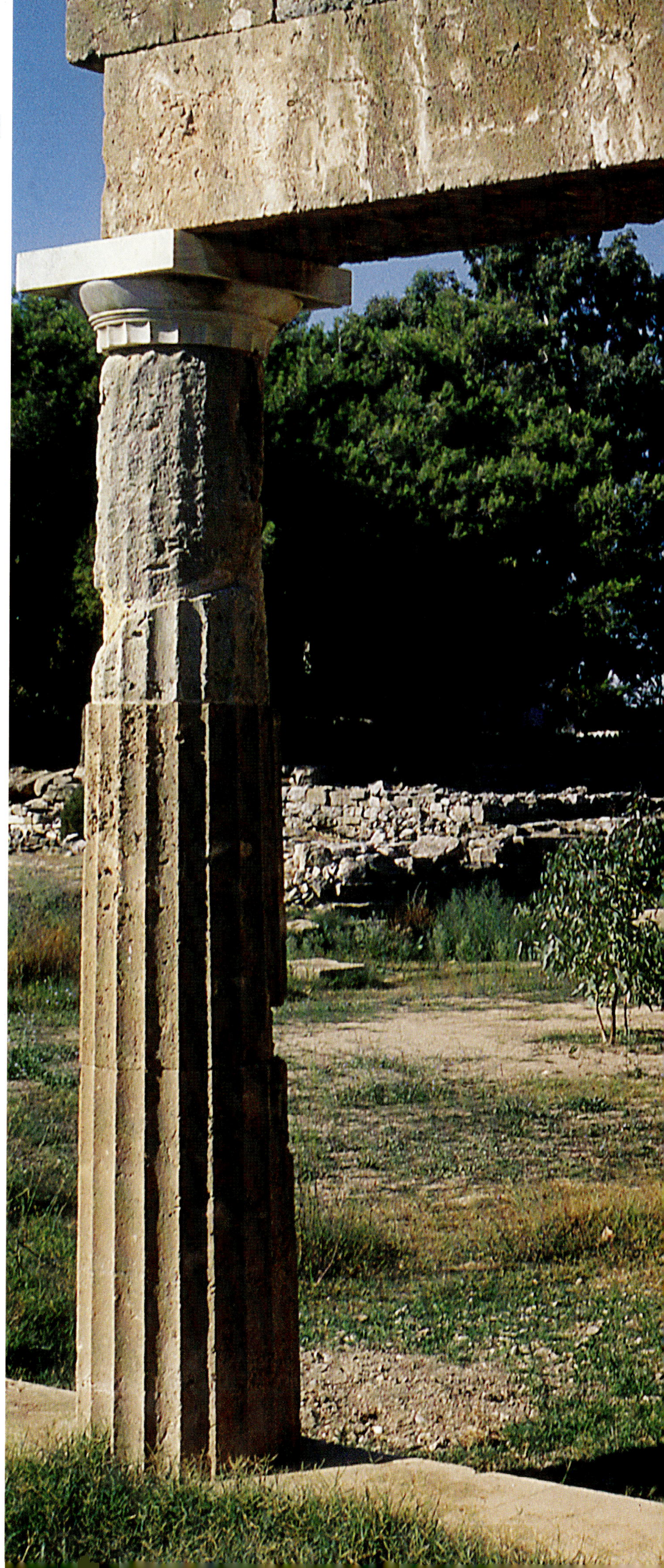

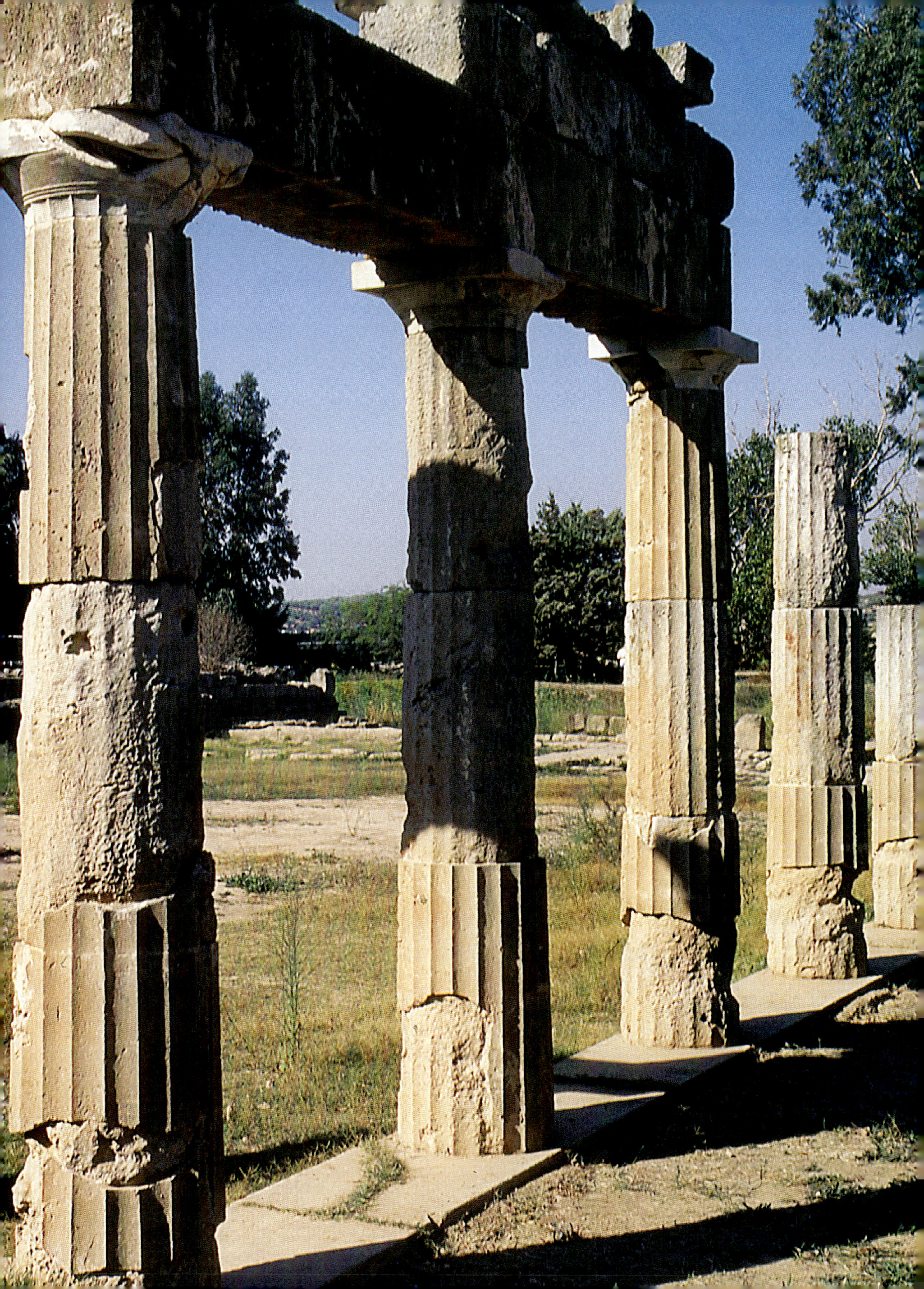

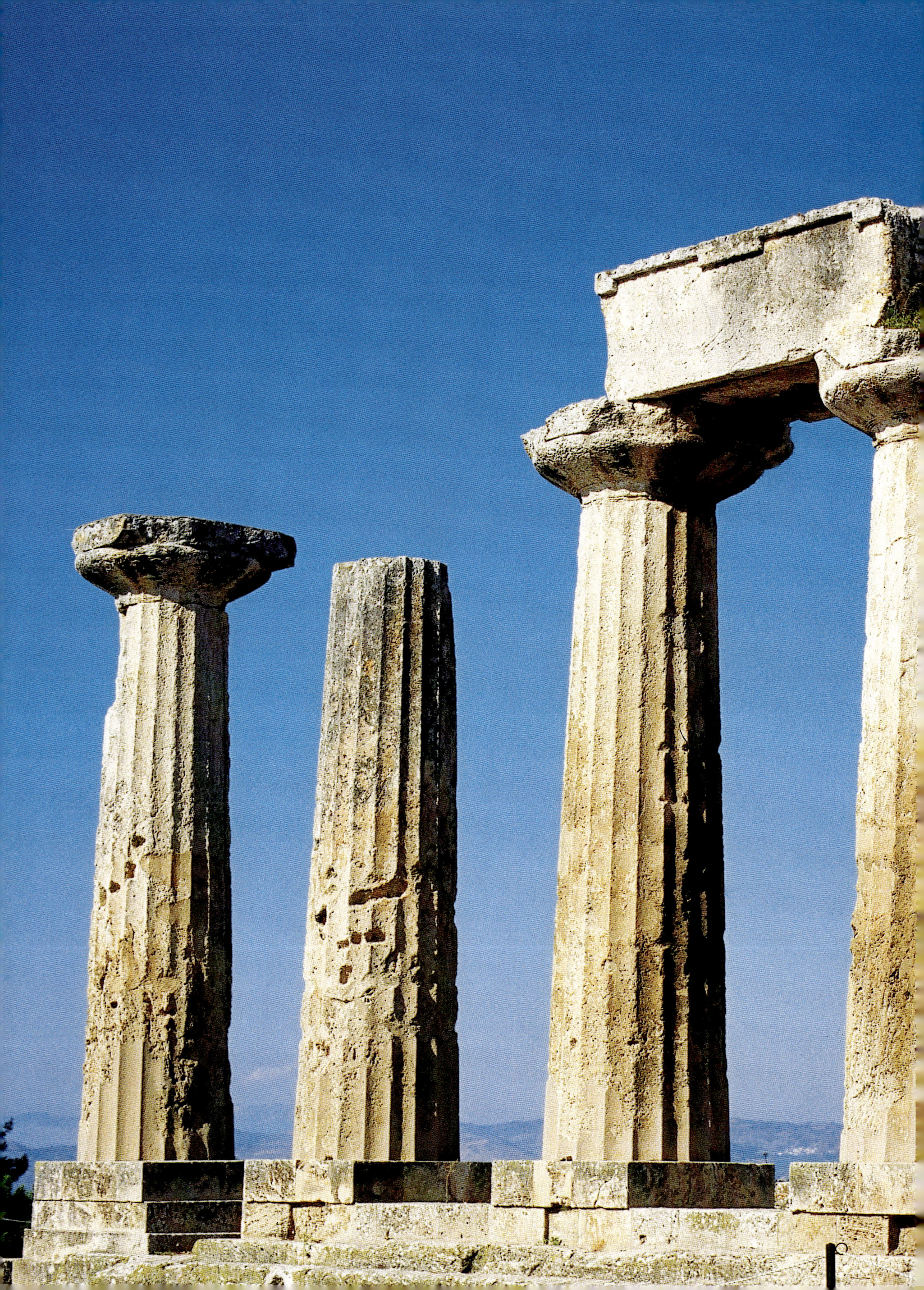

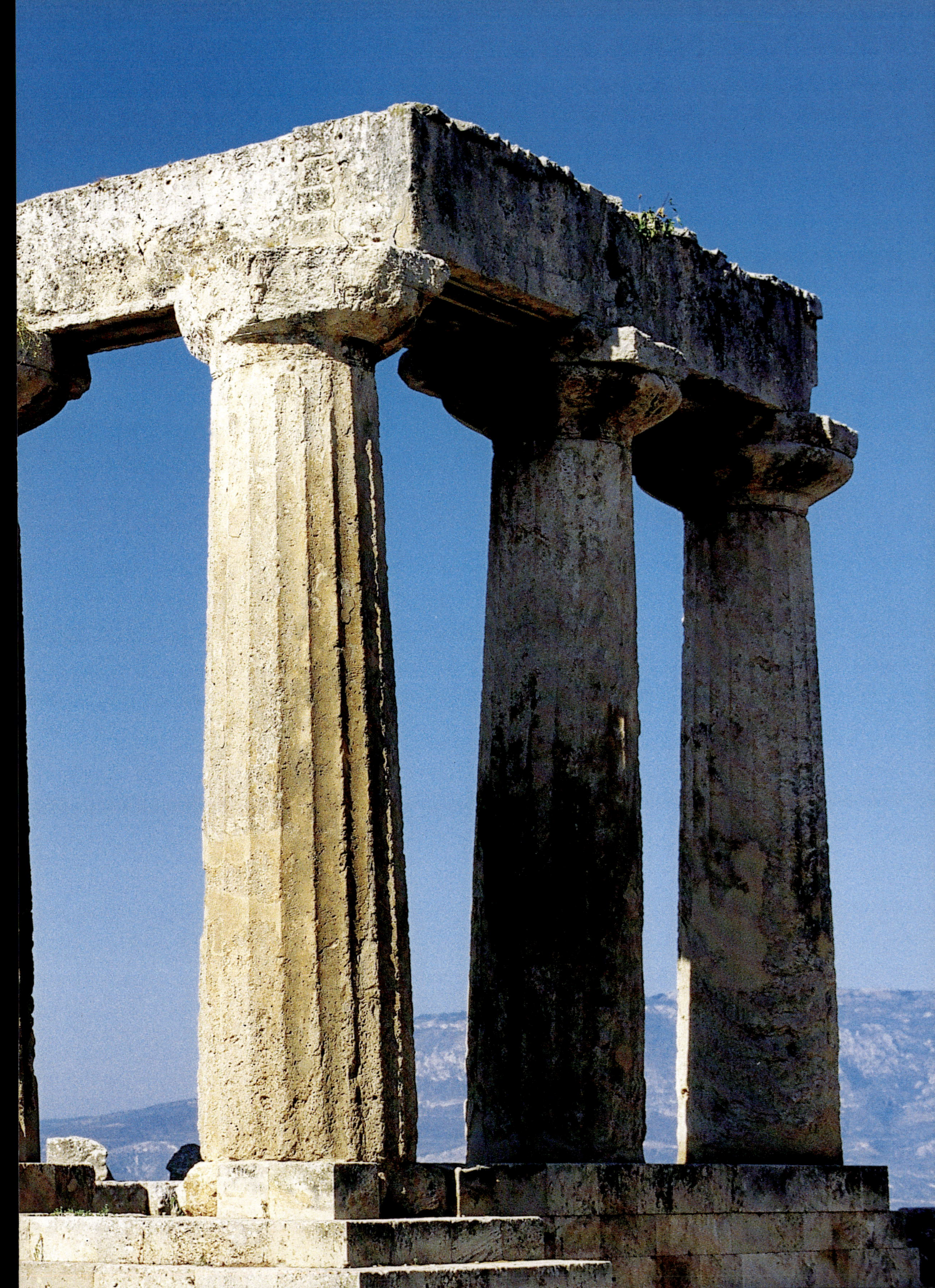

THE TEMPLE AT BASSAE

The temple dedicated to Apollo the healer stands right in the middle of the mountains of Arcadia, 3700 feet above sea level. It is one of the most impressive sites in Greece, and one of the most difficult to get to. The local inhabitants built the sanctuary towards the end of the 5th century BC to thank the god for saving them from the plague. The temple is remarkable in that it has Ionic, Corinthian and Doric columns and its sanctuary faces in an unusual direction.

SACRIFICES

The Greeks sacrificed domestic animals, like sheep, lambs, goats and piglets. Calves, cows and bulls were the most prestigious offerings. The animals were prepared, decked with ribbons and garlands, before being brought in procession to the altar, which was similarly decorated and at the foot of which waited a basket with the ritual knife and a basin to receive the blood. The celebrant lit the fire and sprinkled the animal with sacred water. This caused the animal to react and this movement was held to signify consent; so it agreed to being sacrificed. Some hair was cut from its forehead and flung on the fire: the first fruits of the sacrifice. Thus purified and dedicated the animal's throat was cut over the altar. Then the priest opened the thorax and removed the entrails. He then examined them and by this means said whether the signs for the future were good. Soon the bones covered in animal fat were burning on the fire. These were the parts reserved for the gods. The worshippers ate the flesh in a communal feast. PAGES 118-119

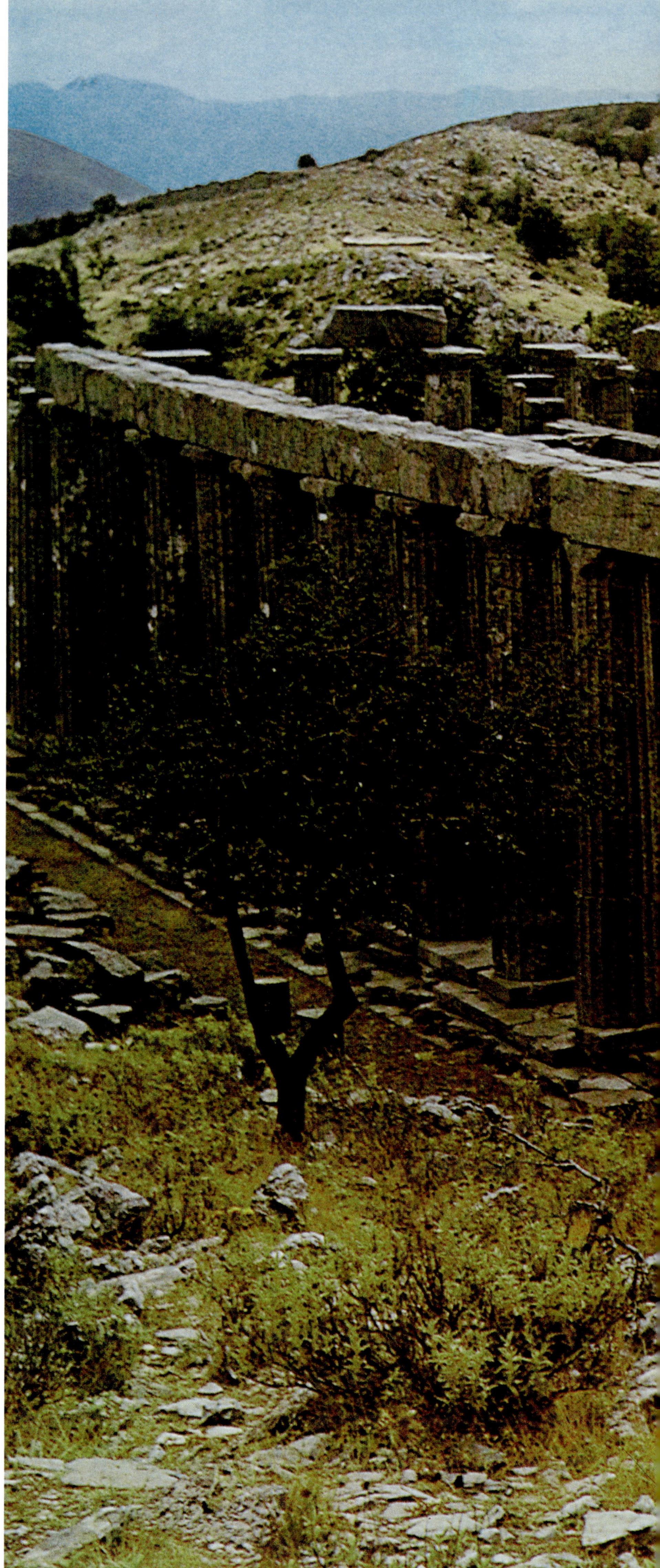

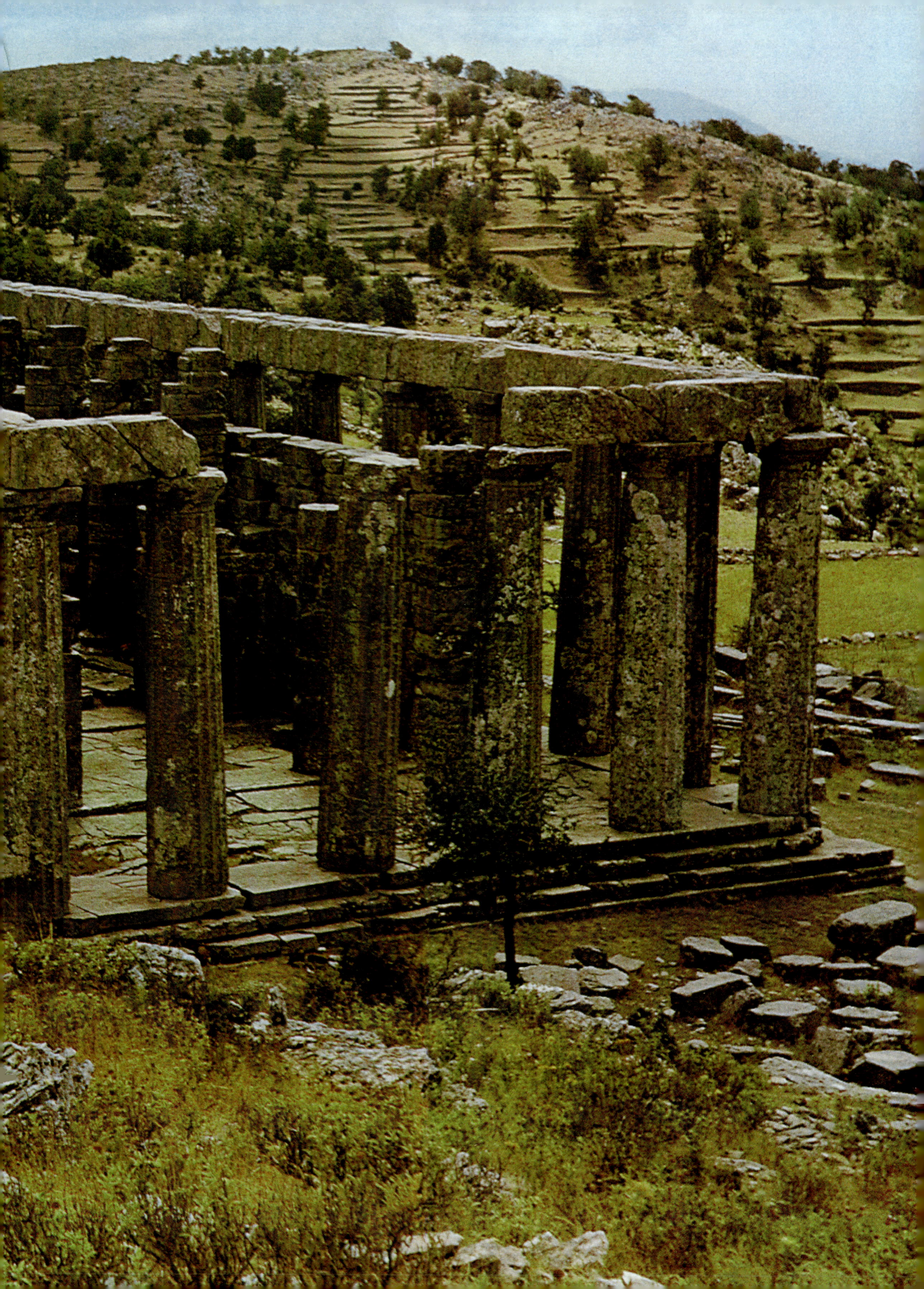

THE RITUALS OF WORSHIP

This bright fresco in Delos shows us the outlines of three people wearing wreaths all solemnly approaching an altar, we don't know if they are priests or ordinary worshippers. They are no doubt coming to honor the god Apollo. The torches above their heads suggest we are in a sacred place. The painting illustrates for us the careful gestures of everyday religious practice. It is impossible to make out if the worshippers are making a libation. That would consist of pouring out wine mixed with water, milk or honeyed water, from a cup or phial. But these figures also seem to be placing an offering, which may or may not be burned on the altar. The first fruits of harvest, corn, fruit or vegetables, but also cakes were often presented as non-blood sacrifices. Traditionally Apollo receives biscuits in the shape of a lyre, a bow or an arrow while those offered to Artemis are shaped like the moon. Dionysus has an appetite for grilled cakes, and Cybele appreciates cakes made from honey or milk. This show of respect to the Immortals is usually made to gain their goodwill. The worshippers are trying to please the god; they tender their gifts with suitable ritual words, hoping the god will grant their request.

SACRIFICING A BULL

The bull was a legendary animal in Crete. He was adored and glorified particularly when big games were held, but was also an animal regularly offered in sacrifice. His special status is apparent in holy sites when we see representations of horns, such as those on view at the entrance to the palace at Knossos. They suggest vigor, force and fertility. Every spring a bull fight was organized. During these festivities young Cretan men tested their daring and their agility by jumping and performing somersaults over the animal or onto his back. One of the animals was then carefully chosen and captured. The priests decorated his horns with garlands of flowers and woolen strips. The victim was then led in procession to the altar, as shown in this picture from a sarcophagus found in the palace of Haghia Triada. The long-horned ox, which originally came from Mesopotamia, attracts our gaze in an unusual way; he seems so peaceful and inoffensive. There were, on the other hand, small wild bulls in Crete and they were aggressive and destructive. During sacrifices the priest placed barley and salt on the animal's head, then killed him with the blow of an axe, or else cut his throat in such a way that his blood spurted out over the altar. FOLLOWING PAGES

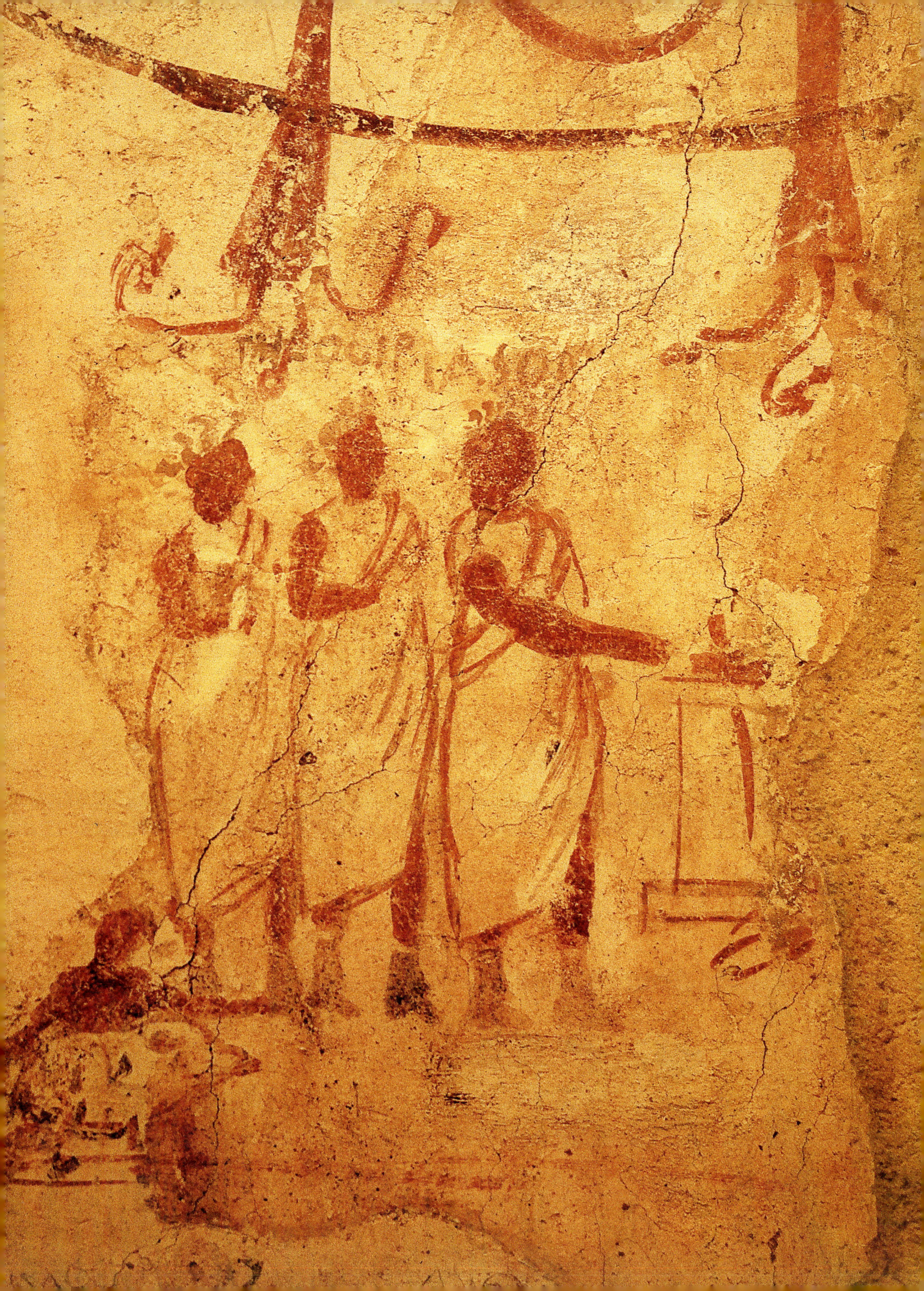

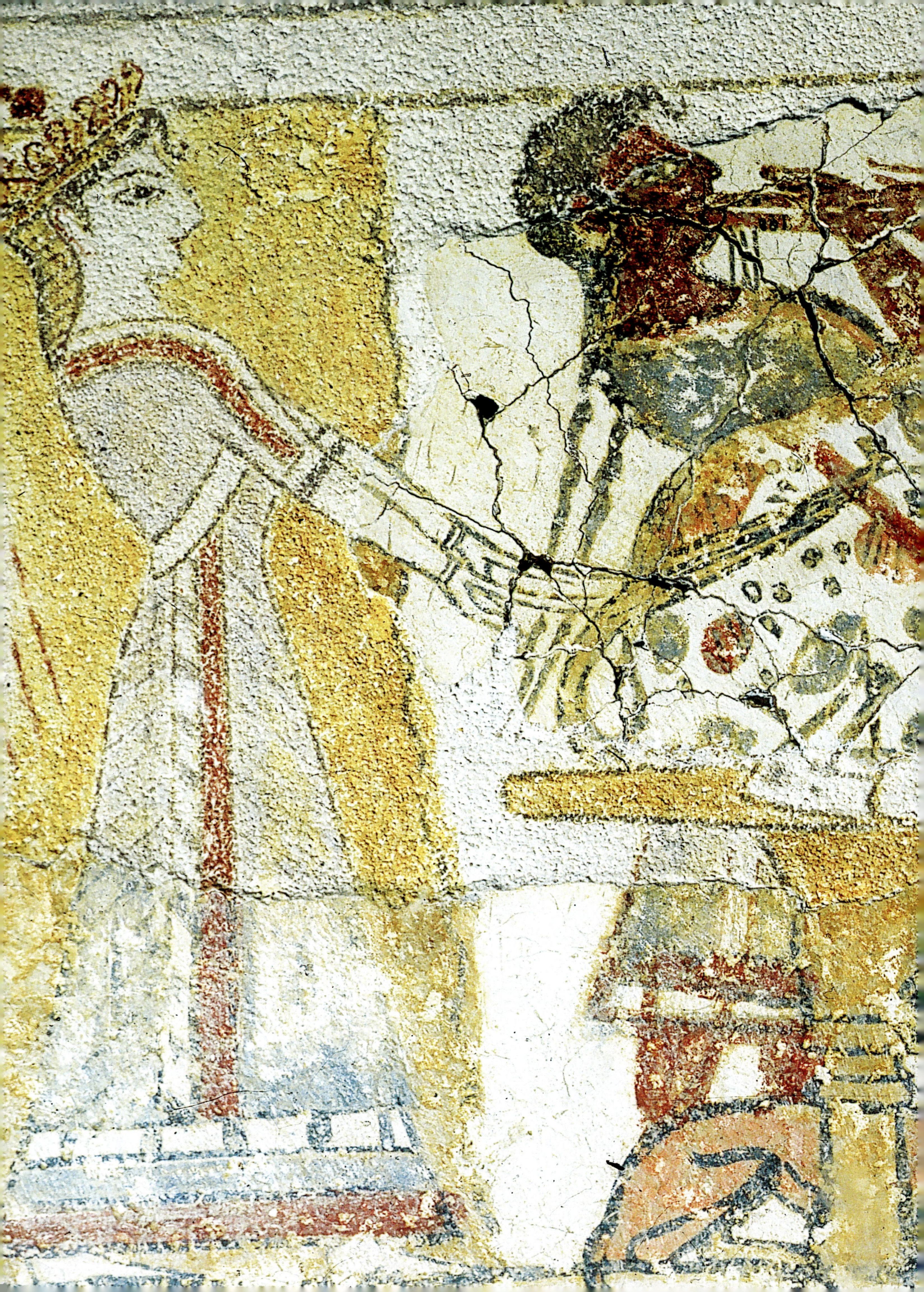

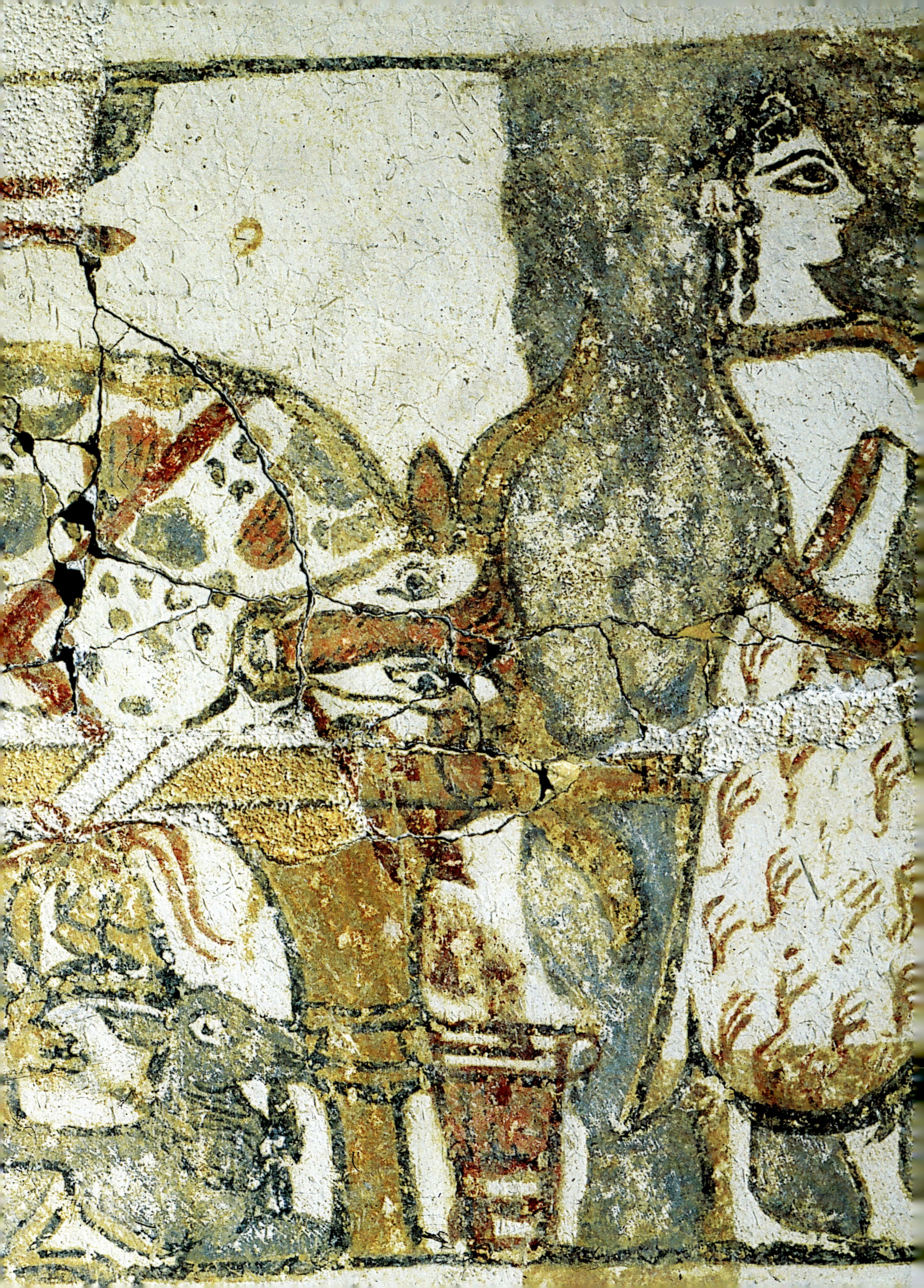

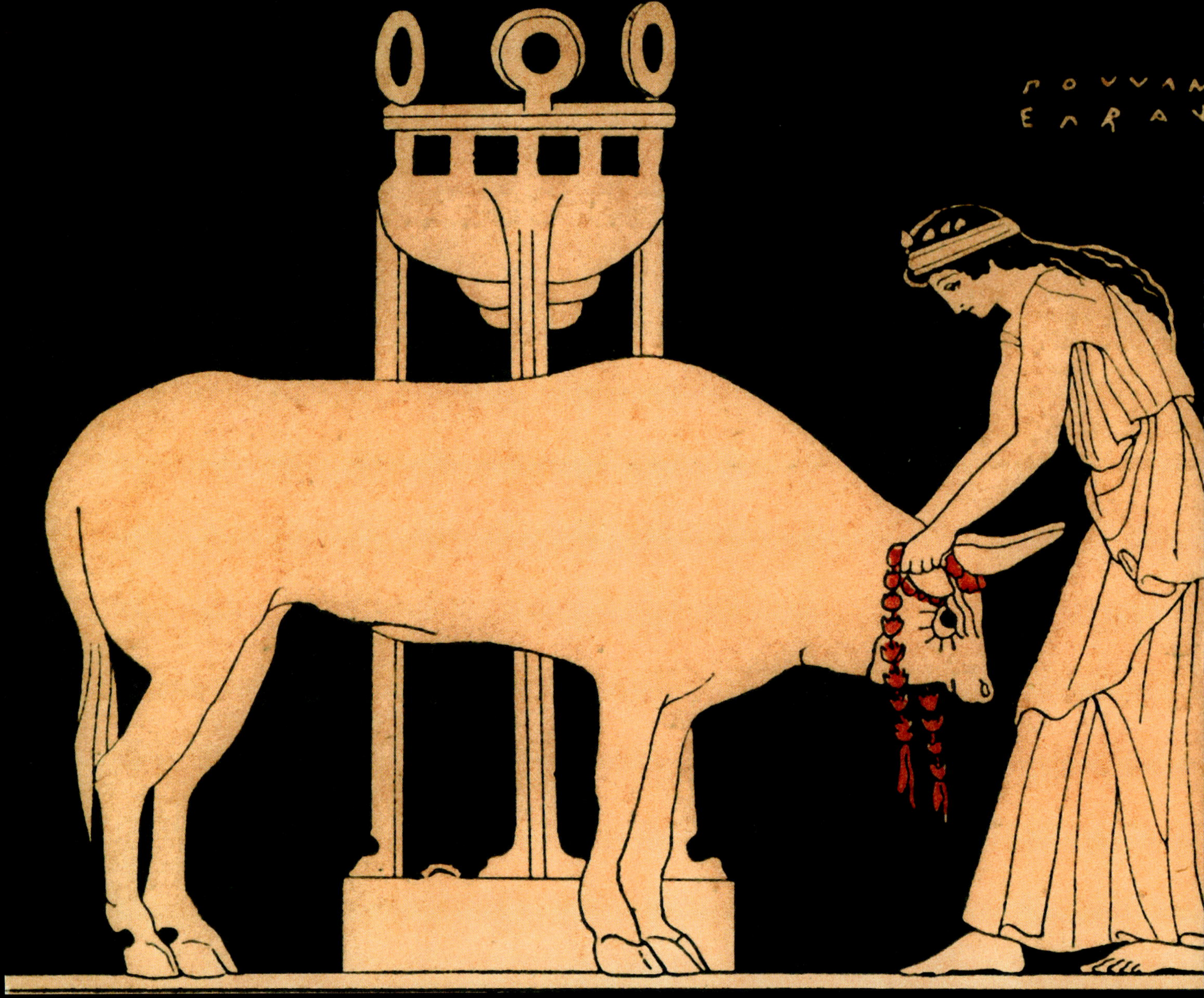

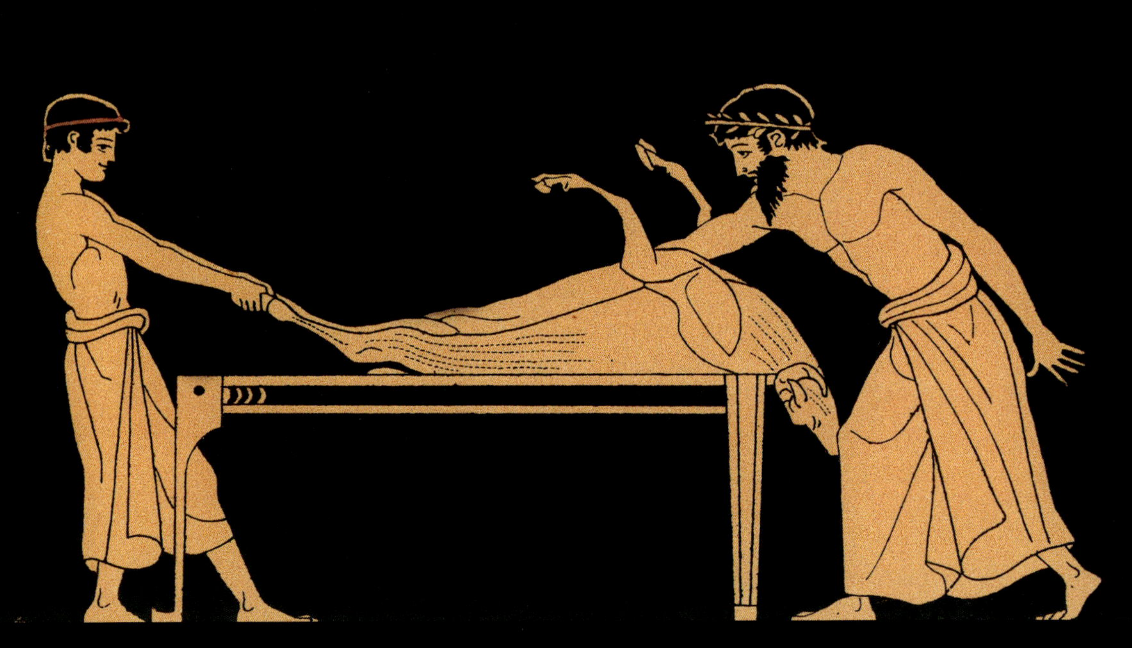

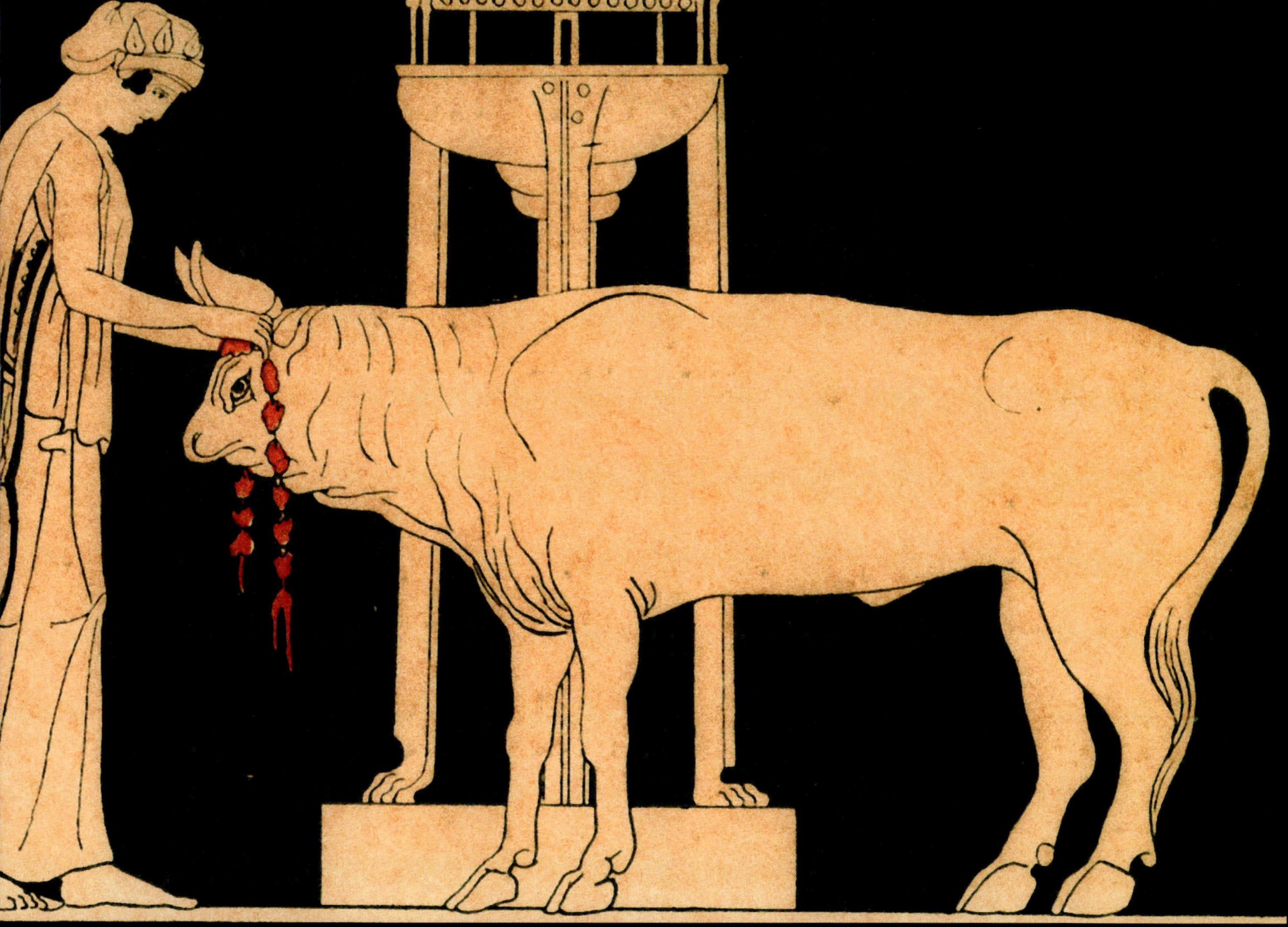

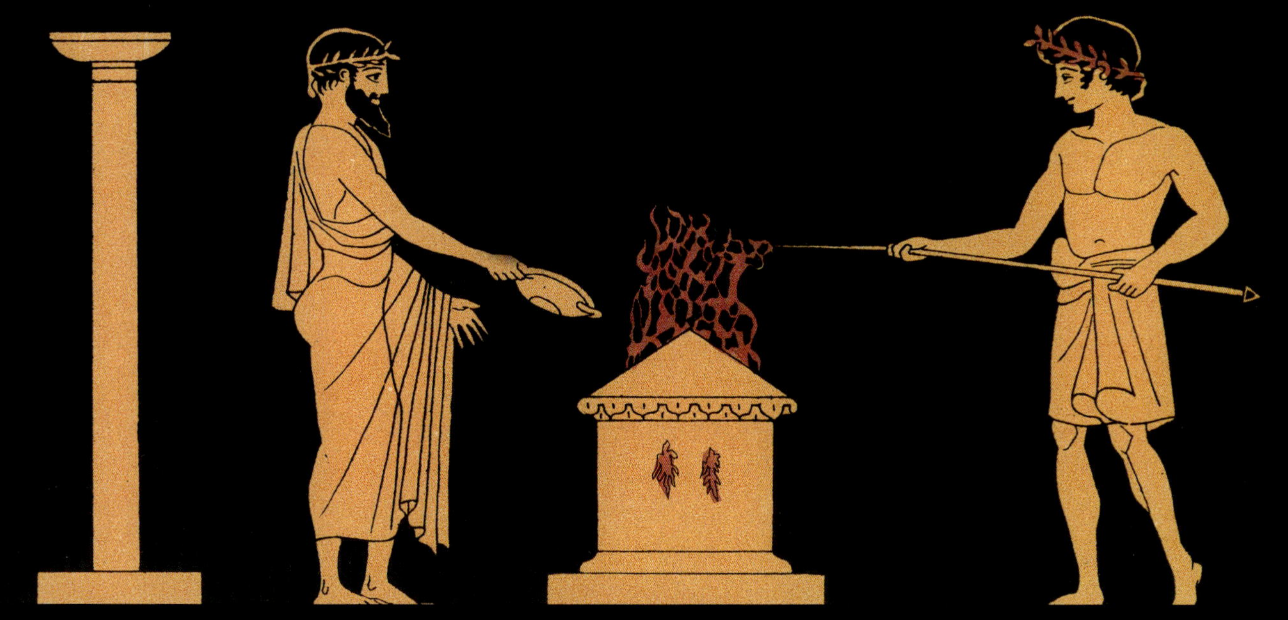

THE GODS HONORED AT ELEUSIS

Eleusis is situated beside the sea near Athens. It was one of the most prestigious sanctuaries in ancient Greece. It was consecrated to the goddess Demeter and to her daughter Persephone.

This mother-daughter couple combines a divinity of vegetation and harvest and a divinity representing the depths of the earth where the seeds germinate and where the dead rest.

Demeter was out searching for her daughter Persephone who had been carried off by Hades when she received hospitality from King Celeus at Eleusis. In gratitude to the king for his kindness Demeter decided to choose that place for the celebration of her mysteries. She asked Celeus to build a temple there and taught him her secret rites. She also gave a winged chariot to his son Triptolemus and ordered him to travel all over the world sowing seeds of corn: he was to teach the arts of agriculture to the human race.

So he was honored at Eleusis along with the Great Goddesses. Other divinities honored there were Athena, Hecate, Aphrodite, Rhea and Iacchus. He was the god who led the procession of candidates for initiation, while priests from the leading local families officiated at the ceremonies. The Mysteries were revealed to the worthy candidates in the Telesterion, a closed building where they were taught the secrets of joy in the afterlife, the promise of resurrection and the hope of a future incarnation. This belief in the immortality of the soul arose from an agricultural mystery in which the gift of corn came from the seed hidden beneath the ground.

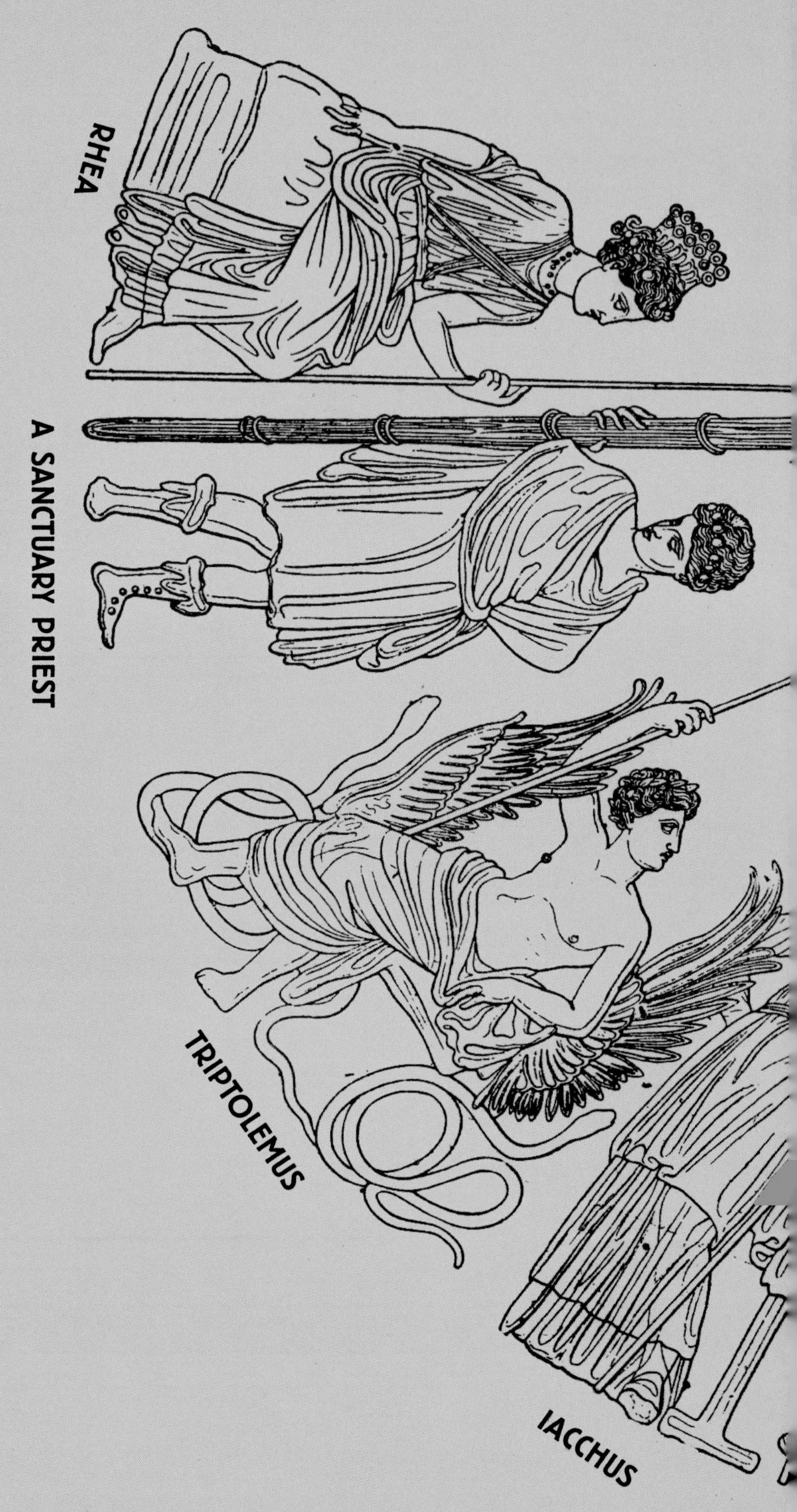

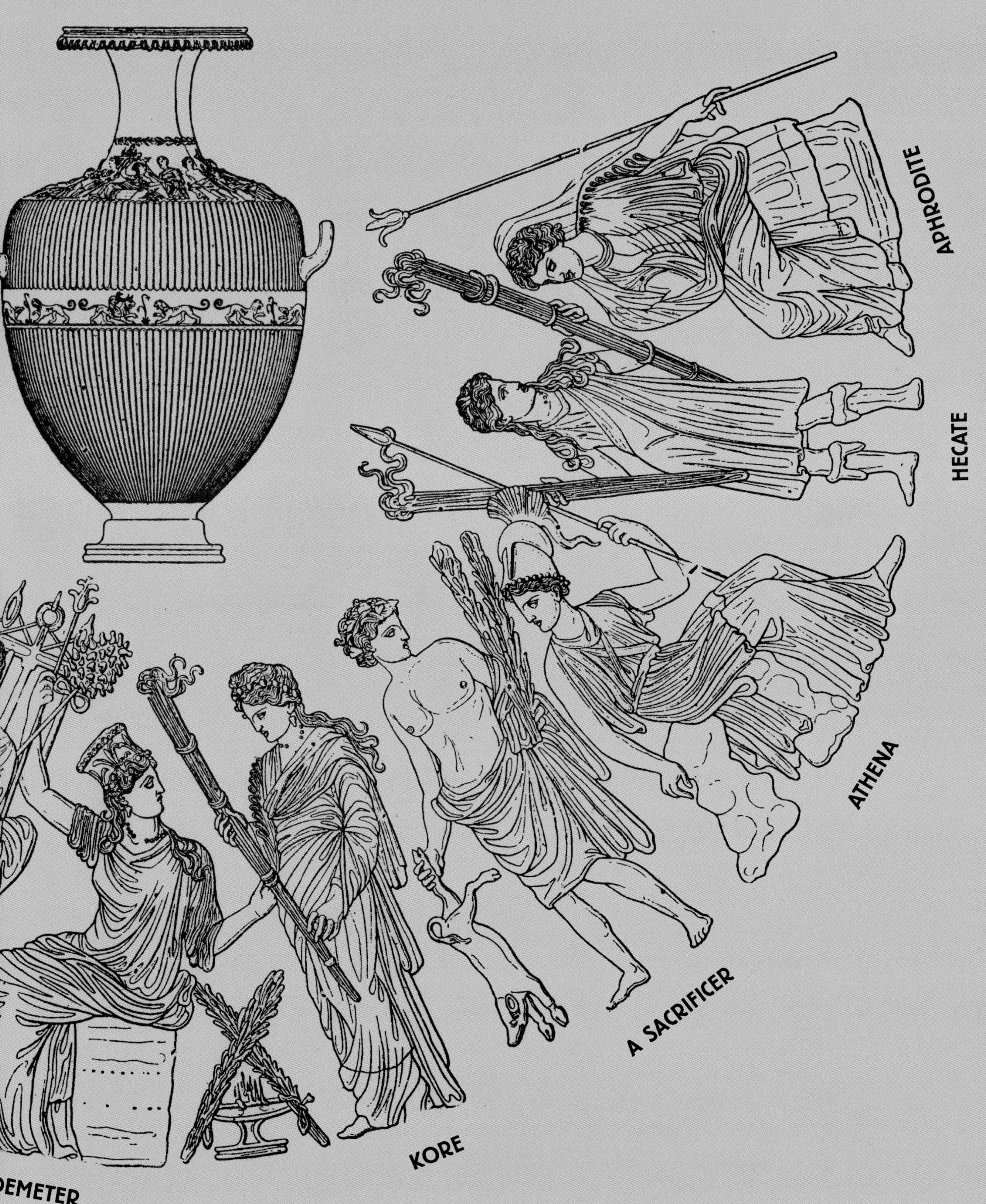
DEMETER
KORE
A SACRIFICER
ATHENA
HECATE
APHRODITE

A CITY TOUR IN CLASSICAL TIMES

Surrounded by its walls the city was the context in which Greek men and women lived their lives. The city was a supportive framework and they strove to make it as agreeable as possible. Temples, statues and altars were everywhere; as they passed by the citizens prayed and made offerings to the gods. Each city had a principal sanctuary; this was dedicated to the city's patron gods, like the high place of the Acropolis in Athens. The city began to get lively at dawn: within its walls they worked, traded, engaged in politics, took their ease, strolled about...

The central square, the agora, was where you gauged the heartbeat of political, economic and social life. It was the symbol of the classical city and was always crowded. Early in the morning the men came to this esplanade. It was a habit that encouraged community living and friendliness. Social links were forged: people conversed with their friends, the latest news was sought, invitations for the evening were issued... The less well off then went to work, the rich got on with politics, pleasure and relaxation.

The morning crowds in the agora allowed people to transact business: the lawyer and doctor saw his clients; contracts and business deals were negotiated here. The banker sat busily at his table. The poor, whether free or slaves, came to be hired out for the day. This was also when the head of the family did his shopping. The daily market was held in the agora. Traders, with their stalls and displays, turned the square into a noisy bazaar. The sellers were allocated places for their stalls depending on what type of produce they sold and laid their wares out on the ground or on trestles. Farmers brought in fruit and vegetables from the surrounding countryside. These commodities stood side by side with stalls selling oil, cheese, wine, pottery or clothes. Foreigners came to sell exotic goods. In Athens Pericles had a special market built for flour; in Megara there was one for perfume. City inspectors saw that the by-laws were observed and controlled the proceedings. They tried to protect the consumer from sharp practice: so fish sellers were forbidden to sprinkle water over their fish in order to make them seem fresher than they were... Traders had a poor reputation, they were always suspected of trying to cheat the customer.

Political life also centered on the agora; it was the symbol of the democratic rule invented in Athens in the 5th century BC. Since it was where everyone met, it was where every citizen came to know what was happening: everyone could read the laws and edicts inscribed on wooden panels, It was where public debates and passionate political discussions took place, where personal opinions were forged. It was here that the citizens educated themselves in their political duties. And citizens could one day be called on to exercise political office.

The most important civic buildings were along the esplanade. By coming here every day, citizens fulfilled their political duties and cast their votes: meetings, assemblies of citizens (ecclesia) or sessions of the courts started at dawn. The richest people sometimes spent all day there. The ecclesia met for a time on the agora, but quickly moved to the Pnyx hill in Athens. The prytanes made up the elected city council and ruled the city; they met and took their meals in the Tholos in the main square. This circular building was also the temple of Hestia, sheltering the sacred fire of the city that must never go out. The Senate House was also on the esplanade; its members were drawn by lot: it had a small temple dedicated to the mother of the gods which also contained the city archives. In the 5th century BC a rectangular hall with tiered seats was added. The Peoples' Court was nearby. Long porticoes (stoa) surrounded the agora; a colonnaded side opened out onto it. It was an excellent place for viewing open-air ceremonies. One could walk there and be sheltered from rain and sun. There were shops inside, craftsmen's workshops and administrative offices.

The agora was shaded by trees and cooled by fountains and thus was an area where one could relax and be entertained. In the afternoon, those who had free time could enjoy the quiet part of the day. They sat there, walked about, dropped in to the hairdresser or the barber, the perfume seller or the shoemaker. They would be sure to meet people they knew for a chat or to exchange the latest gossip. They also listened to philosophers, like Socrates, who met their pupils there. After the day's work the ordinary people of the city enjoyed the shows and entertainment: all over the agora, jugglers, acrobats, mummers, conjurers, clowns and puppeteers amused the crowds. The richer citizens preferred to go to the baths, and then perhaps, they had been invited to a banquet...

The city also provided a stadium, a gymnasium and a palestra (an exercise area). These buildings drew young athletes to train there; their elders also come to admire skill and strength, and the well-muscled bodies of youth. In the 5th century BC these sporting complexes were equipped with fountains, wash basins and even swimming pools. Then in the 4th century BC establishments specifically built as public baths became more frequent. They were built beside the agora in Assos in the Troad. Better off citizens went there regularly and for long periods of time: they chatted, lounged about, had a meal. They took alternate hot and cold baths to make themselves sweat. There were also steam baths and saunas. Boys were employed to sprinkle clients' bodies with water and to rub them with oil. There were special areas for physical exercises. Poorer people stayed there for long periods in the winter to warm up. There was a women's section; this was usually frequented by the poorest section of the population, by slaves and by prostitutes.

Finally, from the 6th century on Greek cities started to build theaters. These were built in connection with the worship of Dionysus: the tyrant Pisistratus introduced the worship of the god to Athens in 534 BC. Religious festivities in honor of this god often took the form of dramatic competitions; so they needed buildings to hold the crowds who came to see the tragedies and comedies. These entertainments became very popular with the Greeks. Usually found in a sanctuary dedicated to Dionysus, the theaters were often built on the side of a hill. The tiered seats, where the audience sat, could be built into the slope, usually in a semicircle. The spectators looked down on a central area, the orchestra, which held the choruses, the musicians and the altar of the god. Beyond that was the stage: where the actors played. These buildings have admirable acoustics. Once a year the Athenians flocked to the theater of Dionysus on the side of the Acropolis to see another form of entertainment: fighting cocks, quail, dogs and cats. The fighting spirit of these animals really impressed the children.

THE CITY OF ASSOS IN THE TROAD FOLLOWING PAGES

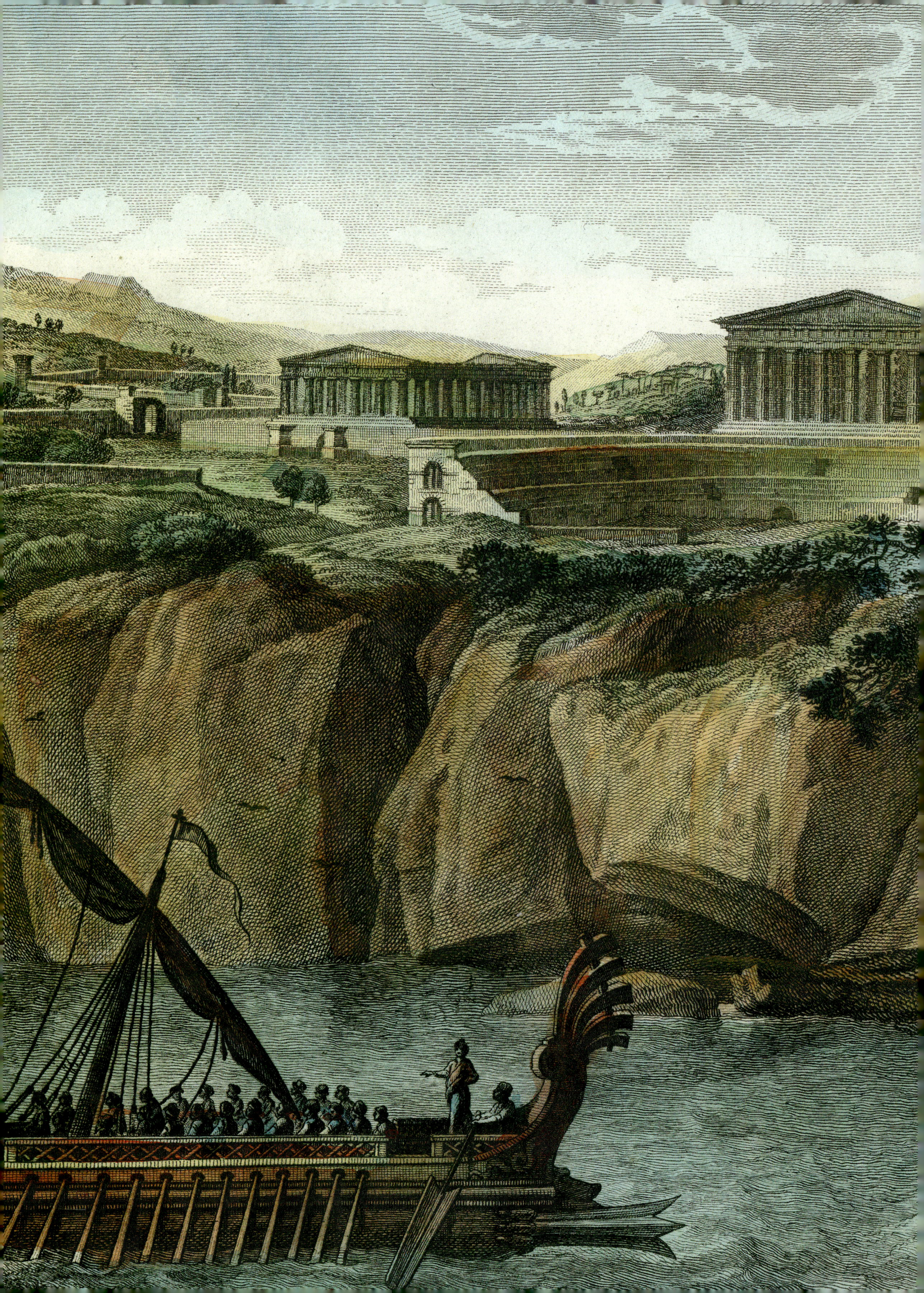

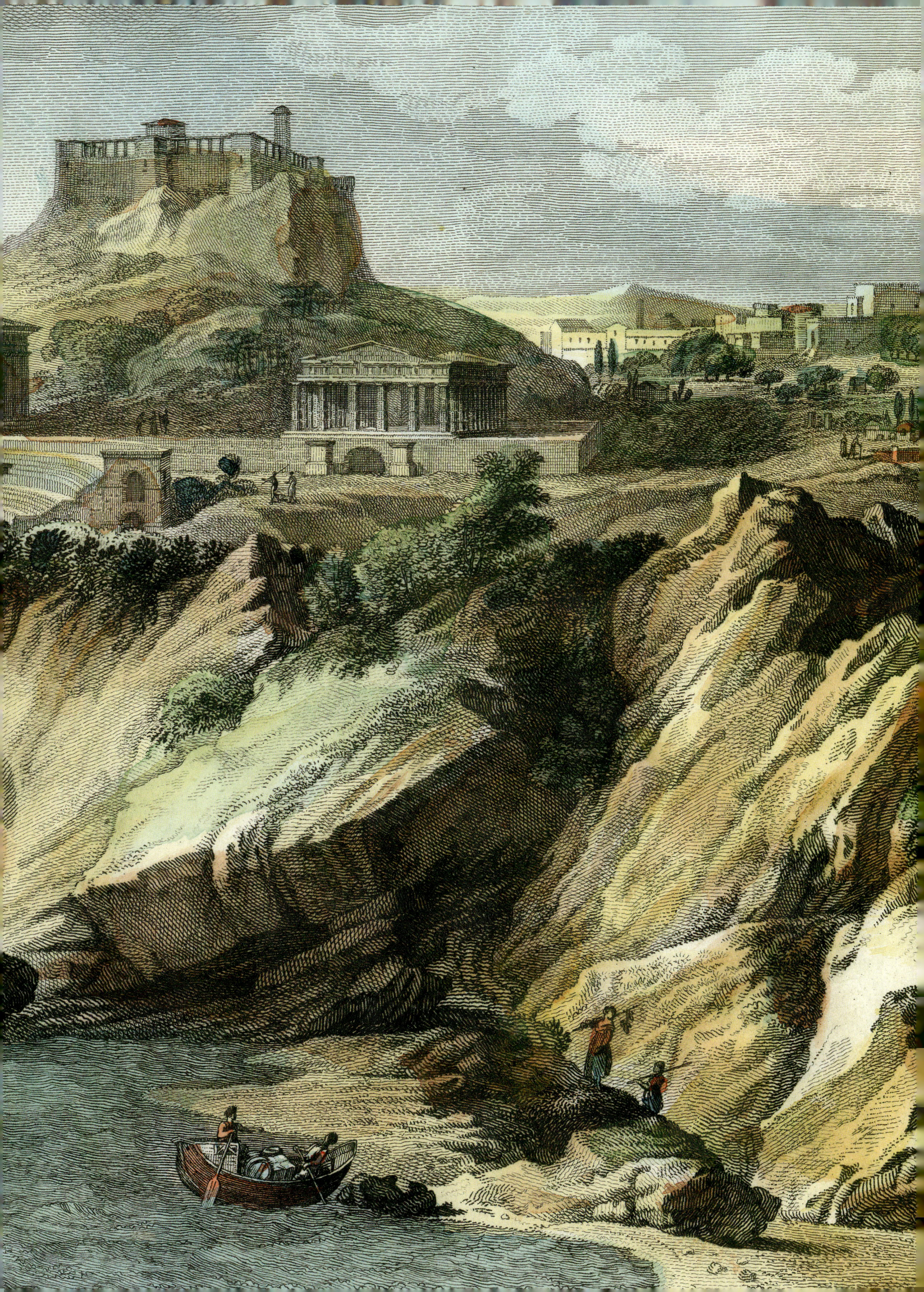

GREEK MONUM

THE ODEON OF PERICLES AT ATHENS

TOMB AT

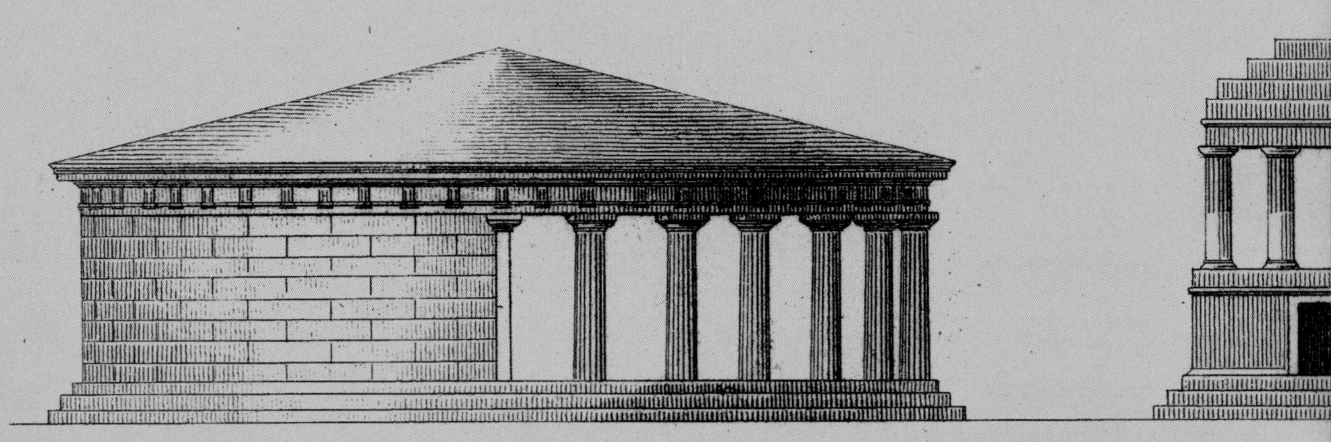

ATHENIAN GATEWAY

TEMPLE BESIDE THE ILISSOS

TEM

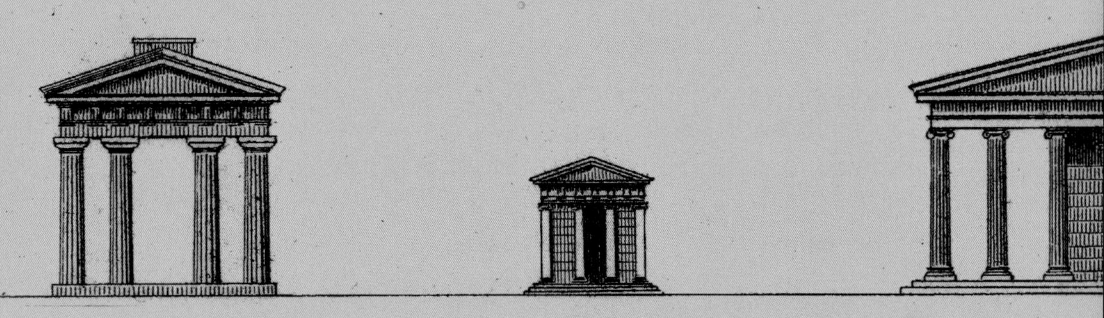

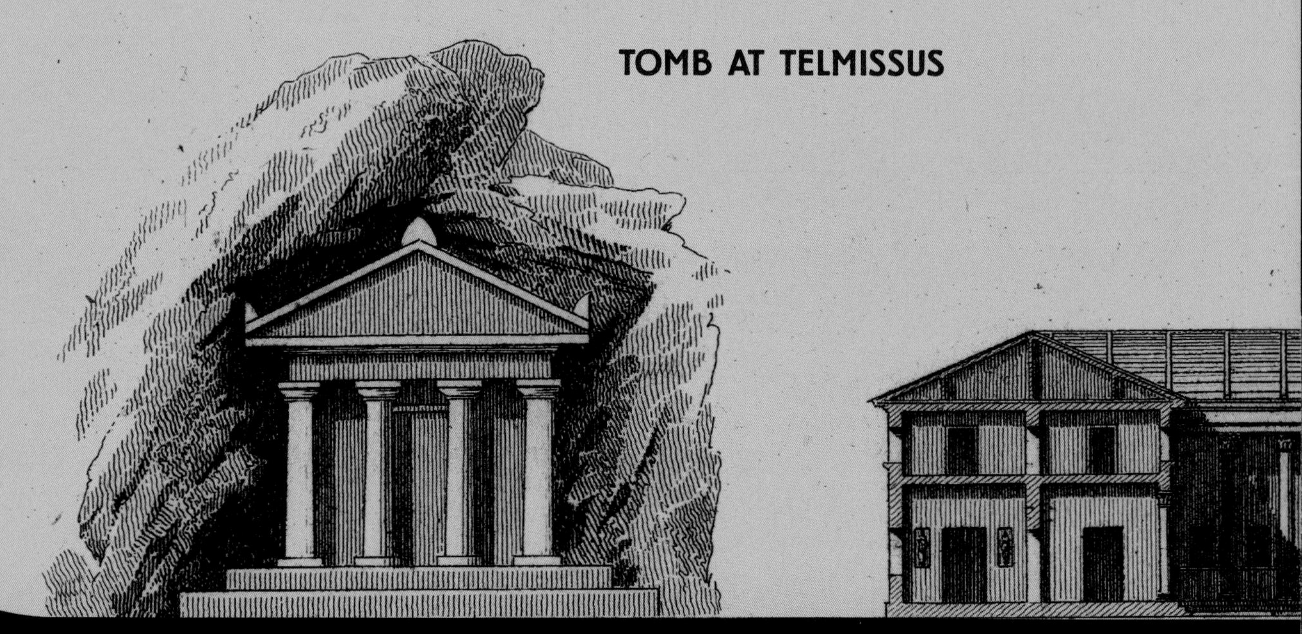

ND BUILDINGS

TEMPLE OF APOLLO DIDYMUS NEAR MILETUS

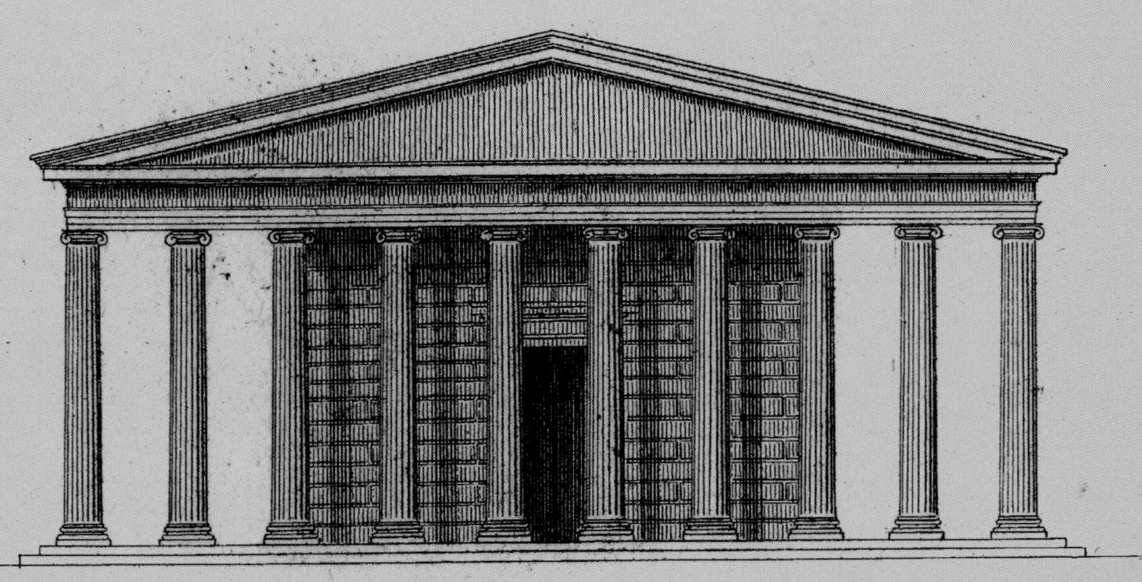

IONYSUS
OS

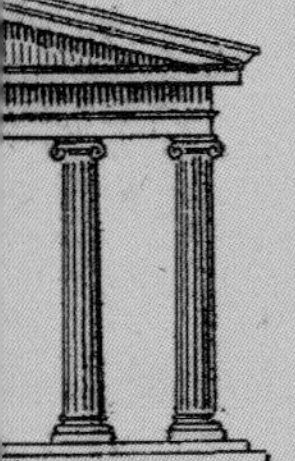

TEMPLE OF AGRAULE
AT THEOS

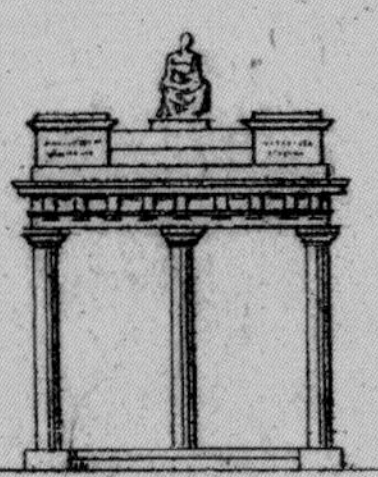

TEMPLE OF ATHENA
AT ATHENS

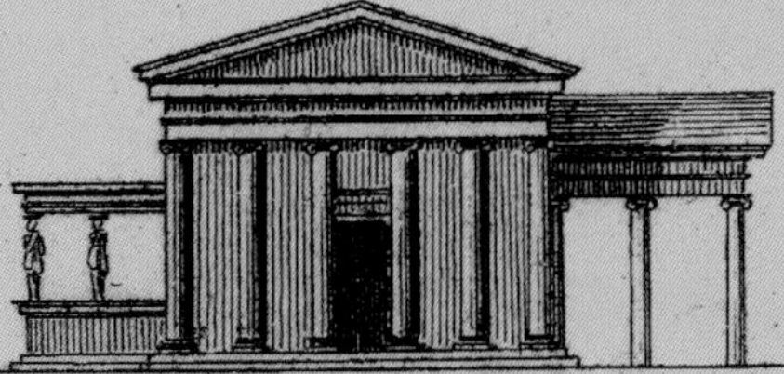

A GREEK HOUSE

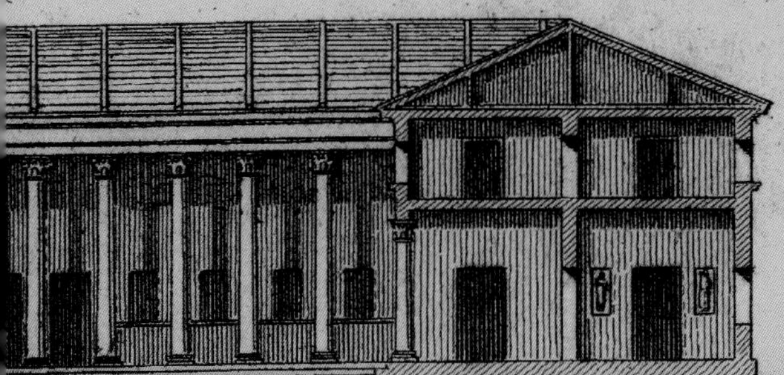

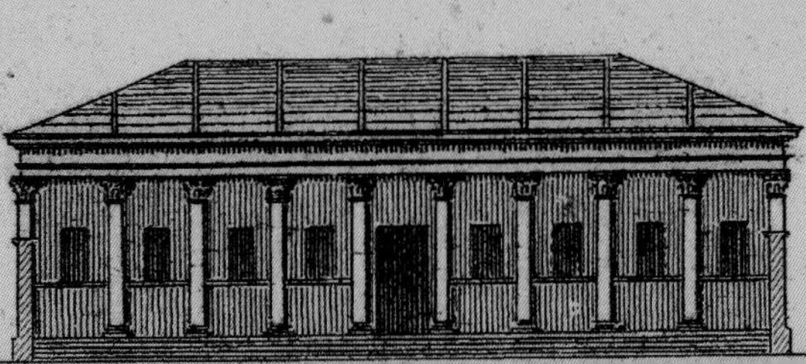

A THE WIFE'S QUARTERS

1 MAIN ENTRANCE OR DOOR TO PUBLIC ROAD
2 PASSAGEWAY, CALLED ITEX BY VITRUVIUS
3 SECOND OR INNER DOORWAY
4 PORTER'S LODGE
5 PERISTYLE
6 DOORWAYS
7 HALLWAY
8 WORK ROOMS
9 BEDCHAMBER OR THALAMUS
10 VISITING CHAMBER OR AMPHITHALAMUS
11 DINING ROOM
12 SERVANTS' QUARTERS
13 PASSAGE BETWEEN WIFE'S AND HUSBAND'S QUARTERS

B THE HUSBAND'S QUARTERS

A HALLWAYS
B GREAT PERISTYLE
C DOORWAYS
D RHODIAN DOORWAY
E FEASTING HALL
F LIBRARY
G PICTURE GALLERY
H DINING ROOM
I AUDIENCE AND RECEPTION ROOMS
K GUEST ROOMS
L STABLES AND YARD
M GARDEN
N PASSAGEWAYS CALLED MEFAULAE

STREET
k
k

PLAN OF A GREEK HOUSE BY VITRUVIUS

STREET

STREET

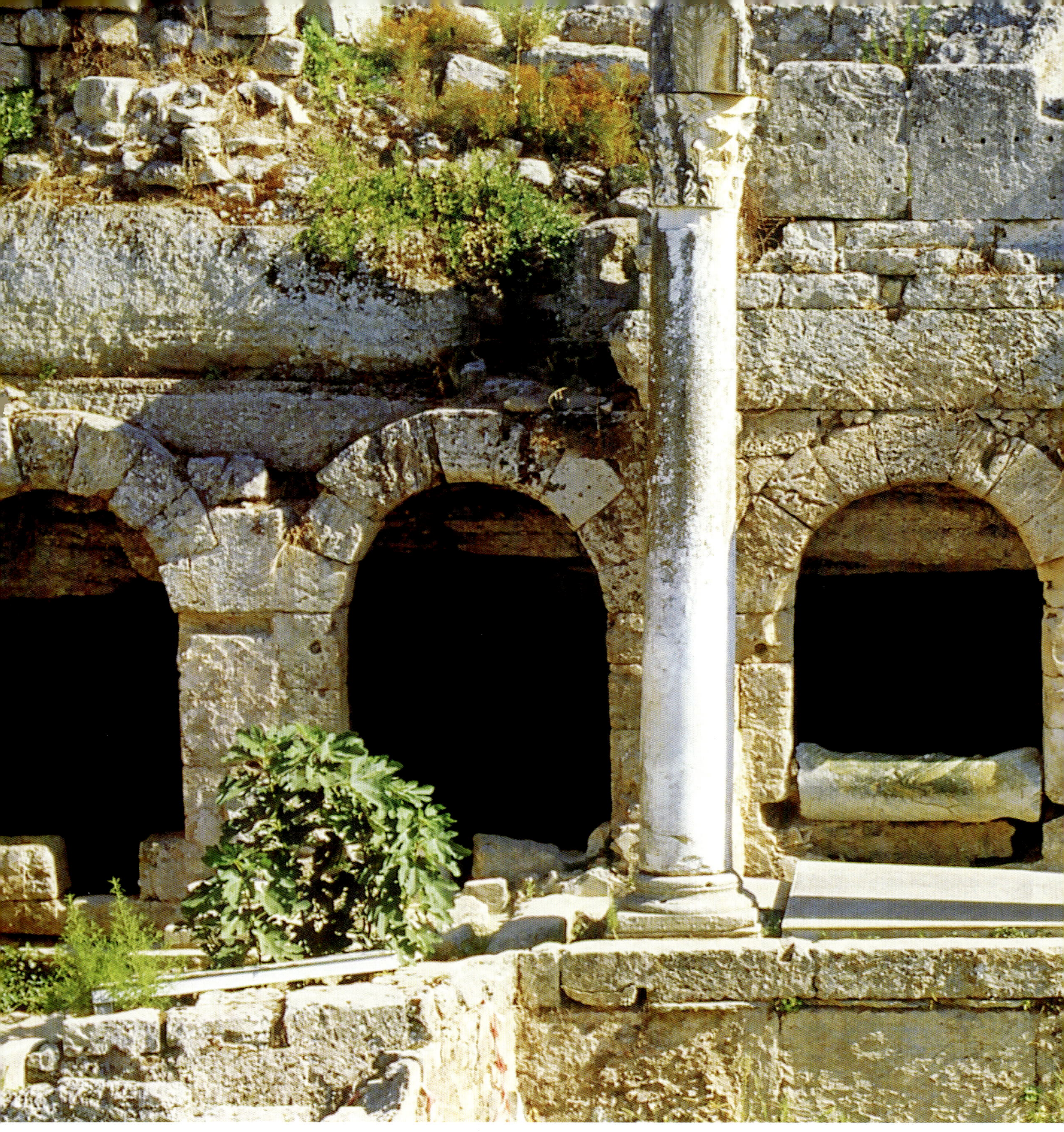

THE FOUNTAIN OF HEROD ATTICUS IN CORINTH

In the 2nd century AD Herod Atticus presented the city of Corinth with one of its finest monuments: a fountain which remained in use until the 19th century.

The great bowl is now full of wild plants and the huge reservoirs beneath the arcades are falling into ruin. However the spring, which still supplies the town's water supply, came into being in ancient times when Sisyphus spotted Zeus kidnapping the daughter of the River Asopus. He resolved to tell the father who the kidnapper was, as long as Asopus gave a spring to his waterless city.

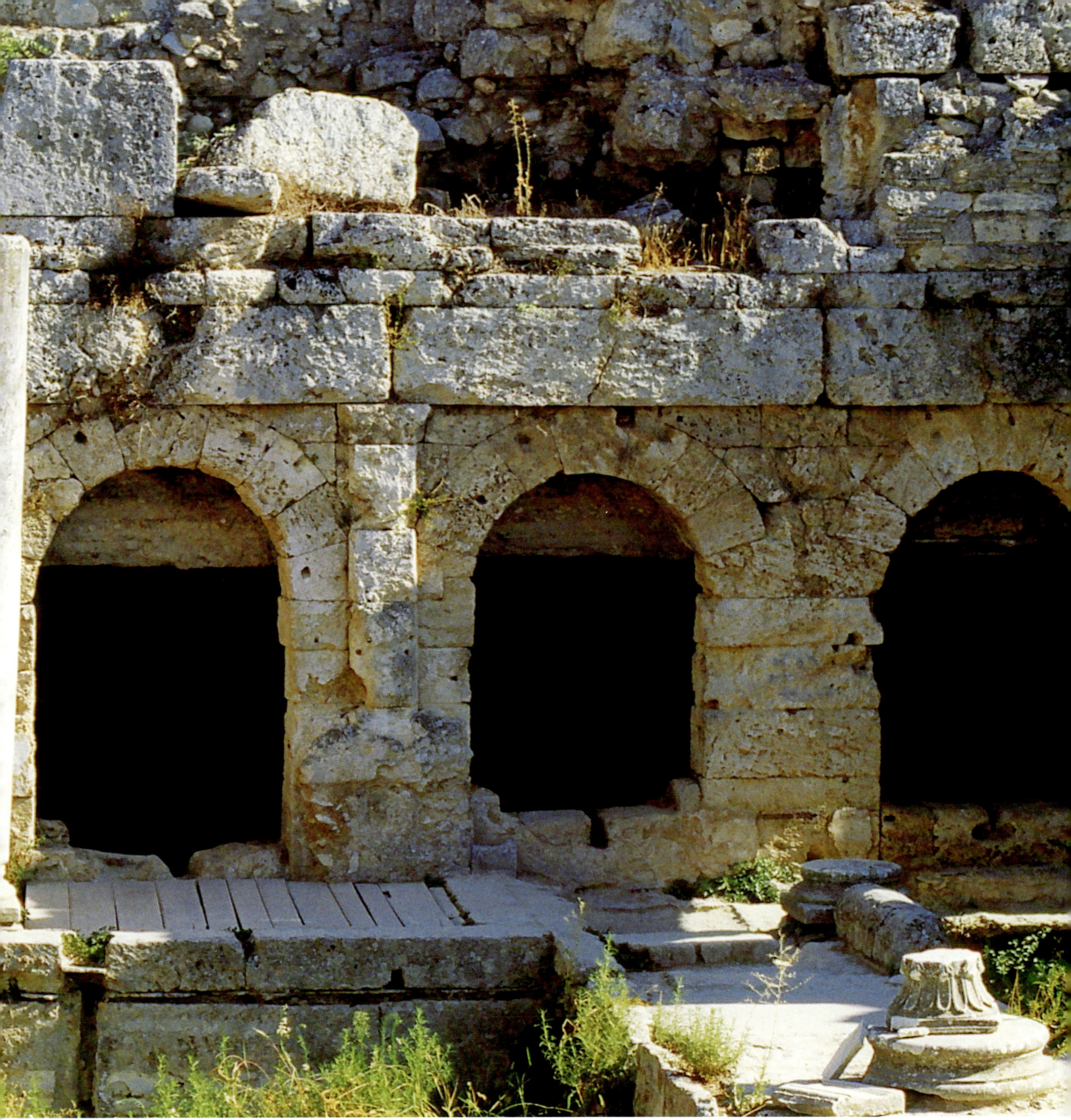

WOMEN'S STYLE

Greek women vied with each other in imagination and skill to dress their long hair, which had to be either curled or waved. They washed it, oiled it and sometimes dyed it. Fashion conscious ladies arranged it in many different ways, each one more stylish than the next: they plaited it or gathered it in a bun, and kept it in place with a hair band, or a headpiece. PAGES 134-135

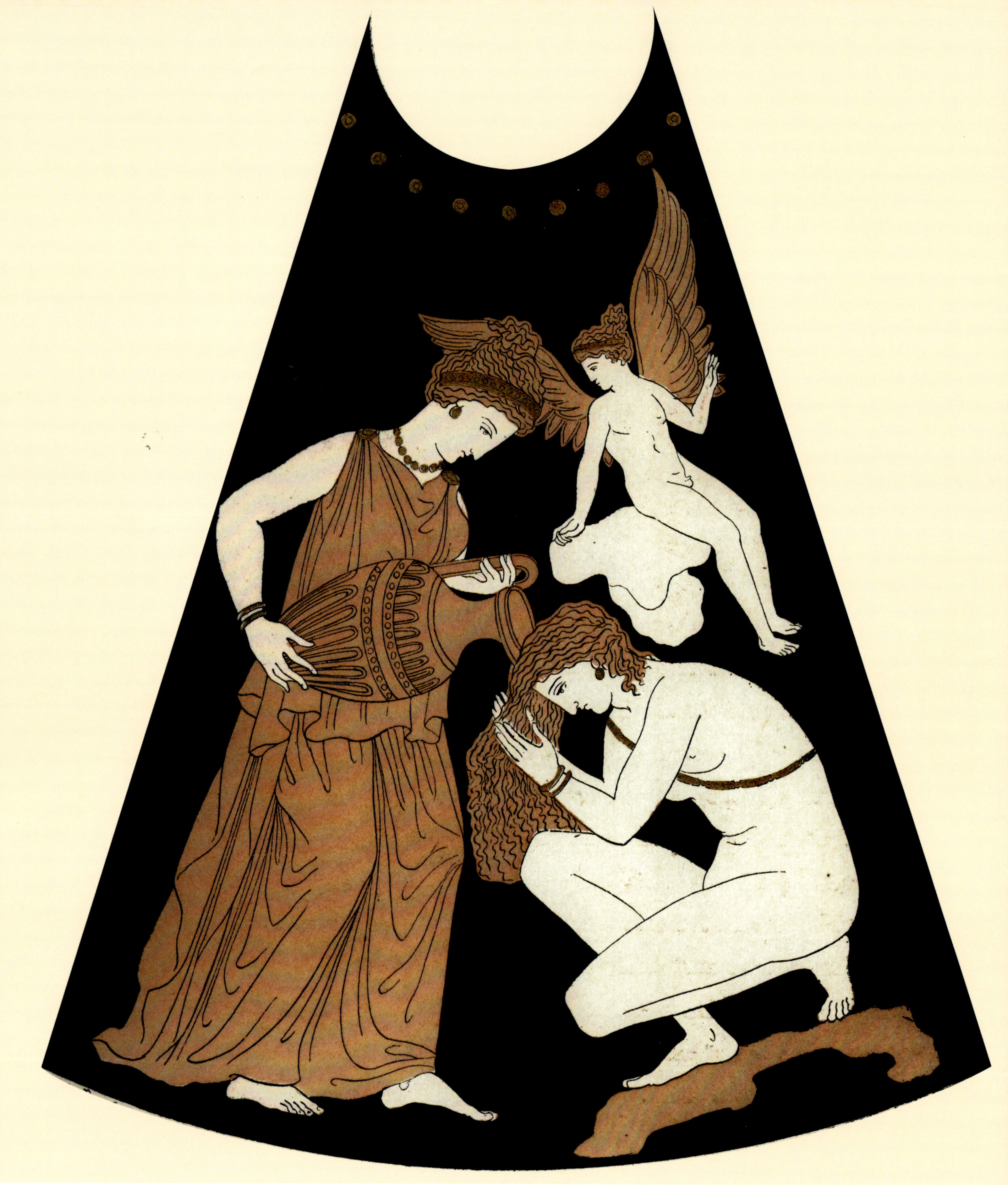

WOMEN DRESSING UP

The Greeks were very conscious of personal hygiene and took great care of their bodies. Women may not have made daily visits to the public baths; nevertheless they spent time at their toilet every day. They washed at home or in the courtyard at a raised basin; the better off had a special washing room

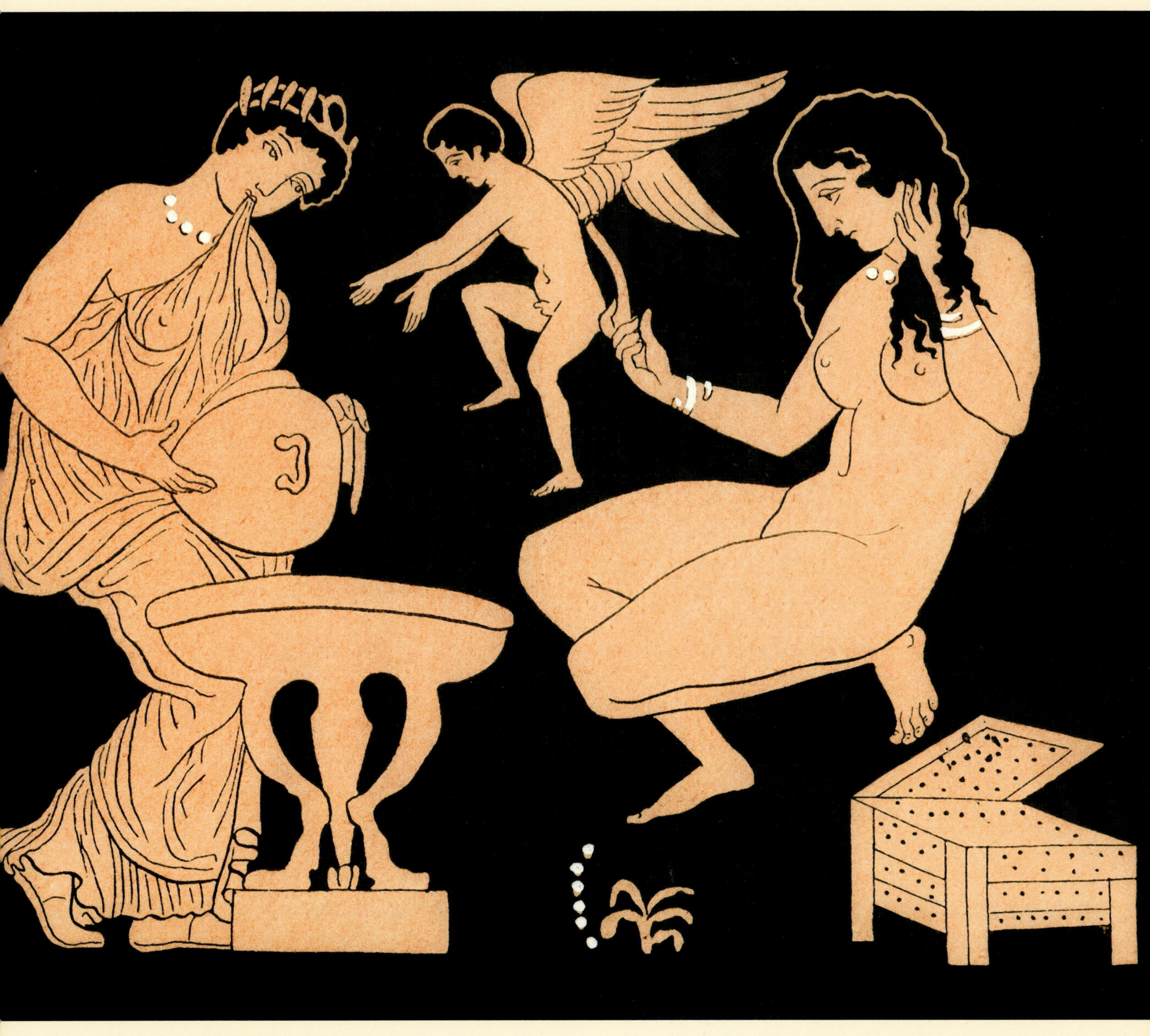

equipped with a bath made of baked clay. Sometimes women met together at the public fountain, chatted, washed and splashed themselves with water. Personal hygiene products were made from chalk, soda and clay. They then rubbed themselves with oil to get rid of the irritation caused. All they then had to do was to titivate themselves, apply perfume and makeup, to style their hair in the latest fashion and put on their finest jewelry.

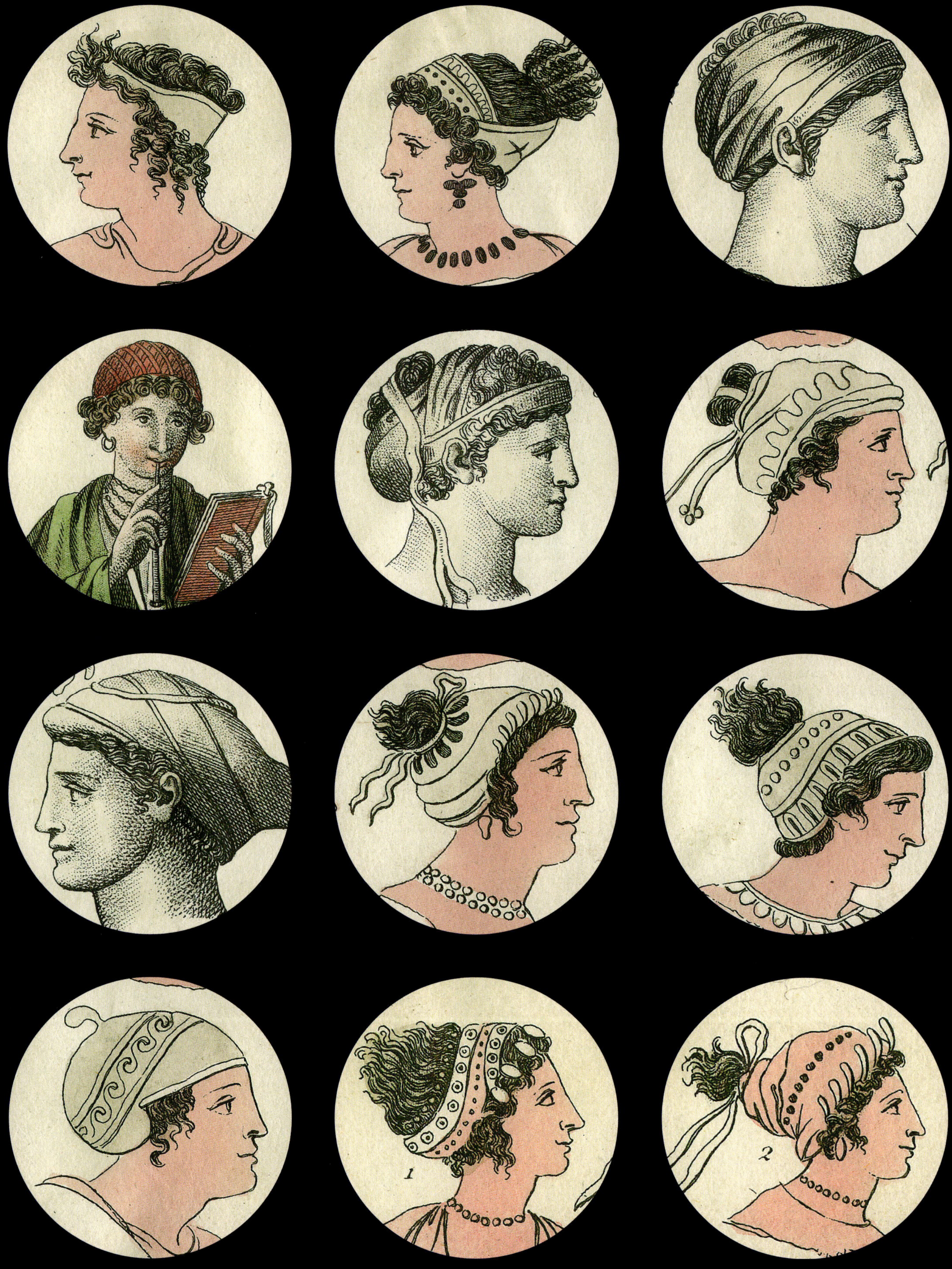

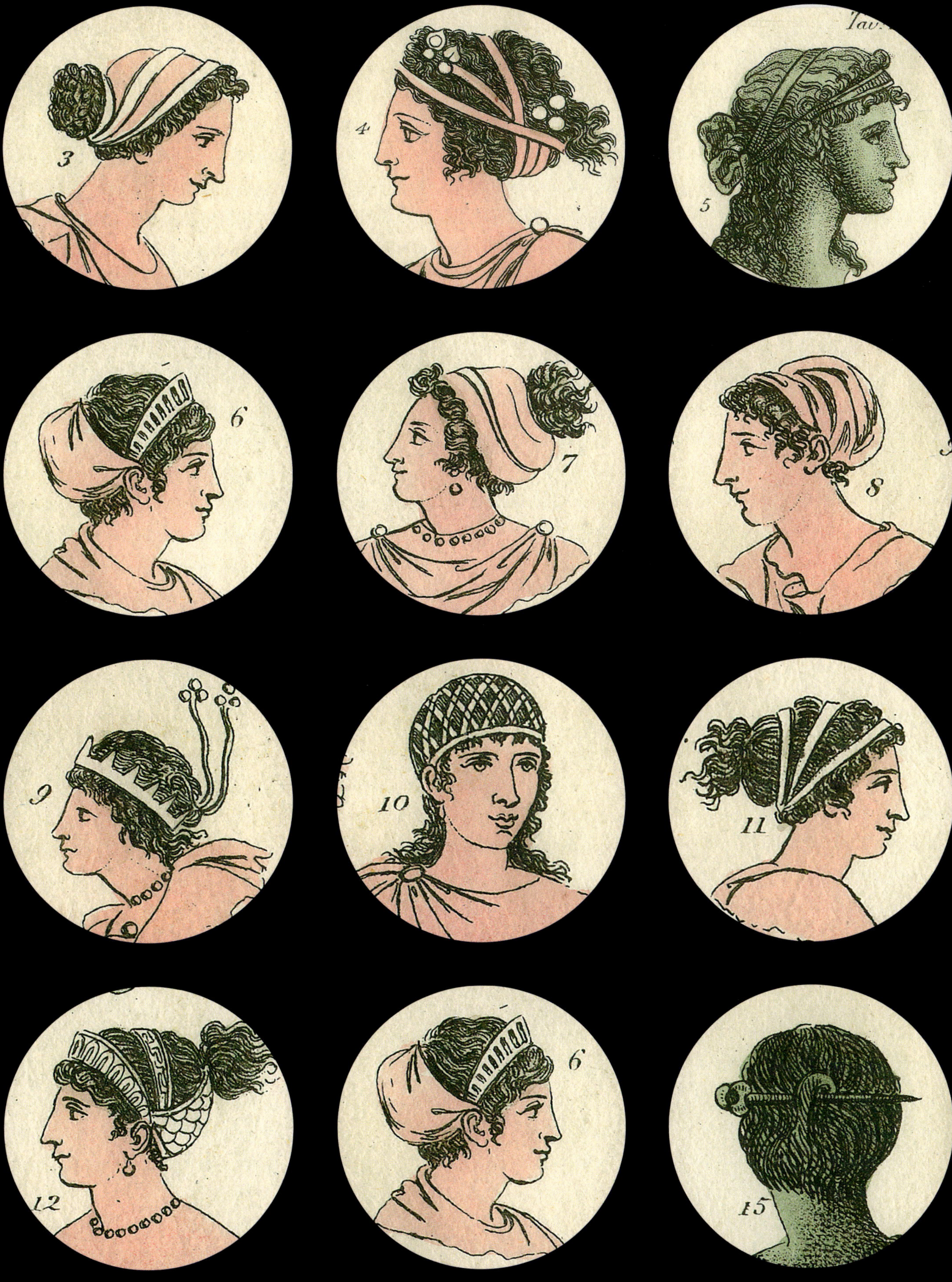

ACTORS AND THE THEATER

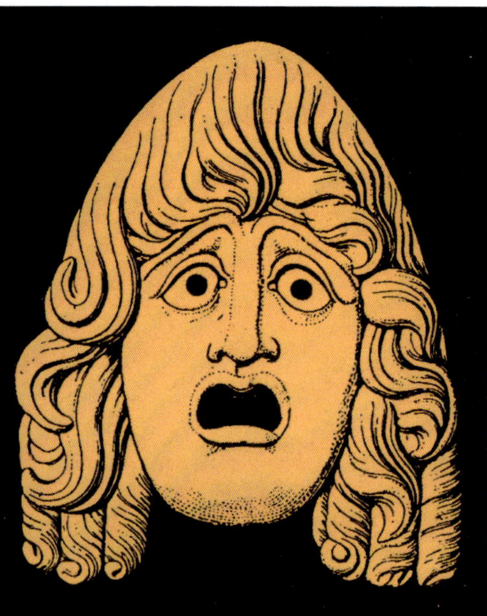

A TRAGIC MASK

Theater was born out of the religious festivals organized in honor of Dionysus by; these gradually became what we now recognize as theatrical plays. To house such a spectacle the first theater was built in Athens in the 5th century BC. At the center was an altar dedicated to the god. The citizen expressed their devotion to Dionysus, by coming to the shows, which were tragedies, comedies and satirical dramas. Even the poorest could attend, because they were supported by a state grant. The actors were all men, playing both male and female roles; they often played several characters in the same play. They got over this difficulty by the way they used a convention of both costumes and masks. In this way actors often wore long robes in various colors which allowed the spectators to tell the identity, sex and social rank of the character being acted. In comedies they tended to put on a short chiton and a huge fake phallus, while padding exaggerated both buttocks and belly. Light sandals allowed them to move quickly and directors used such possibilities to comic effect. In order to appear bigger, tragic actors wore thick-soled laced half boots, which made them a foot taller but which also limited movement. The masks hid the face; in the 2nd century AD Julius Pollux listed 76 models. Comedy used a wide variety of expressions, but satirical drama used only four. Satyrs always had a beard, pointed ears and a bald head. The old masks were made of leather with grimacing faces; we know what they looked like thanks to copies made of baked clay which have been preserved.

A SCENE FROM A COMEDY: HERMES AND ZEUS ARE OFF ON A GALLANT ADVENTURE

FOLLOWING PAGES: **THE THEATER AT DODONA**

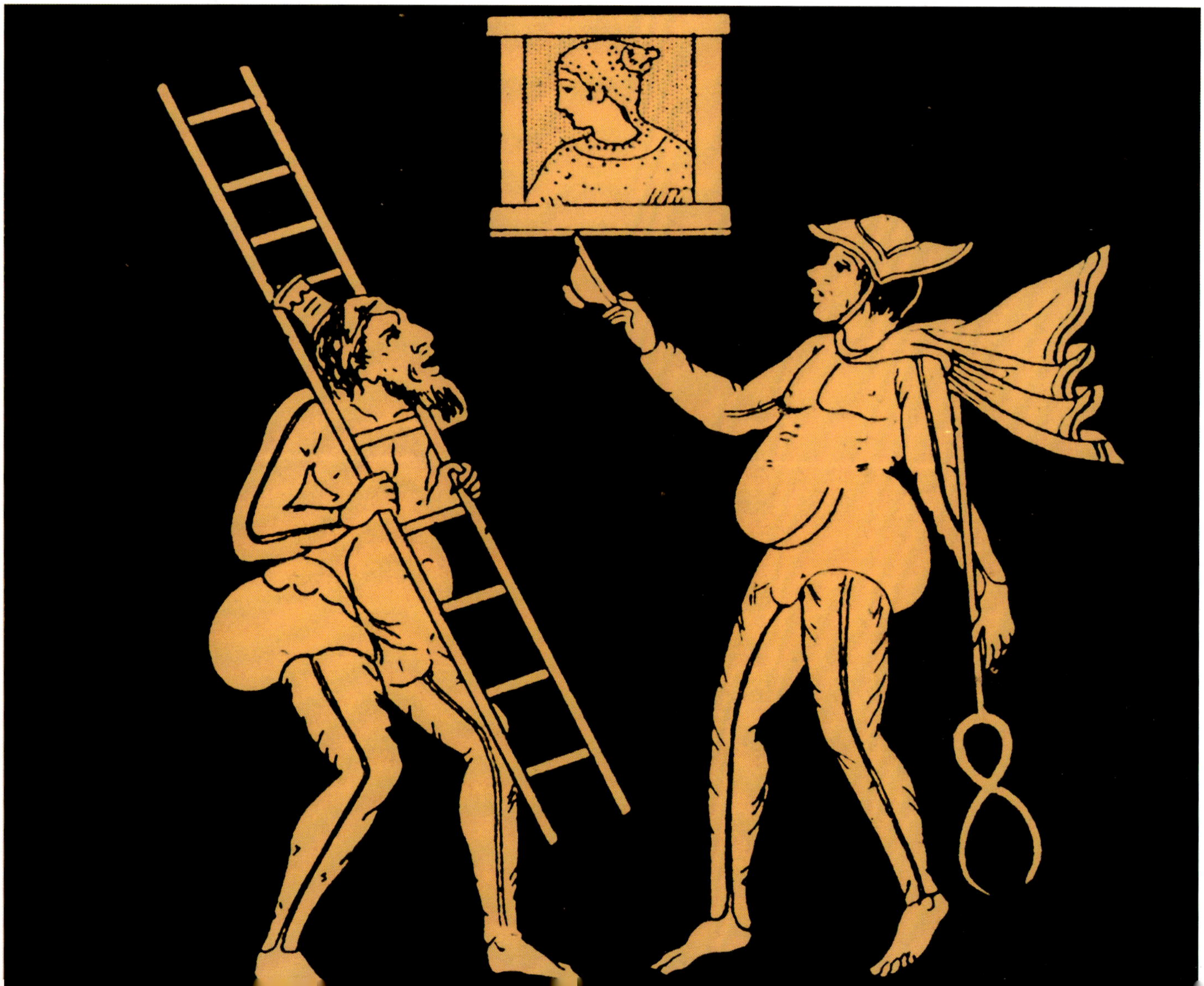

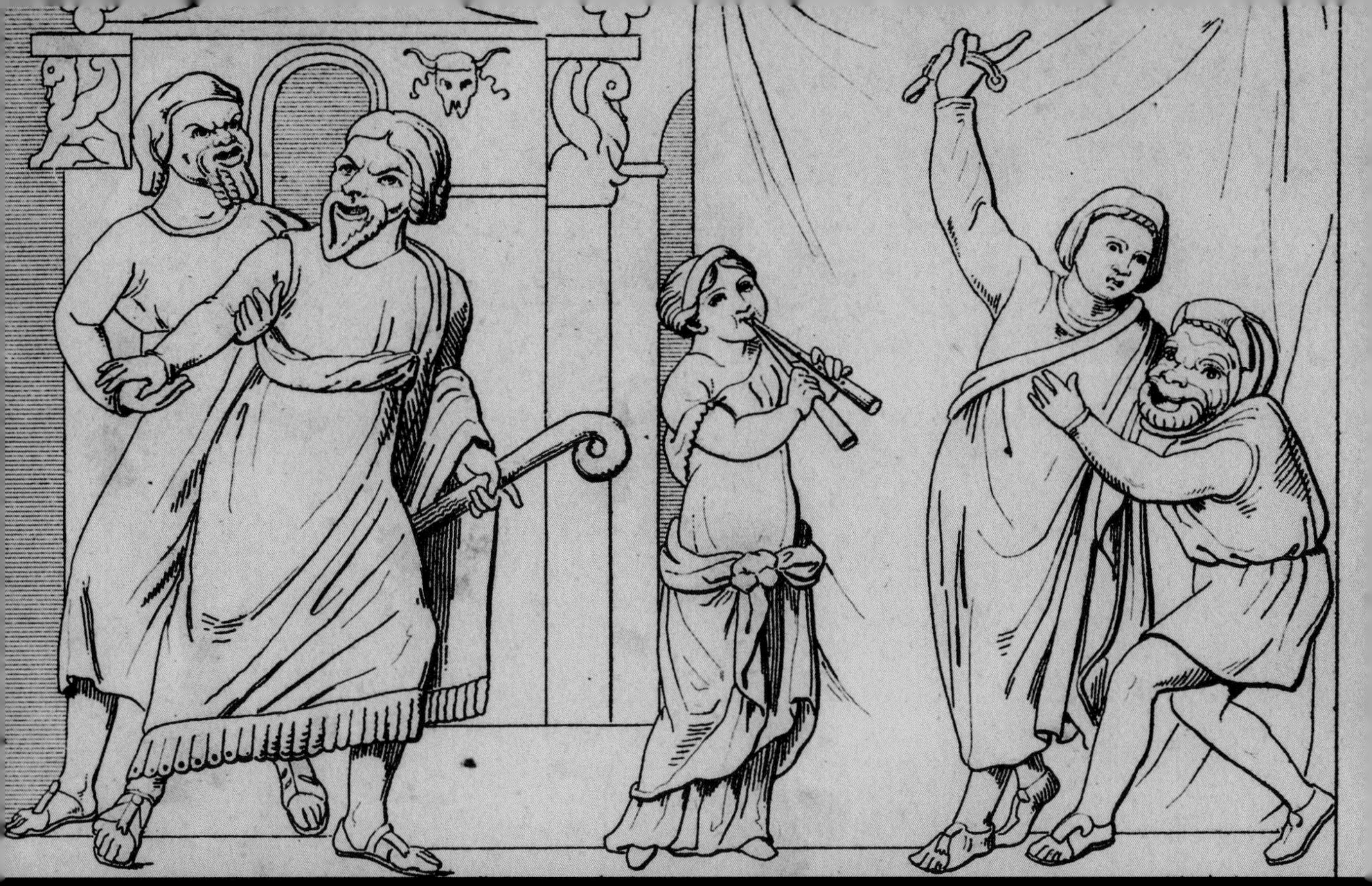

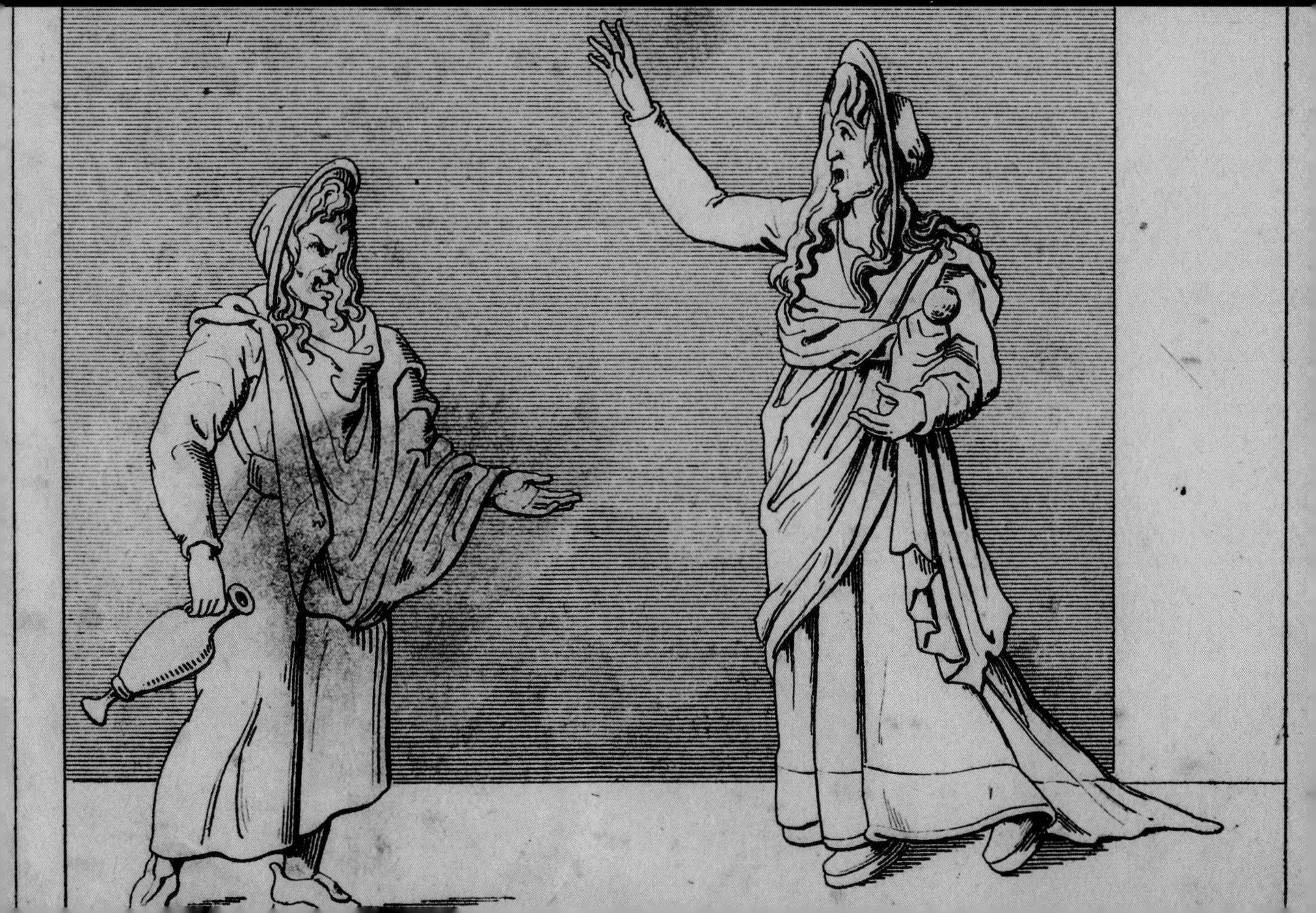

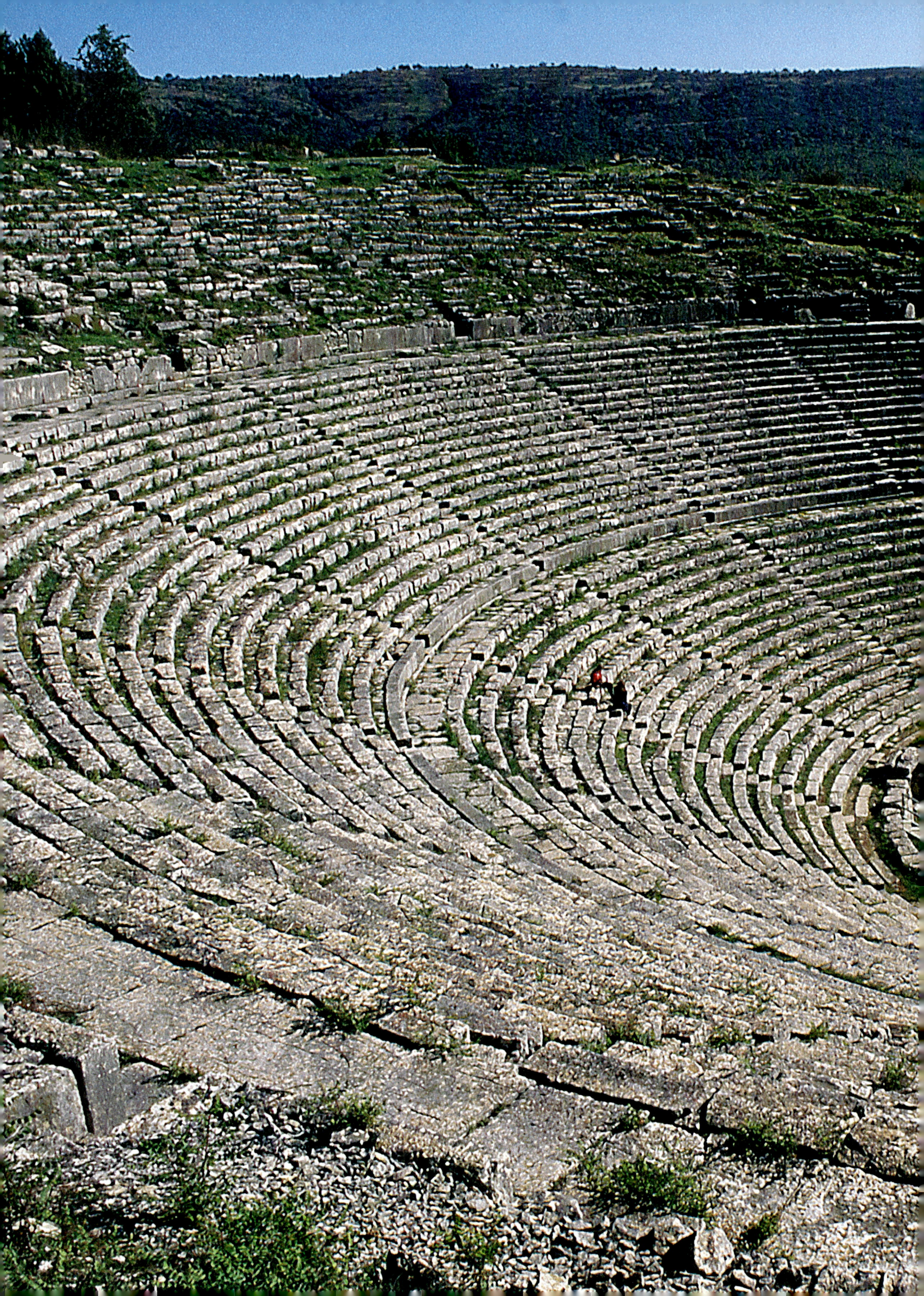

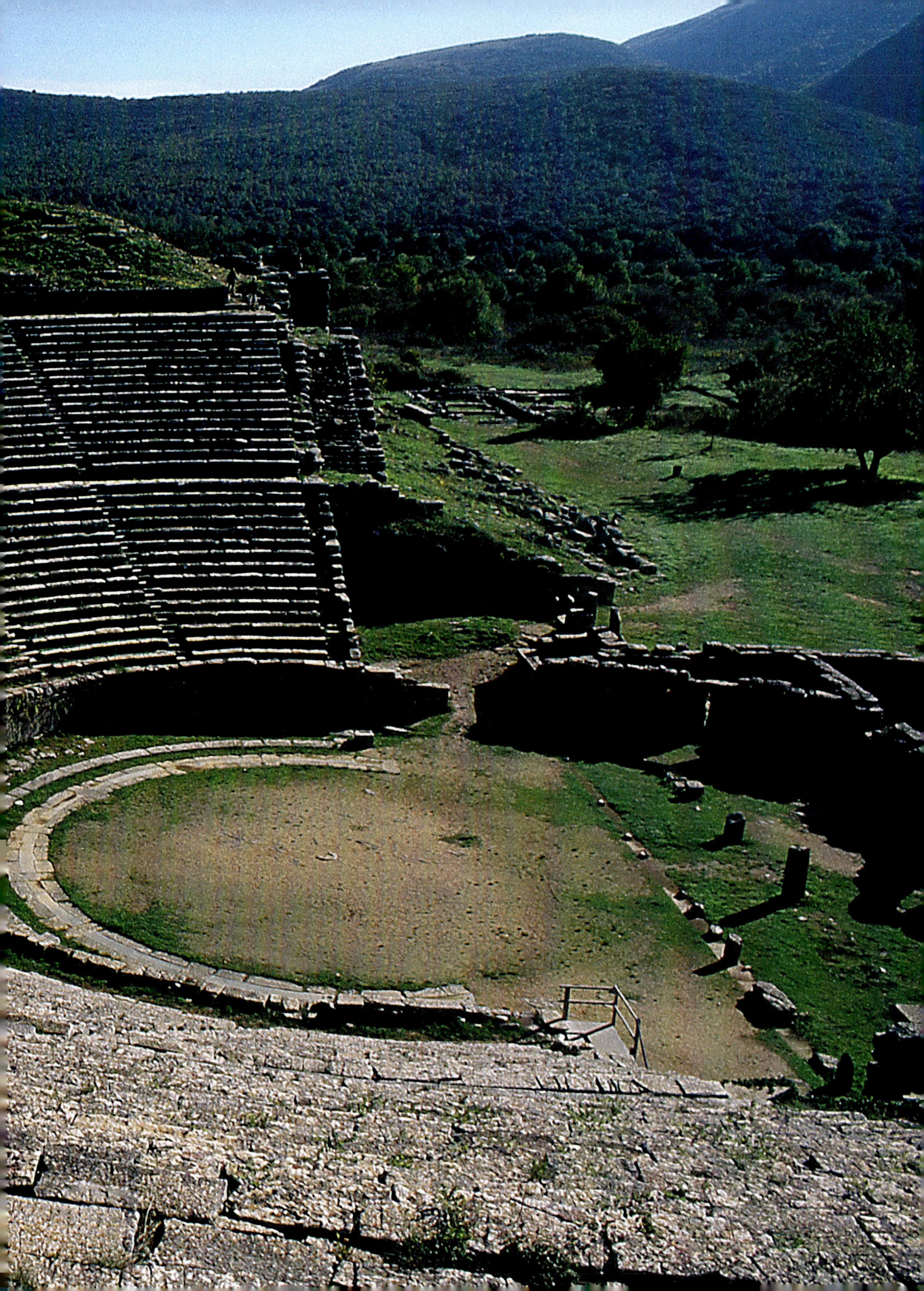

LOOKING OUTWARDS

The Greeks liked to settle on the coast, with their backs to the mountains, looking out over the vast seascape. The sea formed part of every Greek landscape; it encouraged them to travel. It attracted them, intrigued them, calmed them also. They felt close to it, intimate with it, they were unable to travel far from it without feelings of loss and anxiety. This familiarity produced a seafaring nation: fishermen, merchants and adventurers curious about what was over the horizon. Everything was an excuse to travel far from home: war, diplomatic missions, colonization, trade, tourism; or the need to be somewhere else, the thirst to find something different and to explore the world. Hermes and other Immortals traveled with them and they constantly prayed to them; the gods were with them and protected them in all dangerous undertakings, by land or sea.

The Greeks were soon to be acquainted with exile. There was little fertile land and that was owned by the few; some resources were scare or could not be found in Greece. Wars between cities, or conflicts between rival factions within cities, often sent people away, beaten or banished. Accordingly the inhabitants of Messina, having been expelled by the Spartans, went and settled in Italy. Following a famine, part of the population of Chalcis in Euboea set out for the same destination. From then on communities set out to find a fertile and hospitable place and founded new cities and colonies. Their institutions were frequently copied from the mother city, but these young colonies enjoyed political freedom. When deciding where to settle, they of course consulted the oracles, but they also had an eye to the resources offered by nature. Consequently Greek colonies were set up all around the Black Sea (the Pontus Euxinus) so as to benefit from the rich wheat lands of what is now the southern Ukraine. Similar communities were soon spread right around the Mediterranean coasts from Spain to Asia Minor as well as in Africa. The older colonies like Miletus were established in Asia Minor in the 11th century BC. In the 8th century, a huge wave of migrants settled around the western edges of the Mediterranean, Sicily and southern Italy; the region became known as Greater Greece, so many Hellenic peoples had settled there. They founded Syracuse, Tarentum, Cumae and Messina. In the 7th century they settled along the shores of the Black Sea (Byzantium, Olbis). Later they arrived on the coasts of southern France (Phocaea), of Spain (Empuries, Malaga) and of Africa (Cyrene, Naucratis). This tendency, which ran out of steam about the middle of the 6th century BC, turned the Mediterranean into a Greek sea. Those colonies spread Hellenic culture, the foundations on which western civilization was built.

These new cities still traded with the cities of Greece and finds of ancient Greek jars tells us just how vigorous trade was. Colonies, trading posts, emporia (places where goods were stored and where traders, emporoi, gathered) ensured that all cities were well and variously supplied in everything they needed. Greek ports became powerful and wealthy: Piraeus in particular, also Corinth and Aegina. The noisy docksides, swarming with colorful crowds, were piled with produce from all over the known world: corn from Italy, Sicily and Pontus Euxinus, fish from the Hellespont, papyrus, sails and ropes from Egypt, metals from the west; incense and spices came from Syria, ivory from Libya, dates and nuts from Asia Minor, carpets and cushions from Carthage. Skins, precious stones, tools, arms, clothes, pearls and slaves were also imported. Pepper came from emporia on the Eritrean coast of the Red Sea; other exotic goods included tortoise shells and purple dye. Foreign names and foreign goods that gave intrepid travelers itchy feet!

In spite of the dangers threatening them, such as brigands and pirates, the Greeks never thought twice before setting out on the their travels. The roads were crowded! At the time, it was of course easier to go by boat. The huge fleet that, in its day, allowed the Greeks to attack Troy, to defeat the Persians at Salamis in 480 BC and to gain the upper hand in trade all around the Mediterranean also provided a passenger service. There were shuttle services for short journeys, between Salamis and Piraeus for example. For longer journeys, they had to take cargo ships...Travelers did not often go overland. Greece, in any case, did not have a well-developed road network. The country's geography did not lend itself to it; the lines of mountains had few passes and the plains were cut off from each other. There were only rocky roads and narrow paths along the bottoms of the valleys, on the sides of the slopes and on the tracks up to high winter pastureland. Small portions were paved, the sacred way between Eleusis and Athens for example. Travelers went on foot, sometimes on horseback or on a mule, on rare occasions in a chariot or cart. They left early in the morning after offering a sacrifice, carrying a simple bundle. They ate frugally, ideally beside a shaded well: olives, onions, figs and dry biscuit. In the evening they slept beneath a portico unless they were offered hospitality (it was a sacred duty) in a private house.

The Greeks traveled for many reasons. Some professions were by nature always on the move: itinerant artists, actors and acrobats played before the crowds in villages and towns. Salesmen traveled, as did farmers, perched on a donkey, bringing their vegetables to the city markets. The artists were visiting the workshops of established masters to exercise their talents there. Doctors often traveled far to offer their services: in the 6th century BC Democedes of Croton went as far as Persia where he treated King Darius. Heralds and messengers were also on the roads; their job was to report word for word what they had been asked to say. Cities sent ambassadors on diplomatic missions to allies and enemies. These delegations were often involved in intense negotiations before signing an alliance or a peace agreement. On such occasions the delegate was free to seek the desired end in any way he saw fit. Demosthenes was said to be full of wiles and arguments to persuade Philip of Macedon that the Athenian claims over Amphipolis were legitimate.

Piety also brought the faithful and pilgrims out onto the roads as they traveled to the great sanctuaries. They bustled along the roads at the times of the great games and pan Hellenic festivals. Scholars, students and sophists roamed all over the then known world; eager to discover new things they traveled in order to learn or to teach. A stay abroad was an essential part of the wise philosopher's training: Solon apparently visited the court of Croesus in Lydia. Pythagoras and Thales got as far as Egypt. The historians Hecateus of Miletus and Herodotus traveled tirelessly as, later, did Strabo and Pausanias.

Herodotus and Strabo have left impressive ethnological descriptions of the peoples they observed. In the 4th century BC, the Greeks pushed back the frontiers of the known world: Alexander the Great explored Iran and India, while the navigator Pytheas of Aegina explored the shores of western Europe up as far as the North Sea. Tourism was at this time developing in Egypt and in the Near East: people could not stay away once they had read Herodotus.

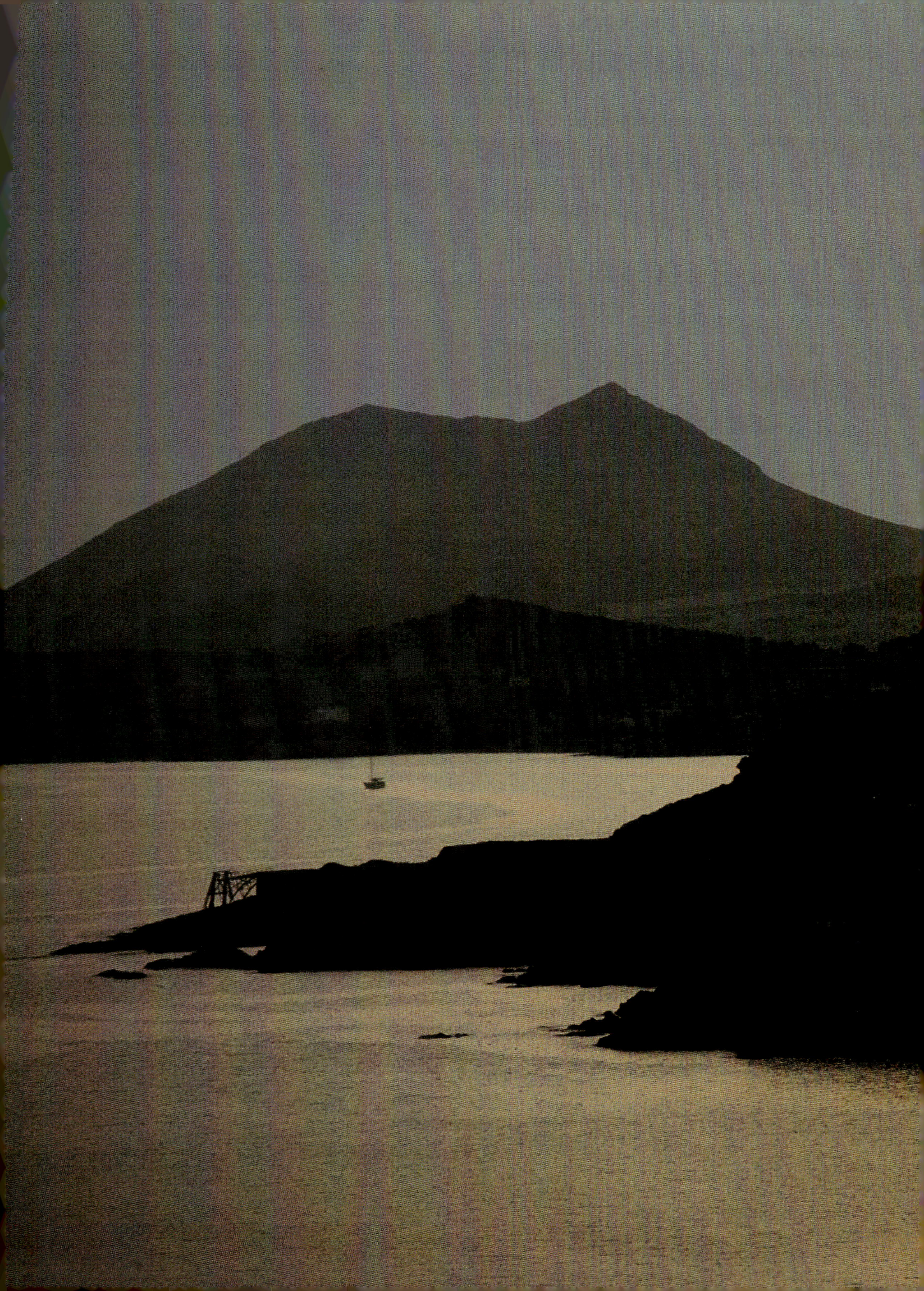

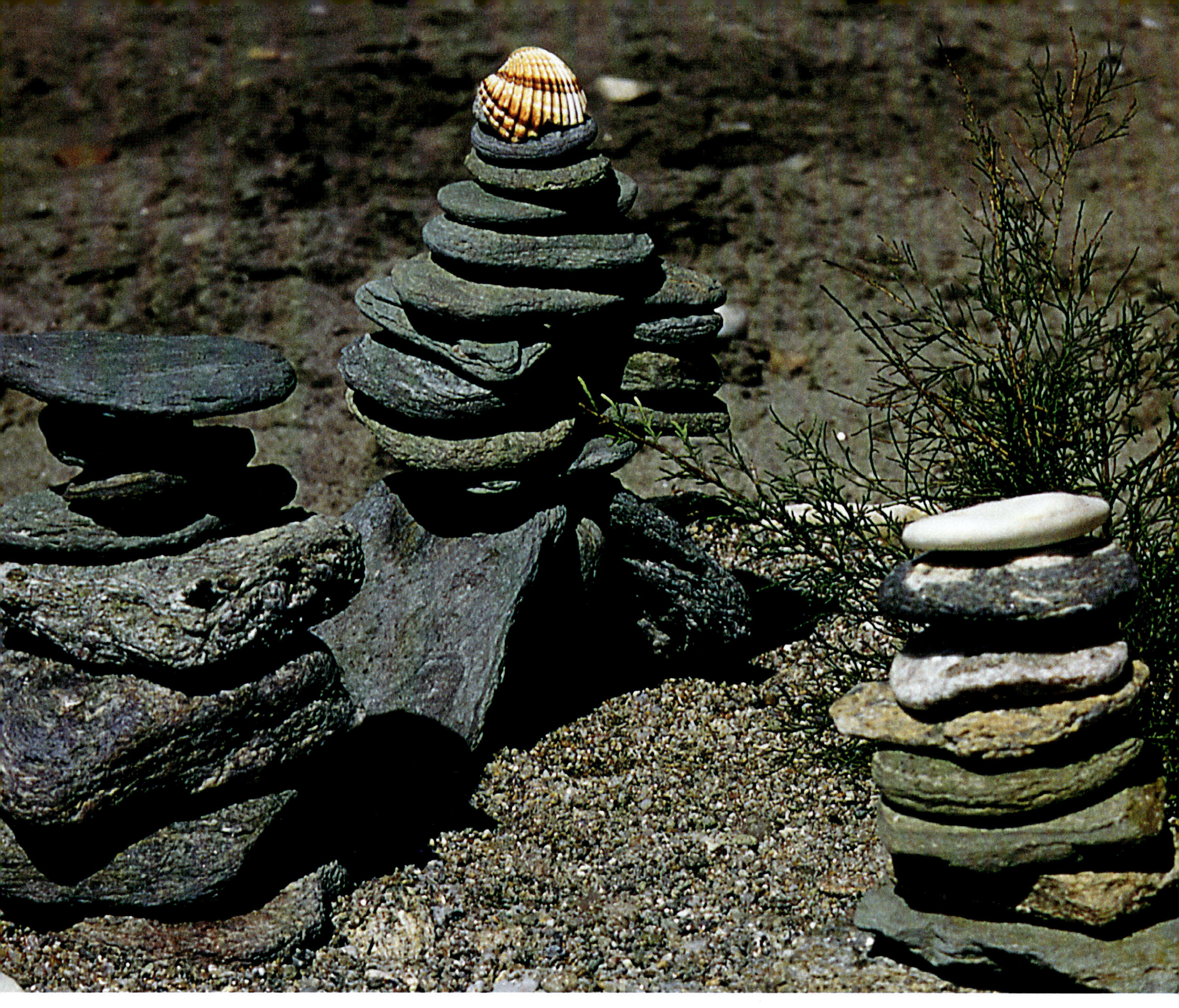

PILES OF STONES IN HONOR OF HERMES

Nothing in the modern Greek landscape is as strange as the piles of small stones, which have been built up by walkers. Such piles are scattered in large numbers all over the summit of the island of Delos. They are signs of the perseverance of those who have made their way up to this place; they remain as a memorial to their pause for contemplation. Such meager monuments are a throw-back to the herms (piles of stones) which the Ancients piled up at roadsides, at crossroads and at striking points in the countryside. They were scattered all over the landscape, they marked out space, and acted as field boundaries. Each passer-by put on a stone and contributed to the cairn. Such an act was held to ensure the protection of Hermes. These acts of homage to the god of travelers became milestones in the Roman period. These monuments are so old that some authors think they are most ancient marks of religious feeling that exist. The worship of Hermes, as expressed by the herms, was both discreet and modest. Passers-by would stop beside a cairn, add a stone and pray. Sometimes they poured out a libation or left a gift of a cake or fruit. These offerings were, in the eyes of the next traveler, a divine gift. There is no doubt that they helped turn the herms into signs of good fortune and gave the god the reputation of bringing good luck and gifts. The piles of stones were often capped by a larger carved stone, and then during the 6th century BC, this became a pillar decorated with an erect phallus.

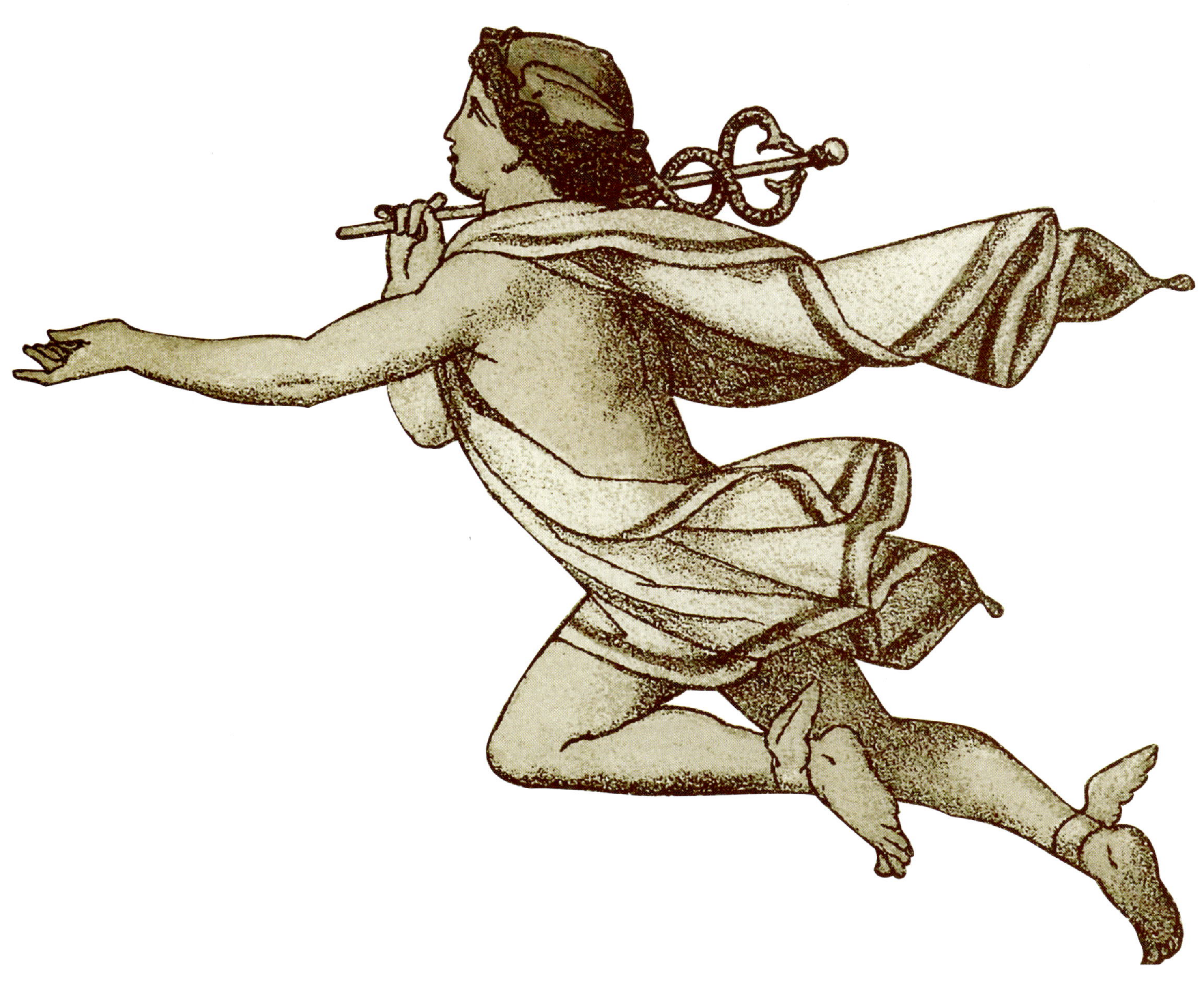

HERMES OR FLUIDITY IN MOVEMENT

Piles of stone called herms were found everywhere in the Greek landscape, so Hermes, the god of travelers, accompanied them whenever they ventured outside of their own city and surrounding area.

He had winged sandals and could move as quickly as lightning, fly above ground and overcome obstacles. He was equally at home in the dimensions of the Olympian gods, of human beings and of the lower regions of Hades. He presided over all travel, all communications and all exchanges. Wherever events and meetings were held, he was there. He was the guide and link between two persons, two regions, two families (marriage), two states of being (from life to death) or two social ranks. He was of mixed origin, at home in two different settings, was vivacious, cunning and looked for immediate effect. He acted by chance, was fickle and sudden.

The benefits and advantages he brought were unexpected and generous. Yet his hybrid origins could be ambiguous and gave Hermes a threatening, troubled and often aggressive air. If travelers saw him as the benevolent and protecting god, the robbers who plagued the roads thought of him as providing their chance to rob passers by and get rich quick!

A MYCENAEAN CHARIOT AND TEAM

This terracotta figure was made in a workshop in the great age of Mycenaean civilization, between 1400 and 1200 BC. It is a statuette of a chariot with two passengers, and drawn by two horses. This means of transport was rare as only the rich could afford it; furthermore the narrow, bumpy roads did not encourage it. However we know it was used by Hellenic Greeks of more recent times.

A HORSE

This fresco, with its ochre and brown tints, is from Delos, nevertheless it seems almost modern in style: the stroke is free and lively, the scene in airy and dynamic. A young man rises effortlessly onto a horse's back, while another is about to follow; they are caught in a joyful moment as they race and play. The three figures seem to be acting together in total harmony. It is a charming warm and happy work with echoes of Minoan wall paintings, when painters liked to show humans in joyful communion with animals and nature: young Cretan acrobats playing with bulls. Trained and tamed, the horse has become the favorite mount of young men. He was the pleasantest and best adapted mount for the narrow, rough and rocky roads of Greece. But the noble animal was a status symbol of the rich! Buying such a companion, maintaining him and looking after him was a luxury only the well-to-do could afford. FOLLOWING PAGES

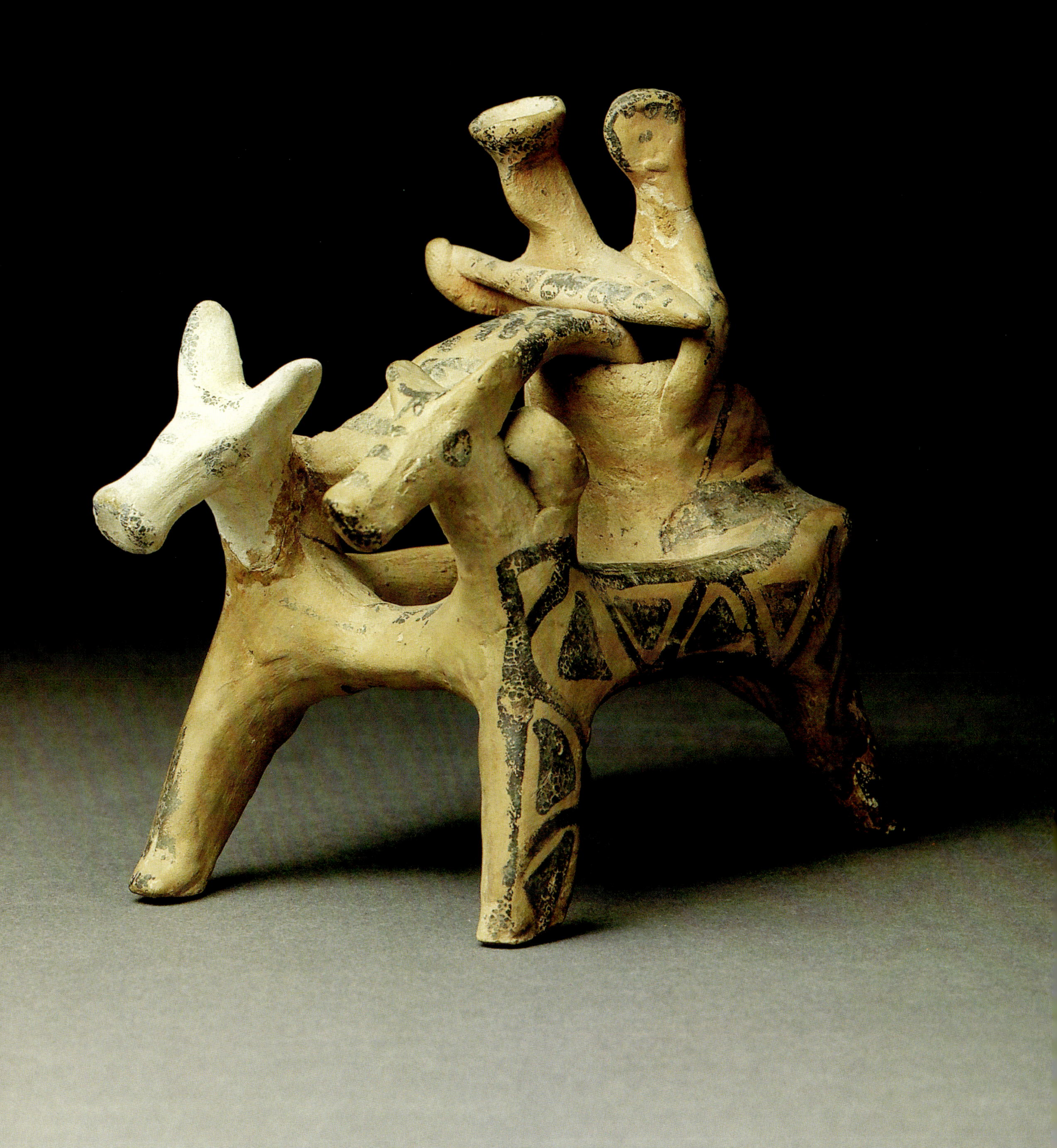

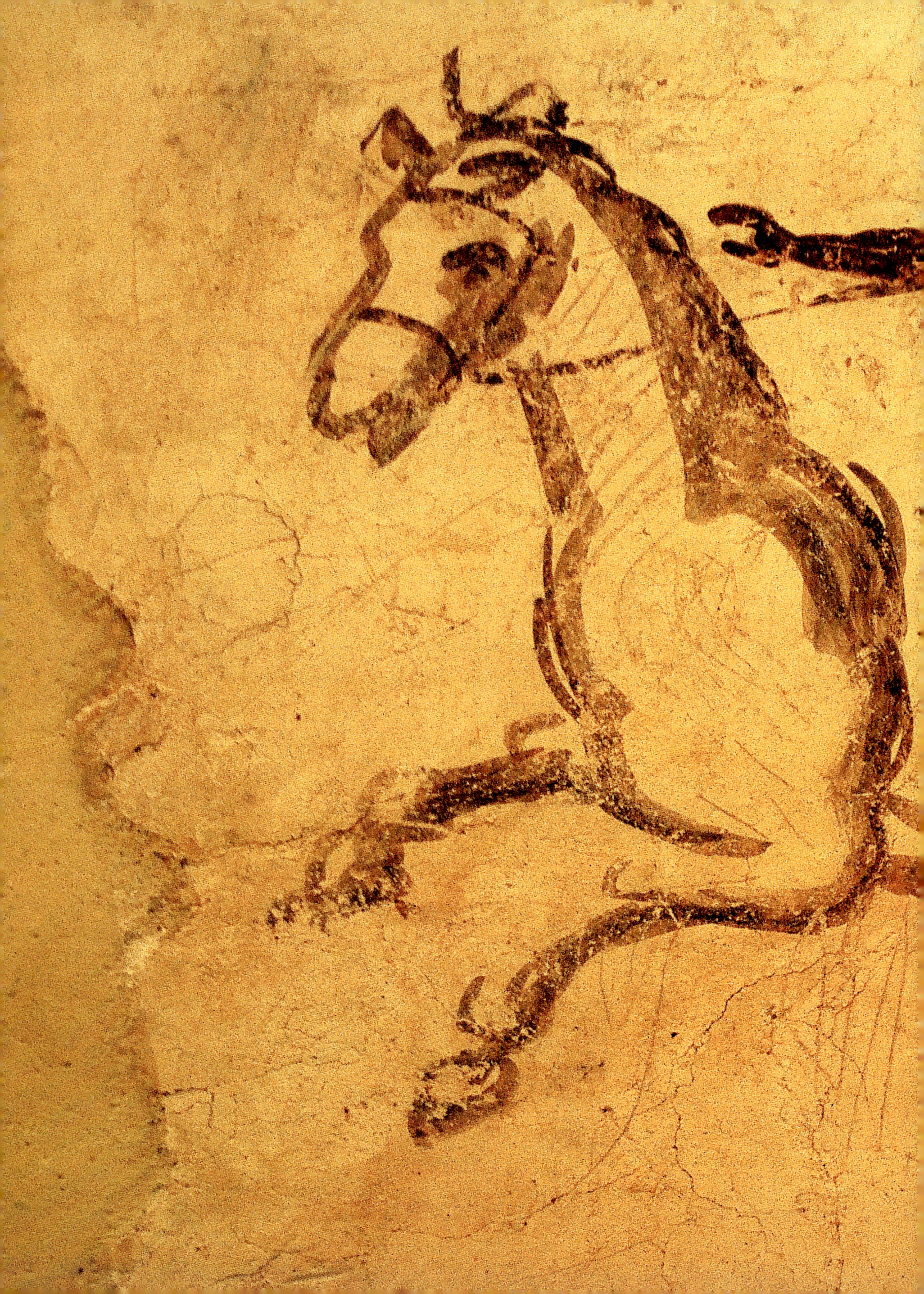

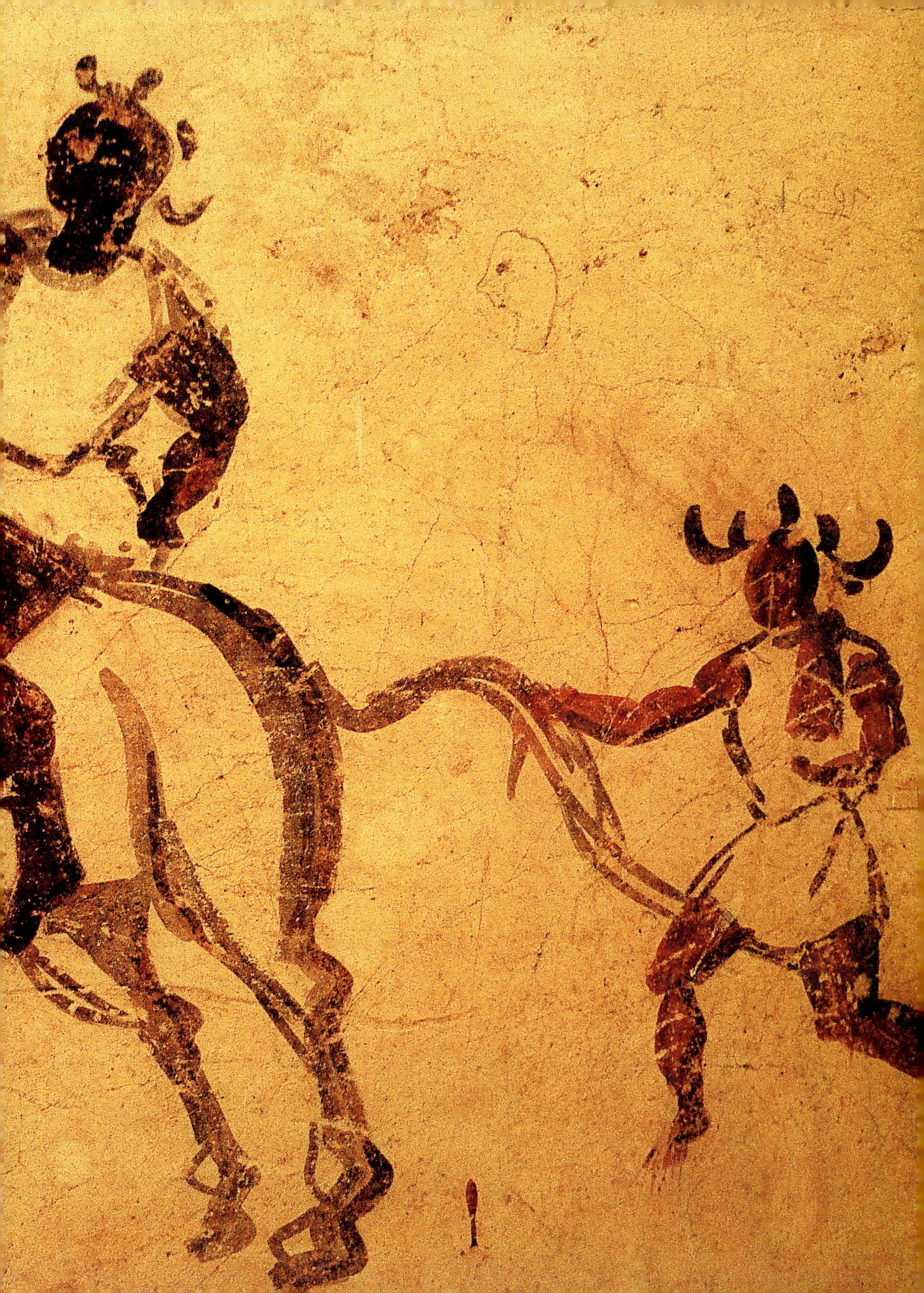

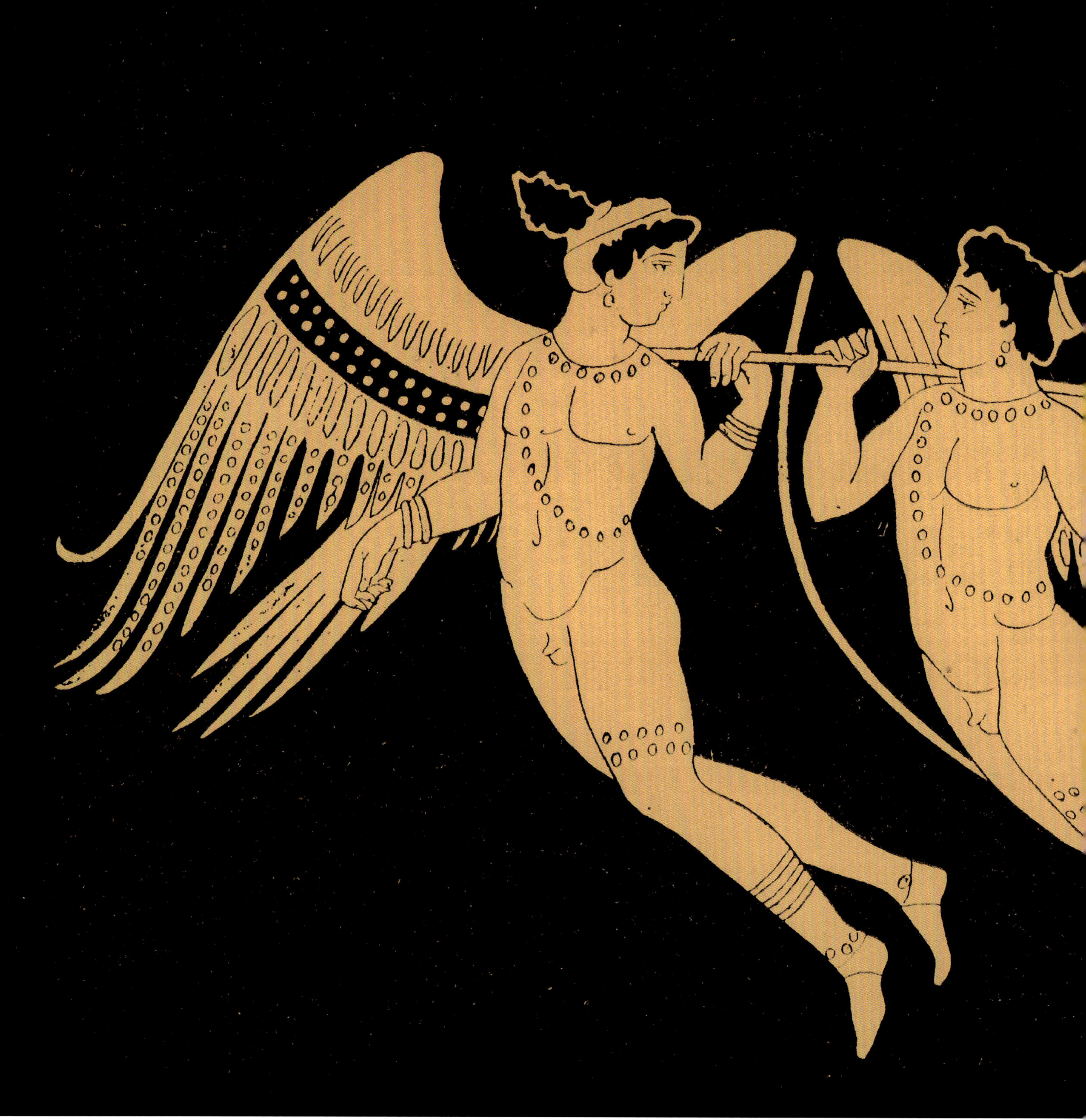

GODS FULL OF SPIRIT

The old legends depict the gods as turbulent and fiery; they loved to travel. They were as mobile as the Greeks themselves. The Hours, the gods of the seasons, opened and closed the doors of Olympus as the gods came and went. Some, like Iris or Hermes, took off in flight, but most traveled in a chariot. The chariots of the gods traveled at dizzying speeds. They were drawn by winged horses, with some exceptions: that of noble and luxury-loving Aphrodite was drawn by two Eros; that of Dionysus by two wild beasts, while the chariot of Poseidon was drawn by two monstrous animals that were half horse and half serpent.

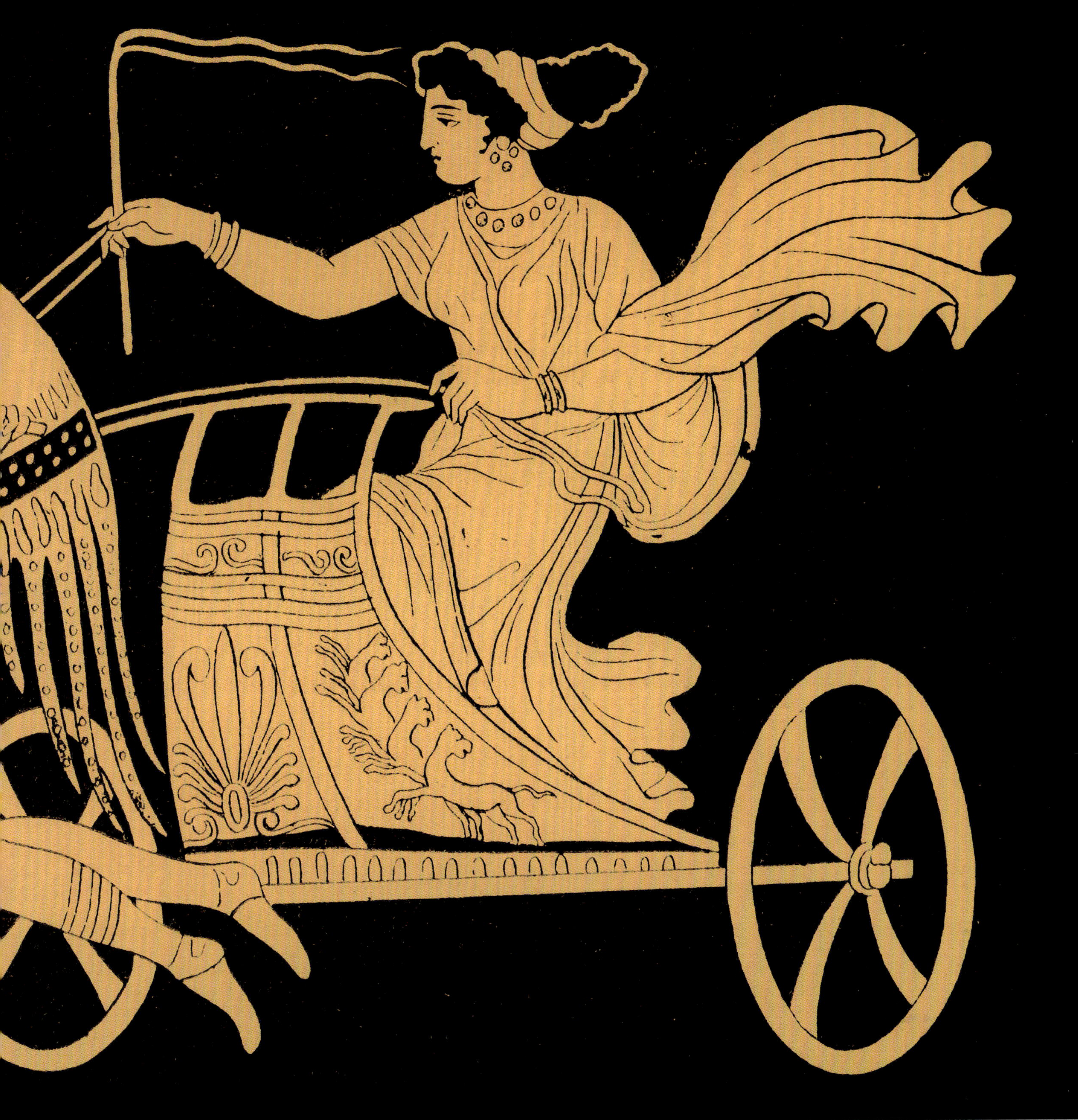

Poseidon who had a special relationship to horses gave the first chargers to the human race and immortal horses to his favorite heroes. He thus gave Pelops, the king of Lydia, winged horses that helped him win a race against Oenomaus and win the hand of Hippodamia. He also gave a winged chariot to Idas and, thanks to it, he carried off his beloved, Marpessa.

When Thetis and Peleus were married, Poseidon brought a magnificent wedding gift: two immortal horses. This team of horses was all the more famous as it would in time draw the chariot of their son Achilles, destined to be the most glorious of all the heroes of the Trojan war. The god also gave Rhesus magnificent horses which might have changed the course of the siege of Troy.

ARTEMIS OF THE EPHESIANS

Greeks spread out all over the Mediterranean basin. The earliest colonies were founded in the 11th century BC in Asia Minor. Ionian immigrants established the city of Ephesus and brought their gods to it. The wet pasturelands and marshy bays, suggested the life-giving richness of the earth. There is no doubt that at such a site the Ancients had venerated a Great Mother goddess. Fascinated by this landscape, with its water, its vegetation and its animals, the Ancients built a sacred enclosure. Here Greek Artemis met with the great Asian goddess and with many breasts and surrounded by stags and dogs, Artemis became a divinity of fertility and nature. The Greeks were so stubborn about rebuilding her temple on the unstable ground of the river mouth that they succeeded in building one of the seven wonders of the ancient world.

GREEK COINS

Coins first appeared in the Greek colonies of Asia Minor in the 7th century BC. They spread to the cities of continental Greece in the 6th century BC. Silver and bronze coins, the drachma and the obole, encouraged the development of the local economy. Soon all these cities were striking coins and trade links developed between the colonies and right across the Mediterranean and Black Seas. For reasons of prestige the great empires like Lydia in the time of Croesus and Persia in the time of Darius struck gold coins. The coins were marked with the city's emblem which allowed them to be identified. The city's patron god, the founding hero or other distinctive marks, both animal and vegetable, could figure on them. Like Athens, Adramytium was represented by the goddess Athena. She is recognizable from her helmet and her shield held across her breast. On the other side she is standing up, holding a statue of victory in her right hand and her shield in her left. She offered protection to the city, but was also used as a display of confidence to those outside. The coins of the city of Myrina show the god Apollo, wearing his laurel wreath. Horses, goats, fabulous animals and serpents appear on the coins of Cyme, Antandros, Assos and Atarnea. FOLLOWING PAGES

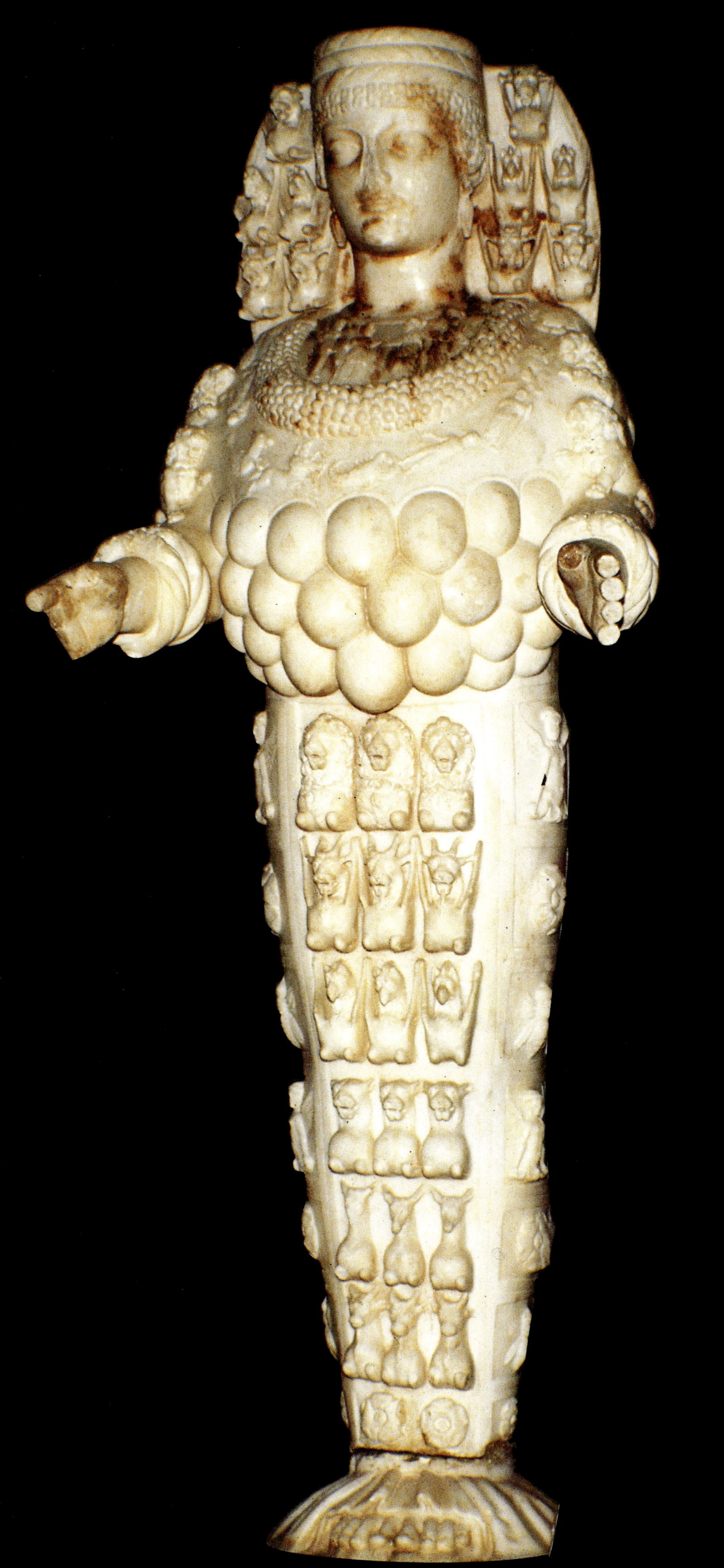

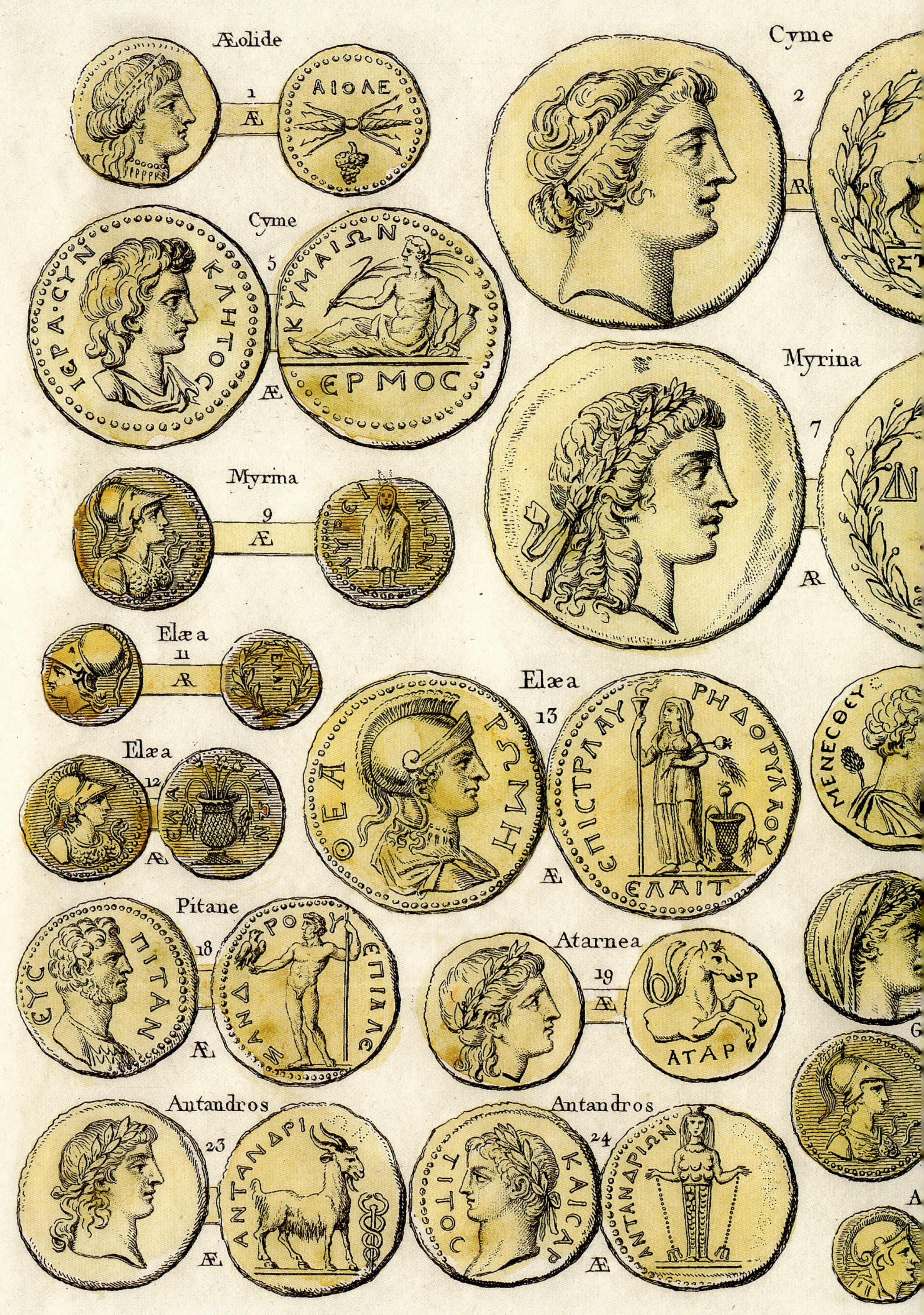
Æolide
1
Æ
ΑΙΟΛΕ
Cyme
2
Æ
Cyme
5
ΙΕΡΑ·CΥΝ
ΚΛΗΤΟC
ΚΥΜΑΙΩΝ
ΕΡΜΟC
Æ
Myrina
7
Æ
Myrina
9
Æ
Elæa
11
Æ
Elæa
13
ΘΕΑ
ΡΩΜΗ
Æ
ΕΠΙCΤΡΛΑΥ
ΡΗΔΟΡΥΛΛΟΥ
ΕΛΑΙΤ
ΜΕΝΕCΘΕΥ
Elæa
12
Æ
Pitane
18
ΕΥC
ΠΙΤΑΝ
Æ
ΡΟΥ
ΕΠΙΔΛΕ
Atarnea
19
Æ
Ρ
ΑΤΑΡ
Antandros
23
ΑΝΤΑΝΔΡΙ
Æ
Antandros
24
ΤΙΤΟC
ΚΑΙCΑΡ
ΑΝΤΑΝΔΡΙΩΝ
Æ

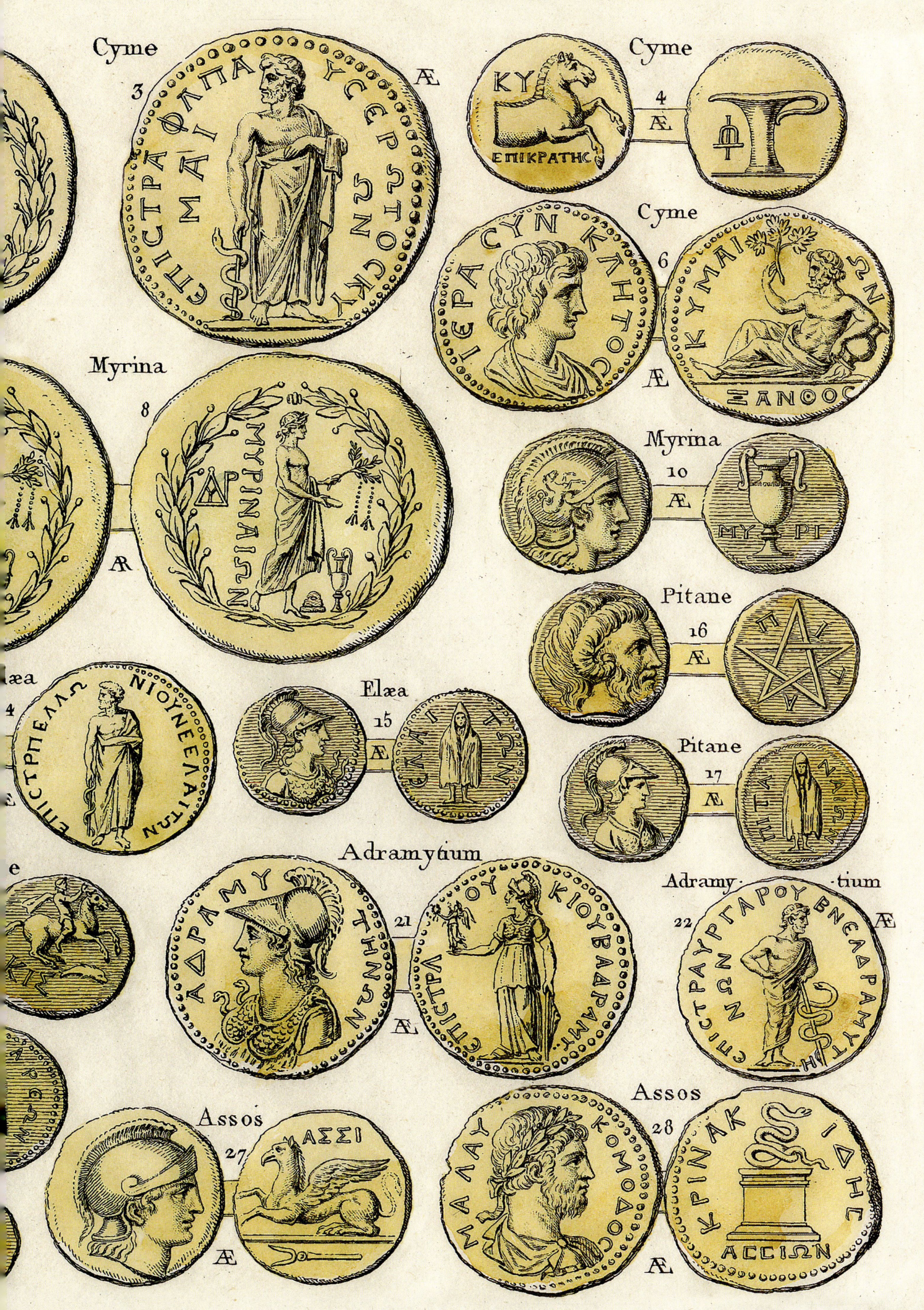
Cyme
3
Æ
Cyme
4
Æ
ΚΥ
ΕΠΙΚΡΑΤΗΣ
Cyme
6
Æ
Myrina
8
Æ
Myrina
10
Æ
ΜΥ ΡΙ
Pitane
16
Æ
Elæa
15
Æ
Pitane
17
Æ
Adramytium
21
Æ
Adramy- -tium
22
Æ
Assos
27
Æ
ΑΣΣΙ
Assos
28
Æ
ΑΣΣΙΩΝ

THE TOMB OF PHILIP II OF MACEDONIA

In the 4th century BC many Greeks classed the Macedonians together with the Persians as 'barbarian' and "the enemy". At about this time Isocrates was calling on all Greeks to come together. He held that being Greek was not a question of language, but a question of education and common values, a fact which was especially obvious during the Pan-Hellenic games. But though the Macedonians might be Greeks, they were still considered outsiders. Their king, Philip II, never tired of promoting his links with the classical Greek cities. He was a man profoundly marked by Hellenic culture and cultivated this image by taking part in the Olympic Games, winning the chariot race in 353 BC. Between 357 and 338 he became master of Greece while trying to preserve the city of Athens which he particularly admired. That city was influenced by Demosthenes, who was hostile to the Macedonian "barbarians", and allied itself with Thebes to oppose the oppressor. But Philip II won the battle of Chaeronea in 338 and became leader of the Pan-Hellenic league. In order to improve his standing with the Greeks he mounted a campaign against the Persians, the traditional common enemy. This great expedition would be successfully concluded after his death by his son, Alexander the Great, who spread Greek ideas far beyond the sphere of the Greek cities and into an immense empire. Following archaeological excavations, the Greeks are rediscovering their roots and the riches of the kingdom of Macedonia, particularly the palace of Vergina and its royal tombs

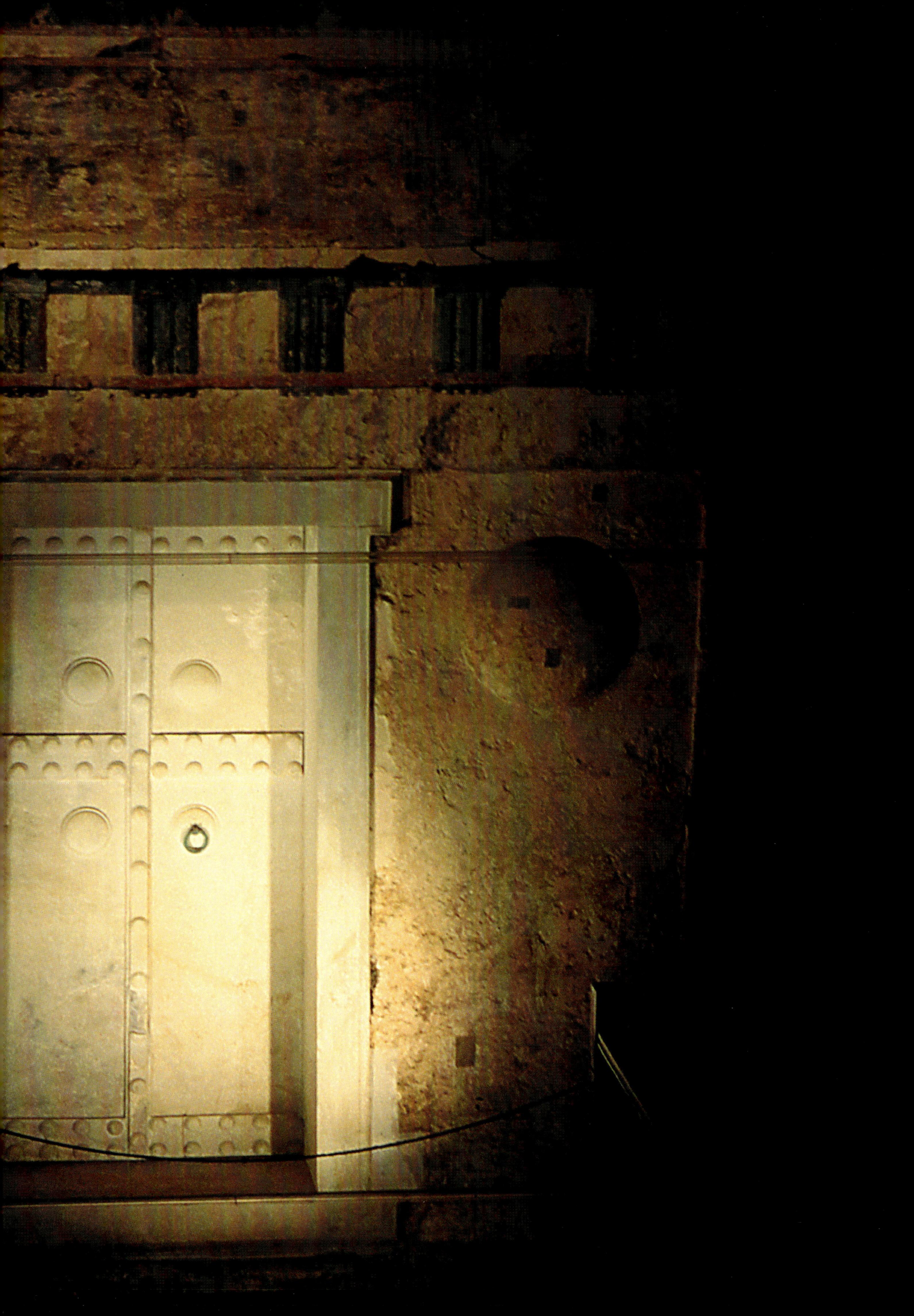

GAMES AND BANQUETS: MOLDING A GREEK IDENTITY

The identity and unity of the Greek people were certainly forged in the rage of battle, but also in the human warmth of dinner parties and sports stadiums. Well before they were conscious of themselves as Hellenes, the Ancients got their sense of identity from their families, their localities, their tribes or their cities. At every level the bonds of community were forged using the same tools: feasting and the sharing of food.

The advantages of eating together are well known! It builds friendships and reinforces cohesion. The practice was already well established amongst friends. The Greeks didn't like to be alone in the evening and issued and accepted invitations. So table arts developed as festive eating increased. They dined lying on a bed, supported by a cushion; food and drink were placed on a small table before each guest. The meal was followed by a symposium, or period of time devoted to drinking, discussion and amusements. Brain-teasers, riddles and other games were enjoyed; one particularly fashionable game involved throwing the dregs of one's drinking goblet at a target. It was believed that the winner would be lucky in love! The evening might also be enlivened by entertainment and performances given by musicians, dancers and acrobats. Women sometimes got together for feasting, but were kept away from their husbands' exuberant festivals. Only courtesans were invited to them!

The family was the cradle of memory, there it was kept alive and from there individuals received their sense of self; family ties also were strengthened by meetings and banquets. Funeral meals were held to commemorate the dead. If resources allowed, they were not restricted to the immediate family, but could involve the whole city. In times of want, being invited to taste the rich offerings of a funeral meal was such a special privilege, that both the family and the person commemorated were unlikely to be forgotten. In Athens there were phratries, kinship groups with both civil and religious duties, rather like an extended family. When they assembled, fathers solemnly presented their new-born children and celebrated the event by sacrificing to the group's gods. At adolescence, young men were ceremonially admitted to the phratry. Such rites of passage introduced new citizens to a reassuring environment and confirmed their sense of identity. It was, of course, another excuse for feasting...

Social cohesion was so important for a city facing persistent threat that offering and receiving hospitality was a political act. In Athens the citizens were divided into ten constituencies or tribes. It was as members of these units that all citizens were called upon to participate in all the great civic events: one ate with one's tribe during public feasts, one voted with one's tribe at elections, one also fought with it in battle. The rich individuals of each tribe were designated by lot to provide the food for the feast. In some places civic duty demanded attendance at the common meal every day! In Sparta, woe betide the poor man who could not make his contribution, he lost his citizenship rights! In Crete the poor were protected from exclusion and continued to partake of the daily banquet. The friendships established at these banquets ensured future support and protection, in battle as well as in politics. Young men listened as their elders discussed the burning questions of the day and were thus trained in the exercise of their civic duties.

At great religious ceremonies the whole city turned out before sitting down to dinner. Celebrating the gods in public assembled the population together to demonstrate its unity, this time in an act of faith. So during the Panathenaean Games, the whole community marched in serried ranks, led by priests and civic dignitaries; the procession route wended its way through the city and thus marked out its boundaries. After the procession, sacrifice was offered to Athena on the Acropolis. Then the citizens ate the meat of the sacrificial victims: the high point was definitely the final banquet...

If these festivals strengthened civic harmony, others widened their audience and celebrated the brotherhood of all Greeks. The so-called Pan-Hellenic sanctuaries welcomed strangers and allowed them to participate in the religious rituals and the subsequent games; this was particularly the case at Olympia, Delphi, on the Isthmus of Corinth and at Nemea. Crowds flocked from every corner of Greece to honor the gods, Zeus, Apollo or Poseidon, and to admire the athletes' performances. Athletic, musical and theatrical competitions, all to the glory of the immortal gods, followed the sacrifices. Races, which drew a large audience, were held in the stadium. Competitors for the pentathlon had to undergo five trials: racing, wrestling, long jump, and throwing of both discus and javelin. According to the philosophers, the range of their talents made them the noblest and most accomplished of champions. Sword fights, wrestling, boxing and pankration, a mixture of wrestling and boxing, were all held in the gymnastic training area, while horse and chariot races were held at the racecourse. At the theatre, there were musical and dramatic competitions for artists.

During these competitions, athletes and spectators camped on the site, amidst a lively fairground atmosphere. Jugglers, mummers, poets and musicians added to the sparkle, sought to attract attention and to entertain the crown. This exhilarating and relaxed mood allowed people to meet and have fun. They ate together and competed honorably. Visitors got to know each other, friendships were forged, and people made contacts from one end of Greece to the other. Old grudges were forgotten, rivalries between small Hellenic communities were laid aside as a truce was declared for the duration of the games. Wars gave way to sporting competitions, where striving for perfection, honesty and virtue was highly valued. From the 7th century BC onwards the games invited all Greeks to look positively on their neighbors.

In 380 BC, during the 100th Olympiad, the Athenian orator Isocrates made a speech called a Panegyric. He praised the union of the Greeks and pleaded for the sort of peace promoted by the games. According to him this burgeoning sense of brotherhood was the best defense against invasion. By overcoming enmity and past grudges, the Greeks had already united against the Persian threat in the 5th century BC. Isocrates invited them to organize even more such occasions in order to promote understanding. What is more he dared dream of a coming together of Greeks and Barbarians. His speech was prophetic. By the Hellenic period, Barbarians steeped in Greek culture were no longer considered outsiders and could take part in the games. However, in times of trouble, these competitions remained the refuge of Hellenic culture. By the second half of the 4th century BC the Greeks were under Macedonian rule and their sense of community had been dealt a harsh blow. In 196 BC the Romans triumphed and, at the Isthmus Games, their general Titus Quinctius Flaminius declared Greece to be free. Such an occasion allowed him to communicate with the widest audience and he was extremely popular. The news was received with delight and enthusiasm.

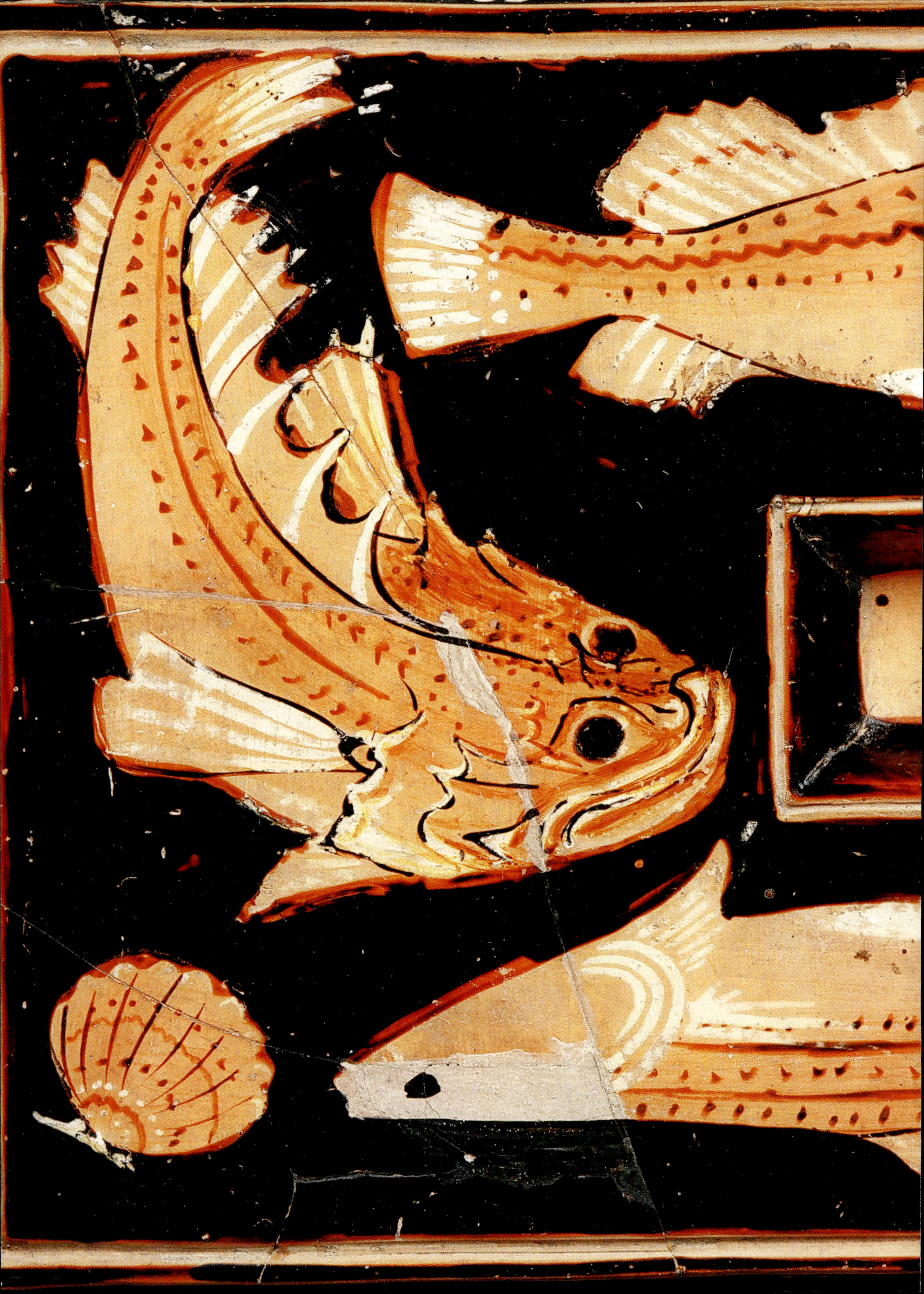

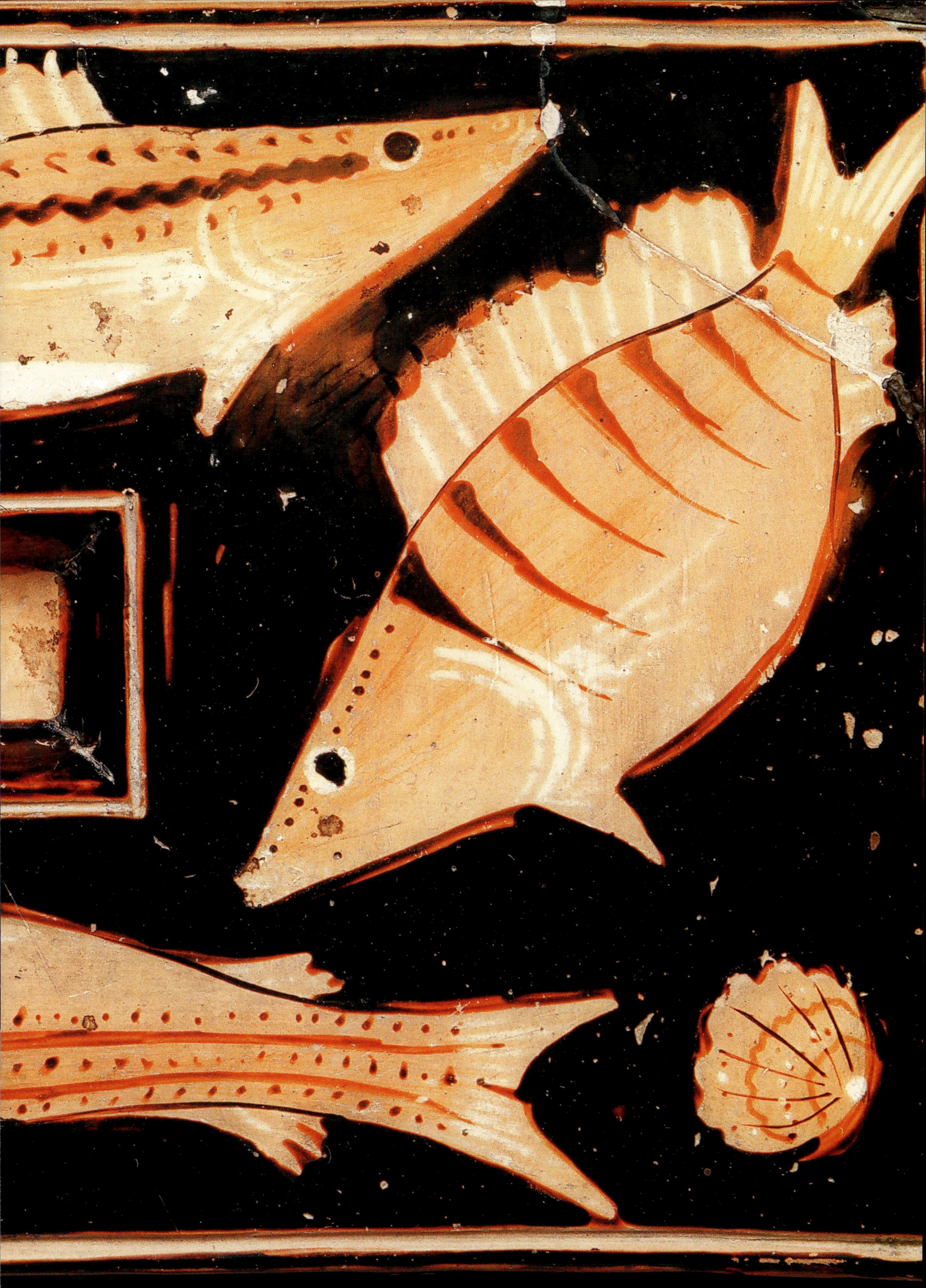

DECORATED HOUSEHOLD UTENSILS

This cooking dish decorated with red figures dates from the third quarter of the 4th century BC. It is ornamented with fish and shells and this remind us how the Greeks were particularly partial to seafood. In fact, whether at rich banquets or during the course of everyday meals, the Greeks ate more fish than meat. They imitated the Phoenicians in turning to the sea in order to exploit its resources. They had mastered the arts of sailing and fishing at a very early period of their history; they became formidable traders and ventured along all the known sea routes. Fish and shellfish were not just eaten on the coast. Fresh or salted, they were also sold inland and in the city markets, such as Athens. Market officials were appointed check the quality of goods on sale and to see that customers were not being sold short. PREVIOUS PAGES

A WOMAN AT HER STOVE

Normally cooking was the work of women and slaves. Professional cooks did not appear until the 4th century BC. We know from works dating from the 2nd and 3rd centuries AD that many books on cookery and gastronomy existed, unhappily none has survived. However Homer, Hesiod and Aristophanes, not to mention archaeology, give us information about Greek cooking. So this baked clay figure from Tanagra in Boeotia (which is dated to the last quarter of the 6th century BC), shows a woman seated at a huge pot. She is boiling a meal over an open fire and stirring it with a spoon. Is she cooking a mutton stew or cooking a dish of eels from the local lake? Eels were considered to be one of the delicacies of Boeotia! However, perhaps our cook is just preparing an ordinary dish, something eaten by humble folk: a mixture of water with barley meal or wheat, often flavored with thyme. Basic foods were made from cornmeal, either as a sort of porridge or cooked as a biscuit or a pancake: according to the Greeks, a people were not civilized unless they ate bread! Basic fare was accompanied by vegetables, usually dried: lentils, chickpeas, beans, but also olives and onions; there were fish, cheese and fruit (figs, grapes and nuts). Meat was rare, and was served at feasts and the banquets of the rich.

A BANQUET

It is going to be a long night! The guests are comfortably settled at the feast: men and courtesans are lying on couches draped with richly decorated covers, their elbows propped up on cushions. They are arranged in pairs on klinê, and converse as they help themselves to the food laid out before them. There are low tables by each couch with drinking cups, bread, cakes and fruit. The arrival of these delicacies signals that the symposium is about to start. This is the second stage of the feast, dedicated to drinking, philosophizing, playing, as well as concerts and entertainments involving dancing, mime and acrobatics. A libation is poured out in honor of Dionysus; this marks the beginning of the symposium and places it under favorable auspices. Dice are thrown to designate a master of ceremonies. His particular role is to decide on the number of cups of wine that each individual must drink. Those who fail are liable to a fine! Slaves are in constant attendance, serving wine mixed with water. The evening's drinking could well end in an orgy. FOLLOWING PAGES

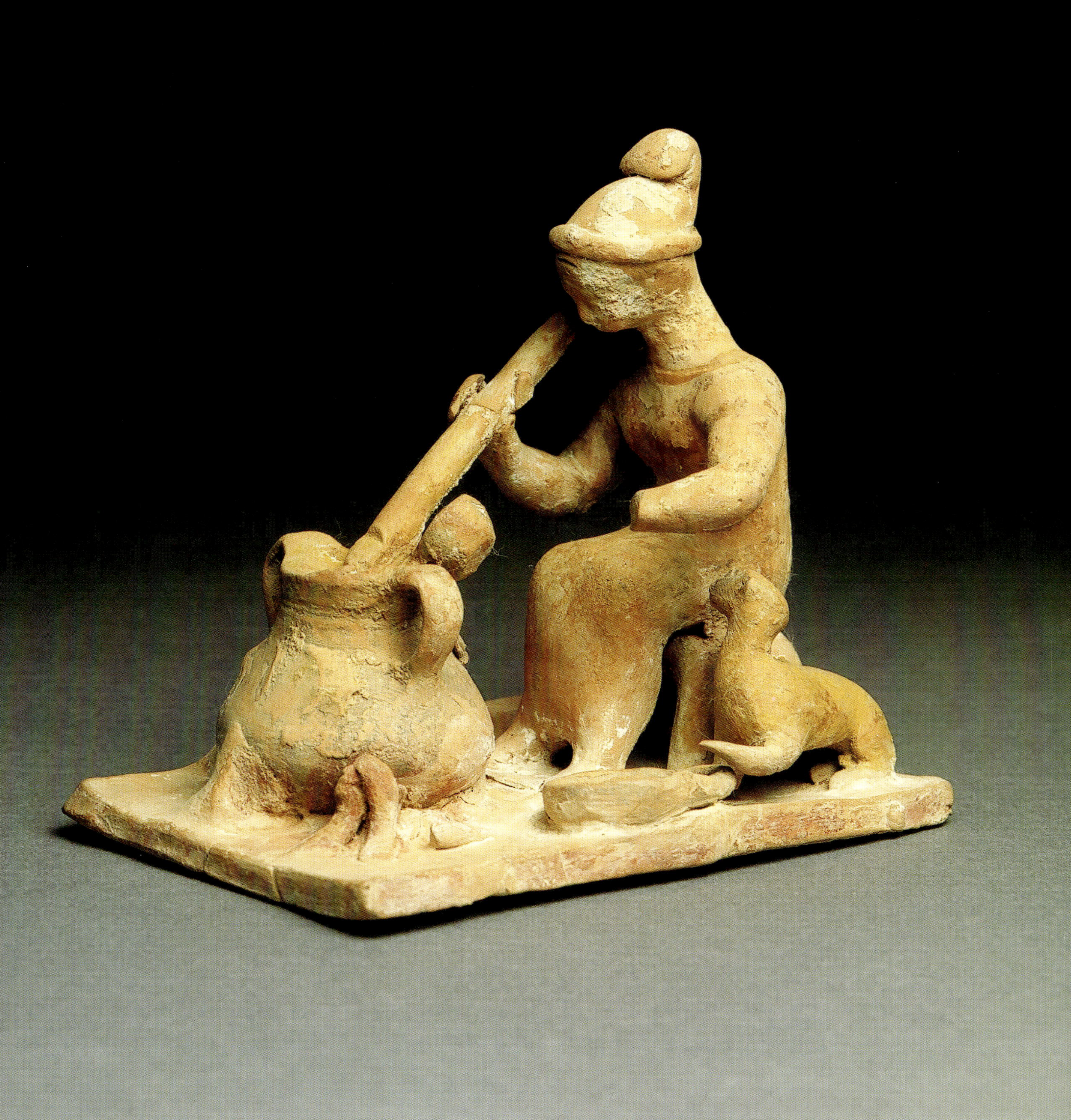

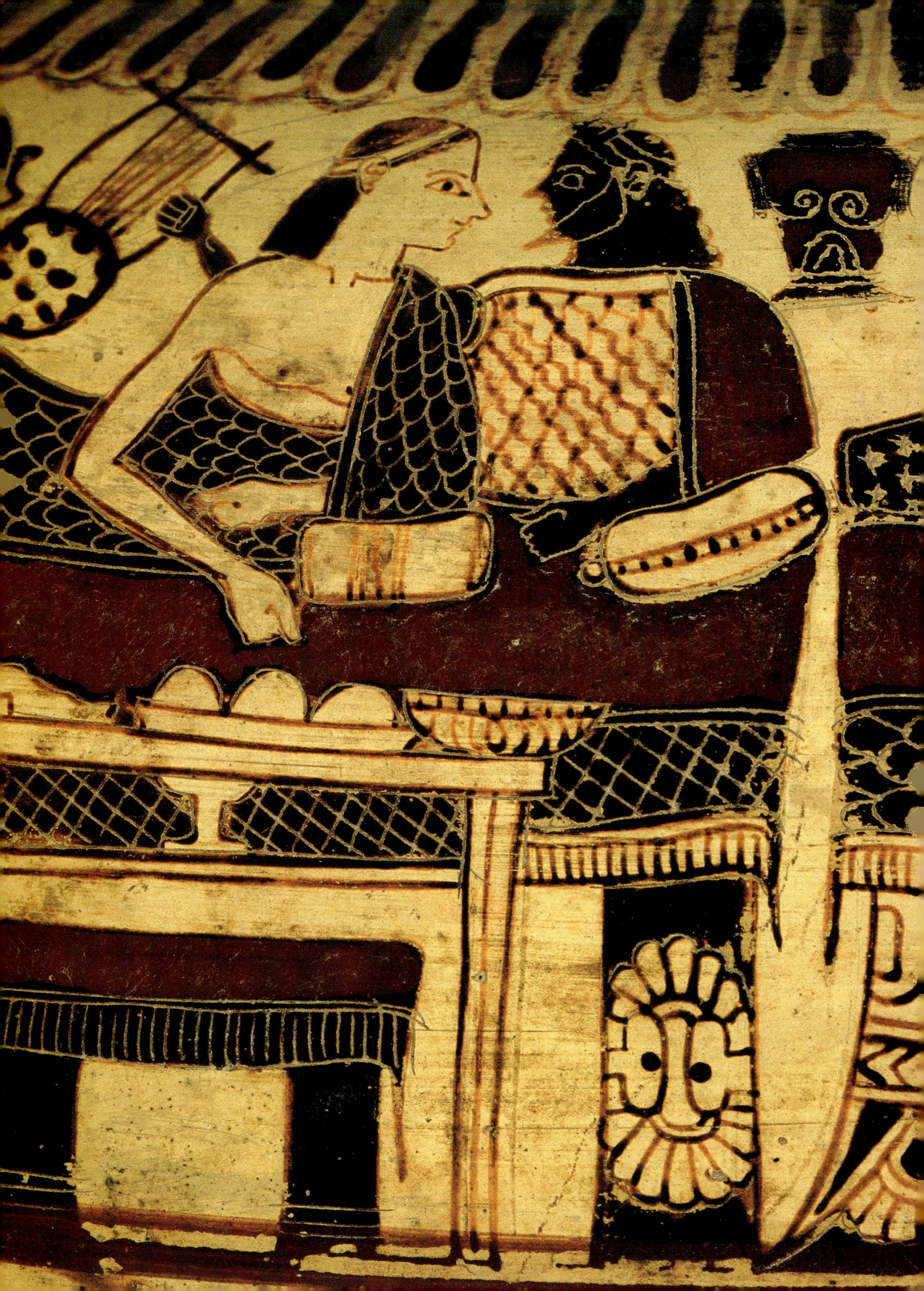

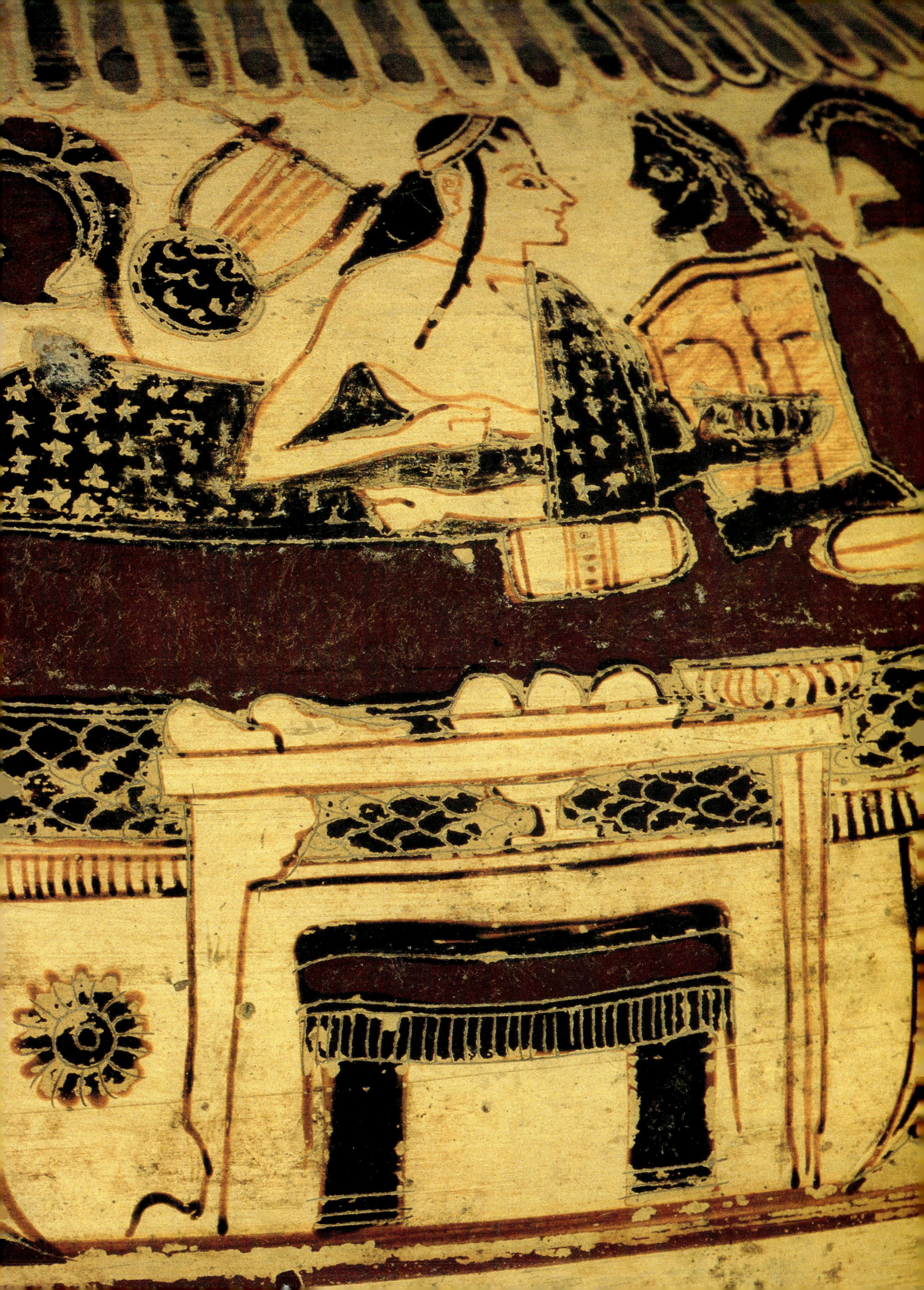

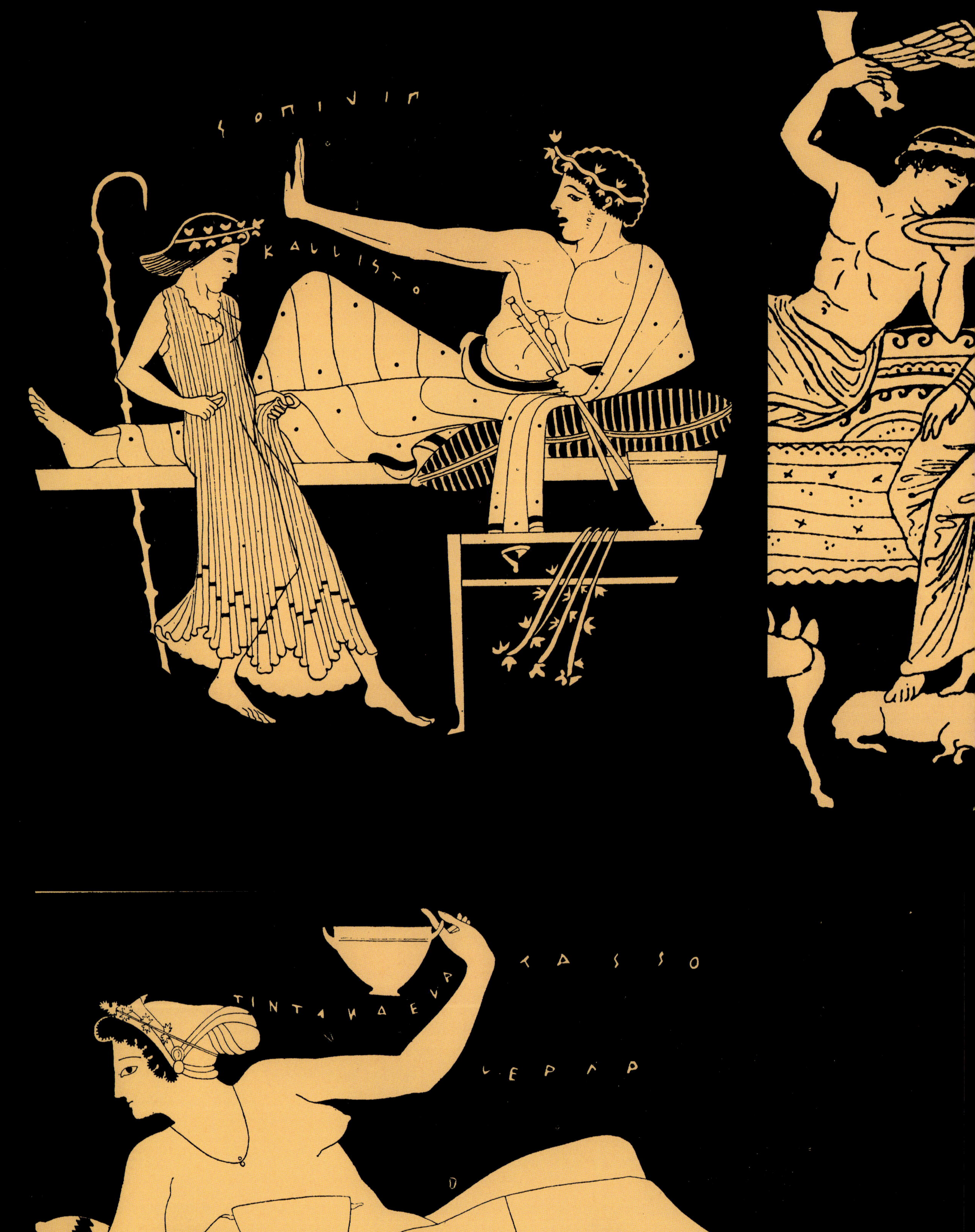
KALLISTO

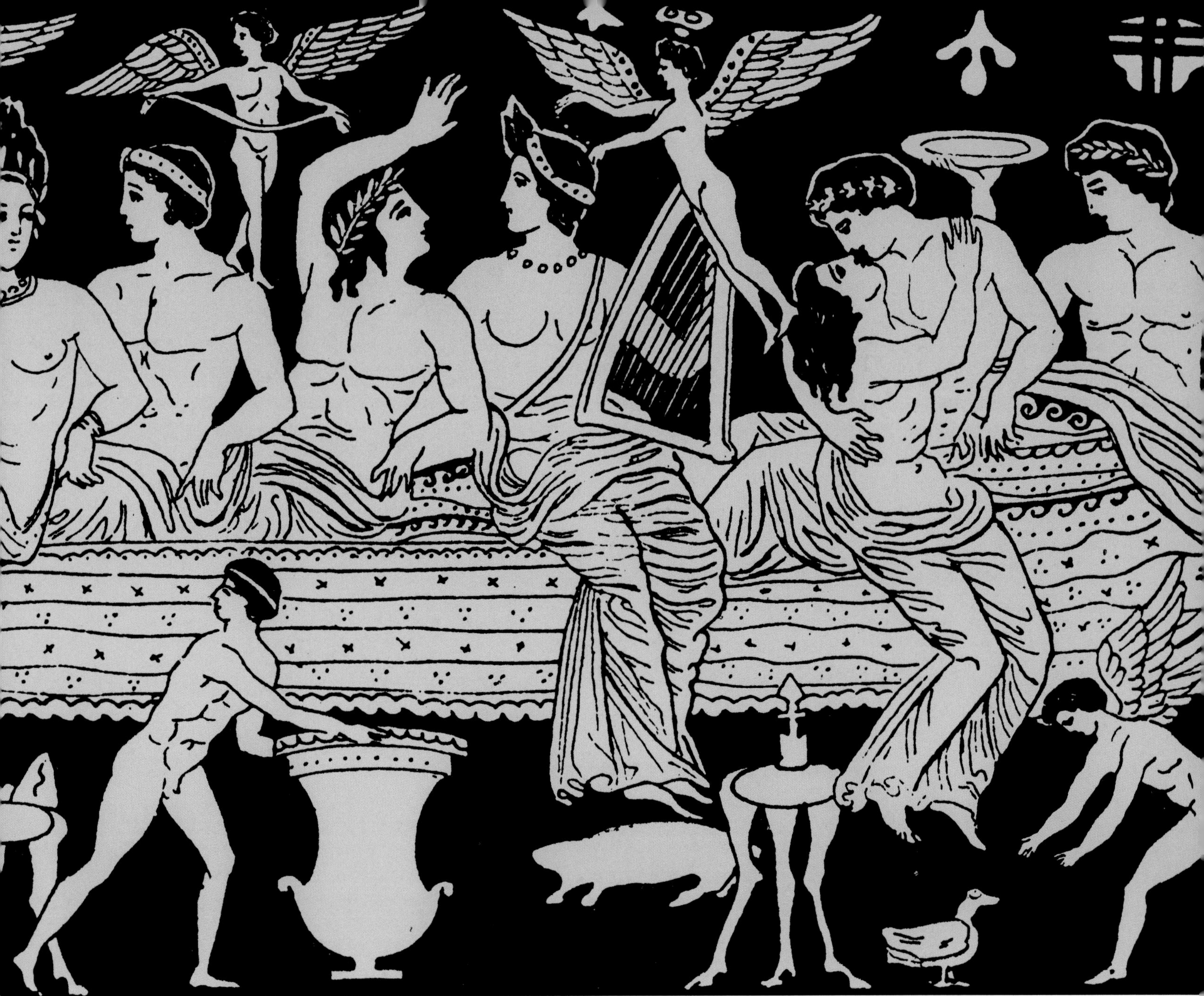

COURTESANS AND LOVERS

Banquets meant wine and other pleasures. Such parties were an occasion for games, private performances and discussions, often ending up in orgies. Hetairai or companion-prostitutes were the only women allowed at these all-male gatherings. The most famous were loved, respected, influential and rich. They had a brilliant social life and became the recognized companions of prominent citizens. So Aspasia of Miletus lived with Pericles, Thaïs with Alexander the Great and Theodotea with Alcibiades. Sexual relations between men were common at banquets; love affairs were frequent, older male lovers helped educated their younger protégés and their relationships were openly acknowledged...

THE KOTTABA PLAYER

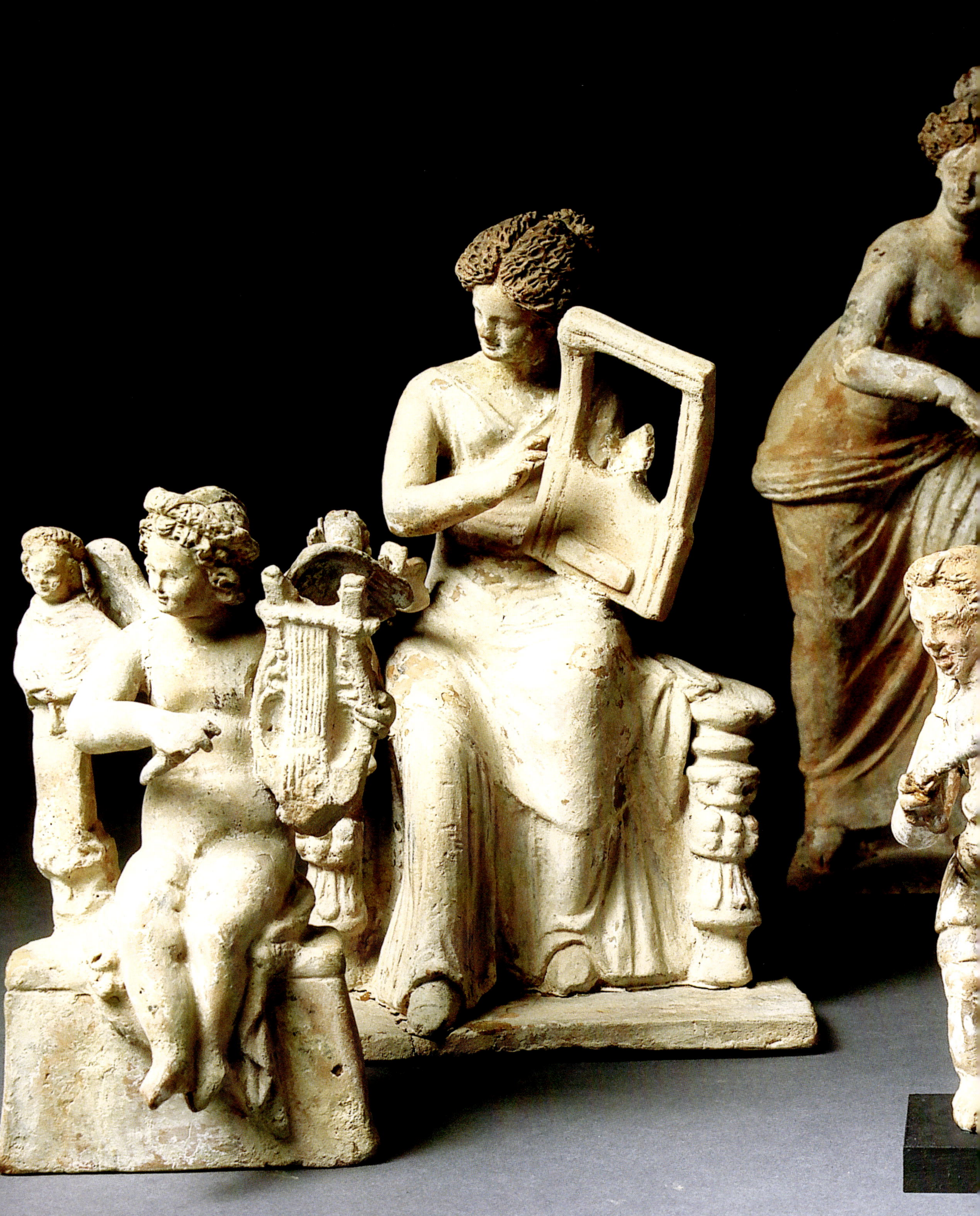

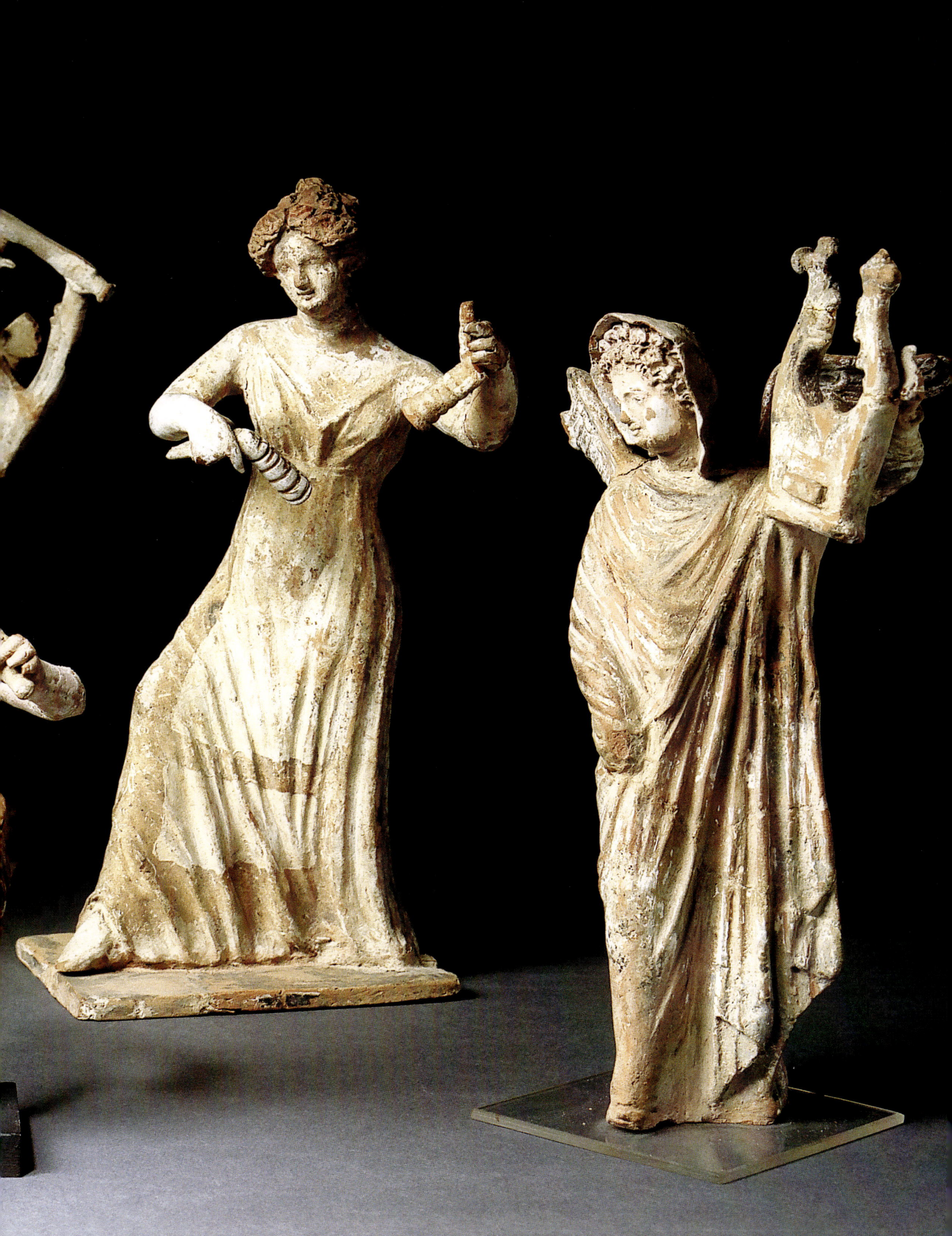

MUSIC

The city of Tanagra in Boeotia was famous for producing statuettes in baked clay: expressive figures of beautiful young women.

These figurines are infused with a harmonious and joyful energy. The musicians and the dwarf are dancing as they play their instruments, a lyre and a rattler. The artists who entertained the guests at banquets were often hetairai. PREVIOUS PAGES

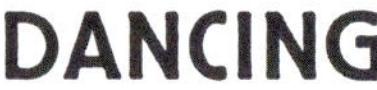

DANCING

Greek philosophers praised dancing as an element in the education of young men. It promoted physical energy amongst the warriors of the future. They also danced at ceremonies in honor of the gods and at theatrical productions.

According to Plato, such dances should not include the excessive and vulgar swaying of the buttocks which were common in comic, satiric and Bacchic dances.

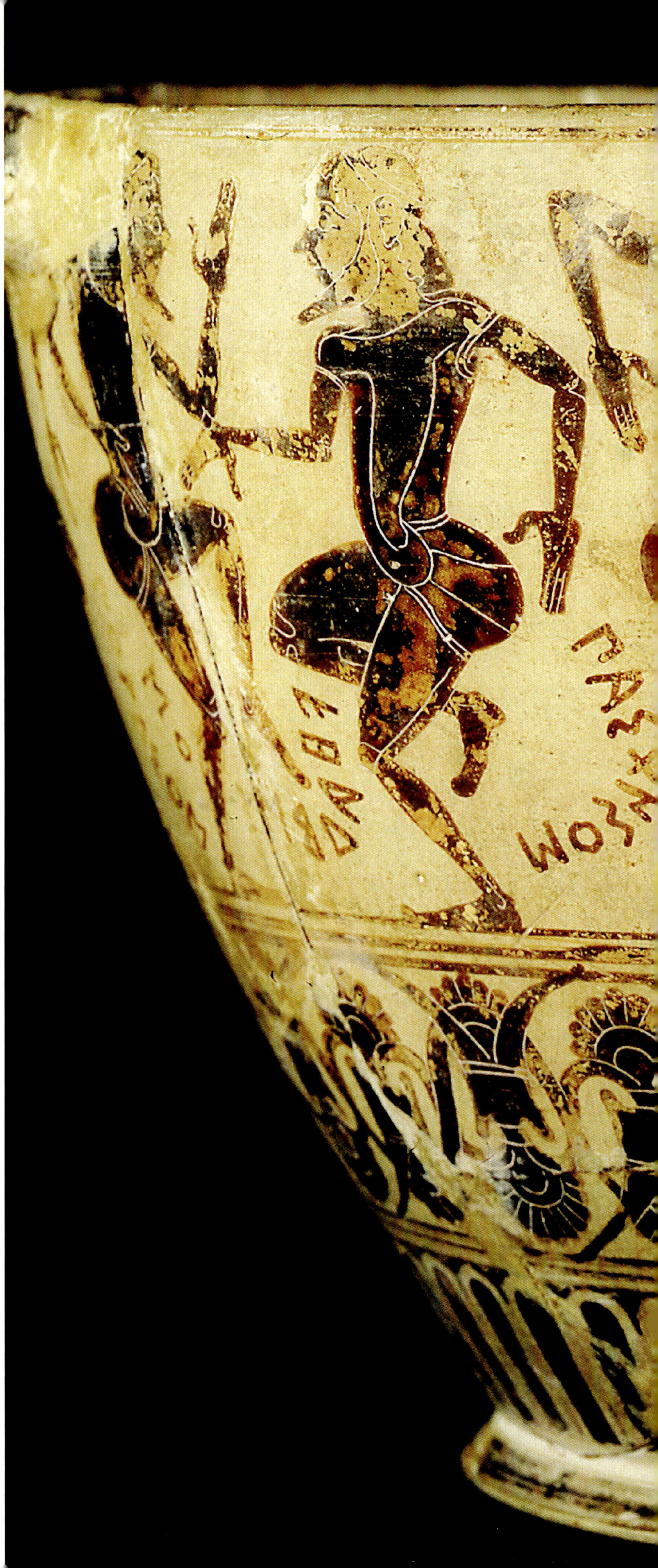

DIONYSIAC CHORUSES

FOLLOWING PAGES

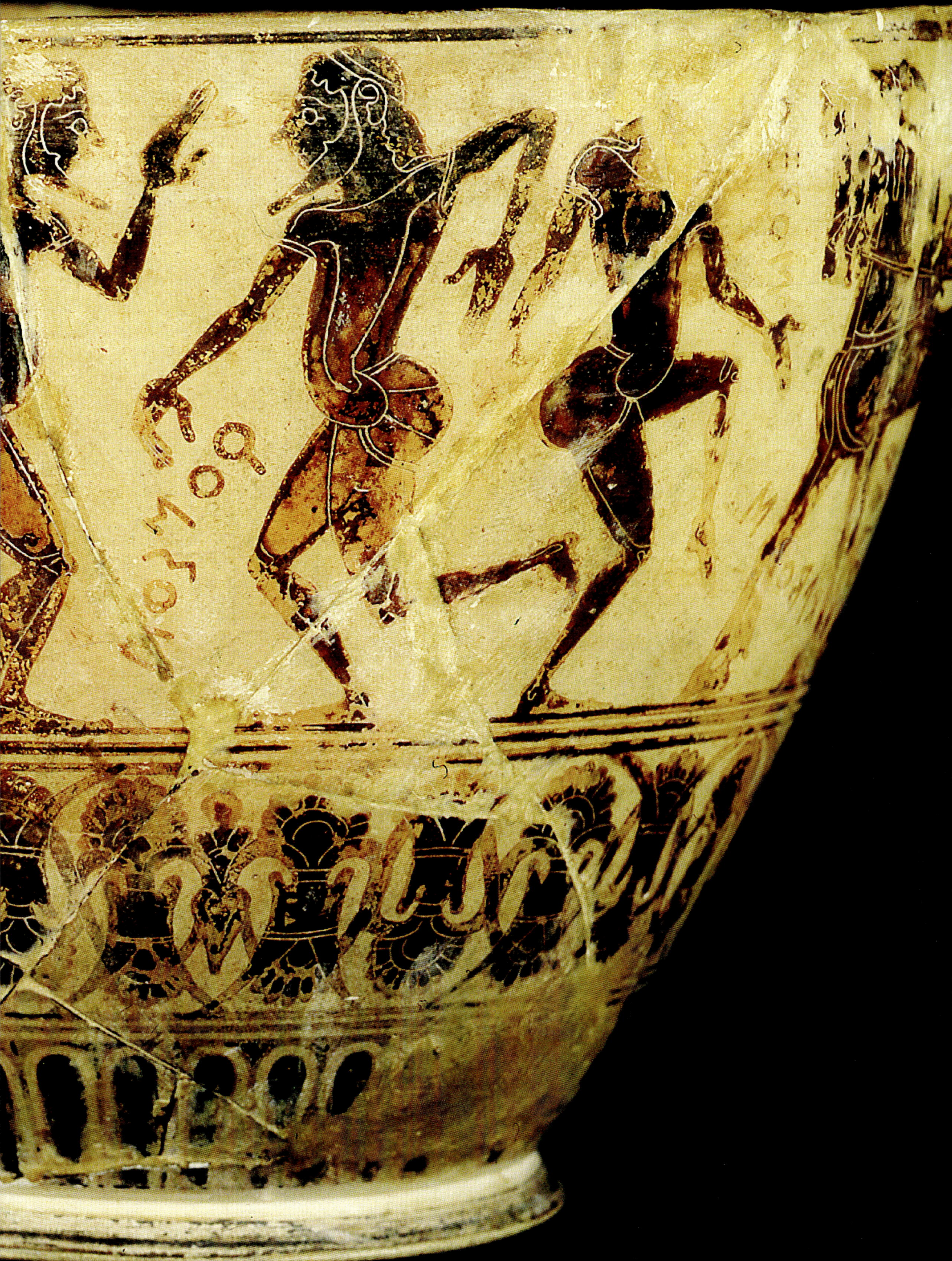

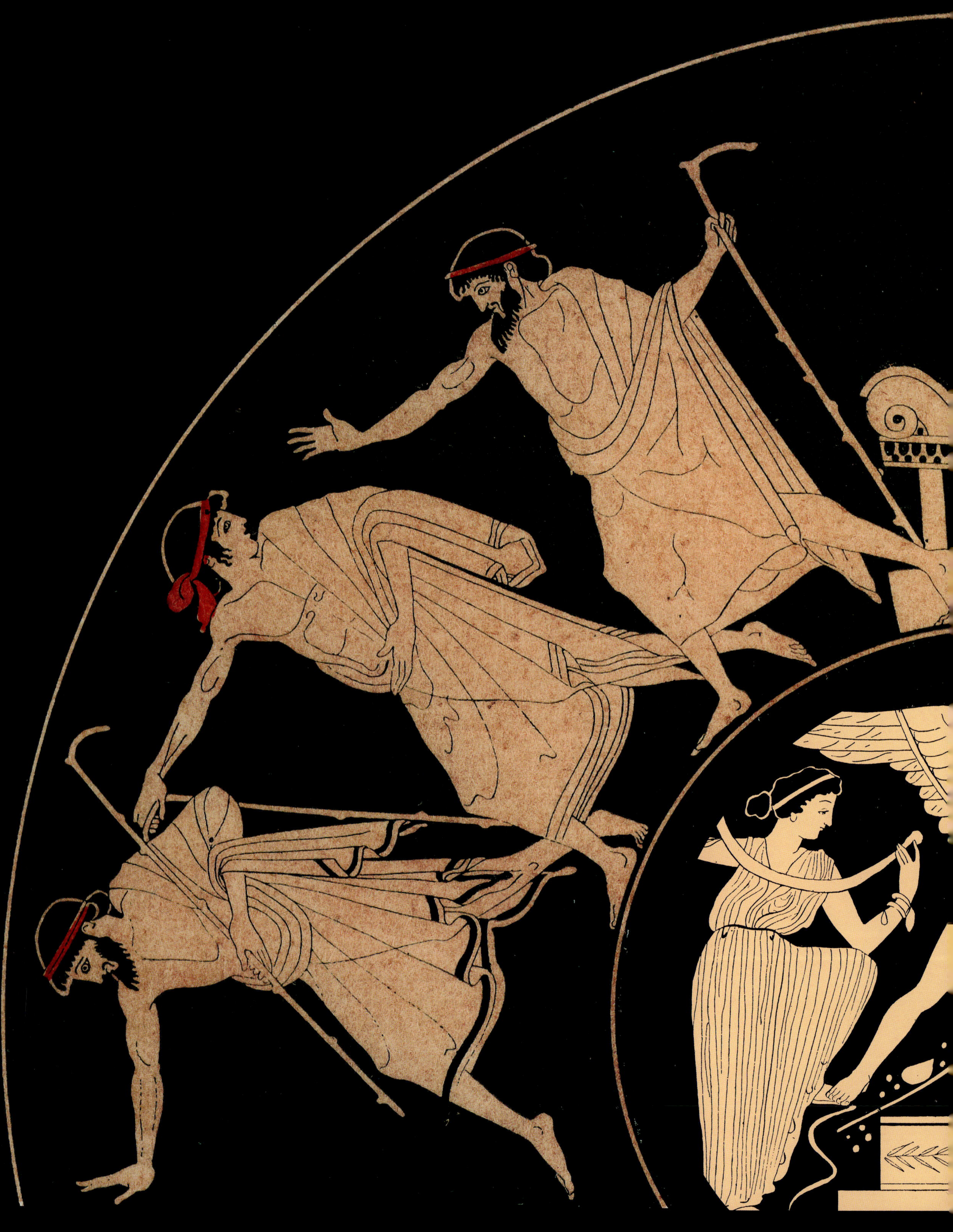

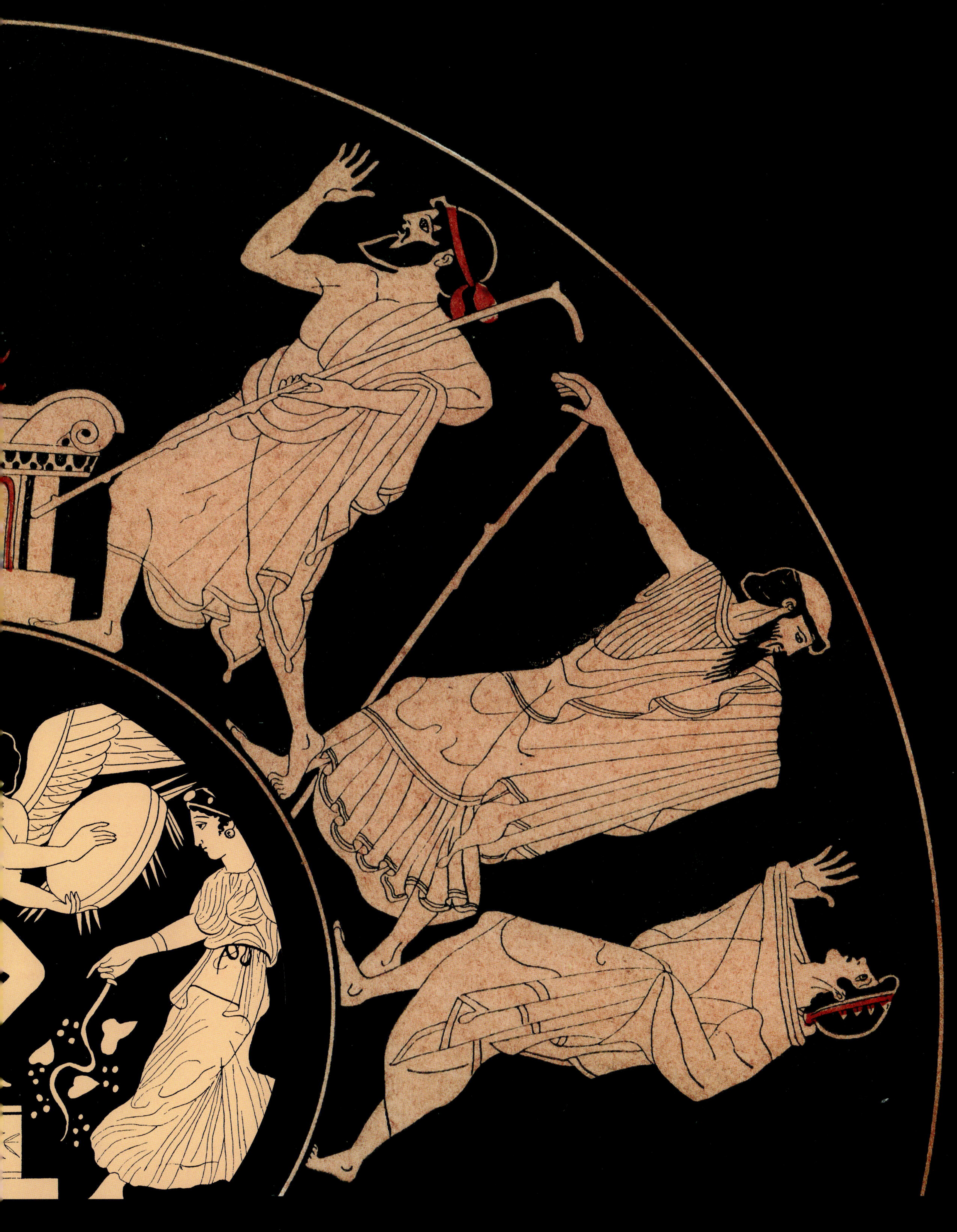

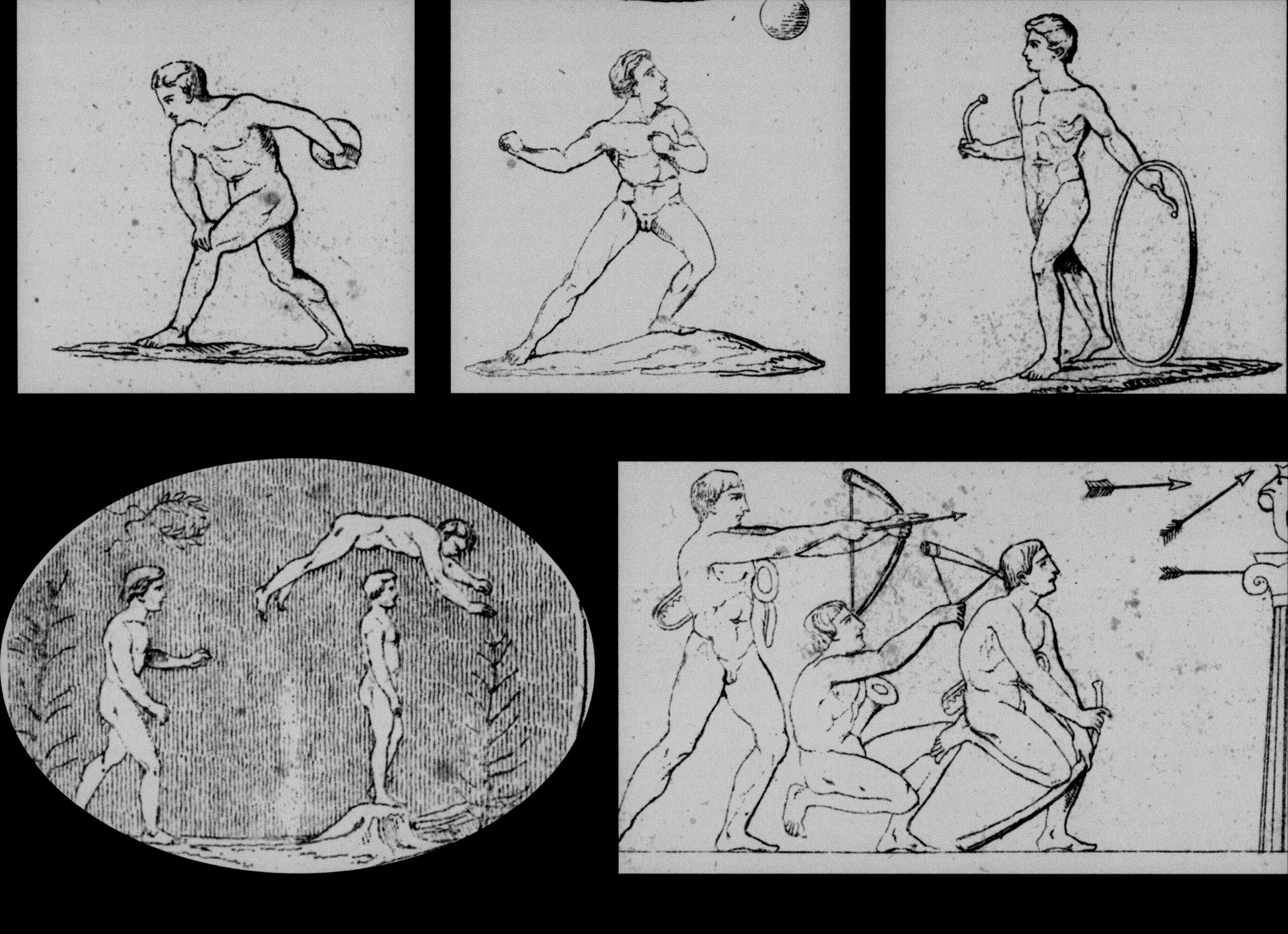

GAMES

Sport occupied an important place in Greek culture. Young people engaged in physical exercise, training every day in the gymnasiums, stadiums and palestras (wrestling courts) for the games organized by the various cities and Pan-Hellenic sanctuaries. The philosophers held that sport encouraged noble and pure values and guided enquirers towards the Beautiful. The athletes' bodies (they competed naked), were admired by all and dignified by artists, who liked to copy athletes engaged in the various sports and model the perfectly muscled body. They admired both technique and beauty, and were particularly inspired by the body's pose, its tension at that very moment, as it threw the shot. It was the same quest when it came to racing: sprinting or long distance. Both were valued, contests being held at the racing track or stadium, which had a standard length, about two hundred yards. Depending on the category, runners did one, two, four or twelve lengths of the track. Boxing, wrestling and pankration, all sports involving fighting, were held at the palestra. Pankration had been invented by Amycus the legendary king of Bithynia. It was definitely the most savage: all blows were allowable. There was a great contest between Amycus and Pollux, one of the Dioscuri. The adversaries wrapped strips of leather studded with lead around their hands. Crafty and quick, Pollux dodged the heavy blows of the giant and struck him repeatedly with incisive right hooks to the face, gradually causing it to swell up and cut. After a prolonged fight, Pollux landed a formidable uppercut which shattered a bone in Amycus' temple and killed him outright.

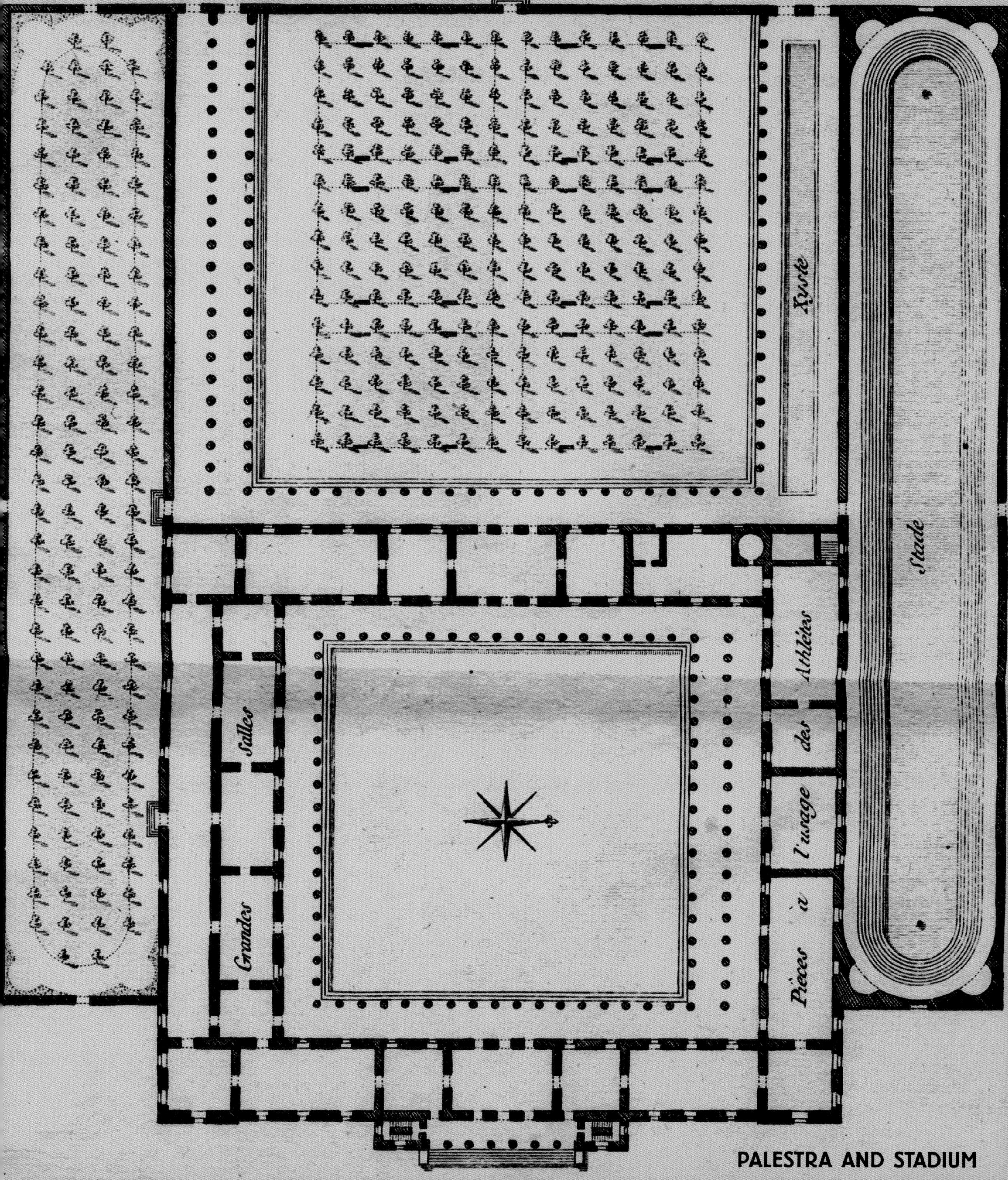

PALESTRA AND STADIUM

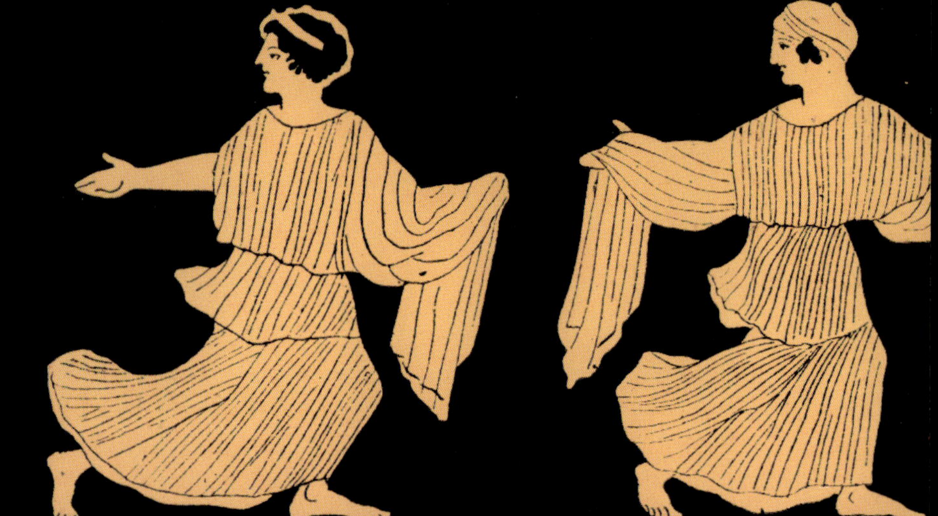

WOMEN'S RACE

PANKRATION

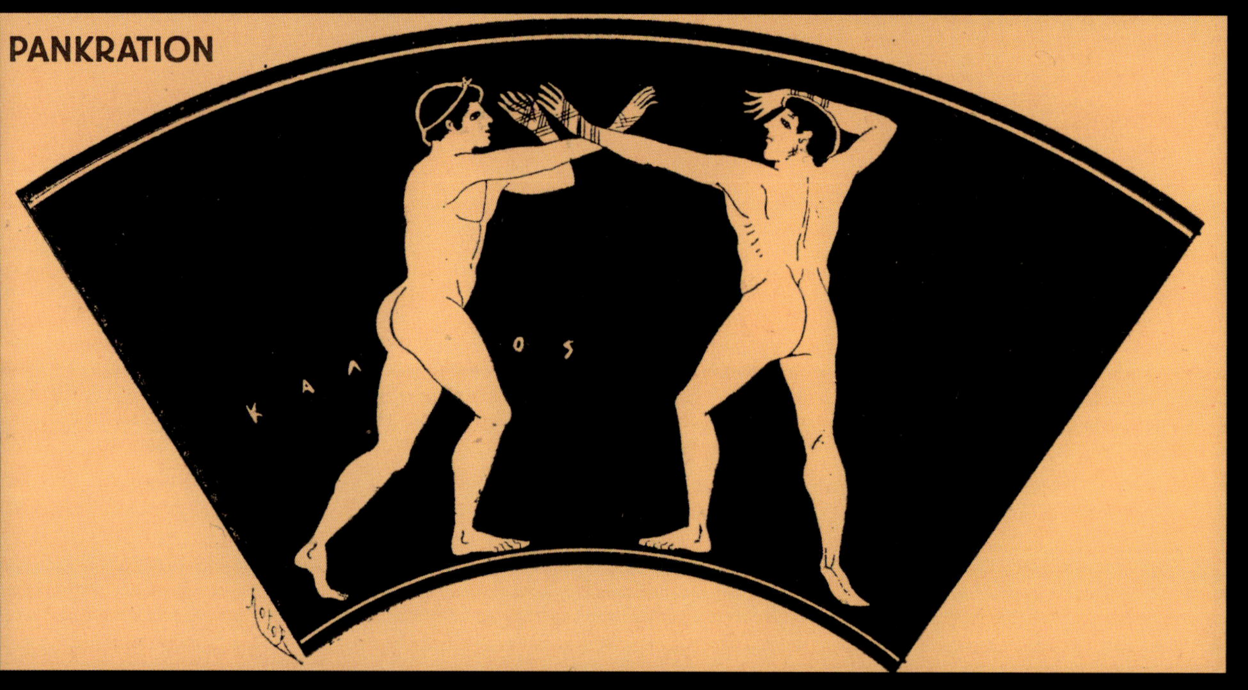

CHARIOT RACE

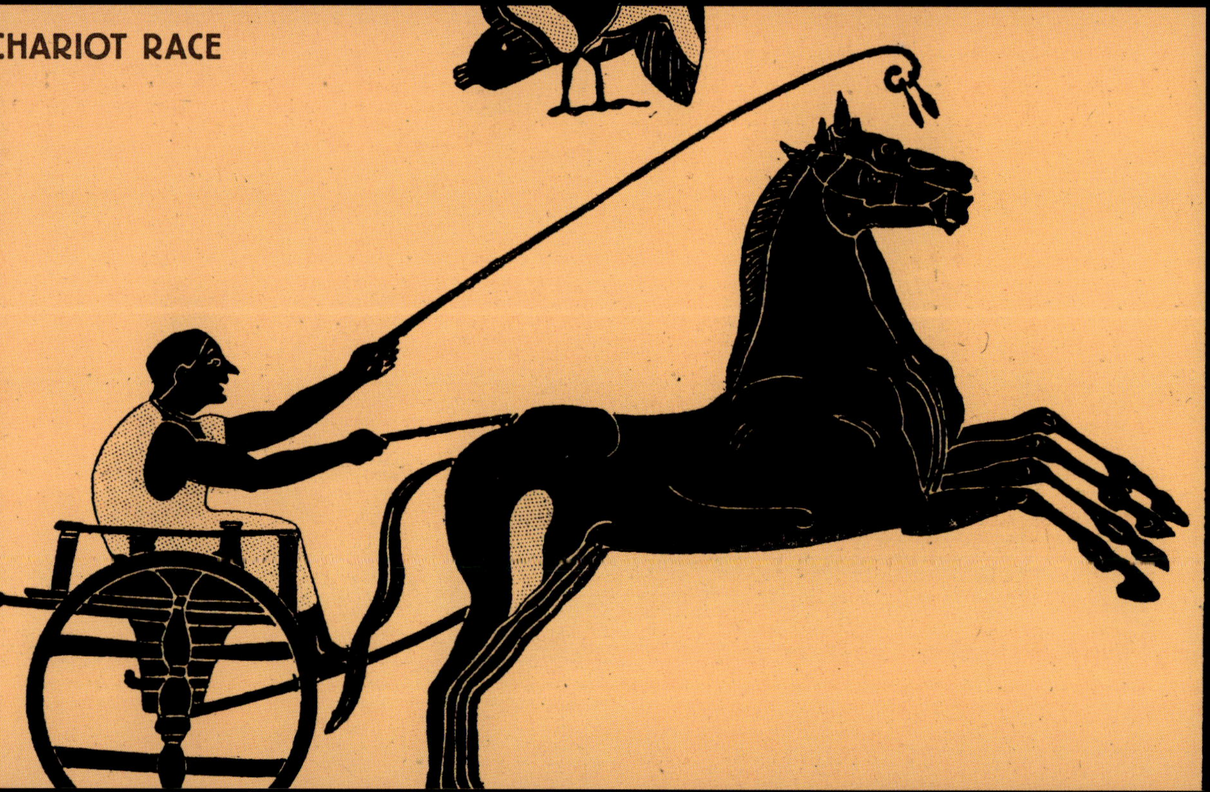

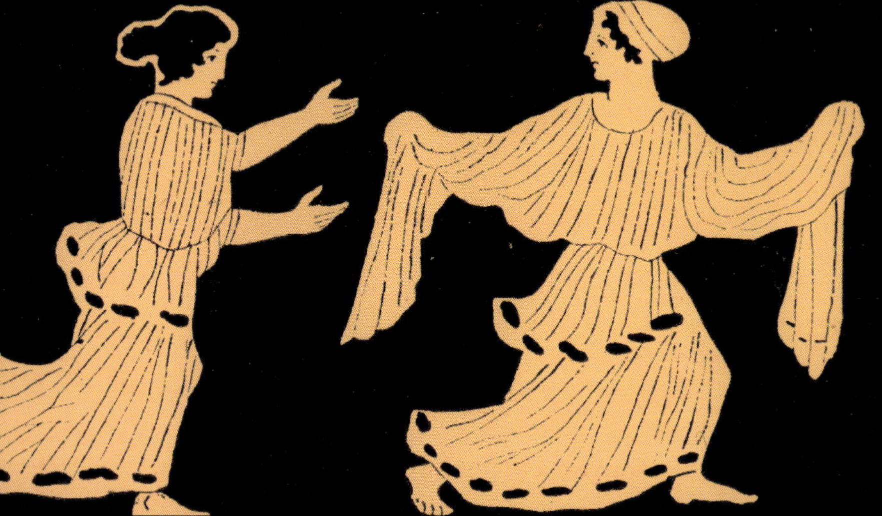

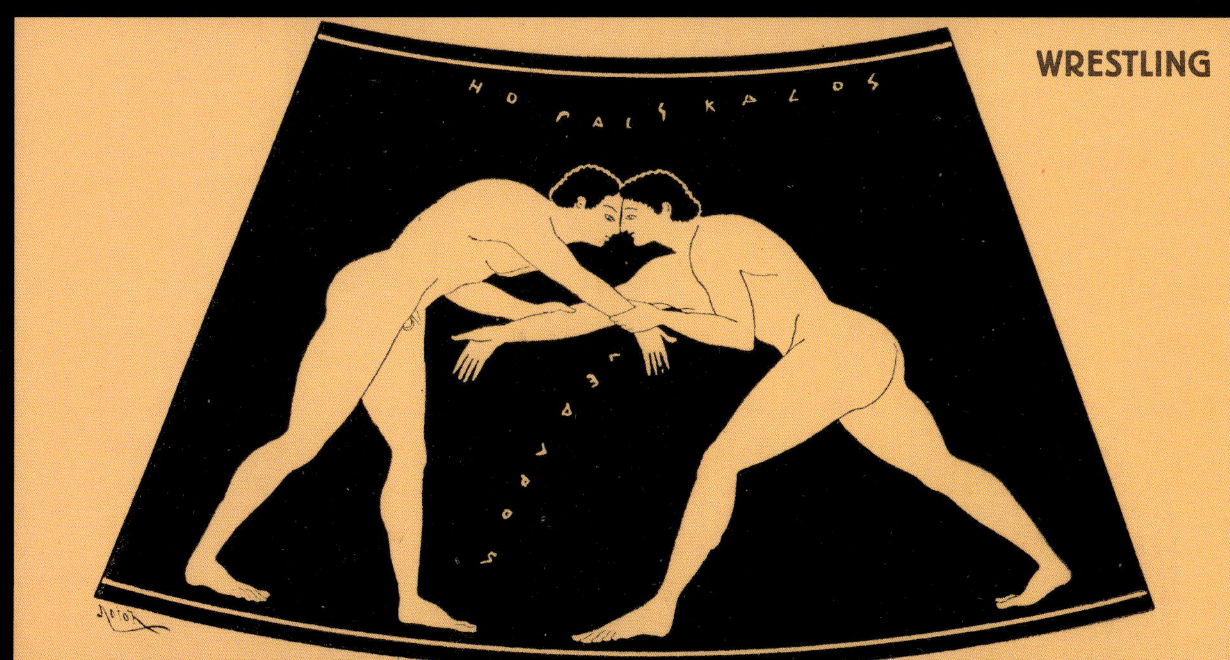

WRESTLING

MEN'S RACE

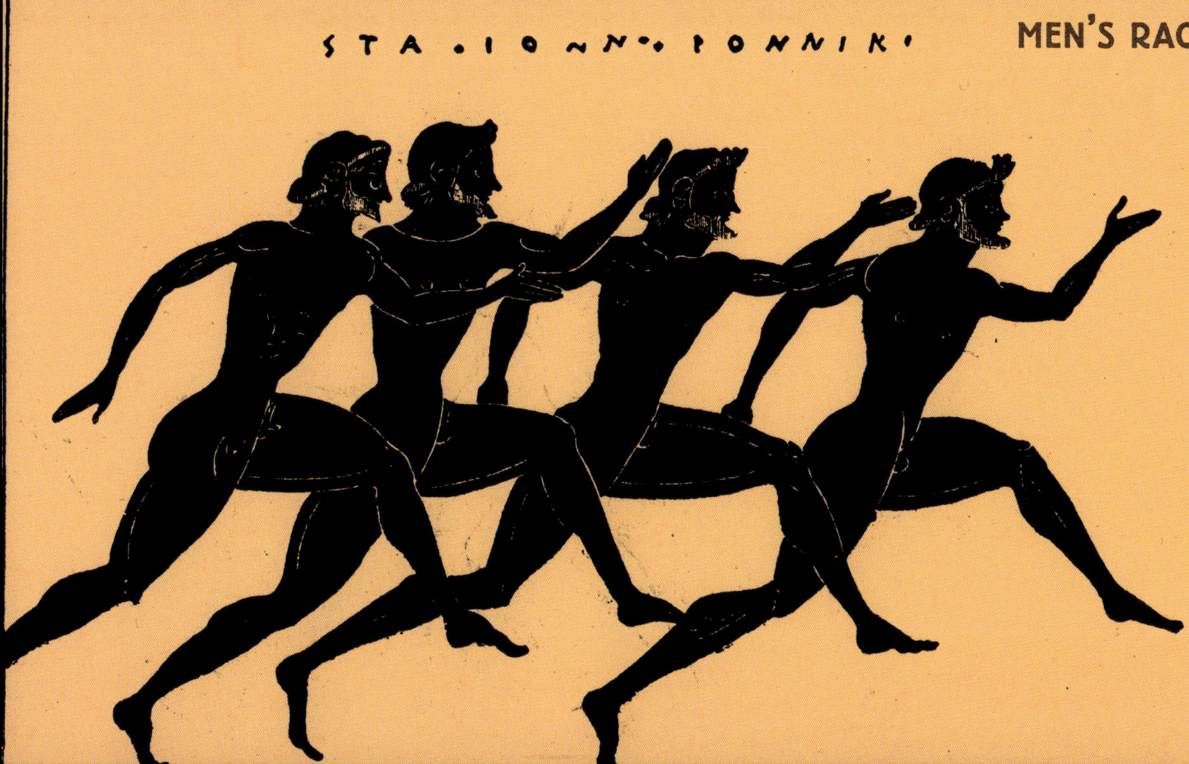

CHRISTIANITY IN GREECE

Christianity traveled speedily to Greece which quickly adopted the new religion. It was brought here by the Apostle Paul in the 1st century. He went to Macedonia, visited Philippi and Salonika and then continued to Athens and Corinth. His visit inspired the first Christian communities in Europe. Patmos, on the other hand, traces the origins of Christianity back to St John the Evangelist who was also the author of the Book of Revelation. He is said to have preached there. Little by little Christianity replaced the worship of the old gods, but it developed in a context of Greek culture and civilization which adopted this new universal ideology and helped it to spread.

In the 4th century the Emperor Constantine legalized the new religion, putting an end to all persecution against Christians; this strengthened its influence all around the Mediterranean basin. Constantine's view was that the new faith would have cohesive social authority and halt the slow disintegration of the Roman Empire. However, because of threats from barbarian invaders along the western borders, Constantine, in 330 AD, removed the imperial capital from Rome to Byzantium, which was renamed Constantinople in his honor. From then on Greece would look towards the eastern city, for it was there that imperial power was exercised. When the barbarians finally overran the Western Roman Empire in 476, Greece remained firmly attached to those eastern lands which maintained the memory and heritage of ancient Rome, and so it became a province of the new Byzantine Empire.

Constantine's successors remained by and large favorable to Christianity. In 393 Theodosius even made it the state religion and simultaneously attacked the symbols of pagan Antiquity: he forbade the worship of the gods, destroyed numerous temples and abolished the Olympic Games. In 529 Justinian closed down the philosophical schools of Athens. These measures did not however force a separation between Christian and Hellenic thought. In fact the Byzantine Empire was built on a number of foundations in a subtle and erudite blend, which gave it prestige and stability. It took its administrative structure and law from Rome; it adopted the Christian faith without however discarding ancient pagan wisdom, since it was in that source that it sought the roots of its cultural, artistic and intellectual life. Europeans are right to think of the Byzantines as Greeks. However since the 7th century their supreme head was referred to, not as imperator, but as basileus, the old Hellenic royal title. What is more, Greek was adopted as the official language of the Byzantine Empire in 630. The language had previously been spoken in eastern lands since the conquests of Alexander the Great and was the obvious social glue binding the various peoples together.

Although Christians, churchmen and political leaders, indeed all members of the educated classes, were steeped in the values and culture of Ancient Greece, they were also deeply aware that Byzantium was the direct inheritor of that classical tradition. Far from abandoning the teachings of pagan philosophers, the Church fathers taught Rhetoric and Philosophy, and favored close links between Christianity and the old civilization. Thus the literary and scientific tradition was saved, copied, studied, commented on and developed by scholars; it thus influenced the artistic efforts of Byzantium and would in time be a foundation for the European

Renaissance. Greece possessed a long tradition of democracy and had long inculcated habits of abstract thought, it was thus ideally placed to provide tools for dialogue and theological questioning. In the collegial exercise of their responsibilities, synods and ecumenical councils of bishops sought to interpret the Scriptures, debate Christian truths in an open and philosophical manner and to stabilize doctrine. So it is not surprising that the Byzantine Empire saw the emergence of so many Christian heresies: Arianism, Nestorianism, Monophysitism or iconoclasm, all of which caused controversy, and disturbed religious and political life. Faced with so much dissention Christianity split; the Schism of 1054 brought about the separation of the Greek Orthodox and the Roman Catholic churches.

Greece experienced the full range of the Byzantine Empire's chaotic history. She enjoyed the golden age of the reign of Justinian (527-566) and then slipped from imperial control when invaded by nomadic Slavs at the end of the 6th century. They settled everywhere in Greece except Thessaloniki which held out against them. Byzantine control was re-established at the end of the 8th century, but more threats were to follow. Arabian pirates frequently attacked the coasts of the Aegean Sea. The great Macedonian dynasty restored peace in the 9th century; it lasted until the middle of the 11th. The Empire was now at its most powerful and shone in every domain. The frontiers were extended, trade was restored and cities became rich: Thessaloniki, for example, with its prestigious fair. Latin countries envied the wealth of the eastern Empire. Intellectual, artistic and monastic life all flourished. The Greek monks and philosophers, Cyril and Methodius invented the Cyrillic alphabet and brought Byzantine religion and culture to the Slavs who converted to Christianity. By the beginning of the 12th century the Byzantine Empire was in decline. It could no longer resist the rapacity of outside forces and crumpled when confronted by Normans and Turks. In 1204 western Crusaders, instead of freeing the Holy Land, attacked Constantinople. The Empire got smaller and broke up into small kingdoms, Nicaea and Epirus are examples. Latin princes shared out the Greek peninsula: the duchies of Athens and Thebes, the Kingdom of Thessaloniki, the principality of Morea in the Peloponnesus. The new Frankish masters set up feudal regimes and built great castles. Meanwhile the Venetians, wishing to control trade routes, occupied strategic positions along the coasts of Thrace and the Peloponnesus, not to mention Crete and the islands of the Aegean and Ionian Seas. But the Byzantines went on the offensive again and re-conquered Constantinople in 1262. The Peloponnesus however, did not return to complete Byzantine control until 1429, before falling to the Turks in 1460.

Byzantines and Latins have given us remarkable examples of architecture and decoration in the monuments they have left on Greek soil. The Byzantines erected churches with marvelous domes, ornamented with frescoes, mosaics and icons all over Greek soil. The first golden age of Byzantium was a high point of basilica building (Nicopolis, Thessaloniki, Amphipolis). There was a fresh outbreak of church building in the 10th century. Churches like those of Daphni, Hosios Loukas and Nea Moni on Khios were built in a new style: the Greek cross. In spite of many troubles, later centuries built sumptuous buildings, like the church of St Demetrios (13th century), the monastery of Pantanassa (15th century) and the Church of the Holy Apostles at Thessaloniki. The internal decoration of these Christian sanctuaries is very rich. The gold of the mosaics shines out from within the domes. The dome is a most holy place; it represents the heavens, the throne of Christ, the creator of all, the master of the universe and the implacable judge with his piercing gaze. He is often surrounded by the gospel writers and the prophets, while nearby we glimpse the calm, reassuring and understanding figure of the Virgin. The upper walls are decorated with frescoes of episodes in the life of Christ.

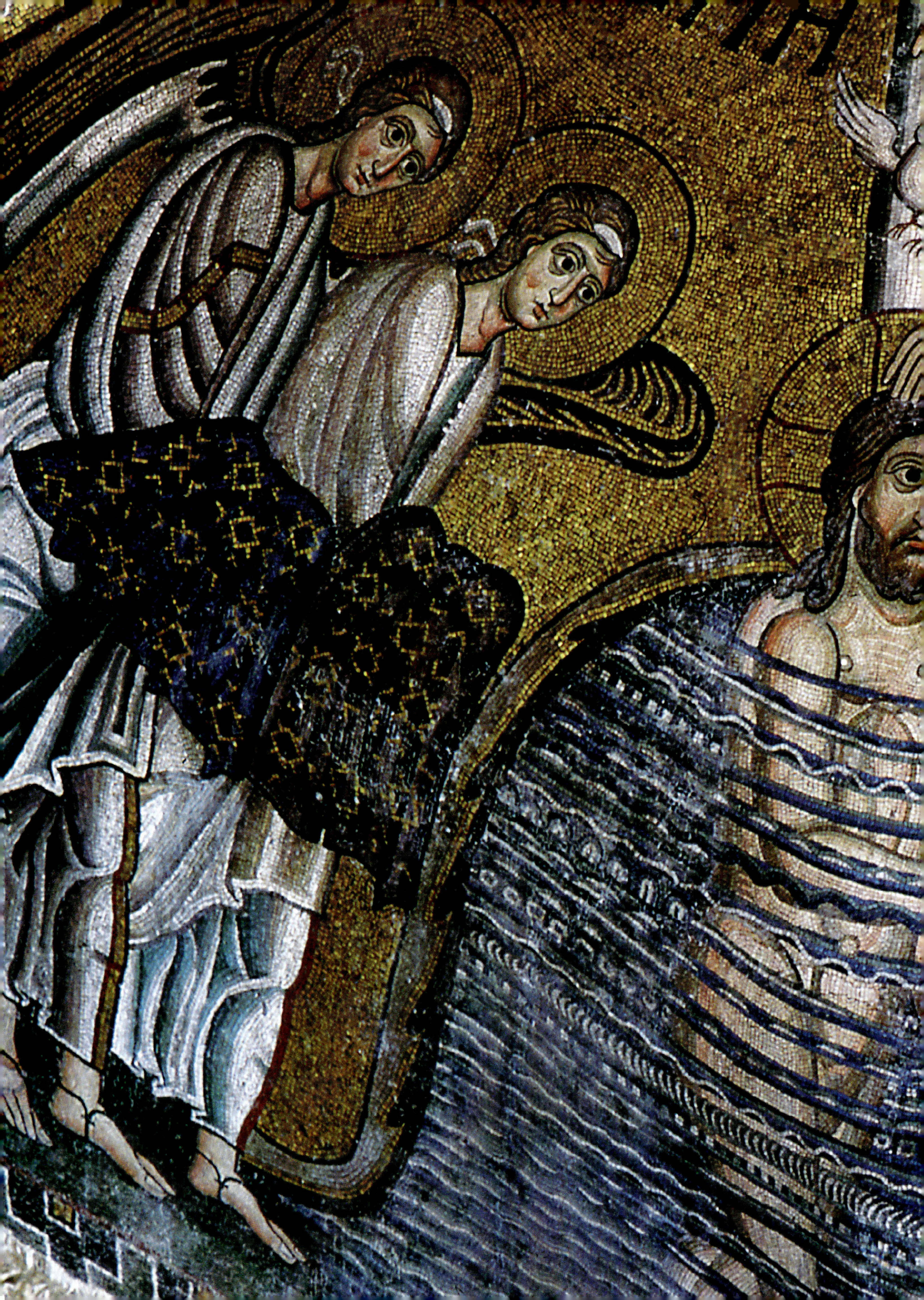

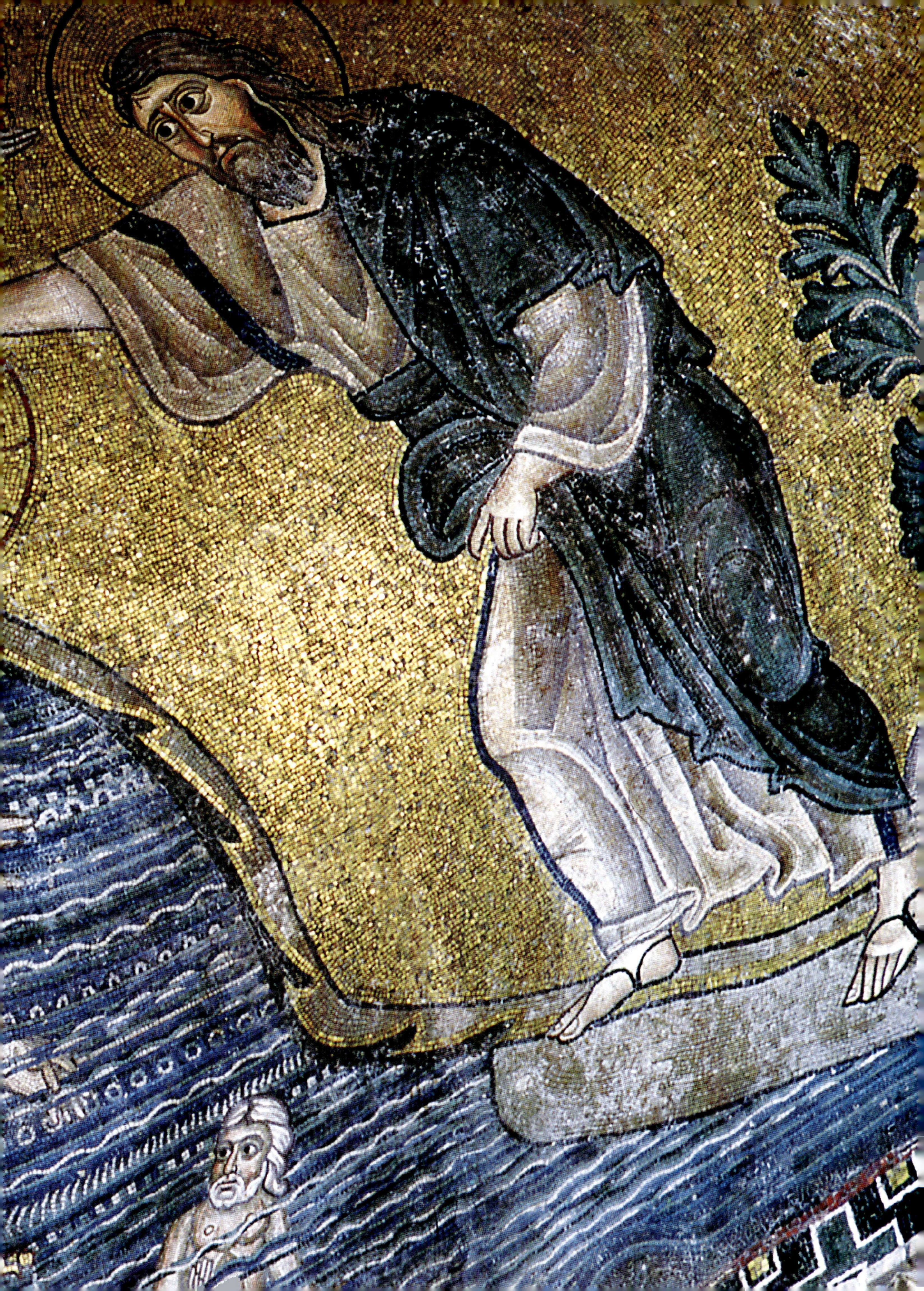

THE BAPTISM OF CHRIST

This fine mosaic with its golden background shows a recurrent and symbolic theme in Byzantine art: the baptism of Christ in the Jordan. The Orthodox commemorate this sacrament on the 6th January. This work is in the Monastery of Hosios Loukas, on the western side of Mount Helikon in central Greece. St Luke's church and its mosaics are considered to be amongst the masterpieces of the second Byzantine age. John the Baptist bows and places his right hand on the head of Jesus, who is standing up to his shoulders in the river. The waters of the Jordan, in accordance with the conventions of Byzantine art, are swelling up with mysterious vital energy. A dove, the symbol of the Holy Sprit, hovers overhead. On the left, two angels look on. In accordance with the Byzantine rite, their hands are veiled as a mark of respect. PREVIOUS PAGES

GERAKI: A CHRIST

Geraki in the Peloponnesus was prosperous in the Middle Ages. We can tell this from the numerous Byzantine churches and chapels, not to mention the 13th century Frankish fortress standing on a promontory of Mount Parnon. This modest village reminds us of the brilliant city of Mystra. On the walls of St Nicholas's chapel a few traces of paint resist the ravages of time. Here the elegant, long and fragile lines of this painting of Christ, his somewhat blurred figure, his faded colors, confer on him a charm that is both moving and majestic.

A SOLDIER MONK

This mosaic comes from Hosios Loukas. This priest-like figure stands unusually still and watchful, ready at any moment to draw his weapon. He reminds us of a time when wars in the name of God were an ever present reality. Monasteries were normally places of relative safety; nevertheless their inhabitants sometimes had to defend themselves from pillage, enemies and pirates. FOLLOWING PAGE LEFT

CHRIST PANTOCRATOR

This mosaic of Christ was made about 1100 AD by artists from Constantinople. Christ, the creator of all, sits enthroned inside the central dome of the church at Daphni. From the sixth century on, the most typical figure in orthodox Christianity was the all-powerful Christ. From the 9th century on, church art was increasingly standardized and such pictures were placed at the top of church domes. Early pictures were of a young and graceful Christ, without a beard; rather like Apollo. These began to disappear in the 4th century and gave way to an adult, oriental Christ, bearded with long, brown hair; he has a severe face; this was the strong influence of monastic asceticism. In western Christianity, Christ is shown as a suffering, understanding and merciful figure; here he is the terrible judge. Like an Old Testament Jehovah, he watches over human behavior from the highest heavens. His angular face, and pronounced shadows, the unevenness of his eyes and raised eyebrows give him a strongly expressive face. The Pantocrator is usually enthroned in majesty, holding the gospel in his left hand and blessing with his right. Here we only see a bust inside a circular medallion representing the heavens, with, around him, the sixteen prophets. Christ has a blue cloak and stands out from the traditional blue background. This mosaic is one of the masterpieces of the second golden age of Byzantine art (11th and 12th centuries). It was at its height following the iconoclastic crisis of the 8th century. FOLLOWING PAGE RIGHT

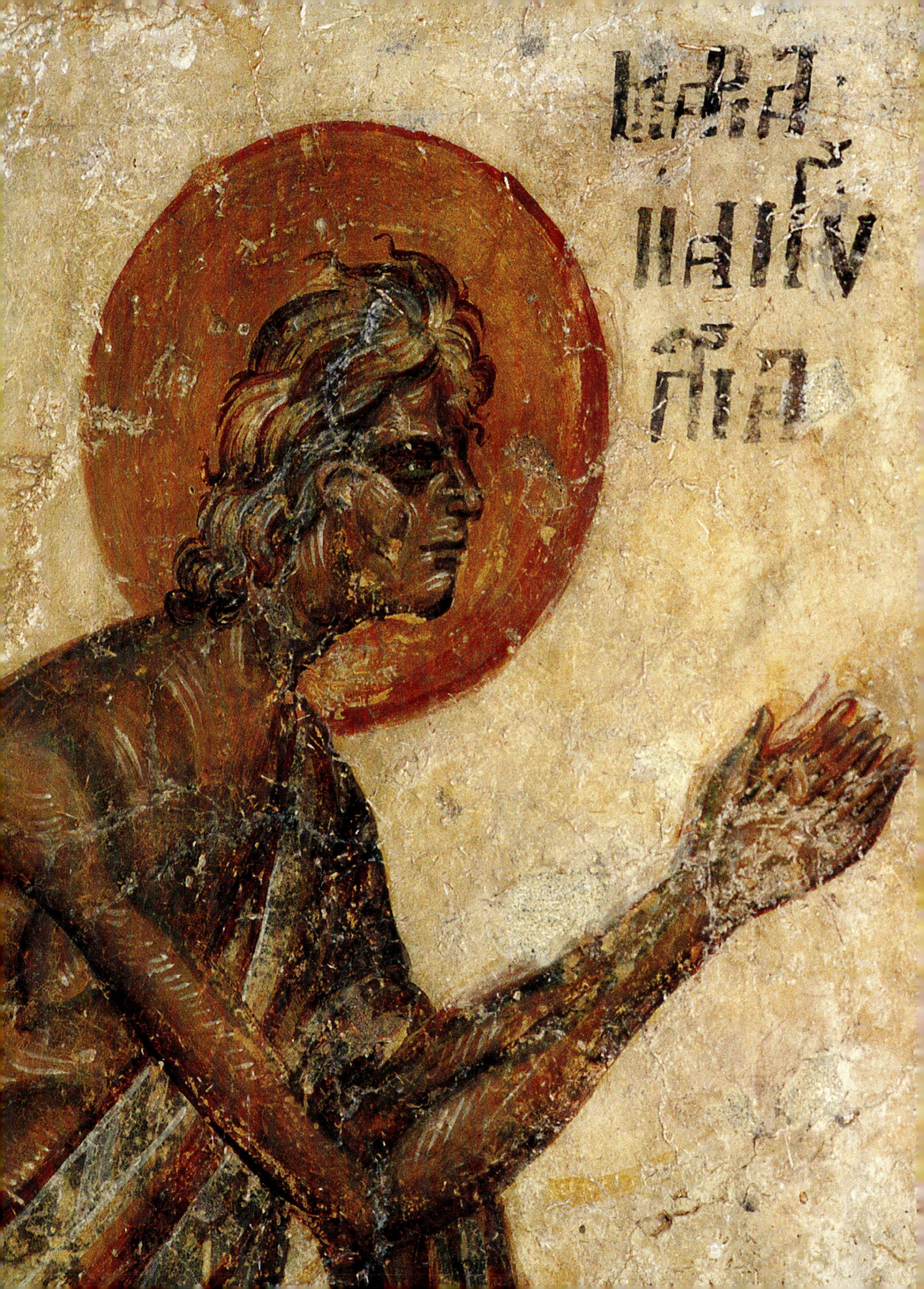

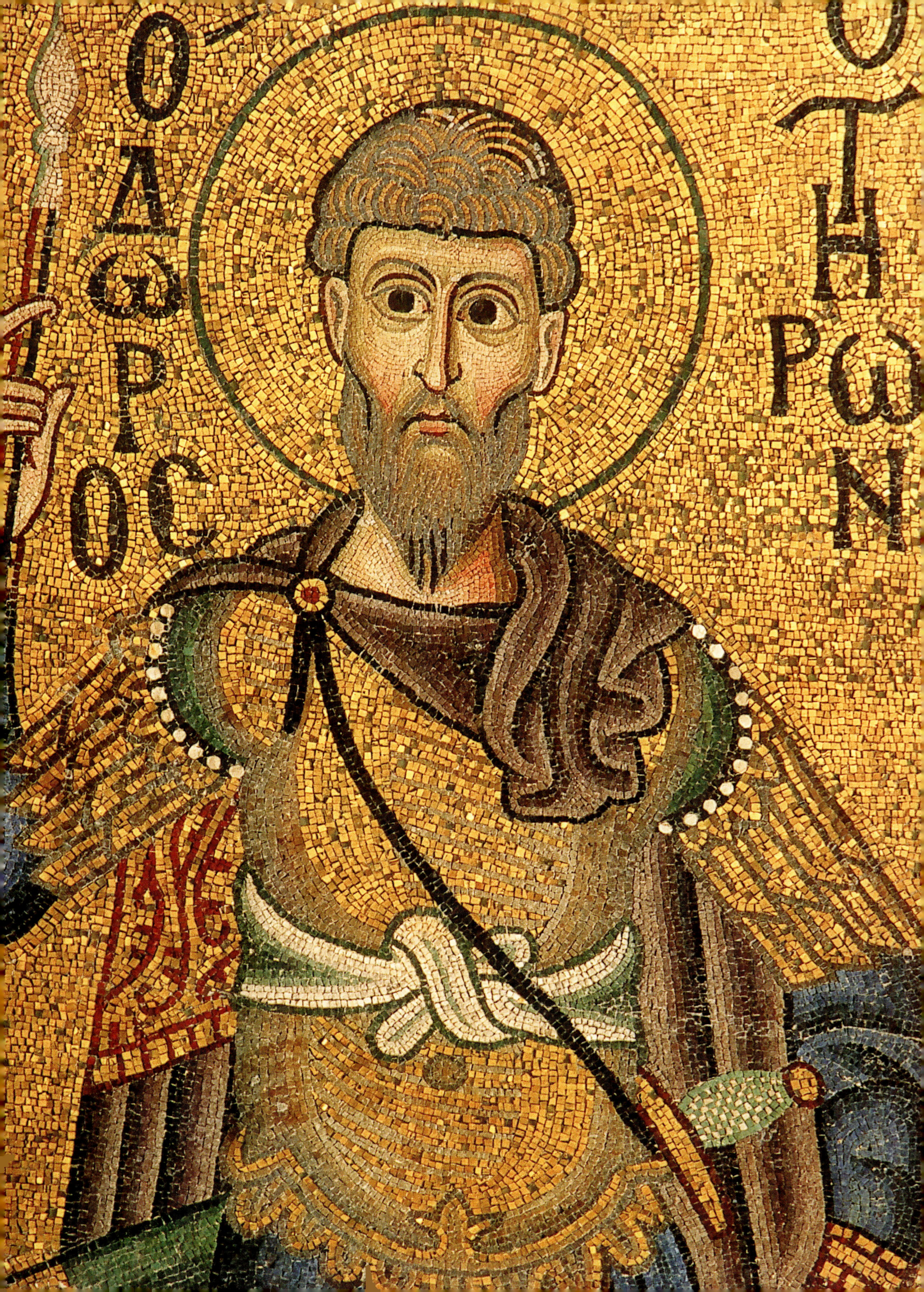
Ο ΤΗΡΩΝ

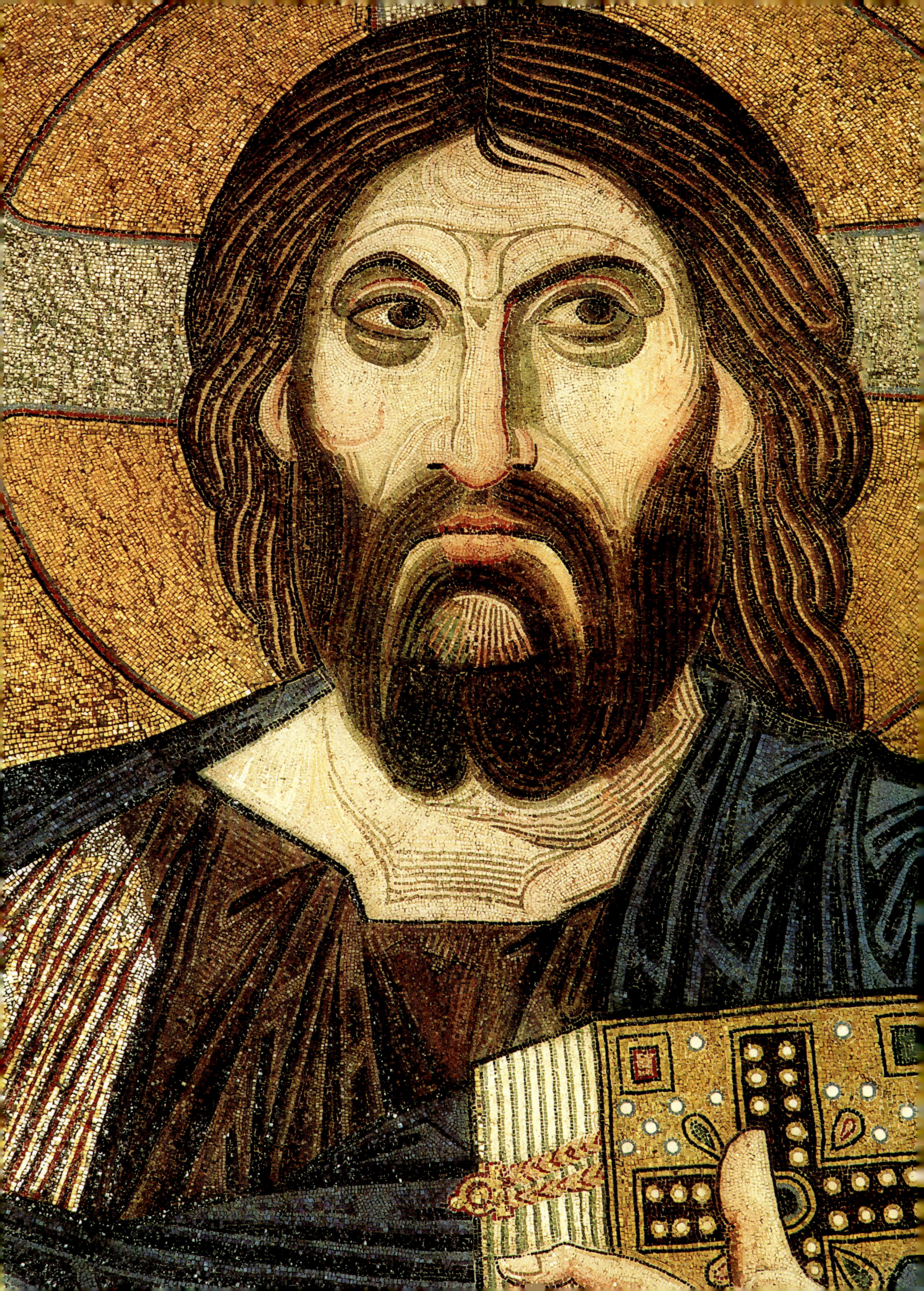

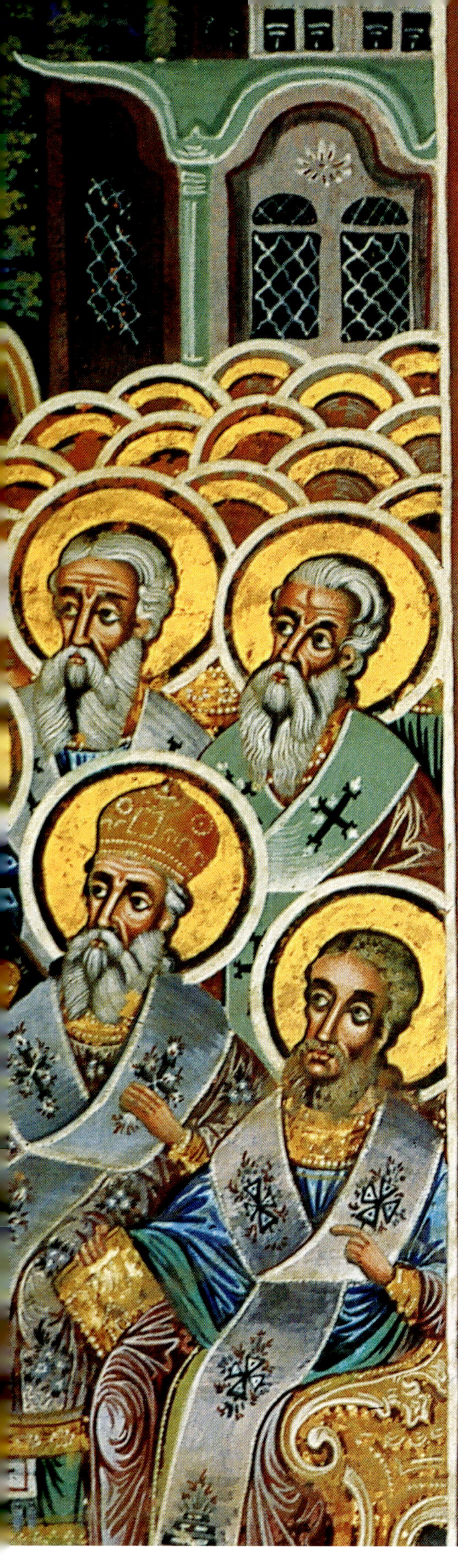

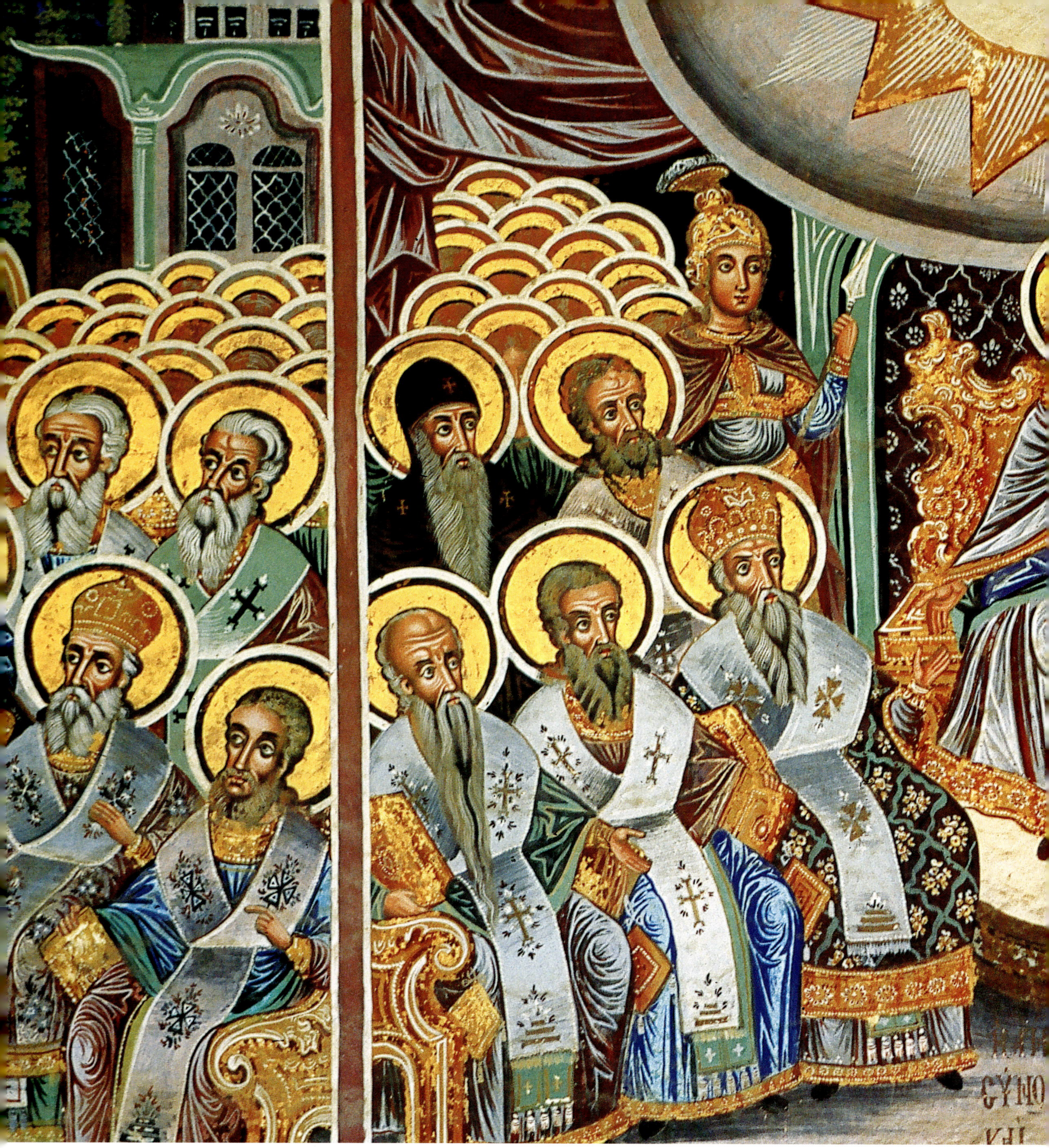

A FRESCO FROM MOUNT ATHOS

In 1856, the English poet, Edward Lear, declared that Mount Athos was the most surprising thing he had ever seen in the course of his travels, with the possible exception of Egypt. It is a mountainous peninsula, ending in a huge precipice. Apart from that cliff, it is a mass of green: chestnut trees and oak trees with, on top of crests and hanging over cliffs, especially beside the sea, magnificent old monasteries. No female of any species is allowed on the peninsula.

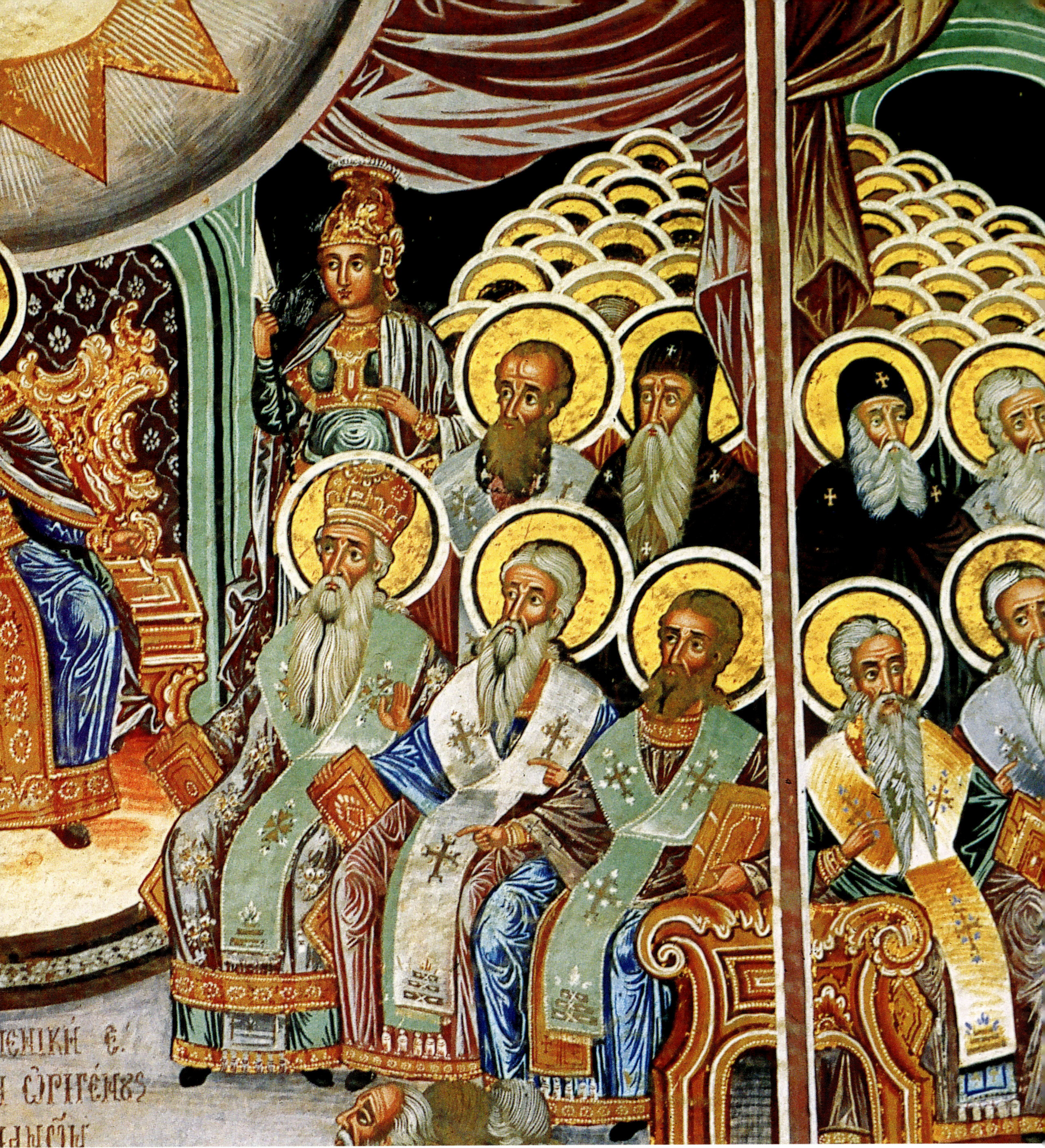

The mountain was dedicated to the contemplative life in 885, by a decree of the Emperor Basil II. But it had already, since the 4th century, been home to many hermits.

The first monastery was founded in 963 by St Athanasius of Trebizond; it is the Great Lavra, and it is here that you will find this fresco. The wall paintings were done much later, between 1535 and 1558. They are the work of a monk named Theophanus who was a famous painter of the Cretan school, as opposed to the Macedonian school, which is represented by the painter Manuel Panselino.

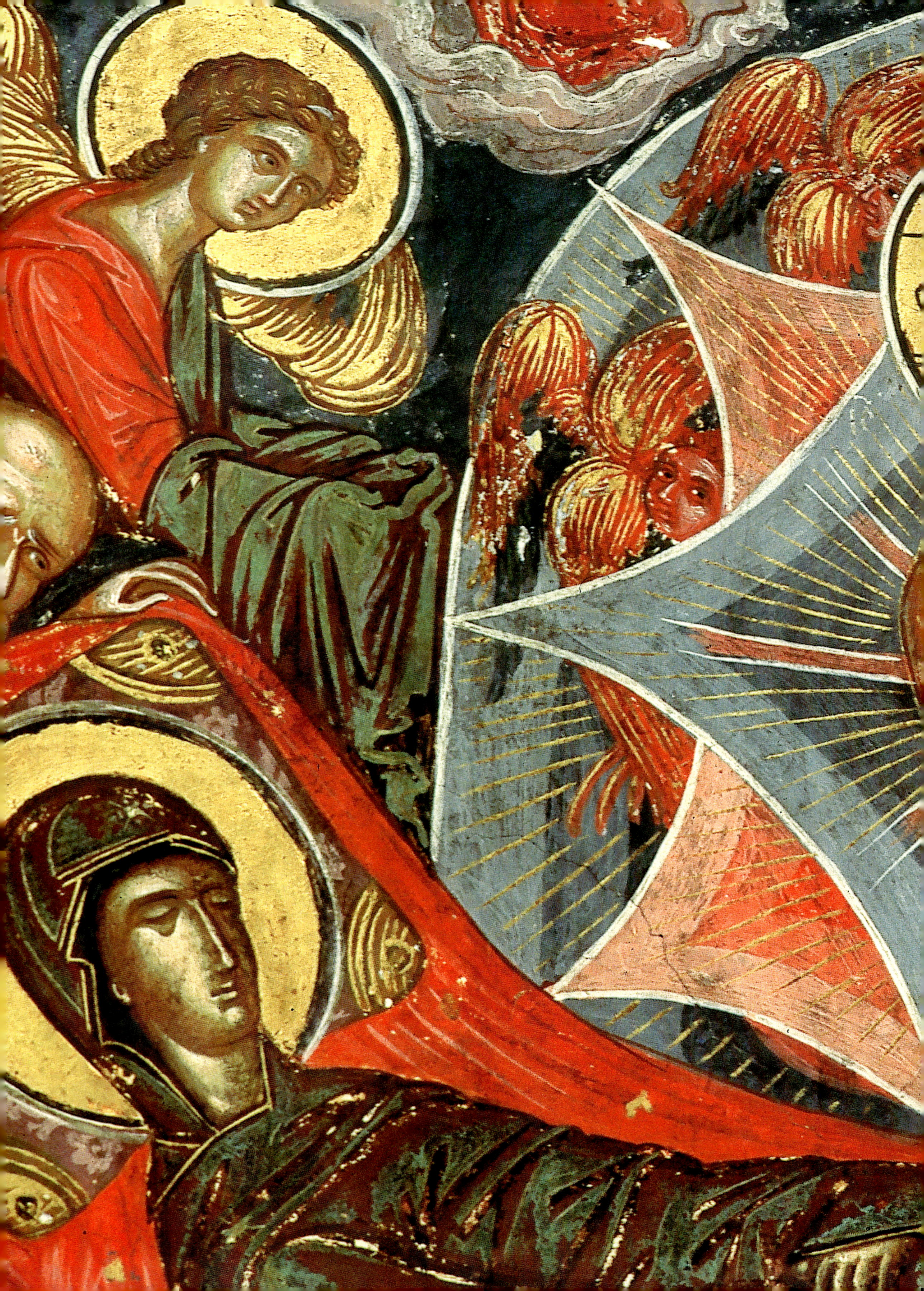

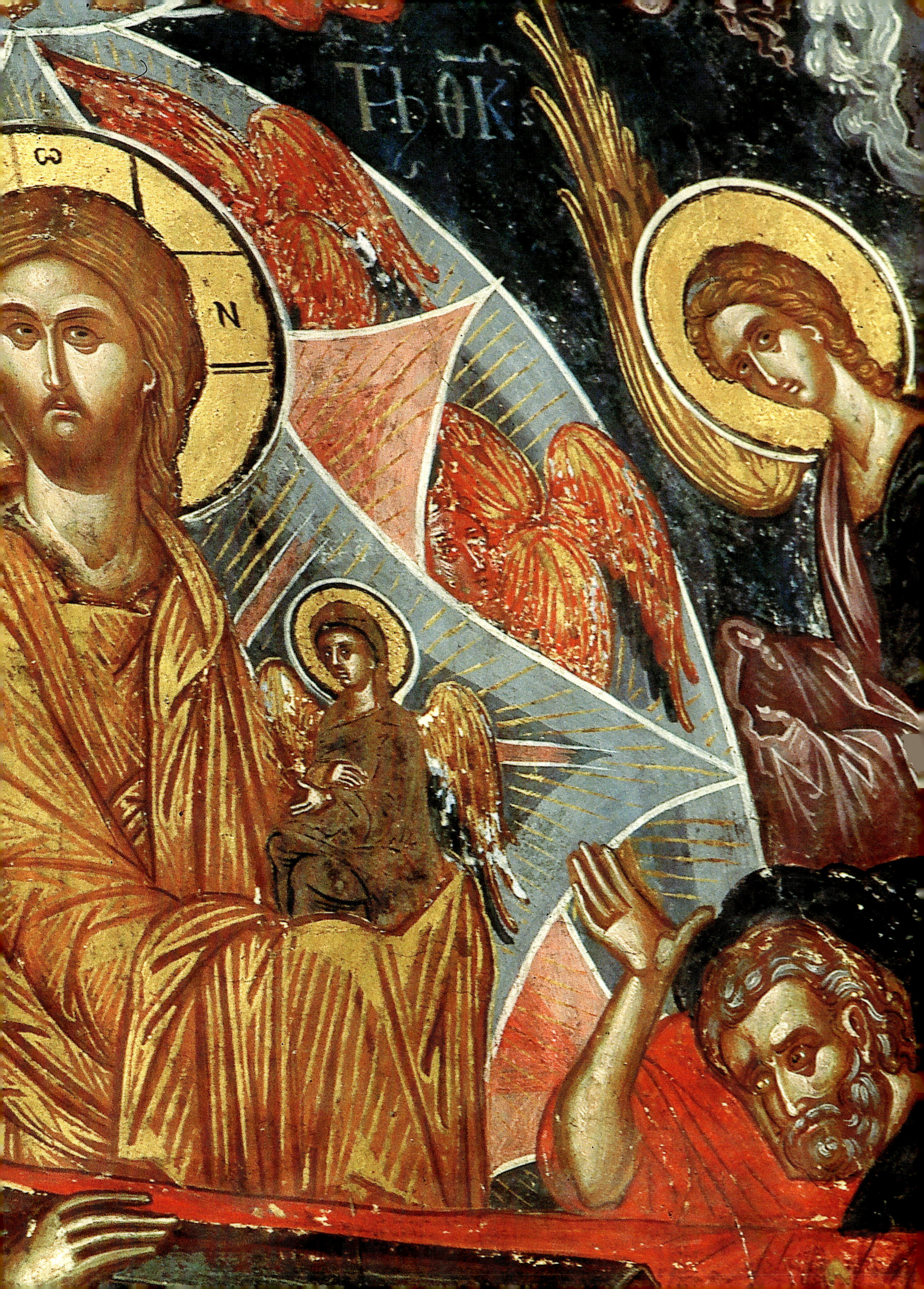

THE DORMITION OF THE VIRGIN

Louis Dupré visited Athens and Constantinople in 1825 and left us this description: "We are going to visit the Meteors. They stand on the very tip of pointed mountain tops, like eagles' nests. The inhabitants of the monasteries lowered a net, shaped like a sack, at the end of a long rope. Mr Hyett chanced going first. He squatted down in the net and, in a few minutes, was raised the 130 feet, by means of a capstan operated by twelve monks... They showed us a chapel, where the arches and walls were painted and gilded, a very clean cloister and several cells."

This fresco comes from the church of the monastery of Varlaam. It was painted between 1548 and 1566. These paintings show a new concern for realism, evidence of the influence of Italy. Christ has come down to earth to stand beside the Virgin; he carries the soul of his mother in his arms. Around her bed are gathered the apostles, while two angels stand, one on either side of Christ; their hands are veiled as a mark of respect. PREVIOUS PAGES

SAINT PANTALEON'S CHAPEL

This tiny 14th century Cretan church is laid out like a basilica with three naves and is typical of Byzantine churches. Its beautiful light-colored stones blend perfectly with the surrounding landscape, and, as in all Orthodox churches, the large number of colored icons, the ex-votos and the smoke from the incense all go to create a warm and welcoming interior.

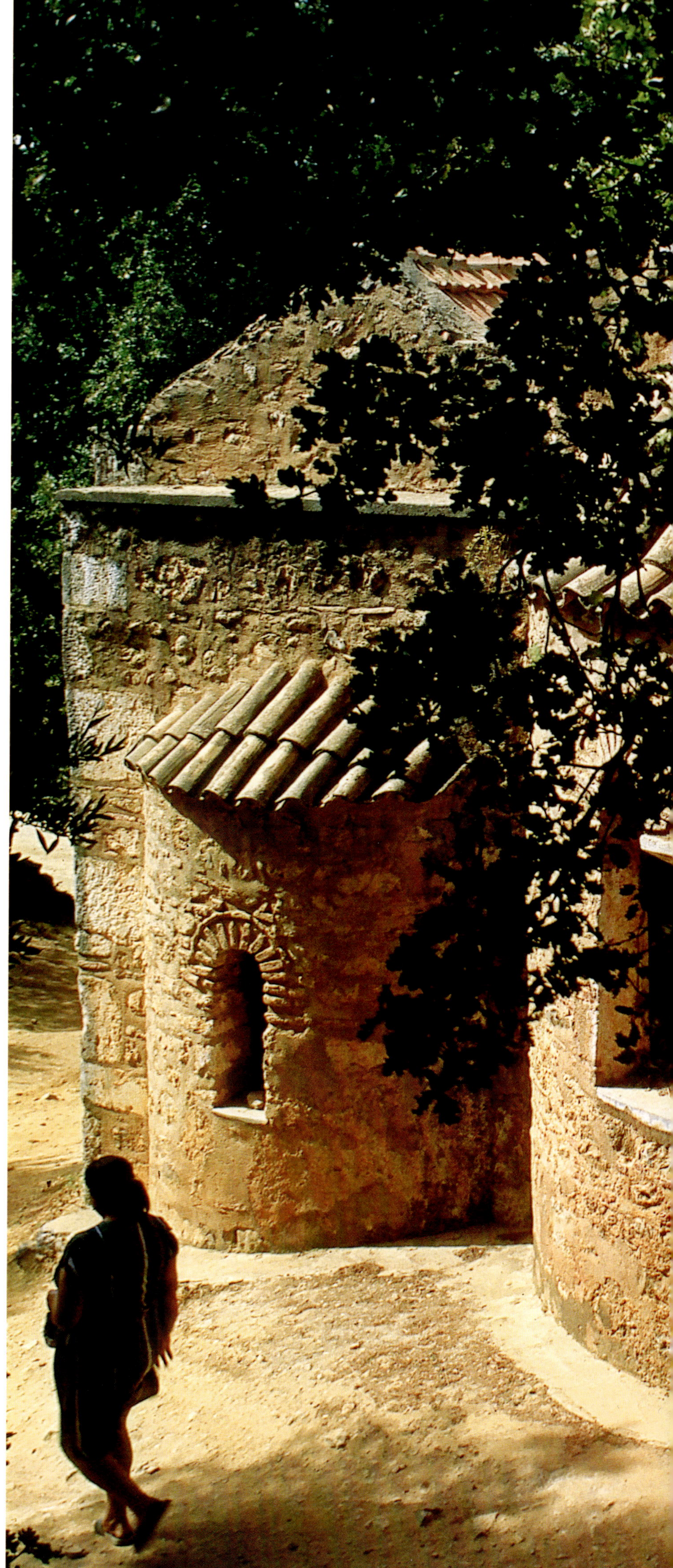

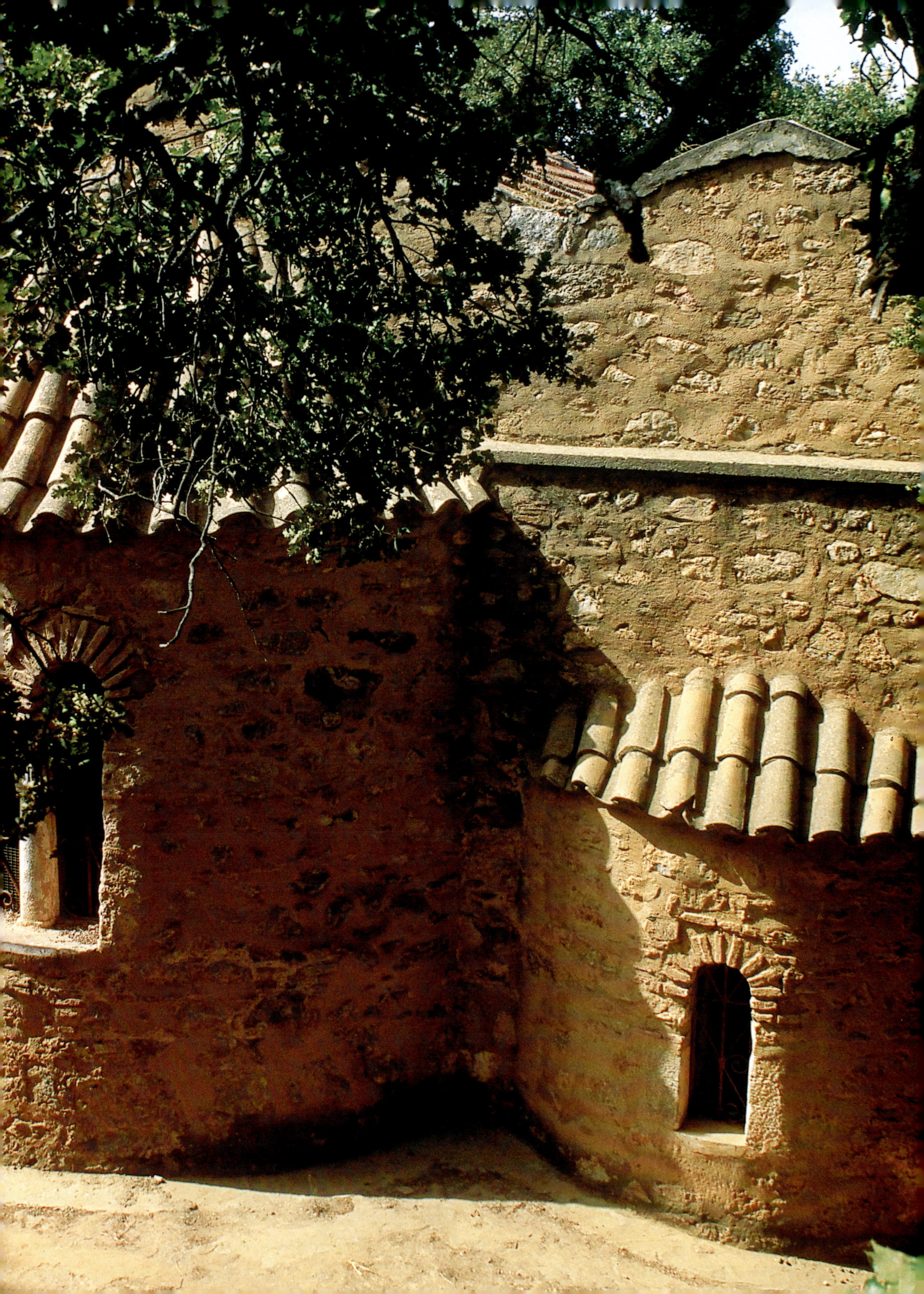

THE CHURCH OF ARKADI

The monastery church of Arkadi has two naves and is a masterpiece of the Cretan Renaissance. It was built in Venetian style with an elegant and richly sculpted façade decorated with double pilasters; over the doors, there are circular bays with spiral decorations and it is surmounted by two obelisks.

The building has a wonderful bell tower. It was built in 1587 and miraculously escaped destruction in 1866, during a gory episode in the course of the fight against the Ottoman occupier.

The civil population had taken refuge in the monastery which was an important stronghold in that struggle.

The monastery was about to be occupied by the Ottoman army. On the 8th November the Prior ordered his monks to set fire to the powder magazine of the besieged convent. He sacrificed the entire Cretan population of the town in order to kill as many enemy soldiers as possible: records tell of 1800 Turks and 850 Cretans killed.

This place is now a national monument and every year a festival commemorates those events. A plaque recalls the incidents: "The flame lit in this crypt, shone from one end to the other over glorious Crete; it was a holy flame, the flame of the people of Crete who sacrificed themselves in the name of liberty."

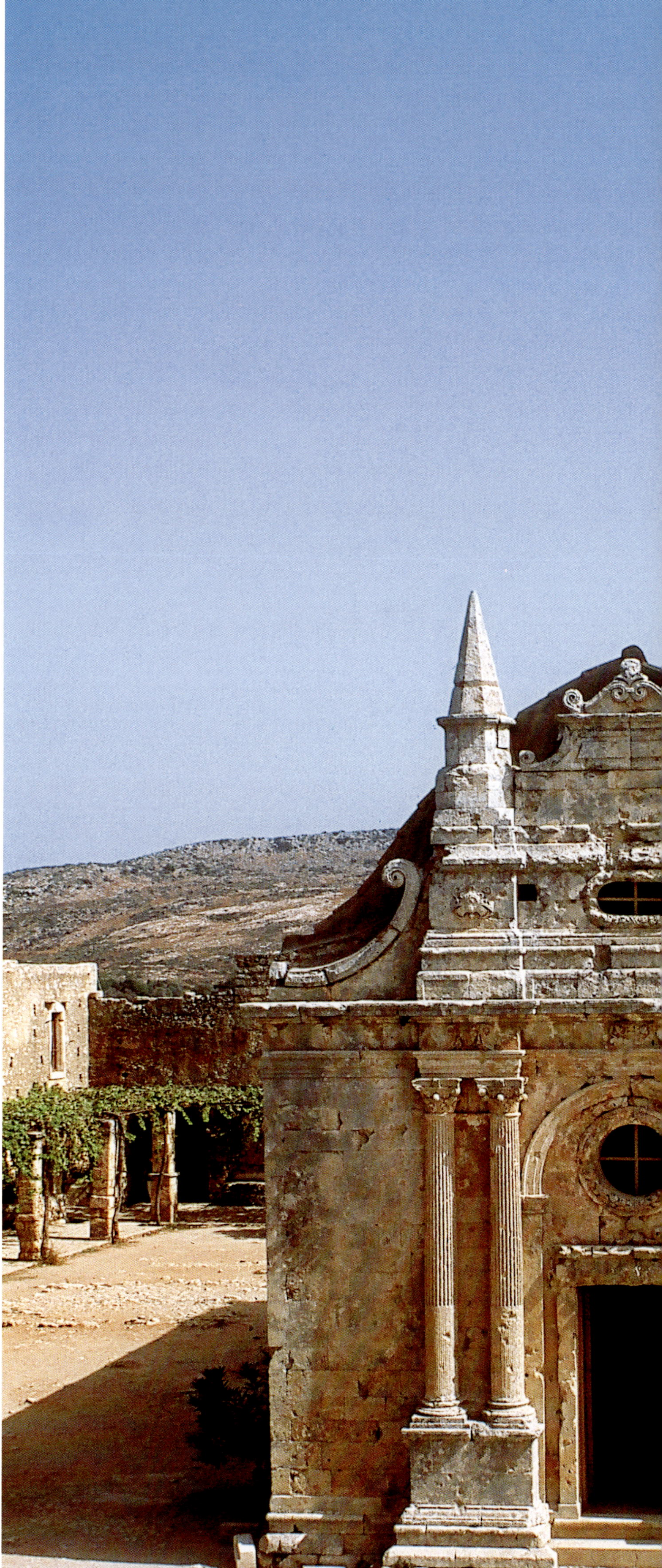

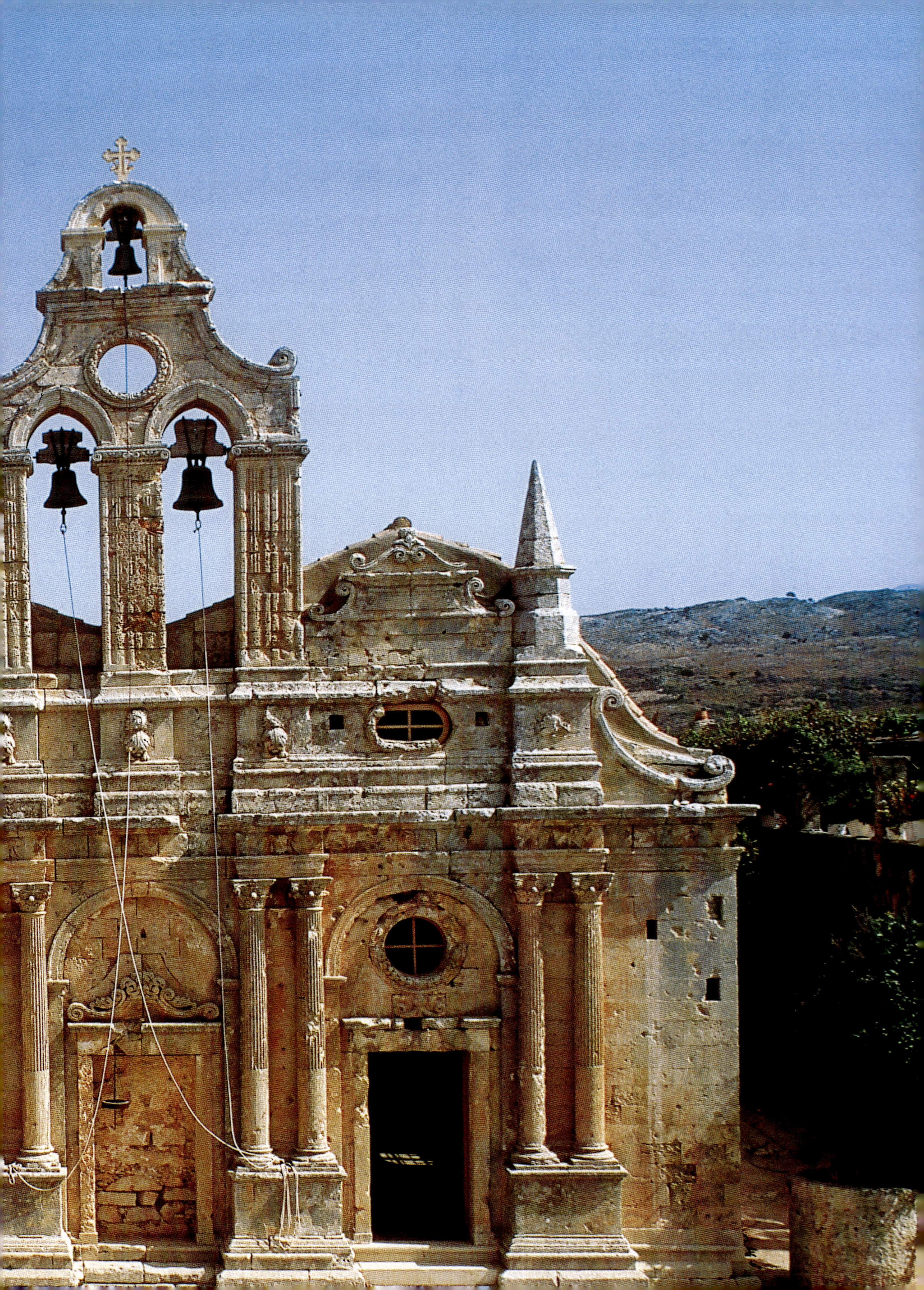

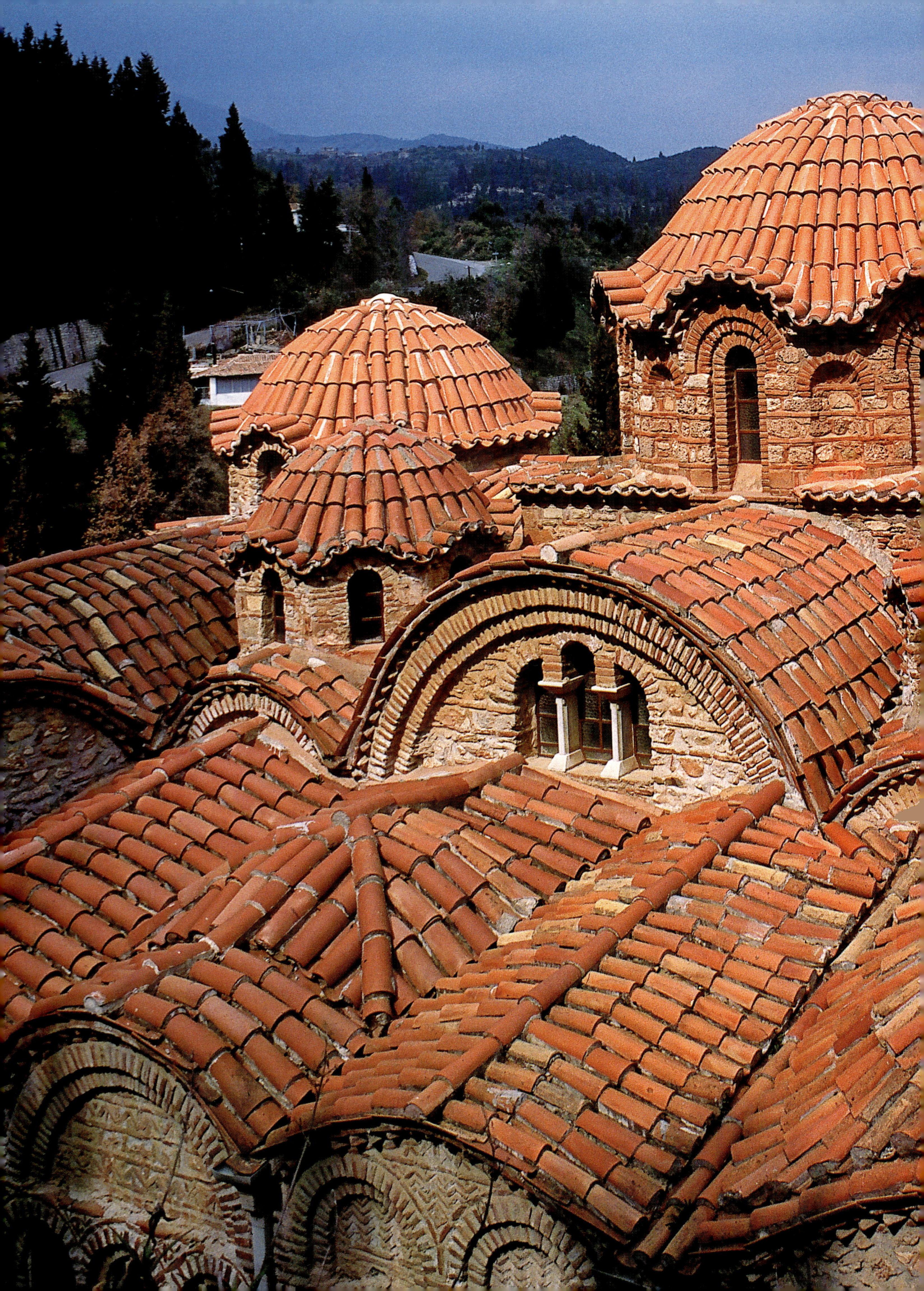

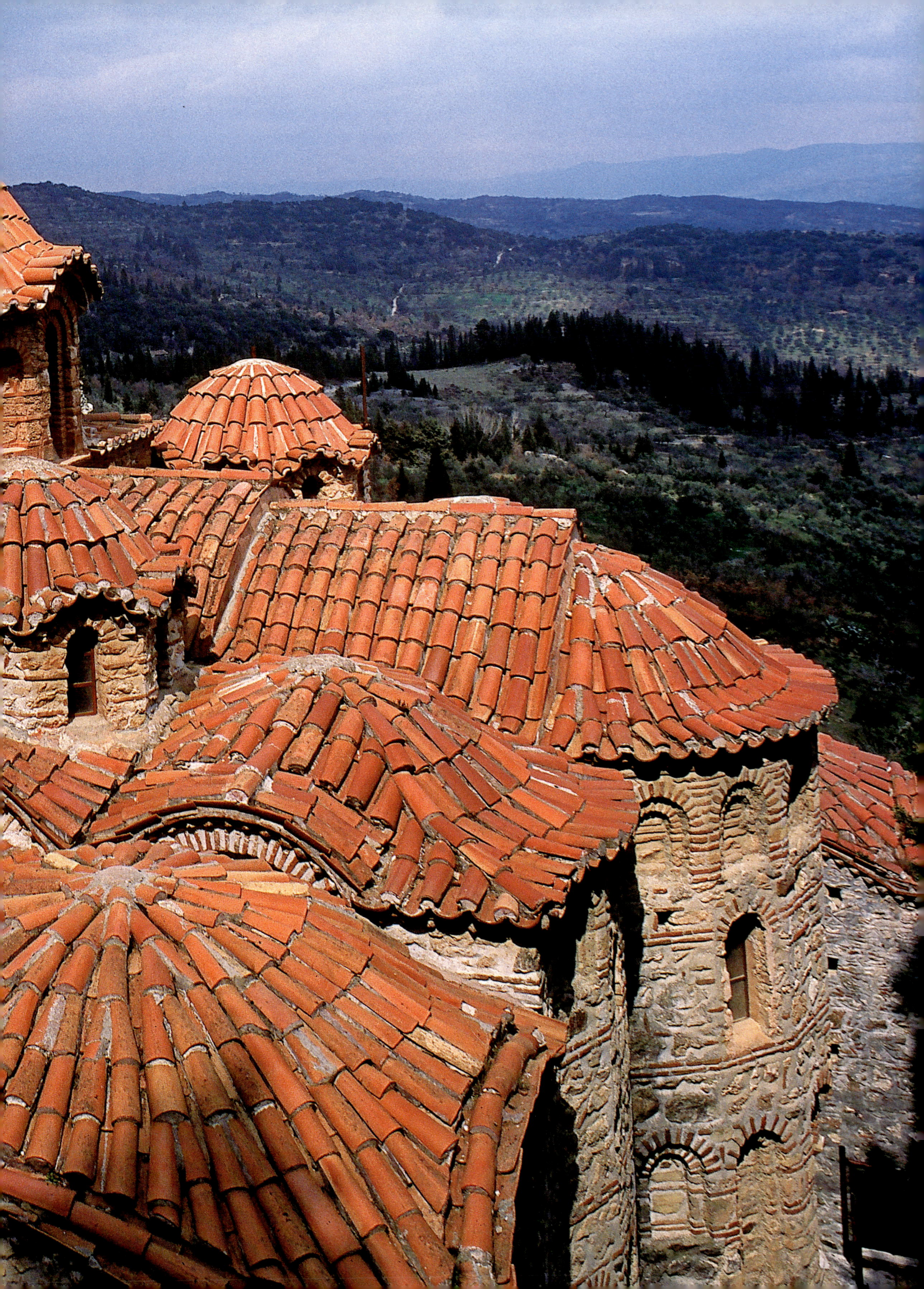

THE DOMES OF MYSTRA

They are the only buildings not to have fallen into ruins in the ancient city of Mystra; the red-tiled domes of the churches dot the side of the hill. These inescapable round shapes of Byzantine architecture are the outcome of a quest. The circle, a mythical shape in the east symbolizing the sky and infinity, is at the heart of every building. This was how architects conceived of buildings that stretched out towards God. The central dome rests upon a drum, which is often octagonal, and it is surrounded by smaller domes. The play of the roof slopes, and the many levels of the roof, add to its charm. The alternating layers of stone and brick confer a harmonious variety of tones to the external walls, which also have niches, arcades, garlands and windows, often with two or three panels. Amongst the most beautiful churches of Mystra are those of the monasteries of Brontochion, Peribleptos and Pantanassa. There is also the Metropolitan church dedicated to St Demetrius (13th to 16th centuries), St Sophia (14th century), and the Evangelistria (late 14th century). PREVIOUS PAGES

AN ICON AT TINOS

This modern example of an Orthodox icon is in the church of Our Lady of the Annunciation overlooking the port of Tinos. This sanctuary hosts an important pilgrimage every year on the 15th August. Pilgrims come from all over Greece to honor the Virgin of Tinos, who is believed to perform miracles. The church is full of icons and ex-votos offered by the faithful: they ask the Virgin's help or thank her for favors received. These ex-votos show eyes, arms or legs from those hoping for a cure, boats from those seeking protection, or a good catch of fish. The church was built and the pilgrimage inaugurated following the discovery, in 1823, of an icon held to have miraculous powers. People come from afar to venerate the icon representing the Virgin of the Annunciation. Over time crowds have tended to come to this place on the 15th of August particularly. That day, which is a feast of the Blessed Virgin, took on a new significance on 15th August 1940 when the torpedo boat 'Elli', present for the ceremonies, was sunk by an Italian submarine, a prelude to the Second World War. The population, spared by two other torpedoes, believed they were miraculously protected and gave thanks to the Virgin.

THE MONASTERY OF VATOPEDI

Mount Athos, (over 6500 feet high), is an unusual enclave in Greek territory. This peninsula in the Khalkidhiki region, is barely separated from the rest of Greece by Xerxes' canal, but is autonomous and administered by Orthodox monks. All females are barred from it. There are numerous monasteries stretching along the coast: Vatopedi is one of them and overlooks a little creek. It was founded in the later 10th century and is particularly rich and imposing. The monks are dressed in long black robes and stove-pipe hats; they are bearded and wear their hair long. Their figures stand out against the bright red walls of the domed church which was built in the early 10th century. This is an idiorhythmic monastery; that is to say each individual monk follows his own routine; each is self regulating and has his own apartment. By contrast, in coenobitic monasteries, the monks live in community, obeying the rules of the house, its timetable and activities. Outside of these structures, hermits live out their faith in the dwellings of their choice. FOLLOWING PAGES

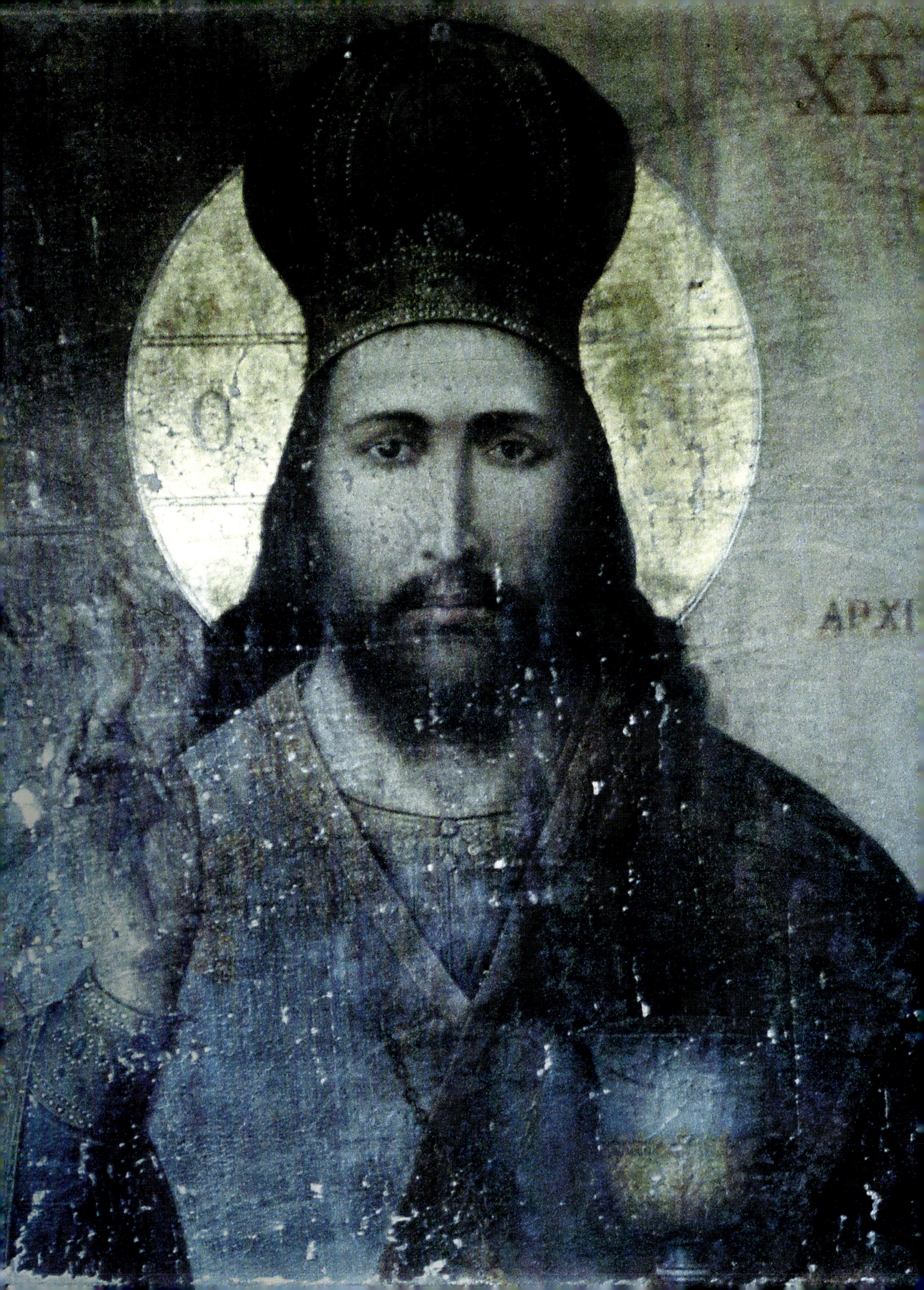
ΧΣ
Ο
ΑΡΧΙ

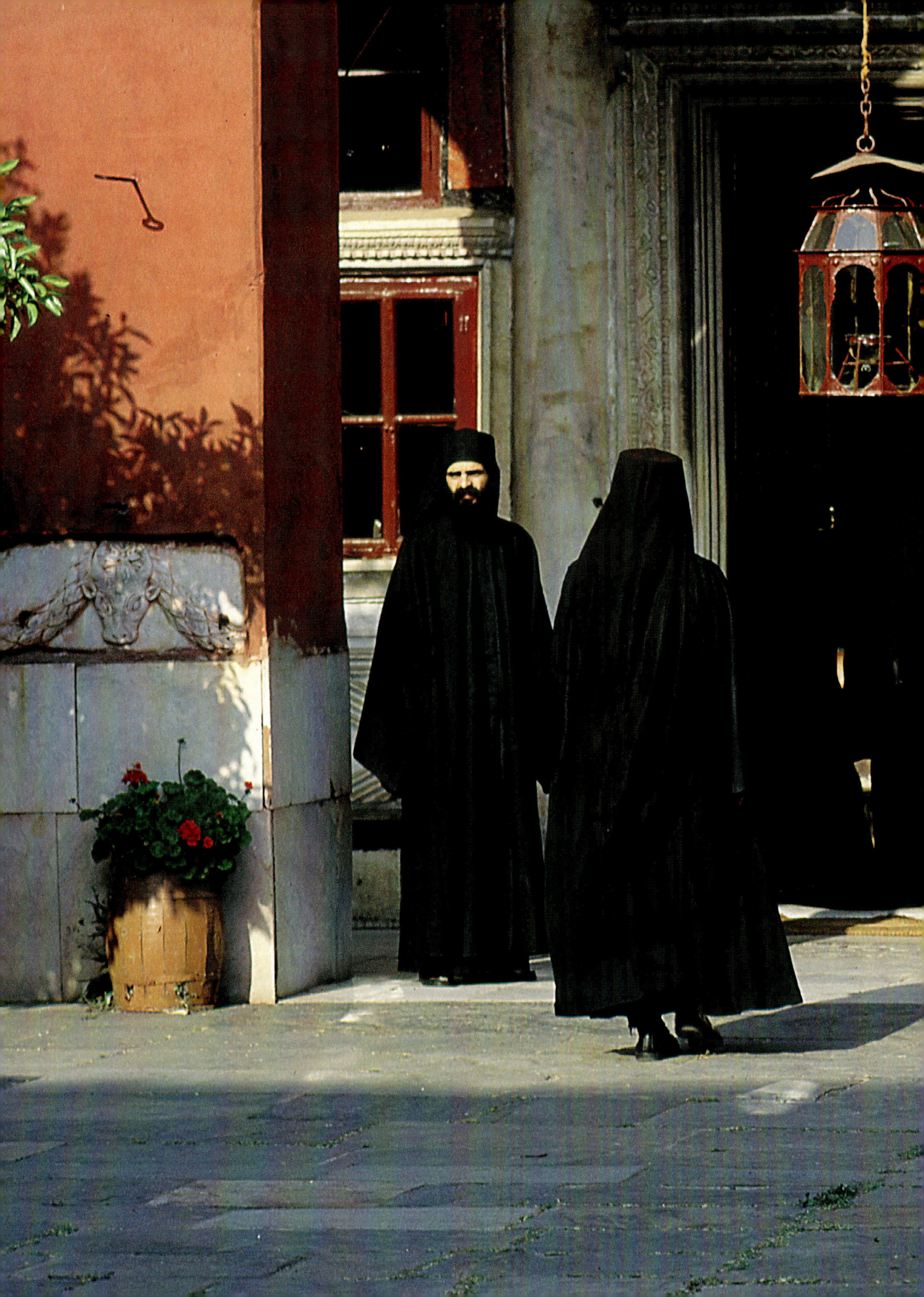

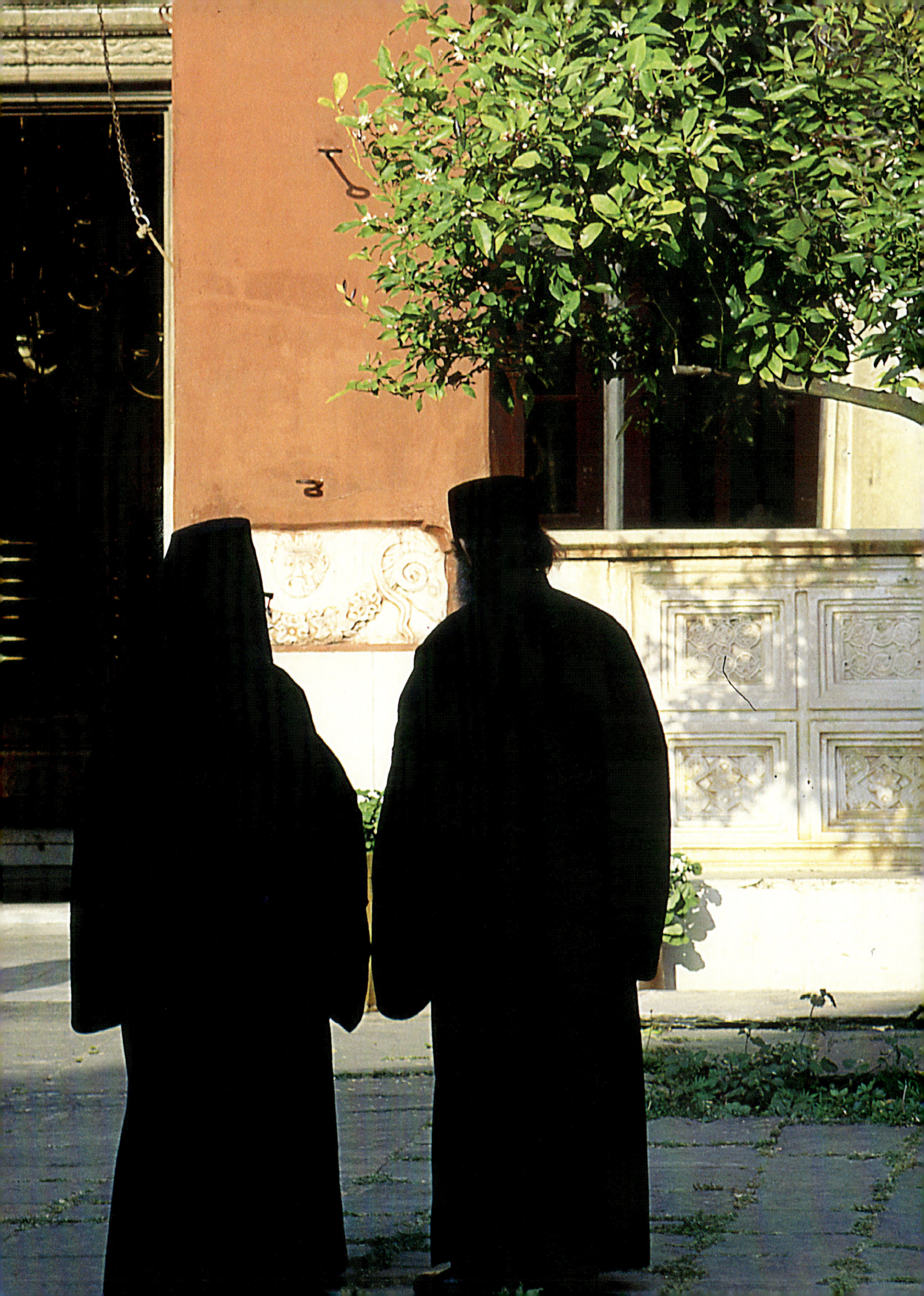

GREECE DURING THE OTTOMAN OCCUPATION

Today there are scarcely any traces left in Greece of the four centuries of Ottoman rule. Since Independence, which was won in 1830, the Greeks have systematically removed the signs of their subjugation. A few cites, however, show marks of that civilization. The upper town of Thessaloniki, surrounded by its ramparts, is distinguished by narrow, winding streets and corbeled houses. This used to be where the Turkish administrators lived. In Kavala, in Ioanina or in Crete, one may still see the tall spire of a minaret. The Turk has become the enemy; earlier he had been given a reserved welcome by Greeks, accustomed to Byzantine or Latin control.

In the 15th century, the Greeks were not happy with their feudal status and submission to the Pope, which had been imposed by western princes. Their resentment made the Muslim victory easier. The Turks had captured Constantinople in 1453, other Byzantine possessions, then Latin lands like the Duchy of Athens in 1456, then Morea in 1460, and Venetian Crete in 1669.

The new masters had wanted to put Greek minds at ease and promised religious tolerance. Islam had, consequently, not threatened the Orthodox Church which kept its property and its authority over the Christian population. What is more the State protected it from the aspirations of the Roman church, which it feared much more than Muslim rule. On the other hand the Orthodox Patriarch had to accept the Sultan's authority and undertake that Christians would be loyal and law-abiding. By means of this privileged position at the heart of the Turkish Empire, the Orthodox Church became an agent of Greek dependence, but at the same time managed to preserve Greek religion, language and traditions.

Once in contact with Ottoman civilization, there were spontaneous conversions to Islam, but only the lower clergy of the Greek provinces were troubled by this. The Turks also managed to attract the services and compliance of the descendants of the Byzantine nobility, Greeks living in the Phanar district of Istanbul. On the other hand many refused to compromise with the conqueror and went into exile; they took with them precious manuscripts, thus initiating the humanist Renaissance in western Europe. But those remaining were given important posts in the Ottoman administration. The inhabitants of Phanar were generally highly educated, politically astute and had profound insights into European affairs; they acted as representatives of the Ottoman government dealing with Russia, France and Britain: they worked as translators, diplomats and ambassadors. These well-off families worked well in the new political setting and were equally prosperous in shipping and commerce. Certainly the powerful Greek families of Istanbul experienced privileges, but both the lay and clerical populations of mainland Greece and the islands, were kept in conditions of inferiority and hardship. The economy had collapsed after the conquest, paralyzing the country. The rural population working the land faced heavy taxation. Strong men emerged in local communities whose job was to collect taxes for the Ottoman authorities; but they abused their power. The situation further deteriorated in the 18th century, when new Muslim dignitaries from the military and landed classes increased their hold over land and people.

The Reverend Thomas Smart Hughes became aware of this oppression while traveling in Greece in 1813; a member of the Ottoman gentry refused to step aside on a road – it would have been an offense to his rank – to allow a donkey piled high with kindling to pass. The animal bumped against him and the arrogant Turk attacked the donkey's owner following behind. He struck him on the face and the unfortunate Greek did not dare utter a complaint for fear of worse reprisals. In the same way, the painter Dodwell told how the Ottoman guards accompanying him threw stones at the Greeks who were intrigued by the artist's activities and stopped to watch him. The French writer Chateaubriand also witnessed uncalled for violence, telling how Turkish forces which had been called upon to deal with a group of bandits, claimed hundreds of victims amongst the local population. These authors tell of submissive Greeks who are but a shadow of their famous ancestors. However revolution was in the air! Some could discern the anger, fire and hope which were smoldering in Greek breasts. Rev. Mr. Hughes tells how his Greek interpreter discovered the works of Lord Byron and, in his enthusiasm, copied out stanzas from *Childe Harold* so that he could show his friends how England supported the Greek cause.

The growth in national feeling was fed by Turkish exactions, and also by the spread of the ideals of the French Revolution. The principles of freedom, justice and nationhood were also encouraged in the Greek people by Orthodox Russia, scheming for the break-up of the Ottoman Empire. At the start of the 19th century the Turkish establishment was by now weakened as it faced both external pressures and internal squabbles; it was "the sick man of Europe". A few isolated revolts had already broken out in Greece: in the Peloponnesus in 1769, for instance. The time was now ripe for insurrection.

This heightening of patriotic feeling was felt in all social classes. Some peasants, exasperated by their oppressed state had already fled to the mountains where they swelled the ranks of gangs of brigands and armed rebels harassing the Turks. They adopted a lifestyle based on heroism and freedom and made full use of the power of their guns. There were also new local elites which sympathized with the poor farmers in their desire for self-government. They had grown out of the 18th century economic boom and had also flourished in maritime trade and small-scale manufacture. This middles class also felt threatened by the Ottoman authorities. Even the cosmopolitan elites of Phanar, which had strong links with European intellectuals and which we have already noted as part of the administrative establishment, set up secret societies. The biggest of these was the 'Friendly Society' of Odessa. Their members were ship-owners, bankers, merchants and writers. They all looked for an independent and liberal Greece. Even the Church, conservative and generally on the government's side, tending to stifle resistance movements, had its dissidents. In fact many priests favored national sentiment, fanned the renewal of Hellenism in the schools and stoked up the fires of rebellion.

The campaign started in 1821 with Alexander Ypsilanti, a former Russian army general, as leader of the Greek Revolution. On the 25th of March, Patriarch Germanos raised the blue standard of insurrection with its white cross. All Greece was alight. By 1824, the Peloponnesus, central Greece and most of the Aegean islands were free. But success was still some way off. The Turks, with their Egyptian allies, got the upper hand again and conducted massacres at Messolongi and Khios; international indignation was aroused. Philhellenism became the first great movement to unite the European peoples in spite of all their differences. Britain, Russia and France intervened in 1827 and their naval victory at Navarino, paved the way for Greek independence in 1830.

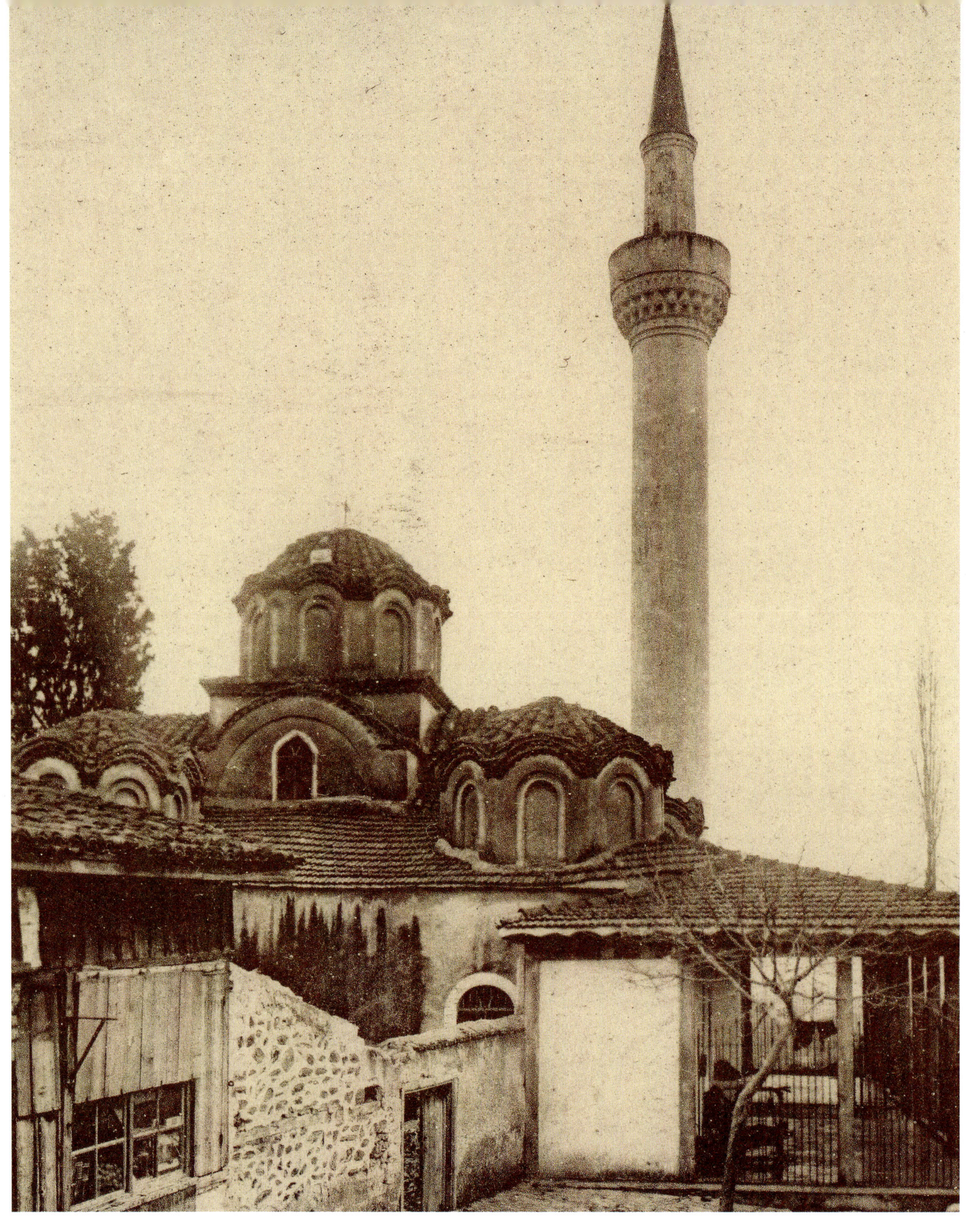

MOSQUES IN GREECE

Mosques flourished in Greece during the period of the Ottoman occupation. Some were built on purpose, but most frequently Byzantine churches were taken over and converted into Muslim places of worship. When Greek independence was won back, the mosques were often turned into factories or stores and the minarets knocked down. However the Mosque of Aslan Pasha, which had been built in 1618 in a corner of the Ioannina Fortress, remained intact. Today it houses the Museum of Popular Art. Some churches which were transformed into mosques kept, alongside their characteristic domes, the tall, slim outline of a minaret, a souvenir of the Ottoman presence. Such was the case with the church of St George at Thessaloniki. ABOVE

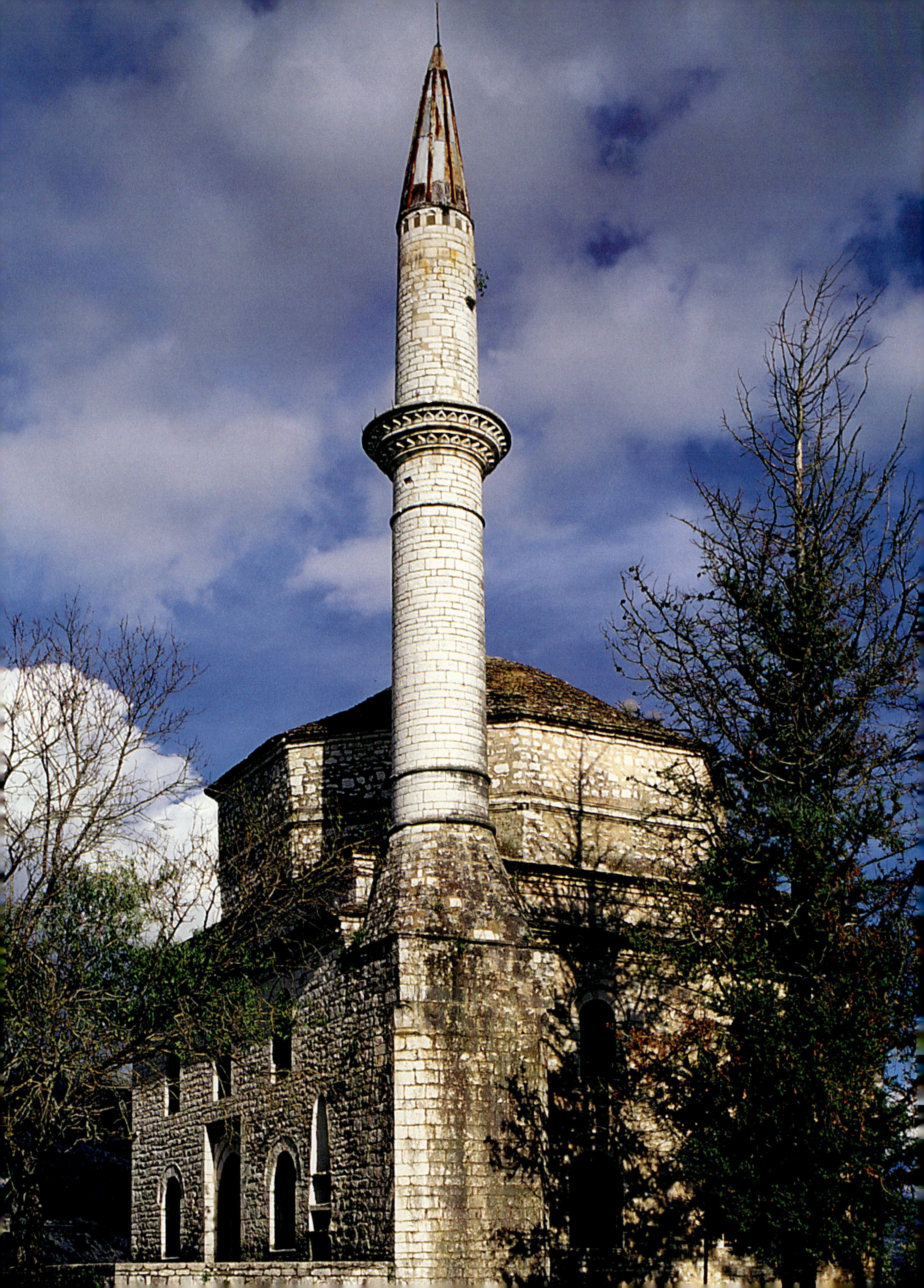

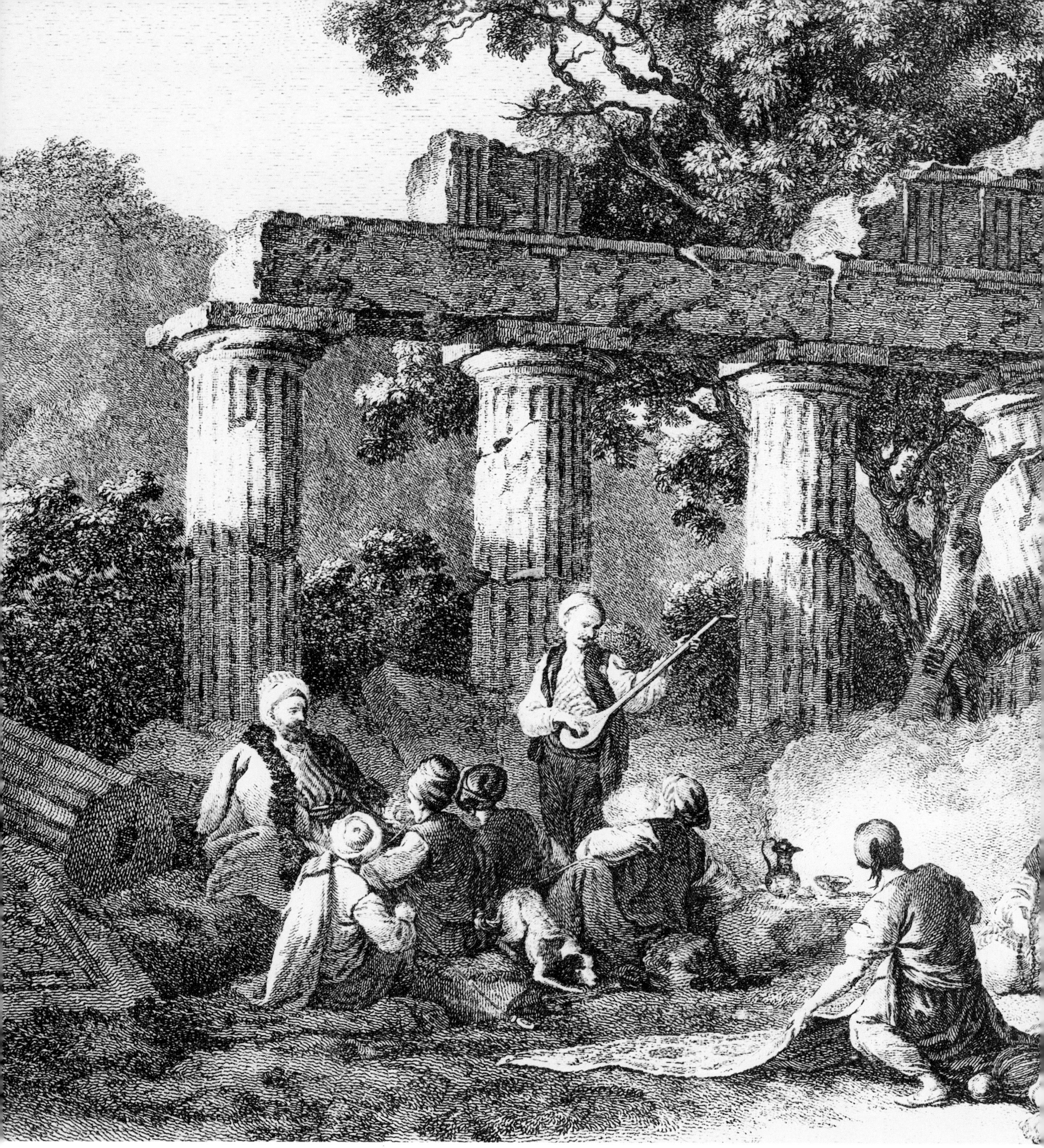

THE RUINS OF THE TEMPLE OF MARS

This engraving is a perfect example of the feelings expressed by artists and travelers in the Romantic period.

They set out to follow the traces of great heroes such as Pericles or Leonidas and found only slaves: mere shadows of their illustrious ancestors. Through their writings and drawings they expressed the sense of a country dying amidst the ruins of its former glory.

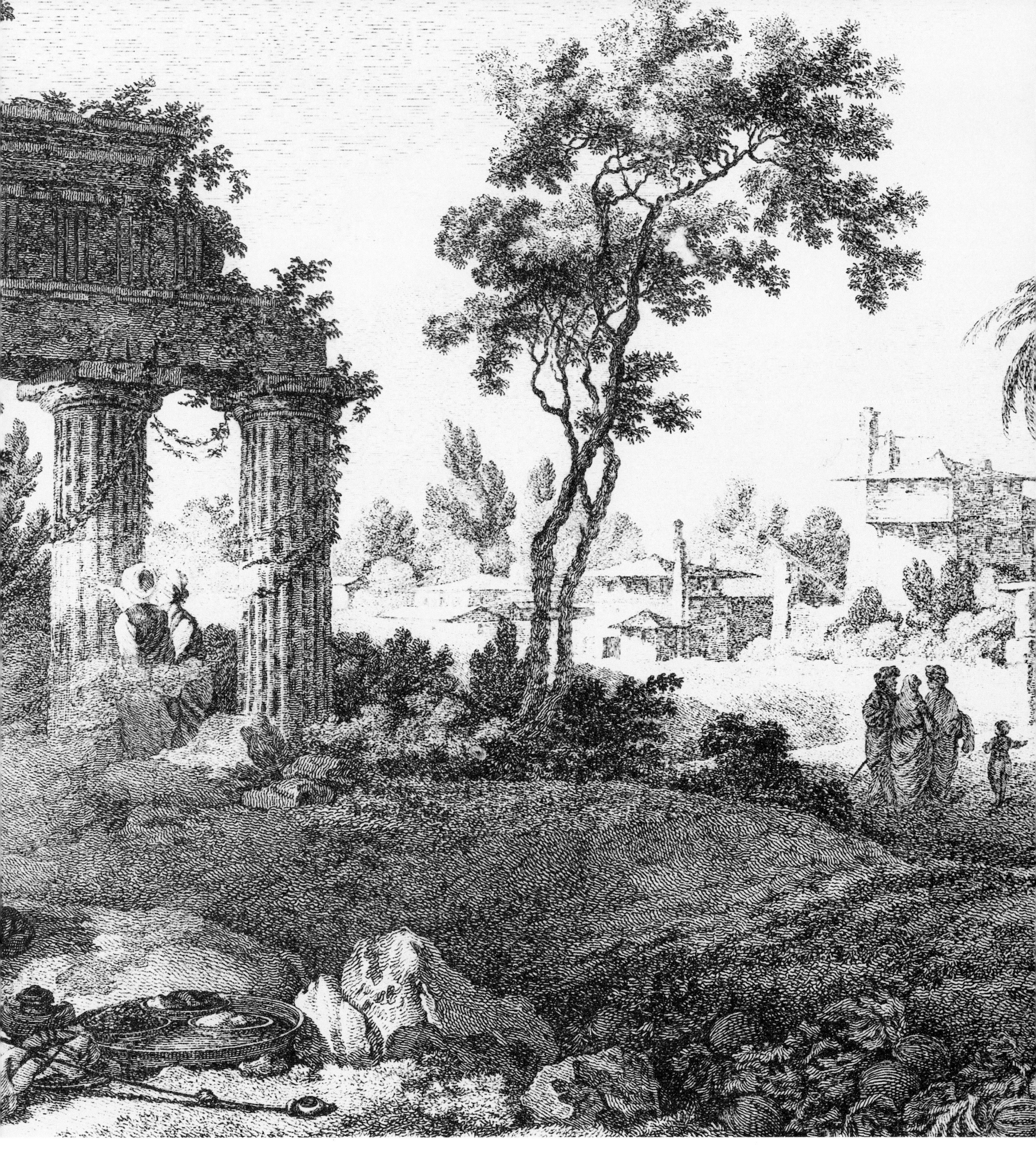

Amongst these ruins the Ottoman Turks reigned as masters. Through their moving flights of oratory, Lord Byron and Chateaubriand impressed upon the conscience of Europe the misfortunes of contemporary Greece. 'We could have heard the citizens applauding the speeches of Demosthenes. But alas, no such sound struck our ears. Just a few whimpers from a people of slaves came from these walls so long accustomed to the voices of a free people… Where are the divine spirits which raised the temple on whose ruins I had been sitting?' (Chateaubriand, *Journey from Paris to Jerusalem*).

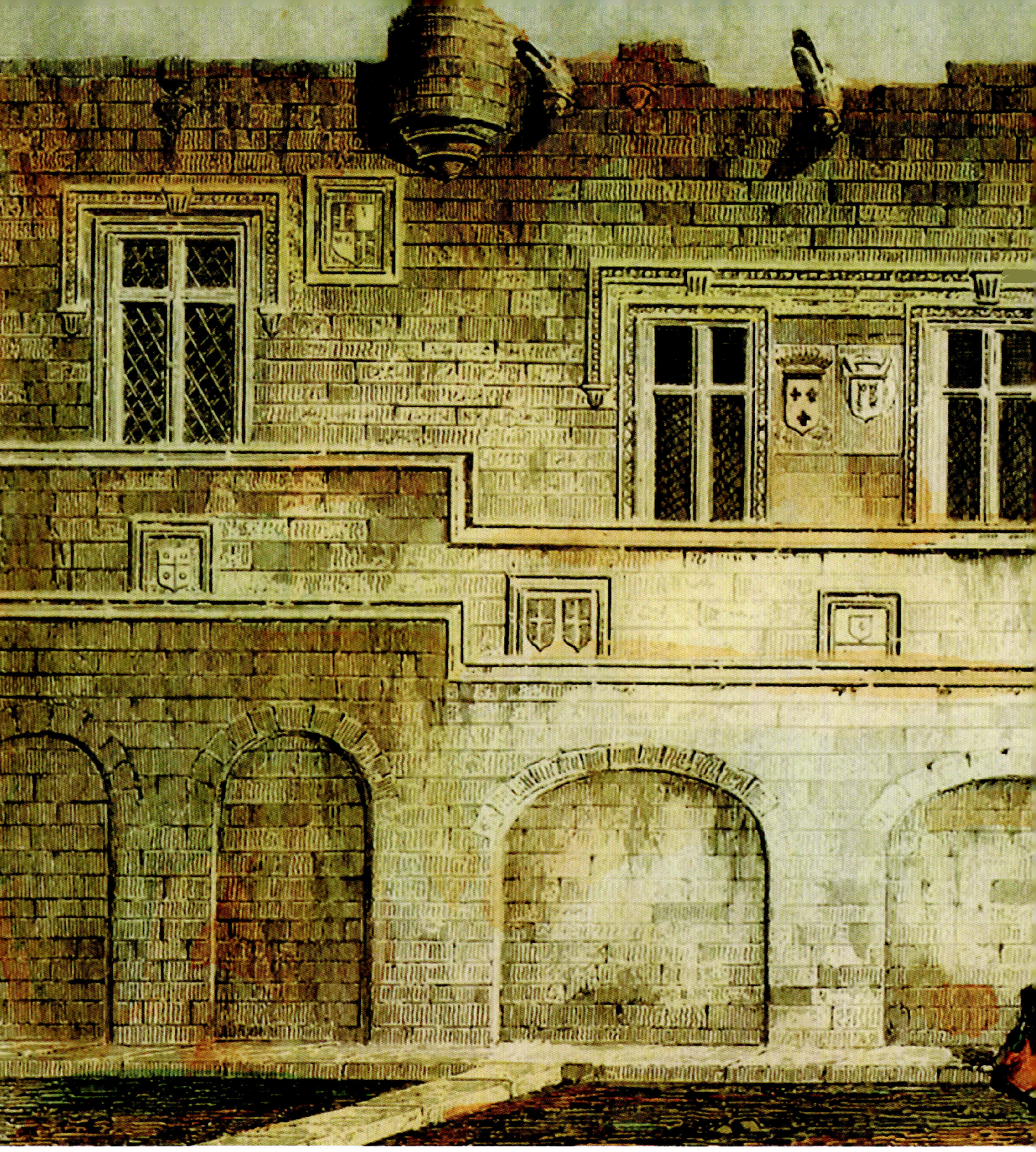

THE PALACE OF THE GRAND MASTERS OF RHODES

In 1309 Rhodes was the stronghold of the religious and military order of the Knights of St John who fought against the Ottomans and fortified the city of Rhodes, leaving striking architectural remains behind them: they were defeated and expelled in 1523. The Turks turned the Grand Masters' palace into a prison. But in 1856 a powder store blew up and destroyed the fortress. The Italians invaded the island in 1912 and restored the palace, often attracting the criticisms of Viollet-le-Duc.

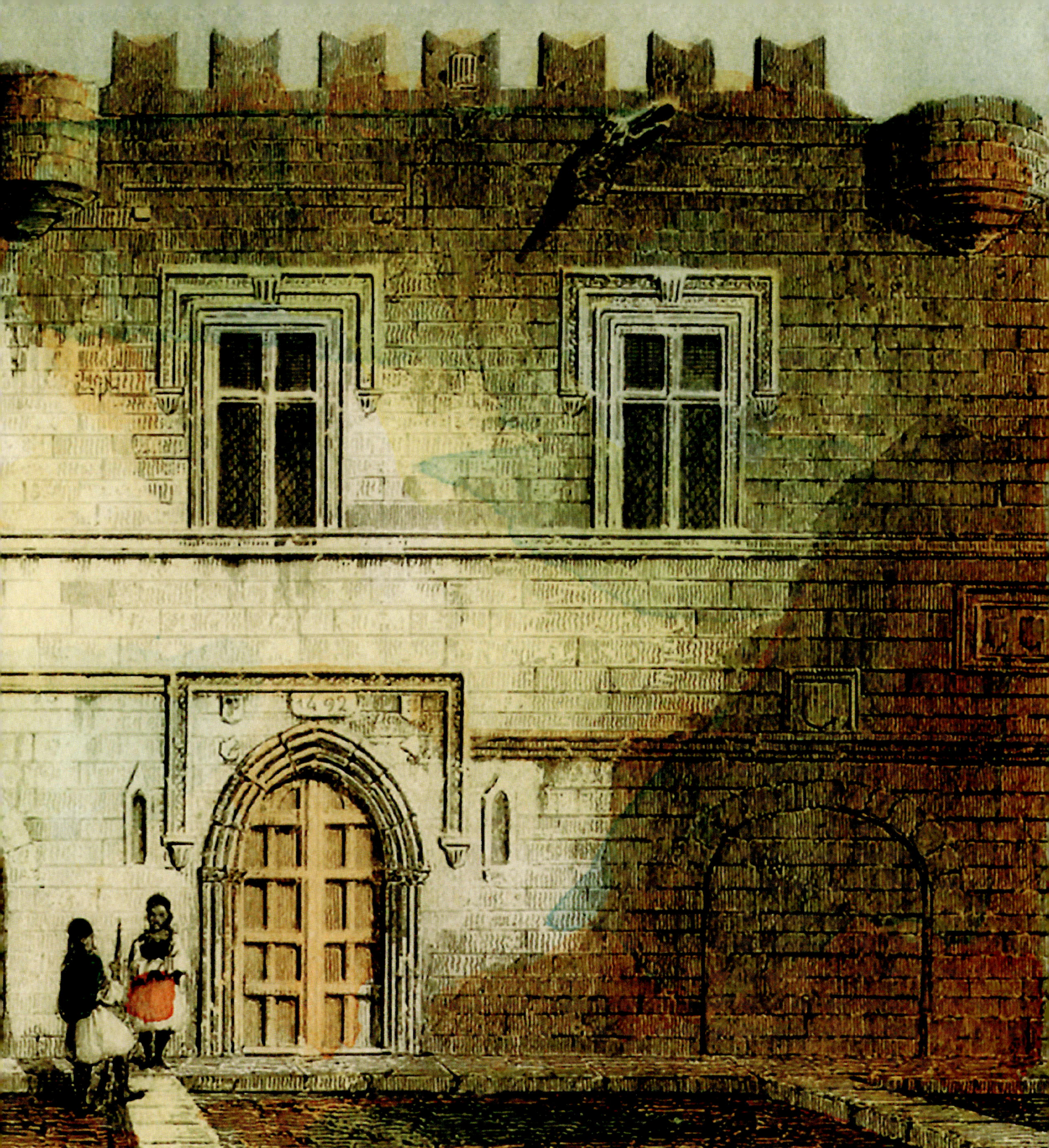

A PUBLIC SQUARE ON KOS

Turkish customs gradually spread throughout the conquered land. This everyday scene could be seen repeated all over Ottoman Greece.

The conquerors were soon imitated by the local gentry as they sat talking and smoking long pipes beneath awnings on the public square. The remains of some pillars may still be seen, together with a minaret in the background.

FOLLOWING PAGES

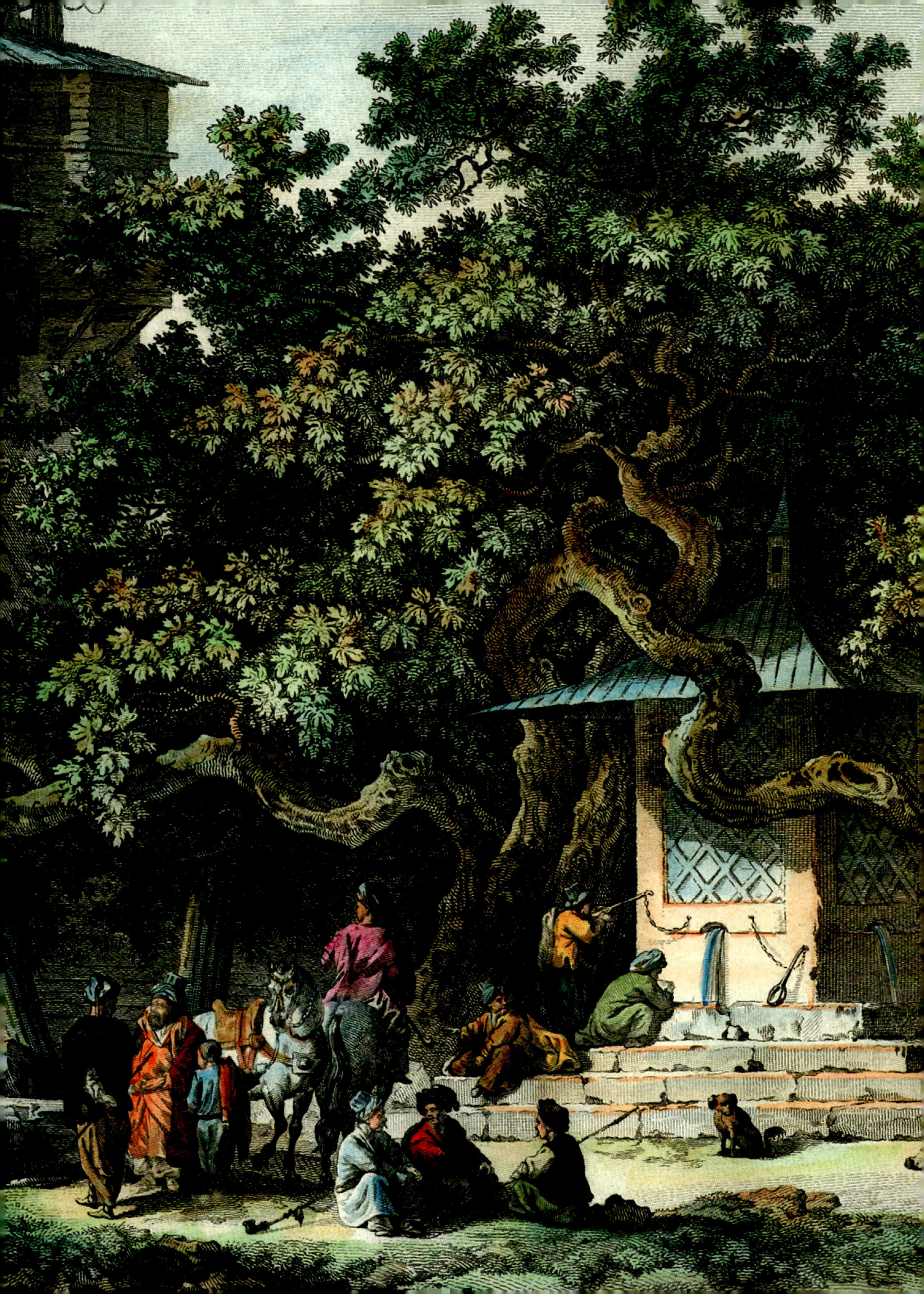

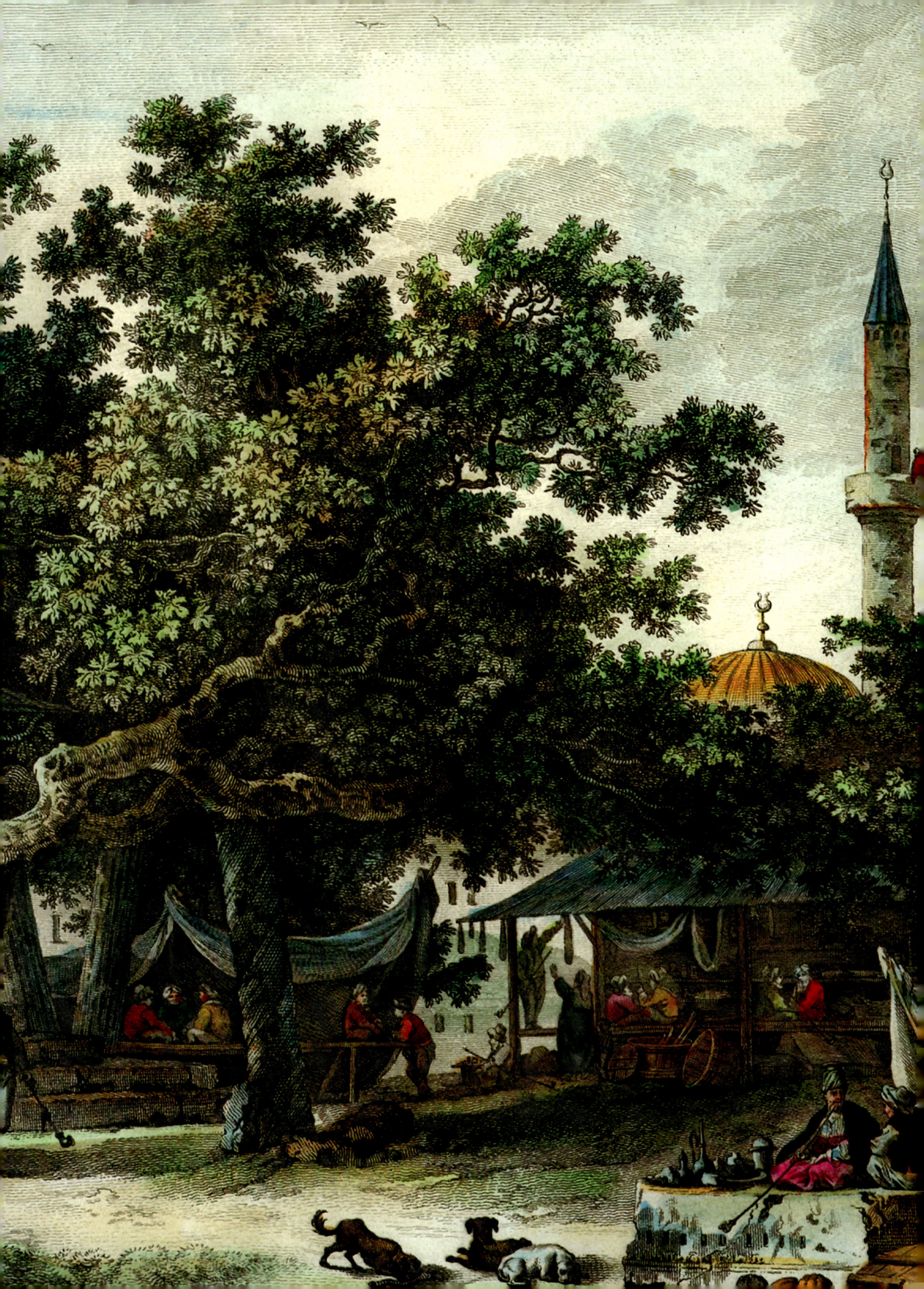

HEROINES OF THE RESISTANCE

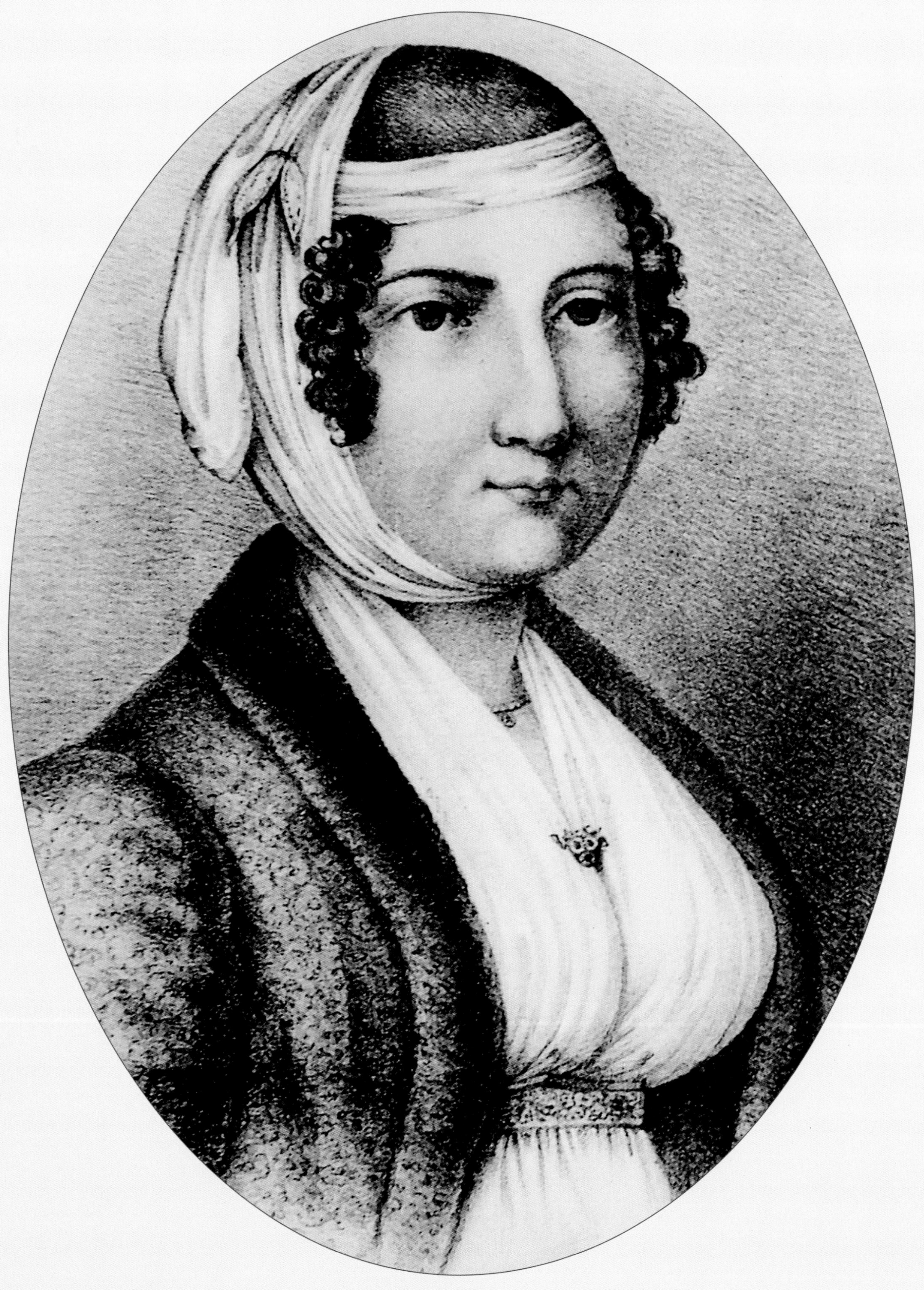

BOUBOULINA

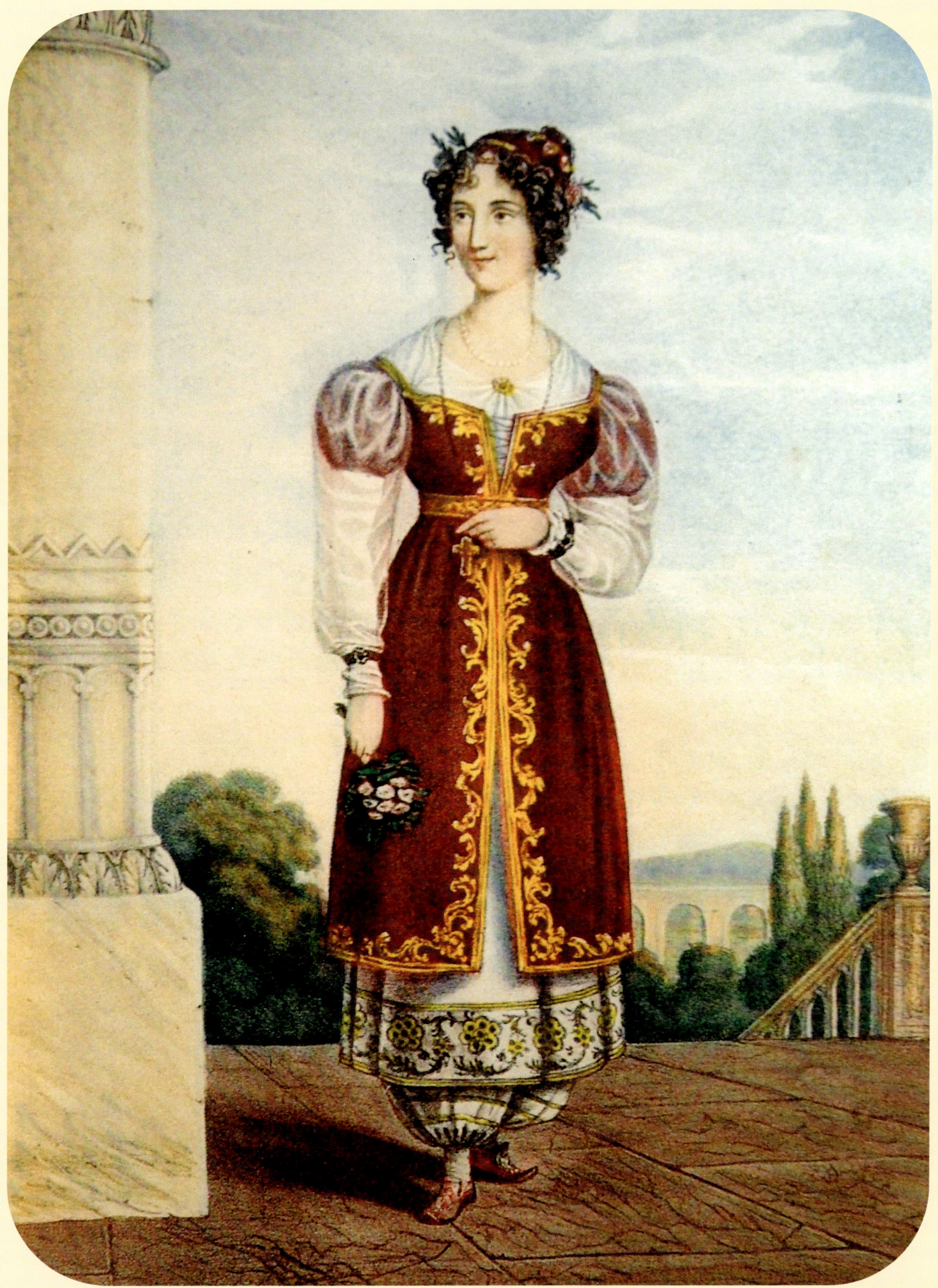

MADO

HEROES OF THE RESISTANCE

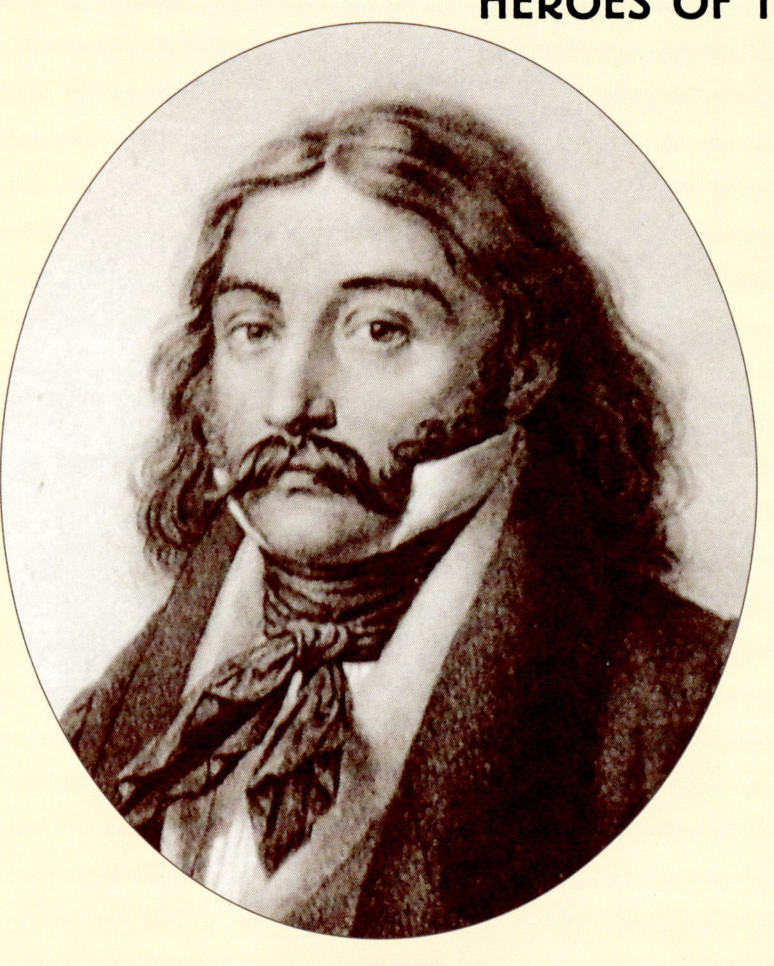

MAVROKORDATO

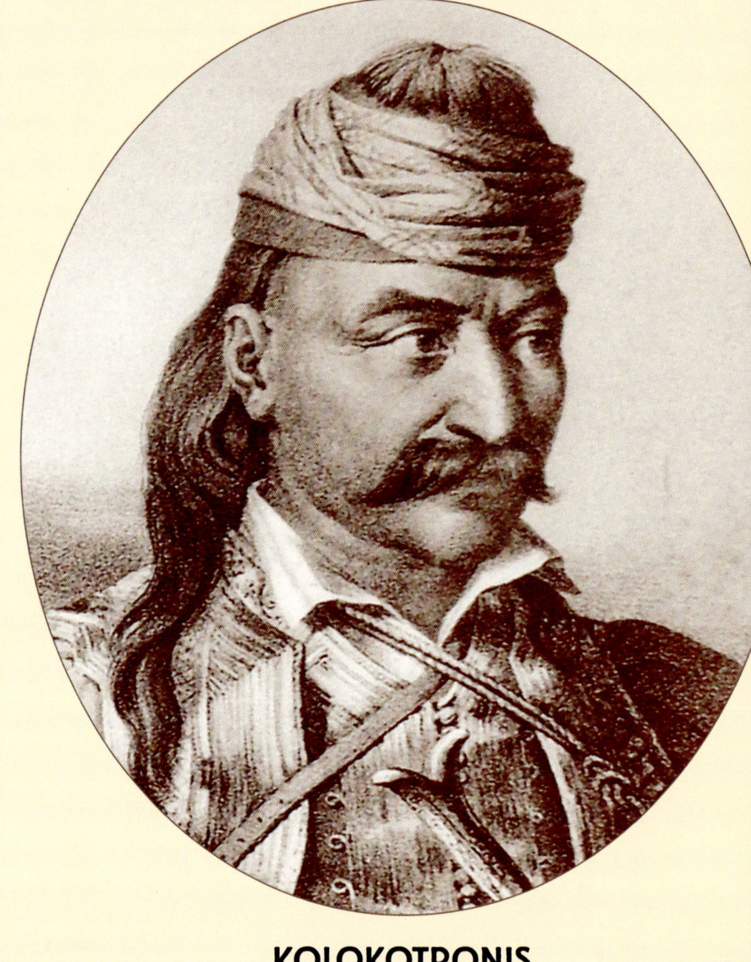

KOLOKOTRONIS

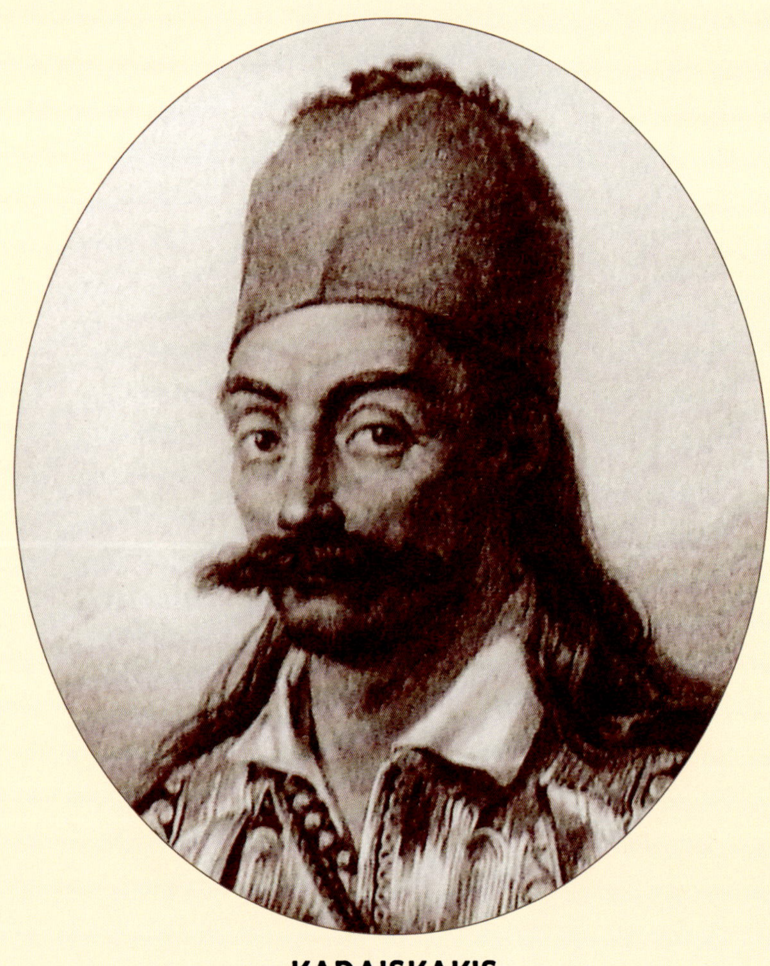

KARAISKAKIS

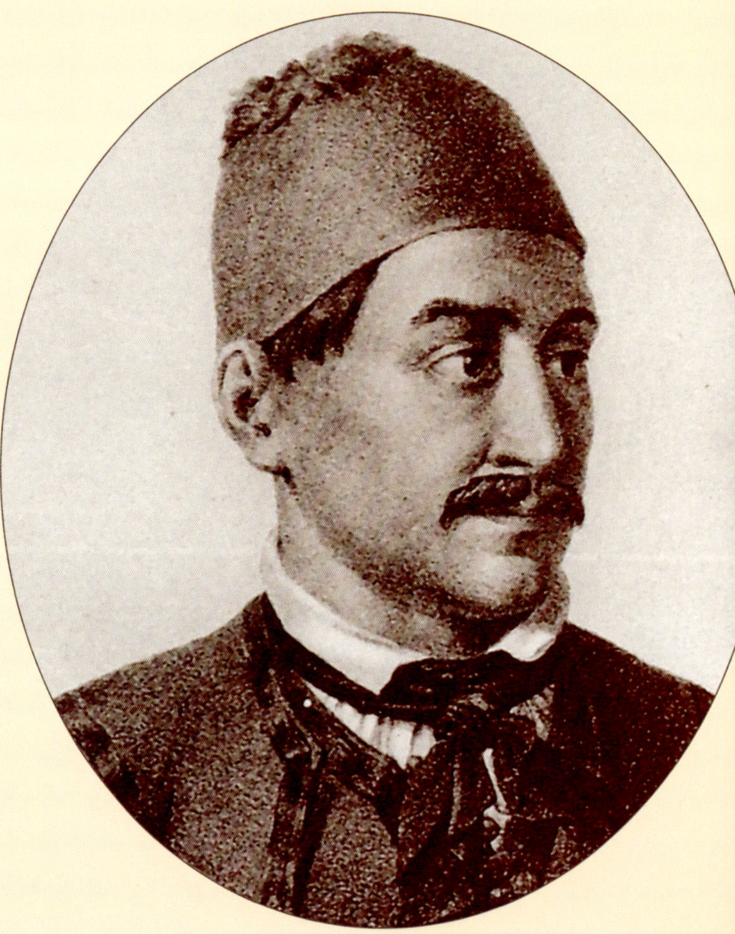

KONDURIOTTIS

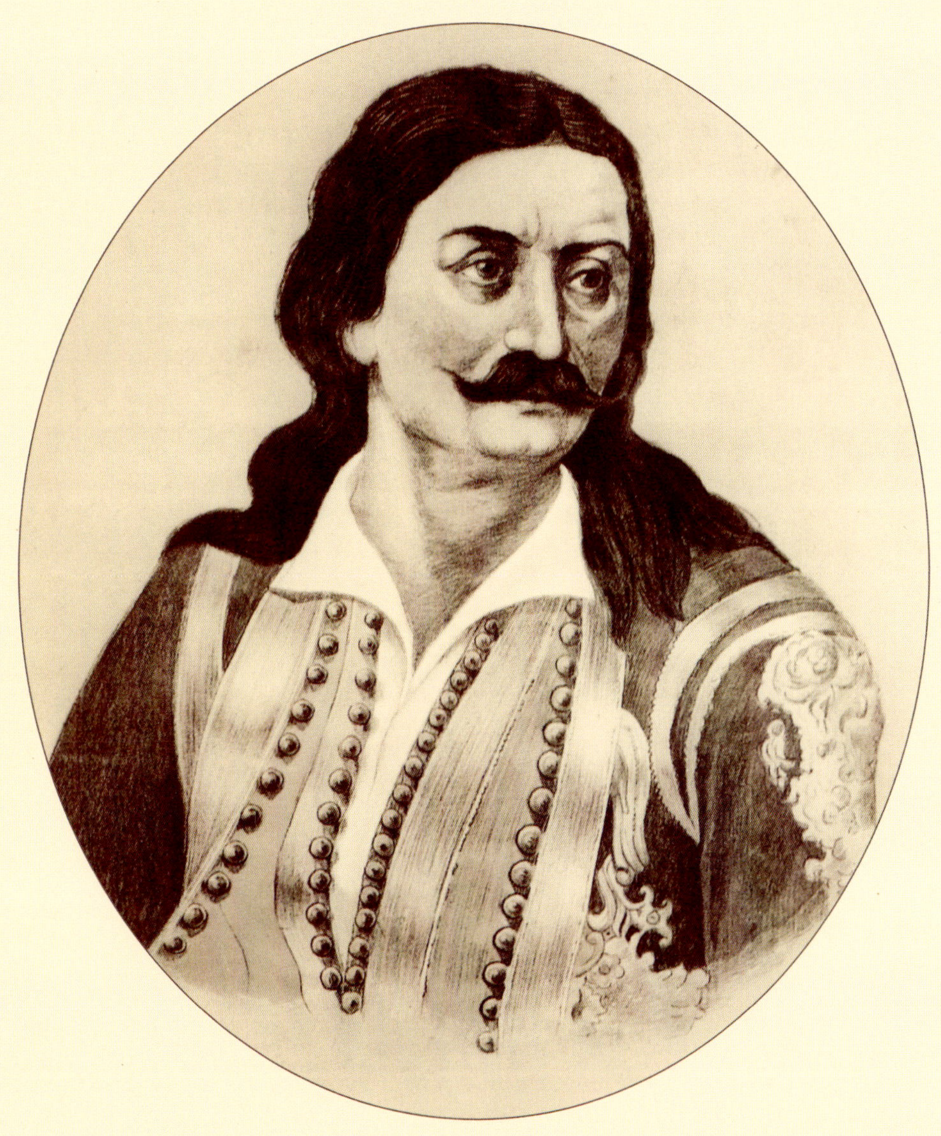

DIAKOS

THE GREEK RESISTANCE

The Ottoman conquest, the arbitrary way power was exercised, together with exploitation and repression, created rebel gangs of armed Greeks who lived on the margins of society. Their numbers increased up to the time of the 1821 Insurrection. These brigands, called "klephtes", controlled the mountains in which they had sought refuge, at Epirus for instance. They were mobile and secretive and waged guerilla warfare against the oppressor. The Turks created a Geek armed militia to fight against them and to maintain order. But the dividing line between the two was vague. Both groups were made up of men accustomed to combat and the use of arms. They also duped the Turkish authorities and enjoyed a certain amount of latitude. The exploits of intrepid and uncatchable brigands were told around the fireside in the evenings. Popular songs celebrated these heroes and painted them in glowing colors: they were freedom-loving adventurers, young, handsome, brave, unruly and impetuous. They were soon participating actively in civil war and became brave 'palikares', freeing Greek regions from the occupier. They were generally from lower-income backgrounds, in direct conflict of interest with the middle classes who wished to control the independence struggle. Portraits of such resistance members were lithographed and distributed all over Europe. Amongst their number were Theodoros Kolokotronis, Athanasius Diakos and George Karaiskakis. Two women also became famous heroines of the War of Independence. Laskarina Bouboulina, who came from the island of Spetses and commanded the Greek fleet during the 1820s, while Mado Mavrogeni fought in numerous battles at the head of a fleet based on the island of Paros.

1687: THE VENETIANS BLOW UP THE PARTHENON, USED AS A MOSQUE BY THE TURKS, AND THEN AS A POWDER STORE

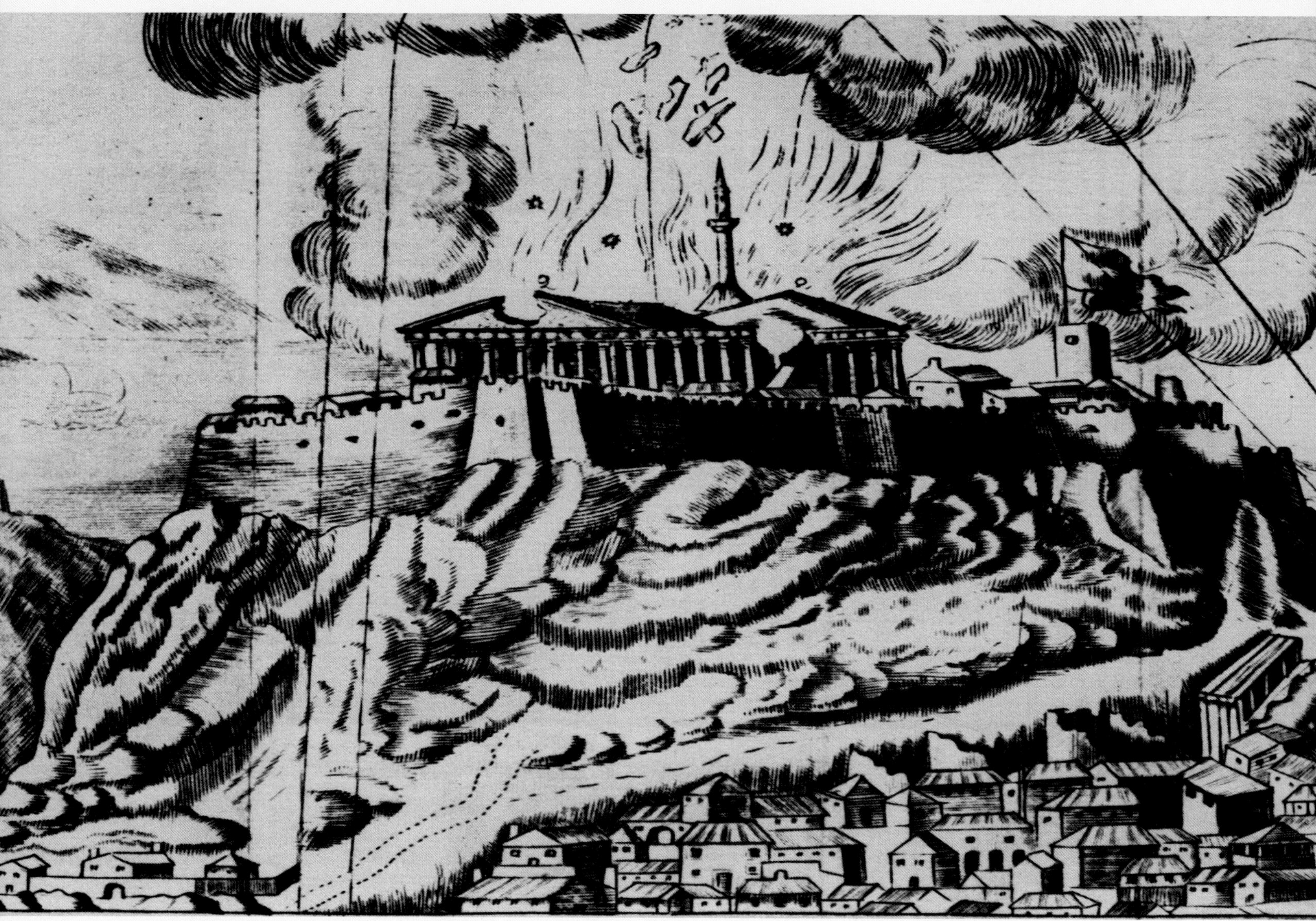

SONGS AS AN EXPRESSION OF THE GREEK SOUL

This became a forceful means of expression with the national re-awakening from the end of the 18th century on. Poetry spoke of revolt against Ottoman authority, the desire for independence, but also portrayed universal human themes like love and death.

EXTRACT FROM THE SONG OF A WIDOW TO HER FAR-OFF SON

'You took away my husband, you made me a widow.
You took away my little birds twelve years ago.
Cursed, be you, foreign soil, and cursed be the Turks
Who distressed my house and dressed me in black.'

DESIRE

'I kissed a red lip and mine was stained with red,
I pressed a handkerchief against it and the handkerchief was stained,
I washed it in the river and the river was stained,
And the edges of the sea and the middle of the Ocean.
The eagle came down to drink and its wings were stained,
And half the sun and all the moon.
I had for you, my love, posted three sentries:
The sun over the mountains, an eagle over the plains
And the wet Northern wind over the ships.
But the sun went down, and the eagle fell asleep
And the wet Northern wind was carried away by the ships.
So Charon found the moment to take you away from me.'

ON THE 20TH AND 21ST OCTOBER 1827 FRENCH, ENGLISH AND RUSSIAN FORCES CRUSHED THE TURKS AT NAVARINO OPENING THE WAY FOR GREEK INDEPENDENCE

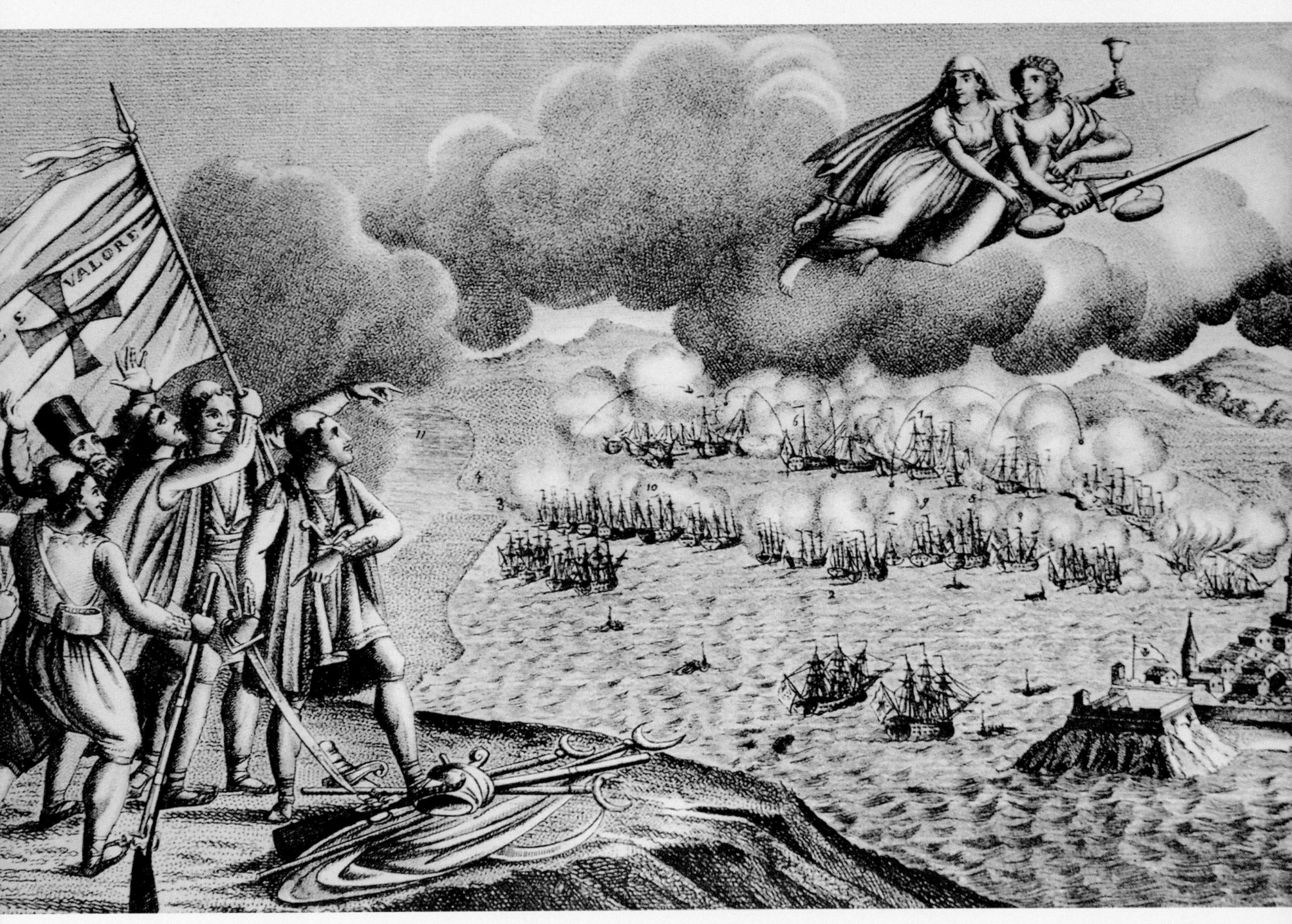

SOLOMOS AND INDEPENDENCE

The poet Solomos (1798-1857) took his inspiration from the Greek War of Independence and the Battle of Missolonghi when he wrote the poem, *The Flag*:

FEMALE COSTUMES FROM ELEUSIS AND MALE COSTUMES FROM METSOVON, LIKE THOSE OF THE *PALIKARES* FREEDOM FIGHTERS

FOLLOWING PAGES

THE FLAG

'Like a sun, like the serene upper air,
Carrying worlds,
From the black cloud and the dark bitumen,
The flagstaff rises up, and at its foot
The throng of brave palikares, and at its peak
the flag.
Murmuring, talking,
And everywhere, waving, the cross
In the wonderful blueness laden with bravery,
And the proud sky looked on admiringly
And earth broke into cheers.
So many voices raised to the light,
Scattering the noble flowers of love,and crying:
'You are invincible, wonderful, revered and holy!'

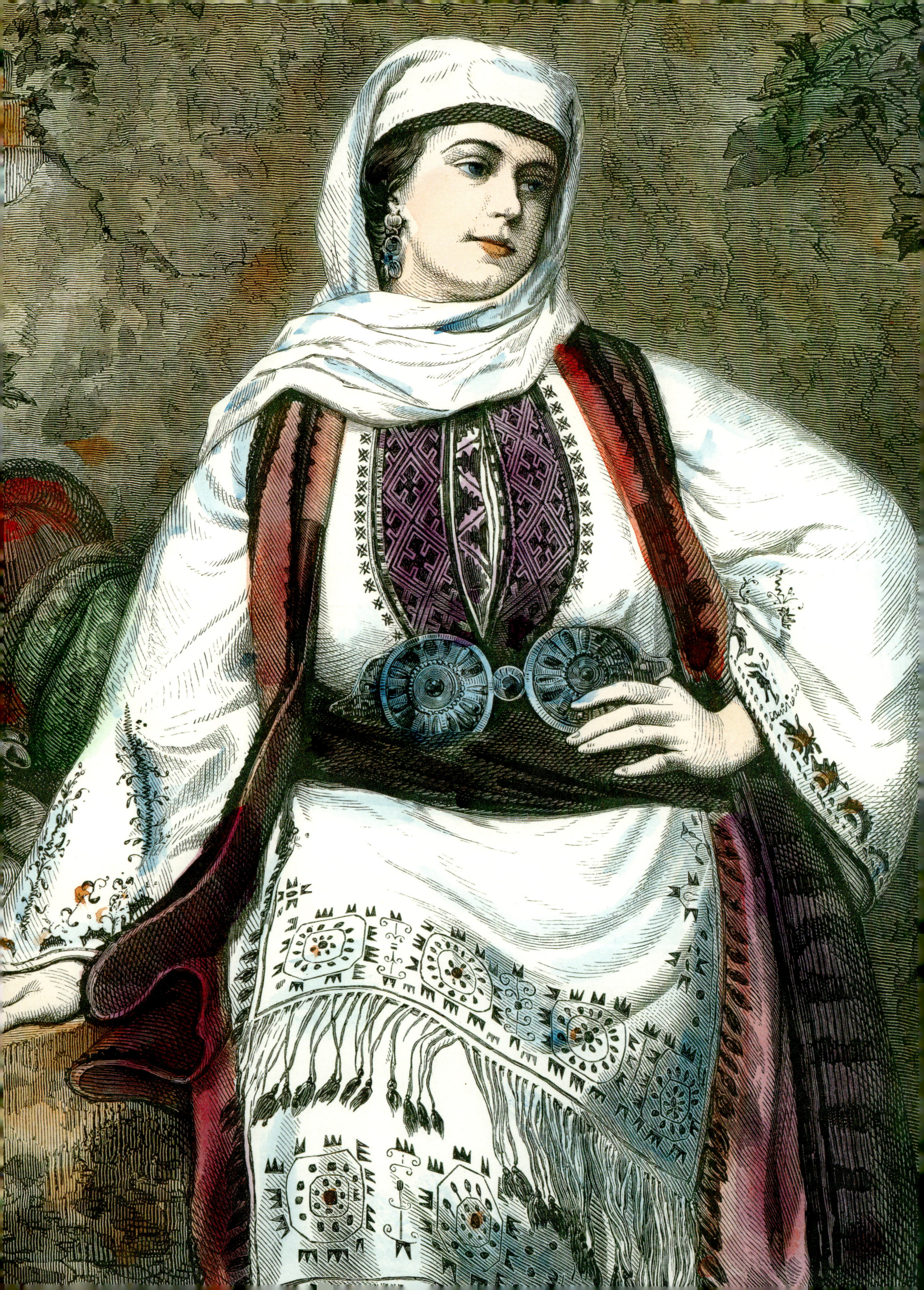

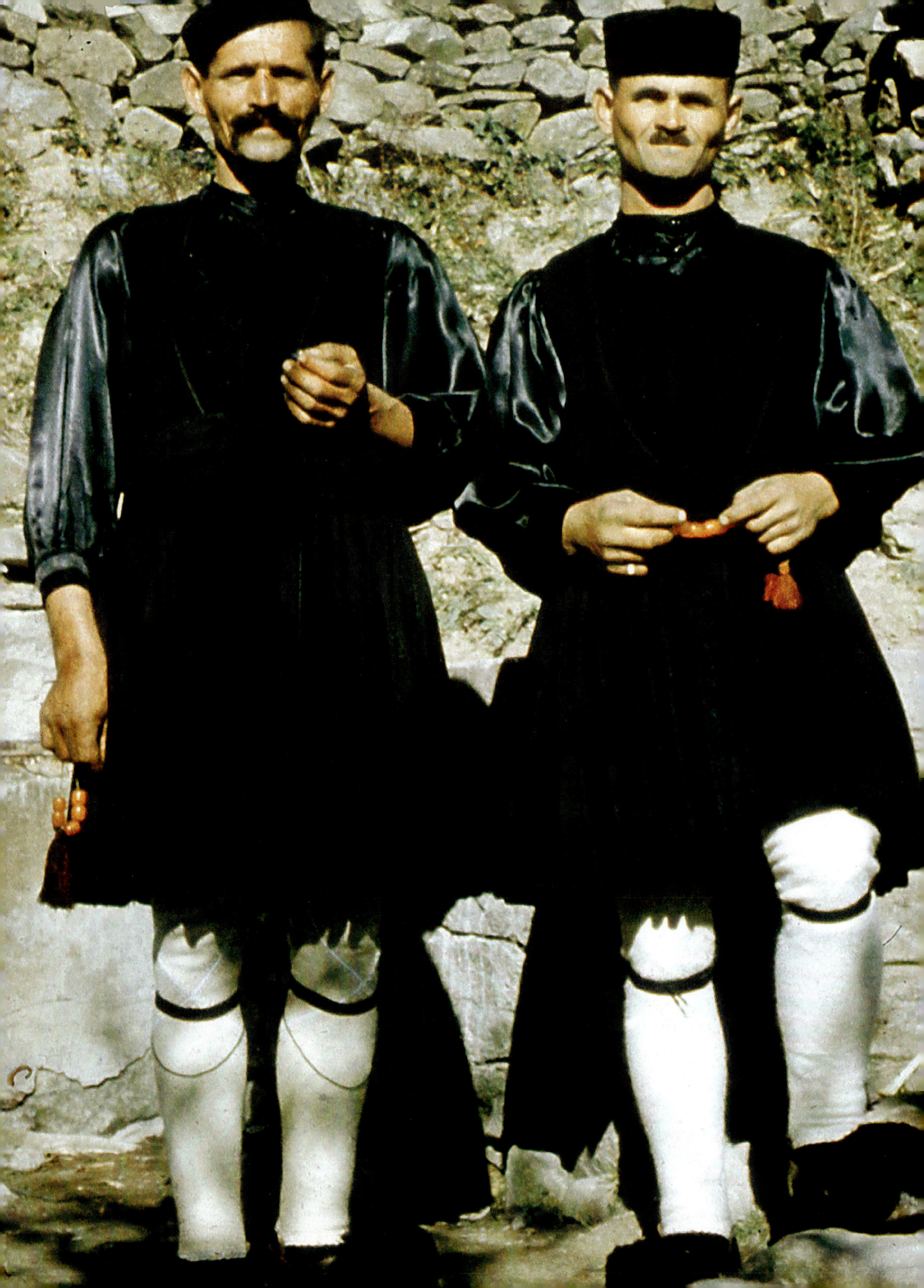

THE GORGES OF THE ERKINA AT LIVADIA

The Erkina, the river flowing through Livadia, the capital of Boeotia, fits narrowly between the Agios Ilias Mountains and Laphystion. This land is cool, bright and green, in sharp contrast with the reputation of these gorges in times past. They were associated with the sinister and menacing oracle of Trophonius and inspired terror in the Ancients. A mocking proverb used to say that only the silent returned with assurance to this place. In fact those who came to consult the oracle often came out shocked and terrorized. The old Turkish bridge crosses the stream just below the sources. They were called the sources of Forgetfulness and of Memory and come out of a cliff full of carved niches with ex-votos. Worshippers drank from one spring and then from the other in order to forget their past and to remember what happened in the god's cave. Having sacrificed to the gods and purified themselves in the water of the river, worshippers went to the cave on Mount Agios Ilias. They entered on foot with honey cakes as offerings in their hands. They sometimes did not come out for several days and then always feet first. Every stage of the ritual resembled a form of initiation in the shape of a descent to the dead. The cave of Trophonius, a hero and god of the earth, was doubtless the entrance to the realm of Hades!

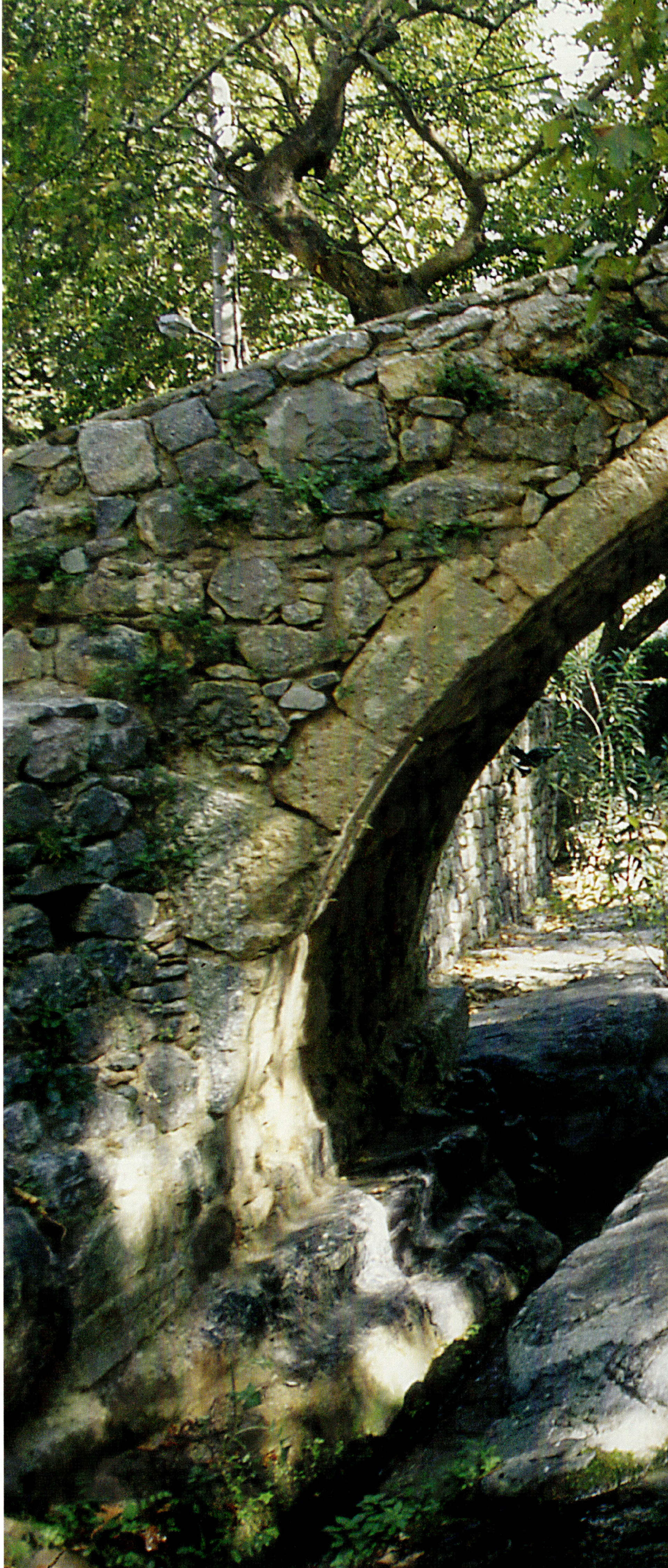

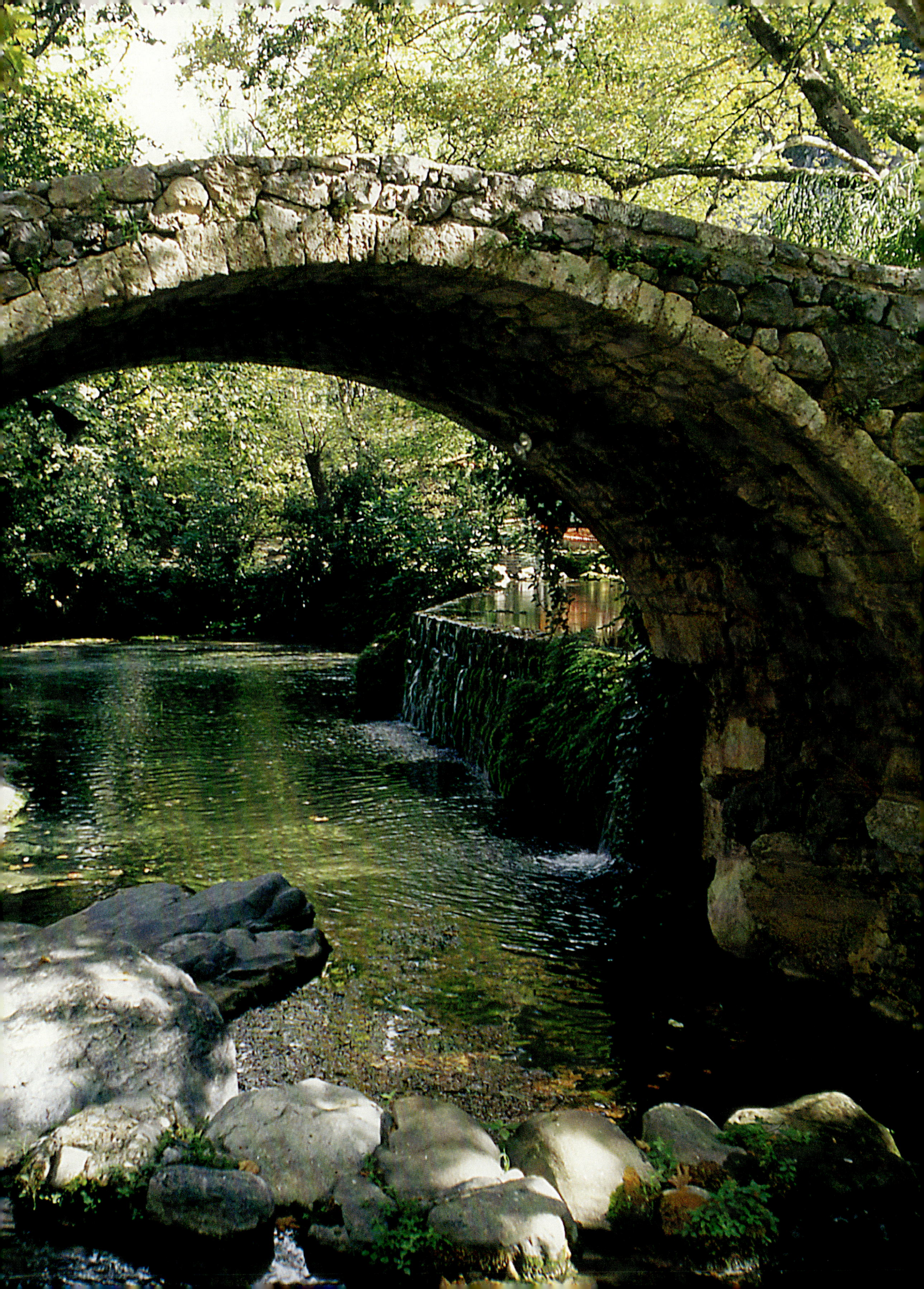

DISCOVERING MODERN GREECE

It doesn't matter what your reasons are for going abroad: if you are looking for a summer of sea, sand and sun, or if you are in love with old stones and ancient ruins, or if you are just curious about whatever it is that happens to fall beneath your gaze, then Greece has something for you! Some come looking for modern, lively resorts, buzzing with festivals and pulsating with nightlife; others seek havens of calm, peace and tranquility. Greece, with its ever-changing landscapes, its multitudes of islands and its long history can satisfy the visitor's every requirement. When setting out to explore a country, one must, of course, seek to satisfy all the senses, here everyone is free to wander, be surprised, pause, turn around, look again and be enchanted…

Planes no longer land on a dusty runway beside the sea, visitors no longer struggle into a decrepit and rusty shed, wondering if they have arrived at the end of the world. Since 2001 travelers in transit walk along the modern antiseptic corridors of Elefterios Venizelos airport; they have to wait until they get out to the Piraeus to feel they are in a different country. Indeed many skip Athens on the way out, and it is only on the way back that they will visit this large city which, truth to tell, does not have a very good reputation. Then they will 'do' the Acropolis or take a stroll in Plaka.

But Athens has many more treasures than that: you must take the time to contemplate the Acropolis from the Hill of the Muses. Up here the air is always fresh and the trees provide shade and a welcome coolness. Up here you get a wonderful view across to the Parthenon and Athena's citadel. It is just as pleasant to walk on the high ground of Strefi Hill or to climb to the top of Lykavettos Hill for dinner. These oases of green are more attractive than the dusty lanes of the Monastiraki district or the streets and steps of Exarcheia. Yet these places too are well worth exploring.

Nevertheless it is frequently at the Piraeus that tourists have their first cultural experience of Greece. Passports at the ready, they are about to set out for the islands and they can now relax. They can sit outside a café on the quays and enjoy the morning sun. They soon become aware of the riot of sound that surrounds them, not to mention the dramas being played out all around them. The music has its own local tone and charm. It is different from what is normal in the west; the songs on the radio have the beguiling and gentle accents of the east. They never totally block out the noises from stalls, kiosks and taverns all around the harbor. They seem to set the tone for the bustle on the quays, as cars and pedestrians scurry to get onto the ferries. Whistles blow and officers in immaculate white uniforms direct the traffic with imperious gestures. The Greeks jostle to get on or off; you would think it was all part of some unfathomable competition! The tourists are dragged along, somewhat bemused by so much commotion. Families call out to each other, their cries mingling with those of the hucksters who endlessly recite the names of their wares, the treats that the Greeks just have to have at all times of the day.

It is at pilgrimage time that the flurry is at its height. As we come up to the 15th of August the ships serving the island of Tinos are packed with pilgrims, many gypsies amongst them. Bright dresses are spread out on highly colored blankets on the decks and gangways. Soon a white splash stretches out in the blue of the sea behind the boat. On the outside decks the travelers enjoy the view and treat every time they arrive into a port as if it were a special event, time for a party.

All journeys in Greece, be they by boat, train, car or bike, are considered to be astounding events and have to be celebrated, one way or another: scattered along the side of the roads you see little chapels commemorating travelers killed in road accidents. They remind travelers of the risks involved in travel and urge them to be careful. At evening time old women sometimes light candles before these memorials. During the night the candles burn in prayer and these enigmatic guardians of the highways keep watch. For those who realize what they are, these will o' the wisps are fretful reminders of risk. As one passes through the countryside numerous domed churches dot the landscape, often built in the most isolated and difficult spots. In the train or on the bus women punctuate their conversations by crossing themselves every time they pass a chapel, a cross or a graveyard, but also every time they talk about something unsafe. The Greeks are expressive and demonstrative about their faith. They still go to church in large numbers, particularly at feasts, and crowds of people go on pilgrimage; they light candles, kiss the icons and kneel down before them in prayer.

On the 15th August in Tinos, many make the pilgrimage in as difficult a manner as they can: on their knees, or crawling along on their tummies. They slowly make their way to the church of Our Lady of the Annunciation, high above the town. These processions are made in fulfillment of vows made to the Blessed Virgin: some are thanking her for a miraculous cure, others asking for her intervention.

You have barely traveled a couple of miles and you find you have strayed from the well known paths and are no longer on the tourist trail; you have passed from a modern, spruced up Greece to a more detached Greece. Take a few steps away from the bustling city districts with their shops and leisure centers, and you find that time has stopped. That is when you discover another side to a country of many contrasts. The countryside and the islands are often forsaken. Villages have grown old and the people have moved away. One passes old shepherds and farmers, perched on a donkey or bent over in a field. They have become the stereotype of a Greece now only seen on post cards. Sometimes they sit beside the road trying to sell their meager harvest of fruit and vegetables. Many houses have been shut up. The brightly painted blues, greens and reds of proud rural houses have lost their luster, and bright colors no longer contrast with their whitewashed walls. But the old faded tones and flaking paint lend them an old fashioned and poignant charm. Doors and windows hang open and you glimpse a crumbling wall, and then you see through them to the sea in the background. Nature is gently taking over and flowers grow over the skeleton of the house. The cities know such districts too, neglected and shabby. Ermoupolis is such a case; it was an old Venetian city with aristocratic buildings. Visiting such places in the midday heat adds to the deadness of these ghost towns. The siesta passes in total silence, blinds down, with an occasional figure glimpsed in the dimness of a village bar.

Café tables set outside, attract the travelers' attention, inviting them to pause beneath the shade of a trellised vine or of a leafy tree, offering the tempting promise of coolness, quiet and conversation. Even the tiniest village has its café. The customers are usually men. The older ones often spend most of the day there. They sit with their backs to the wall, facing the street; they often stay a long time, silent, without moving. They watch the passers-by, and eye the newcomers, fingering a komboloï, which gives them an impression of composure and keeps boredom away. But discussions often become lively and strident. They talk loud and fast, in true Mediterranean style, so that the stranger often thinks a quarrel is about to break out. The men also like to play backgammon. Game follows game and the dice and counters click together on the table; it all adds to the familiar atmosphere of the place. Most drink the famous Greek coffee, it is in fact Turkish coffee, but that is not admitted.

Then it is time for ouzo, and following that they go off to partake of the family meal. Cafés and taverns are at the heart of Greek culture. They are the main social centers. In the evenings the Greeks gather there in family groups or in order to meet friends. Go to the taverns if you want to get to know the delights of Greek cooking. Away from the tourist trail or on the less known islands like Siphnos you will find that all is peaceful, preserved from mass tourism. Take a seat bedside the water and eat grilled fish... or lamb kebabs flavored with lemon... or a traditional salad... it is a real pleasure!

It is best to spend the hottest time of the day in the shade, contemplating the way the light sparkles on the clear water, drinking an iced coffee, playing backgammon, before setting off to bathe once more in the sea...

CORFU

These two little islands are situated on the southern point of Corfu. The first is linked to the land by a long, narrow causeway, and is the home of the 17th century monastery of Vlachernes; the second, Pondikonissi, or Mouse Island, also has a monastery.

Legend saw it as the ship which was turned to stone by Poseidon, because it had carried Ulysses to Ithaca. The god had sworn to avenge himself on the hero and was angry with the people who had helped him.

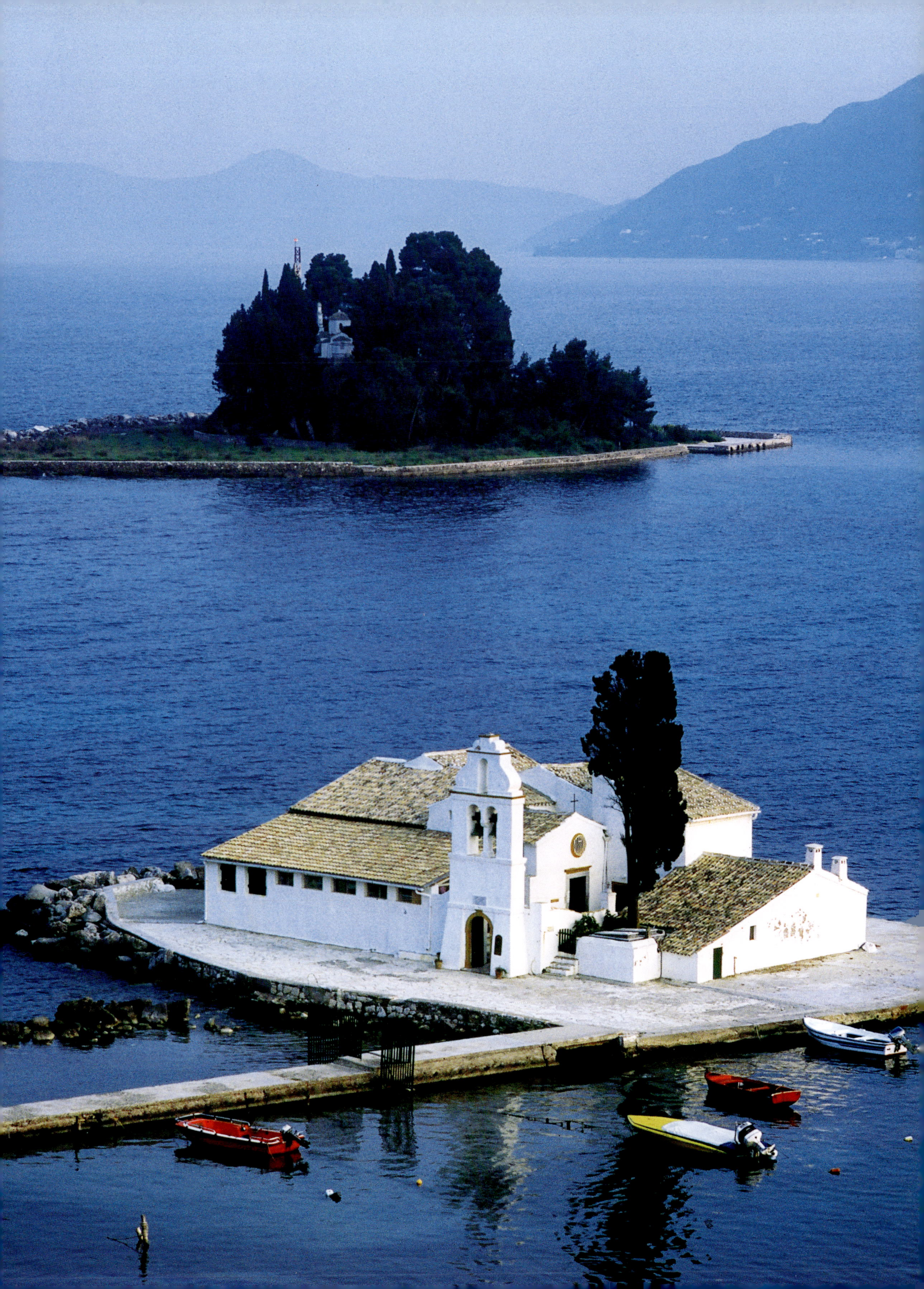

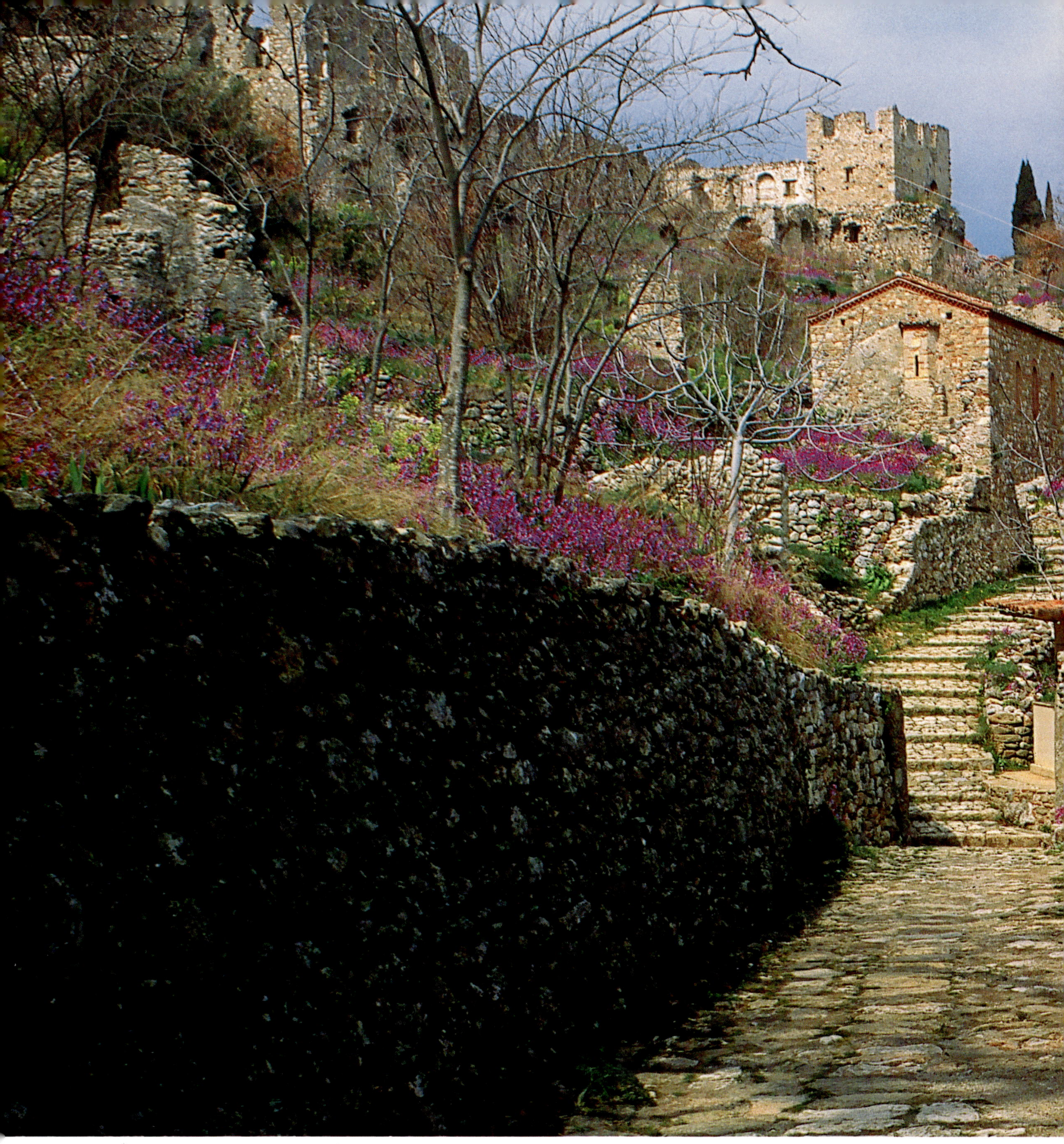

MYSTRA

During the 1830s, a scientific expedition to Morea described it as a ruined town. One could still see the towers of a few churches, some minarets and rows of cypresses like green pyramids. It was crowned by a French fort built on top of a conical rock; the whole site wore a remarkable air of mystery with its castle in ruins and the city abandoned. It was a time when Mystra, the former capital of medieval Morea, was but a shade of its former self. Vegetation has grown over the ruins. Today visitors stroll pensively through a sleeping city. They walk on

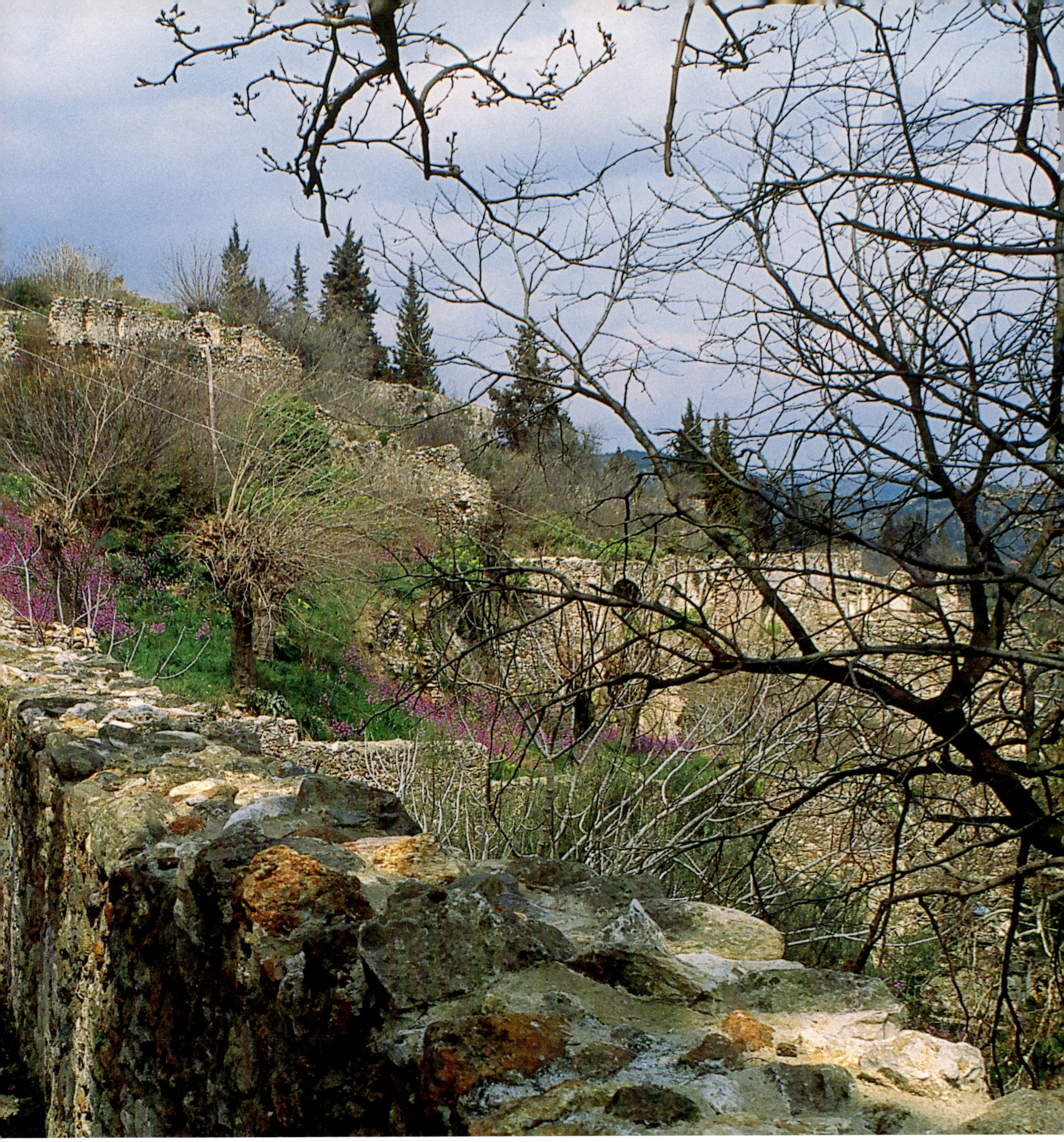

paved streets and admire the remaining churches and frescoes. Mystra inspires respect and contemplation. The memory of the days of the Villehardouin, the local lords, still haunts this ghostly town. There is also the aura left behind by the philosophers and humanists who made it famous.

Gemiste Plethon (1360-1452) was a disciple of Plato and wrote commentaries on his work. He chose to live in Mystra and contributed to its fame. He believed that the powers of the monarch should be reinforced. According to him, the monarch's authority should be based on the middle classes of the town and that the rights of the property-owning classes, that is the Church and the aristocracy, should be limited.

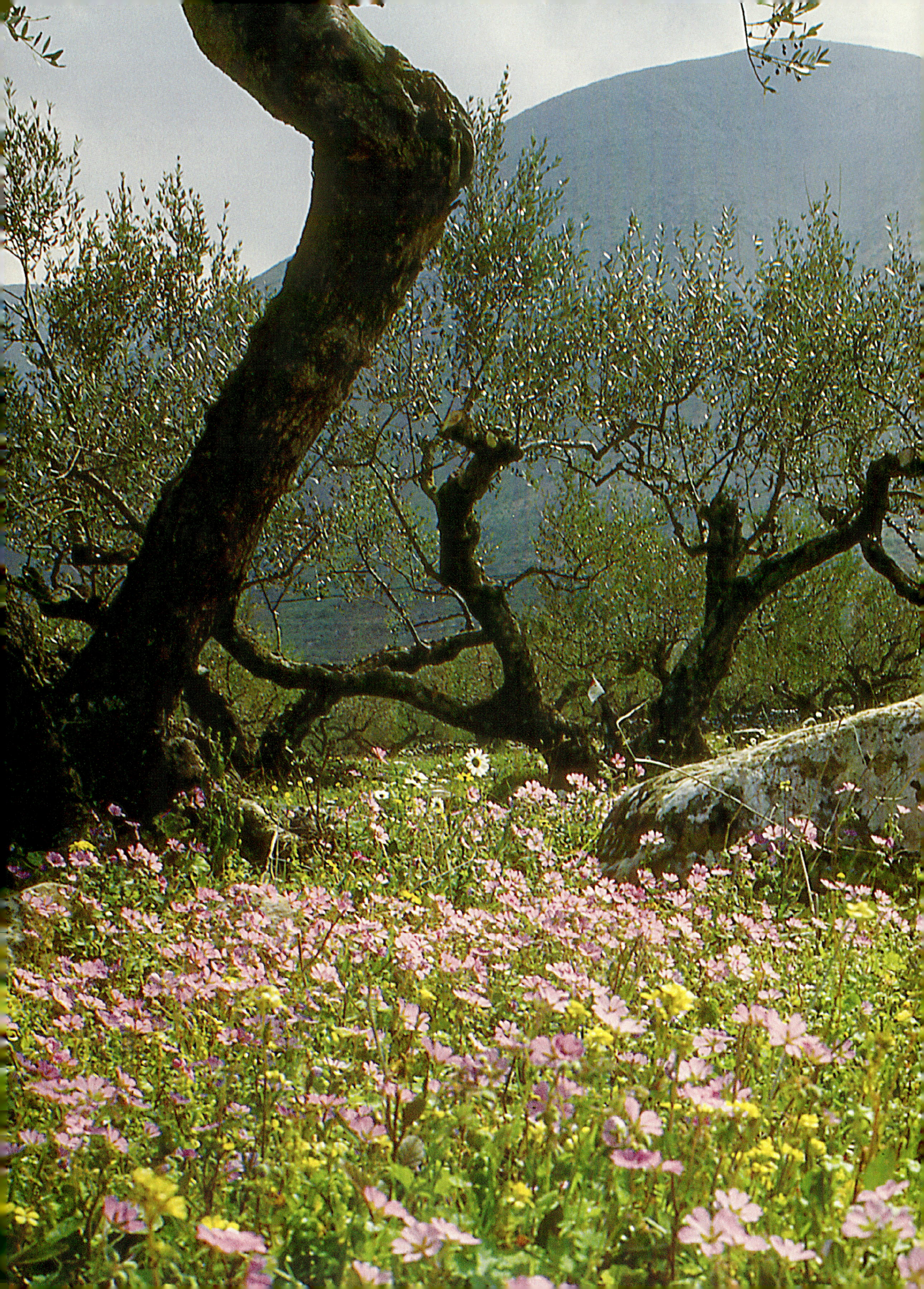

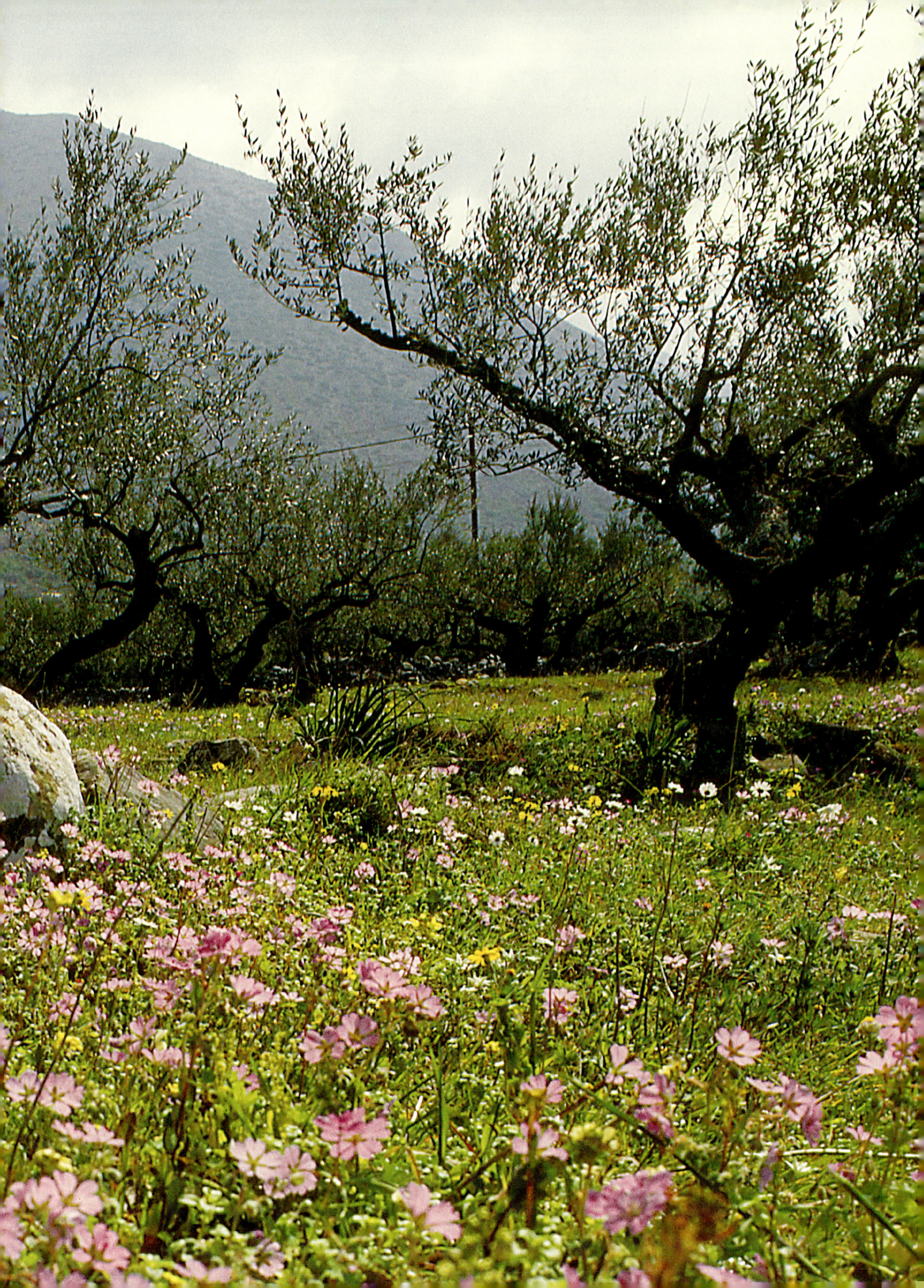

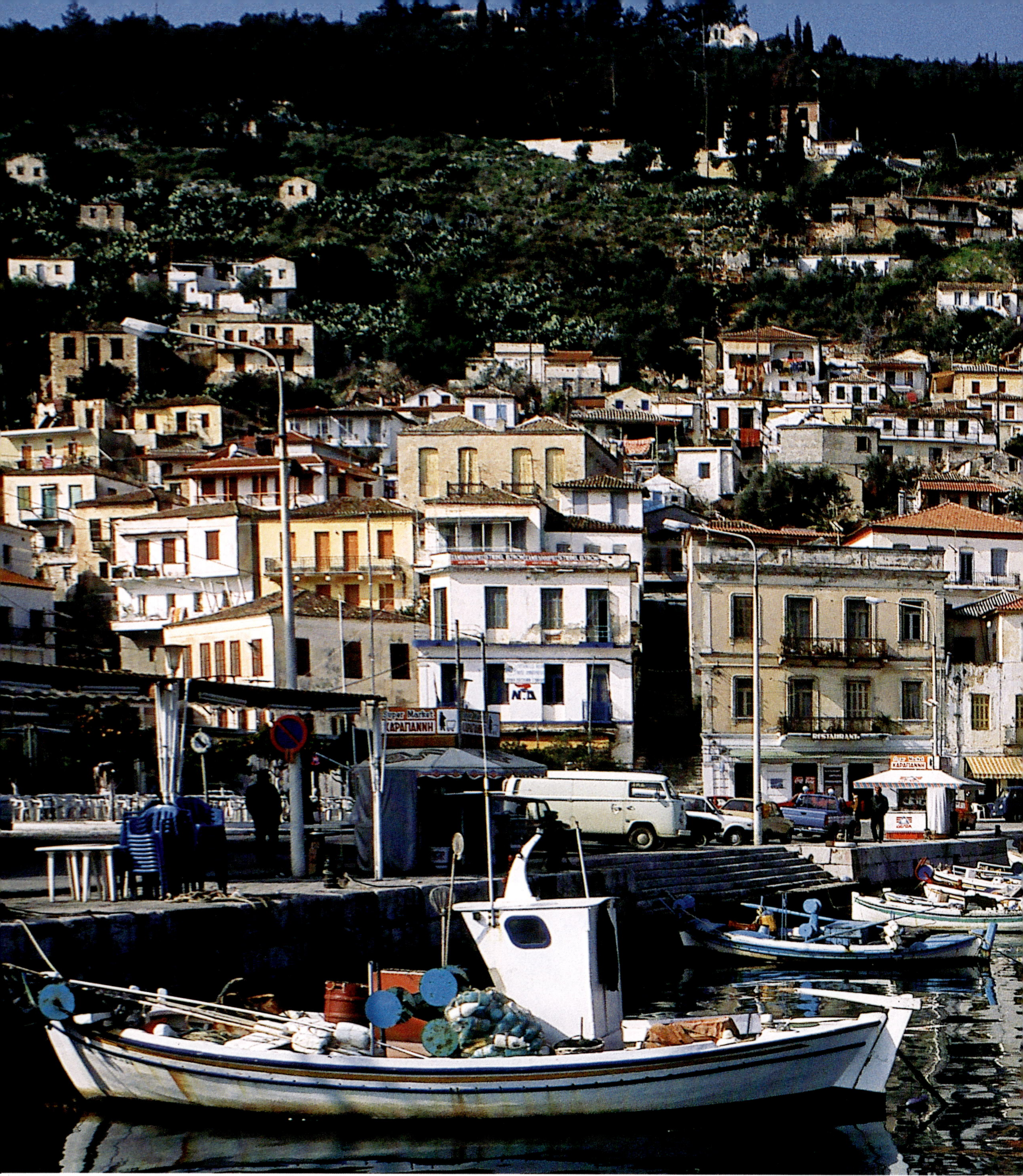

THE PORT OF GITHIO

This port, at the foot of Mount Koumaro, is an ancient site and has been identified with the Phoenician outpost of Kranae, famous for its trade in purple cloth, but it was also famous because it took in Paris and Helen following their flight from Mycenae. From there the lovers took a ship to Cythera and then to Troy.

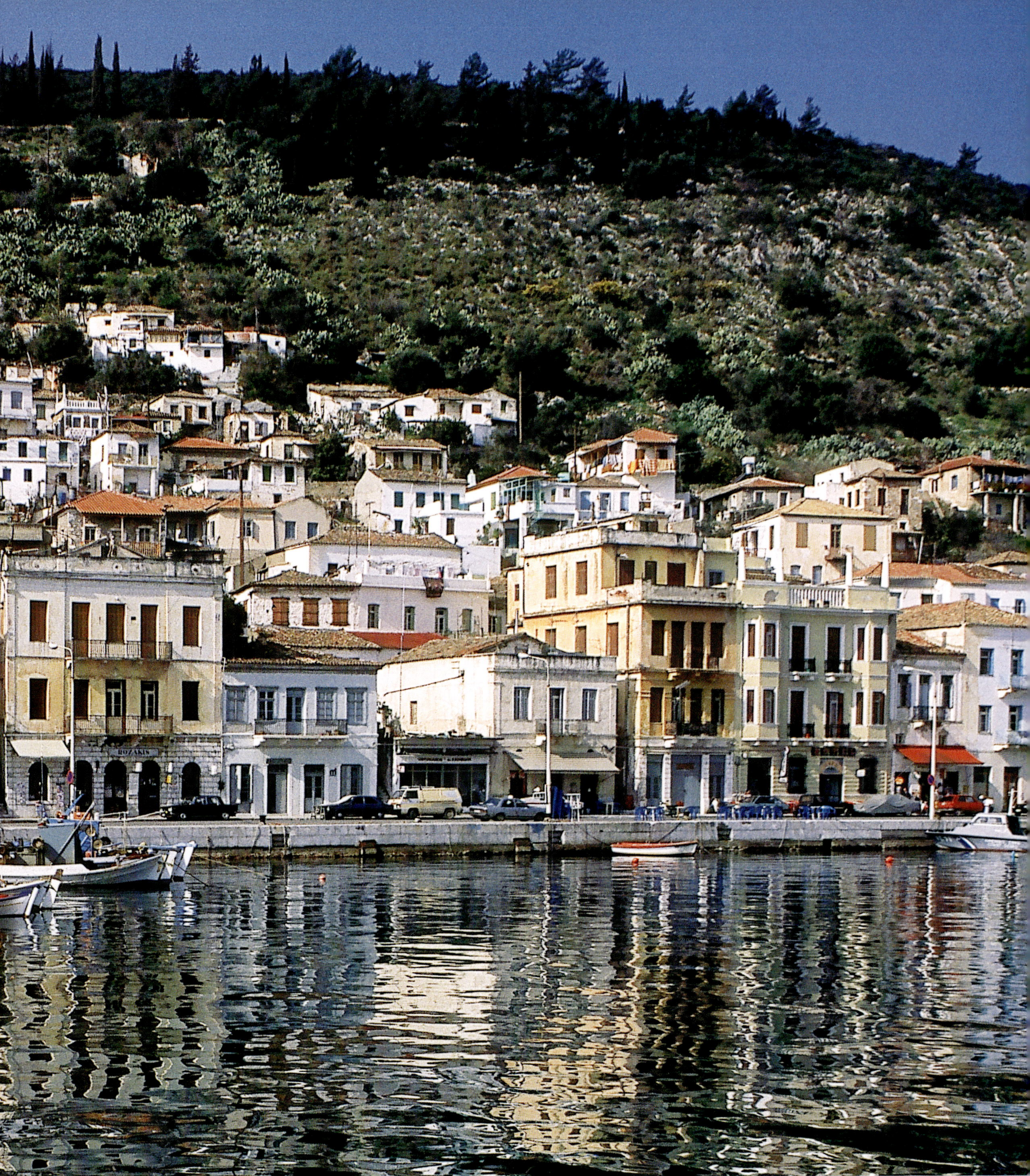

Today Githio is a pretty little seaside resort. The lovely, bright, colored houses on the sea front stretch up the hill opposite the harbor.

Their architecture makes one think of the power the Venetians once wielded in this region. The front is full of taverns and cafés and that is where the Greeks like to walk in the evening.

THE MANI REGION

This picture is quite different from the traditional view of the Mani region. The central peninsula at the bottom of the Peloponnesus is an arid, mountainous region, with bare rocks and little vegetation. However, there are olive trees, and in the spring they are charming, full of color and flowers. Over the centuries this bleak mountain region became an impregnable fortress. The local population was organized in clans and jealously defended its freedom, refusing to be subject to the Ottoman authorities. The spirit of resistance shown by these proud and brave fishermen and mountain farmers won the admiration of Europe. The region also managed to avoid paying Ottoman taxes. In the 16th century, clan chieftains with a taste for vendetta, built themselves fortified towers, and this form of architecture became typical of the area. In 1718 Pasha Kodja tried once again to coax compliance out of the people of the Mani region, by offering gifts. As they were being enticed to recognize his authority, they sent him a gift of two pigs, the only tribute they would consent to. What is more, they advised him to leave quickly if he didn't want to see his fleet burned... PAGES 226-227

A ROADSIDE SCENE IN CRETE

We are far from the bustling cities of the twenty-first century. The countryside lives by its own traditional rhythms. The young have left to find work in the towns. The old remain as guardians of the deserted villages. It is through them that traditional activities, crafts, agriculture and pastoral skills live on. They often sit beside the road to sell their produce to passers-by.

A RURAL SCENE: MAN AND DONKEY

Even today the donkey is the familiar companion of the rural smallholder, and it is not unusual to see a donkey in a field, along a rutted track, or even on a modern road. This old man is bringing fodder to livestock on the donkey's back. It is a typical rural scene in a country with strong contrasts between tradition and modernity. FOLLOWING PAGES

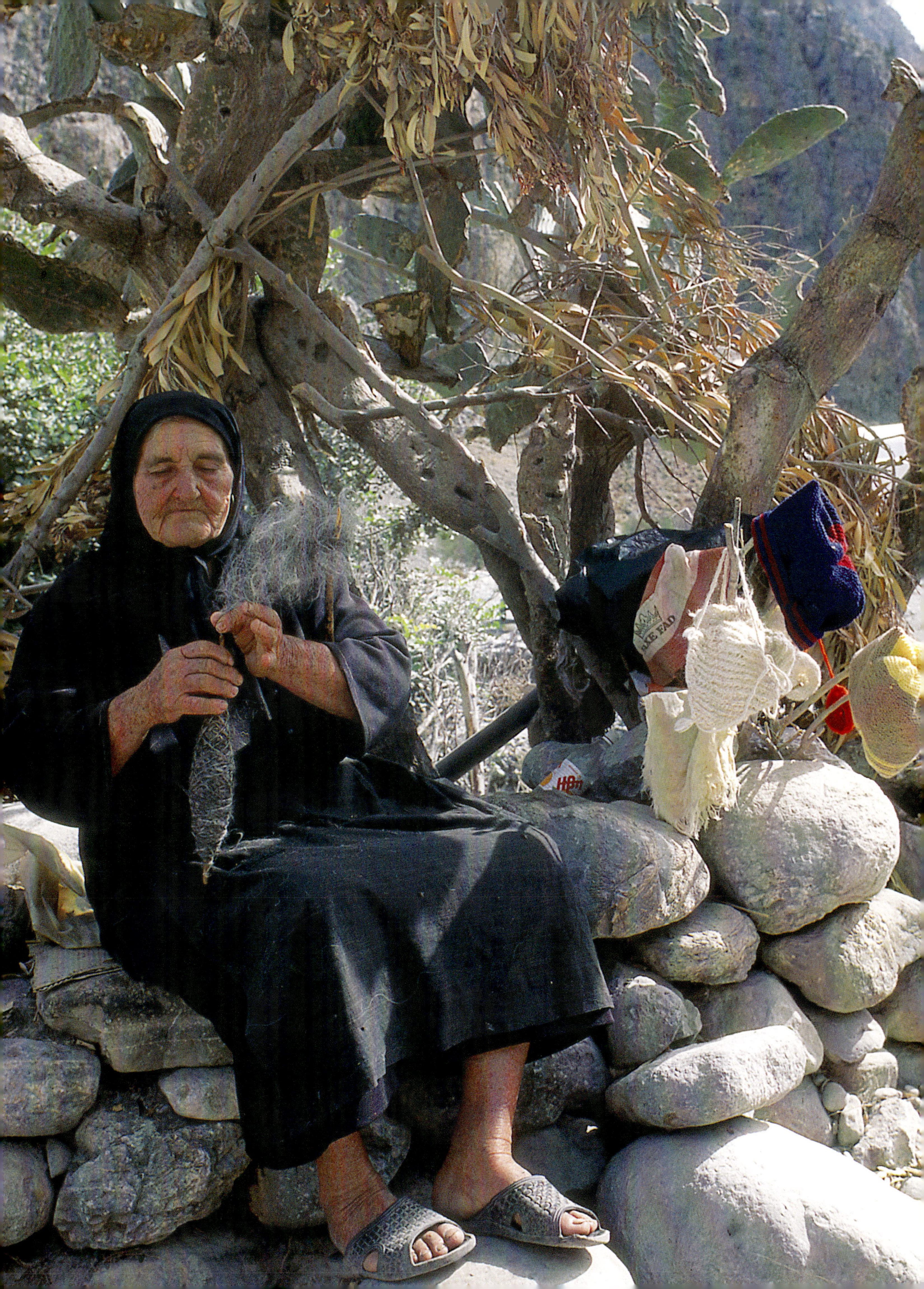

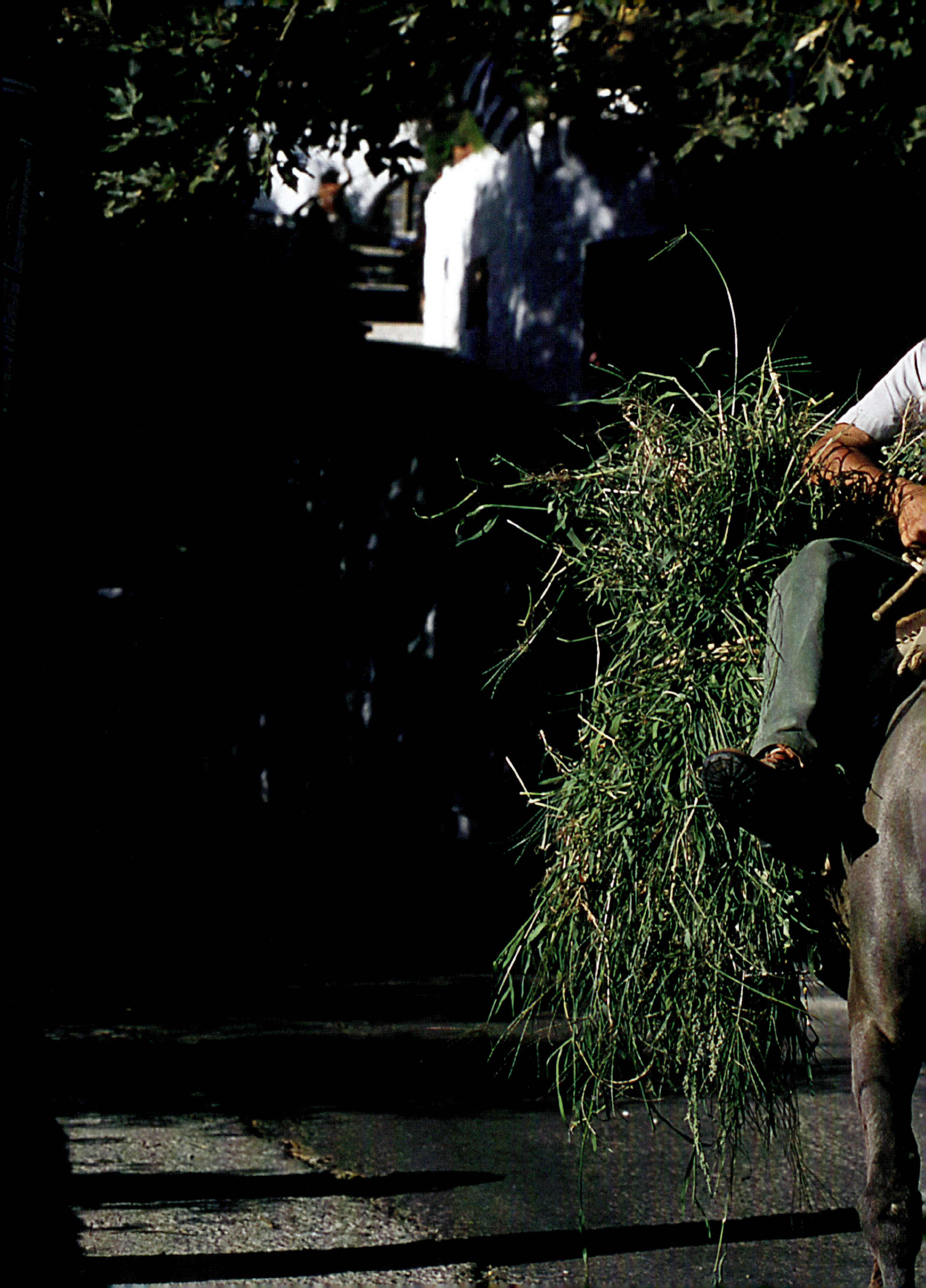

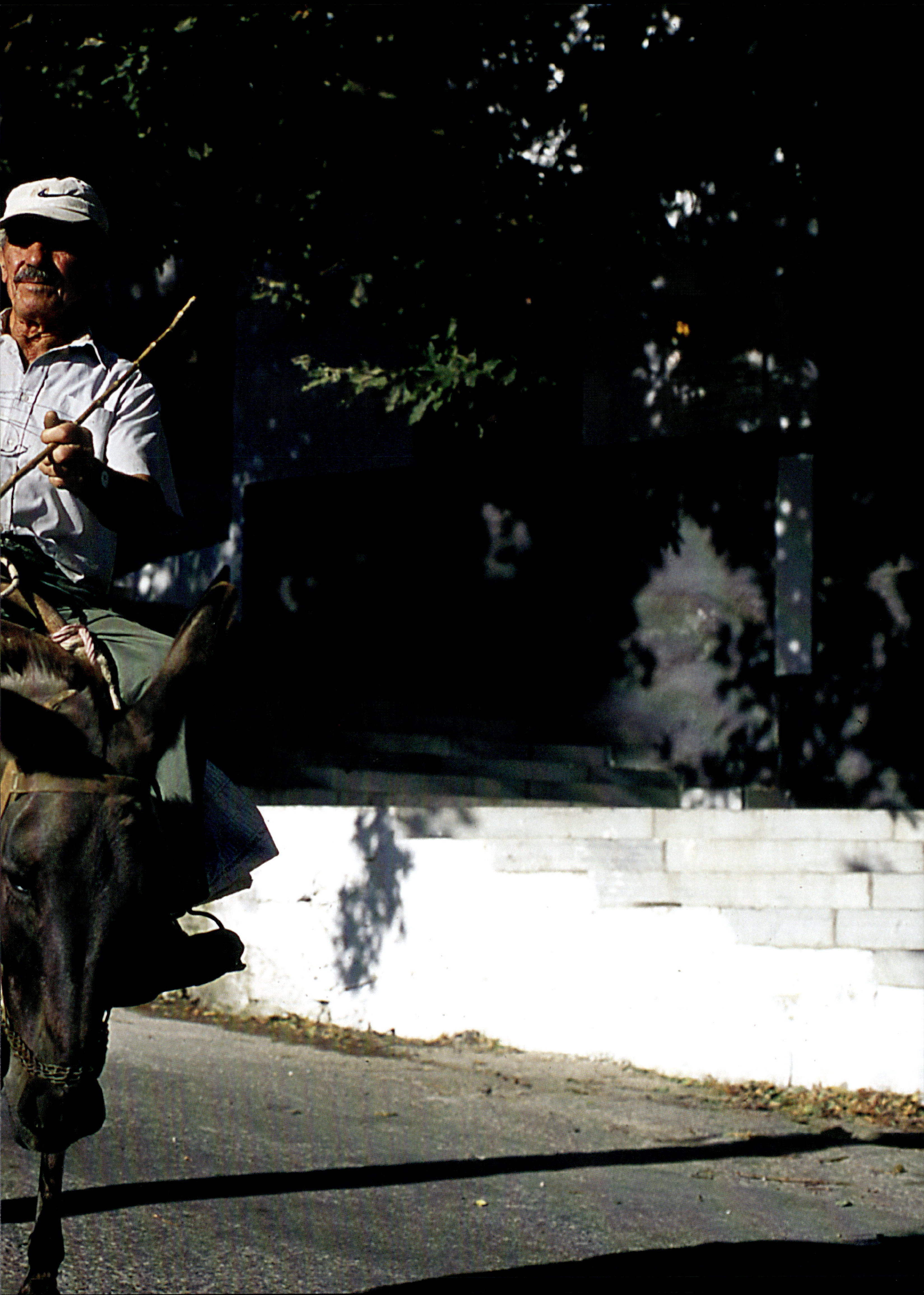

THE FRUIT AND VEGETABLE STALL

Ermoupolis is the most dynamic city of the Cyclades. However its shopping district has many little businesses like this one. The shop signs are old and faded. But the Greeks still like to shop at little stalls and markets, even though the big supermarket chains are also present. This man is patiently waiting for customers to come along. His stall is a mosaic of colors and flavors; fresh fruit in season and vegetables in abundance: peaches, apricots, watermelon, melons, grapes, apples, oranges, lemons or figs beside tomatoes, courgettes, aubergines and cucumbers.

THE OLD PORT AT MYKONOS

There are little white houses, there are taverns and cafés along the quayside, and multicolored boats ride patiently at anchor. This is typical of the charming scenes to be found in all the ports of the Cyclades. The flashes of color from the doors and windows match the warmth and jauntiness of the craft in the harbor. In the background the famous windmills of Mykonos watch over the town like benevolent giants. PAGES 238-239

A PORT AT THE END OF THE PELOPONNESUS

At the very end of the Mani peninsula a tiny port suggests one has come to the end of the world. The whole area around Gerolimenas has a ghostly air. Most of the houses have been abandoned and are in ruins. There is little activity in the port, boats are rare. The women are waiting for the fishermen to return. They have come to buy fish and haggle on the quay. PAGES 240-241

TINOS

Shadows lengthen over the creek. The setting sun lights up the rocks and red earth of the hillside which has, for centuries, been molded into terraces. There are many beaches on the island of Tinos, but this one has no road leading to it. You have to walk across an arid landscape to get to it, follow a track you can barely see, before you can enjoy its charms. A little isolated and abandoned chapel, as well as two trees, offer shelter to the bold adventurer. All the islands have enchanting and peaceful corners, well away from the crowds; the noise of the waves alone disturbs the peace the little chapel watches over. PAGES 242-243

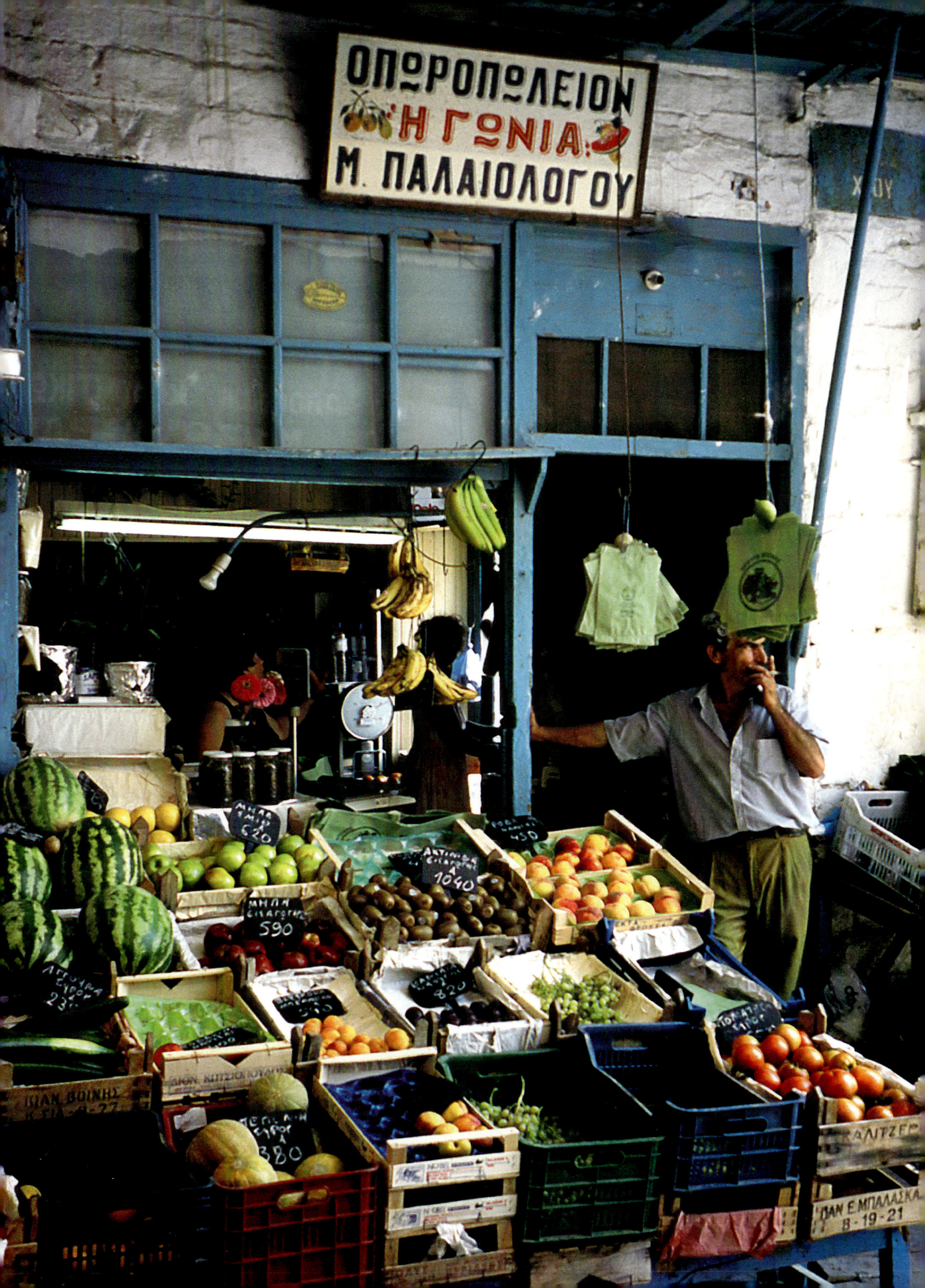
ΟΠΩΡΟΠΩΛΕΙΟΝ
Η ΓΩΝΙΑ
Μ. ΠΑΛΑΙΟΛΟΓΟΥ
ΠΑΝ Ε ΜΠΑΛΑΣΚΑ
8-19-21

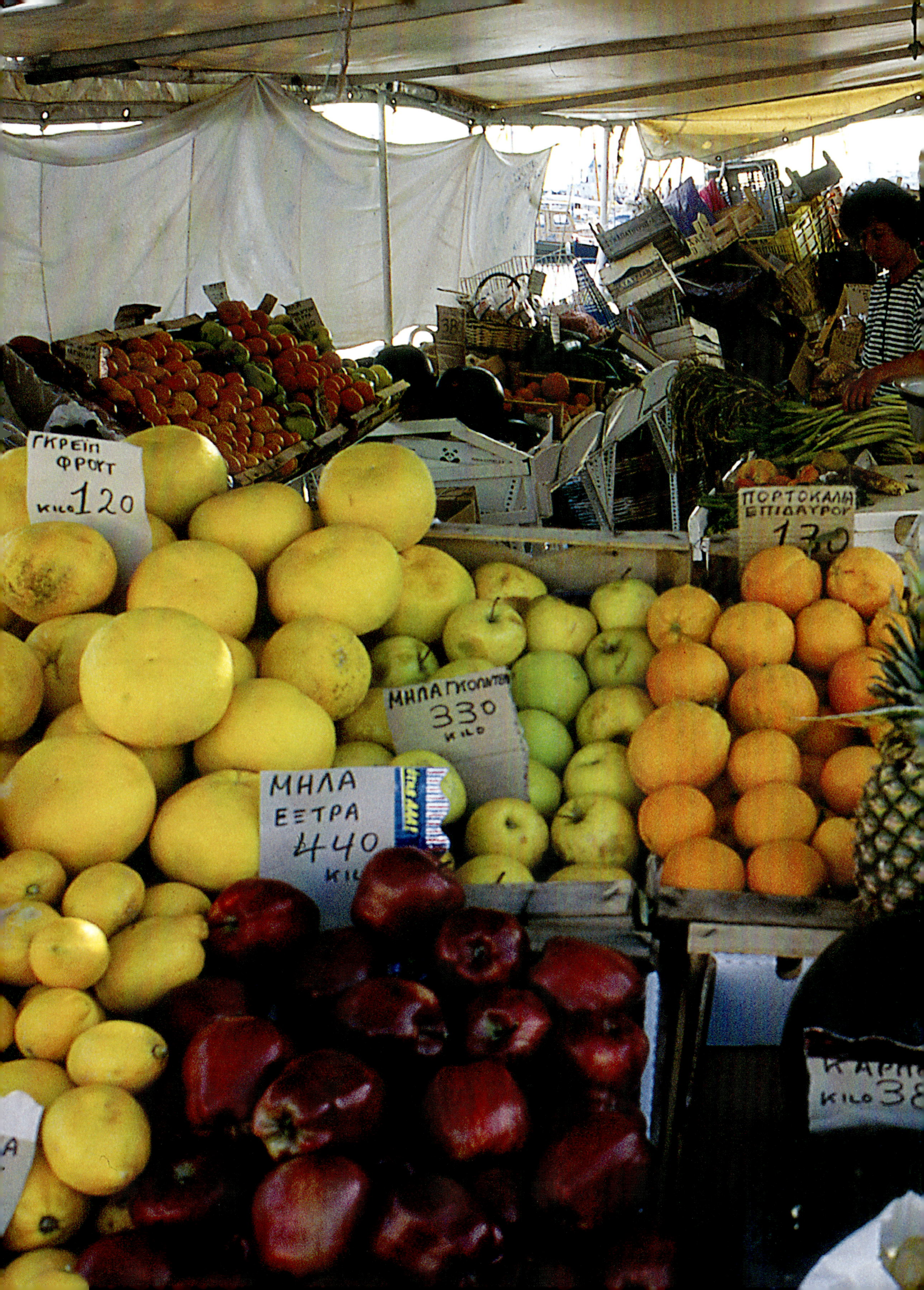
ΓΚΡΕΙΠ ΦΡΟΥΤ
KILO 120
ΠΟΡΤΟΚΑΛΙΑ ΕΠΙΔΑΥΡΟΥ
130
ΜΗΛΑ
330
KILO
ΜΗΛΑ
ΕΞΤΡΑ
440

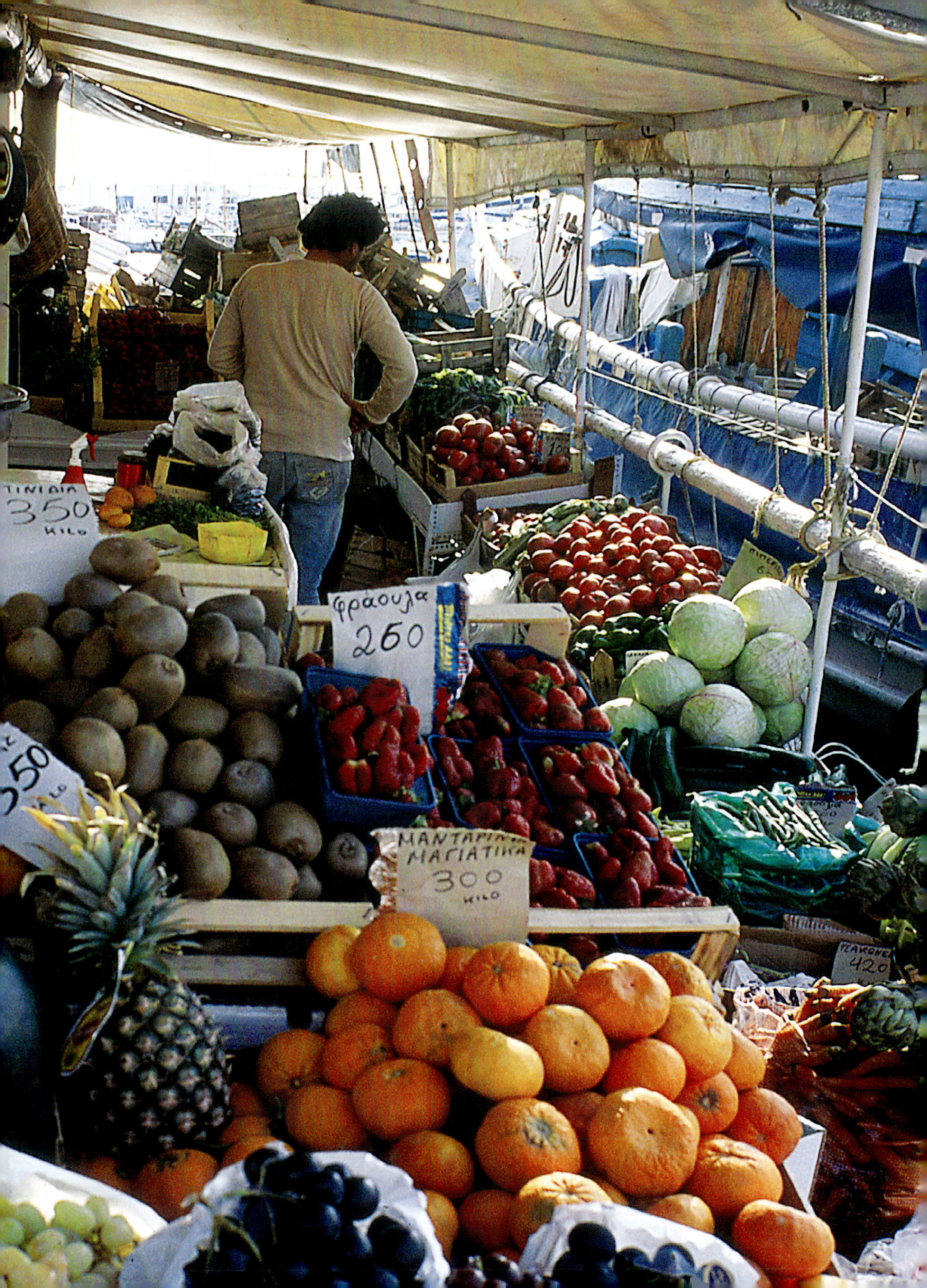
350
KILO
φράουλα
260
ΜΑΓΙΑΤΙΚΑ
300
KILO
420

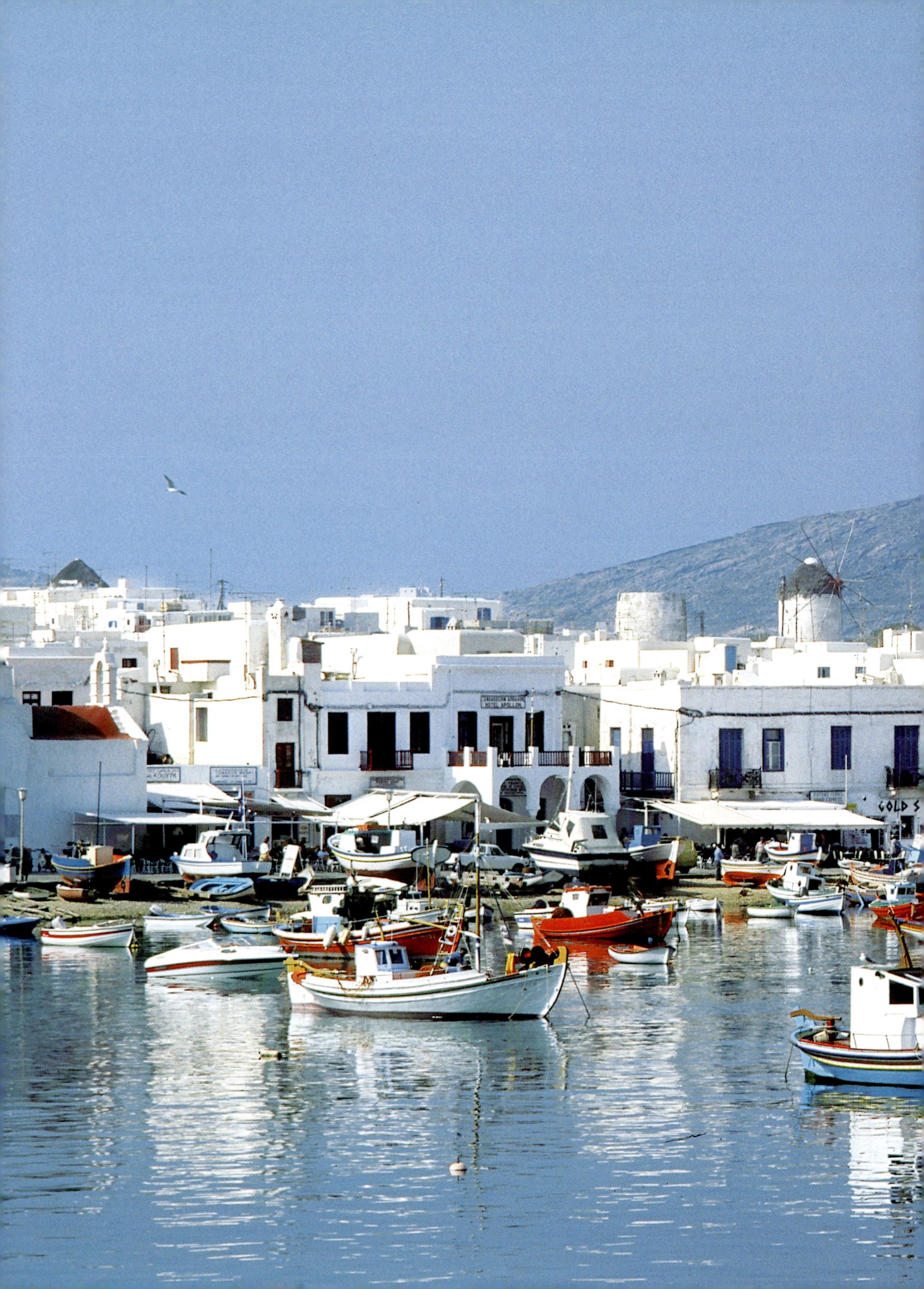

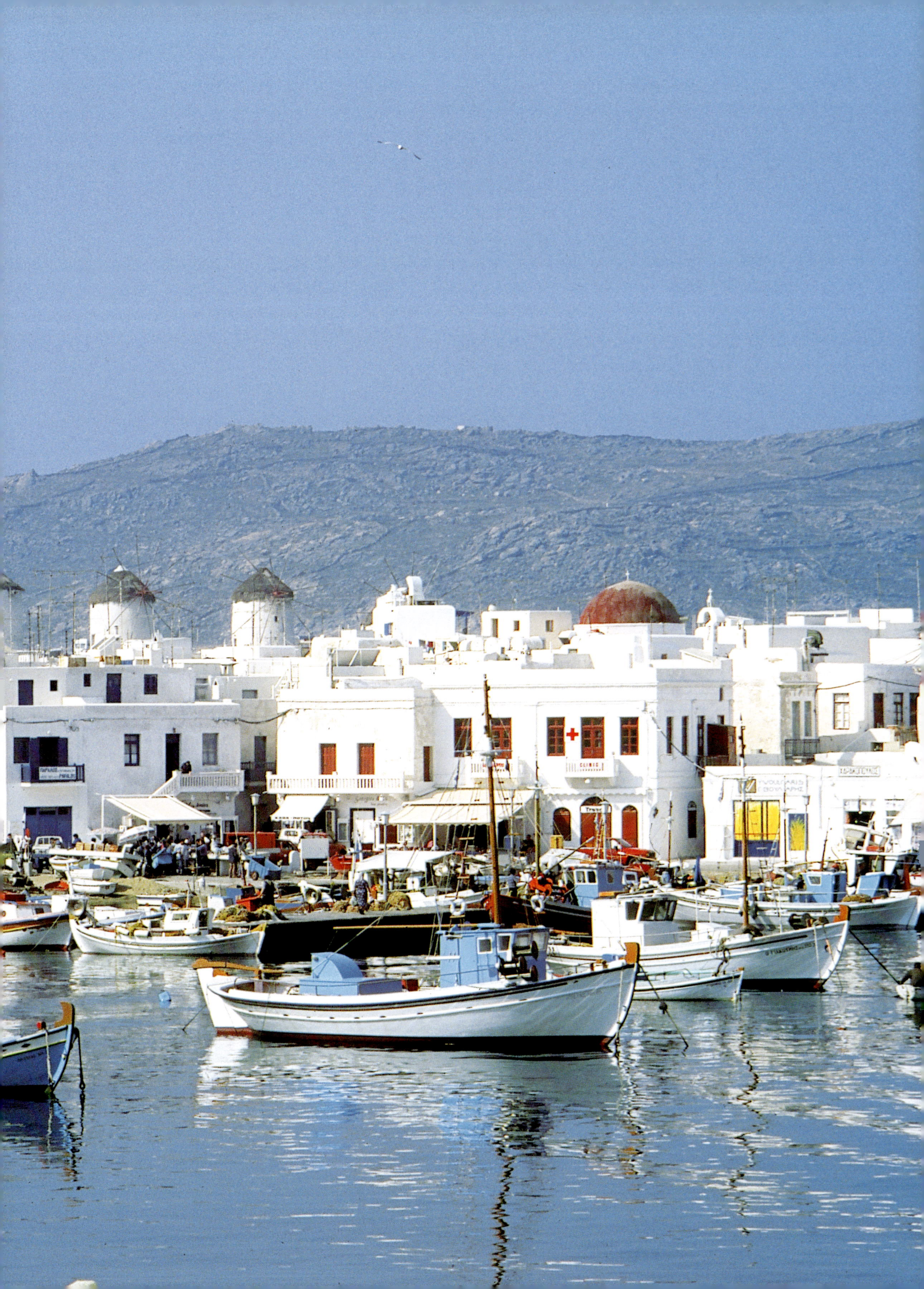

CLINIC

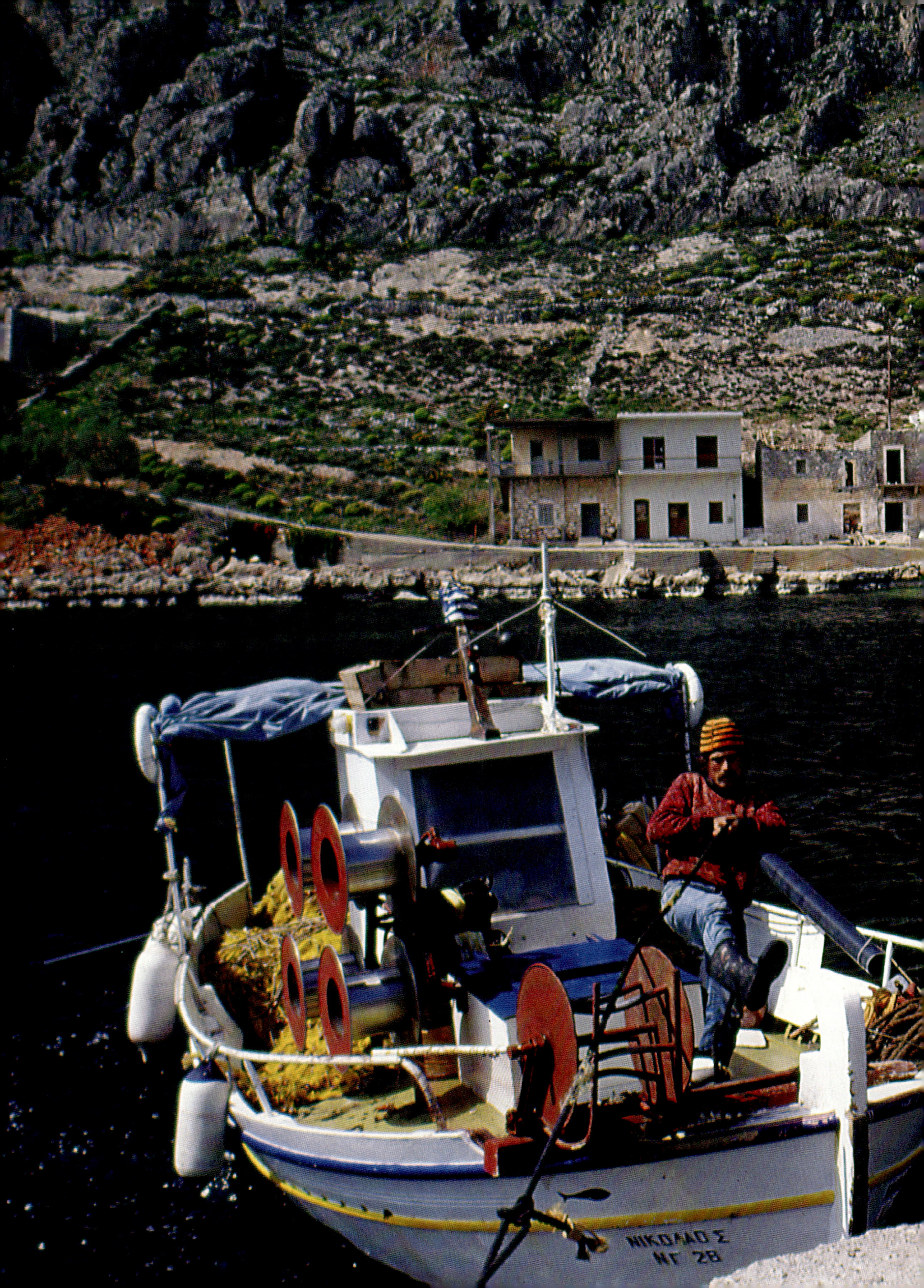
ΝΙΚΟΛΑΟΣ
ΝΓ 28

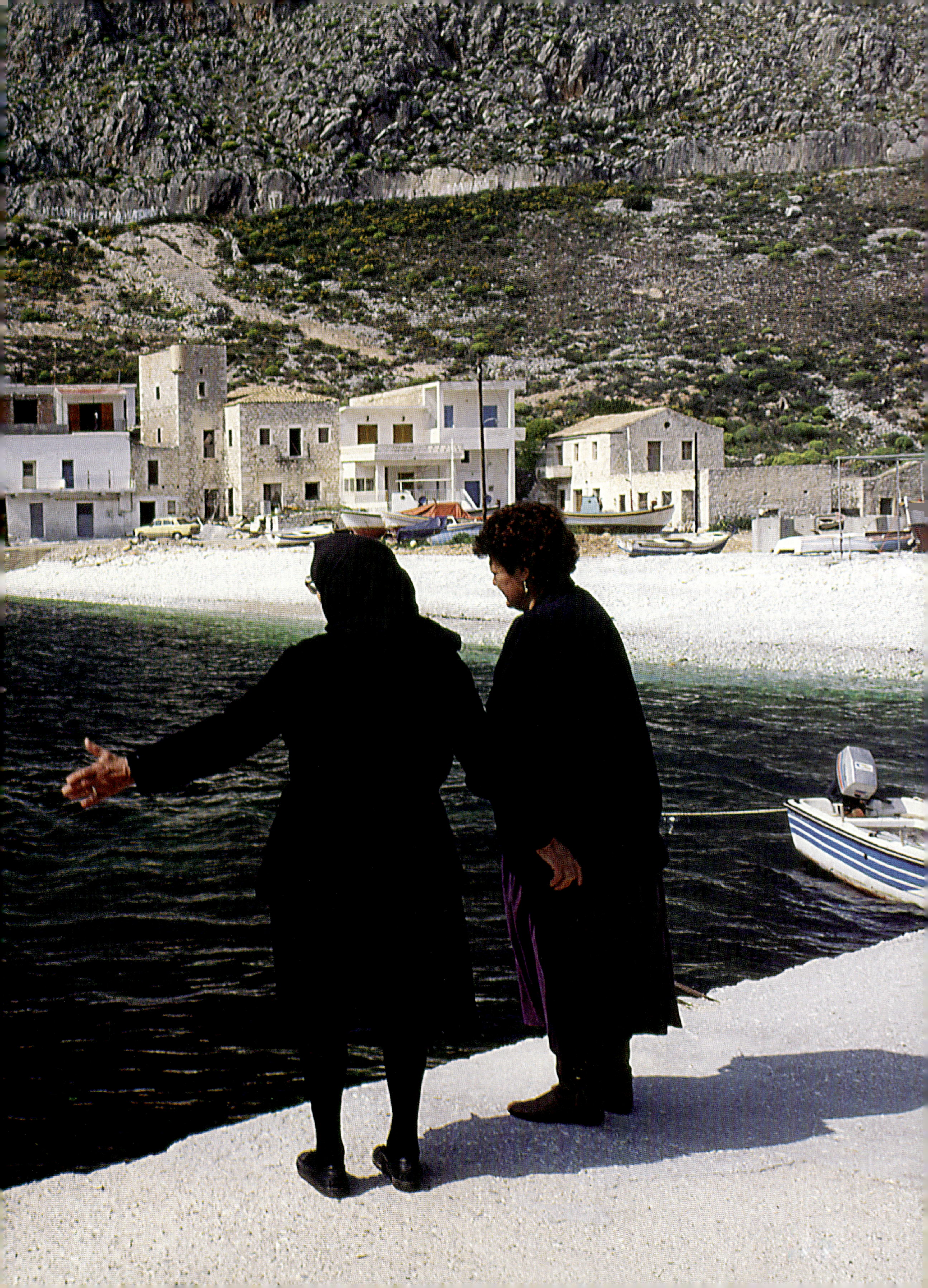

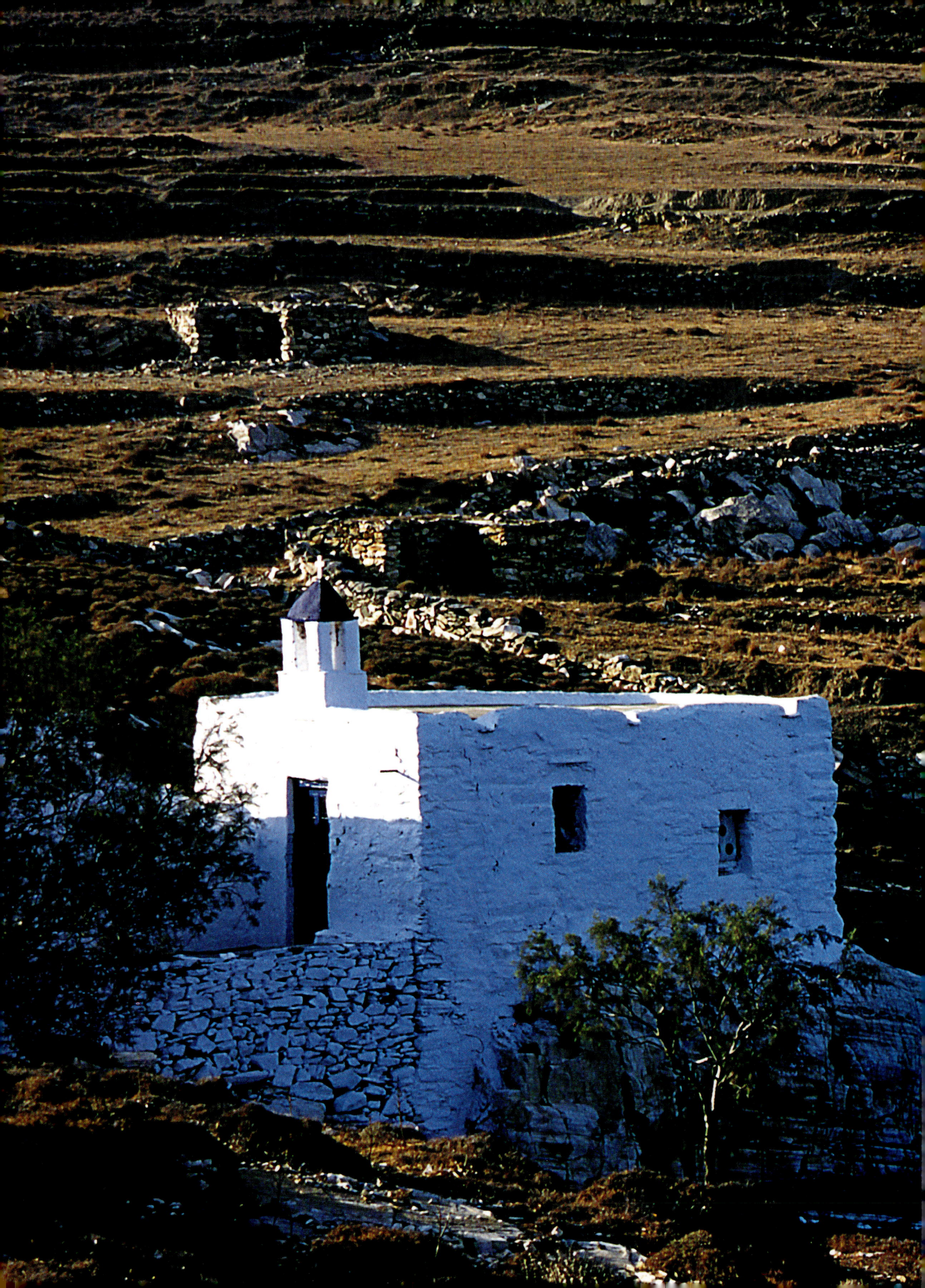

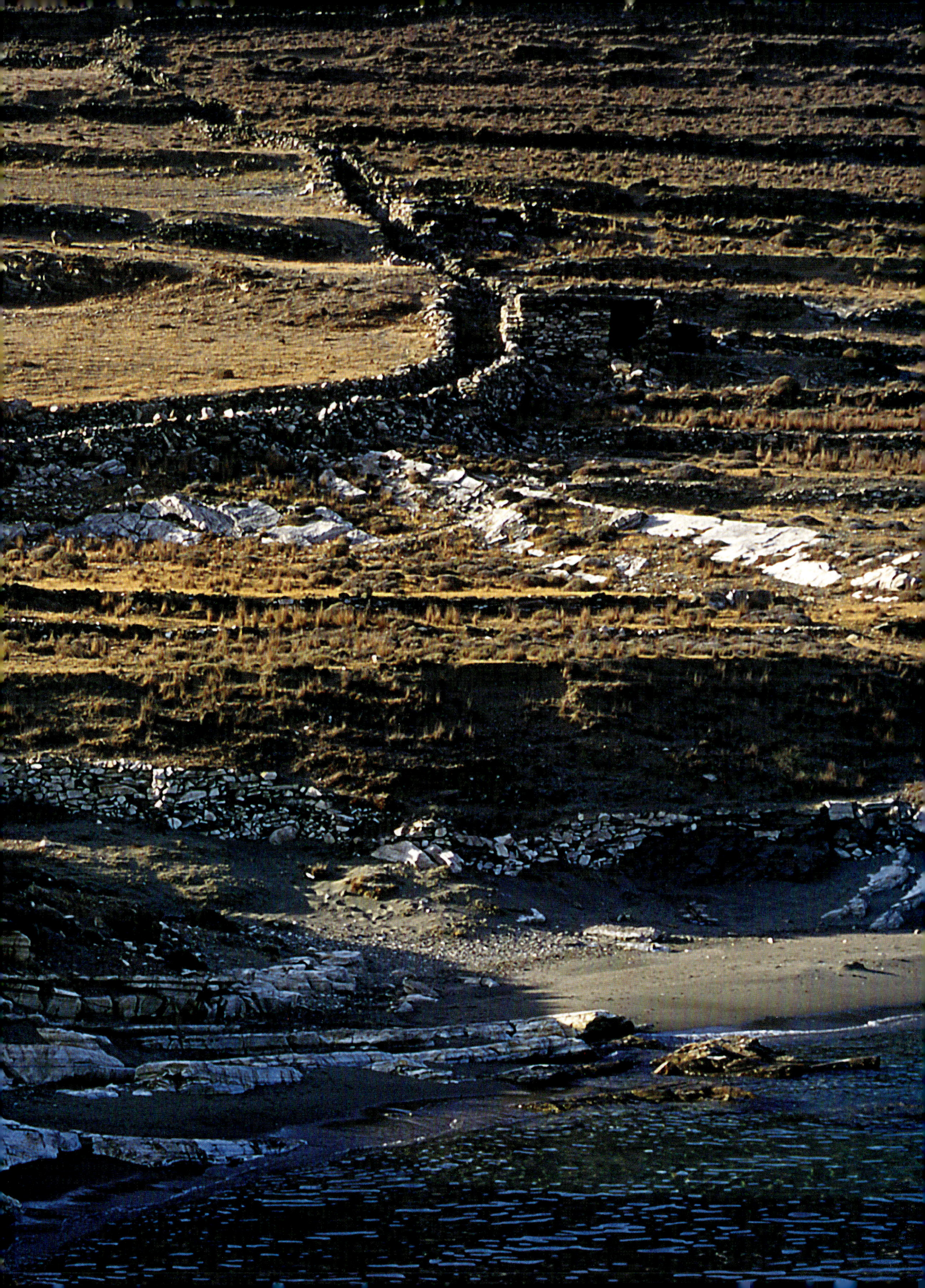

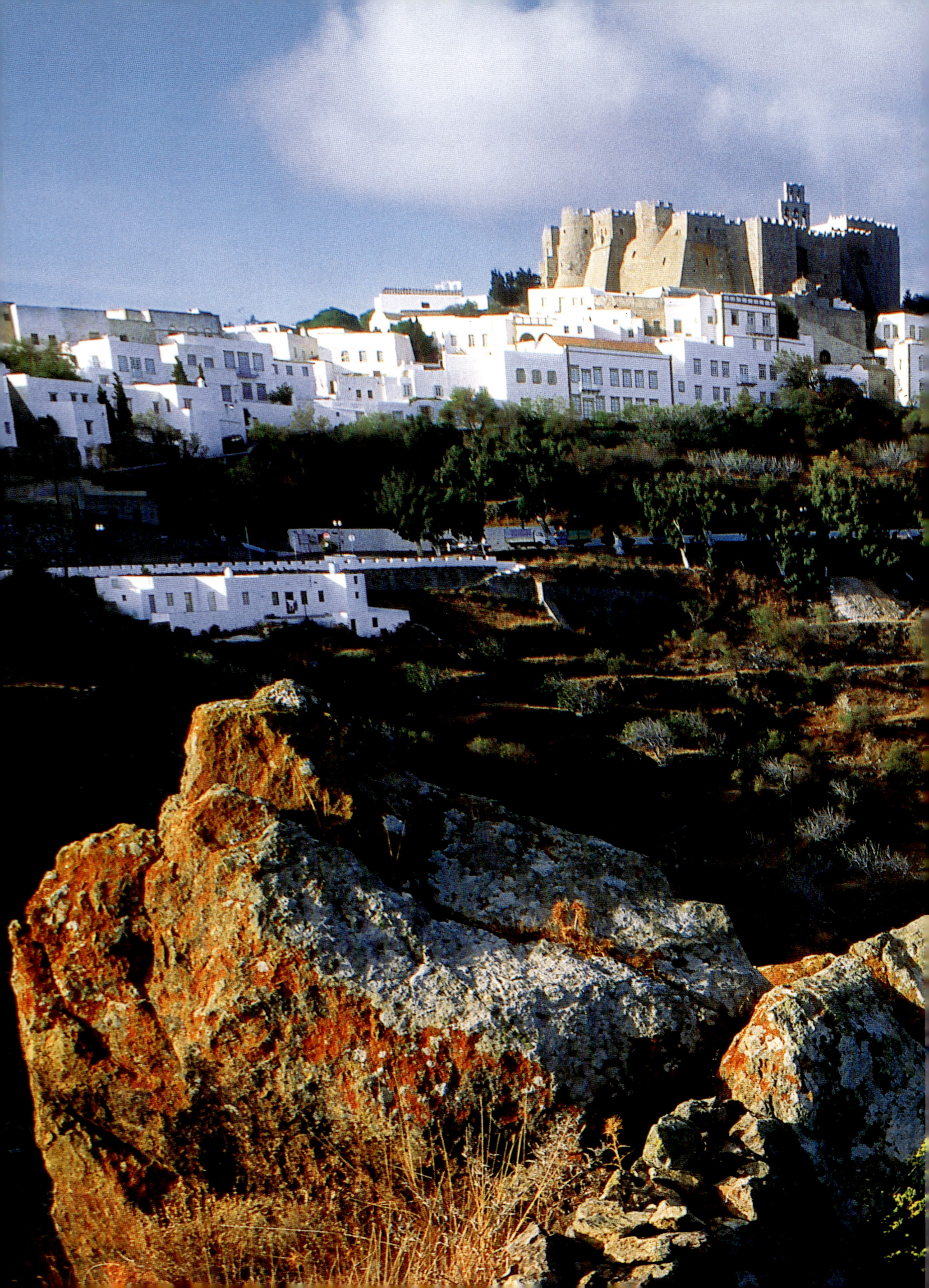

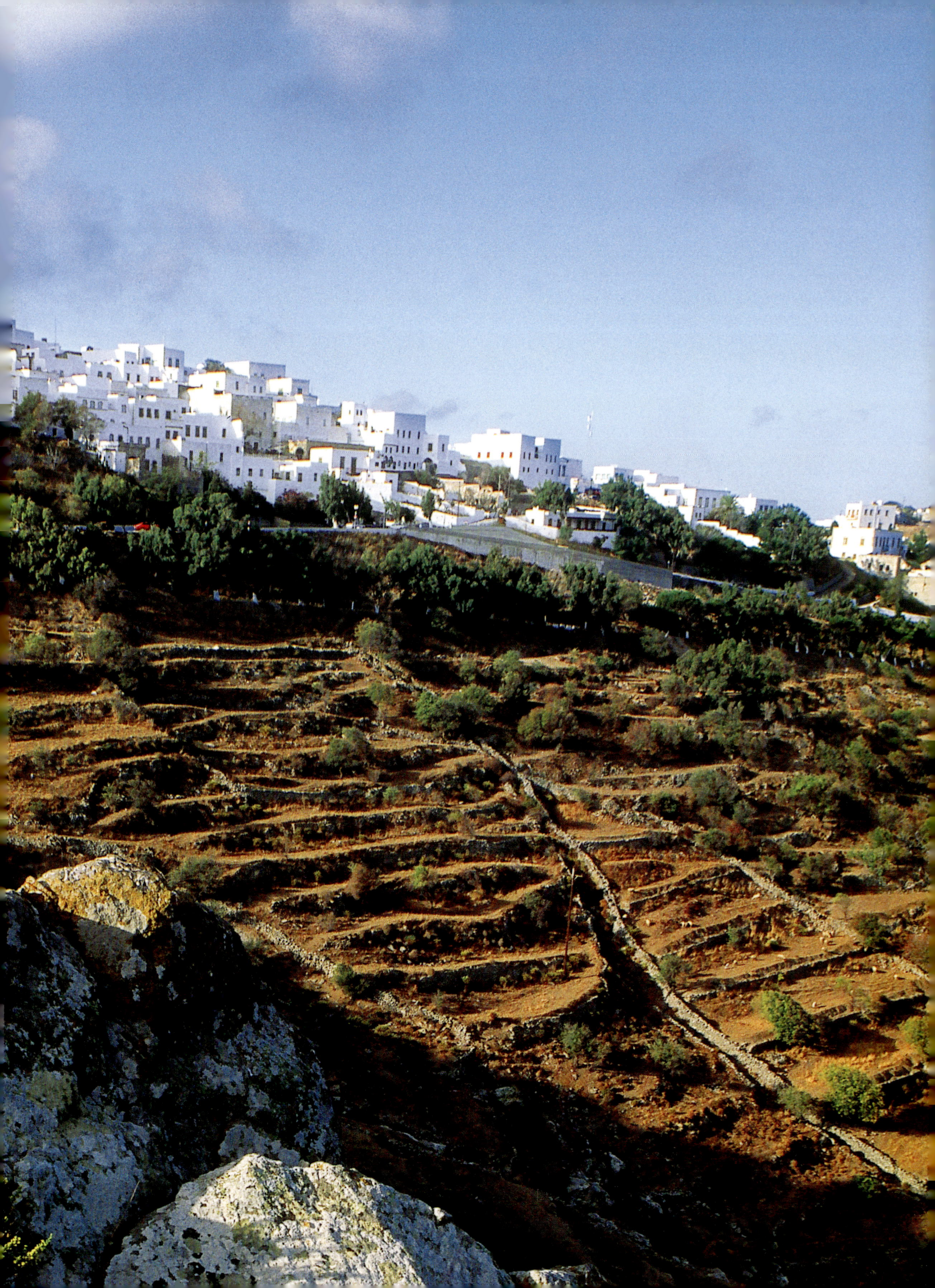

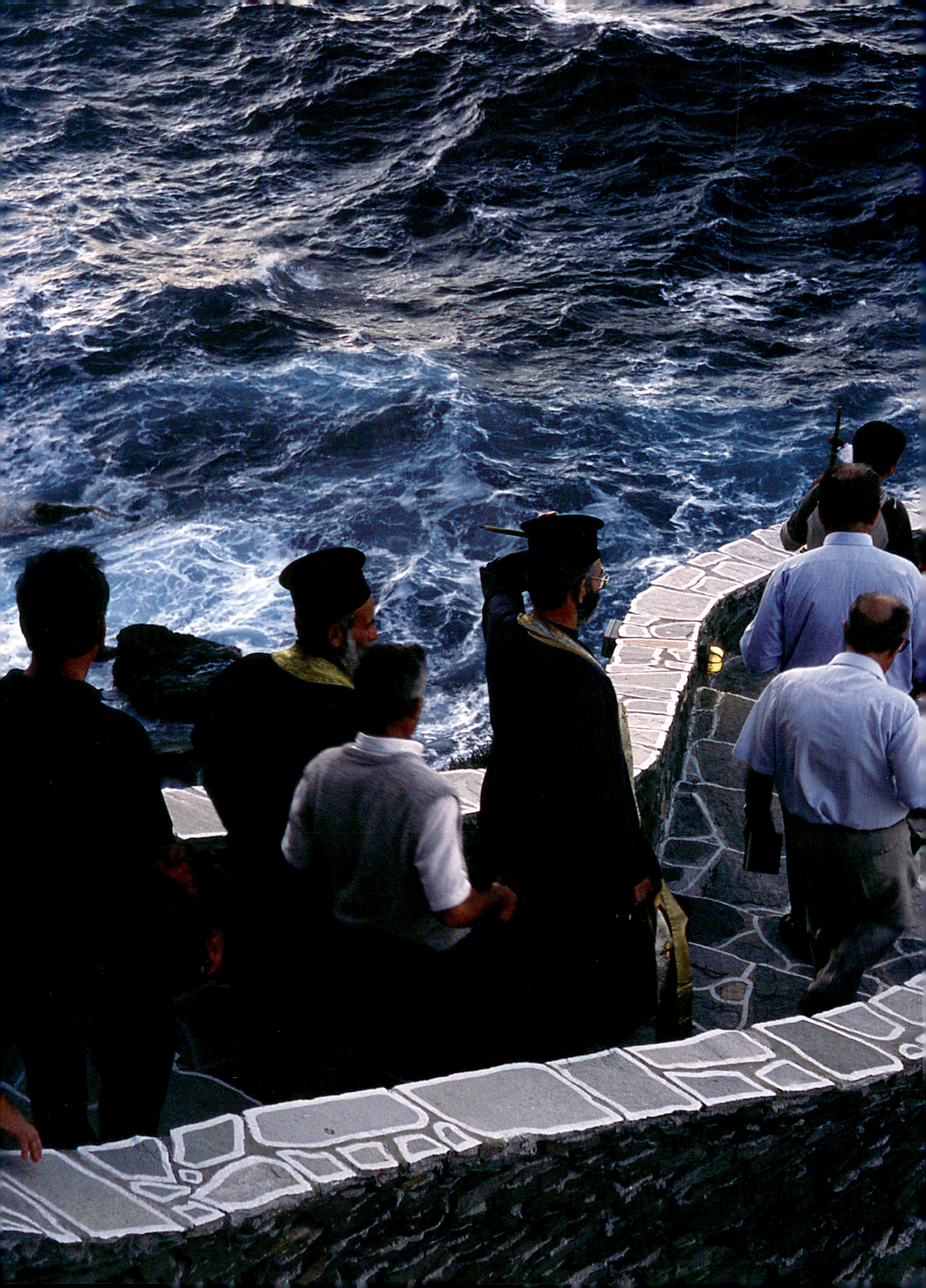

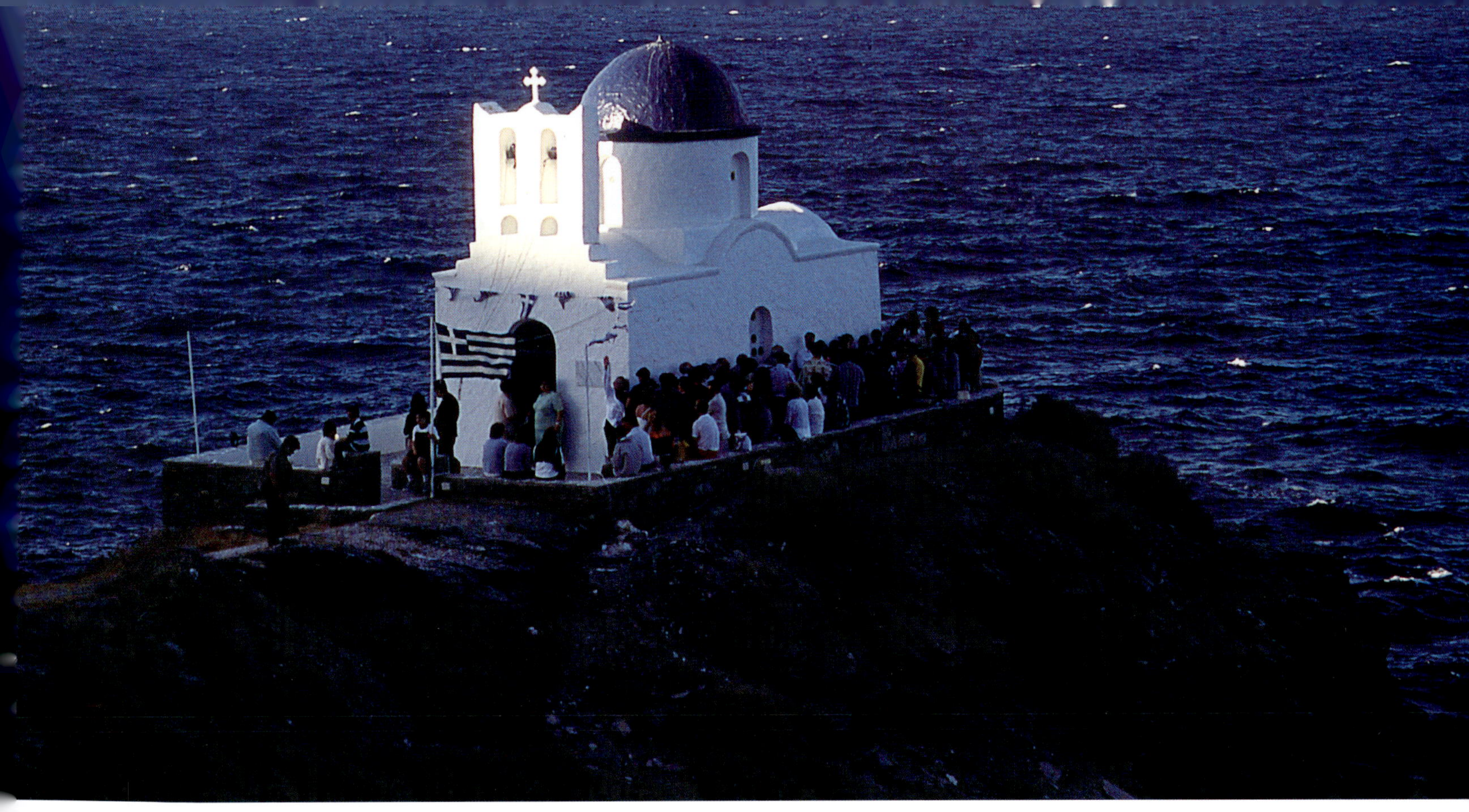

A PILGRIMAGE ON SIFNOS

Just as their devout ancestors went in procession to the temples to honor the gods, so Greeks still take part in pilgrimages: they crowd into the churches on the feast days of the Orthodox Church.

On the island of Sifnos, the faithful and the priests process solemnly along a road which winds around the side of a hill. This wonderful landscape calls you to quiet and meditation. There are steps carved into the rock leading to the little church near the medieval village of Kastro. The chapel stands on top of a rocky headland plunging steeply into the sea. But it is too small to hold everybody, so some sit outside as they follow the service; its sounds blend harmoniously with those of waves and wind.

THE JERUSALEM OF THE AEGEAN SEA

Visitors arriving on the rocky island of Patmos are making a pilgrimage to the very sources of Christianity. It was here that St John the Evangelist was exiled, living in a cave where today the faithful come to pray. In 95 AD, he dictated the Book of the Revelation to his disciple Prochoros.

The Monastery of St John the Divine, which looks like a fortress, sits on top of the hill; while the houses of the upper city creep up its side. The road from the port is steep and difficult, and that alone, not to mention the ramparts of the citadel, must have put off pirates and enemies. Patmos, however, did not get off totally unscathed; in particular it was pillaged by the Venetians under Gardelli on the 19th June 1659. PREVIOUS PAGES

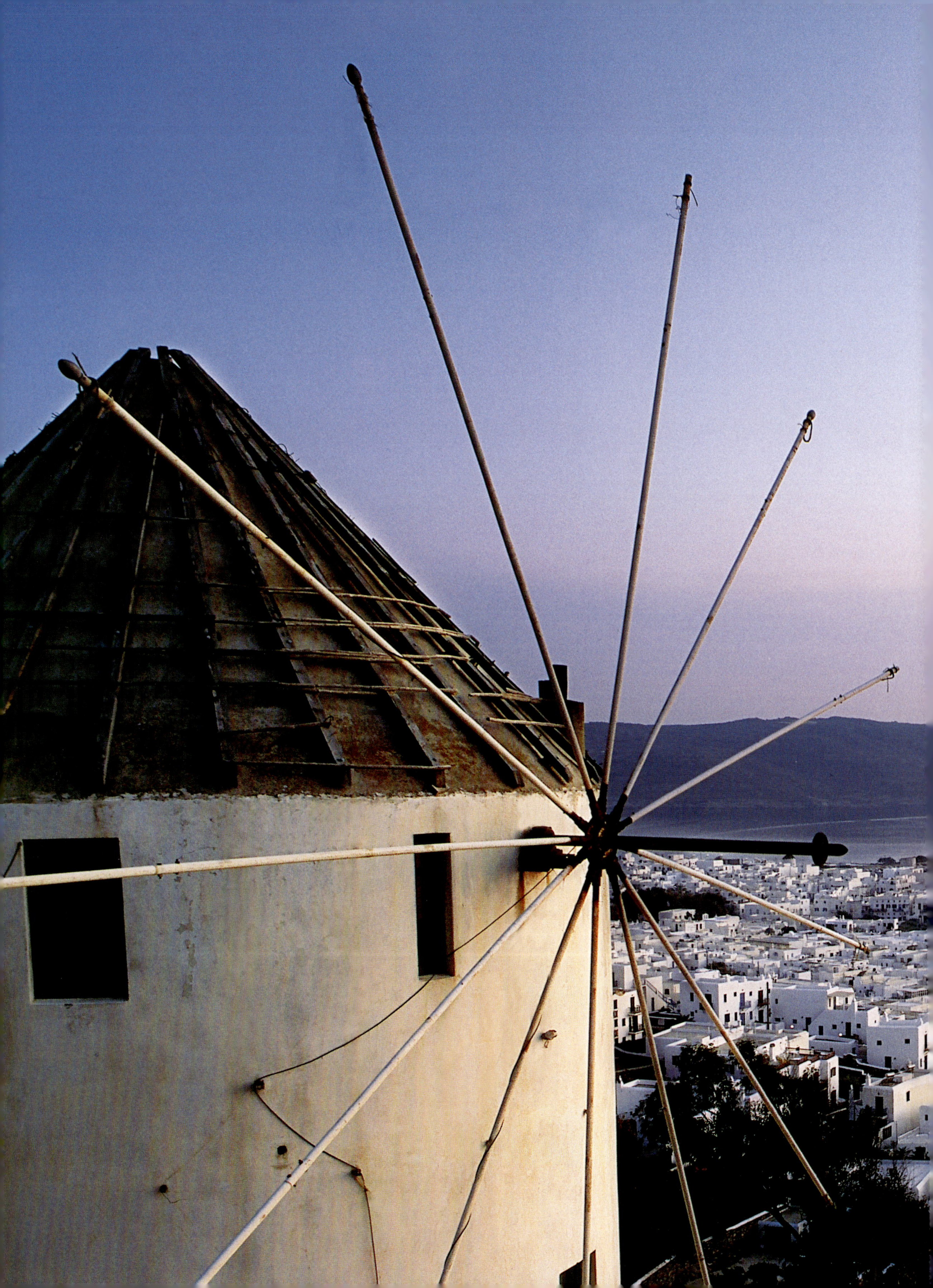

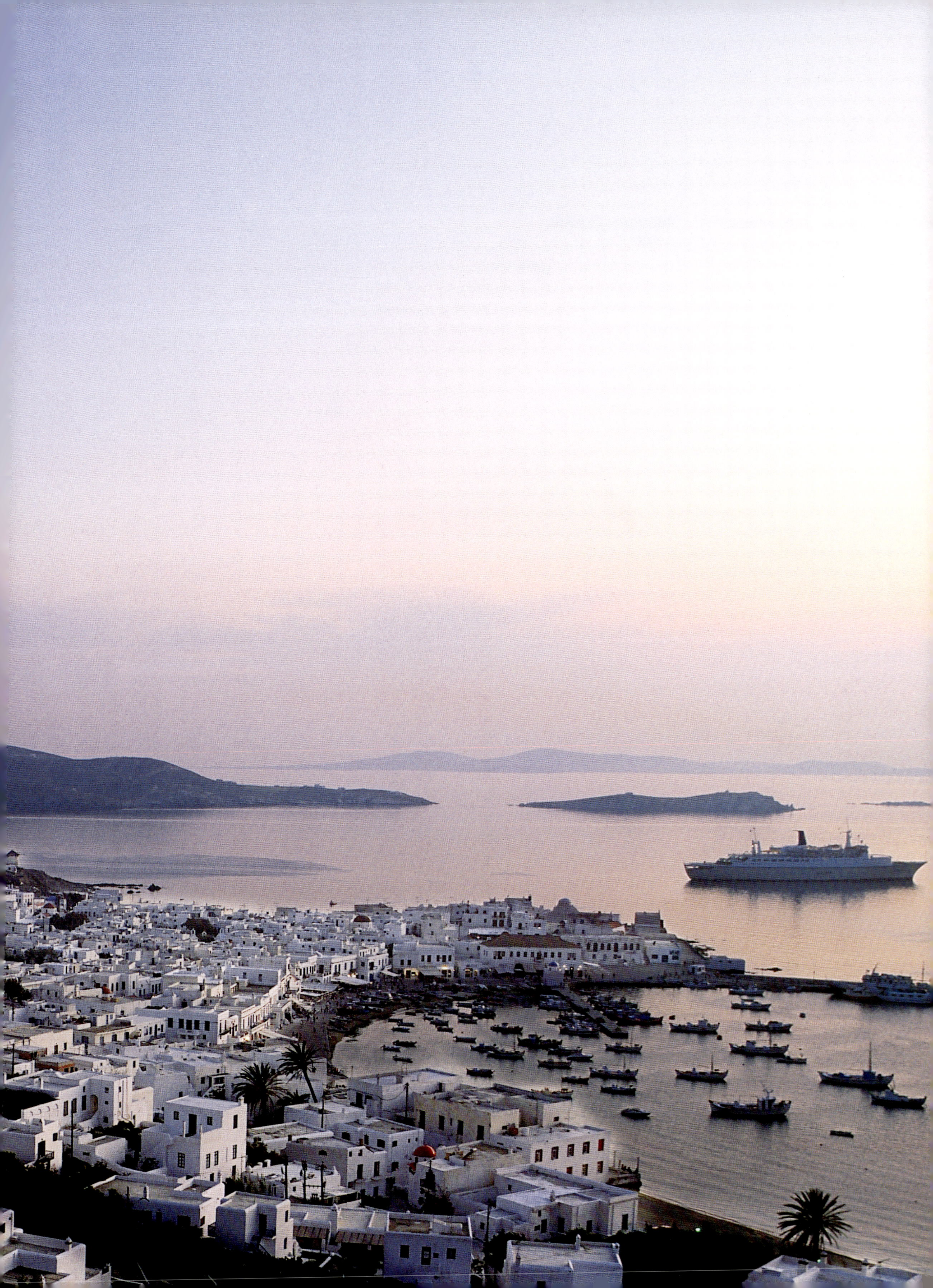

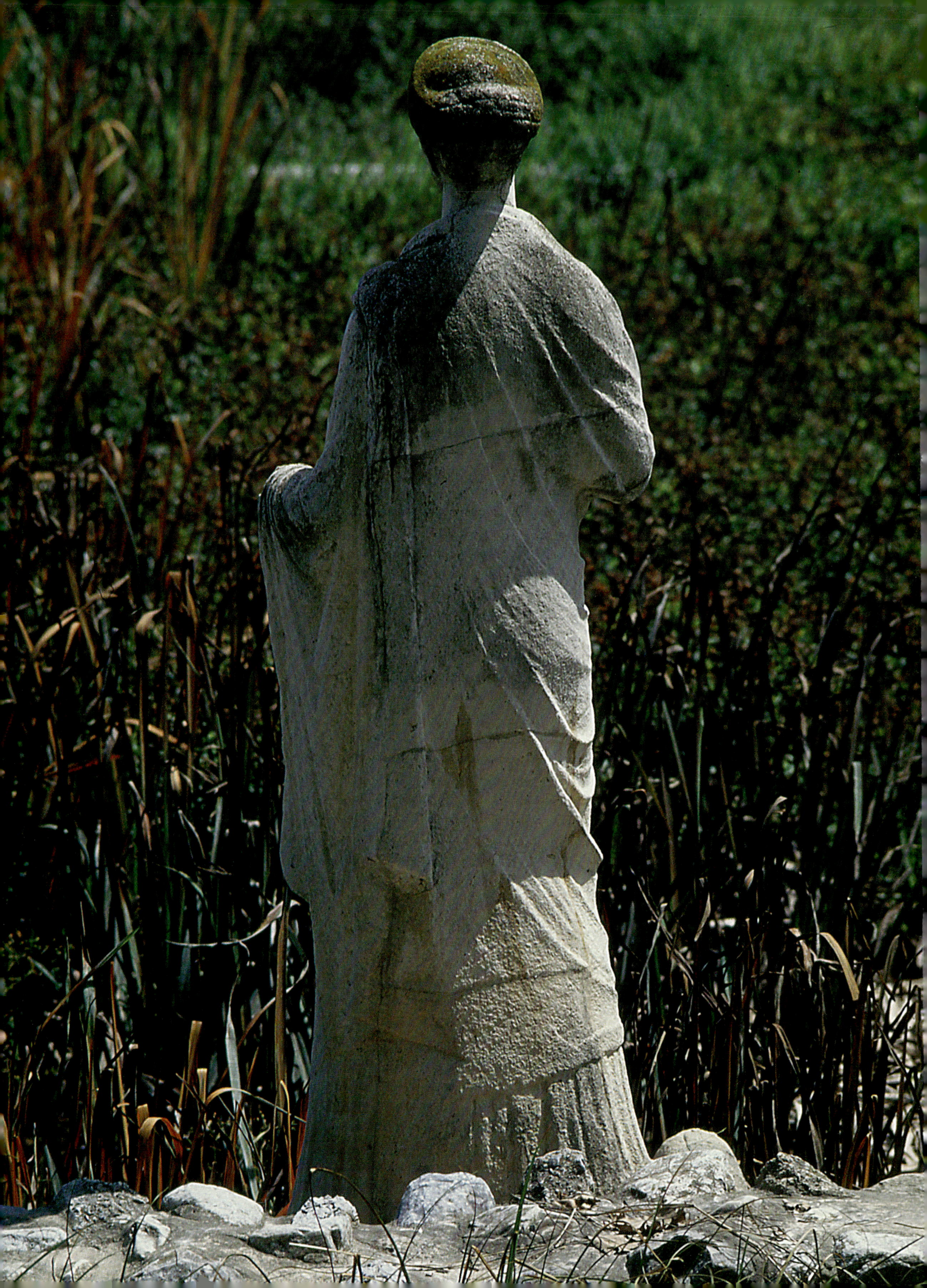

BIBLIOGRAPHY

AESCHYLUS, Works.
BARRÈS Maurice, Le Voyage de Sparte, Librairie Plon, 1922.
BÉRARD Victor, Dans le sillage d'Ulysse, Armand Colin, 1973.
BOUTMY Emile, Le Parthénon et le génie grec, Armand Colin, 1897.
BRASILLACH Robert, Anthologie de la poésie grecque, Stock, 1991.
BRUNEL Pierre, Le mythe d'Electre, Honoré Champion, 1995.
Le mythe de la métamorphose, José Corti, 2004.
BULFINCH Thomas, Greek and Roman Mythology, Dover, 2000.
BYRON Lord, traduction de Amédée Pichot, Œuvres, Furne, 1836.
DIEHL Charles, Excursions archéologiques en Grèce, A. Colin, 1939.
DURRELL Lawrence, Les îles grecques, Albin Michel, 1978.
FLACELIÈRE Robert, La Vie quotidienne dans la Grèce antique, Hachette, 1959.
GIDE André, Thésée, Jacques Schiffrin, 1946.
GODEL Roger, Une Grèce secrète…, Les Belles Lettres, 1960.
GRIMAL Pierre, Dictionary of Classical Mythology, translated by A.R. Maxwell-Hyslop, Oxford University Press, 1986.
HÉRODOTE, L'Enquête, Desrez, 1840.
HESIOD, Theogony.
HOMER, The Iliad, The Odyssey.
IAKOVIDIS, Mycènes, Epidaure, Ekdotike Athenon, Athènes, 1988.
LÉVÊQUE Pierre, La Naissance de la Grèce, Gallimard, 1990. Nous partons pour la Grèce, PUF, 1962.
MAUCLAIR Camille, Le pur visage de la Grèce, Grasset, 1938.
MAULNIER Thierry, Cette Grèce où nous sommes nés, Flammarion, 1964.
MAURRAS Charles, Anthinea, Librairie H. et E. Champion, 1923.
OVID, The Metamorphoses.
PAUSANIAS, Voyage historique de la Grèce, Editions Desrez, 1797.
PETTAZZONI Raffaele, La Religion dans la Grèce antique des origines à Alexandre le Grand, Payot, 1953.
PICARD Charles, La Sculpture antique des origines à Phidias, Librairie Renouard, H. Laurens éditeur, 1923.
PROCOPIOU Angelo, Athènes, cité des dieux, Albin Michel, 1964.
RICHER Jean, Géographie sacrée du monde grec, Bibliothèque des Guides bleus, Hachette, 1967.
ROMILLY Jacqueline de, Problèmes de la démocratie grecque, Hermann, 1983. Pourquoi la Grèce ?, Fallois, 1992.
ROUX G., Delphes, son oracle et ses dieux, Les Belles Lettres, 1976.
SCHLIEMANN Henri, Une vie d'archéologue, les trésors de Mycènes et de Troie, Jean-Cyrille Godefroy, 1982.
SCHMITT PANTEL, Pauline, La cité au Banquet, École française de Rome, 1992.
SPAWFORTH, T. The Complete Greek Temples. Thames & Hudson.
STERN Thomas, Thésée ou la puissance du spectre, Seghers, 1981.
THUCYDIDE, Histoire de la guerre du Péloponnèse, Laffont, 1990.
VIVIER Frédérique, La Grèce, Molière, 1998. Greek Mythology, Grange Books, 2004.

Cover: Detail of the Slaughter of the Giants: Poseidon riding a white horse, red-figured amphora, so-called Milo amphora, Louvre, c.410 BC. Flyleaves: Island of Aegina, Temple of Aphaia. Page 4: Ancient Greece uncovered by Archaeology, Leon Commerre, 1898, Guizot Lecture Hall, University of Paris-Sorbonne. Page 11: Homer and other poets. Page 12: Island of Corfu about 1920. Page 248: Island of Mykonos. Page 250: Dion, Macedonia: a statuette. Photographic credits: Emmanuelle Le Pommelet: 92, 110, 130, 144, 197. Hervé Champollion: 2, 40, 54, 56, 58, 108, 116, 138, 142, 156, 180, 182, 184, 185, 186, 188, 190, 192, 194, 198, 203, 218, 223, 224, 226, 228, 231, 236, 238, 240, 244, 248, 250. Christophe Lefébure: 232, 235, 242, 246, 247, 253. Alain Mahuzier: 85, 86, 88, 90, 95, 98, 99, 112, 115, 148. RMN: 1, 16, 50, 52, 63, 64, 67, 68, 71, 75, 76, 78, 82, 94, 103, 147, 160, 163, 164, 168, 170. ADOC-Photos: 12. Nguyen Thuc Diem: 96, 153. D. R/Private collection: 4, 6, 11, 18-37,42-49, 70, 73, 77, 93, 104-107, 118-121, 124-129, 132-137, 145, 150, 154, 166, 172-177, 202, 204-217. Collaboration: F. B. S.B. Printed in China.

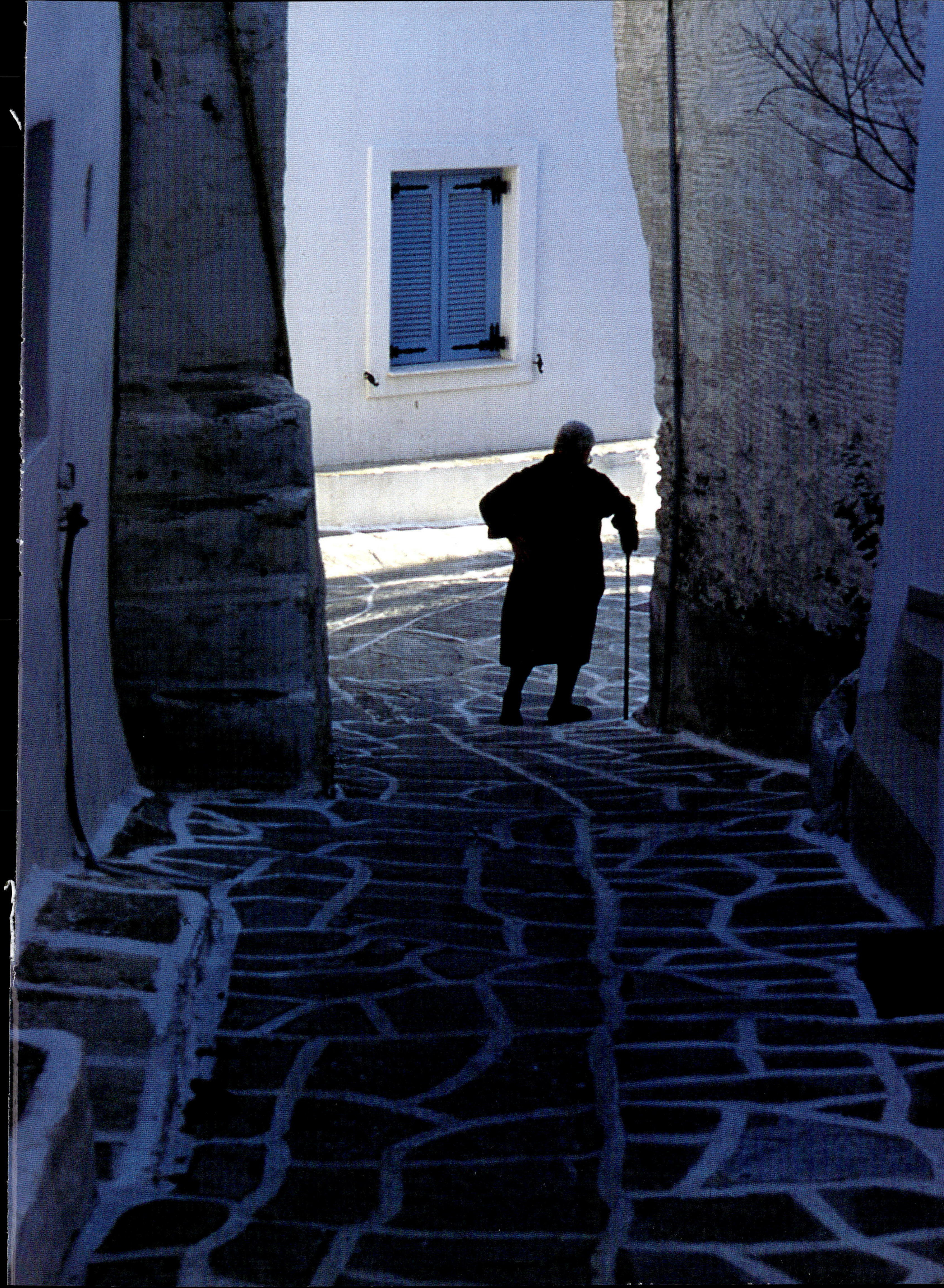

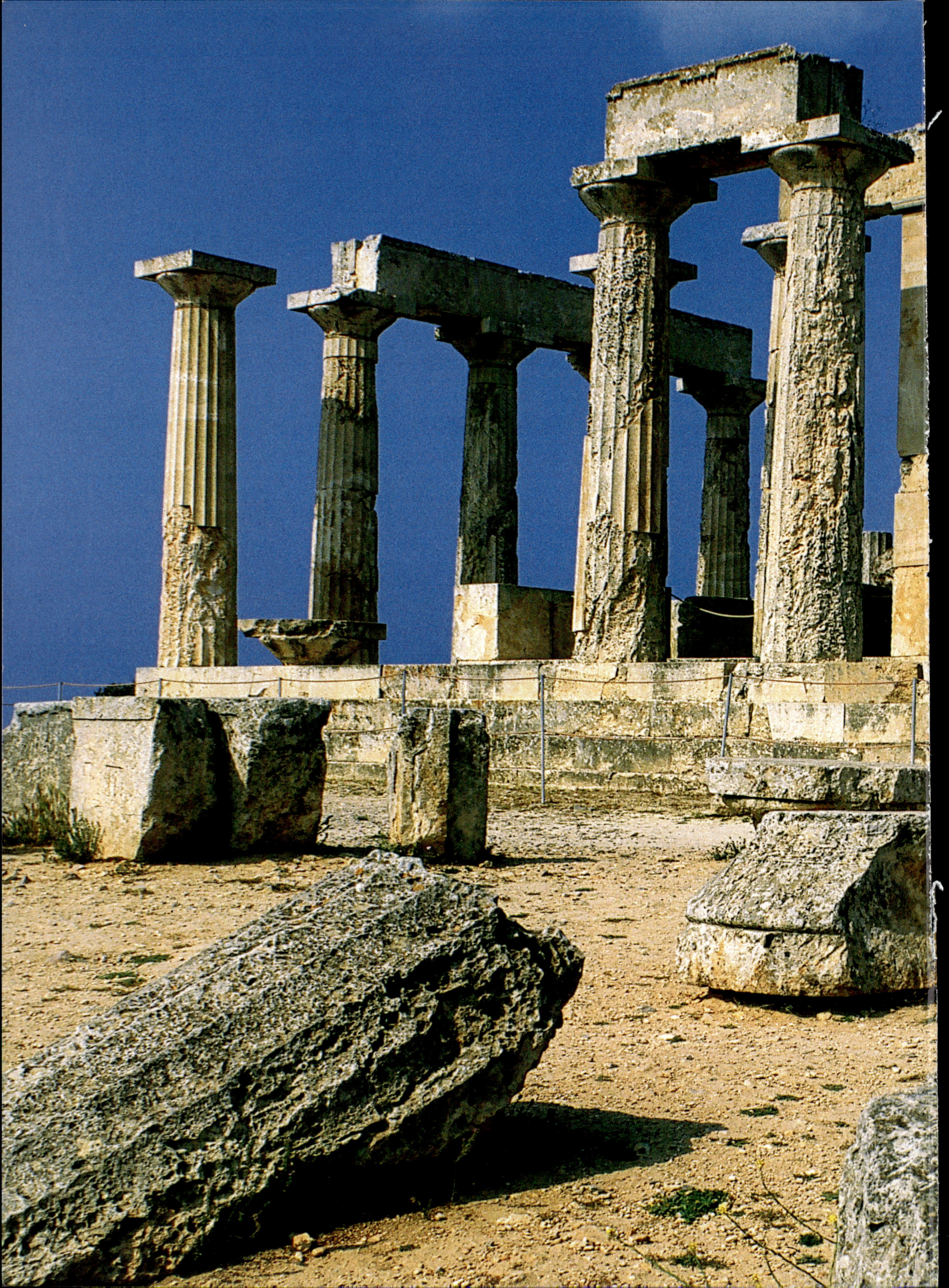